ELEMENTS OF
PURE ECONOMICS

A translation of the Edition Définitive (1926) of
the *Eléments d'économie politique pure*, annotated
and collated with the previous editions

Léon Walras

ELEMENTS OF
PURE ECONOMICS

OR

THE THEORY OF SOCIAL WEALTH

TRANSLATED BY

WILLIAM JAFFÉ

Northwestern University, Evanston, Illinois

ORION EDITIONS

First edition 1954
(Homewood, Ill.: Richard D. Irwin Inc.;
London: George Allen & Unwin Ltd.)

Reprinted 1984 by
ORION EDITIONS
Philadelphia, PA 19107
*By arrangement with George Allen & Unwin Ltd.
and the American Economic Association*

Library of Congress Cataloging in Publication Data

Walras, Léon, 1834–1910.
   Elements of pure economics, or, The theory of social
wealth.

   Translation of: Eleménts d'économie politique pure.
   Reprint. Originally published: Homewood, Ill. : R.D.
Irwin, 1954.
   Includes indexes.
   1. Economics.   I. Title.
HB173.W2213   1984   330   83-19354
ISBN 0-87991-253-7

Manufactured in the United States of America

TRANSLATOR'S FOREWORD

As good wine needs no bush, so Léon Walras's *Eléments d'économie politique pure* needs no prologue. Like most celebrated classics, the *Eléments* is more often cited than read. The fault, if it be a fault, lies not only in the forbidding magnificence of its reputation, but also in the book itself, which needs to be drained to the dregs before it can be truly judged. The distinguishing characteristic of Walras's theory of economic equilibrium is that it is general and has to be taken into account in all its generality to be adequately understood. The argument is progressive, moving deliberately to a premeditated climax, and unless the reader moves with it in sympathy with the author's intention, the meaning is lost. The book is all the more difficult because the theory, though essentially mathematical, is expressed in primitive mathematics and then paraphrased in crabbed prose.

Nevertheless, it was this book that directly inspired Vilfredo Pareto, Enrico Barone, Knut Wicksell, Irving Fisher, Henry Ludwell Moore and Joseph Schumpeter during Walras's own lifetime. The number of economists and econometricians it inspired, directly or indirectly, since Walras's day is legion. Though Walras had indeed laid firm foundations for what came to be known, even before he died, as the School of Lausanne, the fame of the *Eléments* was not suddenly acquired, but has grown slowly, almost imperceptibly, since the first edition was published in the early 1870's. The Walrasian theory did not make its appearance as a "flash of light illuminating a dark and confused landscape", but rather as a penetrating pencil of esoteric rays serviceable only to specialists to whom it gradually revealed a clear design of organic unity inherent in socio-economic phenomena.

Our author, Marie-Esprit Léon Walras,[1] was born on December 16th, 1834, at Evreux, in the Department of Eure, France. His father was Antoine Auguste Walras of Montpellier and his mother Louise Aline *née* Sainte-Beuve of Evreux. His early years were spent in Paris, Lille, Caen and Douai, where his father, an economist in his own right, pursued his career as a teacher of philosophy and rhetoric and as an educational administrator. Léon Walras, having twice failed in the competitive examination to enter the École Polytechnique, found refuge in the École des Mines. Neither the study nor the career of engineering suited the bohemian temperament of his youth. He soon abandoned the École des Mines and turned to literature and

---

[1] I was told by Walras's daughter, the late Mlle Aline Walras, that the final s is sounded in the correct pronunciation of the name.

journalism; but his first published novels enjoyed no real success. In 1858 he was persuaded by his father to consecrate his life to the development of economics as a science. Then began a long and difficult struggle that lasted twelve years until he obtained a position that permitted him to realize his own and his father's dream. This is not the place to recount his intervening trials and tribulations as a journalist, a clerk in a railway office, a managing director of a bank for co-operatives, a newspaper editor, a public lecturer, and a bank employee when his own bank was forced to liquidate. It can be seen that his early experience was by no means entirely academic; he had faced the hard facts of the business world. Indeed, he had received no academic preparation in economics at all. In theoretical economics he had but one teacher, his father. For the rest, he was self-taught; but, as we know from the *Eléments*, he did not depart from the classical tradition, which he criticized only in order to perfect and enlarge its scientific structure. His lack of any officially recognized preparation in economics explains, in some degree, why he never succeeded in winning a teaching post in France. What his native country denied him he found in Switzerland. There he read a paper in 1860 on taxation, and thanks to the remarkable impression he made on that occasion, he was invited ten years later as the first occupant of a newly founded chair in economics at the Faculty of Law of the Academy of Lausanne. From then on, he devoted himself to the elaboration of his theory, to teaching and to writing, while maintaining some contact with the practical world of affairs as a consulting actuary for a large Swiss insurance company. Though he retired from his professorship in 1892, he continued his research and writing until he died on January 5th, 1910, at Clarens, near Lausanne. He deeply appreciated the opportunities for independent scientific endeavour Switzerland afforded him during the last four decades of his life, but he remained a French citizen to the end. Such are the bare outlines of the professional career of Léon Walras, whose private life, rich in human experience and beset with intimate tragedies that would have broken a lesser man, still remains to be told.[1]

[1] Aided by a Fullbright Research Award, I have gathered primary materials for a book, now in preparation, on the Life and Works of Léon Walras. It will be seen, in this fuller account, with what difficulties he had to contend while he produced writings which he recorded in a bibliography listing 129 items! Some of his more important economic contributions are mentioned in the Preface to the Fourth Edition of the *Eléments* translated below. For a detailed discussion of Walras's non-analytical works, dealing mainly with discussions of economic policy, see Marcel Boson's thesis, *Léon Walras, Fondateur de la politique économique scientifique*, Paris, R. Pichon et R. Durand-Auzias, and Lausanne, F. Rouge, 1951. Among the principal published sources on the life of Walras we have "Leone Walras—autobiografia", *Giornale degli economisti*, 2nd series, vol. XXXVII, December 1908, pp. 603–610 with a short preface by Maffeo Pantaleoni; and William Jaffé's "Unpublished Papers and Letters of Léon Walras", *Journal of Political Economy*, vol. XLIII, No. 2, April 1935, pp. 187–207.

As can be seen from the facsimiles (see below pp. 29–34) of the title pages or covers of the five editions of the *Eléments* prepared by Walras, it is now nearly eighty years since the first half-volume of the first edition made its appearance and more than twenty-five years since the posthumously published definitive edition[1] came out. And yet the *Eléments* has never before been translated. Walras himself urged his contemporaries in England and America to translate some of his works, but he was told in 1885 by an English publisher of note that "it is very hard to persuade the English public to read foreign books at all, however good they may be", and in 1906 by an American admirer, an economist of high scientific standing, ". . . I was sure that you underestimated the difficulties of your work and . . . I doubted the wisdom of a translation." The latter remark, it should be emphasized was made not apropos of the *Eléments* itself, but of Walras's simplified version, which has since been published under the title, *Abrégé des éléments d'économie politique pure*, edited by Gaston Leduc, Paris, R. Pichon et R. Durand-Auzias, and Lausanne, F. Rouge, 1938. Up to the present, all that we have had in English of Walras's writings are:[2] (1) "On the Solution of the Anglo-Indian Monetary Problem", a paper translated and read by Professor Herbert Somerton Foxwell before the British Association for the Advancement of Science on September 6th, 1887 and published in the *Transactions* of Section F of that Association, London, 1888, pp. 849–851 (cf. Léon Walras, "*Note sur la solution du problème monétaire anglo-indien*", *Revue d'économie politique*, vol. I, No. 6, November–December 1887, pp. 633–636); (2) "The Geometrical Theory of the Determination of Prices", *Annals of the American Academy of Political and Social Science*, vol. III, No. 1, July 1892, pp. 45–64, which was translated under the supervision of Irving Fisher; and (3) "Walras on Gossen", which was published recently in a book edited by Professor Henry William Spiegel, *The Development of Economic Thought, Great Economists in Perspective*, New York, John Wiley and Sons, and

---

[1] The "Edition définitive" (1926), incorporating Walras's afterthoughts and corrections recorded between 1900 and 1902, is much more a definitive version of the 4th edition than a new edition. It is for that reason that I have referred to the 1926 edition in abbreviation as ed. 4 def.

[2] Walras fared a little better than this in Italian and German, in which languages we find: besides the "Autobiografia" mentioned in footnote 1 of the previous page, both an Italian and a German translation of the four early memoirs described below (p. 36, footnote 2), the first of these translations by Gerolamo Boccardo, appearing under the title "Teoria matematica della ricchezza" in the *Biblioteca dell' Economista*, Series III, vol. II, Turin, Unione tipografica editrice, 1878, pp. 1289–1388, and the second by Ludwig von Winterfeld, under the title *Mathematische Theorie der Preisbestimmung der wirtschaftlichen Güter*, Stuttgart, Enke, 1881; and an article,"Un nuovo ramo della matematica, dell'applicazione delle matematiche all'economia politica", *Giornale degli economisti*, vol. III, no. 1, April 1876, pp. 1–40, which, like the "Autobiografia", had never been published in the original French from which it was translated by Boccardo. Since Walras's death, we have also the *Theorie des Geldes*, Jena, Gustav Fischer, 1922, a translation by Richard Kerschagl and Stephan Raditz of Walras's *Théorie de la monnaie*, Lausanne, Corbaz, 1886.

London, Chapman and Hall, 1952, pp. 471–488, where it is described as a translation "in slightly abridged form" of Walras's article "Un économiste inconnu, H. H. Gossen", which first appeared in the *Journal des économistes*, Series 4, vol. 30, No. 4, April 1885, pp. 68–90, with a rectificatory letter in the following issue No. 5, May 1885, pp. 260–261.

The idea of translating the *Eléments* first occurred to me as the result of a conversation I had long ago with my friend, the late Henry Schultz, who made me painfully aware of the complete unreliability of the secondary sources from which, up to that time, I had drawn all I knew about the Walrasian theory. On looking more closely into the matter, I discovered that authors of unquestioned eminence who cited the original work often missed its true meaning. I felt that an integral translation was needed and ventured upon the task. Those who know how many years I have devoted to it may not be aware of the number of successive versions I discarded before I dared to offer the present one for publication. With the proverbial taunt, *traduttore traditore*, forever ringing in my ears, I can only hope that the passages where I have unwittingly betrayed the master's thought are outnumbered by those in which I have succeeded in my attempt to clarify it.

The purpose of this translation is two-fold: to bring a great classic to students who have too little French to read the original and to furnish scholars interested in the history of economic analysis with an instrument of research. Hence the Notes which are found at the end of this volume and which are referred to in the translation by references enclosed in square brackets. These brackets, it will be observed, are used everywhere to apprise the reader of the translator's deliberate intrusions, whether they be Note references or additional words and phrases inserted in the text to elucidate obscure passages.

I have contributed two sets of Notes: Translator's Notes, referred to by number; and Collation Notes, referred to by letter. On the utility of the former, the reader alone can decide, but he would do well to bear in mind the dictum of Dr. Johnson: "It is impossible for an expositor not to write too little for some, and too much for others. He can only judge what is necessary by his own experience; and how long soever he may deliberate, will at last explain many lines which the learned will think impossible to be mistaken, and omit many for which the ignorant will want his help." On the need for the Collation of Editions, I think every student of Walras will agree with Professor Arthur W. Marget's observation that "a proper understanding of Walras's system requires a study of the various transformations through which that system passed, and the various refinements which were added in the successive editions of the *Eléments* and the rest of

Walras's writings". Doubtless, it would have been better to compile a complete variorum edition, but that was obviously not feasible in the case of a translation. Anyone fortunate enough to find copies of the rarer early editions could, with the aid of my Table of Corresponding Sections, Lessons and Parts, trace in detail the successive changes in particular passages. In my Collation of Editions, I have not attempted to give the earlier versions of every change, for some were trivial or purely stylistic, while others were so extensive that an additional volume would have been necessary to quote them textually. I have had to resort to a compromise: obviously minor changes are ignored; all major changes that are not too unwieldly are recorded by quotation from the original French of the earlier editions and can be compared with the French of the last edition which is now readily available;[1] all extensive changes are described.

Besides the translation of the entire text of the "Edition définitive" with its two Appendices, the present volume contains a translation of an additional Appendix III which appeared in the 3rd edition (1896) only. Despite its withdrawal from the subsequent editions, the transient appearance of this Appendix, entitled "Note on Mr. Wicksteed's Refutation of the English Theory of Rent", still constitutes a noteworthy event in the history of the marginal productivity theory, if for no other reason, for the controversy it has stirred up.

The Indexes also have been added, and only the summaries found at the head of each Leçon in the original have been subtracted. These, however, were adapted, not translated, to make up my analytical table of contents.

While the geometric Figures in the translation were reproduced from the five folded plates located at the end of the 4th edition (the reproduction in the definitive edition not being clear enough), the originals were subjected to a slight modification. Walras's Figures were often crowded with curves, probably for the sake of economy, to enable him to use one Figure to illustrate several separate arguments. In my arrangement, the Figures are dispersed so that each is placed in its immediate context and consists only of those curves that are relevant to the adjacent discussion. I have also labelled the axes.

The pristine "exuberance of algebraic foliage", to use Edgeworth's apt phrase, has been retained as in the original.

"Yet sit and see,
"Minding true things, by what their mock'ries be."

---

[1] A new reprint ("nouveau tirage") of the "Edition définitive" of the *Eléments d'économie politique pure* was published by the Librairie Générale de Droit et de Jurisprudence, R. Pichon et R. Durand-Auzias, 20 rue Soufflot, Paris 5e, in 1952.

The few changes made in the notation were typographically unavoidable.

Not only in the mathematical presentation, but also in the translation of the text, I have made no attempt to modernize the book. So far as I was able, I tried to translate the prose into the English of Walras's contemporaries. The *Eléments* translated into the technical jargon current in our day would be a misleading anachronism. In the final stages of this literary task, I have been ably seconded by my wife, Olive Caroline Jaffé, who suggested felicitous renderings of many difficult and intricate passages, though she had never read a treatise on economics before. Moreover, in the proof-reading stage, it was she who verified the entire translation by checking it against the original. In an important sense, she might well be regarded as a co-translator, though responsibility for defects in this work must remain entirely mine.

I am greatly indebted to fellow economists who aided me with their counsel and encouragement; to Northwestern University, its Graduate School, the Social Science Research Council and the American Philosophical Society for their generous contributions in support of the project; and to the succession of students and clerical assistants who helped prepare the manuscript. I must, in particular, express my profound gratitude to my colleague, Professor James Washington Bell, Secretary of the American Economic Association, who has been to me what Louis Ruchonnet was to Walras. When courage flagged, it was his patient and friendly prompting that gave me strength to go on. To Dean Simeon E. Leland of the College of Liberal Arts of Northwestern University I owe grateful acknowledgement for his indefatigable efforts in obtaining for me further opportunities to pursue my researches at home and abroad. In the earlier stages of the work, I benefited greatly from the invaluable criticisms and suggestions offered by Dr. C. Oswald George, now with the Board of Trade in England as a Chief Statistician. In the later stages, I received much helpful advice from my colleague, Professor Robert H. Strotz in Evanston, Illinois, and, while I was in Paris, from M. G. Th. Guilbaud and the other members of the staff of the Institut de Science Economique Appliquée of which Professor François Perroux is Director. I wish also to express my appreciation to M. Jean Charles Biaudet, Librarian, and to M. Charles Roth, Keeper of Manuscripts, of the Bibliothèque Cantonale et Universitaire de Lausanne, where I was able to consult the archives containing Walras's scientific correspondence and papers. M. Roth very kindly proof-read the multilingual passages in my Notes. Finally, I feel bound to acknowledge the co-operation of all my colleagues in the Department of Economics of Northwestern University.

Although Walras did not live to see an English translation of his major work, I like to think of him in the Valhalla of intellectual warriors, happy in the knowledge that a translation of his *Eléments* is appearing under the joint auspices of the Royal Economic Society and the American Economic Association, and rejoicing now as he did in 1892 when the American Economic Association elected him an honorary member in recognition of his "eminent services to the Science of Political Economy".

WILLIAM JAFFÉ

Lausanne, Switzerland
June 16, 1953

CONTENTS

PART I

Object and Divisions of
Political and Social Economy

§1. Need for a definition of Political Economy. §2. Physiocrats' definition too broad. §3. Adam Smith's two aims of Political Economy: (1) to provide a plentiful subsistence for the people, (2) to supply the State with a sufficient revenue. §4. Both aims equally important, but neither the subject matter of economic science. §5. Smith's two aims differentiated; material well-being and justice. §6. J. B. Say's conception of Political Economy. §7. Naturalistic point of view inadequate for refutation of socialism; choice of systems of production or distribution based on principles of expediency or justice. §8. J. B. Say's division of subject purely empirical. §9. Blanqui's and Garnier's corrections incomplete.

§10. Charles Coquelin's distinction: art prescribes and directs; science observes, describes and explains. §11. Distinction between science and art *vs.* distinction between theory and practice. §12. Science enlightens art; art puts science to use. §13. Relationship between arts and sciences. §§14–15. Coquelin's distinction excellent, but inadequate. §16. Science, the study of facts. §17. *Natural* and *human* phenomena distinguished; both, the subject matter of *pure science.* §18. Human *industry* and human *institutions* distinguished. §19. Industrial phenomena, the subject matter of applied science or *art*; institutional phenomena, the subject matter of moral science or *ethics.* §20. The *true*, the *useful*, and the *good* as the respective criteria of science, art and ethics.

PART II

Theory of Exchange of Two Commodities for Each Other

prices p_a and p_b. §45. Effective demand and offer of (A) and (B): D_a, O_a, D_b, O_b; theorem: $O_b = D_a p_a$ and $O_a = D_b p_b$; demand, the principal fact; offer, the accessory fact. §46. Theorem: $\dfrac{D_a}{O_a} = \dfrac{O_b}{D_b}$. §47. Case of equality between offer and demand; market equilibrium. §48. Case of inequality; rise or fall in price; effect on demand. Effect on offer?

§49. Effective demand diminishes as price rises. §§50–51. Individual demand as a function of price; curves and equations. §52. Curves and equations of total demand. §53. Demand curves as implicit offer curves. §54. Hyperbolas of total existing quantity. §55. Demand curves situated between these hyperbolas and co-ordinate axes. §56. Problem of exchange in two-commodity market. §57. Geometric solution. §58. Algebraic solution. §59. The two solutions combined by construction of explicit offer curves. §§60–61. Law of effective offer and effective demand, or law of establishment of equilibrium prices.

§§62–63. Discussion restricted to case of continuous curves with single maximum. §64. Case of non-intersection between demand and offer curves: no solution. §65. Case of triple intersection: three solutions. §§66–68. Stable and unstable equilibria. §69. Case of coincidence of one demand curve with hyperbola of total existing quantity. §70. Case of coincidence of both demand curves with hyperbolas.

§71. Intercept of individual demand curve on quantity axis: *extensive utility*. §72. Slope of individual demand curve; its intercept on price axis: *intensive utility*. §73. Influence of *initial stock*. §74. Assumption of measurability of utility; utility or want curves. §75. *Effective utility* and *rareté* as functions of *quantity consumed*; geometric representation. §76. Object of exchange: to maximize satisfaction of wants. §77. Exchange of o_b of (B) for d_a of (A)

demand functions; equations of exchange. §110. Geometrical representation precluded; algebraic statement. §111. Conditions of general equilibrium. §§112–114. Assume $p_{c,b} = \alpha \dfrac{p_{c,a}}{p_{b,a}}$, where $\alpha > 1$; arbitrage. §115. Assume $\alpha < 1$. §116. Generalized equations of offer and demand.

§117. Generalized case of holders of several commodities. §118. Individual offer and demand functions derived from equations of exchange and maximum satisfaction for each party. §§119–122. Case of offer equal to quantity possessed, determinate. §123. System of $m-1$ equations expressing equality between total demand and total offer in m-commodity market. §124. Transition to empirical establishment of equilibrium prices in multi-commodity market. §125. Prices expressed in *numéraire*; general equilibrium implied. Prices cried at random; rule-of-thumb determination of individual demands and offers. §§126–127. Case of inequality between total demand and total offer; price adjustments. §128. Consequent adjustments in total demand and total offer. §§129–130. Rise (or fall) in price when total demand is greater (or less) than total offer.

§131. Analysis of exchange in multi-commodity market. §132. At equilibrium, ratio of *raretés* of any two commodities the same for all traders. §§133–134. Proportionality of *raretés* to values in exchange; qualifications. §135. Average *raretés*. §136. Absolute values in exchange are arbitrary and indeterminate. §137. Price changes caused by changes in utility and in quantity possessed. §138. Stability in price considered as result of mutually compensating changes in utility and quantity possessed.

§139. Redistributions of commodities among traders; the value of individual holdings and the total existing quantities of commodities unaffected by exchange. §§140–144. Necessary consequence of (1) individual offer and demand functions derived from condition of maximum satisfaction, (2) equality between values of commodities offered and commodities demanded by each individual, (3) equality between total demand and total offer of each and every commodity. §145. *Numéraire*, the standard commodity. §146. Rational *vs.* popular conception of price; error of popular conception. §147. The standard defined as the quantity, not the value of *numéraire*. *Numéraire* as the measuring rod of value and wealth. §§148–150. Money, the medium of exchange.

PART IV
Theory of Production

§200. Assume *n* types of productive services, *m* types of final products. §201. *Rareté* functions of consumers' services and final
products; value of services offered=value of products demanded;
condition of maximum satisfaction; equations of individual offer of
services and individual demand for products. §202. Equations
(1) of total offer of services; equations (2) of total demand for
products. §203. *Coefficients of production.* Equations (3) expressing
equality between demand and offer of services; equations (4) expressing equality between selling prices and costs of products. §204.
Coefficients of production provisionally assumed constant. §205.
Raw materials eliminated from equations. §206. $2m+2n+1$
equations equal to number of unknowns. §207. Solution in
practice; emergence of equilibrium *ab ovo*; process of groping;
hypothetical use of *tickets*.

§208. Assume: (1) value of services bought=value of products sold
by entrepreneurs, (2) prices of productive services cried at random.
§209. Cost of production equations; assume random quantities
produced. §210. Selling prices of products; entrepreneur's profit or
loss. §§211–212. Process of groping towards equality between
selling price and cost of production. §213. Demand for product
serving as *numéraire*; cost of production of *numéraire*-product equal
to unity, a necessary condition of equilibrium. §214. Assume
quantity of services employed=quantity of services sold to entrepreneurs; case of inequality between demand and offer of services.
§215. Effective demand and offer of services; demand for services by
entrepreneurs and consumers; price adjustments. §§216–217.
Process of groping towards equality between demand and offer of
services. §218. Demand for the product serving as *numéraire*. §219.
Process of groping towards equality between cost of production of
numéraire-product and unity. §220. Law of establishment of
equilibrium prices of products and services.

§221. Analysis of free competition in production. §222. Free
competition as a precept. §223. *Laisser-faire* policy undemonstrated;

exceptions to principle not usually admitted: public services, natural monopoly, redistribution of property. §§224–226. Values in exchange of services proportional to their *raretés*. §227. Law of variation of equilibrium prices of products and services. §§228–230. Purchase and sales curves of services; price curves of products.

PART V

Theory of Capital Formation ['Capitalisation'] and Credit

§231. The capital goods market; dependence of prices of capital goods on prices of their services. §232. *Net income* from capital goods=*gross income*−(depreciation+insurance); prices of capital goods proportional to their net incomes. §233. *Rate of net income* defined. §234. Assume: (1) newly manufactured capital goods exchanged against excess of aggregate income over aggregate consumption, (2) equality between selling prices of capital goods and their costs of production. §235. *Credit*; the loan of money savings and the demand for new capital goods. §§236–237. Assume quantities of land and persons given. §238. Assume quantity of capital goods proper unknown; capitalized net income=cost of production of capital goods proper at equilibrium. §§239–240. Income $\gtreqless$ consumption. §241. Income−consumption $\gtreqless$ depreciation+insurance of capital goods proper. §242. Hypothetical commodity (E) defined as perpetual net income; price of (E); individual demand for (E); aggregate excess of income over consumption=aggregate demand for (E)×price of (E)=aggregate demand for new capital goods×price of capital goods. §243. $2l+2$ equations equal to number of unknowns.

§244. Value of services offered=value of products and net income demanded; equations of maximum satisfaction; equations of individual offer of services and individual demand for products and net income. §245. Equations (1) of total offer of services; equations (2) of total demand for products. §246. Equation (3) of aggregate excess of income over consumption. §247. Equations (4) expressing

PART VI
Theory of Circulation and Money

PART VII

*Conditions and Consequences of Economic Progress.
Critique of Systems of Pure Economics*

and circulating capital. §319. Assumption of fixed annual period; table of hypothetical aggregate values of elements of production. §320. Relationship of circulating capital to annual aggregate output. §321. Consumption and reproduction of circulating capital. §322. Continuous market; oscillatory convergence towards equilibrium; *crises.*

§323. Laws of price variations in a progressive economy. §324. Variability of coefficients of production in a progressive economy: diminishing land-coefficients, increasing capital-coefficients. Indefinite progress defined: decreasing *raretés* with increasing population. *Technical* vs. *economic* progress. §325. The production function. §326. *Theory of marginal productivity*, the theory of the determination of coefficients of production consistent with minimum cost of production. §327. Condition of economic progress: increase in capital proper must precede and exceed increase in population. §§328–329. Malthusian theory of population. §330. Commodity prices not necessarily variable in progressive economy. §331. Assume land fixed; population doubled, capital more than doubled, output less than doubled. §332. Characteristics of new equilibrium: rise in rent, fall in interest charges, nearly constant wages. §333. Fall in rate of net income. §334. Constant price of capital goods; rise in price of land and personal faculties. §335. Essential characteristic of economic progress: rise in price of land-services.

§336. The *"Tableau économique"*. §337. Distribution of aggregate annual output among *productive, proprietary* and *sterile* classes. §338. Industrial class not unproductive; Physiocratic error due to identification of wealth with materiality. §§339–340. Contribution of industrial class to net product and to initial capital investment. §341. Absence of theory of determination of prices in *"Tableau économique"*.

§342. Alleged fundamental distinction between indefinitely reproducible and non-reproducible products. §343. Indefinitely reproducible products non-existent. §344. Price-determining costs non-existent. §345. Influence of price of productive services on price of products; case of extinct productive services. §§346–348. Cases of specialized and unspecialized services: no antithesis. §349. Mill's confusion between timeless cost function and increase in production over time.

PART VIII
Price Fixing, Monopoly, Taxation

Appendices

Notes

ÉLÉMENTS

D'ÉCONOMIE POLITIQUE

PURE

PAR

LÉON WALRAS

Professeur d'Economie politique à l'Académie de Lausanne.

———— ◊∞ ————

**Objet et divisions de l'économie politique et sociale.
Théorie mathématique de l'échange.
Du numéraire et de la monnaie.**

———— ∞◊∞ ————

LAUSANNE
IMPRIMERIE L. CORBAZ & Cⁱᵉ ÉDITEURS

PARIS		BALE
GUILLAUMIN & Cⁱᵉ, ÉDITEURS		H. GEORG, LIBRAIRE-ÉDITEUR
11, rue Richelieu.		Même maison à Genève.

1874
Tous droits réservés.

(COVER)

ÉLÉMENTS

D'ÉCONOMIE POLITIQUE

PURE

PAR

LÉON WALRAS

Professeur d'Économie politique à l'Académie de Lausanne.

———— ∞∞ ————

**Théorie naturelle de la production et de la consommation
de la richesse.
Conditions et conséquences du progrès économique.
Effets naturels et nécessaires des divers modes d'organisation
économique de la société.**

———— ∞∞ ————

LAUSANNE

IMPRIMERIE L. CORBAZ & Cie, ÉDITEURS

PARIS	BALE
GUILLAUMIN & Cie, ÉDITEURS	H. GEORG, LIBRAIRE-ÉDITEUR
11, rue Richelieu.	Même maison à Genève.

1877

(COVER)

ÉLÉMENTS

D'ÉCONOMIE POLITIQUE

PURE

ou

THÉORIE DE LA RICHESSE SOCIALE

PAR

LÉON WALRAS

Professeur d'Économie politique à l'Académie de Lausanne,
Membre de l'Institut international de Statistique.

———

DEUXIÈME ÉDITION
REVUE, CORRIGÉE ET AUGMENTÉE

———

LAUSANNE

F. ROUGE, ÉDITEUR
Rue Haldimand, 4.

<table>
<tr><td>PARIS</td><td>LEIPZIG</td></tr>
<tr><td>GUILLAUMIN & Cie, ÉDITEURS</td><td>VERLAG VON DUNCKER & HUMBLOT</td></tr>
<tr><td>Rue Richelieu, 14.</td><td>Dresdnerstrasse, 17.</td></tr>
</table>

—

ÉLÉMENTS

D'ÉCONOMIE POLITIQUE

PURE

OU

THÉORIE DE LA RICHESSE SOCIALE

PAR

LÉON WALRAS

TROISIÈME ÉDITION

LAUSANNE

F. ROUGE, ÉDITEUR
Librairie de l'Université.

PARIS | LEIPZIG
F. PICHON, IMPRIMEUR-ÉDITEUR | VERLAG VON DUNCKER & HUMBLOT
Rue Soufflot, 24. | Dresdnerstrasse, 17.

1896

ÉLÉMENTS

D'ÉCONOMIE POLITIQUE

PURE

ou

THÉORIE DE LA RICHESSE SOCIALE

PAR

LÉON WALRAS

———

QUATRIÈME ÉDITION

———

LAUSANNE	PARIS
F. ROUGE, LIBRAIRE-ÉDITEUR	F. PICHON, IMPRIMEUR-ÉDITEUR
4, rue Haldimand, 4.	24, rue Soufflot, 24.

1900

ÉLÉMENTS

D'ÉCONOMIE POLITIQUE

PURE

ou

THÉORIE DE LA RICHESSE SOCIALE

PAR

LÉON WALRAS

———

ÉDITION DÉFINITIVE
REVUE ET AUGMENTÉE PAR L'AUTEUR

———

PARIS

R. PICHON et R. DURAND-AUZIAS
Editeurs, 20, rue Soufflot.

LAUSANNE

F. ROUGE, LIBRAIRE-ÉDITEUR
4, rue Haldimand, 4.

1926
—

PREFACE TO THE FOURTH EDITION

This fourth edition of the *Elements of Pure Economics* is the definitive edition.[1] In June of 1874 I wrote the following lines which I feel I must reproduce from the Preface of my first edition:

To the enlightened initiative of the Council of State of the Canton of Vaud, which organized a competitive examination in 1870 to fill a chair of political economy newly instituted at the Faculty of Law of the Academy of Lausanne, and particularly to the confidence and benevolence of M. Louis Ruchonnet, Head of the Department of Public Instruction and Public Worship, Member of the Swiss National Council, who, since inviting me to enter this competition for the chair I now occupy, has never wavered in his kind encouragement, I owe it that I am now able to start publishing a treatise on the elements of political and social economy, conceived on a new plan, elaborated according to an original method, and reaching conclusions which, I venture to say, differ in several respects from those of current economic science.

This treatise is made up of the following three Books, each constituting a volume to be published in two instalments:

Book One: THE ELEMENTS OF PURE ECONOMICS or *The Theory of Social Wealth*; [containing in the first instalment:] Part I. Object and divisions of political and social economy.—Part II. Mathematical theory of exchange.—Part III. On *numéraire* and money.—[and in the second instalment:] Part IV.—Natural theory of the production and the consumption of wealth.—Part V. Conditions and consequences of economic progress.—Part VI. Natural and necessary effects of different kinds of economic systems of society.

Book Two: ELEMENTS OF APPLIED ECONOMICS or *The Theory of the Agricultural, Industrial, and Commercial Production of Wealth*.

Book Three: ELEMENTS OF SOCIAL ECONOMICS or *The Theory of the Distribution of Wealth via Property and Taxation.*[2]

I am now offering the first instalment of the first volume. It contains a mathematical solution of the problem of the determination of current prices and also a scientific formulation of the law of offer and demand in the case of the exchange of any number of commodities for one another. I am well aware that the notations used will at first appear somewhat cumbersome; but I beg the reader not to be discouraged by this complexity, for it is inherent in the subject and constitutes its only mathematical difficulty. This system of notation once mastered, the system of economic phenomena is, to a certain degree, understood.

This half-volume was completely written and almost completely printed, and I had already submitted a paper to the Académie des sciences morales et

[1] When the standing type matter of the present volume was stored for eventual replating, I inserted on pp. 376 and 414 [pp. 386 and 418 in the translation] only two notes bearing the same date as this note (1902) and I made small alterations [in the text] required by these insertions.

[2] Books Two and Three were replaced by the following two volumes: *Etudes d'économie sociale* (1896) and *Etudes d'économie politique appliquée* (1898). I have been compelled to make this substitution in order to bring my work as near as possible to completion. [Both of these books were published by F. Rouge et Cie in Lausanne and by R. Pichon et Durand-Auzias in Paris. Second editions (virtually reprints) of the two books were prepared by Professor Gaston Leduc and brought out in 1936 by the same publishers.]

politiques in Paris[1] on the basic principle of the theory expounded in my forth-coming book, when, a month ago, my attention was drawn to a work on the same subject, entitled: *The Theory of Political Economy*, Macmillan & Co., 1871, by W. Stanley Jevons, Professor of Political Economy at Manchester. Mr. Jevons applies mathematical analysis to pure economics, especially to the theory of exchange, very much as I do; and, what is really remarkable, he founds the whole application of mathematics to economics on a fundamental formula which he calls the equation of exchange and which is rigorously identical with the formula which serves as my point of departure and which I call the *condition of maximum satisfaction*.

Mr. Jevons's main purpose was to develop a general, philosophical exposition of the new method and to lay the foundations for the application of this method not only to the theory of *exchange*, but also to the theories of *labour*, *rent*, and *capital*. For my part, I have done my utmost in the present half-volume to give a very thorough account of the *mathematical theory of exchange*. As is only proper, therefore, I acknowledge Mr. Jevons's priority so far as his formula is concerned, without relinquishing my right to claim originality for certain important deductions of my own. I shall not enumerate these points which competent readers will readily discover. I need only add that, as I see it, Mr. Jevons's work and my own, far from being mutually competitive in any harmful sense, really support, complete, and reinforce each other to a singular degree. This is my considered opinion, in token of which I strongly recommend this eminent English economist's excellent book to all who have not yet read it.

The second instalment of the first edition was published in 1877. In it I developed a theory of the determination of the prices of productive services (wages, rent, and interest) and a theory of the determination of the rate of net income, both very different from those of Jevons.[2]

In 1879 Jevons, who had meanwhile become a professor at University College, London, published the second edition of his *Theory of Political Economy*. On pp. xxxv–xlii of his Preface to this edition he partly conceded to Gossen, a German, the priority of discovering the starting-point of mathematical economics, which, as stated above, I had already conceded to Jevons. I have written an article on Gossen, entitled "Un économiste inconnu, Hermann-Henri Gossen", in the *Journal des Economistes* for April and May 1885, in which I described his life and work, and endeavoured to determine what remained as my own contribution, after making due allowance

[1] See the *Compte-rendu des séances et travaux de l'Académie* for January 1874, or the *Journal des Economistes* for April and June 1874.
[2] Part I of the first edition of the *Eléments d'économie politique pure* was summarized in two memoirs entitled: *Principe d'une théorie mathématique de l'échange* and *Equations de l'échange*, the first having been submitted to the Académie des sciences morales et politiques in Paris in the month of August 1873, and the second to the Société Vaudoise des sciences naturelles at Lausanne in December 1875. Part II was summarized before its publication in two memoirs entitled: *Equations de la production* and *Equations de la capitalisation et du crédit*, both submitted to the Société Vaudoise des sciences naturelles, the first in January and February and the second in July 1876. These four memoirs were translated into Italian under the title of *Teoria matematica della ricchezza sociale* (Biblioteca dell'Economista, 1878) and into German under the title of *Mathematische Theorie der Preisbestimmung der wirthschaftlichen Güter* (Stuttgart, Verlag von Ferdinand Enke, 1881).

for the contributions of my two predecessors.[1] At the end of
Lesson 16 of this present volume the reader will find a paragraph in
which I revert to this matter. He will there see that once again, in
1872, the importance of considering *rareté* in the [theory of] exchange
was rediscovered and stressed, independently of the three of us, by
Carl Menger, a professor of economics at the University of Vienna.

I readily acknowledge Gossen's priority with respect to the utility
curve and Jevons's priority with respect to the equation of maximum
utility in exchange, but these economists were not the source of my
ideas. I am indebted to my father, Auguste Walras, for the fundamental principles of my economic doctrine; and to Augustin Cournot
for the idea of using the calculus of functions in the elaboration of this
doctrine. I have publicly acknowledged this fact in my first essays
and on every suitable occasion ever since. Now I should like to
explain how this doctrine was conceived, evolved, and completed in
the successive editions of the present work.

Though I have since made improvements in several points of
detail, yet, viewed as a whole, my solution of the equations of
exchange, production, capital formation and credit has remained
very much the same [as when first published].

In the theory of exchange, the rudimentary proof of the theorem
of *maximum utility of commodities* was supplemented by : (1) a proof
making use of the usual notations of the infinitesimal calculus which
is applicable to the case of continuous utility curves, in order to
prepare the way for the subsequent proof of the theorem of the
maximum utility of new capital goods, and (2) a proof applicable to
the case of discontinuous curves.

In the theory of production, I no longer represented the preliminary groping towards equilibrium as it takes place effectively, but
I assumed, instead, that it was done *by means of tickets* ['*sur bons*']
and then carried this fiction through the remainder of the book.

In the theory of capital formation, instead of setting down the
savings function empirically, I deduced it rationally from the equations of exchange and maximum satisfaction; and in a new theorem
I established the proposition that the condition of a uniform rate of
net income was also the condition of maximum utility relative to new
capital goods. When I published my first edition I was conscious of
only one of the two problems of maximum utility involving the
services of new capital goods, namely the problem connected with
an individual's distribution of his income among his various wants,
under the assumption that the quantities of the capital goods were
given by the nature of things or determined at random. This I have
called the problem of the *maximum utility of commodities*, the

---

[1] This article was republished in my *Etudes d'économie sociale*.

mathematical solution of which is found in the proportionality of the *raretés* to the prices of the services of capital goods. It was in the course of preparing the second edition that I became aware of another problem, namely, the problem which arises when we seek to determine the quantities of [the different kinds of] new capital goods consistent with the maximum effective utility of their services and which pertains to the distribution by the economy as a whole of its excess of income over consumption among the diverse opportunities for new investment. I have called this the problem of the *maximum utility of new capital goods*, the mathematical solution of which is found in the proportionality of the *raretés* to the prices of the capital goods themselves. It follows that the double maximum is attained when the prices of the services are proportional to the prices of the capital goods. Subject only to one reservation, this is precisely what results from the working of free competition.

Chiefly, however, it was my theory of money that underwent the most important changes as a result of my research on the subject from 1876 to 1899.[1] In the first and second editions [of the *Eléments*] the Lessons on money were made up partly of pure theory, and partly of applied theory; but the latter having been eliminated from the third and fourth editions I shall speak only of the former, and particularly of the underlying idea of this theory, namely, the solution of the problem of the value of money. In the first edition, this solution was founded on a consideration of the "circulation to be cleared" ["circulation à desservir"], which I had borrowed from the economists. In the second and subsequent editions, however, I based the solution on the concept of a "desired cash balance" ["encaisse désirée"], which I had already used in my *Théorie de la monnaie* [1886]. Nevertheless, I continued in the second and third editions, as in the first, to write the equation of offer and demand for money apart from the other equations and as empirically given. In the present edition this equation is deduced rationally from the equations of exchange and maximum satisfaction as well as from the equations showing equality between the demand and offer of circulating capital goods. In this way, the *theory of circulation and money*, like the *theories of exchange, production, capital formation and credit*, not only posits, but solves the relevant system of equations. The six Lessons in which this theory is developed give the

---

[1] Some of these research articles are in the realm of pure theory, and have, accordingly, been included in the present volume, viz. my "Note sur le 15½ légal", "Théorie mathématique du bimétallisme", "De la fixité de valeur de l'étalon monétaire" (*Journal des Economistes*, for December 1876, May 1881, and October 1882 respectively), and my "Equations de la circulation" (*Bulletin de la Société Vaudoise des sciences naturelles*, 1899). The other articles belong to the realm of applied theory and have been republished in my *Etudes d'économie politique appliquée*, e.g. "D'une méthode de régularisation de la variation de valeur de la monnaie" (1885), "Théorie de la monnaie" (1886), and "Le problème monétaire" (1887–1895).

solution of the fourth major problem of pure economics, that of circulation.

I have made some slight changes in the number, order, and titles of the main Parts of my book in order to indicate more clearly the logical sequence of the four problems. In particular, I have placed the theory of circulation immediately after that of capital formation and immediately before a special Part into which I moved my studies of *economic progress and systems of pure economics*. In this last Part, I included the *theory of marginal productivity*, that is, the theory of the determination of the coefficients of production which were thenceforth considered as unknowns and no longer as given quantities of the problem.

In consequence of these changes, the table of contents of this volume is as follows:

ELEMENTS OF PURE ECONOMICS or *Theory of Social Wealth*

This volume, despite the aforementioned changes, is, as I have already said, simply the definitive edition of the book that I first published in 1874–1877. By this I mean that my doctrine is the same today as it was then, a doctrine which was perfectly understood by a few mathematicians, who were also economists. It can be summarized in the following manner.

[1 Reprinted in this translation from ed. 3. This appendix was omitted from the subsequent editions.]

Pure economics is, in essence, the theory of the determination of prices under a hypothetical régime of perfectly free competition.[1] The sum total of all things, material or immaterial, on which a price can be set because they are *scarce* (i.e. both *useful* and *limited in quantity*), constitutes *social wealth*. Hence pure economics is also the theory of *social wealth*.

Among the things that make up social wealth a distinction must be made between *capital goods* or *durable goods* which can be used more than once, and *income goods* or *non-durable goods* ['biens fongibles'] which cannot be used more than once. Capital goods comprise *land, personal faculties*, and *capital goods* proper. Income goods comprise not only *consumers' goods* and *raw materials* which are, for the most part, material things, but also the successive uses of capital goods, i.e. their *services*, which are, in most instances, immaterial things. The services of capital goods which have a direct utility are called *consumers' services* and are put in the same class as consumers' goods. Those services of capital goods which have only indirect utility are called *productive services* and are put in the same class as raw materials. That, in my opinion, is the key to the whole of pure economics. The failure to make the distinction between capital goods and income goods, and particularly the refusal to include the immaterial services of capital goods in the same class of social wealth as material income goods preclude the possibility of a scientific theory of the determination of prices. If, however, the proposed distinction and classification are accepted, then it becomes possible to arrive successively at: (1) a determination of the prices of consumers' goods and services by means of *the theory of exchange*; (2) a determination of the prices of raw materials and productive services by means of the *theory of production*; (3) a determination of the price of fixed capital goods by means of the *theory of capitalization*; and (4) a determination of the prices of circulating capital goods by means of the *theory of circulation*. I shall now proceed to show how this is done.

First, let us imagine a market in which only consumers' goods and services are bought and sold, that is to say, exchanged, the *sale of any service* being effected by the *hiring out of a capital good*. Once the *prices* or the ratios of exchange of all these goods and services have been cried at random in terms of one of them selected as the *numéraire*, each party to the exchange will *offer* at these prices those goods or services of which he thinks he has relatively too much, and

---

[1] This means a régime of free competition among sellers of services who underbid one another and among buyers of products who outbid one another. Free competition among entrepreneurs is, as I explain in § 188, not the only means of bringing selling price into equality with cost of production. It is the part of applied economics to inquire whether free competition is always the best means.

he will *demand* those articles or services of which he thinks he has relatively too little for his consumption during a certain period of time. The quantities of each thing effectively demanded and offered having been determined in this way, the prices of those things for which the demand exceeds the offer will *rise*, and the prices of those things of which the offer exceeds the demand will *fall*. New prices having now been cried, each party to the exchange will offer and demand new quantities. And again prices will rise or fall until the demand and the offer of each good and each service are equal. Then the prices will be *current equilibrium prices* and exchange will effectively take place.

We pose the problem of production by enlarging the scope of the problem of exchange to include the fact that consumers' goods are products resulting either from a combination of productive services alone or from the application of these services to raw materials. In order to take this fact into account, we must think of the *land-owners, workers,* and *capitalists* as sellers of [productive] services and buyers of consumers' goods and services, standing face to face with sellers of products and buyers of productive services and raw materials. These latter sellers and buyers are the *entrepreneurs* who seek a profit by transforming productive services into products consisting either of raw materials which they sell to one another, or of consumers' goods which they sell to the land-owners, workers, and capitalists from whom they buy productive services. In this connection it will help us to gain a better understanding of the phenomena under consideration if we imagine two markets instead of one. Let one of these markets be the *services market*, where services are offered exclusively by land-owners, workers, and capitalists, and demanded, in so far as they are [directly] consumable services, by the selfsame land-owners, workers, and capitalists, and, in so far as they are productive services, by entrepreneurs. Let the other be the *products market*, where products are offered exclusively by entrepreneurs, and demanded, in so far as they are raw materials, by the selfsame entrepreneurs, and, in so far as they are consumers' goods, by land-owners, workers, and capitalists. At prices cried at random in these two markets, the land-owners, workers, and capitalists, in their capacity as consumers, will offer services and demand consumers' goods and services in order to procure the largest possible sum total of utility in the period considered. At the same time the entrepreneurs, in their capacity as producers, will offer products and demand productive services or raw materials to be delivered during this same period, in the measure required by the coefficients of production in the form of productive services. These entrepreneurs will expand output whenever the selling price of the products exceeds the cost of the productive services involved in their production; and they will reduce their output whenever the cost of these productive services exceeds the selling price. On each market, prices rise whenever demand exceeds supply, and fall whenever supply exceeds demand. The current equilibrium prices are those at which the demand and the supply of each service or product are equal and at which the *selling price* of each product is equal to the *cost of production*, i.e. the cost of the productive services employed.

In order to pose the problem of capital formation, we must assume that there are land-owners, workers, and capitalists who *save*, that is to say, who do not demand consumers' goods and services up to the total value of the services they offer, but demand *new capital goods* instead for part of this value. We must also assume that over against those who create savings, there are entrepreneurs who produce new capital goods in lieu of raw materials or consumers' goods. Given, therefore, a certain sum of savings on the one hand, and certain quantities of newly manufactured capital goods on the other hand, these savings and these new capital goods are exchanged against each other on the *capital goods market*, in a ratio which depends, in conformity with the mechanism of competition, on the prices of the consumers' and productive services yielded by the capital goods, these prices being determined by virtue of the theories of exchange and of production. Hence we have a certain rate of income, and for each capital good a certain selling price, which is equal to the ratio of the price of its service to the rate of income. The manufacturers of new capital goods, like those of consumers' goods, expand or contract their output according as the selling price exceeds the cost of production or the cost of production exceeds the selling price.

Once we have the rate of income [from capital goods], we can obtain not only the price of newly manufactured fixed capital goods, but also the price of old fixed capital goods (viz. land, personal faculties, and already existing capital goods proper) by dividing the prices of their services (i.e. rent, wages, and interest) by the rate of income. There remains, then, only to find the price of circulating capital and to see what becomes of all these prices when the *numéraire* is also money. This is the object of the problem of circulation and money.

We shall see in this fourth edition how the inclusion of the "desired cash balance" made it possible for me to state and solve this problem within this static framework in exactly the same terms and in precisely the same way as I solved the preceding problems. All I had to do was first to represent the circulating capital as rendering a *service of availability*, either *in kind* or *in money*; and then to look upon the offer of all such services as coming exclusively from capitalists, and the demand as coming, in part, so far as these services are *consumers' services*, from land-owners, workers, and capitalists in their pursuit of maximum satisfaction, and in part, so far as these services are *productive services*, from entrepreneurs to the extent of their need for certain coefficients of production in the form of services of availability. Thus the current prices of these services are determined exactly like the prices of all other services. Moreover, the prices of the circulating capital and of money are determined, in consequence, as ratios of the prices of their services of availability to the rate of income, the price of money, *qua* money, being established as an inverse function of its quantity.

This whole theory is mathematical. Although it may be described in ordinary language, the proof of the theory must be given mathematically. The proof rests wholly on the theory of exchange; and the theory of exchange can be summed up in its entirety in the following double condition of market equilibrium: first, that each party to the exchange attain maximum utility and secondly, that, for each and every commodity the aggregate quantity demanded equal the aggregate quantity offered by all parties. It is only with the aid of mathematics that we can understand what is meant by the condition of maximum utility, for, by attributing to each trading party an equation or curve relative to each consumers' good or service, in order to express the *rareté*, i.e. *the intensity of the last want satisfied*, as a decreasing function of the *quantity consumed*, mathematics enables us to see that a given party will obtain the greatest possible total satisfaction of his wants if he demands and offers commodities in such quantities when certain prices are cried that the *raretés* of these commodities are proportional to their prices upon completion of the exchange. Nor can we understand without mathematics why or how current equilibrium prices are arrived at not only in exchange, but also in production, capital formation and circulation, by raising the price of services, products and new capital goods, when demand exceeds supply, and by lowering the price in the contrary case. Mathematics renders all this intelligible, first of all by deducing from the *rareté* functions not only the functions which express the *offer* of services and the *demand* for services, products and new capital goods with a view to maximizing the satisfaction of wants, but also the equations which express equality between the demand and supply of these services, products and new capital goods; secondly, by combining these equations with other equations, those which express equality between the selling price and the cost of production of products and new capital goods and those which express uniformity in the rate of income from all new capital goods; and, finally, by demonstrating: (1) that the aforementioned problems of exchange, production, capital formation, and circulation are determinate problems, in the sense that the number of equations entailed is exactly equal to the number of the unknowns, and (2) that the upward and downward movement of market prices in conjunction with the effective flow of entrepreneurs from enterprises showing a loss to enterprises showing a profit is purely and simply a method of groping towards a solution of the equations involved in these problems.

Such is the system I am presenting in this volume with proofs which I have worked out as meticulously as I could. This system had already been published and demonstrated in the four memoirs that make up my *Théorie mathématique de la richesse sociale*, 1873–1876, and in the first edition of my *Eléments d'Economie Politique Pure*, 1874–1877. As soon as I had mastered the underlying principle of my theory as a whole, I felt it my duty to communicate it to the Académie des sciences morales et politiques in Paris; and I drafted the first of the four above-mentioned memoirs for this purpose. In that study I took the case of the exchange in kind of two commodities for each other and showed, at one and the same time, how the solution of the problem of maximum satisfaction of wants for each exchanging party is given by the proportionality of the intensities of the last wants satisfied to the values in exchange, and how the solution of the problem of the determination of the respective current prices of the two commodities is arrived at by a rise in price when demand exceeds offer and by a fall in price when offer exceeds demand. The Académie gave this paper a very bad and most discouraging reception. I grieve for this learned body, and I venture to say that after the double misfortune of awarding a prize to Canard and slighting Cournot, it might, in its own interest, have profited by this opportunity to establish its competence in economics a little more brilliantly. So far as I am concerned, the cold reception I had from the Académie actually brought me good luck, for since that time the doctrine I espoused twenty-seven years ago has gained wide acceptance both in form and content.

Everyone competent in the field knows that the theory of exchange based on the proportionality of prices to *intensities of the last wants satisfied* (i.e. to *Final Degrees of Utility* or *Grenznutzen*), which was evolved almost simultaneously by Jevons, Menger and myself, and which constitutes the very foundation of the whole edifice of economics, has become an integral part of the science in England, Austria, the United States, and wherever pure economics is developed and taught.

From the moment the principle of the theory of exchange found a place in the science, it was inevitable that the principle of the theory of production would soon follow, which it most effectively did. In the second edition of his *Theory of Political Economy* Jevons became aware of a point he had missed in the first edition, namely, that if the *Final Degree of Utility* determines the prices of products, it must also determine the prices of the productive services, i.e. the rent, wages, and interest, because the selling prices of products and the costs of the services employed in producing them tend towards equality under a régime of free competition. In May 1879 Jevons wrote ten remarkable pages at the close of the preface to his second edition (pp. xlviii–lvii), in which he clearly stated that the formula of the English school, in any case the school of Ricardo and Mill, must be reversed, for the prices of productive services are determined by the prices of their products and not the other way round. This fruitful suggestion was not immediately taken up in England; in fact, there was at first a reaction against Jevons's idea and in favour of the Ricardian cost of production theory. Nevertheless, the Austrian economists, having arrived independently at the conception of *Grenznutzen* in their theory of value in exchange, also carried this idea to its logical consequence in the theory of production. They established exactly the same relation between the value of *Produkte* and the value of *Produktivmittel* that I established between the value of products, on the one hand, and the value of raw materials and productive services, on the other

Our agreement is not so perfect, however, as regards the theory of capital formation, on which Carl Menger published an article entitled "Zur Theorie des Kapitals" in vol. XVII of the *Jahrbücher für Nationalökonomie und Statistik*. Menger's views were amplified by von Böhm-Bawerk, a professor at Innsbruck, in a book, entitled *Kapital und Kapitalzins*, 1884–1889, where he deduces the phenomenon of interest on capital from the difference between the value of a present good and that of a future good.[1] I must state plainly that on this point Böhm-Bawerk and I part company; and I should like to explain briefly why I cannot accept his theory. Such an explanation calls, however, for a mathematical formulation, if not of the entire theory in question, at least of the theory of the determination of the rate of interest which it implies.[2]

Let us open the first treatise on business finance that comes to hand, and we learn there that a thing worth A for spot delivery will only be worth

$$A' = \frac{A}{(1+i)^n}$$

[1] Menger's article and Böhm-Bawerk's book were very carefully reviewed in the *Revue d'économie politique* November–December 1888 and March–April 1889.

[2] The next paragraph is reprinted without any changes from my preface to the second edition written in May 1889 [pp. xxi–xxiii]. It will be seen that although in the text of that edition I still wrote the savings function as empirically given, even then I called attention in the preface to a way of establishing it rationally as a successively increasing and decreasing function of the rate of net income.

for future delivery n years from date, given the annual rate of interest i. Nevertheless, if we propose to use this formula as the basis of an economic theory of the determination of the rate of interest, we must first be told how A is determined, and then we have to be shown the market on which i is deduced from A' in conformity with the above equation. I have looked in vain for such a market. And that is why I persist in deriving i, if we disregard depreciation and insurance, from the equation

$$\frac{D_k p_k + D_{k'} p_{k'} + D_{k''} p_{k''} + \ldots}{i} = F_e(p_t \ldots p_p \ldots p_k, p_{k'}, p_{k''} \ldots p_b, p_c, p_d \ldots i)$$

in which p_k, $p_{k'}$, $p_{k''}$, i.e. the prices of the services of the capital goods (K), (K'), (K'') ..., are determined by the theories of exchange and production; D_k, $D_{k'}$, $D_{k''}$ ..., i.e. the quantities manufactured of these new capital goods, are determined by the condition of equality between their selling price and their cost of production or by the condition of uniformity of rate of income (which is also the condition of their maximum utility); and, finally,

$$F_e(p_t \ldots p_p \ldots p_k, p_{k'}, p_{k''} \ldots p_b, p_c, p_d \ldots i),$$

i.e. the [aggregate] amount of savings, is determined by the comparison which each saver makes, at the current price of services and products, between the utility for him of 1 to be consumed immediately and the utility for him of i to be consumed year in year out. The left-hand side of the above equation constitutes the supply of new capital goods in terms of *numéraire*, and is manifestly a decreasing function of i. The right-hand side constitutes the demand for new capital goods in terms of *numéraire*, and is a function of i which first increases and then decreases as i increases. The demanders are either the savers themselves or entrepreneurs who borrow savings in the form of money capital. Equality between the two sides of the equation is achieved through an increase or decrease in the price of new capital goods brought about by a fall or a rise in i, according as the demand is greater or less than the supply. The alert reader will notice immediately that this is exactly what takes place through fluctuations on the stock exchange where titles to property in new capital goods are exchanged against savings at prices proportional to their incomes. He will perceive, moreover, that my theory of capital formation, the whole of which, let me repeat, is based on the logically prior theories of exchange and production, is indeed what a theory of this kind ought to be, viz. the abstract expression and rational explanation of facts of the real world. While I am on this subject, may I remark to what extent my theorem of maximum utility of new capital goods confirms my whole system of pure economics. Admittedly, it is no great discovery to state that society realizes a gain in utility by withdrawing capital from an employment where it yields a lower interest in order to invest it in an employment where it yields a higher interest; but it seems to me that to have demonstrated mathematically so plausible and even so evident a truth argues strongly in favour of the definitions and methods of analysis by which this truth was reached.

The final decision in this controversy must eventually be left to mathematicians. Even today there are a few to whom I would confidently take my case. Soon after publication, Jevons's theory and my own were translated into Italian, as were the earlier essays of Whewell and Cournot. Then, in Germany, Gossen's book, at first unnoticed, was added to the already known works of von Thünen and

Mangoldt. Since that time a considerable number of books on mathematical economics have appeared in Germany, Austria, England, Italy, and the United States.[1] The school which is gradually coming into being will have no difficulty in discerning which system, among so many, should constitute the science. As for those economists who do not know any mathematics, who do not even know what is meant by mathematics and yet have taken the stand that mathematics cannot possibly serve to elucidate economic principles, let them go their way repeating that "human liberty will *never* allow itself to be cast into equations" or that "mathematics ignores frictions which are *everything* in social science" and other equally forceful and flowery phrases. They can never prevent the theory of the determination of prices under free competition from becoming a mathematical theory. Hence, they will always have to face the alternative either of steering clear of this discipline and consequently elaborating a theory of applied economics without recourse to a theory of pure economics or of tackling the problems of pure economics without the necessary equipment, thus producing not only very bad pure economics but also very bad mathematics. If the reader will turn to Lesson 40, he will find samples of these theories that are just as mathematical as mine, but that differ from mine in this, that I feel constrained to have always as many equations as there are unknowns in my problems, while the illustrious authors of the theories cited in Lesson 40 allow themselves sometimes to determine one and the same unknown by means of two equations and sometimes to use a single equation to solve for two, three, and even four unknowns. It is very unlikely, at least so I hope, that such procedures will continue indefinitely to stand in the way of a method which promises to convert pure economics into an exact science.

In any case, the establishment sooner or later of economics as an exact science is no longer in our hands and need not concern us. It is already perfectly clear that economics, like astronomy and mechanics, is both an empirical and a rational science. And no one can reproach our science with having taken an unduly long time in becoming rational as well as empirical. It took from a hundred to a hundred and fifty or two hundred years for the astronomy of Kepler to become the astronomy of Newton and Laplace, and for the mechanics of Galileo to become the mechanics of d'Alembert and Lagrange. On the other hand, less than a century has elapsed between the publication of Adam Smith's work and the contributions

[1] These books are listed with earlier writings on the same subject in Professor Irving Fisher's *Bibliography of Mathematical Economics*, which was inserted as an appendix to Mr. T. N. Bacon's translation of Cournot's *Researches into the Mathematical Principles of the Theory of Wealth*. The translation was published in an American collection of Economic Classics [edited by W. J. Ashley; N.Y., Macmillan, 1897, reprinted 1927, pp.173–213].

of Cournot, Gossen, Jevons, and myself. We were, therefore, at our post, and have performed our duty. If nineteenth-century France, which was the cradle of the new science, has completely ignored it, the fault lies in the idea, so bourgeois in its narrowness, of dividing education into two separate compartments: one turning out calculators with no knowledge whatsoever of sociology, philosophy, history, or economics; and the other cultivating men of letters devoid of any notion of mathematics. The twentieth century, which is not far off, will feel the need, even in France, of entrusting the social sciences to men of general culture who are accustomed to thinking both inductively and deductively and who are familiar with reason as well as experience. Then mathematical economics will rank with the mathematical sciences of astronomy and mechanics; and on that day justice will be done to our work.

Lausanne, June 1900.   L.W.

PART 1

*Object and Divisions
of Political and Social Economy*

Lesson 1

DEFINITIONS OF POLITICAL ECONOMY
ADAM SMITH; J. B. SAY

1. In beginning a course or treatise on political economy, the first step is to define the science, setting forth its object, divisions, nature and scope. I have no thought of evading this obligation; but I must point out that it takes longer and is more difficult to fulfil than one might suppose. A satisfactory definition of political economy is still wanting. Of all the definitions proposed thus far, not one has met with the general and final assent which is the mark of established scientific truths. I shall quote and criticize the most significant of these definitions, and I shall endeavour to present my own. In performing this task, I shall find occasion to bring in certain names, titles of books and dates that should be known.

2. Quesnay and his disciples form the first important group of economists. Having a common doctrine they constitute a school. They themselves call their doctrine *Physiocracy*, that is to say, the natural government of society; and for this reason they are known today as Physiocrats. Besides Quesnay, who wrote the *Tableau économique* (1758), the principal Physiocrats are Mercier de la Rivière, author of *L'ordre naturel et essentiel des sociétés politiques* (1767), Dupont de Nemours, author of *Physiocratie ou constitution naturelle du gouvernement le plus avantageux au genre humain* (1767–1768), the Abbé Baudeau, and Le Trosne. Turgot belongs to a separate category. It is evident from the titles of their books that the Physiocrats enlarged instead of narrowing the scope of the science. The theory of the natural government of society is not so much political economy as it is social science. Thus the term Physiocracy implies too wide a definition.

3. Adam Smith in his *Inquiry into the Nature and Causes of the Wealth of Nations*, published in 1776, made the first attempt to organize the subject matter of political economy as a distinct branch of study, and he did this with remarkable success. It was not, however, until he came to the introduction to Book IV of the *Wealth of Nations*, where he treats "Of Systems of Political Economy", that it occurred to him to frame a definition of the science. And this is the definition he gives there:

Political economy, considered as a branch of the science of a statesman or legislator, proposes two distinct objects: first, to provide a plentiful revenue or subsistence for the people, or more properly to enable them to provide such a revenue or subsistence for themselves; and secondly, to supply the state or commonwealth with a revenue sufficient for the public services. It proposes to enrich both the people and the sovereign.[1]

This definition, coming from the reputed "father of political economy", deserves careful consideration, especially since he set it down not at the beginning but well on towards the middle of his *Inquiry*, when he had presumably acquired a complete grasp of his subject. There are two important observations that I should like to make in this connection.

4. To provide a plentiful revenue for the people and to supply the State with a sufficient income are incontestably most worthy aims. If political economy helps to achieve this double purpose, it renders a signal service. But it seems to me that this is not, strictly speaking, the object of a science. Indeed the distinguishing characteristic of a science is the complete indifference to consequences, good or bad, with which it carries on the pursuit of pure truth. Thus when the geometer states that an *equilateral triangle is at the same time equiangular* and when the astronomer states that *the planets move in an elliptical orbit at one of the foci of which is the sun*, they are making statements which are scientific in the strict sense of the term. It is possible that the first of these two truths, like all the other truths of geometry, may yield results of inestimable value to carpentry, stone cutting, and to every type of architecture or construction; it is possible that the second and the whole body of astronomical truths may be of the greatest service to navigation; still neither the carpenter, nor the mason, nor the architect, nor the navigator, nor even those who work out the theories of carpentry, stone cutting, architecture, or navigation are scientists or creators of science strictly speaking. Now the two lines of action of which Adam Smith speaks are analogous, not to those of the geometer and the astronomer, but to those of the architect and the navigator. Thus if political economy were simply what Adam Smith said it was, and nothing else, it would certainly be a very interesting subject, but it would not be a science in the narrow sense of the term. It must be pointed out that political economy is not quite what Adam Smith thought. The primary concern of the economist is not to provide a plentiful revenue for the people or to supply the State with an adequate income, but to pursue and master purely scientific truths. That is precisely what economists do when they assert, for example, that *the value of a thing tends to increase as the quantity demanded increases or as the quantity supplied decreases, and that this value tends to diminish under contrary conditions*; that *the rate of interest declines in a progressive economy*; that *a tax levied on ground rent falls exclusively on the land-owner without*

affecting the prices of the products of the land. In making statements such as these, economists are working in a pure science. Adam Smith did something of this sort himself. His disciples, Malthus and Ricardo, did more—the former in his *Essay on the Principles of Population* (1798) and the latter in his *Principles of Political Economy and Taxation* (1817). Hence Adam Smith's definition is incomplete, because it fails to mention the aim of political economy considered as a science strictly speaking. Indeed, to say that the object of political economy is to provide a plentiful revenue and to supply the State with an adequate income is like saying that the object of geometry is to build strong houses and that the aim of astronomy is to navigate the high seas in safety. This, in short, is to define a science in terms of its applications.

5. My first observation on Adam Smith's definition had to do with the object of the science. Now I have another, no less important observation to make concerning the nature of the science.

To provide an income for the people and to supply the State with a sufficient revenue are two operations of equal importance and delicacy, but very distinct in character. The first operation consists in placing agriculture, industry and trade in such and such determinate conditions. According as these conditions are favourable or unfavourable, the agricultural, industrial and commercial output will be abundant or scanty. It has been observed, for example, that in times gone by, industry languished and stagnated under a system of guilds, trade regulations and price fixing. It is evident today that under the opposite system of freedom of enterprise and freedom of trade, industry grows and prospers. Say what we will about the shortcomings of the earlier situation and the merits of the present order, our judgement is founded solely on considerations of material advantage; justice does not come in question one way or the other. The problem of supplying the State with sufficient revenue is an entirely different matter. In fact, this operation consists in deducting from individual incomes the amounts necessary to make up the community income. This takes place under good or bad conditions. The character of these conditions is determined not only by the sufficiency or insufficiency of the State's revenue, but also by the fairness or unfairness with which individuals are treated. They are treated fairly if each contributes his proportional share, and unfairly if some are sacrificed while others are given special privileges. Thus in the past some classes were exempt from taxation, while certain other classes bore the entire burden. Today such a system is considered flagrantly unjust. Thus the aim in procuring a plentiful revenue for the people is practical expediency, whereas in supplying the State with a sufficient revenue the aim is equity. Practical expediency and fairness, or material well-being and justice, are two very different orders of consideration.[2] Adam Smith ought to have stressed this difference by saying, for example, that the aim of political economy is to set forth first the conditions for the production of a *plentiful* social income and second the conditions for an *equitable* division of this income between individuals and the State. Such a definition would have been an improvement, but it would still pass by the really scientific aspect of political economy.[a]

6. Jean Baptiste Say, the most illustrious of the immediate successors of Adam Smith, said of his predecessor's definition, "I prefer to say that the aim of political economy is to show the ways in which wealth is produced, distributed and consumed."[3] Say's work, the first edition of which appeared in 1803 while the second, banned by Consular censorship, was not published until after the fall of the First Empire, is entitled *Traité d'économie politique, ou simple exposition de la manière dont se forment, se distribuent et se consomment les richesses*.[4] This definition and the time-honoured divisions of the subject which it sets up have been widely approved and generally adopted by economists. They may be regarded as classic. I venture, however, to reject them for the very reasons that have contributed to their success.

7. It is evident at a glance that J. B. Say's definition is not only different from Adam Smith's, but, from a certain point of view, is its exact opposite. According to Adam Smith's view, the whole of political economy is an *art* rather than a *science* (§4); while, according to Say, it is entirely a *natural* science. From Say's definition it would seem that the *production*, *distribution*, and *consumption* of wealth take place, if not spontaneously, at least in a *manner* somehow independent of the will of man, and as though political economy consisted entirely of a *simple exposition* of this manner of production, distribution and consumption.

What has proved so pleasing and at the same time so misleading to economists in this definition is precisely its characterization of the whole of political economy as a natural science pure and simple. Such a point of view was particularly useful to them in their controversy with the socialists. Every proposal to reorganize production, every proposal to redistribute property was rejected *a priori* and practically without discussion, not on the grounds that such plans were contrary to economic well-being or to social justice, but simply because they were artificial arrangements designed to replace what was natural. Moreover, this naturalistic viewpoint had been taken over from the Physiocrats by J. B. Say and was inspired by the formula, *laissez-faire, laissez-passer*, which summarizes the Physiocratic doctrine relating to industry and trade. Such an attitude led

Proudhon to hurl the epithet *fatalistic* at this school of economists. To appreciate fully the incredible lengths to which they carried their conclusions, one should read certain articles in the *Dictionnaire de l'économie politique*, such as those of Charles Coquelin on "Concurrence", "Economie politique" and "Industrie" or André Cochut's article on "Morale".[5] There are very revealing passages in these articles.

Unfortunately, convenient as this point of view is, it is mistaken. If men were nothing more than a superior species of animal, like bees that live and work together instinctively, then, to be sure, the description and explanation of social phenomena in general and of the production, distribution and consumption of wealth in particular would be a natural science. Indeed, it would be a branch of natural history, viz. the natural history of man, a sequel to the natural history of bees. But this is not the case at all. Man is a creature endowed with reason and freedom, and possessed of a capacity for initiative and progress. In the production and distribution of wealth, and generally in all matters pertaining to social organization, man has the choice between better and worse and tends more and more to choose the better part. Thus man has progressed from a system of guilds, trade regulations and price fixing to a system of freedom of industry and trade, i.e. to a system of *laisser-faire, laisser-passer*; he has progressed from slavery to serfdom and from serfdom to the wage system. The superiority of the later forms of organization over the earlier forms lies not in their greater naturalness (both old and new are artificial, the newer forms more so than the old, since they came into existence only by supplanting the old); but rather in their closer conformity with material well-being and justice. The proof of such conformity is the only justification for adhering to a policy of *laisser-faire, laisser-passer*. Moreover, socialistic forms of organization should be rejected if it can indeed be shown that they are inconsistent with material well-being and justice.

8. J. B. Say's definition is therefore inaccurate and inferior to Adam Smith's which was only incomplete. I contend, furthermore, that the divisions of the subject that follow from Say's definition are purely empirical. Though the theory of property and the theory of taxation are simply two aspects of one and the same theory of the distribution of wealth in human society, the first representing this society as composed of separate individuals and the second representing it as a collectivity in the shape of the State, and though both the theory of property and the theory of taxation are so intimately dependent on ethical principles, yet Say separates the two, throwing the theory of property in with the theory of production, and the theory of taxation in with the theory of consumption, treating both

from an exclusively economic point of view. On the other hand, the theory of value in exchange, which bears so clearly the mark of a natural science, is included by Say in his theory of distribution. Say's disciples, it is true, have taken his arbitrary categories none too seriously, and with no less arbitrariness some classify the theory of value in exchange under the theory of production while others classify the theory of property under the theory of distribution. This is the sort of political economy which is being fashioned and taught today. Is that not reason enough to hold that the structure is cracked and the façade deceptive and that in such a case it is the right and the primary duty of the economist carefully to formulate a philosophy of his science?

9. Even though some of Say's students dimly perceived the defectiveness of his definition, they did nothing to remedy it.

Adolphe Blanqui has written:

In Germany and France economists have gone furthest outside the true field which today is generally assigned to political economy. Some have attempted to make it a universal science; others have tried to confine it to narrow, trivial limits. The present conflict in France between these two opposite schools turns upon the question whether political economy should be considered as an explanation of what is or as a programme of what ought to be. In other words, is political economy a natural science or a moral science? In our view, it is both. . . . [3]

Blanqui thus approves J. B. Say's definition for the very reason that serves so well to condemn it.

Later, Joseph Garnier wrote:

Political economy is at one and the same time a natural and a moral science. From these two points of view, it sets forth that which is and that which ought to be according to the natural course of things and in conformity with the idea of justice. [3]

Consequently Garnier proposes to modify J. B. Say's definition by making a slight addition to it. Thus he says:

Political economy is the science of wealth, that is, the science which seeks to determine how wealth *is* and *ought to be* produced, exchanged, distributed and utilized as rationally (naturally and equitably) as possible, both in the interest of individuals and in the interest of the whole community. [3]

Garnier here makes an earnest and most praiseworthy effort to get out of the rut into which his school had fallen. It is strange that he did not immediately perceive how fantastic and incoherent was the result of this interweaving and fusion of two separate definitions into one. This is a curious example of that absence of philosophy among French economists which offsets and nullifies so many of their intellectual qualities, among which the most outstanding are clarity and precision. [6] How could political economy be simultaneously a natural science and a moral science? How is such a science to be understood? On the one hand, we have a moral science the aim of which is to determine how wealth *ought to be* distributed as equitably as possible; and on the other hand, we have a natural science the aim of which is to determine how wealth *is* produced as naturally as possible. In short, Say's definition clearly leads us back to Adam Smith's (§5); and in all this discussion the true conception of a natural science eludes us as much as ever.

We shall undertake to look for it on our own account. If necessary we shall divide political economy into a natural science, a moral science and an art. To this end we shall first of all distinguish between science, art and ethics.[b]

SCIENCE, ART AND ETHICS DISTINGUISHED

10. Several years ago Charles Coquelin, author of a reputable *Traité du crédit et des banques*,[1] and one of the most active and esteemed contributors to the *Dictionnaire de l'économie politique*,[2] observed in this dictionary under "Economie Politique" that political economy had yet to be defined. In support of this assertion he cited not only the definitions of Adam Smith and J. B. Say which I quoted earlier, but also those of Sismondi, Storch and Rossi. He pointed out the differences among them and declared that not one had gained final acceptance. Coquelin went so far as to prove that the authors of these definitions were the first to depart from them in their own works. Then he very wisely observed that before defining political economy we must ask whether it is a science or an art, or whether it may not be both one and the other simultaneously. The first thing he did was to distinguish clearly between the two. Coquelin's discussion of this subject is remarkably apt, and since the problem raised is still where he left it, we shall do well to quote him.

An art (he says) consists . . . of a set of precepts or rules to be followed, a science consists of knowledge of certain phenomena or relationships which have been observed or discovered. . . . Art advises, prescribes and directs; science observes, describes and explains. When an astronomer observes and describes the course of the stars, he is engaged in scientific work; but when after making his observations he deduces from them rules of navigation he is creating an art. . . . Thus the observation and description of real phenomena is science, while the formulation of precepts and the prescription of rules is art.

11. Coquelin, in a footnote, adds a remark which clarifies the distinction and which deserves to be quoted.

The very real distinction (he says) which we have made between science and art has nothing to do with the distinction which, rightly or wrongly, is made between theory and practice. There are theories of art just as there are theories of science, but only of the former can it be said that they are sometimes in conflict with practice. The rules that an art prescribes are general rules, and it is not unreasonable to suppose that these rules, however sound, may be at variance with practice in particular cases. The same cannot be said of science which lays down no rules, gives no advice and formulates no precepts, but which simply observes and explains. In what way could science ever come into conflict with practice?

12. Having thus differentiated between art and science, Coquelin clearly indicates their respective roles and their relative importance.

Far be it from us to find it deplorable or strange that men try to infer rules of action for everyday life from such scientific truths as are founded on accurate observation and careful deduction. It is not a good thing for scientific truths to remain sterile, and the only way to make them useful is to make them the basis for art. As we have already noted, there is a close relationship between science and art. Science clarifies art with its fund of knowledge, it helps to perfect the technique, illumine the path and direct the course of art. Without the aid of science, art could only grope in the dark, stumbling at each step. From another point of view, without art the truths which science has discovered would remain sterile; it is art which makes them fruitful. Almost invariably the principal driving force behind the scientist's labours is the practical application of his discoveries. Man rarely studies solely for the pleasure of knowing. Generally his work has a utilitarian end in view which can only be attained by means of an art.

13. None the less Coquelin insists that a distinction must be drawn between science and art. In support of his position he makes a further remark which deserves mention.

It is all the more important (he says) to emphasize the distinction which we have just made between science and art, because they are far from coinciding at all points, however much they really have in common. The contributions of any one science can sometimes find use in many different arts. For example, geometry, the science of space relations, illuminates and guides the work of the engineer, the surveyor, the artilleryman, the navigator, the ship-builder, the architect, etc. Chemistry is of assistance not only to the pharmacist but also to the dyer and to a host of other industrial callings. Conversely, any one art can make use of the information furnished by several sciences. Thus, to cite only one example, medicine, or the art of healing, draws upon the contributions of anatomy, physiology, chemistry, physics, botany, etc.

14. To conclude, Charles Coquelin endeavours to show how appropriate and fruitful this distinction between art and science can be when applied to the definition of political economy and to the classification of its subject matter. And he adds:

From now on, shall we attempt to draw a sharper line between art and science by giving them different names? No. It is enough for us to have made clear that there is a distinction. Time and a better understanding of the subject will do the rest.

This reserve is astonishing. It is strange that a writer, after having hit upon so good an idea, should thus voluntarily forgo the pleasure and the honour that he might have had in following it through. And it is stranger still that Coquelin should have failed utterly, in the genuine attempt which he made, despite his professions to the contrary, to bring about a separation between economic art and economic science in the course of his discussion of the true object of political economy. So unsuccessful was he that, far from dispelling the confusion to which he had called attention, he deepened the confusion by mistaking elements of art for those of science and by sticking to a conception of industrial phenomena too deeply imbued with the naturalistic and Physiocratic point of view—a view which I condemned in J. B. Say (§7) and from which his followers have never been able to free themselves. Certainly he is lost in utter confusion when he asks: *Is economic science a study of wealth or of industry, the source of wealth?* or when he inquires: *Why has wealth rather than human industry been taken as the subject matter of political economy?* and *what have been the consequences of this error?* and finally when he declares that *the established characteristic of economic science* is that *it is a branch of the natural history of mankind.* He could not possibly have gone further astray despite all his elaborate precautions.

15. Such results are likely to lead to the conclusion that the very idea of a distinction between art and science is not as appropriate to our purpose as it seems. And yet this distinction is perfectly applicable to political economy. There is a theory of wealth, that is, a theory of exchange and value in exchange, which is a science, and a theory of the production of wealth, that is, a theory of agriculture, industry and trade, which is an art. Once this has been pointed out, only a moment's reflection is necessary to convince anyone who is free from sectarian prejudice. We must hasten to add, however, that the distinction, while valid, is incomplete because the distribution of wealth is left out.

This is immediately apparent as soon as we recall Blanqui's observation that political economy may be considered both as an *explanation of what is* and *as a programme of what ought to be.* Now, what ought to be, should be considered as such either from the point of view of expediency or material well-being, or from the point of view of equity or justice. What ought to be from the point of view of material well-being is the concern of applied science or art; while what ought to be from the point of view of justice is the concern of moral science or ethics. Blanqui and Garnier are evidently thinking of what ought to be from the standpoint of justice since they speak of political economy as a moral science and are preoccupied with right and justice and with fairness in the distribution of wealth (§9). Coquelin, however, evidently missed this point of view, for, while calling attention to the distinction to be made between art and science, he failed to announce the need to distinguish between art and ethics.[a] Let us, on our side, not overlook anything. Let us take up the whole question in its entirety and follow the distinction through rationally, completely and definitively.[b]

16. We have to distinguish between science, art and ethics. In other words, we must sketch the general philosophy of science in

order to arrive at the particular philosophy of political and social economy.

A truth long ago demonstrated by the Platonic philosophy is that science does not study corporeal entities but universals of which these entities are manifestations. Corporeal entities come and go, but universals remain for ever. Universals, their relations, and their laws, are the object of all scientific study. Moreover, the various sciences can differ only with respect to their subject matter, or the facts they study. Thus, in order to classify sciences, we must classify facts.

17. Now, the first point to notice is that we may divide the facts of our universe into two categories: those which result from the play of the blind and ineluctable forces of nature and those which result from the exercise of the human will, a force that is free and cognitive. Facts of the first category are found in nature, and that is why we call them *natural* phenomena. Facts of the second category are found in man, and that is why we call them *human* phenomena. Alongside the many blind and ineluctable forces of the universe there exists a force which is self-conscious and independent, namely, the will of man. It may be that this force is not quite as self-conscious and independent as it supposes itself to be. It is only after a study of the will of man that we can tell. For our immediate purpose such a study would be of secondary interest. The essential point is that, at least within certain limits, the human will is self-conscious and independent. This is what makes its operations so profoundly different from those of other forces. Obviously all one can do about manifestations of the forces of nature is to identify, verify and explain them; but in dealing with the workings of the human will, not only is it possible to identify, verify and explain them, but having done that, one can then control them.[e] This clearly follows from the fact that natural forces are not at all conscious of their actions, nor can they possibly act in any other way than they do; whereas the human will is conscious of its acts and can act in several ways. The operations of the forces of nature constitute the subject matter of what is called *pure natural science* or *science* properly speaking. The operations of the human will constitute, in the first place, the subject matter of what is called *pure moral science* or *history*, and, in the second place, as will be seen presently, the subject matter of a study to which another name, either art or ethics, is attached. Thus, without going any further, we arrive at a justification for Coquelin's distinction between science and art (§10). Art "advises, prescribes and directs", inasmuch as it deals with phenomena originating in the exercise of the human will, which, being free and cognitive, at least up to a certain point, is capable of receiving advice, of having such and such a course of

action prescribed to it, and of being directed. Science "observes, describes and explains", inasmuch as it deals with phenomena originating in the play of natural forces, the operations of which, being blind and ineluctable, are not amenable to anything but observation, description and explanation.

18. In this way, we come anew upon an understanding of the distinction between science and art, not, as Coquelin did, empirically, but methodically after taking into account the freedom and cognitive nature of the human will. Our next task is to distinguish between art and ethics. It is by starting again from a consideration of the freedom and cognitive nature of the human will, or at least from some consequence of its freedom and percipience, that we shall find a principle which, by dividing human phenomena into two categories, leads to the distinction between art and ethics.

The fact that man's will is cognitive and free makes it possible to divide every entity in the universe into two great classes: *persons* and *things*. Whatsoever is not conscious of itself and not master of itself is a thing. Whatsoever is conscious of itself and master of itself is a person. Man, being both self-conscious and self-directing, is a person. Man alone is a person; minerals, plants and animals are things.

From the rational point of view, the purpose of things is under the dominion of the purpose of persons. Since a thing is neither self-conscious nor self-directing, it is not responsible for the pursuit of its ends or for the fulfilment of its destiny. Being just as incapable of evil as it is of good, it is always completely innocent and can be likened to a pure mechanism. In this respect animals do not differ from minerals and plants: an animal's instinct is a blind and ineluctable force like any other natural force. A person, on the other hand, just because he is conscious of himself and master of himself, is charged with responsibility for the pursuit of his ends and for the fulfilment of his destiny. If he succeeds, he has merit; if not, he takes blame. He has, therefore, an unlimited faculty for *subordinating* the purpose of things to his own purpose. This faculty, in all its length and breadth, is invested with a particular character. It is not only a moral power, it is a right. This is the basis of the right of persons over things.

But while the purpose of all things is under the dominion of the purpose of all persons, no one person's destiny is ever subordinated to the destiny of any other person. If there were only one man in the world he would be master of all things. Since this is not the case, as long as every man in the world is just as much a person as anyone else, each equally responsible for the pursuit of his ends and for the fulfilment of his destiny, all these ends and aims have to be mutually *co-ordinated.* Here we have the origin of the reciprocation of rights and duties among persons.

19. It will be seen from the foregoing that a fundamental distinction must be drawn in the realm of human phenomena. We have to place in one category those phenomena which are manifestations of the human will, i.e. of human actions in respect to natural forces. This category comprises the relations between persons and things. In another category we have to place the phenomena that result from the impact of the human will or of human actions on the will or actions of other men This second category comprises the relations between persons and persons. The laws of these two classes of phenomena are essentially different The object of bringing the human will to bear upon natural forces, that is to say, the object of relations between persons and things, is the subordination of the purpose of things to the purpose of persons. The object of exercising the human will on the will of others, in other words, the object of relations between persons and persons, is the mutual co-ordination of human destinies.

Translating this distinction into appropriate definitions, I call the sum total of phenomena of the first category *industry*, and the sum total of phenomena of the second category *institutions*. The theory of industry is called *applied science* or *art*; the theory of institutions *moral science* or *ethics*.

It is, therefore, a necessary and sufficient condition for any phenomenon to be classified under the heading of industry and for the theory of this phenomenon to be some art or other, that the phenomenon in question originate in the exercise of the human will and that it consist of a relationship between persons and things designed to subordinate the purpose of things to the purpose of persons. This characteristic, it will be noted, is common to all the arts cited in the above-mentioned examples, be it architecture, shipbuilding, or navigation. Thus, architecture implies the use of wood and stone in the erection of houses; shipbuilding calls to mind the use of hemp for rope-making, and wood and iron in the construction of vessels; and navigation indicates ways of trimming, setting and manœuvring sails. The sea bears the vessels, the wind fills the sails, and the stars in the heavens point the way to the navigator.

Moreover, for any phenomenon to be classified under the heading of institutions and for the theory of this phenomenon to constitute a branch of ethics, it is necessary and sufficient that this phenomenon too originate in the exercise of the human will and, besides, that it consist of a relationship between persons and persons designed for the mutual co-ordination of the destinies of the persons concerned. So, for example, in matters pertaining to marriage and the family, it is ethics which determines the role and position of husband and wife and of parents and children.

20. Such, then, are the distinguishing characteristics of science, art and ethics. Their respective *criteria* are the *true*; the *useful*, meaning material well-being; and the *good*, meaning justice. Now, let us ask whether in a comprehensive study of wealth and related phenomena there is subject matter for only one of the above categories of intellectual inquiry, for two of them, or for all three? We shall look into this question in the following Lesson which deals with an analysis of the concept of wealth.[d]

Lesson 3

SOCIAL WEALTH. THREE CONSEQUENCES OF SCARCITY. VALUE IN EXCHANGE AND THE PURE THEORY OF ECONOMICS

21. By *social wealth* I mean all things, material or immaterial (it does not matter which in this context), that are *scarce*,[1] that is to say, on the one hand, *useful* to us and, on the other hand, only available to us *in limited quantity*.

Since this definition is fundamental, I am going to scrutinize its terms.

I say that things are useful whenever they can be put to any use at all; whenever they are seen to be capable of satisfying a want. In this connection, there is no need to consider the subtle shades of meaning classified in ordinary language under terms ranging from the necessary to the useful, from the useful to the agreeable, from the agreeable to the superfluous. For present purposes, necessary, useful, agreeable and superfluous simply mean more or less useful. Furthermore, we need not concern ourselves with the morality or immorality of any desire which a useful thing answers or serves to satisfy. From other points of view the question of whether a drug is wanted by a doctor to cure a patient, or by a murderer to kill his family is a very serious matter, but from our point of view, it is totally irrelevant. So far as we are concerned, the drug is useful in both cases, and may even be more so in the latter case than in the former.

I say that things are available to us only in a limited quantity whenever they do not exist in such quantities that each of us can find at hand enough completely to satisfy his desires. There are a certain number of utilities in this world, which, when present at all, are available to us in unlimited quantities. Such are atmospheric air, the light and warmth of the sun in daytime, and water, which exists in such quantities in lakes, rivers and streams, that no one need go without; everyone can take as much as he wishes from the water's edge. These things, though useful, are generally not scarce and are consequently not items of social wealth. Under exceptional circumstances they may become scarce, and then they do become part of social wealth.

22. From this one can see in what sense the words *scarce* and *scarcity* are used here. They are given scientific meaning like the word *velocity* in mechanics and the word *heat* in physics. The

65

mathematician and the physicist do not oppose velocity to slowness and heat to cold as is done in ordinary language. To the mathematician slowness means only less velocity; to the physicist cold means less heat. In the language of science, a body has velocity as soon as it moves at all; it has heat whenever it has any temperature at all. In the same way, scarcity and abundance are not opposed for our purposes. In political economy, however abundant a thing may be, it is scarce whenever it is useful and limited in quantity, just as in mechanics a body has velocity whenever it travels a given distance within a given time.[a] Does this mean that scarcity is a ratio of utility to quantity, i.e. the utility per unit of quantity, in the same manner that velocity is the ratio of distance passed over to the time taken to pass over it, i.e. the distance travelled per unit of time? We shall leave this question in suspense for the moment since we shall come back to it later.[2] For the present let us note that three consequences follow from the limitation in quantity, or from the scarcity, of useful things.

23. (1) Useful things limited in quantity are *appropriable*. Useless things are not appropriated, for it never occurs to anyone to appropriate things which cannot be put to any use. Useful things which exist in unlimited quantities, are also not amenable to appropriation. In the first place, however much one might wish to do so, this kind of thing cannot possibly be seized as a whole and brought under control, because there is too much of it. It cannot be withdrawn in its entirety from the public domain. In the second place, what would be the good of setting aside a small fraction of such a thing, since the remainder, which would still be the greater part, would be at everyone's disposal? Should an individual wish to make a profit out of what he sets aside, where would the demand for it come from, since everyone can always help himself to as much as he wants? Should he wish to reserve the appropriated fraction for his own use later on, what would be the sense of laying up stocks of a thing of which he is always sure to find as much as he wants? Why should anyone store up atmospheric air (I mean under ordinary conditions), since he will never have occasion to give it to anyone else and needs only to inhale whenever he wants to breathe? On the other hand, useful things which exist only in limited quantity are capable of being appropriated and actually are appropriated. In the first place, these things are amenable to seizure and control, in view of the fact that it is physically possible for a certain number of individuals to gather the entire existing quantity of such a thing for themselves, with none of it left in the public domain. In the second place, those who do this reap a double advantage: not only do they assure themselves of a supply which can be reserved for their own use and satisfaction; but,

if they are unwilling or unable to consume all of their original supply themselves, they are also in a position to exchange the unwanted remainder for other scarce utilities which they do care to consume. To pursue this line of thought further would lead into matters which do not concern us here. For the present we need only note that *appropriation* (and consequently the *ownership of property*, which is legalized appropriation, or appropriation in conformity with justice) is applicable to all of social wealth and nothing but social wealth.

24. (2) We have just intimated that useful things limited in quantity are *valuable and exchangeable*. Once all things that can be appropriated (that is, all scarce things and nothing else) have been appropriated, they stand in a certain relationship to each other, a relationship which stems from the fact that each scarce thing, in addition to its own specific utility, acquires a special property, namely, that of being exchangeable against any other scarce thing in such and such a determinate ratio. An individual owning any one of these scarce things can, by giving it up, acquire some other scarce thing which he lacks. He can get what he does not possess only on condition that he surrender some other scarce object which he has in his possession. If he has nothing to give in exchange, he will have to do without what he lacks. Such is the phenomenon of *value in exchange*, which, like the phenomenon of property, applies to all social wealth and nothing but social wealth.

25. (3) Useful things limited in quantity are *things that can be produced and multiplied by industry*. In other words, they are reproducible. I mean by this that it is worth while producing them and increasing their quantity as much as possible by regular and systematic efforts. Besides these things the world contains certain useless things (not to speak of harmful ones), such as weeds and animals for which man has found no use. They call for no action from us, apart from a systematic attempt to discover in them properties which will take them out of the class of useless things and render them useful. Then there are things that are useful, but unlimited in quantity. We ought to make sure that we are making use of them, but evidently we need not give any thought to increasing their quantity. Finally, there are useful things that are limited in quantity. These are the scarce things. It is obvious that only things in this last category need be examined and acted upon with a view to making their quantity less limited than it is; and it is equally obvious that without exception, everything in this category can and should be so examined and acted upon. Taking the definition of social wealth given above, as the sum total of scarce things, we may now state that *industrial production*, that is, *industry*, like appropriation and value in exchange, is applicable to all social wealth, and nothing but social wealth.

26. *Value in exchange, industry* and *property* are, then, the three generic phenomena or the three orders or groups of specific facts which result from the limitation in quantity of utilities or the scarcity of things. All three are bound up with the whole of social wealth and nothing else. Now we see how vague it is, how loose, how unphilosophical, perhaps even wrong, to say, as Rossi did, for instance, in his opening remarks on political economy, that its object is to study social wealth. From what point of view shall we study it? Shall we do it from the point of view of *value in exchange*, that is, from the point of view of the influences of purchase and sale to which social wealth is subject? Or shall we do it from the point of view of *industrial production*, that is, from the point of view of the conditions which favour or hinder the increase in quantity of social wealth? Or, finally, shall we do it from the point of view of *property*, the object of which is social wealth, that is to say, from the point of view of the conditions which render the appropriation of social wealth legitimate or illegitimate? We must make up our minds. Above all, we must be exceedingly careful not to study social wealth from all three points of view at once or from any two of them simultaneously; for, as we shall find later, nothing could be more incongruous.[b]

27. We have seen *a priori* how scarce things, once appropriated, acquire value in exchange (§24). We need only look around us to establish *a posteriori* the fact of exchange as a generic phenomenon.

All of us in our daily life make exchanges by a series of special acts known as purchases and sales. Some of us sell land or the use of land, or the fruits thereof; some sell houses, or the use of houses; some sell at retail industrial products or merchandise previously bought at wholesale; some sell consultations, others legal pleading, still others works of art and there are those who sell days or hours of labour. All receive money in return. With this money, we buy now bread, wine and meat; now clothes; now shelter, now furniture, jewels, horses and carriages, now raw materials or labour, now merchandise, now land, and now stocks or bonds of all sorts of businesses.

Exchange is carried on in the market. The places where exchanges of any special kind are transacted are regarded as special markets. Thus one speaks of the European market, the French market, the Parisian market; Le Havre is a market for cotton; Bordeaux a market for wines; public markets are markets for fruit, vegetables, wheat and other cereals; the stock exchange is a market for industrial securities.

Consider for example, the wheat market. Let us suppose that, at a certain moment, five hectolitres of wheat are being exchanged for 120 francs, i.e. for 600 grammes of silver 0·900 fine. We say then:

"Wheat is worth 24 francs a hectolitre." This is how the phenomenon of value in exchange makes its appearance.

28. Wheat is worth 24 francs a hectolitre. We observe, first of all, that this fact partakes of the character of a *natural* phenomenon. This particular value of wheat in terms of money, that is to say, this price of wheat, does not result either from the will of the buyer or from the will of the seller or from any agreement between the two. Though the seller would like to sell at a higher price, he cannot do so, because the wheat *is not worth any more*. Moreover, if he refused to sell at 24 francs a hectolitre, the buyer would readily find a number of other sellers willing to sell at this price. The buyer would be only too pleased to buy at a lower price; but he cannot do so, because the wheat *is not worth any less*. Furthermore, if he refused to buy at 24 francs a hectolitre the seller would readily find a number of other buyers willing to pay that price.

Thus any value in exchange, once established, partakes of the character of a natural phenomenon, natural in its origins, natural in its manifestations and natural in essence. If wheat and silver have *any value at all*, it is because they are scarce, that is, useful and limited in quantity—both of these conditions being natural. If wheat and silver have a *definite value* with respect to each other, it is because they are, each of them, more or less scarce, that is, more or less useful and more or less limited in quantity—again the same two natural conditions mentioned above.

This does not mean that we have no control over prices. Because gravity is a natural phenomenon and obeys natural laws, it does not follow that all we can do is to watch it operate. We can either resist• it or give it free rein, whichever we please, but we cannot change its essence or its laws. It is said[3] we cannot command nature except by obeying her.[c] This applies also to value. In the case of wheat, for example, we could either raise its price by destroying part of its supply, or lower the price by eating rice or potatoes or some other foodstuff in place of wheat. We could even fix the price of wheat by decree at 20 francs instead of 24 francs a hectolitre. In the first instance, we should be acting upon the causes of the phenomenon of value in such a way as to substitute one natural value for another natural value. In the second instance, we should be acting directly upon the phenomenon itself, substituting an artificial value for a natural one. It would even be possible, in an extreme case, to abolish value altogether by abolishing exchange. If, however, exchanges do take place, we cannot prevent them from giving rise to or tending to give rise to certain exchange values, naturally under given conditions of supply and demand, in short, of scarcity.

29. Wheat is worth 24 francs a hectolitre. We observe, now, that

this phenomenon is *mathematical* in character as well. The value of wheat in terms of money, or the price of wheat, was 22 or 23 francs yesterday. A short while before it was 23 francs 50 centimes or 23 francs 75 centimes. Soon it will be 24 francs 25 centimes or 24 francs 50 centimes. Tomorrow it will be 25 or 26 francs. But at this present moment, today, it is 24 francs, *neither more nor less*. This phenomenon is so clearly mathematical in character that I shall proceed immediately to state it in terms of an equation and thereby give it its true expression.

The hectolitre being taken as the quantitative unit of measure for wheat, and the gramme as the quantitative unit of measure for silver, we can say with utmost precision that, if 5 hectolitres of wheat are exchanged for 600 grammes of silver, it means that "5 hectolitres of wheat *have the same value* as 600 grammes of silver", or that "the *value in exchange* of 5 hectolitres of wheat *equals* the *value in exchange* of 600 grammes of silver", or finally, that "5 times the value in exchange of 1 hectolitre of wheat equals 600 times the value in exchange of 1 gramme of silver".

Accordingly, let v_b be the value in exchange of 1 hectolitre of wheat and let v_a be the value in exchange of 1 gramme of silver 0·900 fine. Using ordinary mathematical notations, we obtain the equation:

$$5v_b = 600v_a,$$

and, if we divide both sides of the equation by 5, we obtain

$$v_b = 120v_a. \qquad ..(1)$$

If we agree to conform to the practice of this hypothetical market selected for our example, and choose as the unit of measure of value, not the value in exchange of 1 gramme of silver, but the value in exchange of 5 grammes of silver 0·900 fine, called a franc, that is to say, if we postulate that

$$5v_a = 1 \text{ franc,}$$

it follows that

$$v_b = 24 \text{ francs.} \qquad ..(2)$$

In form (1), precisely as in form (2), the equation is an exact translation of the following phrase, or, as I should prefer to put it, the scientific representation of the following fact: "Wheat is worth 24 francs a hectolitre."

30. Value in exchange is thus a magnitude, which, as we now see, is measurable. If the object of mathematics in general is to study magnitudes of this kind, the theory of value in exchange is really a branch of mathematics which mathematicians have hitherto neglected and left undeveloped.

It must be evident to the reader from the previous discussion that I do not claim that this science constitutes the whole of economics. Force and velocity are also measurable magnitudes, but the mathematical theory of force and velocity is not the whole of mechanics. Nevertheless, pure mechanics surely ought to precede applied mechanics. Similarly, given the *pure theory of economics*, it must precede *applied economics*; and this pure theory of economics is a science which resembles the physico-mathematical sciences in every respect. This assertion is new and will seem strange; but I have just proved it to be true, and I shall elaborate the proof in what follows.

If the pure theory of economics or the theory of exchange and value in exchange, that is, the theory of social wealth considered by itself, is a physico-mathematical science like mechanics or hydrodynamics, then economists should not be afraid to use the methods and language of mathematics.

The mathematical method is not an *experimental* method; it is a *rational* method. Are the sciences which are strictly speaking natural sciences restricted to a pure and simple description of nature, or do they transcend the bounds of experience? I leave it to the natural scientists to answer this question.[d] This much is certain, however, that the physico-mathematical sciences, like the mathematical sciences, in the narrow sense, do go beyond experience as soon as they have drawn their type concepts from it. From real-type concepts, these sciences abstract ideal-type concepts which they define, and then on the basis of these definitions they construct *a priori* the whole framework of their theorems and proofs. After that they go back to experience not to confirm but to apply their conclusions. Everyone who has studied any geometry at all knows perfectly well that only in an abstract, ideal circumference are the radii all equal to each other and that only in an abstract, ideal triangle is the sum of the angles equal to the sum of two right angles. Reality confirms these definitions and demonstrations only approximately, and yet reality admits of a very wide and fruitful application of these propositions. Following this same procedure, the pure theory of economics ought to take over from experience certain type concepts, like those of exchange, supply, demand, market, capital, income, productive services and products. From these real-type concepts the pure science of economics should then abstract and define ideal-type concepts in terms of which it carries on its reasoning. The return to reality should not take place until the science is completed and then only with a view to practical applications. Thus in an ideal market we have ideal prices which stand in an exact relation to an ideal demand and supply. And so on. Do these pure truths find frequent application? To be sure, the scholar has a right to pursue science for its own sake, just as the geometer has the right (which, in fact, he exercises every day) to study the most singular properties of geometric figures, however fantastic, if he finds that they excite his curiosity. We shall see, however, that the truths of pure economics yield solutions of very important problems of applied economics and social economics, which are highly controversial and very little understood.

As to mathematical language, why should we persist in using everyday language to explain things in the most cumbrous and incorrect way, as Ricardo has often done and as John Stuart Mill does repeatedly in his *Principles of Political Economy*, when these same things can be stated far more succinctly, precisely and clearly in the language of mathematics?[e]

Lesson 4

INDUSTRY AND APPLIED ECONOMICS.
PROPERTY AND SOCIAL ECONOMICS

31. Only useful things limited in quantity can be produced by industry and all things that industry produces are scarce (§ 25). In fact we may be certain that industry does nothing but produce scarce things and that it endeavours to produce them all.

This phenomenon of industrial production now needs to be described in some detail. Useful things limited in quantity, besides suffering from the drawback (for such it is) of this limitation, sometimes lie under the additional disadvantage of having only an indirect rather than a direct utility. Fleece is unquestionably a useful thing, but before it can be used to satisfy a need, like our need for clothing, it must undergo two preliminary industrial operations, one converting the wool into cloth, and the other fashioning the cloth into clothing. A moment's reflection is sufficient to show beyond doubt that the number of those things which are limited in quantity, but useful only in an indirect sense, is very large. It follows that industry has a twofold aim: first, to increase the number of useful things which exist only in limited quantities, and second, to transform indirect utilities into direct utilities.

Thus we now have a clear-cut idea of the object of industry which was defined earlier, in general terms, as the sum total of relations between persons and things designed to subordinate the purpose of things to the purpose of persons.[1] It is obvious that man makes contact with all things in order to make use of them, and it is equally obvious that the constant aim of these contacts is the increase and transformation of social wealth.

32. In pursuing this twofold aim, man performs two distinct classes of operations.

(1) The first consists of industrial operations in the narrow sense, that is, *technical* operations. For example, agriculture increases the number of plants and animals which are used for food and clothing; extractive industries augment the quantity of mineral products out of which instruments and tools are made; manufacturing industries convert textile fibres into linen, woollen and cotton fabrics, and minerals into all kinds of machines; engineering industries build factories and railways. Clearly, these operations, which, in a limited and specific sense, consist in the augmentation and transformation of social wealth, possess, moreover, the well-defined characteristics

73

of relations between persons and things designed to subordinate the purpose of things to the purpose of persons. These operations make up our first class of industrial phenomena which are the objective of a first group of applied sciences or arts, namely the *technical arts*.

(2) The second class of operations are those related to the *economic* organization of industry, properly speaking.

In fact, the first class of operations described above would constitute the whole of industry and would be the objective of all the arts, were it not for an essential fact which confronts us at this point, namely man's physiological aptitude for the *division of labour*. If all men were destined to be independent of each other in their endeavours to satisfy their wants, each individual would have to look after himself by increasing, as he saw fit, the quantity of useful things which do not exist in unlimited quantity and by transforming indirect utilities into direct utilities as it suited him. Each would have to be in turn his own farmer, his own spinner, his own baker, his own tailor, and so on. Man's condition, under such circumstances, would not be very different from that of brute beasts, for industry in the narrow sense, i.e. technical industry, would be very rudimentary without the developments which it owes to the division of labour. Conceivably, industry might still exist[a] in the first or technological sense, but not in the economic sense.

There is nothing in real life that corresponds to the conditions [of individual isolation] we have momentarily assumed. Not only does man possess a physiological aptitude for the division of labour, but, as we shall see, this aptitude is an indispensable condition of his very existence and his subsistence. Far from being independent, the destinies of all men are bound together in the pursuit of the satisfaction of wants. This, however, is not the place to examine the nature and origin of the division of labour. For the present we are interested only in noting the existence of this phenomenon, just as we previously noted the existence of man's moral freedom and ethical personality. The phenomenon does indeed exist, for instead of each of us increasing the quantity of scarce things solely for our own individual accounts, instead of each of us converting indirect into direct utilities only to the extent to which we are individually concerned, we split up this task into specialized occupations. Some of us are ploughmen by specialty and nothing but ploughmen, others are spinners by specialty and nothing but spinners, and so on. This constitutes, we repeat, the division of labour. The existence of this phenomenon is perfectly obvious even from a fleeting glance at human society. And it is this phenomenon alone which engenders industry in the economic sense.

33. Two problems arise in this connection. In the first place,

whether there is any division of labour or not, industrial production must be not only *abundant*, but also properly *proportioned*. It is necessary to avoid producing too much of some scarce things while producing too little of others. It is also necessary to avoid converting some indirect utilities into direct utilities on too large a scale while converting others in insufficient quantity. If each man were at once his own farmer, his own manufacturer and his own engineer, he would ply each trade to just that extent and in just such a manner as he saw fit. But if the various occupations are specialized, there must not be, for example, too many manufacturers and too few farmers.

In the second place, whether there is any division of labour or not, the distribution of social wealth among the members of a community must be *equitable*. Social disorder is as much to be eschewed as economic disorder. If each individual produced everything that he consumed and consumed nothing that he had not himself produced, not only would he adjust his production to his wants, but the amount of his consumption would be limited by the extent of his production. But it is important that the specialization of occupations should not result in making it possible for those who have produced little to consume much, while others, who have produced much, consume little.

The significance of these two problems is perfectly obvious, and the direction which the various solutions to these problems have taken is well known. The object of the guild system was, clearly, to assure proper apportionment in production. It is claimed for the system of freedom of trade and freedom of enterprise—for what is called the system of *laisser-faire, laisser-passer*—that it harmonizes apportionment with abundance. We shall see whether this is so. The earlier systems of slavery and serfdom had the obvious disadvantage of forcing some classes of the community to work for the benefit of other classes. Our present system of private property and taxation is reputed to have put a complete end to this exploitation of man by man. We shall look into this later.

34. For the present we need only take cognizance of the two problems, and examine their nature after defining their object. It is absolutely impossible for us, whatever Charles Coquelin and the economists of his school may say, to include the question of the production of social wealth, any more than the question of its distribution, within the scope of natural science.[2] The will of man is free to influence the production, as well as the distribution, of social wealth. The only difference is that in distribution, man's will is guided by considerations of justice, whereas in production his will is guided by considerations of material well-being. Moreover,

technical production and economic production, as we have defined them, are not unlike in essence. The two phenomena are, in fact, closely connected and interrelated, each being complementary to the other. Not only are they both human and not natural, but they are also both industrial and not social phenomena, for economic production as well as technical production are manifestations of relations between persons and things with a view to the subordination of the purposes of things to the purposes of persons.

Thus the theory of the economic production of social wealth, that is, of the organization of industry under a system of the division of labour, is an applied science. For this reason we shall call it *applied economics*.[b]

35. We have seen that all useful things limited in quantity and nothing else are appropriable (§23). This is evident from everyday observation. Useless things are disregarded; useful things unlimited in quantity are left to the common domain; but scarce things are withdrawn from the common domain and are no longer available to the first-comer.

The appropriation of scarce things or of social wealth is a phenomenon of human contrivance and not a natural phenomenon. It has its origins in the exercise of the human will and in human behaviour and not in the play of natural forces.

It is surely not within our power to make useful things unlimited in quantity appropriable, or to make useful things limited in quantity inappropriable. But once the conditions of appropriation are fulfilled in the nature of things, it is within our power to determine whether this appropriation shall be carried on in one way rather than in another. Obviously, this power does not reside in each of us individually but in all of us taken collectively. We are dealing here with a human phenomenon that is shaped, not by the separate will of each individual, but by the collective activity of society as a whole. As a matter of fact, human initiative always has exerted and always will exert a modifying influence on the phenomenon of appropriation to suit its own purpose. In early societies, the appropriation, or distribution of social wealth, that took place under a system of division of labour, was effected by force, cunning and chance, but not altogether irrationally. The boldest, the strongest, the cleverest, the luckiest had the lion's share, the others had what was left over, which amounted to little or nothing. But in the history of property as in the history of government, the human race has slowly and steadily progressed from initial confusion towards an ultimate, principled order. To sum up, while nature makes things appropriable, mankind determines and carries out the appropriation.

36. Moreover, the appropriation of things by persons or the distribution of social wealth among men in society is a moral and not an industrial phenomenon. It is a relationship among persons.

Surely, the purpose of our contact with scarce things is to appropriate them; and often it is only after long and persistent efforts that we succeed in achieving this end. This, however, is an aspect of the problem to which we have already adverted and with which we are not at present concerned. For the time being, we shall consider the distribution of social wealth *per se*, without alluding either to the antecedent circumstances or the natural conditions of the phenomenon. An example will make my meaning clear.

I imagine a tribe of savages and a deer in a forest. The deer is a useful thing limited in quantity and hence subject to appropriation. This point once granted, nothing more needs to be said about it. To be sure, before the deer can be actually appropriated it has to be hunted and killed. Again, this side of the question need not detain us, nor need we stop to consider such correlated problems as arise in connection with the need to dress the deer and prepare it in the kitchen. Quite apart from all these aspects of man's relation to the deer, yet another question claims our attention; for whether the deer is still running about in the forest or has been killed, the question is: who shall have it? That is the point of view from which we are considering the problem of appropriation, for when it is looked at in this way, appropriation is seen to involve a relationship among persons. We need only carry our illustration one step further to make this clear. "The deer belongs to the one who has killed it!" cries a young and active member of the tribe, adding, "If you are too lazy or if your aim is not good enough, so much the worse for you!" An older, weaker member replies: "No! The deer belongs to all of us to be shared equally. If there is only one deer in the forest, and you happen to be the first to catch sight of it, that is no reason why the rest of us should go without food." Obviously we are here confronted with a phenomenon which is fundamentally social and which gives rise to questions of justice or of the mutual co-ordination of human destinies.

37. Thus the mode of appropriation depends on human decisions, and according as those decisions are good or bad, so will the mode of appropriation be good or bad. If good, there will be a mutual co-ordination of human destinies; justice will rule. If bad, the destiny of some will be subordinated to the destiny of others; injustice will prevail. What mode of appropriation is good and just? What mode of appropriation does reason commend as compatible with the requirements of moral personality? This is the problem of property.

Property consists in fair and rational appropriation, or rightful appropriation. While appropriation by itself is an objective fact, pure and simple, property, on the other hand, is a phenomenon involving the concept of justice; it is a right. Between the objective fact and the right, there is a place for moral theory. This is an essential idea, which must not be misconstrued. It is entirely beside the point to find fault with the natural conditions of appropriation or to list the different ways in which men have distributed social wealth in different places and at different times throughout history. It is, however, very much to the point to scrutinize these various systems of distribution from the standpoint of justice, originating in the moral personality of man, or from the standpoint of equality and inequality; to inquire in what respects all past systems were, and all present systems still are, defective, and to describe the only good system.

38. From the very beginning of human society and from the first appearance of social wealth, the problem of the distribution of this wealth has been subject to debate. It has always been discussed on its true plane [that of justice], and there it should remain. Of all the systems of distribution which have ever been devised, the two most prominent are communism and individualism, which have had as their respective champions the two greatest minds of antiquity, Plato and Aristotle. Now, what do these systems stand for? Communism says, "Goods ought to be appropriated collectively. Nature has given them to all men, not only to men living today but to posterity as well. To divide these goods among individuals is to alienate the patrimony of the community and to despoil future generations. It exposes those born after this division to the danger of finding themselves stripped of the resources which Providence meant for them and thwarted in both the pursuit of their ends and the fulfilment of their destiny." In reply, individualism argues, "Goods ought to be appropriated individually. Nature has made men unequal in virtue and talent. To compel the industrious, the skilful, the thrifty to throw the fruits of their labour and of their saving into a common pile is to rob them for the benefit of the lazy, the incompetent and the thriftless. It relieves all men of responsibility for the proper or improper pursuit of their ends and for the moral or immoral fulfilment of their destinies." I shall not pursue this argument further. Which is right, communism or individualism? Are not both of them both right and wrong at the same time? We do not need to decide this dispute here. For the present I prefer to abstain from adding anything by way of judgement or further amplification of the two opposing doctrines. All I had in mind was to make clear what exactly is the object of the problem of property considered from the

broadest and most comprehensive point of view. This object consists essentially in establishing human relations arising from the appropriation of social wealth so as to achieve a mutual co-ordination of human destinies in conformity with reason and justice. Appropriation being in essence a moral phenomenon, the theory of property must be in essence a moral science. *Ius est suum cuique tribuere* —justice consists in rendering to each that which is properly his. If any science has for its object to render to each what is properly his, if, therefore, any science espouses justice as its guiding principle, surely it must be the science of the distribution of social wealth, or, as we shall designate it, *social economics*.

39. There remains, however, one difficulty to which I wish to call attention at this point.[c]

The theory of property defines the mutual relations established between man and man with respect to the appropriation of social wealth, and determines the conditions of the equitable distribution of social wealth within a community. In this connection, men are considered in the capacity of moral personalities. The theory of industry, on the other hand, defines those relations between man and things which aim at the increase and transformation of social wealth, and determines the conditions of an abundant production of social wealth within a community. Here men are considered in the capacity of specialized workers. The conditions determined by the theory of property are moral conditions deducible from the premise of justice; while those determined by the theory of industry are economic conditions deducible from the premise of material welfare. In the one case as in the other we are dealing with social conditions, or with guiding principles for the organization of society. But are these two orders of consideration in conflict with each other, or do they mutually support each other? If, for example, both the theory of property and the theory of industry agree, on grounds of justice, in repudiating slavery or in repudiating communism, then all is well. Suppose, however, that one of these condemns slavery or advocates communism on grounds of justice while the other advocates slavery or condemns communism on grounds of material welfare. Then there would be a conflict between moral science and applied science. Is such a conflict possible? If it appears so, what should be done?

We shall come back to this problem later and then give it the attention it deserves. It is a question of the relation of ethics to economics which was hotly debated by Proudhon and Bastiat, among others, around 1848. In his *Contradictions économiques* Proudhon argued that there is a conflict between justice and material well-being.[3] Bastiat in his *Harmonies économiques* defended the opposite thesis.[4] I think that neither proved his point. I shall take up Bastiat's proposition again and defend it in a different way. At all events, if the problem exists, it must be solved and not concealed by confusing two distinct sciences, namely, the theory of property, which is a moral science, and the theory of industry, which is an applied science.[d]

Theory of Exchange of Two Commodities for Each Other

Lesson 5

THE MARKET AND COMPETITION. PROBLEM OF EXCHANGE OF TWO COMMODITIES FOR EACH OTHER

40. In our general introductory survey we defined social wealth (§21) as the sum total of all things, material or immaterial, that are scarce, i.e. that are both useful and limited in quantity. We proved that all scarce things and nothing else have value and are exchangeable. Here we shall proceed differently. Starting with a definition of *social wealth* as the sum total of all things, material or immaterial, which are valuable and exchangeable, we shall prove that all valuable and exchangeable things, to the exclusion of everything else, are useful and at the same time limited in quantity. Up to this point we reasoned from cause to effect, but now we shall reason from effect to cause. It is clear that once the close connection between scarcity and value in exchange has been demonstrated, we may reason in whichever direction we please. I think, however, that in a systematic study of any general phenomenon like value in exchange, an inquiry into its nature should precede the investigation of its origin.

41. *Value in exchange* is a property, which certain things possess, of not being given or taken freely, but of being bought and sold, that is, of being received and conveyed in return for other things in definite quantitative proportions.[1] The buyer of a thing is the seller of that which he gives in exchange. The seller of a thing is the buyer of that which he takes in exchange. In other words, every exchange of one thing for another is made up of a double purchase and a double sale.

Things that are valuable and exchangeable are also known as *commodities*. The *market* is a place where commodities are exchanged. Thus the phenomenon of value in exchange manifests itself in the market, and we must go to the market to study value in exchange.

Value in exchange, when left to itself, arises spontaneously in the market as the result of competition. As buyers, traders make their *demands* by *outbidding* each other. As sellers, traders make their *offers* by *underbidding* each other. The coming together of buyers and sellers then results in giving commodities certain values in exchange, sometimes rising, sometimes falling, sometimes stationary. The more perfectly competition functions, the more rigorous is the manner of arriving at value in exchange. The markets which are best organized from the competitive standpoint are those in which purchases and sales are made by auction, through the instrumentality of stockbrokers, commercial brokers or criers acting as agents who centralize transactions in such a way that the terms of every exchange are openly announced and an opportunity is given to sellers to lower their prices and to buyers to raise their bids. This is the way business is done in the stock exchange, commercial markets, grain markets, fish markets, etc. Besides these markets, there are others, such as the fruit, vegetable and poultry markets, where competition, though not so well organized, functions fairly effectively and satisfactorily. City streets with their stores and shops of all kinds—baker's, butcher's, grocer's, tailor's, shoemaker's, etc.—are markets where competition, though poorly organized, nevertheless operates quite adequately. Unquestionably competition is also the primary force in setting the value of the doctor's and the lawyer's consultations, of the musician's and the singer's recitals, etc. In fact, the whole world may be looked upon as a vast general market made up of diverse special markets where social wealth is bought and sold. Our task then is to discover the laws to which these purchases and sales tend to conform automatically. To this end, we shall suppose that the market is perfectly competitive, just as in pure mechanics we suppose, to start with, that machines are perfectly frictionless.

42. We shall see, now, how competition works in a well-organized market. Let us go into the stock exchange of a large investment centre like Paris or London. What is bought and sold in such places are titles to property in shares of very important kinds of social wealth, such as fractions of State and municipal loans or shares of railways, canals, metallurgical plants, etc. Our first impression on entering such an exchange is that of confused uproar and chaotic movement. Once, however, we are informed of what is going on, this clamour and bustle become perfectly comprehensible.

Let us take, for example, trading in 3 per cent French Rentes on the Paris Stock Exchange and confine our attention to these operations alone.

The three per cents, as they are called, are quoted at 60 francs. At this price, brokers who have received some orders to sell at 60 francs and other orders [authorizing them to sell] *at less* than 60 francs, will offer a certain quantity of 3 per cent Rentes, that is, a certain number of certificates each yielding 3 francs annually payable by the French State. We shall apply the term *effective offer*[2] to any offer made, in this way, of a definite amount of a commodity at a definite price. *Per contra,* the brokers who have received some orders to buy at 60 francs and others [authorizing them to buy] *at more* than 60 francs will demand a certain quantity of 3 per cent Rentes, when 60 francs is quoted. We shall apply the term *effective demand* to any such demand for a definite amount of a commodity at a definite price.

We have now to make three suppositions according as the demand is *equal to, greater than,* or *less than* the offer.

First Supposition. The quantity demanded at 60 francs is equal to the quantity offered at this same price. Each broker, on either the buying or the selling side, finds another broker with an exactly equivalent counter-proposal to sell or to buy.[3] Exchange takes place.[a] The rate of 60 francs is maintained. The market is in a *stationary state* or in *equilibrium*.

Second Supposition. The brokers with orders to buy can no longer find brokers with orders to sell. This is a clear indication that the quantity of three per cents demanded at 60 francs is greater than the quantity offered at that price. Theoretically, trading should come to a halt.[a] Brokers who have orders to buy at 60 francs 05 centimes *or who have orders to buy at higher prices* make bids at 60 francs 05 centimes. They raise the market price.

Two results follow from this bidding: first, those buyers who would have bought at 60 francs but who refuse to buy at 60 francs 05 centimes, withdraw; second, those sellers who are willing to sell at 60 francs 05 centimes but who previously refused to sell at 60 francs, come forward. These buyers and sellers will now give orders to this effect to their brokers if they have not already done so. Then, in consequence of a two-sided movement, the difference between effective demand and effective offer is reduced. If equality between effective offer and effective demand is restored, the *rise in price* ceases. Otherwise, the price continues to go up from 60 francs 05 centimes to 60 francs 10 centimes, and from 60 francs 10 centimes to 60 francs 15 centimes until offer equals demand. A new stationary state is thus found at a higher price.

Third Supposition. Brokers with orders to sell can no longer find brokers with orders to buy. This is a clear indication that the quantity of three per cents offered at 60 francs is greater than the quantity demanded at that price. Trading stops.[a] Brokers who have orders to sell at 59 francs 95 centimes *or who have orders to sell at lower prices* make offers at 59 francs 95 centimes. They lower the price.

Two results follow: first, the withdrawal of those who would have sold at 60 francs but who refuse to sell at 59 francs 95 centimes; second, the advent of those who are willing to buy at 59 francs 95 centimes but who previously refused to buy at 60 francs. The difference between offer and demand is reduced. The price *falls*, if it has to, from 59 francs 95 centimes to 59 francs 90 centimes and from 59 francs 90 centimes to 59 francs 85 centimes until equality between offer and demand is restored. Thus a new equilibrium is found at a lower price.

Suppose now, that at the same time that this sort of trading is going on in 3 per cent French Rentes, similar trading is taking place in the securities of other governments, English, Italian, Spanish, Turkish and Egyptian, and in stocks and bonds issued by railways, ports, canals, mines, gas works, other factories, banks, credit institutions, etc.; suppose that all this trading proceeds by conventional shifts in price of 5 centimes, 25 centimes, 1 franc 25 centimes, 5 francs, or 25 francs, according to the value of the securities; and suppose that besides *cash* transactions there are *future* transactions, some *firm* and others *optional*, then the tumult of the stock market resolves itself into a veritable symphony in which each player plays his part.

43. We shall study value in exchange as it arises under such competitive conditions. Economists, generally speaking, have fallen all too frequently into the error of studying value in exchange under unusual circumstances. They are always talking about diamonds, Raphael's paintings, and concert recitals given by famous singers. De Quincey, whom John Stuart Mill quotes,[4] imagines two men "on Lake Superior in a steam boat". One owns "a musical snuff-box"; the other, who is "making his way to an unsettled region 800 miles ahead of civilization", suddenly realizes that "in the hour of leaving London" he had forgotten to buy one of these instruments possessing "a magic power ... which lulls your agitations of mind"; and, "when the last knell of the clock has sounded, which summons you to buy now or to forfeit for ever", he buys the musical snuff-box from his fellow-passenger for 60 guineas. Of course, our theory should cover all such special cases. The general laws of the market should apply to the diamond market, the market for Raphael's paintings and to the market for tenors and sopranos. These laws should even apply to a market like the one Mr. De Quincey imagines, in which there is a single buyer, a single seller, one commodity and only one minute in which to make the exchange.[5] But logic demands that we consider general before special cases, and not the other way round. What physicist would deliberately pick cloudy weather for astronomical observations instead of taking advantage of a cloudless night?[b]

44. I have cited the example of buying and selling securities for gold and silver on the stock market in order to give an introductory idea of the phenomenon of exchange and the mechanism of competition. Securities, however, are a very special kind of commodity. Furthermore, the use of money in trading has peculiarities of its own, the study of which must be postponed until later, and not interwoven

at the outset with the general phenomenon of value in exchange. Let us, therefore, retrace our steps and state our observations in scientific terms. We may take any two commodities, say oats and wheat, or, more abstractly, (A) and (B). I put the letters A and B in parentheses whenever I wish to indicate that these letters do not represent *quantities*, which are the only things that can be used in equations, but rather kinds or species or, as one might say in philosophical terms, *essences*.

Let us now imagine a market to which some people come holding commodity (A), ready to exchange part of it in order to procure commodity (B); while others come holding commodity (B), ready to exchange part of their (B) in order to procure commodity (A). Since the bidding will have to start at some point or other, we shall suppose that a broker offers to give up n units of (B) for m units of (A) in accordance, let us say, with the closing rate of exchange of the preceding day. This bid will conform to the equation of exchange

$$m v_a = n v_b$$

in which v_a is the value in exchange of one unit of (A) and v_b is the value in exchange of one unit of (B) (§29).[6]

Let us define *prices* in general as ratios between values in exchange or as relative values in exchange. In general, also, let us designate the price of (B) in terms of (A) by p_b and the price of (A) in terms of (B) by p_a. If, then, we denote, in the particular case we are dealing with, the quotients of the ratios $\dfrac{m}{n}$ and $\dfrac{n}{m}$ by μ and $\dfrac{1}{\mu}$ respectively, it follows from the above equation that

$$\frac{v_b}{v_a} = p_b = \frac{m}{n} = \mu,$$

$$\frac{v_a}{v_b} = p_a = \frac{n}{m} = \frac{1}{\mu};$$

and from these two that

$$p_b = \frac{1}{p_a}, \qquad p_a = \frac{1}{p_b}.$$

Thus: *Prices, or ratios of values in exchange,*[c] *are equal to the inverse ratios of the quantities exchanged.*

The price of any one commodity in terms of another is the reciprocal of the price of the second commodity in terms of the first.

If (A) were oats ['avoine'] and (B) wheat ['blé'], and a broker had offered to exchange 5 hectolitres of wheat for 10 hectolitres of oats, then the bid price of wheat in terms of oats would be 2, and that of oats in terms of wheat would be 1/2. We have already observed that there is always a double sale and a double purchase in every exchange transaction; correspondingly there is also a double price. It is of the utmost importance that the invariable reciprocal nature of the relationship between the two prices in any exchange be fully understood, and the use of algebraic symbols is particularly useful in this connection because it makes this reciprocal relationship stand out in the clearest possible relief. Furthermore, it is seen that these symbols have the advantage of being conducive to a clear and precise formulation of general propositions. That is why we shall continue to use them.

45. Let D_a, O_a, D_b and O_b be the effective demand and offer of commodities (A) and (B) at their respective prices $p_a = \dfrac{1}{\mu}$ and $p_b = \mu$.

Between the quantities demanded, quantities offered and prices there is a fundamental relationship, which we must examine before we do anything else.

Effective demand and effective offer are, as we have seen, the demand and the offer of a given quantity of a commodity at a given price. Consequently, to say that a quantity D_a of (A) is demanded at the price p_a is, *ipso facto*, the same thing as saying that a quantity O_b of (B), equal to $D_a p_a$, is being offered. For example, to say that there is a demand for 200 hectolitres of oats at the price 1/2 in terms of wheat is, by virtue of that fact alone, the same as saying that 100 hectolitres of wheat are being offered. It follows that in general the relationship between D_a, p_a and O_b can be expressed by the equation

$$O_b = D_a p_a.$$

In like manner, to say that a quantity O_a of (A) is offered at the price p_a is, *ipso facto*, the same thing as saying that a quantity D_b of (B), equal to $O_a p_a$, is being demanded. For example, to say that 150 hectolitres of oats are being offered at the price of 1/2 in terms of wheat is, by virtue of that fact alone, the same as saying that there is a demand for 75 hectolitres of wheat. It follows that in general the relations between O_a, p_a and D_b can always be expressed by the equation

$$D_b = O_a p_a.$$

It could be proved, in like manner, that D_b, O_b, p_b, O_a and D_a are related according to the following equations:

$$O_a = D_b p_b,$$
$$D_a = O_b p_b;$$

but it would be superfluous to do so, since these last two equations follow from the two previous ones together with the equation $p_a p_b = 1$.

Thus: *The effective demand for or offer of one commodity in exchange for another is equal respectively to the effective offer of or demand for the second commodity multiplied by its price in terms of the first.*

Evidently, any two of the four quantities, D_a, O_a, D_b and O_b, will determine the other two. For the present we shall assume that the quantities offered, O_b and O_a, are determined by the quantities demanded, D_a and D_b respectively, and not the other way round. Indeed, demand ought to be considered as the principal fact and offer as the accessory fact where two commodities are exchanged for each other in kind. No one ever makes an offer simply for the sake of offering. The only reason one offers anything is that one cannot demand anything without making an offer. Offer is only a consequence of demand. Consequently, to begin with, we shall confine ourselves to the indirect relationship between offer and price, and study direct relationships only in so far as they subsist between demand and price. At prices p_a and p_b, D_a and D_b are demanded, whence we deduce that $O_a = D_b p_b$ and $O_b = D_a p_a$ are being offered.

46. This being so, if we let

$$D_a = \alpha O_a,$$

then we may make any one of three suppositions, according as $\alpha = 1$, $\alpha > 1$ or $\alpha < 1$. But, before going into that, let us state a final theorem.

If in the above equation we substitute for D_a and O_a the values given by the equations

$$D_a = O_b p_b$$

and

$$O_a = D_b p_b,$$

we obtain

$$O_b = \alpha D_b.$$

Thus: *Given two commodities, the ratio of the effective demand of either one of them to its effective offer is equal to the ratio of the effective offer of the other to its effective demand.*

This theorem may be deduced as follows:[7]

$$D_a = O_b p_b,$$

$$D_b = O_a p_a,$$

$$D_a D_b = O_a O_b;$$

or, in like manner:

$$O_a = D_b p_b,$$
$$O_b = D_a p_a,$$
$$O_a O_b = D_a D_b.$$

In either case it follows that

$$\frac{O_b}{D_b} = \frac{D_a}{O_a} = \alpha.$$

It is to be observed that if the effective demand for and effective offer of (A) are equal, the effective offer of and effective demand for (B) will also be equal. We see, too, that if the effective demand for (A) is greater than its effective offer, then the effective offer of (B) will be proportionately greater than its effective demand. Finally, if the effective offer of (A) is greater than its effective demand, then the effective demand for (B) will be proportionately greater than its effective offer. This is the meaning of the above theorem.

47. Now suppose that $\alpha = 1$, $D_a = O_a$, and $O_b = D_b$; that the quantities demanded and quantities offered of each of the two commodities (A) and (B) are equal at their respective prices, $p_a = \frac{1}{\mu}$ and $p_b = \mu$; and that each buyer and each seller finds a corresponding seller and a corresponding buyer with the exact counterpart of his bid or offer. The market will be in equilibrium. At the equilibrium prices $\frac{1}{\mu}$ and μ, the quantity $D_a = O_a$ of (A) will be exchanged for the quantity $O_b = D_b$ of (B), and at the close of the market, each party to the exchange will go his own way.

48. But let $\alpha \gtrless 1$, $D_a \gtrless O_a$ and $O_b \gtrless D_b$. How then can equality between the demand for and the offer of each of the two commodities be reached?[d]

The first idea that comes to mind is to repeat purely and simply the line of reasoning which we developed earlier in our discussion of Rentes in the stock exchange. But that would be an egregious error.[e] What we had in our example drawn from the stock exchange were buyers and sellers of Rentes, that is, of securities the value of which depended both on the particular yield of these securities and on the general rate of return on capital. As we shall see later, the only possible result that could follow from a rise in the price of Rentes would be a decrease in the demand for them and an increase in their offer; and the only possible result that could follow from a fall in their price would be an increase in the demand for them and decrease in their offer. In our present example, traders exchange nothing but (A) and (B), which are assumed to possess direct utility and to be the only commodities which can be exchanged for each other in the market. This circumstance alters everything.

To be sure, it will still be necessary to raise p_a (or lower p_b), whenever D_a is greater than O_a, or, contrariwise, to raise p_b (or lower p_a) whenever D_b is greater than O_b. Moreover, there is no doubt that our previous reasoning about demand still holds good. As the price increases, demand cannot increase; it can only decrease.[8] Moreover, as price decreases, demand cannot decrease; it can only increase.[7] Let us imagine a trader holding 12 hectolitres of wheat who offers 5 of them for 10 hectolitres of oats, or, in other words, who demands 10 hectolitres of oats at the price 0·50 in terms of wheat. At this price 0·50 of oats, in terms of wheat, he could have bought as many as 24 hectolitres of oats, but his own need for wheat compels him to restrict his demand for oats to 10 hectolitres. At the price 0·60, he could purchase at most 20 hectolitres of oats; and it must be admitted that, in view of his own wheat requirements, he would have to content himself with an amount of oats at most equal to, but more likely less than, the 10 hectolitres which he had been able to get when [in consequence of the lower price] he was better off.[9] Thus a rise in p_a, which is the same thing as a fall in p_b, can only decrease D_a and increase D_b. *Per contra*, a rise in p_b, which is the same thing as a fall in p_a, can only decrease D_b and increase D_a. But what will happen to O_a and O_b? It is impossible to tell. O_a is equal to the product of D_b multiplied by p_b. Now, if either one of the two factors, say p_b, decreases or increases, the other factor must increase or decrease in consequence. Likewise O_b is equal to the product of D_a multiplied by p_a. As p_a increases or decreases, D_a must decrease or increase in consequence. How can we tell, then, whether we are approaching equilibrium?[9]

Lesson 6

CURVES OF EFFECTIVE OFFER AND EFFECTIVE DEMAND. THE ESTABLISHMENT OF EQUALITY BETWEEN OFFER AND DEMAND

49. Since we are assuming here that there is only an indirect or mediate relation between price and effective offer, whereas the relation between price and effective demand is direct and immediate, we shall be concerned primarily with the latter relationship.

Let us consider, for this purpose, one of the holders of wheat. Let this particular individual own wheat, but no oats. He wishes to retain a certain quantity of wheat for his own use, but is prepared to give up the rest in exchange for oats for his horses. As to the respective quantities that he will retain and give up, these depend on the price of oats and on the quantity of oats that he will demand having regard to its price. We shall now see how this works out. At the price zero, if he has to give zero hectolitres of wheat for one hectolitre of oats, in other words, if oats are to be had gratis, our holder of wheat will take all the oats he wants, that is, enough for all the horses he has and even for the horses he is likely to acquire, seeing that horses cost nothing to feed. He will not have to give up any wheat at all in exchange. At each successive price, 1/100, 1/10, 1/5, 1/2 . . . (if our holder of wheat is called upon to give up 1/100, 1/10, 1/5, 1/2 . . . hectolitres of wheat for one hectolitre of oats), he will reduce his demand more and more. At the prices: 1, 2, 5, 10, or more (if he has to give up 1, 2, 5, 10, or more hectolitres of wheat to obtain one hectolitre of oats) he will cut down his demand still further. At the same time, the quantity of wheat which he offers in exchange will always equal the quantity of oats he demands multiplied by the price of oats. Finally, at some price, more or less high, say at 100 (if our holder of wheat has to give up 100 hectolitres of wheat for 1 hectolitre of oats), he will not demand any oats at all, for at that price he will no longer be able or willing to keep a single horse. Clearly, once this price has been reached, he will not offer any wheat in exchange. From this it follows that the effective demand for oats diminishes continuously as the price increases, for the effective demand starts at a certain figure when the price is zero and finally vanishes altogether when the price reaches a certain height. As for the corresponding effective offer of wheat, this starts at zero, increases, attains at least one maximum, then decreases and returns to zero.

50. All holders of wheat display similar, but not identical, tendencies in their bidding. This is equally true of all the holders of oats on their side. In general, every holder of a commodity, who comes to the market with the intention of exchanging some of this commodity in return for a quantity of some other commodity, has in mind a *trader's schedule*,[1] either virtual or actual, which can be rigorously determined.

Having recourse now to algebraic notations, let us say that holder (1) of a quantity q_b of commodity (B) comes to the market to exchange a quantity o_b of (B), in return for a quantity d_a of (A) which he is ready to take in conformity with the equation

$$d_a v_a = o_b v_b,$$

and that he leaves the market carrying away a quantity d_a of (A) and a quantity y of (B), such that $y = q_b - o_b = q_b - d_a \dfrac{v_a}{v_b}$. In any case, the quantities q_b, $\dfrac{v_a}{v_b}$ or p_a, d_a and y are always related as follows:

$$q_b = y + d_a p_a.$$

The individual we are considering knows what his q_b is, but he does not know, before he reaches the market, what $\dfrac{v_a}{v_b}$ or p_a will be. He is, however, certain to discover it as soon as he arrives. And when he has found out what p_a is, he will immediately have to decide how great d_a is to be; and hence, by virtue of the above equation, y will finally be determined.

If our individual [holder of q_b] goes to the market in person, his trader's schedule for the time being may be virtual rather than actual, that is to say, he may not make up his mind what his demand d_a will be until he knows the price p_a. Even under these circumstances, a trader's schedule nevertheless exists. But if he were prevented from going to the market himself, or if, for one reason or another, he had to entrust his business to a friend or give his orders to a broker, he would have to anticipate all possible values of p_a from zero to infinity and determine accordingly all the corresponding values of d_a, which he will find some means of representing. Now anyone at all familiar with mathematics knows that there are two ways of representing this schedule mathematically.

51. Let there be two co-ordinate axes, as drawn in Fig. 1: a horizontal *price axis*, Op, and a vertical *demand axis*, Od.[2] On the price axis, starting at the origin O, I lay off the lengths Op'_a, Op''_a, . . . representing various possible prices of oats in terms of wheat, or of (A) in terms of (B). On the other axis, beginning at the same

origin O, I measure the length $Oa_{d,1}$, representing the quantity of oats or (A) which our holder of wheat or (B) will demand at the price zero. On lines drawn through the points $p'_a, p''_a, \ldots$ parallel to the vertical demand axis I lay off the lengths $p'_a a'_1, p''_a a''_1, \ldots$ representing the quantities of oats or (A) which will be demanded at the prices $p'_a, p''_a, \ldots$ respectively. The length $Oa_{p,1}$ represents the price at which our holder of wheat or (B) will not demand any oats or (A) at all.

Having done this, we may represent the demand schedule in the mind of holder (1) of commodity (B) either geometrically by the

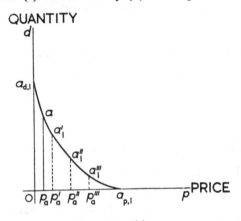

FIG. 1[3]

curve $a_{d,1} a_{p,1}$ drawn through the points $a_{d,1}, a'_1, a''_1, \ldots a_{p,1}$ or algebraically by the equation of this curve, $d_a = f_{a,1}(p_a)$.[a] Both the curve $a_{d,1} a_{p,1}$ and the equation $d_a = f_{a,1}(p_a)$ are empirical. Following the same procedure, we obtain the curves $a_{d,2} a_{p,2}, \ a_{d,3} a_{p,3} \ldots$ (Fig. 2) or their corresponding equations $d_a = f_{a,2}(p_a), d_a = f_{a,3}(p_a) \ldots$ which represent geometrically or algebraically the demand schedules in the minds of all the other holders of (B), Messrs. (2), (3), $\ldots$.

52. If, at this juncture, we add up, so to speak, all these partial [or individual demand] curves, $a_{d,1} a_{p,1}, \ a_{d,2} a_{p,2}, \ a_{d,3} a_{p,3}, \ \ldots$ by joining to one another all the ordinates corresponding to each abscissa, we obtain a total [or aggregate demand] curve $A_d A_p$ (Fig. 3) representing geometrically the demand schedule of all the holders of (B) taken together. Moreover, if we sum up all the individual [demand] equations, we obtain an aggregate equation,

$$D_a = f_{a,1}(p_a) + f_{a,2}(p_a) + f_{a,3}(p_a) + \ldots = F_a(p_a),$$

which represents the above schedules algebraically. This gives us the *demand curve* or the *demand equation* of (A) in exchange for (B) as a function of the price of (A) in terms of (B). In like manner, we could derive the demand curve or the demand equation of (B) in exchange for (A) as a function of the price of (B) in terms of (A).

There is nothing to indicate that the individual demand curves $a_{d,1}a_{p,1}$ and so on, or the individual demand equations $d_a=f_{a,1}(p_a)$ and so on, are *continuous*, in other words, that an infinitesimally small increase in p_a produces an infinitesimally small decrease in d_a. On the contrary, these functions are often discontinuous. In the case

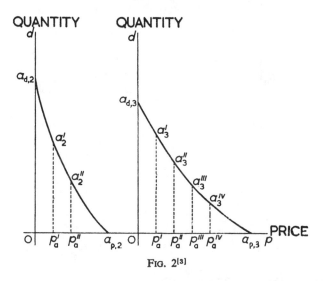

FIG. 2[3]

of oats, for example, surely our first holder of wheat will not reduce his demand gradually as the price rises, but he will do it in some intermittent way every time he decides to keep one horse less in his stable. His individual demand curve will, in reality, take the form of a step curve passing through the point *a* as in Fig. 4. All the other individual demand curves will take the same general form. And yet the aggregate demand curve A_dA_p (Fig. 3) can, for all practical purposes, be considered as continuous by virtue of the so-called *law of large numbers*.[4] In fact, whenever a very small increase in price takes place, at least one of the holders of (B), *out of a large number of them*, will then reach the point of being compelled to keep one horse less, and thus a very small diminution in the total demand for (A) will result.

53. Under these conditions, the curve A_dA_p (Fig. 3) shows the quantity of (A) effectively demanded as a [continuous] function of

the price of (A). For example, at the price $p_{a,m}$, which is represented by the abscissa $Op_{a,m}$ of the point A_m, the effective demand is $D_{a,m}$, which is represented by the ordinate $OD_{a,m}$ of the same point A_m. Moreover, when the effective demand for (A) in exchange for (B) is $D_{a,m}$ at the price $p_{a,m}$, the effective offer of (B) in exchange for (A) is, *ipso facto*, $O_{b,m} = D_{a,m} p_{a,m}$ (§45), which is represented by the area

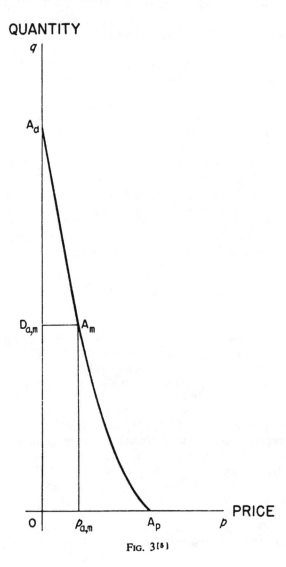

QUANTITY

FIG. 3[5]

of the rectangle $OD_{a,m}A_m p_{a,m}$ with a base of $Op_{a,m}$ and an altitude $OD_{a,m}$. Thus the curve $A_d A_p$ shows simultaneously the demand for (A) and the offer of (B) as a function of the price of (A) in terms of (B). Likewise the curve $B_d B_p$ (Fig. 5) shows simultaneously the demand for (B) and the offer of (A) as a function of the price of (B) in terms of (A).

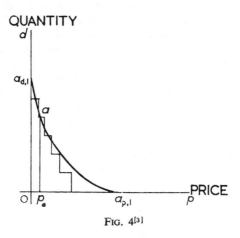

FIG. 4[3]

54. Let Q_b [i.e. a magnitude numerically equal to the area of the rectangle $O\beta Q_b p_{a,m}$ of Fig. 5] be the total quantity of (B) in the market in the hands of holders of (B), and let an equilateral hyperbola, $xy = Q_b$, with the axes as asymptotes, be drawn through the point Q_b. Let the line $p_{a,m}A_m$ be extended until it meets the hyperbola at the point Q_b, and let the line βQ_b be drawn parallel to the x or price axis. Q_b is the area of the rectangle $O\beta Q_b p_{a,m}$ which represents the total quantity of (B) brought to the market. $D_{a,m}$ multiplied by $p_{a,m}$ is the area of the rectangle $OD_{a,m}A_m p_{a,m}$ representing that part of the total quantity of (B) which is exchanged for (A) at the price $p_{a,m}$ of (A). It follows that $Y = Q_b - D_{a,m} p_{a,m}$, or the area of the rectangle $D_{a,m}\beta Q_b A_m$, represents that part, which is withheld from sale and taken back from the market by the original holders of (B) at the price just mentioned, $p_{a,m}$ of (A). Moreover, in all cases the quantities Q_b, p_a, D_a and Y are invariably related by the equation:

$$Q_b = Y + D_a p_a.$$

Thus, when $xy = Q_b$, when, in other words, the curve passing through the point Q_b is the *hyperbola of the total existing quantity* of (B), the curve $A_d A_p$ is the boundary line between that part of (B) which is

exchanged for (A) and that part of (B) which is withheld from sale
depending on the price of (A) in terms of (B). Naturally, the same
general relationship could be found between the curve B_dB_p and the
hyperbola of the total existing quantity of (A), $xy=Q_a$, which we
might have been drawn in Fig. 5.

55. Demand curves are, therefore, enclosed by hyperbolas of total
existing quantity. It may be added that, in general, demand curves
meet the co-ordinate axes and are not asymptotic to them.

Demand curves generally intersect their demand axes, because the
quantity of any good which an individual will take is ordinarily
finite even when the price is zero. If oats were obtainable absolutely
free of charge, some individuals might keep ten and others a hundred
horses, but no one would keep an infinite number of horses and
consequently no one would demand an infinite quantity of oats.
Now the sum total of the separate quantities of oats demanded at
the price zero, being the sum of finite quantities, would itself have to
be a finite quantity.

Demand curves usually intersect their price axes, because the price
of any commodity may conceivably be set so high, though short of
infinity, that no one at all will demand even an infinitely small
quantity of it.[b] We cannot, however, make any absolute assertions
to that effect. It is perfectly possible for a case to arise where
all or a part of commodity (B) is offered *unconditionally at whatever
price it can fetch*.[6] In that case the demand curve A_dA_p will
coincide, in whole or in part, with the hyperbola passing through Q_b
or with some other hyperbola closer to the axes. Hence, in order to
keep our minds open to all contingencies, we shall consider demand
curves capable of taking all possible positions between the co-
ordinate axes and the hyperbolas of total existing quantity.[c]

56. Now that we have described the nature of the direct and
immediate relationship which connects the effective demand for a
commodity with its price in terms of another commodity, we shall
proceed to set forth a mathematical expression of this relationship.

Thus, in the case of commodity (A), we may represent this
relationship geometrically by the curve A_dA_p, or algebraically by the
equation (§52) of this curve

$$D_a=F_a(p_a).$$

In the case of commodity (B), we may represent the relationship
either geometrically by the curve B_dB_p or algebraically by the
equation of this curve

$$D_b=F_b(p_b).$$

Moreover, having also described the nature of the indirect and

QUANTITY

QUANTITY

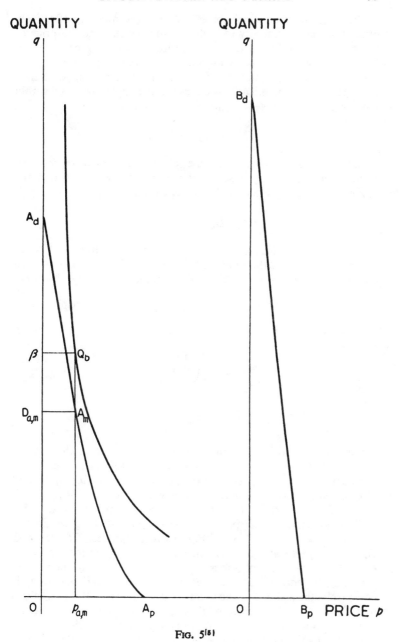

FIG. 5[5]

mediate relationship which exists between the quantity effectively
offered of one commodity in exchange for another and the price of
the other commodity in terms of the first, we shall proceed to set
forth a mathematical expression for this relationship as well.

In the case of the commodity (A), the relationship in question may
be represented geometrically by a series of rectangles inscribed within
the curve $B_d B_p$, or algebraically by the equation (§53)

$$O_a = D_b p_b = F_b(p_b) p_b.$$

In the case of commodity (B), the relationship may be represented
either geometrically by a series of rectangles inscribed within the
curve $A_d A_p$, or algebraically by the equation

$$O_b = D_a p_a = F_a(p_a) p_a.$$

From these formulas it is a very simple matter to deduce
others to represent the relation between the effective offer of each
commodity and its price in terms of the other commodity. It is only
necessary to substitute $\dfrac{1}{p_a}$ for the price p_b and $\dfrac{1}{p_b}$ for the price p_a in
the last two equations by virtue of the relation $p_a p_b = 1$. We then
obtain

$$O_a = F_b\left(\frac{1}{p_a}\right)\frac{1}{p_a}$$

and

$$O_b = F_a\left(\frac{1}{p_b}\right)\frac{1}{p_b}.$$

Possessing all these elements, we are ready to solve the general
problem of the exchange of two commodities for each other. This
problem may be stated as follows: *Given two commodities, (A) and
(B), and the demand curve of each in terms of the other, or the equations
of these curves, to determine their respective equilibrium prices.*

57. Geometrically the problem consists in inscribing within the
two curves $A_d A_p$ and $B_d B_p$ of Fig. 6 two rectangles, $OD_a A p_a$ and
$OD_b B p_b$ respectively, such that their bases [prices] are reciprocals of
each other, while their altitudes are so related that the altitude of the
first OD_a is equal[7] to the area of the second $OD_b \times Op_b$ and,
conversely, the altitude of the second OD_b is equal to the area of the
first $OD_a \times Op_a$. The bases of these two rectangles, Op_a and Op_b,
represent equilibrium prices, inasmuch as at these prices the demand for (A), represented by the altitude OD_a equals the offer of

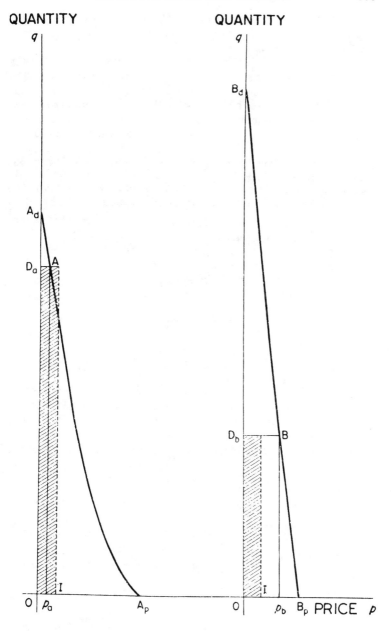

FIG. 6[8]

(A) represented by the area $OD_b \times Op_b$ and the demand for (B) represented by the altitude OD_b equals the offer of (B) represented by the area $OD_a \times Op_a$ (§47).

In saying that *the altitude of either rectangle is equal to the area of the other*, I have been equating terms that are not homogeneous. But under the circumstances homogeneity is not necessary, since the condition that the bases be reciprocals of each other implies the predetermination of a common unit, say OI, which was used in the construction of both curves. To make the point still clearer, I might add that the height of each rectangle should contain as many of these predetermined units of length as the other rectangle contains similar units of area; or, alternatively, that the area of each rectangle should equal the area of a rectangle having the same altitude as the other rectangle but with a base one unit in length. [See shaded areas in Fig. 6.] It follows, moreover, from the terms of the problem that the base of either rectangle is equal to the inverse ratio of the altitude of that rectangle to the altitude of the other,[9] and to the direct ratio of the area of that rectangle to the area of the other.[10]

58. Algebraically the problem consists in finding the two roots, p_a and p_b, of one of the following pairs of equations:

$$\begin{cases} F_a(p_a)=F_b(p_b)p_b \\ p_a p_b=1 \end{cases}$$

or

$$\begin{cases} F_a(p_a)p_a=F_b(p_b) \\ p_a p_b=1, \end{cases}$$

or, alternatively, of two equations which are expressions of equality between D_a and O_a and between D_b and O_b respectively:

$$\begin{cases} F_a(p_a)=F_b\left(\dfrac{1}{p_a}\right)\dfrac{1}{p_a} \\ F_a\left(\dfrac{1}{p_b}\right)\dfrac{1}{p_b}=F_b(p_b). \end{cases}$$

59. Moreover, the geometric and algebraic methods may be combined into one. Starting with the known curves $A_a A_p$ and $B_a B_p$ or their equations

$$D_a=F_a(p_a)$$

and

$$D_b=F_b(p_b),$$

respectively, let us now draw the curves KLM and NPQ (Fig. 7) with the equations

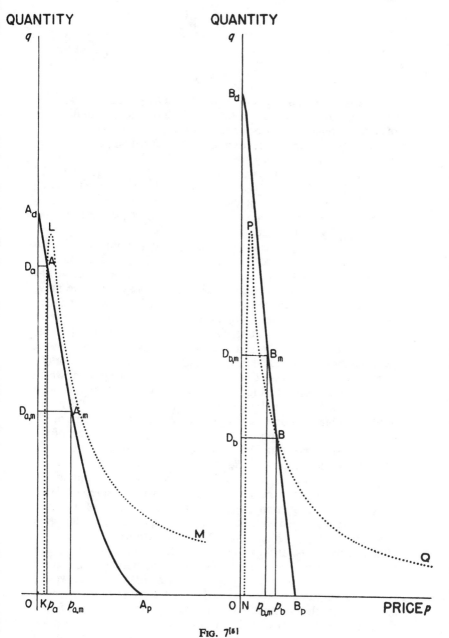

FIG. 7[5]

$$O_a = F_b \left(\frac{1}{p_a}\right) \frac{1}{p_a}$$

and

$$O_b = F_a \left(\frac{1}{p_b}\right) \frac{1}{p_b}.$$

KLM will intersect $A_d A_p$ at the point A, and NPQ will intersect $B_d B_p$ at the point B, i.e. at those very points which give us the [equilibrium] rectangles we have described above (§57).

It is easy to interpret the meaning of the dotted curves, KLM and NPQ, and to see how they are drawn.

The first curve KLM is an *offer curve* of (A), no longer identified with the demand curve of (B) which represented the offer of (A) as a function of p_b by means of the areas of inscribed rectangles constructed on the co-ordinate axes, but distinct, depicting this same offer of (A) by the ordinates as a function of p_a.

The curve starts [at the extreme right] from [an ordinate of] zero for an infinitely high price of (A) in terms of (B), corresponding to an infinitesimally small price of (B) in terms of (A). In other words, KLM is asymptotic to the price axis. The curve rises as we move along it [from the extreme right] towards the origin, with each fall in the price of (A) in terms of (B) corresponding to a rise in the price of (B) in terms of (A). It reaches its maximum [ordinate] at the point L the abscissa of which represents a price of (A) in terms of (B) such that its reciprocal $p_{b,m}$, i.e. the price of (B) in terms of (A) measured by the abscissa $Op_{b,m}$ of the point B_m is the price at which the rectangle inscribed within $B_d B_p$ is a maximum. Then the curve KLM falls as we move along it [to the left of L] towards the origin until its ordinate becomes zero again at a price of (A) in terms of (B) represented by the length OK, this price being the reciprocal of the price of (B) in terms of (A) measured by the abscissa OB_p of the point B_p where the curve $B_d B_p$ meets the price axis.

Similarly, the second curve NPQ is an offer curve of (B), no longer identified with the demand curve of (A) which represented the offer of (B) as a function of p_a by means of the areas of inscribed rectangles constructed on the co-ordinate axes, but distinct, depicting this same offer of (B) by the ordinates as a function of p_b.

This curve starts [at the extreme right] from [an ordinate of] zero for an infinitely high price of (B) in terms of (A), corresponding to an infinitesimally small price of (A) in terms of (B). In other words, NPQ is asymptotic to the price axis. The curve rises as we move along it [from the extreme right] towards the origin, with each fall in the price of (B) in terms of (A) corresponding to a rise in the price of (A) in terms of (B). It reaches its maximum [ordinate] at the point P, the abscissa of which represents a price of (B) in terms of (A) such that its reciprocal $p_{a,m}$, i.e. the price of (A) in terms of (B) measured by the abscissa $Op_{a,m}$ of the point A_m, is the price at which the rectangle inscribed within A_dA_p is a maximum. Then the curve NPQ falls as we move along it [to the left of P] towards the origin until its ordinate becomes zero again at a price of (B) in terms of (A) represented by the length ON, this price being the reciprocal of the price of (A) in terms of (B) measured by the abscissa OA_p of the point A_p where the curve A_dA_p meets the price axis.

It is obvious that the shapes of the curves KLM and NPQ are intimately related to the shapes of B_dB_p and A_dA_p respectively. If we had supposed the latter curves to be different, the former, too, would have been entirely different. At all events, in the diagram we have just been discussing (Fig. 7), the curve B_dB_p passes, while falling from left to right, through the point B_m [corner of the maximum inscribed rectangle] *before* cutting the dotted curve NPQ at a point where NPQ is rising as we move along it [leftwards] *from its zero ordinate* [at the extreme right] *to its maximum ordinate at P*; and, consequently, the curve A_dA_p passes, while it too falls from left to right, through the point A_m [corner of the maximum inscribed rectangle] *after* cutting the dotted curve KLM at a point where KLM is falling as we move along it [leftwards] *from its maximum ordinate L to its zero ordinate* [at the extreme left].

60. Now, under these circumstances, it is evident that if the two curves A_dA_p and KLM intersect at the point A, then the curve A_dA_p lies *below* the curve KLM *to the right* of this point and *above* the curve KLM *to the left*; and it is likewise evident that if the two curves B_dB_p and NPQ intersect at the point B, then the curve B_dB_p lies *below* the curve NPQ *to the right* of this point and *above* the curve NPQ *to the left*.

Thus, since $p_a=\dfrac{1}{\mu}$ and $p_b=\mu$ are, by hypothesis, the prices at which $D_a=O_a$ and $O_b=D_b$, it follows that at all prices of (A) in terms of (B) higher than p_a, corresponding to prices of (B) in terms of (A) lower than p_b, $O_a>D_a$ and $D_b>O_b$. Conversely, at all prices of (A) in terms of (B) lower than p_a, corresponding to prices of (B) in terms of (A) higher than p_b, $D_a>O_a$ and $O_b>D_b$. In the first case, the equilibrium price could only be restored by an increase in p_b corresponding to a decrease in p_a; whereas in the second case, equilibrium price could only be restored by an increase in p_a, corresponding to a decrease in p_b.

We are now ready to formulate in the following terms *the law of effective offer and effective demand or the law of the establishment* [*or emergence*][11] *of equilibrium prices* in the case of the exchange of two commodities for each other: *Given two commodities, for the market to be in equilibrium with respect to these commodities, or for the price of either commodity to be stationary in terms of the other, it is necessary and sufficient that the effective demand be equal the effective offer of each commodity. Where this equality does not obtain, in order to reach equilibrium price, the commodity having an effective demand greater than its effective offer must rise in price, and the commodity having an effective offer greater than its effective demand must fall in price.*[12]

Such is the law that we might have been tempted to formulate earlier, immediately after our study of the stock exchange [13] (§42), but it was necessary first to develop a rigorous demonstration (§48).

61. We are now in a position to see clearly what the mechanism of market competition is. It is the practical solution, reached through a rise or fall in prices, of the same problem of exchange to which we have just given a theoretical and mathematical solution; but it must be understood that we do not have the slightest idea of substituting one solution for the other. The rapidity and reliability of the practical solution leave no room for improvement. It is a matter of daily experience that even in big markets where there are neither brokers nor auctioneers, the current equilibrium price is determined within a few minutes, and considerable quantities of merchandise are exchanged at that price within half or three quarters of an hour. In fact, the theoretical solution would be absolutely impracticable in almost every case. On the other hand, it is no valid objection against our method to speak of the difficulty of deriving [empirical] curves or equations of exchange. Whether there is any advantage to be found in constructing all or part of either the demand or the offer curve of a given commodity in certain cases, and whether it is possible or impossible to do so, are questions on which we reserve judgement entirely. For the moment, we are examining the problem of exchange in general, and the [abstract] conception, pure and simple, of curves of exchange is sufficient and at the same time indispensable.[d]

Lesson 7

DISCUSSION OF THE SOLUTION OF THE PROBLEM OF EXCHANGE OF TWO COMMODITIES FOR EACH OTHER

62. To recapitulate: given two commodities (A) and (B), and given the following equations connecting their effective demands with their respective prices:

$$D_a = F_a(p_a)$$

and

$$D_b = F_b(p_b),$$

the equilibrium price is determined either by the equation

$$D_a v_a = D_b v_b,$$

or, on substitution of the values of D_a and D_b [from the first two equations given above], by the equation

$$F_a(p_a)v_a = F_b(p_b)v_b,$$

which can be written in the form

$$F_a(p_a) = F_b\left(\frac{1}{p_a}\right)\frac{1}{p_a}, \qquad \qquad ..(1)$$

or in the form

$$F_a\left(\frac{1}{p_b}\right)\frac{1}{p_b} = F_b(p_b), \qquad \qquad ..(2)$$

according as we wish to solve for p_a or p_b. Equation (1) expresses the fact that $D_a = O_a$, and equation (2) that $O_b = D_b$.

In §59 we have already given a [geometrical] solution to the above equation in both forms (1) and (2) by the intersection of curve $D_a = F_a(p_a)$ by curve $O_a = F_b\left(\frac{1}{p_a}\right)\frac{1}{p_a}$, and the intersection of curve $O_b = F_a\left(\frac{1}{p_b}\right)\frac{1}{p_b}$ by curve $D_b = F_b(p_b)$; but this solution requires further elucidation.

63. We shall not discuss the solution of all possible cases, for that would be both tedious and premature. We shall restrict ourselves to the relatively simple, general cases portrayed in Fig. 7 of the previous Lesson.[a] In this diagram we assumed that the curves $A_d A_p$ and

107

$B_d B_p$ were continuous and that no more than one maximum rectangle could be inscribed within each, as the co-ordinates (p_a, D_a) and (p_b, D_b) [of the upper right-hand corners] of these rectangles were allowed to move along their respective curves between the points where the price of the commodity is zero and the demand for the commodity falls to zero. We need only consider that portion of each of these curves which falls within the first quadrant, where we shall confine our attention, in the one case, to the segment between the points A_d and A_p, and, in the other case, to the segment between the points B_d and B_p. This clearly follows from the very nature of the phenomenon of exchange. Under these assumptions, KLM and NPQ must be continuous curves having only one maximum ordinate each. Even in so narrowly defined a case as this there is material for an interesting discussion.

64. We have been assuming all along that each of the two pairs of intersecting curves, $A_d A_p$ and KLM on the one hand, and $B_d B_p$ and NPQ on the other, had only one point of intersection: point A for the first pair and point B for the second.[1] We must, however, note, to begin with, that it is possible for these curves to have no point of intersection at all. If, for example, $B_d B_p$ converged on the price axis to the left of the point N, it would not intersect the curve NPQ. In that case the curve KLM would start [from K] on the price axis at a point situated to the right of the point A_p and it would not intersect the curve $A_d A_p$.[2] There would be no solution.

There is nothing surprising in this eventuality. It occurs whenever no one holding (B) is willing to give A_p units of (B) for 1 unit of (A), or 1 unit of (B) for $\frac{1}{A_p}$ [$=ON$] units of (A); while, at the same time, no one at all can be found holding (A) who is willing to give $\frac{1}{A_p}$ [$=ON$] units of (A) for 1 unit of (B), or 1 unit of (A) for A_p units of (B).[3] Obviously, under these circumstances the bids and offers would be such that no transaction could take place. To be sure, at any price of (A) in terms of (B) below A_p, corresponding to some price of (B) in terms of (A) above $\frac{1}{A_p}$ [$=ON$], there would be a number of demanders of (A) offering (B) in exchange, but no one would demand (B) in exchange for (A). Also, at any price of (B) in terms of (A) below $\frac{1}{A_p}$ [$=ON$], corresponding to some price of (A) in terms of (B) above A_p, there would be a number of demanders of (B) offering (A) in exchange, but no one would demand (A) in exchange for (B).

65. The above case having been thoroughly explored, a close examination of the shape of the curves reveals the further possibility that they may have several points of intersection.[b] If, for example, the two commodities (A) and (B) were such that the demand for (A) in terms of (B) continued to be represented, as before, by the curve $A_d A_p$, while the demand for (B) in terms of (A), however, was represented by the curve $B'_d B'_p$ [Fig. 8(b)], then the new curve $B'_d B'_p$ would intersect the curve NPQ at three points: B, B' and B''. In this case, the former offer curve of (A), KLM, would be replaced by the curve $K'L'M'$ [Fig. 8(b)] which would intersect the curve $A_d A_p$ at three points: A, A' and A'', the point A corresponding to the point B, the point A' to the point B' and the point A'' to the point B''. There would then be three different solutions to the problem of exchange of two commodities, (A) and (B), for each other, since there would be three systems of pairs of rectangles inscribed within the curves $A_d A_p$ and $B'_d B'_p$, each rectangle of any pair being so related to the other that its base was the reciprocal of the other, while its altitude was equal to the area of the other. Do all three solutions, however, have the same significance?

66. Taking first thóse two of the three pairs of rectangles which are identified by the points A' and B' for one pair and A'' and B'' for the other, we find that the situation in both these cases is precisely the same as that which we described earlier in the case of the pairs of rectangles designated by the points A and B in Fig. 7 where we had a unique solution (§60). The curve $A_d A_p$ lies *below* the curve $K'L'M'$ *to the right*, and *above* the curve $K'L'M'$ *to the left* of the point A' at which the two curves $A_d A_p$ and $K'L'M'$ intersect. Likewise the curve $B'_d B'_p$ lies *below* the curve NPQ *to the right*, and *above* the curve NPQ *to the left* of the point B' at which two curves $B'_d B'_p$ and NPQ intersect. Moreover, the curve $A_d A_p$ lies *below* the curve $K'L'M'$ *to the right*, and *above* the curve $K'L'M'$ *to the left* of the point A''; while the curve $B'_d B'_p$ again lies *below* the curve NPQ *to the right*, and *above* the curve NPQ *to the left* of the point B''.

In both instances, to the right of the point of equilibrium, *the offer of the commodity in question is greater than the demand for it*, which must result in a *fall* in price, that is, in a return to the point of equilibrium. Again, in both instances, *to the left* of the point of equilibrium, *the demand for the commodity in question is greater than its offer*, which must result in a *rise* in price, that is, in a movement towards the point of equilibrium. Such an equilibrium is exactly similar to that of a suspended body of which the centre of gravity lies directly beneath the point of suspension, so that if this centre of gravity were displaced from the vertical line beneath the point of suspension, it would automatically return to its original position

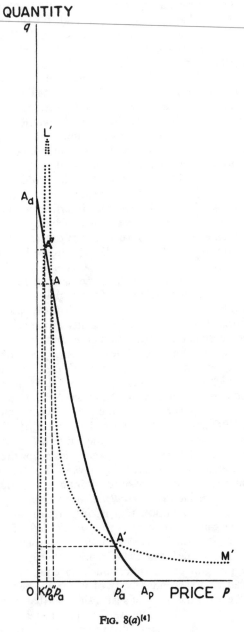

FIG. 8(a)[4]

QUANTITY

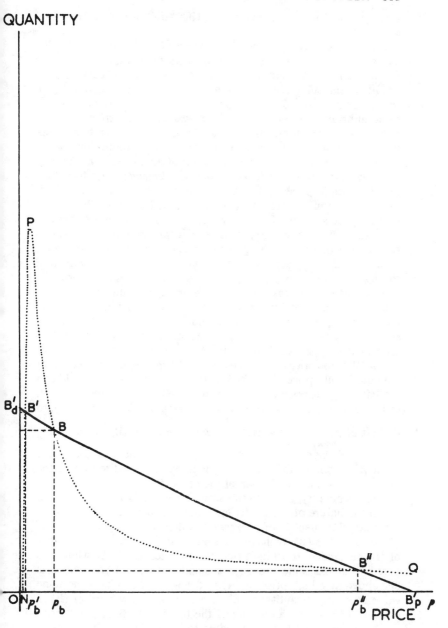

FIG. 8(b)[4]

through the force of gravitation. This equilibrium is, therefore, *stable.*[5]

67. The same is not true of the points A and B of Fig. 8. The curve A_dA_p lies *above* the curve $K'L'M'$ *to the right*, and below the curve $K'L'M'$ *to the left* of the point A. Likewise, the curve $B'_dB'_p$ lies *above* the curve NPQ *to the right*, and *below* the curve NPQ *to the left* of the point B. Hence, in this case, *to the right* of the point of equilibrium, *the demand for the commodity in question is greater than its offer*, which must lead to a *rise* in price, that is, to a movement farther and farther away from the point of equilibrium. And, in this same case, *to the left* of the point of equilibrium, *the offer of the commodity in question is greater than the demand for it*, which must lead to a *fall* in price, that is, to a movement once again away from the point of equilibrium. This equilibrium is exactly similar to that of a suspended body of which the point of suspension lies directly beneath the centre of gravity, so that if this centre of gravity once leaves the vertical line above the point of suspension, it does not return automatically but keeps on moving farther and farther away until through the force of gravitation it reaches the position vertically beneath the point of suspension. Such an equilibrium is *unstable*.

68. As a matter of fact, only the systems of rectangles identified by the letters A', B' and A'', B'' give solutions of the problem, for the system designated by A, B merely marks the boundary separating each of the respective fields of the two solutions. To the right of $p_b=\mu$,[6][c] the price of (B) in terms of (A) moves in the direction of the equilibrium price p''_b, which is the abscissa of the point B''; to the left of p_b, the price of (B) in terms of (A) moves in the direction of the price p'_b, which is the abscissa of the point B'. Conversely, to the left of $p_a=\dfrac{1}{\mu}$,[d] the price of (A) in terms of (B) moves in the direction of the equilibrium price p''_a, which is the abscissa of the point A''; while to the right of p_a it moves in the direction of the price p'_a, which is the abscissa of the point A'.

This eventuality, as is readily seen, corresponds to a situation in which the nature of the two commodities is such that it is possible for a large[e] quantity of (A), which is demanded at a low price of (A) in terms of (B), to have the same value as a small[f] quantity of (B) demanded at a high price of (B) in terms of (A), while it is possible, at the same time, for a small quantity of (A), which is demanded at a high price of (A) in terms of (B), to have the same value as a large quantity of (B) demanded at a low price of (B) in terms of (A). Then, according as the bidding starts at a low price of (A) in terms of (B) corresponding to a high price of (B) in terms of (A), or at a low price of (B) in terms of (A) corresponding to a high price of (A) in terms of (B), it will culminate in the first or the second of the two equilibria. We shall see later[7] whether such a contingency may also arise when several commodities are exchanged for one another through the medium of a *numéraire* and money.[g]

69. Thus far in our discussion we have assumed that the demand curves $A_d A_p$, $B_d B_p$ and $B'_d B'_p$ have intercepts on both the co-ordinate axes. We must now examine the extreme case where the demand curves coincide with hyperbolas of total existing quantity and are, therefore, asymptotic to these axes. [8][h]

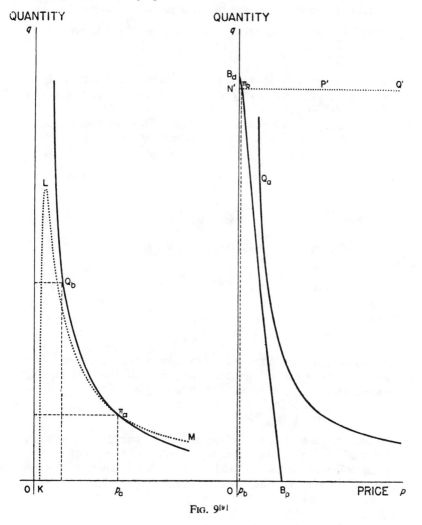

FIG. 9[g]

For example, if A_dA_p coincided with the hyperbola $D_ap_a=Q_b$, so that all of commodity (B) were offered unconditionally at whatever price it could fetch,[10] equation (1) [§62] would become[11]

$$Q_b\frac{1}{p_a}=F_b\left(\frac{1}{p_a}\right)\frac{1}{p_a},$$

which represents the intersection of the hyperbola passing through Q_b with the curve *KLM* at the point π_a in Fig. 9. I am leaving out of account the solution given by the equation $\frac{1}{p_a}=0$ or $p_a=\infty$.

Under these circumstances, equation (2) [§62] would become[12]

$$Q_b=F_b(p_b),$$

which represents the intersection at the point π_b of the curve B_dB_p with the straight line $N'P'Q'$ drawn parallel to the price axis at a distance $ON'=Q_b$.

70. Finally, if both commodities were offered unconditionally at whatever price they could fetch, we should have the equations [13]

$$Q_b\frac{1}{p_a}=Q_a$$

and

$$Q_b=Q_a\frac{1}{p_b},$$

from which we obtain the following values of p_a and p_b:

$$p_a=\frac{Q_b}{Q_a}$$

and

$$p_b=\frac{Q_a}{Q_b}.$$

In this case, the two commodities would be exchanged for each other at a rate exactly equal to the inverse ratio of the total existing quantities, that is, according to the following equation:

$$Q_av_a=Q_bv_b.$$

Moreover, it is easily seen that the equality described above between the total existing quantities and the quantities exchanged of the two commodities is tantamount to equality between the effective demand for and the effective offer of both of them.[4]

Lesson 8

UTILITY CURVES OR WANT CURVES. THE
THEOREM OF MAXIMUM UTILITY OF
COMMODITIES

71. Our study of the nature of exchange up to this point makes it possible for us now to examine the cause of this phenomenon. If, in fact, prices result mathematically from demand curves, the causes and primary conditions that generate and affect demand curves will also generate and affect prices.[a]

Let us, therefore, return to the individual demand curves, and take, for example, the curve $a_{d,1}a_{p,1}$ (Fig. 1 in §51), which represents geometrically the demand schedule of holder (1) of (B) for (A). To begin with, let us see what circumstance determines the position of the point $a_{d,1}$ where the curve starts its descent from the demand axis. The length $Oa_{d,1}$ represents the quantity of (A) effectively demanded by the above-mentioned individual at the price zero, that is to say, it represents the quantity which he would consume if commodity (A) were obtainable free of charge But upon what does this quantity generally depend? It depends upon a certain kind of utility of the commodity which we shall call *extensive* utility,[1] because it is found in the capacity of the particular kind of wealth under consideration to fill wants that are more or less extensive or numerous, depending upon the number of people that feel them and the strength with which they feel them[2]—in a word, because more or less of the commodity would be consumed even if no sacrifice at all had to be made to procure it. This first attribute of utility is simple and absolute, in the sense that the extensive utility of (A) does not influence anything but the demand curves of (A), and the extensive[3] utility of (B) does not influence anything but the demand curves of (B). Furthermore, extensive utility is a measurable quantity, inasmuch as it consists in *the quantity that will be taken at the price zero*, and this quantity can be measured.

72. Extensive utility, however, does not describe the whole of utility; it is only one attribute. There is another attribute which reveals itself to us as soon as we turn our attention to the circumstances which determine the slope of the curve $a_{d,1}a_{p,1}$ and consequently the position of the point $a_{p,1}$, where the curve meets the price axis. The slope of the curve is simply a ratio of two quantities, viz. the increase in price and the resulting diminution in demand. Upon what does this ratio generally depend? It depends upon

115

another type of utility of the commodity which we shall call *intensive utility*,[4] because it is found in the capacity of this type of wealth to fill wants that are more or less intense or urgent in proportion to the number of people who continue to feel these wants and the persistence with which each person feels them notwithstanding the expensiveness of the commodity—in a word, because the magnitude of the sacrifice which must be made to procure it affects the quantity consumed of the commodity. Unlike the first attribute of utility,

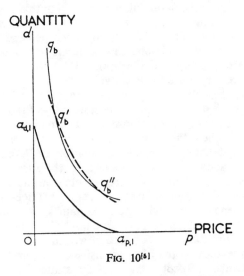

Fig. 10[5]

this second attribute is complex and relative, inasmuch as the slope of the demand curves of each of the two commodities, (A) as well as (B), is determined by both the intensive utility of (A) and the intensive utility of (B). Thus, the slope of the demand curve, which can be very simply defined in terms of mathematics as *the limit of the ratio of a decrease in demand to an increase in price*, still remains for us a complex relation between the intensive utilities of the two commodities exchanged.

73. There is still another factor which affects the slope of the demand curve for (A), $a_{d,1}a_{p,1}$, and that is the original stock, q_b, of commodity (B) in the possession of holder (1). In general, an individual demand curve lies below the hyperbola of the individual's initial stock, in the same way that an aggregate demand curve lies below the hyperbola of total existing quantity.[6] As the hyperbola of an individual's original stock moves towards or away from the origin of the co-ordinate axes, the individual demand curve will

move along with it, shifting as it would under the influence of changes in intensive utilities. The diagram (Fig. 10) faithfully portrays this necessity in the one instance as in the other.

74. The above analysis is incomplete; and it seems impossible, at first glance, to pursue it further, because intensive utility, considered absolutely, is so elusive, since it has no direct or measurable relationship to space or time, as do extensive utility and the quantity of a commodity possessed. Still, this difficulty is not insurmountable. We need only assume that such a direct and measurable relationship does exist, and we shall find ourselves in a position to give an exact, mathematical account of the respective influences on prices of extensive utility, intensive utility and the initial stock possessed.

I shall, therefore, assume the existence of a standard measure of intensity of wants or intensive utility, which is applicable not only to similar units of the same kind of wealth but also to different units of various kinds of wealth.[7] With this in mind, let us draw two co-ordinate axes, one vertical, Oq, and the other horizontal, Or, as in Fig. 11.[b] On the vertical axis Oq, starting at the point O, I lay off successive lengths, $Oq', q'q'', q''q''' \ldots$, which represent the units of (B) which holder (1) would successively consume in a certain interval of time if he had these units at his disposal. I am assuming that, during this interval, the utility, both extensive and intensive, remains *fixed* for each party, which makes it possible for me to include time implicitly in the expression of utility. Were this not the case and had I supposed utility to be a *variable* functionally related to time, then time would have had to figure explicitly in the problem. And we should then have passed from economic *statics* to economic *dynamics*.

All the successive units of (B) consumed by holder (1), from the first unit which fills his most urgent want to the last after which satiety sets in, have a diminishing intensive utility for him. Our problem is to find a mathematical expression for this diminution. If commodity (B) is such that it is naturally consumed in [whole] units like pieces of furniture or articles of clothing, I lay off, as in Fig. 11, on the horizontal axis, Or, and on lines drawn parallel to this axis through the points $q', q'', \ldots$ the lengths $O\beta_{r,1}, q'r'', q''r''' \ldots$, which represent respectively the *intensive utilities* of each of the successive units consumed. I then draw in the rectangles $Oq'R'\beta_{r,1}, q'q''R''r''$, $q''q'''R'''r''' \ldots$, and obtain the curve $\beta_{r,1}R'r''R''r'''R''' \ldots$, which is a discontinuous curve. If, on the other hand, commodity (B) could be consumed in infinitely small morsels, like food, the intensive utility would diminish not only from one unit to the next but also from the first to the last fraction of each unit, and the discontinuous curve $\beta_{r,1}R'r''R''r'''R''' \ldots$ would resolve itself into the continuous curve $\beta_{r,1} r'' r''' \ldots \beta_{q,1}$. Similarly, I could construct the curve $\alpha_{r,1} \alpha_{q,1}$ of Fig. 12 for commodity (A). Whether the curve be continuous or discontinuous, I postulate that intensive utilities always diminish from that of the first unit or fraction of a unit consumed to that of the last unit or fraction of a unit consumed.

QUANTITY

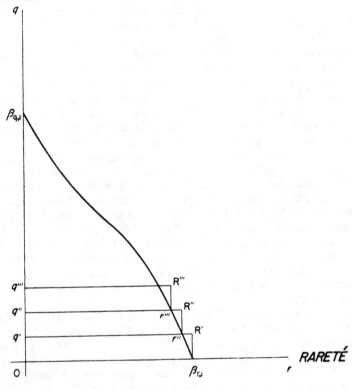

FIG. 11[8]

The lengths $O\beta_{q,1}$ and $O\alpha_{q,1}$ [Fig. 12] represent the *extensive utilities* of commodities (B) and (A) respectively for holder (1), i.e. the extent of holder (1)'s wants for commodities (B) and (A). The areas $O\beta_{q,1}\beta_{r,1}$ and $O\alpha_{q,1}\alpha_{r,1}$ represent the *virtual utilities* of commodities (B) and (A) respectively for the same holder, or the sum of holder (1)'s wants for (B) and for (A), in terms of both their extensive and intensive dimensions. The curves $\alpha_{r,1}\alpha_{q,1}$ and $\beta_{r,1}\beta_{q,1}$ are, therefore, holder (1)'s *utility curves* or *want curves* for commodities

(A) and (B). But that is not all, for these curves have a double character which we have still to consider.

75. If we let the term *effective utility* designate the sum total of wants satisfied by any given *quantity consumed* of a commodity, these wants being measured in terms of both their extensive and intensive

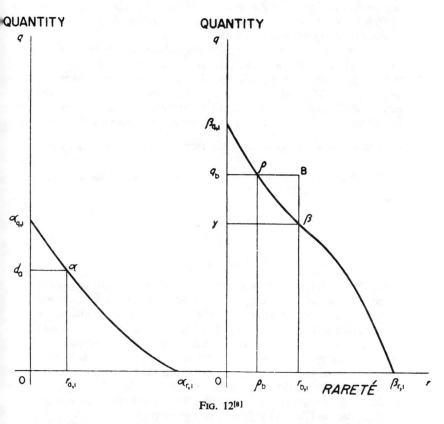

FIG. 12[8]

dimensions, then the curve $\beta_{r,1}\beta_{q,1}$ becomes our individual's curve of effective utility, considered [in respect of the enclosed area] as a function of the quantity of (B) which he consumes. For example, in case he consumes the quantity q_b of (B) represented by the length Oq_b, the effective utility is represented by the area $Oq_b\varrho\beta_{r,1}$. If, now, we let the term *rareté*[9] designate the intensity of the last want satisfied by any given *quantity consumed* of a commodity, then the curve $\beta_{r,1}\beta_{q,1}$ becomes our individual's *rareté* curve, considered [in respect of the ordinate] as a function of the quantity of (B) which he consumes. Thus, in case he consumes a quantity q_b of (B), represented by the length Oq_b, the rareté is ϱ_b, represented by the length $q_b\varrho = O\varrho_b$. Similarly, the curve $\alpha_{r,1}\alpha_{q,1}$ is, at one and the same time, a curve of effective utility and a rareté curve, both being functions of the quantity of (A) consumed.[c] Hence I call one of the co-ordinate axes the rareté axis and the other the quantity axis. We must postulate, I repeat, that rareté increases as the quantity possessed decreases, and vice versa.

Analytically, if we are given effective utilities as functions of the quantities consumed according to the equations $u = \Phi_{a,1}(q)$ and $u = \Phi_{b,1}(q)$, then the raretés are designated by the derivatives, $\Phi'_{a,1}(q)$ and $\Phi'_{b,1}(q)$. If, on the other hand, we are given the raretés as functions of the quantities consumed, according to the equations $r = \phi_{a,1}(q)$ and $r = \phi_{b,1}(q)$, then the effective utilities are designated by the definite integrals from 0 to q: $\int_o^q \phi_{a,1}(q)dq$ and $\int_o^q \phi_{b,1}(q)dq$. We then have for u and r the mutually related expressions[d]

$$u = \Phi(q) = \int_o^q \phi(q)dq,$$

and

$$r = \Phi'(q) = \phi(q).$$

76. If, on the basis of these considerations, the extensive and intensive utility of commodity (A) for holder (1) of (B) is represented geometrically by the continuous curve $\alpha_{r,1}\alpha_{q,1}$ and algebraically by the equation of this curve $r = \phi_{a,1}(q)$, while the extensive and intensive utility of commodity (B) for this same holder is represented geometrically by the continuous curve $\beta_{r,1}\beta_{q,1}$ and algebraically by the equation of this curve, $r = \phi_{b,1}(q)$; and if the quantity q_b, represented by the length Oq_b, is the initial quantity of (B) which holder (1) possesses, let us see whether we can determine accurately what his demand for (A) will be at any given price.[e]

It follows from the way in which we have set up our want curves and from the properties we have ascribed to curves drawn in this way that if holder (1) were to reserve all of his q_b units of (B) for his own consumption, he would gratify a sum total of wants represented by the area $Oq_b\varrho\beta_{r,1}$. This is not, however, what our holder of (B) would ordinarily do, because, more often than not, he would be able to gratify a larger sum total of wants by consuming only part of his (B) and exchanging the rest for some quantity of (A) at the current price. If, for example, when the price of (A) in terms of (B) is p_a, our holder keeps back only y units of (B) represented by Oy in Fig. 12, and if he exchanges the rest, $o_b = q_b - y$, represented by yq_b, for d_a units of (A), represented by Od_a, he will be able to gratify a sum total of wants represented by the two areas, $Oy\beta\beta_{r,1}$ and $Od_a\alpha\alpha_{r,1}$ which may be larger than the previous sum total. If we suppose that his object in trading is to gratify the greatest possible sum total of wants, then, surely, d_a is determined for a given p_a by the condition that the sum of the two areas, $Oy\beta\beta_{r,1}$ and $Od_a\alpha\alpha_{r,1}$ be maximized.[7] Now the condition of such a maximum is that the ratio of the intensities $r_{a,1}$ and $r_{b,1}$ of the last wants satisfied by the quantities d_a and y, i.e. the ratio of their respective *raretés* upon completion of this exchange, be equal to the price p_a.[10]

77. Suppose this condition to be satisfied; then we have the simultaneous equations

$$o_b = q_b - y = d_a p_a,$$

$$r_{a,1} = p_a r_{b,1}.$$

Eliminating p_a, we obtain[11]

$$d_a r_{a,1} = o_b r_{b,1}.$$

If we replace d_a, o_b, $r_{a,1}$ and $r_{b,1}$ by the corresponding [geometrical] lengths by which they are represented in Fig. 12, namely Od_a, $q_b y$, $d_a\alpha$ and $y\beta$ respectively, we have

$$Od_a \times d_a\alpha = q_b y \times y\beta.$$

Thus the areas of the two rectangles, $Od_a\alpha r_{a,1}$ and $yq_b B\beta$, are equal. But it is evident from the very nature of the curves $\alpha_{r,1}\alpha_{q,1}$ and $\beta_{r,1}\beta_{q,1}$, that, on the one hand,

$$\text{area } Od_a\alpha\alpha_{r,1} > Od_a \times d_a\alpha,$$

while, on the other hand,

$$q_b y \times y\beta > \text{area } yq_b \varrho\beta.$$

Therefore

$$\text{area } Od_a\alpha\alpha_{r,1} > \text{area } yq_b \varrho\beta.$$

It is clear that the exchange of a quantity o_b of (B) for a quantity d_a of (A) is advantageous for our holder of (B), because the area of satisfaction he acquires thereby is greater than the area of satisfaction he relinquishes. This, however, is not sufficient, for we have still to show that the particular exchange transaction we have been considering is more advantageous for our holder than any other exchange transaction involving the relinquishment of a smaller or greater quantity of (B) than o_b in return for a [correspondingly] smaller or greater quantity of (A) than d_a.

78. For this purpose, let us picture the entire transaction involving the exchange of o_b of (B) for d_a of (A) as if it were made up of a succession of s piecemeal exchanges each of equal size. As our holder of (B) keeps selling $\frac{o_b}{s}$ of (B) and buying $\frac{d_a}{s}$ of (A) on each of s successive occasions, according to the equation of exchange

$$\frac{o_b}{s} = \frac{d_a}{s} p_a,$$

he will decrease his *rareté* of (A) and increase his *rareté* of (B). In that way the ratio of these *raretés*, which started out by being higher than the price p_a, becomes equal to this price. Now I say, in the first place, that under these conditions each and every piecemeal exchange transaction is advantageous to our holder, though the advantage diminishes steadily from the first transaction to the sth.

In Fig. 13 we mark off two lengths: Od'_a measured above the origin O of the first curve, on the vertical segment Od_a, and $q_b y'$ measured below the point q_b of the second curve on the vertical segment, $q_b y$, in order to represent respectively the quantities $\frac{d_a}{s}$ of (A) and $\frac{o_b}{s}$ of (B) exchanged in the first piecemeal transaction. Upon the completion of this first transaction, the ratio of the *raretés*, though diminished, is still, by hypothesis, higher than the price. Designating these *raretés* by r_a and r_b, we have

$$r_a > p_a r_b,$$

which, by virtue of the preceding equation, gives us[12]

$$\frac{d_a}{s} r_a > \frac{o_b}{s} r_b.$$

Replacing $\frac{d_a}{s}$, $\frac{o_b}{s}$, r_a and r_b by the corresponding lengths Od'_a, $q_b y'$, $d'_a \alpha'$ and $y' \beta'$, which represent them geometrically, we obtain:

$$Od'_a \times d'_a \alpha' > q_b y' \times y' \beta'.$$

But from the very nature of the want curves we observe that, on the one hand,

$$\text{area } Od'_a \alpha' \alpha_{r,1} > Od'_a \times d'_a \alpha'$$

while, on the other hand,

$$q_b y' \times y' \beta' > \text{area } y' q_b \varrho \beta'.$$

It follows *a fortiori* that

$$\text{area } Od'_a\alpha'\alpha_{r,1} > \text{area } y'q_b\varrho\beta'.$$

Hence the first piecemeal exchange of $\dfrac{O_b}{s}$ of (B) for $\dfrac{d_a}{s}$ of (A) is advantageous to our holder. It can be shown in like manner that the next $s-2$ piecemeal exchanges are advantageous, for the ratio of *raretés*

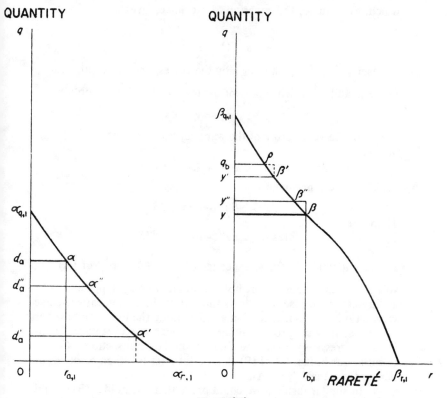

QUANTITY   QUANTITY

FIG. 13[13]

after each transaction, though diminishing, will still, by hypothesis, be greater than the price. Evidently the advantageousness [of each successive transaction to holder (1)] diminishes with every diminution in the ratios of the *raretés*.

Now, again in Fig. 13, let us mark off the length $d_a d''_a$ directly below the point d_a on the vertical segment $d_a O$ of the first curve and the length yy'' directly above the point y on the vertical segment yq_b

of the second curve, to represent respectively the same quantities exchanged, $\frac{d_a}{s}$ of (A) and $\frac{o_b}{s}$ of (B), as before, this time, however, in the last piecemeal transaction. Upon completion of this final transaction, the diminished ratio of the *raretés* is, by hypothesis, equal to the price; and we have

$$r_{a,1}=p_a r_{b,1},$$

which, by virtue of the equation of exchange, gives us:

$$\frac{d_a}{s} r_{a,1}=\frac{o_b}{s} r_{b,1}.$$

Replacing $\frac{d_a}{s}$, $\frac{o_b}{s}$, $r_{a,1}$ and $r_{b,1}$ by the corresponding lengths $d_a d''_a$ yy'', $d_a\alpha$ and $y\beta$ which represent them geometrically, we obtain

$$d_a d''_a \times d_a\alpha = yy'' \times y\beta.$$

But from the very nature of the want curves we observe that, on the one hand,

$$\text{area } d''_a d_a\alpha\alpha'' > d_a d''_a \times d_a\alpha,$$

while, on the other hand,

$$yy'' \times y\beta > \text{area } yy''\beta''\beta.$$

Therefore

$$\text{area } d''_a d_a\alpha\alpha'' > \text{area } yy''\beta''\beta.$$

Hence, the final piecemeal exchange of $\frac{o_b}{s}$ of (B) for $\frac{d_a}{s}$ of (A) will still be advantageous to our holder. Since we may suppose s to be as large as we please, it follows that all of the piecemeal exchange transactions, without exception and including the final one however small that may be, are advantageous, though the advantage diminishes progressively from the first to the sth transaction. Consequently, our holder (1) of (B) should not offer less than o_b of (B) or demand less than d_a of (A).

79. In similar fashion, we could prove that our holder (B) should not offer more than o_b of (B) or demand more than d_a of (A), because, beyond this limit where o_b of (B) has been exchanged for d_a of (A), all piecemeal exchange transactions without exception, even including the first however small we may suppose it to be, would be disadvantageous, and increasingly so with each further transaction. The proof of this is logically implied in the demonstration we have just given in the previous section. In fact, if, after the limit marked by the equality of the ratio of the *raretés* with the price p_a has been reached, we continue to diminish the *rareté* of (A) and

to increase the *rareté* of (B) by the exchange of any quantity whatsoever of (B) for a quantity of (A) of equal value in terms of (B), we encounter the inequality

$$r_a < p_a r_b,$$

which may be expressed as

$$r_b > p_b r_a.$$

It follows from the demonstration given above that, under these conditions, we get closer and closer to maximum satisfaction by exchanging a certain quantity of (A) for a certain quantity of (B) up to the point where

$$r_{b,1} = p_b r_{a,1},$$

or where

$$r_{a,1} = p_a r_{b,1}.$$

80. Holder (1) of (B) will, therefore, offer exactly o_b of (B) and will demand exactly d_a of (A), neither more nor less, at the price p_a of (A) in terms of (B), if these are the quantities for which we have the relation $r_{a,1} = p_a r_{b,1}$.

In general terms: *Given two commodities in a market, each holder attains maximum satisfaction of wants, or maximum effective utility, when the ratio of the intensities of the last wants satisfied [by each of these goods], or the ratio of their* raretés, *is equal to the price. Until this equality has been reached, a party to the exchange will find it to his advantage to sell the commodity the* rareté *of which is smaller than its price multiplied by the* rareté *of the other commodity and to buy the other commodity the* rareté *of which is greater than its price multiplied by the* rareté *of the first commodity.*

It is possible, of course, that a party to the exchange may find it to his advantage to offer the entire amount of whichever one of the two commodities he possesses to start with or to demand none at all of the other commodity. We shall come back to this point presently. [14][g]

81. If, in the equation

$$r_{a,1} = p_a r_{b,1},$$

we replace $r_{a,1}$ and $r_{b,1}$ by their equivalents, then[15]

$$\phi_{a,1}(d_a) = p_a \phi_{b,1}(y) = p_a \phi_{b,1}(q_b - o_b)$$
$$= p_a \phi_{b,1}(q_b - d_a p_a).$$

This last equation gives d_a as a function of p_a. If we suppose the equation to be solved for the first of the two variables, this relation reduces to

$$d_a = f_{a,1}(p_a).$$

This is the equation of the curve $a_{d,1}a_{p,1}$ [Fig. 1] which represents holder (1)'s demand for (A) in exchange for (B). This equation would be mathematically determinable if the equations $r=\phi_{a,1}(q)$ and $r=\phi_{b,1}(q)$[h] were determinable. It is precisely because these last equations are not determinable that $d_a=f_{a,1}(p_a)$ remains empirical.[f]

The problem which was to be solved may now be stated as follows: *Given two commodities (A) and (B), given each party's utility or want curves for these commodities, and given the initial stock which each party possesses, to determine the demand curves.*[j]

82. We shall do well to reformulate this solution in the customary notation of the infinitesimal calculus.[k]

Let d_a be the quantity of (A) which will be demanded, and $o_b=d_ap_a$ be the quantity of (B) which will be offered at the price p_a of (A) in terms of (B); and, consequently, let q_b-o_b be the quantity of (B) which will be retained, so that we have

$$d_ap_a+(q_b-o_b)=q_b, \qquad ..(1)$$

where q_b is the initial stock of (B) possessed by a given holder.

Moreover, let $u=\Phi_{a,1}(q)$ and $u=\Phi_{b,1}(q)$ be the two equations denoting the effective utilities of (A) and (B) respectively for our individual as functions of the quantities consumed; and let

$$\Phi_{a,1}(d_a)+\Phi_{b,1}(q_b-o_b)$$

be, therefore, the total effective utility to be maximized. Since the derivatives of the Φ functions are essentially decreasing, the maximum which our party to the exchange seeks will be found when the algebraic sum of the differential increments of utility with respect to the quantities consumed of each of the two commodities is zero. For, if we suppose these increments to be unequal and opposite in sign, our party will find it to his advantage to demand more or less of the commodity of which the differential increment is larger or smaller and to offer in return more or less of the commodity of which the differential increment is smaller or larger. The condition of maximum satisfaction of wants can now be expressed by the equation[16]

$$\Phi'_{a,1}(d_a)\,dd_a+\Phi'_{b,1}(q_b-o_b)\,d(q_b-o_b)=0.$$

Now, on the one hand, the derivatives of the functions of effective utility with respect to the quantities consumed are none other than the *raretés* [§75]; while, on the other hand, the algebraic sum of the products of the prices of the two commodities in terms of one of them multiplied by the differentials of the quantities consumed is, by virtue of equation (1),[1] equal to zero according to the equation[17]

$$p_a dd_a + d(q_b - o_b) = 0.$$

It follows from this that[18]

$$\phi_{a,1}(d_a) = p_a \phi_{b,1}(q_b - d_a p_a).$$

I have explained the process of differentiation for the benefit of those readers who are not familiar with it. Others will see immediately that by differentiating either of the following two expressions with respect to d_a:

$$\Phi_{a,1}(d_a) + \Phi_{b,1}(q_b - d_a p_a)$$

or

$$\int_o^{d_a} \phi_{a,1}(q) dq \; + \; \int_o^{q_b - d_a p_a} \phi_{b,1}(q) dq,$$

we obtain[19]

$$\phi_{a,1}(d_a) - p_a \phi_{b,1}(q_b - d_a p_a) = 0$$

or

$$\phi_{a,1}(d_a) = p_a \phi_{b,1}(q_b - d_a p_a).$$

It will be readily seen also that the root of this derived equation always corresponds to a maximum and not a minimum, because the functions $\Phi'_{a,1}(q)$ or $\phi_{a,1}(q)$ and $\Phi'_{b,1}(q)$ or $\phi_{b,1}(q)$ are by their nature decreasing and the second derivative

$$\phi'_{a,1}(d_a) + p_a^2 \phi'_{b,1}(q_b - d_a p_a)$$

is necessarily negative.[m]

83. It is presupposed in the above demonstration that the utility curves are continuous. Let us now turn to those cases where one or more of the utility curves are discontinuous. Strictly speaking there are three possibilities: the case of the exchange of a commodity with a continuous utility curve for a commodity with a discontinuous utility curve, the case of the exchange of a commodity with a discontinuous utility curve for a commodity with a continuous utility curve, and the case of the exchange of two commodities both of which have discontinuous utility curves. We shall, nevertheless, confine our attention to the first case, since, as we shall see later on, the chosen commodity to the value of which the values of all other commodities are referred and by means of which all other commodities are purchased, can and must have a continuous utility curve.

Accordingly let $\beta_{r,1}\beta_{q,1}$ [Fig. 14] be the utility curve of commodity (B) for holder (1) of (B), as before, and let q_b be his original stock of (B). Furthermore, let a step curve passing through the points **a** and **a'''** be the utility curve of commodity (A) for this individual. If commodity (A) cannot be bought otherwise than in whole units, and if p_a is its price [per unit] in terms of (B), it follows that commodity (B) will be sold only in parcels equal to p_a. If, after our individual has attained maximum satisfaction by exchange, the segments $d_a d''_a$ and $d_a d'''_a$ represent respectively the last unit of (A) bought and the first unit unbought, and if, at the same time, the segments yy'' and yy''' represent respectively the final parcel of (B) sold, and the first parcel unsold, then two inequalities result:[20]

$$\text{area } yy''\beta''\beta < d_a\mathbf{a}$$

and

$$\text{area } yy'''\beta'''\beta > d'''_a\mathbf{a}'''.$$

Let us designate by m'' and m''' two intermediate lengths, the first shorter than $y\beta$ and longer than $y''\beta''$, and the second longer than $y\beta$ but shorter than $y'''\beta'''$; and let these lengths be such that upon multiplying m'' and m''' by $yy''=yy'''=p_a$ we obtain two areas equal respectively to $yy''\beta''\beta$ and $yy'''\beta'''\beta$. Thus m'' and m''' will represent respectively the average intensities of utility of the final parcel of (B) sold and of the first parcel unsold. We may now express the above two inequalities, which together determine d_a, the demand for (A), as:

$$d_a\mathbf{a}=p_a m''+\varepsilon''$$

and

$$d'''_a\mathbf{a}'''=p_a m'''-\varepsilon'''.$$

From these two equations we readily derive[21]

$$\frac{d_a\mathbf{a}+d'''_a\mathbf{a}'''}{m''+m'''} = p_a+\frac{\varepsilon''-\varepsilon'''}{m''+m'''}.$$

Now $m''+m'''$ is very nearly equal to $2y\beta$,[22] and $\dfrac{\varepsilon''-\varepsilon'''}{m''+m'''}$ is quite small.[23] Consequently, our last equation closely approximates

$$\frac{\dfrac{d_a\mathbf{a}+d'''_a\mathbf{a}'''}{2}}{y\beta} = p_a.$$

Thus: *Once maximum satisfaction has been attained in the case of an exchange of a commodity with a continuous utility curve for a commodity with a discontinuous utility curve, the ratio of the average of the intensities of the last want satisfied and the first want not satisfied by the commodity bought to the intensity of the last want satisfied by the commodity sold is very nearly equal to the price.*[n]

I say very nearly, because not only is it possible for the product $p_a \times y\beta$, in other words for the price of (A) in terms of (B) multiplied by the intensity of the last want satisfied by (B), to be unequal to the average of the intensities of the last want satisfied and the first want not satisfied by (A), but it may also happen that this product is greater or smaller than each of the two quantities averaged. In fact, of necessity

$$\text{area } yy''\beta''\beta < p_a \times y\beta$$

and

$$d_a\mathbf{a} > \text{area } yy''\beta''\beta$$

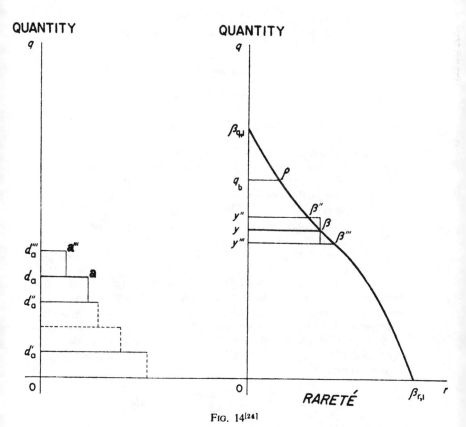

FIG. 14[24]

but it is not necessary that

$$d_a \mathbf{a} > p_a \times y\beta;$$

and if indeed

$$d_a \mathbf{a} < p_a \times y\beta,$$

then $d_a \mathbf{a}$ and $d'''_a \mathbf{a}'''$, which is $< d_a \mathbf{a}$, will both be less than $p_a \times y\beta$. Similarly, it is necessarily true that

$$\text{area } yy'''\beta'''\beta > p_a \times y\beta$$

and that

$$d'''_a \mathbf{a}''' < \text{area } yy'''\beta'''\beta;$$

but it is not necessary that

$$d'''_a \mathbf{a}''' < p_a \times y\beta;$$

and if indeed

$$d'''_a \mathbf{a}''' > p_a \times y\beta,$$

then $d'''_a \mathbf{a}'''$ and $d_a \mathbf{a}$, which is $> d'''_a \mathbf{a}'''$, will both be greater than $p_a \times y\beta$.

84. Let us return to the two inequalities:

$$\text{area } yy''\beta''\beta < d_a \mathbf{a},$$

and

$$\text{area } yy'''\beta'''\beta > d'''_a \mathbf{a}'''.$$

As p_a diminishes, the left-hand sides of both the above inequalities diminish.[25] The [sign of the] first inequality remains unchanged, but, after a certain point, the [sign of the] second inequality will be reversed and d_a will increase by at least one unit. As p_a increases, the left-hand sides of both the above inequalities increase. The [sign of the] second inequality then remains unchanged, but, after a certain point, the [sign of the] first inequality will be reversed and d_a will decrease by at least one unit. The demand curve for (A) is thus descending and discontinuous.

Analytically, a given price p_a of (A) in terms of (B) having been cried, according as our individual demands $1, 2 \ldots$ units of (A) to fill wants with intensities $r_1, r_2 \ldots$[26] respectively, thereby acquiring effective utilities of (A) measured by the same magnitudes $r_1, r_2 \ldots$, he will retain the quantities $q_b - p_a$, $q_b - 2p_a \ldots$ of (B) and relinquish effective utilities of (B)[o] measured by the numerical value of the integrals[27]

$$\int_{q_b - p_a}^{q_b} \phi_{b,1}(q)dq, \qquad \int_{q_b - 2p_a}^{q_b - p_a} \phi_{b,1}(q)dq \ldots .$$

Furthermore, the demand, d_a, which will yield maximum satisfaction is determined simultaneously by the following two inequalities

$$\int_{q_b-d_a p_a}^{q_b-(d_a-1)p_a} \phi_{b,1}(q)dq < r_{d_a},$$

and

$$\int_{q_b-(d_a+1)p_a}^{q_b-d_a p_a} \phi_{b,1}(q)dq > r_{d_a+1}.$$

In this way d_a could be mathematically determined for all values of p_a, and a descending, discontinuous curve could be drawn representing the demand for (A) in exchange for (B) as a function of price.[28]

DISCUSSION OF DEMAND CURVES. GENERAL FORMULA FOR THE MATHEMATICAL SOLUTION OF THE PROBLEM OF EXCHANGE OF TWO COMMODITIES FOR EACH OTHER

85. Since the individual demand equation

$$d_a = f_{a,1}(p_a),$$

when solved for d_a, becomes[1]

$$\phi_{a,1}(d_a) = p_a \phi_{b,1}(q_b - d_a p_a),$$

we may discuss the equation in the latter form.

First let $p_a = 0$. The equation then reduces to

$$\phi_{a,1}(d_a) = 0,$$

the root of which is $d_a = \alpha_{q,1} = Oa_{d,1}$ [Fig. 15].

We conclude: *Given two commodities in a market, when the price of one of them is zero, the quantity of this commodity which will be demanded by each holder of the other commodity will equal the quantity necessary for the complete satisfaction of all his wants for it; that is, it will equal the extensive utility of the commodity in question.*

This necessarily follows from §71. The curve $a_{d,1}a_{p,1}$ starts at the point $\alpha_{q,1}$.

86. If, on the other hand, we let $d_a = 0$, the [individual] demand equation becomes

$$\phi_{a,1}(0) = p_a \phi_{b,1}(q_b),$$

the root of which is $p_a = \dfrac{\phi_{a,1}(0)}{\phi_{b,1}(q_b)} = \dfrac{\alpha_{r,1}}{\varrho_b} = Oa_{p,1}$ [Fig. 15].

We conclude: *The quantity demanded of one of the two commodities [in the market] by a holder of the other commodity becomes zero, whenever the price of the commodity demanded is equal to or greater than the ratio of the intensity of his maximum want for it to the intensity of the last want which can be satisfied by the quantity possessed of the commodity offered.*

132

This, too, follows necessarily, since in this case the last parcel of (B) which holder (1) consumes, say $\frac{o_b}{s}$, yields him the satisfaction

$\frac{o_b}{s} \varrho_b$, while this same parcel of (B) if exchanged for $\frac{d_a}{s}$ of (A) at the

price p_a, would yield him no more satisfaction than $\frac{d_a}{s} \alpha_{r,1} = \frac{o_b}{s} \frac{\alpha_{r,1}}{p_a}$

which is equal to or less than $\frac{o_b}{s} \varrho_b$.

87. Now that we have formulated the price condition which must be fulfilled if holder (1) of (B) is to refrain from demanding any of (A) at all, let us see how to formulate the necessary price condition under which our holder will not retain any of (B) at all. We must now rewrite equation

$$\phi_{a,1}(d_a) = p_a \phi_{b,1}(q_b - d_a p_a) \qquad \qquad ..(1)$$

by setting

$$d_a p_a = q_b, \qquad \qquad ..(2)$$

so that equation (1) becomes

$$\phi_{a,1}(d_a) = p_a \phi_{b,1}(0), \qquad \qquad ..(3)$$

the root of which is

$$p_a = \frac{\phi_{a,1}(d_a)}{\phi_{b,1}(0)} = \frac{\varrho_a}{\beta_{r,1}} .$$

We conclude: *The holder of one of the two commodities will offer all he possesses of that commodity whenever the price of the commodity demanded in exchange is equal to or less than the ratio of the intensity of the last want which can be satisfied by the commodity demanded to the intensity of the maximum want satisfied by the commodity to be offered.*

This, again, is necessarily true because in the case under consideration, the first parcel of (B), say $\frac{o_b}{s}$, which holder (1) might have consumed, would yield him no more than $\frac{o_b}{s} \beta_{r,1}$ in satisfaction, while

this same parcel of (B) if exchanged for $\frac{d_a}{s}$ of (A) at the price p_a

will yield him a satisfaction $\frac{d_a}{s} \varrho_a = \frac{o_b}{s} \frac{\varrho_a}{p_a}$ which is equal to or

greater than $\frac{o_b}{s} \beta_{r,1}$.

88. If we multiply equations (2) and (3), member for member, and divide both sides by p_a so as to eliminate it, we obtain

$$d_a \phi_{a,1}(d_a) = q_b \phi_{b,1}(0).$$

Or if we replace q_b and $\phi_{b,1}(0) = \beta_{r,1}$ by the corresponding [geometrical] lengths which represent them in Fig. 15, namely, Oq_b and $O\beta_{r,1}$ respectively, we obtain

$$d_a \phi_{a,1}(d_a) = Oq_b \times O\beta_{r,1}.$$

The condition which this equation defines may be translated into the following terms: *For the offer of one of the two commodities to equal the quantity possessed of that commodity, it must be possible to inscribe within the want curve of the commodity to be demanded a rectangle with an area equal to the area of another rectangle so*

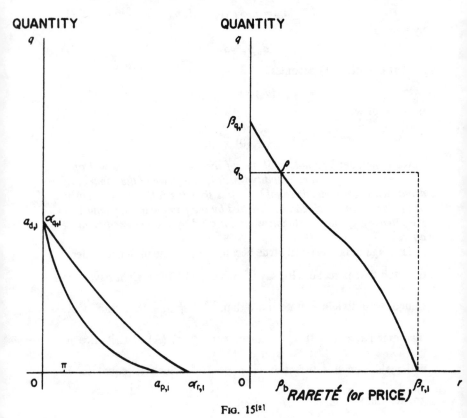

Fig. 15[2]

constructed that its height is measured by the quantity possessed of the commodity to be offered and its base by the intensity of the maximum want for the same commodity.

This condition is not always satisfied; actually, it is not satisfied in our example. We may, however, substitute another condition for it. In fact, [the solution of] equations (1) and (2) is represented by the point of intersection of the hyperbola of the quantity possessed of (B), $d_a p_a = q_b$, with the individual demand curve for (A), $d_a = f_{a,1}(p_a)$. These two curves do not always meet; for example, they do not meet in the case of the holder whose trader's schedule we are considering [Fig. 10].

89. This observation brings us to another very important point. Suppose the condition defined by the above equation were satisfied and suppose the demand curve [broken curve in Fig. 10] were to meet the hyperbola of the quantity possessed at the points q'_b and q''_b. The offer of (B) would then be equal to the quantity possessed q_b at prices represented by the abscissas of the points q'_b and q''_b and at all prices in between. It seems from the two equations or the two curves that, at prices in between those indicated by the abscissas of the points q'_b and q''_b, the offer of (B) would have to exceed q_b, the quantity possessed of (B). But since a holder cannot offer a greater quantity than he possesses, we must obviously introduce the constraint that $q_b - d_a p_a$ cannot be a negative quantity. This constraint is taken into account if we reformulate the condition as follows: *For the offer of one of the two commodities to equal the quantity possessed, the hyperbola of the quantity possessed and the demand curve of the other commodity must meet. Between points of intersection of these two curves the hyperbola of the quantity possessed becomes the demand curve.*

90. If, under the assumption that the curves $\alpha_{r,1}\alpha_{q,1}$ and $\beta_{r,1}\beta_{q,1}$ of Fig. 15 are fixed, q_b is allowed to decrease, ϱ_b will increase and consequently $\dfrac{\alpha_{r,1}}{\varrho_b} = Oa_{p,1}$ will decrease. When $q_b=0$, then $\varrho_b=\beta_{r,1}$, and the ratio $\dfrac{\alpha_{r,1}}{\varrho_b}$ becomes identical with $\dfrac{\alpha_{r,1}}{\beta_{r,1}} = O\pi$. The demand curve $a_{d,1}a_{p,1}$ will then coincide with the segments $a_{d,1}O$ and $O\pi$ of the co-ordinate axes.

We conclude: *If the utility [curves] of the two commodities are assumed to be fixed for an individual holding one of them, and if the quantity possessed of that commodity is allowed to decrease, the point where the demand curve for the other commodity meets the price axis moves in the direction of the origin of the co-ordinate axes. When the quantity possessed [of the commodity held] is zero, the demand curve* [*of the other commodity*] *coincides with segments of the co-ordinate axes consisting of that portion of the quantity axis which measures the extensive utility of the commodity demanded and that portion of the price axis which is equal in length to the ratio of the maximum intensive utilities of the two commodities.*

91. On the other hand, if q_b were to increase, ϱ_b would decrease and consequently $\dfrac{\alpha_{r,1}}{\varrho_b} = Oa_{p,1}$ would increase. When $q_b = \beta_{q,1}$, then $\varrho_b = 0$, and the ratio $\dfrac{\alpha_{r,1}}{\varrho_b}$ would become infinitely large. The distance of the point $a_{p,1}$[3] from the point O would then become infinite.

We conclude: *If the utility* [*curves*] *of the two commodities are assumed to be fixed for an individual holding one of them, and if the quantity possessed of that commodity is allowed to increase, the point where his demand curve for the other commodity meets the price axis moves away from the origin of the co-ordinate axes. When the quantity possessed* [*of the commodity held*] *equals its extensive utility, the demand curve* [*of the other commodity*] *becomes asymptotic to the price axis.*

Clearly, this must be so. It is apparent, moreover, that we were right in refraining from making any premature assertions about the form of the aggregate demand curves in §55. We are now in a position to affirm that these curves always intersect the demand axis, since no commodity ever has an infinite aggregate extensive utility. On the other hand, the asymptotic relation of aggregate demand curves to the price axis may be considered a common and frequent fact, since it occurs as soon as any one individual among all the holders of a commodity has as much as he wants of it for complete satisfaction.[a] It follows from this that aggregate offer curves often start at the origin.[1]

92. Up to this point we assumed that every party to the exchange was a holder of no more than one commodity, either commodity (A) or commodity (B). We must now take up the particular case where one and the same individual is a holder of two commodities (A) and (B), and we have to express such an individual's trading schedule mathematically. Actually, we are bound to do this, because, all

---

[1] It would be appropriate here to supplement the discussion of demand and offer curves by a demonstration of the double proposition, deducible from the negative inclination of utility curves, that the demand curve is always negatively inclined and that the offer curve alternately rises and falls from zero to zero (at infinity) as price increases. The first part was laid down as a sort of postulate in §48, and the second was deduced from the first in §49. The proofs for both parts will be developed for the general case, i.e. for the case of the exchange of any number of commodities for one another and for the case of holders of several commodities, in Appendix I, GEO-METRICAL THEORY OF THE DETERMINATION OF PRICES, §1: THE EXCHANGE OF SEVERAL COMMODITIES FOR ONE ANOTHER. [This note appears first in ed. 4.]

things considered, the second case is the general case, and the case previously studied a special case which can be found by equating one of the quantities possessed in the general case to zero. We did not begin our study of the problem of the exchange of two commodities for each other with the more general case, because it would have rendered our reasoning too complicated. With the aid of the theorem of maximum satisfaction, however, it is possible now to arrive at an easy and simple solution of the problem.

Let us suppose that holder (1) of (B) has the same wants for (A) and (B) as before, which can be expressed by the equations $r=\phi_{a,1}(q)$ and $r=\phi_{b,1}(q)$[b] of the want curves $\alpha_{r,1}\alpha_{q,1}$ and $\beta_{r,1}\beta_{q,1}$ of Fig 16, and that he comes to the market, no longer with a zero quantity of (A) and a quantity q_b of (B), which was represented in Fig. 12 by Oq_b, but rather with a quantity $q_{a,1}$ of (A) now represented by $Oq_{a,1}$ and a quantity $q_{b,1}$ of (B) represented by $Oq_{b,1}$. We shall see

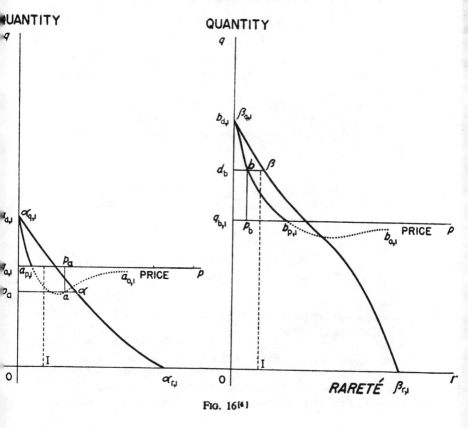

FIG. 16[a]

how to express his demand for (B) as a function of the price p_b and his demand for (A) as a function of the price p_a.

If at a price p_b of (B) in terms of (A), represented by the length $q_{b,1}p_b$, our individual demands a quantity d_b of (B) represented by the length $q_{b,1}d_b$, he will have to offer a quantity o_a of (A), represented by the length $q_{a,1}o_a$, such that the relation between p_b, d_b and o_a is defined by the equation

$$o_a = d_b p_b.$$

In this case, the intensity of the last want satisfied by (B) being r_b, represented by the length $d_b\beta$, and the intensity of the last want satisfied by (A) being r_a, represented by the length $o_a\alpha$, we have, by virtue of the theorem of maximum satisfaction (§80),

$$r_b = p_b r_a,$$

or, if we substitute equivalent values for r_b and r_a,

$$\phi_{b,1}(q_{b,1} + d_b) = p_b \phi_{a,1}(q_{a,1} - o_a) \qquad \qquad ..(4)$$
$$= p_b \phi_{a,1}(q_{a,1} - d_b p_b).$$

This gives us the equation of the demand curve of (B), $b_{d,1}b_{p,1}$, as a function of the price of (B) in terms of (A), referred to $q_{b,1}q$ and $q_{b,1}p$ as axes.

Likewise, if at a price p_a of (A) in terms of (B) our individual demands a quantity d_a of (A), he will have to offer a quantity o_b of (B), such that the relation between p_a, d_a and o_b, is defined by the equation

$$o_b = d_a p_a.$$

Then the intensity of the last want satisfied by (A) being r_a, and the intensity of the last want satisfied by (B) being r_b, we have

$$r_a = p_a r_b,$$

or

$$\phi_{a,1}(q_{a,1} + d_a) = p_a \phi_{b,1}(q_{b,1} - o_b) \qquad \qquad ..(5)$$
$$= p_a \phi_{b,1}(q_{b,1} - d_a p_a).$$

Thus we derive the equation of the demand curve of (A), $a_{d,1}a_{p,1}$, which is a function of the price of (A) in terms of (B), referred to $q_{a,1}q$ and $q_{a,1}p$ as axes.

93. The discussion of the two equations (4) and (5) under various suppositions, as when the price is zero, or when the demand is zero, or when the quantity offered equals the quantity possessed, or when the quantity possessed either increases or decreases, would be exactly similar to the previous discussion [in §§85–91]. There is nothing to

be gained in repeating the argument, except as it relates to a special question which it is important to settle.

If in equation (4) we set $d_b=0$, that equation becomes

$$\phi_{b,1}(q_{b,1})=p_b\,\phi_{a,1}(q_{a,1}).$$

Remembering that $p_a p_b=1$, we may write this equation in the form

$$\phi_{a,1}(q_{a,1})=p_a\,\phi_{b,1}(q_{b,1}),$$

which would also be the equation we should obtain by setting $d_a=0$ in equation (5).

We conclude: *If the demand for one of the two commodities is zero at a certain price, the demand for the other commodity is also zero at the corresponding price* [*of the second commodity in terms of the first*].

94. This proposition, however, is only a corollary, of a more general theorem.

In order to transform equation (4), expressing the demand for (B) as a function of the price of (B) in terms of (A), into an equation of the offer of (A) as a function of the price of (A) in terms of (B), we need only substitute $o_a p_a$ for d_b and $\dfrac{1}{p_a}$ for p_b. We should then have

$$\phi_{a,1}(q_{a,1}-o_a)=p_a\,\phi_{b,1}(q_{b,1}+o_a p_a),$$

which is the same as equation (5) with $-o_a$ in the place of d_a. Thus equation (5) of the demand for (A) becomes an equation of the offer of (A) for negative values of d_a. We could demonstrate similarly that equation (4) of the demand for (B) becomes an equation of the offer of (B) for negative values of d_b. Hence, prices being positive by their very nature, when d_b is *positive*, $o_a=d_b p_b$ is positive and consequently $d_a=-o_a$ is *negative*; and when d_b is *negative*, $o_a=d_b p_b$ is negative and consequently $d_a=-o_a$ is *positive*. We could demonstrate in like manner that when d_a is *positive*, d_b is *negative* and when d_a is *negative*, d_b is *positive*.

We conclude: *If the demand for one of the two commodities is positive at a given price, the demand for the other is negative, that is, its offer is positive at the corresponding price* [*of the second in terms of the first*].

In fact, a holder of both commodities can only demand one of them by offering the other in exchange. It follows from this that if he neither demands nor offers any quantity at all of one of these commodities, he neither offers nor demands any of the other. This, it is easy to see, is the case where the ratio of the *raretés* of the two commodities are exactly equal to the price of one in terms of the other and maximum effective utility is immediately realized.

95. The segments of the curves in Fig. 16 from $a_{d,1}$ to $a_{p,1}$ and from $b_{d,1}$ to $b_{p,1}$ are, therefore, demand curves, the points $a_{p,1}$ and $b_{p,1}$ being reciprocals of each other.[5] The segments from $a_{p,1}$ to $a_{o,1}$ and from $b_{p,1}$ to $b_{o,1}$, that are dotted and lie below the axes $q_{a,1}p$ and $q_{b,1}p$ in the same diagram, are offer curves. The joint demand and offer curves for each commodity, when referred to the Or axis, constitute a curve of the total quantity (i.e. the sum of the quantities retained and acquired) of that commodity, considered as a function of its price. The joint curve has a minimum which corresponds to the maximum quantity offered of each commodity in exchange for the other.

96. To sum up, if, for simplicity, we designate by x_1 and y_1 the positive or negative quantities of commodities (A) and (B) which party (1), having regard to the price, will add to his initial holdings, $q_{a,1}$ and $q_{b,1}$, of these commodities, then his exchange schedule will result from the following two equations, one of exchange[6] and the other of maximum satisfaction:

$$x_1 v_a + y_1 v_b = 0$$

and

$$\frac{\phi_{a,1}(q_{a,1}+x_1)}{\phi_{b,1}(q_{b,1}+y_1)} = \frac{v_a}{v_b}.$$

From the above equations either we can eliminate y_1 and solve for x_1 as a function of p_a, or we can eliminate x_1 and solve for y_1 as a function of p_b. The formulae we obtain in this way,[7] viz.

$$\phi_{a,1}(q_{a,1}+x_1) = p_a \phi_{b,1}(q_{b,1}-x_1 p_a)$$

and

$$\phi_{b,1}(q_{b,1}+y_1) = p_b \phi_{a,1}(q_{a,1}-y_1 p_b),$$

are general formulae which need only to be suitably developed to express the same individual's trading schedule in the case of the exchange of several commodities for one another.

It is important to note that for such values of p_a as will render any negative x_1 [numerically] larger than $q_{a,1}$, the first of the above two equations must be replaced by $x_1 = -q_{a,1}$, and in that case the value of y_1 is given by the equation $y_1 p_b = q_{a,1}$. In like manner, for such values of p_b as will render any negative y_1 [numerically] greater than $q_{b,1}$, the second of these equations must be replaced by $y_1 = -q_{b,1}$, and in that case the value of x_1 is given by $x_1 p_a = q_{b,1}$.[8]

97. These equations, when solved for x_1 and y_1, and appropriately adapted to satisfy the above-mentioned restrictions, take the form[9]

$$x_1 = f_{a,1}(p_a) \quad \text{and} \quad y_1 = f_{b,1}(p_b).$$

Similarly, we could deduce the following expressions for the trading schedules of individuals (2), (3) . . .

$$x_2 = f_{a,2}(p_a) \quad \text{and} \quad y_2 = f_{b,2}(p_b)$$
$$x_3 = f_{a,3}(p_a) \quad \text{and} \quad y_3 = f_{b,3}(p_b)$$

. . . .

The equality between the [aggregate] effective demand and offer of each of the two commodities (A) and (B) could be expressed by either of the following equations:[10]

$$X = f_{a,1}(p_a) + f_{a,2}(p_a) + f_{a,3}(p_a) + \ldots = F_a(p_a) = 0,$$

or

$$Y = f_{b,1}(p_b) + f_{b,2}(p_b) + f_{b,3}(p_b) + \ldots = F_b(p_b) = 0.$$

For example, we could derive p_a from the first of these equations, and then p_b from the equation

$$p_a p_b = 1,$$

and thus obtain a value of p_b which would necessarily satisfy the second of the above equations, since it is evident that

$$X v_a + Y v_b = 0,$$

whence it follows that if $F_a(p_a) = 0$ for a given value of p_a, then $F_b(p_b) = 0$ for the corresponding value of $p_b \left[= \dfrac{1}{p_a} \right]$.

This solution is analytical. It could also be formulated geometrically. The sum of the positive x's [for given values of p_a] would make up the demand curve for (A), and the sum of the positive y's [for given values of p_b] the demand curve of (B).[11] From these two demand curves we could derive the curves representing the offer of the two commodities which would be the same thing as the sums of the negative x's and y's taken positively.[12] The intersection of these [demand and offer] curves would determine the current prices.[c]

98. This would give us a mathematical solution of our problem. In the market the solution would be reached as follows.

Once any two prices that are reciprocals of each other, say p_a and p_b, are cried, $x_1, x_2, x_3 \ldots$ and $y_1, y_2, y_3 \ldots$ will be determined naturally without recourse to mathematical calculation, and yet in such a way as to satisfy the condition of maximum satisfaction. This would be sufficient to determine X and Y. Now, if $X = 0$, then also $Y = 0$, and the prices would be equilibrium prices. But generally $X \gtrless 0$ and consequently $Y \lesssim 0$.[13] The first of these inequalities may be written as

$$D_a \gtrless 0_a$$

in which D_a designates the sum of the positive x's and O_a the sum of the negative x's taken positively. The problem is to bring D_a into equality with O_a.

So far as D_a is concerned, this quantity is positive when $p_a=0$, and it diminishes indefinitely as p_a increases, becoming zero for a given value of p_a somewhere between zero and infinity. O_a, on the other hand, is zero when $p_a=0$ and even for certain positive values of p_a; then it increases as p_a increases, but not indefinitely, for it passes through at least one maximum and finally decreases as p_a continues to increase, becoming zero for $p_a=\infty$. Under these conditions, provided that D_a does not fall to zero before O_a ceases to be zero, in which case there is no solution,[14] there is a certain value of p_a at which O_a and D_a are equal. To find this value, p_a must increase when $D_a>O_a$ and decrease when $D_a<O_a$. We recognize here the law of effective offer and demand.[d]

Lesson 10

RARETÉ, THE CAUSE OF VALUE IN EXCHANGE

99. In the last analysis, the utility curves and the quantities possessed constitute the necessary and sufficient data for the establishment of current or equilibrium prices. From these data we proceed, first of all, to the mathematical derivation of individual and aggregate demand curves in view of the fact that each party to an exchange seeks the greatest possible satisfaction of his wants.[a] And then, from the individual or aggregate demand curves, we derive mathematically the current equilibrium prices since there can be only one price in the market, namely the price at which total effective demand equals total effective offer, that is to say, since each trader must give up quantities which stand in a definite ratio to the quantities received and vice versa.

Thus: *The exchange of two commodities for each other in a perfectly competitive market is an operation by which all holders of either one, or of both, of the two commodities can obtain[b] the greatest possible satisfaction of their wants consistent witn the condition that the two commodities are bought and sold at one and the same rate of exchange throughout the market.*[1]

The main object of the theory of social wealth is to generalize this proposition by showing, first, that it applies to the exchange of several commodities for one another as well as to the exchange of two commodities for each other, and secondly, that, under perfect competition, it applies to production as well as to exchange. The main object of the theory of production of social wealth is to show how the principle of organization of agriculture, industry and commerce can be deduced as a logical consequence of the above proposition. We may say, therefore, that this proposition embraces the whole of pure and applied economics.

100. If we let v_a and v_b be values in exchange of commodities (A) and (B) such that the ratios between them constitute the current equilibrium prices, and if we let $r_{a,1}, r_{b,1}, r_{a,2}, r_{b,2}, r_{a,3}, r_{b,3} \ldots$ be the *raretés* of these commodities, i.e. the intensities of the last wants satisfied for holders (1), (2), (3) . . . after the exchange, then by virtue of the theorem of maximum satisfaction we have

$$\frac{r_{a,1}}{r_{b,1}} = p_a \qquad \text{and} \qquad \frac{r_{b,1}}{r_{a,1}} = p_b$$

for holder (1);

143

$$\frac{r_{a,2}}{r_{b,2}}=p_a \qquad \text{and} \qquad \frac{r_{b,2}}{r_{a,2}}=p_b$$

for holder (2);

$$\frac{r_{a,3}}{r_{b,3}}=p_a \qquad \text{and} \qquad \frac{r_{b,3}}{r_{a,3}}=p_b$$

for holder (3); and so on. It follows, then, that

$$p_a=\frac{r_{a,1}}{r_{b,1}}=\frac{r_{a,2}}{r_{b,2}}=\frac{r_{a,3}}{r_{b,3}}= \ldots$$

and

$$p_b=\frac{r_{b,1}}{r_{a,1}}=\frac{r_{b,2}}{r_{a,2}}=\frac{r_{b,3}}{r_{a,3}}= \ldots,$$

which can be rewritten as follows:[c]

$$v_a \;\; : v_b$$
$$:: r_{a,1} : r_{b,1}$$
$$:: r_{a,2} : r_{b,2}$$
$$:: r_{a,3} : r_{b,3}$$
$$:: \ldots \ldots$$

It should be observed that if any of these commodities are of such a nature that they can be consumed in whole units only and their utility curves are discontinuous, then some of the terms in the above table of *raretés* will have to be proportional terms specially underlined, to indicate, as we have seen above in §83, that they are close approximations of the arithmetical mean of the intensities of the last wants satisfied and of the first wants unsatisfied.[d]

It is also possible that one of the two terms may be missing in one or more of the ratios of the *raretés*. For example, it may happen that at the price p_a holder (2) does not want any of (A) at all. Then there would be no *rareté* of (A) for holder (2) because no want would be satisfied by (A) so far as he was concerned. Consequently the term $r_{a,2}$ would have to be replaced by $p_a r_{b,2}$ which would be greater than $\alpha_{r,2}$ or the intensity of the first want which holder (2) has for (A) (§86). It may also happen that at the price p_a holder (3), for example, demands all the (A) he can get unconditionally at whatever price he must pay, in other words, he may offer all he possesses of (B). Then there would be no *rareté* of (B) for holder (3), because no want would be satisfied by (B) so far as he was concerned. Then the term $r_{b,3}$ would have to be replaced by $p_b r_{a,3}$[e] which would be greater than $\beta_{r,3}$ or the intensity of the first want which holder (3) has for

(B) (§87).[1] We could introduce the convention of putting the terms $p_a r_{b,2}$ and $p_b r_{a,3}$ in parentheses as they are entered in the above tables.[2] This would be tantamount to defining *rareté* as the intensity of the last want which *is* or which *might have been* satisfied.

Subject to these two reservations, we may formulate the following proposition:

Current prices or equilibrium prices are equal to the ratios of the raretés.

In other words:

Values in exchange are proportional to the raretés.

101. As regards the exchange of two commodities for each other, we have now reached the goal we set ourselves when we began our study of the mathematical theory of exchange (§40). We undertook at that point, to deduce *rareté* from value in exchange, instead of deducing value in exchange from scarcity, as we did in Part I where the object and divisions of political and social economy were discussed. In fact, the *rareté* defined in Part II as the intensity of the last want satisfied is precisely the same thing as the *scarcity* we had defined earlier in §21 in terms of the twin conditions of utility and limitation in quantity. There could not possibly be a last want satisfied if there were no want, that is to say, if a commodity had neither extensive nor intensive utility, or if it were *useless*. Moreover, the intensity of the last want satisfied would be zero if a commodity which possessed a utility curve were so plentiful that its quantity exceeded its extensive utility, as would be the case, for example, if it were unlimited in quantity. Thus the *rareté* we have been discussing in the last lessons turns out to be synonymous with the *scarcity* [also 'rareté' in French] we mentioned earlier. There is only this difference: *rareté* is taken to be a measurable magnitude which is not only inevitably associated with value in exchange but is also, of necessity, proportionate to this value, in the same way that weight is related to mass. If, therefore, it is certain that *rareté* and value in exchange are two concomitant and proportional phenomena, it is equally certain that *rareté* is the cause of value in exchange.[3]

Value in exchange, like weight, is a *relative* phenomenon; while *rareté*, like mass, is an absolute phenomenon. If, of the two commodities, (A) and (B), one of them became useless, or, though useful, became unlimited in quantity, that commodity would no longer be scarce and would cease to have value in exchange. Under these circumstances, the other commodity too would lose its value in exchange, but it would not stop being scarce; it would only be more or less scarce and have a determinate *rareté* for each of the holders of the commodity.

I say for each of the holders of this commodity—and I wish to emphasize this point—because there is no such thing as *the rareté* of commodity (A) or *the rareté* of commodity (B), or as the ratio of the *rareté* of (A) to the *rareté* of (B) or of the *rareté* of (B) to the *rareté* of (A); there are no other *raretés* than the *raretés* of (A) or (B) for holders (1), (2), (3) . . . of these commodities, and it is only for these holders that there are ratios of *raretés* of (A) to *raretés* of (B) or of *raretés* of (B) to those of (A). *Rareté* is *personal* or *subjective*; value in exchange is *real* or *objective*.[g] It is only with respect to a given individual that we can define *rareté* in terms of *effective utility* and *quantity possessed* in a manner strictly analagous to the definition of *velocity* in terms of *distance passed over* and *the time taken to pass over it*, so that *rareté* defined as *the derivative of effective utility with respect to the quantity possessed* corresponds exactly to *velocity* defined as *the derivative of distance passed over to the time taken to pass over it*.

If we were looking for something that we might call *the rareté* of commodity (A) or of commodity (B), we should have to take the *average rareté*, which would be the arithmetical average of the *raretés* of each of these commodities for all parties to the exchange after the exchange was completed. This conception of an *average rareté* is no more far-fetched than that of an average height or an average life span in a given country. For certain purposes it may even be more useful. These average *raretés* would themselves be proportional to the [corresponding] values in exchange.[d]

102. The theorist has the right to assume that the underlying price determinants are invariant over the period he has chosen to use in his formulation of the law of equilibrium prices. But, once this formulation has been completed, it is his duty to remember that the forces that underlie prices are by their nature variable, and consequently he must formulate the law of the variation of equilibrium prices. This now remains to be done. Fortunately, the second formulation follows immediately from the first, for the forces underlying the establishment of prices are the very forces that underlie the variation of prices, viz. the utilities and the quantities possessed of the commodities considered. These forces are, therefore, the primary causes and conditions of the variation of prices.[h]

If we suppose that in the same market where (A) and (B) were previously traded at the above-mentioned current prices, $\frac{1}{\mu}$ of (A) in terms of (B) and μ of (B) in terms of (A), the trading now takes place at different current prices, $\frac{1}{\mu'}$ of (A) in terms of (B) and μ' of (B) in terms of (A), then we may posit that this change in price is the result of one, or more, of the following four causes:

1. A change in the utility of commodity (A).

2. A change in the quantity of commodity (A) possessed by one or more holders.

3. A change in the utility of commodity (B).

4. A change in the quantity of commodity (B) possessed by one or more holders.

These circumstances, which are absolute, could be determined under ideal conditions. In practice, of course, this determination may prove to be more or less difficult; but there is no reason to regard it as impossible in theory. By putting questions to each and every individual about the elements that enter into the making of his individual demand curve, the problem might be solved by direct investigation. A case may conceivably arise, where one of the causes of a change in price impresses the investigators as the primary cause in one sense or another. For example, if we suppose a rise in price from μ to μ' to coincide with the discovery of a remarkable new property in commodity (B) or with a catastrophe destroying part of the supply of this commodity, we could not possibly avoid associating one or the other of these events with the rise in price. Such inescapable inferences are not beyond the bounds of possibility. By their aid the primary causes and conditions of variations in prices are often determined.

103. Let us suppose that equilibrium is established and that the several parties to the exchange possess whatever quantities of (A) and (B) are necessary to yield them maximum satisfaction at the reciprocal prices $\frac{1}{\mu}$ of (A) in terms of (B) and μ of (B) in terms of (A). This condition of maximum satisfaction is fulfilled as long as prices are equal to the ratios of the *raretés*, and it ceases the moment this equality is destroyed. Let us inquire, then, how variations in utility and in the quantity possessed disturb the condition of maximum satisfaction and let us investigate the consequences of such a disturbance.[d]

Variations in utility may occur in very different ways: there may be an increase in intensive utility and a decrease in extensive utility or vice versa, and so on. We must, therefore, take care how we enunciate general propositions in this respect. For example, we shall restrict our use of the expressions *increase in utility* and *decrease in utility* to shifts in the want curve which entail an increase or decrease in *rareté*, i.e. in the intensity of the last want satisfied after the completion of exchange. With this in mind, let us suppose an increase in the utility of (B), or in other words, a shift in the want curve of (B) resulting in an increase in the *rareté* of (B) for certain parties. These individuals will no longer derive maximum satis-faction [by maintaining the *status quo*]. Hence, they will find it to their advantage to demand (B) by offering some of their (A) at the current reciprocal prices $\dfrac{1}{\mu}$ and μ. Inasmuch as the offer was equal to the demand for each of the two commodities at the prices $\dfrac{1}{\mu}$ and μ [before the increase in the utility of (B) for some of the traders], there will now be an excess of demand over offer in the case of (B) and an excess of offer over demand in the case of (A) at these same prices, and hence a rise in p_b and a fall in p_a. It follows also that the other traders [for whom the utility of (B) had not increased] will no longer derive maximum satisfaction [from the previously determined quantities of (A) and (B) which they consume]. They will find it, therefore, to their advantage, when the price of (B) becomes greater than μ and the price of (A) less than $\dfrac{1}{\mu}$, to offer some of their (B) and to demand (A) in exchange. Equilibrium will be re-established when the demand and offer of the two commodities are equated at a new price of (B) higher than μ and at a new price of (A) lower than $\dfrac{1}{\mu}$. Thus an increase in the utility of (B) for some of our individuals will finally result in a rise in the price of (B).

If there had been a decrease in the utility of (B), it would obviously entail a fall in the price of (B).

A glance at the want curves is sufficient to show that an increase or decrease in the quantity possessed will result in a decrease or an increase in *rareté*. Moreover, we have just seen that price decreases or increases as *rareté* decreases or increases. Consequently, the effect of changes in the quantity possessed is exactly the opposite of the effect of changes in utility. We may now enunciate the law we have been looking for in the following terms:[4]

Given two commodities in a market in a state of equilibrium,[4] *if, all other things being equal, the utility of one of these two commodities increases or decreases for one or more parties, the value of this commodity in relation to the value of the other commodity, i.e. its price, will increase or decrease.*

If, all other things being equal, the quantity of one of the two commodities in the hands of one or more holders increases or decreases, the price of this commodity will decrease or increase.

We should point out, however, before going any further, that although a change in prices necessarily implies a change in the forces underlying these prices, it does not follow that stability of prices necessarily implies stability of the forces behind them. Indeed we may also enunciate, without further demonstration, the following double proposition:

Given two commodities, if both the utility and the quantity of one of these two commodities in the hands of one or more traders or holders vary in such a way that their raretés remain unchanged, then the value of this commodity in relation to the value of the other commodity, i.e. its price, will not change.

If the utility and the quantity of both commodities in the hands of one or more parties or holders vary in such a way that the ratios of their raretés remain unchanged, then the prices of the two commodities will not change. [k]

PART III[a]

Theory of Exchange of Several Commodities for One Another

Lesson 11

PROBLEM OF EXCHANGE OF
SEVERAL COMMODITIES FOR ONE ANOTHER.
THE THEOREM OF GENERAL EQUILIBRIUM

104. We shall now pass from the study of the exchange of two commodities, (A) and (B), for each other to a study of the exchange of several commodities, (A), (B), (C), (D) . . ., for one another. In this connection, all we need to do is to return to the case in which each party to the exchange is a holder of only one commodity and then generalize our formulae in a suitable way.[a]

From now on, let $D_{a,b}$ designate the effective demand for (A) in exchange for (B), $D_{b,a}$ the effective demand for (B) in exchange for (A), $p_{a,b}$ the price of (A) in terms of (B) and $p_{b,a}$ the price of (B) in terms of (A). To relate the four unknowns $D_{a,b}$, $D_{b,a}$, $p_{a,b}$, and $p_{b,a}$ we have two equations of effective demand

$$D_{a,b} = F_{a,b}(p_{a,b}),$$
$$D_{b,a} = F_{b,a}(p_{b,a}),$$

and two equations expressing equality between effective demand and effective offer:[b]

$$D_{b,a} = D_{a,b}p_{a,b},$$
$$D_{a,b} = D_{b,a}p_{b,a}.$$

As we have already seen, the first two of these equations can be represented geometrically by two curves, and the last two by inscribing two rectangles within these curves such that the base of each is equal to the inverse ratio of its altitude to the altitude of the other or to the direct ratio of its area to the area of the other (§57).

105. Now, leaving the case of two commodities (A) and (B), we shall take the case of three commodities (A), (B), and (C). We shall imagine, therefore, some people coming to a market with commodity (A), of which they are prepared to give up one part for commodity (B) and another part for commodity (C); while others come to the same market with commodity (B) of which they are prepared to give up one part for commodity (A) and another part for commodity (C); and still others come with commodity (C) of which they are prepared to give up one part for commodity (A) and another part for commodity (B).

Under this supposition, let us take one of these people, say a holder of (B), and let us develop the reasoning which we outlined earlier in

§50 in a way that is appropriate to the new situation. We shall find that here again the trader's schedule of this individual can be rigorously determined.

In fact, every holder of a quantity q_b of commodity (B), who comes to the market prepared to exchange a certain quantity $o_{b,a}$ of (B) for a certain quantity $d_{a,b}$ of (A) according to the equation of exchange

$$d_{a,b}v_a = o_{b,a}v_b,$$

as well as a certain quantity $o_{b,c}$ of (B) for a certain quantity $d_{c,b}$ of (C) according to the equation of exchange

$$d_{c,b}v_c = o_{b,c}v_b,$$

will take away from the market a quantity $d_{a,b}$ of (A), a quantity $d_{c,b}$ of (C) and a quantity y of (B) equal to

$$q_b - o_{b,a} - o_{b,c} = q_b - d_{a,b}\frac{v_a}{v_b} - d_{c,b}\frac{v_c}{v_b}$$

In general, the quantities q_b and $\frac{v_a}{v_b}$ or $p_{a,b}$, $d_{a,b}$ and $\frac{v_c}{v_b}$ or $p_{c,b}$, $d_{c,b}$ and y will always be related by the equation

$$q_b = y + d_{a,b}p_{a,b} + d_{c,b}p_{c,b}.$$

Before he reaches the market, our trader does not know what $\frac{v_a}{v_b}$ or $p_{a,b}$ and what $\frac{v_c}{v_b}$ or $p_{c,b}$ will be; but he is sure to find out as soon as he gets there. Once he discovers how high $p_{a,b}$ and $p_{c,b}$ are, he will decide upon the quantities $d_{a,b}$ and $d_{c,b}$ accordingly, whence a certain value of y results by virtue of the above equation. Surely, we must admit that the determination of $d_{a,b}$ is impossible unless $p_{c,b}$ is known as well as $p_{a,b}$ and that the determination of $d_{c,b}$ is impossible unless $p_{a,b}$ is known as well as $p_{c,b}$. At the same time, we have to agree that, when both $p_{a,b}$ and $p_{c,b}$ are known, this very knowledge makes possible the determination of $d_{a,b}$ and $d_{c,b}$.

106. Now, again, nothing could be easier than to indicate mathematically the direct relationship of $d_{a,b}$ and $d_{c,b}$, i.e. the effective demand for (A) and (C) in exchange for (B), to $p_{a,b}$ and $p_{c,b}$, i.e. prices of these commodities. This relationship, which amounts to the trader's schedule of the individual we are considering, is rigorously defined by the two equations, $d_{a,b} = f_{a,b}(p_{a,b}, p_{c,b})$ and $d_{c,b} = f_{c,b}(p_{a,b}, p_{c,b})$. In like manner, we could obtain equations to express the several trader's schedules of all other holders of (B) for

(A) and (C). Then, simply by adding these equations of individual demand, we obtain two equations of total demand

$$D_{a,b}=F_{a,b}(p_{a,b},\ p_{c,b}),$$
$$D_{c,b}=F_{c,b}(p_{a,b},\ p_{c,b}),$$

which express the trader's schedules of all holders of (B) taken together.

Similarly, we could obtain two equations of total demand

$$D_{a,c}=F_{a,c}(p_{a,c},\ p_{b,c}),$$
$$D_{b,c}=F_{b,c}(p_{a,c},\ p_{b,c}),$$

which express the trader's schedules of all holders of (C) taken together.

Finally, using the same procedure, we could obtain two equations of total demand

$$D_{b,a}=F_{b,a}(p_{b,a},\ p_{c,a}),$$
$$D_{c,a}=F_{c,a}(p_{b,a},\ p_{c,a}),$$

which express the trader's schedules of all holders of (A).

107. We have, besides, two equations of exchange of (B) for (A) and of (B) for (C)

$$D_{b,a}=D_{a,b}p_{a,b},$$
$$D_{b,c}=D_{c,b}p_{c,b}.$$

We have, also, two equations of exchange of (C) for (A) and of (C) for (B):

$$D_{c,a}=D_{a,c}p_{a,c},$$
$$D_{c,b}=D_{b,c}p_{b,c}.$$

And, last of all, we have two equations of exchange of (A) for (B) and of (A) for (C):

$$D_{a,b}=D_{b,a}p_{b,a},$$
$$D_{a,c}=D_{c,a}p_{c,a}.$$

Thus we have in all twelve equations relating the following twelve unknowns: the six prices of the three commodities each expressed in terms of the other two, and the six total quantities of the three commodities which are exchanged for one another.

108. Now let us suppose a market in which there are m commodities: (A), (B), (C), (D). . . . It is readily seen that by using, in this case, exactly the same reasoning which we used first in the case of two commodities and then in the case of three commodities and which it would be otiose to repeat here, we can immediately write,

first, the $m-1$ equations of effective demand for (B), (C), (D) . . . in exchange for (A)

$$D_{b,a}=F_{b,a}(p_{b,a},\ p_{c,a},\ p_{d,a}\cdot\cdot\cdot),$$
$$D_{c,a}=F_{c,a}(p_{b,a},\ p_{c,a},\ p_{d,a}\cdot\cdot\cdot),$$
$$D_{d,a}=F_{d,a}(p_{b,a},\ p_{c,a},\ p_{d,a}\cdot\cdot\cdot),$$
$$\cdot\quad\cdot\quad\cdot\quad\cdot\quad\cdot\quad\cdot\quad\cdot\quad\cdot\quad\cdot\quad\cdot\quad\cdot$$

then, the $m-1$ equations of effective demand for (A), (C), (D) . . . in exchange for (B)

$$D_{a,b}=F_{a,b}(p_{a,b},\ p_{c,b},\ p_{d,b}\cdot\cdot\cdot),$$
$$D_{c,b}=F_{c,b}(p_{a,b},\ p_{c,b},\ p_{d,b}\cdot\cdot\cdot),$$
$$D_{d,b}=F_{d,b}(p_{a,b},\ p_{c,b},\ p_{d,b}\cdot\cdot\cdot),$$
$$\cdot\quad\cdot\quad\cdot\quad\cdot\quad\cdot\quad\cdot\quad\cdot\quad\cdot\quad\cdot\quad\cdot\quad\cdot$$

then, the $m-1$ equations of effective demand for (A), (B), (D) . . . in exchange for (C)

$$D_{a,c}=F_{a,c}(p_{a,c},\ p_{b,c},\ p_{d,c}\cdot\cdot\cdot),$$
$$D_{b,c}=F_{b,c}(p_{a,c},\ p_{b,c},\ p_{d,c}\cdot\cdot\cdot),$$
$$D_{d,c}=F_{d,c}(p_{a,c},\ p_{b,c},\ p_{d,c}\cdot\cdot\cdot),$$
$$\cdot\quad\cdot\quad\cdot\quad\cdot\quad\cdot\quad\cdot\quad\cdot\quad\cdot\quad\cdot\quad\cdot\quad\cdot$$

then, the $m-1$ equations of effective demand for (A), (B), (C) . . . in exchange for (D)

$$D_{a,d}=F_{a,d}(p_{a,d},\ p_{b,d},\ p_{c,d}\cdot\cdot\cdot),$$
$$D_{b,d}=F_{b,d}(p_{a,d},\ p_{b,d},\ p_{c,d}\cdot\cdot\cdot),$$
$$D_{c,d}=F_{c,d}(p_{a,d},\ p_{b,d},\ p_{c,d}\cdot\cdot\cdot),$$
$$\cdot\quad\cdot\quad\cdot\quad\cdot\quad\cdot\quad\cdot\quad\cdot\quad\cdot\quad\cdot\quad\cdot\quad\cdot$$

and so on. In all we have $m(m-1)$ equations.

109. In addition, we can evidently write, without further explanation, the $m-1$ equations of exchange of (A) for (B), (C), (D) . . .

$$D_{a,b}=D_{b,a}p_{b,a}, \qquad D_{a,c}=D_{c,a}p_{c,a}, \qquad D_{a,d}=D_{d,a}p_{d,a}\cdot\cdot\cdot$$

the $m-1$ equations of exchange of (B) for (A), (C), (D) . . .

$$D_{b,a}=D_{a,b}p_{a,b}, \qquad D_{b,c}=D_{c,b}p_{c,b}, \qquad D_{b,d}=D_{d,b}p_{d,b}\cdot\cdot\cdot$$

the $m-1$ equations of exchange of (C) for (A), (B), (D) . . .

$$D_{c,a}=D_{a,c}p_{a,c}, \qquad D_{c,b}=D_{b,c}p_{b,c}, \qquad D_{c,d}=D_{d,c}p_{d,c}\cdot\cdot\cdot$$

the $m-1$ equations of exchange of (D) for (A), (B), (C) . . .

$$D_{d,a}=D_{a,d}p_{a,d}, \qquad D_{d,b}=D_{b,d}p_{b,d}, \qquad D_{d,c}=D_{c,d}p_{c,d}\cdot\cdot\cdot$$

and so on. In all we have again $m(m-1)$ equations.

These $m(m-1)$ equations of exchange along with the $m(m-1)$ equations of effective demand make a total of $2m(m-1)$ equations.

These equations connect precisely $2m(m-1)$ unknowns, for there are $m(m-1)$ prices and $m(m-1)$ total quantities exchanged when the m commodities are considered two at a time.

110.[c] In the special case of the exchange of two commodities for each other, and in the special case of the exchange of three commodities for one another, the problem can be solved either geometrically or algebraically, because in both these cases the demand functions[d] can be represented geometrically. In the first of these special cases, the demand functions are functions of one variable[e] and can be represented by two curves. In the second, the demand functions are functions of two variables [f] and can be represented by six surfaces in space. In the first case we obtain a geometrical solution of the problem (of equilibrium) simply by inscribing rectangles within the curves; while in the second case we arrive at a geometrical solution by inscribing rectangles within curves obtained by the intersection of the six surfaces by planes.[1]

In the general case, however, the demand functions are functions of $m-1$ variables which are too numerous to be represented in space. It seems, therefore, that the problem when generalized can only be formulated and solved algebraically, not geometrically.[1] It should be recalled, moreover, that what we have in mind throughout this volume is not to pose and solve the problem in question as if it were a real problem in a given concrete situation, but solely to formulate scientifically the nature of the problem which actually arises in the market where it is solved empirically.[g] From our point of view, not only is the algebraic solution as good as the geometrical solution; but we may go so far as to say that in adopting the analytical form of mathematical expression we are using a form that is general and scientific *par excellence*.

111.[h] The problem of the exchange of several commodities for one another now appears to be solved. Actually, it is only half solved. Under the conditions described above, there would indeed be a certain equilibrium in the market so far as the prices of commodities taken two at a time were concerned; but that equilibrium would be an imperfect equilibrium. *We do not have* perfect *or general market equilibrium unless the price of one of any two commodities in terms of the other is equal to the ratio of the prices of these two commodities in terms of any third commodity.* This remains to be proved. Let us begin by selecting three commodities out of the total number, say (A), (B) and (C), and let us suppose that the price $p_{c,b}$ is greater or smaller than the ratio of $p_{c,a}$ to $p_{b,a}$, and see what will happen.

---

[1] A geometrical solution is nevertheless given below in Appendix I, entitled *A Geometrical Theory of the Determination of Prices*. [This note appears first in ed. 4.]

In order to fix our ideas, we shall imagine that the place which serves as a market for the exchange of all the commodities (A), (B), (C), (D) ... for one another is divided into as many sectors as there are pairs of commodities exchanged. We should then have $\dfrac{m(m-1)}{2}$ special markets, each identified by a signboard indicating the names of the two commodities exchanged there as well as their prices or rates of exchange which are mathematically determined in accordance with the system of equations developed above. For example, we should read: "Exchange of (A) for (B) and (B) for (A) at the reciprocal prices $p_{a,b}$ and $p_{b,a}$"; "Exchange of (A) for (C) and (C) for (A) at the reciprocal prices $p_{a,c}$ and $p_{c,a}$"; and "Exchange of (B) for (C) and (C) for (B) at the reciprocal prices $p_{b,c}$ and $p_{c,b}$". Under these assumptions, if each holder of (A) who wanted (B) and (C) simply traded his (A) for (B) and (C) on the first two of the above specially designated markets, if each holder of (B) who wanted some (A) and (C) simply traded his (B) for (A) and (C) on the first and third of these markets, and if each holder of (C) who wanted (A) and (B) simply traded his (C) for (A) and (B) on the last two of these markets, then equilibrium would remain unchanged [even though $p_{c,b}$ might be greater or less than the ratio of $p_{c,a}$ to $p_{b,a}$]. It is easy to show, however, that neither the holders of (A), nor those of (B), nor those of (C) will trade in this way. They will all go about it in another way which is more to their advantage.

112. Let us suppose, as we did before, that

$$p_{c,b} = \alpha \frac{p_{c,a}}{p_{b,a}},$$

or that

$$\frac{p_{c,b}\,p_{b,a}\,p_{a,c}}{\alpha} = 1,$$

where α is first assumed >1.[2]

It follows from this equation that the true price of (C) in terms of (B) will not be $p_{c,b}$ but $\dfrac{p_{c,b}}{\alpha}$,[3] in view of the fact that for $\dfrac{p_{c,b}}{\alpha}$ units of (B) it is possible first to obtain $\dfrac{p_{c,b}\,p_{b,a}}{\alpha}$ units of (A) on the (A, B) market at the price $p_{a,b} = \dfrac{1}{p_{b,a}}$ of (A) in terms of (B), and then to trade these $\dfrac{p_{c,b}\,p_{b,a}}{\alpha}$ units of (A) on the (A, C) market for $\dfrac{p_{c,b}\,p_{b,a}\,p_{a,c}}{\alpha} = 1$ unit of (C) at the price $p_{c,a} = \dfrac{1}{p_{a,c}}$ of (C) in terms of (A).

It follows also that the true price of (B) in terms of (A) will not be $p_{b,a}$ but $\dfrac{p_{b,a}}{\alpha}$, in view of the fact that for $\dfrac{p_{b,a}}{\alpha}$ units of (A) it is possible first to obtain $\dfrac{p_{b,a}p_{a,c}}{\alpha}$ units of (C) on the (A, C) market at the price $p_{c,a}=\dfrac{1}{p_{a,c}}$ of (C) in terms of (A), and then to trade these $\dfrac{p_{b,a}p_{a,c}}{\alpha}$ units of (C) on the (B, C) market for $\dfrac{p_{b,a}p_{a,c}p_{c,b}}{\alpha}=1$ unit of (B) at the price $p_{b,c}=\dfrac{1}{p_{c,b}}$ of (B) in terms of (C).

And finally it follows that the true price of (A) in terms of (C) will not be $p_{a,c}$ but $\dfrac{p_{a,c}}{\alpha}$, in view of the fact that for $\dfrac{p_{a,c}}{\alpha}$ units of (C) it is possible first to obtain $\dfrac{p_{a,c}p_{c,b}}{\alpha}$ units of (B) on (B, C) market, at the price $p_{b,c}=\dfrac{1}{p_{c,b}}$ of (B) in terms of (C) and then to trade these $\dfrac{p_{a,c}p_{c,b}}{\alpha}$ units of (B) on the (A, B) market for $\dfrac{p_{a,c}p_{c,b}p_{b,a}}{\alpha}=1$ unit of (A) at the price $p_{a,b}=\dfrac{1}{p_{b,a}}$ of (A) in terms of (B).

113. In order to clarify this point with the aid of concrete numbers, let us suppose that $p_{c,b}=4$, $p_{c,a}=6$, and $p_{b,a}=2$, which makes $\alpha=1\cdot33$.[4] From the equation

$$\frac{4\times2\times\frac{1}{6}}{1\cdot33}=1$$

we see that the true price of (C) in terms of (B) will not be 4, but $\dfrac{4}{1\cdot33}=3$, in view of the fact that for 3 units of (B) [intended for the eventual purchase of (C)] it is possible first to obtain $3\times2=6$ units of (A) on the (A, B) market, where the price of (A) in terms of (B) is $\frac{1}{2}$; and then to trade these 6 units of (A) on the (A, C) market for $6\times\frac{1}{6}=1$ unit of (C), since the price there of (C) in terms of (A) is 6.

We see also from the above equation that the true price of (B) in terms of (A) will not be 2, but $\dfrac{2}{1\cdot33}=1\cdot50$, in view of the fact that for $1\cdot50$ units of (A) [intended for the eventual purchase of (B)] it is possible first to obtain $1\cdot50\times\frac{1}{6}=\frac{1}{4}$ of a unit of (C) on the (A, C) market, where the price of (C) in terms of (A) is 6; and then to trade this $\frac{1}{4}$ of a unit of (C) on the (B, C) market for $\frac{1}{4} \times 4 = 1$ unit of (B), since the price there of (B) in terms of (C) is $\frac{1}{4}$.

And finally we see that the true price of (A) in terms of (C) will not be $\frac{1}{8}$, but $\dfrac{1}{6 \times 1 \cdot 33} = \frac{1}{8}$, in view of the fact that for $\frac{1}{8}$ of a unit of (C) [intended for the eventual purchase of (A)] it is possible first to obtain $\frac{1}{8} \times 4 = \frac{1}{2}$ of a unit of (B) on the (B, C) market, where the price of (B) in terms of (C) is $\frac{1}{4}$; and then to trade this $\frac{1}{2}$ of a unit of (B) on the (A, B) market for $\frac{1}{2} \times 2 = 1$ unit of (A), since the price there of (A) in terms of (B) is $\frac{1}{2}$.

114. Clearly, no one of the holders of (A), or (B), or (C) will hesitate to resort to the expedient of substituting the indirect exchange of (A) against (C) and (C) against (B) for the direct exchange of (A) against (B); or the indirect exchange of (B) against (A) and (A) against (C) for the direct exchange of (B) against (C); or the indirect exchange of (C) against (B) and (B) against (A) for the direct exchange of (C) against (A). This indirect exchange is called *arbitrage*. As to the gains the trading parties realize by arbitrage, they will distribute them as they please according to their various wants, by purchasing a little more of one commodity or another in order to procure the largest possible sum total of satisfactions. The condition of this maximum, it is well to point out, is that the ratios of the intensities of the last wants satisfied be equal to the real prices resulting from arbitrage operations.[5] But we shall not go into that now, for it suffices to note at this point that the supplementary demand [entailed in arbitrage operations] is part and parcel of the principal demand: when the holders of (A) exchange (A) against (C) and (C) against (B) but never (A) directly against (B); when the holders of (B) exchange (B) against (A) and (A) against (C) but never (B) directly against (C); and when the holders of (C) exchange (C) against (B) and (B) against (A) but never (C) directly against (A). Consequently, on the (A, B) market there will inevitably be a demand for (A) and an offer of (B), but no demand for (B) nor offer of (A); whence a fall in $p_{b,a}$. On the (A, C) market there will inevitably be a demand for (C) and an offer of (A), but no demand for (A) nor offer of (C); whence a rise in $p_{c,a}$. And on the (B, C) market there will inevitably be a demand for (B) and an offer of (C), but no demand for (C) nor offer of (B); whence a fall in $p_{c,b}$.

115. It is evident from this that in the case where $p_{c,b} > \dfrac{p_{c,a}}{p_{b,a}}$, the market equilibrium will neither be final nor general and arbitrage operations will be effected with the result that $p_{c,b}$ will fall, $p_{c,a}$ will rise and $p_{b,a}$ will fall. It is evident, also, that if the case were such

that $p_{c,b} < \dfrac{p_{c,a}}{p_{b,a}}$, there would be arbitrage operations in the market, resulting in a rise in $p_{c,b}$, a fall in $p_{c,a}$ and a rise in $p_{b,a}$. In this second case we should find that

$$p_{c,b} = \alpha \frac{p_{c,a}}{p_{b,a}},$$

or

$$\alpha p_{b,c} p_{a,b} p_{c,a} = 1$$

where $\alpha < 1$, in consequence of which the true price of (B) in terms of (C) would be $\alpha p_{b,c}$, provided that (C) was traded for (A) and (A) for (B); the true price of (A) in terms of (B) would be $\alpha p_{a,b}$, provided that (B) was traded for (C) and (C) for (A); and the true price of (C) in terms of (A) would be $\alpha p_{c,a}$, provided that (A) was traded for (B) and (B) for (C). Clearly, what has been said about the prices of (A), (B) and (C) is equally true of the prices of any three commodities whatsoever. Hence, if one wished to leave arbitrage operations aside and at the same time to generalize the equilibrium established for pairs of commodities in the market, it would be necessary to introduce the condition that the price of either one of any two commodities [chosen at random] expressed in terms of the other be equal to the ratio of the prices of each of these two commodities in terms of any third commodity.[4] In other words, the following equations would have to be satisfied:

$$p_{a,b} = \frac{1}{p_{b,a}}, \qquad p_{c,b} = \frac{p_{c,a}}{p_{b,a}}, \qquad p_{d,b} = \frac{p_{d,a}}{p_{b,a}} \ldots$$

$$p_{a,c} = \frac{1}{p_{c,a}}, \qquad p_{b,c} = \frac{p_{b,a}}{p_{c,a}}, \qquad p_{d,c} = \frac{p_{d,a}}{p_{c,a}} \ldots$$

$$p_{a,d} = \frac{1}{p_{d,a}}, \qquad p_{b,d} = \frac{p_{b,a}}{p_{d,a}}, \qquad p_{c,d} = \frac{p_{c,a}}{p_{d,a}} \ldots$$

. . . .

and so forth. We should have, in all, $(m-1)(m-1)$ equations of general equilibrium, which contained implicitly $\dfrac{m(m-1)}{2}$ equations expressing the reciprocal relationship between prices. The commodity in terms of which the prices of all the others are expressed is the 'numéraire' [or *standard commodity*[6]].

116. It goes without saying that the change to these $(m-1)(m-1)$ conditions calls for a reduction of our previously developed system of equations of demand and exchange by an equal number of equations. This is precisely the reduction which is effected when a single general

market is substituted for the several special markets [§111] in such a way that the equations of exchange expressing equality between the demand and offer of each commodity in terms of and in exchange for each of the other commodities[1] taken separately are replaced by the following equations of exchange expressing equality between the demand and offer of each commodity in terms of and in exchange for all the other commodities taken together:

$$D_{a,b}+D_{a,c}+D_{a,d}+ \ldots =D_{b,a}p_{b,a}+D_{c,a}p_{c,a}+D_{d,a}p_{d,a}+ \ldots$$
$$D_{b,a}+D_{b,c}+D_{b,d}+ \ldots =D_{a,b}p_{a,b}+D_{c,b}p_{c,b}+D_{d,b}p_{d,b}+ \ldots$$
$$D_{c,a}+D_{c,b}+D_{c,d}+ \ldots =D_{a,c}p_{a,c}+D_{b,c}p_{b,c}+D_{d,c}p_{d,c}+ \ldots$$
$$D_{d,a}+D_{d,b}+D_{d,c}+ \ldots =D_{a,d}p_{a,d}+D_{b,d}p_{b,d}+D_{c,d}p_{c,d}+ \ldots$$

. . . .

and so on, in all m equations. But these m equations reduce to $m-1$ equations. If we insert the values of the prices found in the general equilibrium equations[7] and then designate the prices of (B), (C), (D) . . . in terms of (A) simply by p_b, p_c, p_d . . ., and the above equations become:

$$D_{a,b}+D_{a,c}+D_{a,d}+ \ldots =D_{b,a}p_b+D_{c,a}p_c+D_{d,a}p_d+ \ldots$$
$$D_{b,a}+D_{b,c}+D_{b,d}+ \ldots =D_{a,b}\frac{1}{p_b}+D_{c,b}\frac{p_c}{p_b}+D_{d,b}\frac{p_d}{p_b}+ \ldots$$
$$D_{c,a}+D_{c,b}+D_{c,d}+ \ldots =D_{a,c}\frac{1}{p_c}+D_{b,c}\frac{p_b}{p_c}+D_{d,c}\frac{p_d}{p_c}+ \ldots$$
$$D_{d,a}+D_{d,b}+D_{d,c}+ \ldots =D_{a,d}\frac{1}{p_d}+D_{b,d}\frac{p_b}{p_d}+D_{c,d}\frac{p_c}{p_d}+ \ldots$$

. . . .

And now, adding together all but the first of these m equations, after multiplying both sides of the first of the remaining $m-1$ equations by p_b, both sides of the second of these $m-1$ equations by p_c, both sides of the third by p_d . . ., and then cancelling out identical terms on both sides of the sum, we end up with the first equation of the above system.[8] The first equation, may, therefore, be omitted, and the whole system reduces to the remaining $m-1$ equations. Thus, we have finally $m-1$ equations of exchange to which we add the $m(m-1)$ equations of demand and the $(m-1)(m-1)$ general equilibrium equations, making a total of $2m(m-1)$ equations [§111] the roots of which are the $m(m-1)$ prices of the m commodities in terms of one another and the $m(m-1)$ total quantities of the m commodities which are exchanged for one another. In this way, given the equations of demand, the prices are determined mathematically. Now there remains only to show—and this is the essential point—that the problem of exchange for which we have just given a theoretical solution is the selfsame problem that is solved empirically on the market by the mechanism of free competition. Before proceeding to this demonstration, however, we shall examine the case where the parties to the exchange come to the market each holding several commodities. This is the general case which the theorem of maximum satisfaction will enable us to deal with quite simply and easily.

THE GENERAL FORMULA OF THE MATHEMATICAL SOLUTION OF THE PROBLEM OF EXCHANGE OF SEVERAL COMMODITIES FOR ONE ANOTHER. THE LAW OF THE ESTABLISHMENT OF COMMODITY PRICES

117.[a] In the case of the exchange of any number of commodities for one another, as in the case of the exchange of two commodities for each other, the individual effective demand equations are mathematically determined by the condition of maximum satisfaction of wants. What, exactly, is this condition of maximum satisfaction? It always consists in the attainment of equality between the ratio of the *raretés* of any two commodities[b] and the price of one in terms of the other, for otherwise it would be advantageous to make further exchanges of these commodities for each other (§80). If each of the parties to the exchange is a holder of one commodity only, and if, in order to furnish an occasion for arbitrage transactions, the $m(m-1)$ prices of the m commodities are cried as ratios of exchange between the commodities taken two at a time without reference to the condition of general equilibrium, then maximum satisfaction will be achieved by each party when the ratios of the *raretés* of the several commodities demanded to the *rareté* of the one commodity originally held are equal, not to prices as they are first cried, but to the true prices arrived at by arbitrage. But if each party is the holder of several commodities and if, in this case, the prices of $m-1$ of the m commodities are cried in terms of the mth, which is selected as the *numéraire*, in order to prevent arbitrage operations from taking place, then, provided that the price of one of any pair of the m commodities in terms of the other is equal to the ratio of their prices in terms of the *numéraire*, it is evident that maximum satisfaction will be achieved by each trader when the ratios of the *raretés* of the commodities not used as the *numéraire* to the *rareté* of the commodity so used equal the prices cried.

118. Now let party (1) be a holder of $q_{a,1}$ of (A), $q_{b,1}$ of (B), $q_{c,1}$ of (C), $q_{d,1}$ of (D).... Let $r=\phi_{a,1}(q)$, $r=\phi_{b,1}(q)$, $r=\phi_{c,1}(q)$, $r=\phi_{d,1}(q)$... be his equations of utility or want for commodities (A), (B), (C), (D)... during a given period of time.[c] Let p_b, p_c, p_d... be the respective prices of commodities (B), (C), (D)... in terms of (A).

164

And let x_1, y_1, z_1, w_1... be the quantities of (A), (B), (C), (D)... respectively which our individual will add to the original quantities held $q_{a,1}$, $q_{b,1}$, $q_{c,1}$, $q_{d,1}$... at prices p_b, p_c, p_d.... These additions may be positive and consequently represent quantities demanded; or they may be negative so as to represent quantities offered. Inasmuch as the individual trader cannot possibly demand any of these commodities without offering in return a quantity of other commodities having the same value, we can be sure that if some of the quantities x_1, y_1, z_1, w_1... are positive, others are bound to be negative, and that the following relationship between these quantities will always hold:

$$x_1 + y_1 p_b + z_1 p_c + w_1 p_d + \ldots = 0.$$

If we suppose maximum satisfaction to have been attained, the above quantities will evidently be related by the following system:[1]

$$\phi_{b,1}(q_{b,1} + y_1) = p_b \phi_{a,1}(q_{a,1} + x_1),$$
$$\phi_{c,1}(q_{c,1} + z_1) = p_c \phi_{a,1}(q_{a,1} + x_1),$$
$$\phi_{d,1}(q_{d,1} + w_1) = p_d \phi_{a,1}(q_{a,1} + x_1),$$
$$\cdot \quad \cdot \quad \cdot \quad \cdot \quad \cdot \quad \cdot \quad \cdot \quad \cdot \quad \cdot \quad \cdot \quad \cdot \quad \cdot$$

constituting in all $m-1$ equations, which together with the preceding equation give us a system of m equations. We may suppose that $m-1$ of the m unknowns, x_1, y_1, z_1, w_1..., are eliminated one after another from these equations so that we are left with only one equation[d] expressing the mth unknown as a function of the prices.[2] We should then have the following equations of demand or offer of (B), (C), (D)... by party (1):

$$y_1 = f_{b,1}(p_b, p_c, p_d \ldots)$$
$$z_1 = f_{c,1}(p_b, p_c, p_d \ldots)$$
$$w_1 = f_{d,1}(p_b, p_c, p_d \ldots)$$
$$\cdot \quad \cdot \quad \cdot \quad \cdot \quad \cdot \quad \cdot \quad \cdot \quad \cdot$$

while his demand or offer of (A) is given by the equation

$$x_1 = -(y_1 p_b + z_1 p_c + w_1 p_d + \ldots).$$

Similarly, in the case of parties (2), (3)... we could derive the following equations of demand or offer of (B), (C), (D)...:

$$y_2 = f_{b,2}(p_b, p_c, p_d \ldots)$$
$$z_2 = f_{c,2}(p_b, p_c, p_d \ldots)$$
$$w_2 = f_{d,2}(p_b, p_c, p_d \ldots)$$
$$\cdot \quad \cdot \quad \cdot \quad \cdot \quad \cdot \quad \cdot \quad \cdot \quad \cdot$$

$$y_3 = f_{a,3}(p_b, p_c, p_d \ldots)$$
$$z_3 = f_{c,3}(p_b, p_c, p_d \ldots)$$
$$w_3 = f_{d,3}(p_b, p_c, p_d \ldots)$$
$$\cdot \quad \cdot \quad \cdot \quad \cdot \quad \cdot \quad \cdot \quad \cdot \quad \cdot$$

and so forth, while their respective demands or offers of (A) are given by the equations:

$$x_2=-(y_2p_b+z_2p_c+w_2p_d+\ldots)$$
$$x_3=-(y_3p_b+z_3p_c+w_3p_d+\ldots)$$

$$\cdots\cdots\cdots\cdots\cdots\cdots$$

In this way everyone's trading schedule could be deduced from the utility which the various commodities have for him and from his original stocks of these commodities. Before proceeding further, however, we have a very important observation to make at this juncture.

119. It is possible for y_1 to be negative at certain values of p_b, p_c, $p_d\ldots$, which is the case when party (1) offers commodity (B) instead of demanding it. It is even possible for y_1 to be equal to $-q_{b,1}$, when party (1) does not retain any of commodity (B) at all for himself. If we enter this value of y_1 in the system of $m-1$ equations of maximum satisfaction, we have

$$\phi_{b,1}(0)=p_b\phi_{a,1}(q_{a,1}+x_1),$$
$$\phi_{c,1}(q_{c,1}+z_1)=p_c\phi_{a,1}(q_{a,1}+x_1),$$
$$\phi_{d,1}(q_{d,1}+w_1)=p_d\phi_{a,1}(q_{a,1}+x_1),$$

$$\cdots\cdots\cdots\cdots\cdots\cdots$$

Substituting the values for p_b, p_c, $p_d\ldots$ derived from the above equations into

$$x_1+z_1p_c+w_1p_d+\ldots=q_{b,1}p_b,$$

we obtain[3]

$$x_1\phi_{a,1}(q_{a,1}+x_1)+z_1\phi_{c,1}(q_{c,1}+z_1)+w_1\phi_{d,1}(q_{d,1}+w_1)+\ldots$$
$$=q_{b,1}\phi_{b,1}(0).$$

This equation expresses a condition which can be translated into the following terms: *For the offer of one of the commodities to be equal to the quantity possessed of that commodity, it must be possible to inscribe such rectangles within the segments of the utility curves enclosing the areas which lie just above the bounded areas representing the wants [already] satisfied by the quantities possessed of the commodities to be demanded, that the sum of their areas is equal to the area of a rectangle the altitude of which represents the original stock of the commodity to be offered and the base the maximum intensity of want for that commodity.*[4]

This condition may or may not be satisfied. If it is, party (1)'s offer of (B) may, under certain circumstances,[5] be equal to the quantity $q_{b,1}$ which he holds to start with. In any case, the offer can never be greater than this quantity. The essential point which follows from this is that the demand or offer equation of (B) must be replaced by $y_1 = -q_{b,1}$ for all values of p_b, p_c, p_d... which make y_1 negative and greater than $q_{b,1}$ in this equation.

120. But that is not all. In the first place, the same conclusion applies to the demand or offer equations of (C), (D)... for such values of p_b, p_c, p_d... which make z_1, w_1... negative and larger than $q_{c,1}$, $q_{d,1}$.... In the second place, it is precisely when these equations have to be replaced by $z_1 = -q_{c,1}$, $w_1 = -q_{d,1}$..., that the demand or offer equation of (B) must be changed in consequence.

For example, if $z_1 = -q_{c,1}$, the system of equations determining party (1)'s demand or offer of (B) would be the following:[6]

$$x_1 + y_1 p_b + w_1 p_d + ... = q_{c,1} p_c,$$
$$\phi_{b,1}(q_{b,1} + y_1) = p_b \phi_{a,1}(q_{a,1} + x_1),$$
$$\phi_{d,1}(q_{d,1} + w_1) = p_d \phi_{a,1}(q_{a,1} + x_1),$$

. . . .

$m - 1$ equations in all, from which we could suppose $m - 2$ unknowns, such as x_1, w_1..., to be eliminated one after another, so that only one equation expressing y_1 as a function of p_b, p_c, p_d... would remain.[e] The procedure is the same when $w_1 = -q_{d,1}$.... It will be readily understood, without further demonstration, that the same procedure would apply not only in the case where offer equals the quantity possessed of one of the commodities (C), (D)..., but also in the case where this equality holds for two, three, four..., or, generally speaking, for any number of these commodities.

121. We have said nothing so far about the equation of the demand or offer of the *numéraire* commodity (A), because this equation takes on a special form. Evidently it too must be replaced by $x_1 = -q_{a,1}$ for values of p_b, p_c, p_d... which would make x_1 negative and greater than $q_{a,1}$. In that case, moreover, the system of equations determining party (1)'s demand or offer of (B) would be the following:

$$y_1 p_b + z_1 p_c + w_1 p_d + ... = q_{a,1},$$
$$p_b \phi_{c,1}(q_{c,1} + z_1) = p_c \phi_{b,1}(q_{b,1} + y_1),$$
$$p_b \phi_{d,1}(q_{d,1} + w_1) = p_d \phi_{b,1}(q_{b,1} + y_1),$$

. . . .

in all, as before, $m - 1$ equations from which we could suppose $m - 2$ unknowns such as z_1, w_1... to be eliminated one after another, so that only one equation expressing y_1 as a function of p_b, p_c, p_d... would remain.[f]

122.[g] Undoubtedly, it would be more or less difficult to set out the demand and offer equations in such a way as to satisfy the restrictions described above; but it is none the less certain—and this is the important point—that, once certain prices, say p'_b, p'_c, p'_d... of

(B), (C), (D)... in terms of (A), have been cried, the quantities to be offered and demanded of all the commodities in question, even when we take into account the fact that offer may equal quantity possessed, are perfectly determinate. This is what we have to prove.

Let $q=\psi_{a,1}(r)$, $q=\psi_{b,1}(r)$, $q=\psi_{c,1}(r)$, $q=\psi_{d,1}(r)$... be the utility equations of party (1) for commodities (A), (B), (C), (D)..., which are to be solved now for the quantities rather than the *raretés*. Upon the completion of all the exchange transactions, we have not only

$$q_{a,1}+x'_1=\psi_{a,1}(r'_{a,1}),$$
$$q_{b,1}+y'_1=\psi_{b,1}(r'_{b,1}),$$
$$q_{c,1}+z'_1=\psi_{c,1}(r'_{c,1}),$$
$$q_{d,1}+w'_1=\psi_{d,1}(r'_{d,1}),$$
$$\cdots\cdots\cdots\cdots$$

but also[7]

$$q_{a,1}+p'_b q_{b,1}+p'_c q_{c,1}+p'_d q_{d,1}+\cdots$$
$$=\psi_{a,1}(r'_{a,1})+p'_b\psi_{b,1}(p'_b r'_{a,1})+p'_c\psi_{c,1}(p'_c r'_{a,1})$$
$$+p'_d\psi_{d,1}(p'_d r'_{a,1})+\cdots$$

by virtue of the condition of equality of the values of the quantities exchanged and the condition of maximum satisfaction (§118). This last equation can be solved for $r'_{a,1}$.[8] Knowing $r'_{a,1}$, we have $r'_{b,1}$, $r'_{c,1}$, $r'_{d,1}$... and consequently x'_1, y'_1, z'_1, w'_1.... The only commodities which will be retained or acquired are those for which the intensity of the first want to be satisfied is greater than the product of price times $r'_{a,1}$.[9]

If $r'_{a,1}$ is greater than the intensity of his first want for (A), party (1) will neither demand nor retain any of the commodity serving as the *numéraire*.

123. The equations of the demand or offer of (A), (B), (C), (D)... by parties (1), (2), (3)... having been appropriately set out *ex hypothesi* in such a way as to satisfy the restrictions described above, let X, Y, Z, W... designate respectively the sums $x_1+x_2+x_3+\cdots$, $y_1+y_2+y_3+\cdots$, $z_1+z_2+z_3+\cdots$, $w_1+w_2+w_3+\cdots$ and let F_b, F_c, F_d... designate respectively the sums of the functions $f_{b,1}$, $f_{b,2}$, $f_{b,3}\cdots f_{c,1}$, $f_{c,2}$, $f_{c,3}\cdots f_{d,1}$, $f_{d,2}$, $f_{d,3}\cdots$. Since the condition of equality between the demand and the offer of (A), (B), (C), (D)... is expressed by the equations $X=0$, $Y=0$, $Z=0$, $W=0$... in the general case under discussion, we have the following equations for the determination of current equilibrium prices:[10]

$$F_b(p_b, p_c, p_d\cdots)=0,$$
$$F_c(p_b, p_c, p_d\cdots)=0,$$
$$F_d(p_b, p_c, p_d\cdots)=0,$$
$$\cdots\cdots\cdots\cdots$$

making up, in all, $m-1$ equations. Moreover, since p_b, p_c, p_d... are by their nature positive, it is evident that, if the above equations are satisfied, i.e. if $Y=0$, $Z=0$, $W=0$..., we also have[h]

$$X=-(Yp_b+Zp_c+Wp_d+...)=0.$$

124.[i] Thus $m-1$ prices of $m-1$ of the m commodities are determined mathematically in terms of the mth commodity which serves as the *numéraire*, when the following three conditions are satisfied: first that each and every party to the exchange obtain the maximum satisfaction of his wants, the ratios of his *raretés* then being equal to the prices; second that each and every party give up quantities that stand in a definite ratio to the quantities received and vice versa, there being only one price in terms of the *numéraire* for each commodity, namely the price at which total effective demand equals total effective offer; and third that there be no occasion for arbitrage transactions, the equilibrium price of one of any two commodities in terms of the other being equal to the ratio of the prices of these two commodities in terms of any third commodity.[j] Now let us see in what way this problem of the exchange of several commodities for one another to which we have just given a scientific solution is also the problem which is empirically solved in the market by the mechanism of competition.

125. First of all, what actually takes place in the market is that the $m(m-1)$ prices of m commodities in terms of one another are reduced through the employment of a *numéraire* to $m-1$ prices of $m-1$ of the m commodities in terms of the mth. This mth commodity is the *numéraire*. The $(m-1)(m-1)$ prices of the remaining commodities in terms of one another are presumed to be equal to the ratios of the prices of the commodities in terms of the *numéraire* in comformity with the condition of general equilibrium. Let p'_b, p'_c, p'_d..., of (B), (C), (D)... in terms of (A) be $m-1$ prices cried in this way, at random. At these prices each party to the exchange decides upon his demand or offer of (A), (B), (C), (D).... These decisions which are arrived at after some deliberation, but without refined calculation, are made as if they were reached by the mathematical solution of the system of equations of demand and offer and of maximum satisfaction subject to suitable constraints. Let x'_1, x'_2, x'_3... y'_1, y'_2, y'_3... z'_1, z'_2, z'_3... w'_1, w'_2, w'_3... be positive or negative, representing the individual demands or offers corresponding to the prices p'_b, p'_c, p'_d.... If the total demand equalled the total offer of each and every commodity, if, in other words, we immediately had $Y'=0$, $Z'=0$, $W'=0$... and, in consequence, $X'=0$, the exchange would take place at these prices and the problem would be solved. Generally, however, the total demand will not

equal the total offer of each and every commodity, so that we have $Y'\gtreqless0$, $Z'\gtreqless0$, $W'\gtreqless0$... and, in consequence, $X'\gtreqless0$. What will happen on the market then? If the demand for any one commodity is greater than the offer, the price of that commodity in terms of the *numéraire* will rise; if the offer is greater than the demand, the price will fall.[11] What must we do in order to prove that the theoretical solution is identically the solution worked out by the market? Our task is very simple: we need only show that the upward and downward movements of prices solve the system of equations of offer and demand by a process of groping ['par tâtonnement'].[12]

126. Let us recall that we have the equation[13]

$$X'+Y'p'_b+Z'p'_c+W'p'_d+\ldots=0,$$

which can be written

$$D'_a-O'_a+(D'_b-O'_b)p'_b+(D'_c-O'_c)p'_c+(D'_d-O'_d)p'_d+\ldots=0,$$

where D'_a, D'_b, D'_c, D'_d... designate the sums of the positive x's, y's, z's, w's... and O'_a, O'_b, O'_c, O'_d... designate the sums of the negative x's, y's, z's, w's... taken positively, the corresponding prices being p'_b, p'_c, p'_d.... We observe that, since p'_b, p'_c, p'_d... are positive by their very nature, if some of the quantities $X'=D'_a-O'_a$, $Y'=D'_b-O'_b$, $Z'=D'_c-O'_c$, $W'=D'_d-O'_d$... are positive, others will be negative, and conversely, if some of these quantities are negative, others will be positive.[k] This means that if at the prices p'_b, p'_c, p'_d... the total demand for some commodities is greater (or smaller) than their offer, then the offer of some of the other commodities must be greater (or smaller) than the demand for them.

127. Let us now consider the inequality[1]

$$F_b(p'_b, p'_c, p'_d\ldots)\gtreqless0,$$

and let us rewrite it in this form

$$\Delta_b(p'_b, p'_c, p'_d\ldots)\gtreqless\Omega_b(p'_b, p'_c, p'_d\ldots),$$

where the function Δ_b is the sum of the positive y's, or D_b, and the function Ω_b is the sum of the negative y's, or O_b. Leaving p_c, p_d... to one side since these prices are assumed to have been previously determined, so that p_b alone remains to be determined, let us try to find how p_b must be adjusted between zero and infinity for the demand for (B) to equal its offer. Although neither the function F_b nor the functions Δ_b and Ω_b are known, we can, nevertheless, derive sufficient information for present purposes from the foregoing study of exchange to tell us how p_b can be brought to a value which, if it exists at all, will make the F_b function equal zero or the Δ_b and Ω_b functions equal to each other.

128. Starting, now, with the function Δ_b, which is the demand

function of (B) in exchange for (A), (C), (D)..., we know that it is positive when $p_b=0$, i.e. at zero prices of (B) in terms of (A), (C), (D).... In fact, at these [zero] prices the total effective demand for (B) will be equal to the excess of the total extensive utility of (B) over the total quantity of (B) possessed, and this will be a positive excess if commodity (B) is scarce and forms part of social wealth. If p_b is allowed to increase in such a way that the various prices of (B) in terms of (A), (C), (D)... all rise in the same proportion, the function Δ_b will decrease since it is a sum of decreasing functions. In fact, commodity (B) will become dearer and dearer in relation to commodities (A), (C), (D)...; and it is unthinkable, under this hypothesis, that the demand for (B) should increase. It can only diminish. Moreover, we can always suppose the value of p_b, that is to say the prices of (B) in terms of (A), (C), (D)..., to be so high, infinite if need be, that the demand for (B) is zero.

Turning our attention, next, to the function Ω_b, which is the offer function of (B) in exchange for (A), (C), (D)..., we know that it is zero for $p_b=0$, and even for certain positive values of p_b, i.e. for the zero price and even certain positive prices of (B) in terms of (A), (C), (D).... Indeed, just as we may suppose prices of (B) in terms of (A), (C), (D)... so high that the demand for (B) is zero, so we may imagine prices of (A), (C), (D)... in terms of (B) so high that the demand for these commodities is zero, in which case the offer of (B) must be zero. If p_b is allowed to increase in such a way that the various prices of (B) in terms of (A), (C), (D)... all rise in the same proportion, the function Ω_b will first increase and then decrease, since it is a sum of functions which first increase and then decrease. In this case, the commodities (A), (C), (D)... will become cheaper and cheaper in relation to commodity (B), and the demand for them will conform to the successive changes in the offer of (B). But this offer will not increase indefinitely; it passes through at least one maximum value which cannot be greater than the total quantity possessed. The offer of (B) must then diminish and return to zero if p_b is infinite, that is, if (A), (C), (D)... are free goods.

129. Under these conditions there exists a certain value of p_b at which D_b and O_b are equal, except in the case where D_b falls to zero before O_b starts to rise above zero, in which case there is no solution. Such a case, however, will not occur as long as there are any parties to the exchange who are holders of more than one commodity.[m] In order to find the [equilibrium] value of p_b, p'_b will have to rise whenever $Y'>0$, i.e. whenever $D'_b>O'_b$ at that price; and p'_b will have to fall whenever $Y'<0$, i.e. whenever $O'_b>D'_b$ at that price. Thus we arrive at the equation

$$F_b(p''_b, p'_c, p'_d...)=0.$$

Once this operation has been carried out, the inequality[1]

$$F_c(p'_b, p'_c, p'_d \ldots) \gtreqless 0$$

becomes

$$F_c(p''_b, p'_c, p'_d \ldots) \gtreqless 0;$$

but this inequality can be turned into

$$F_c(p''_b, p''_c, p'_d \ldots) = 0$$

by increasing or decreasing p'_c according as $Z \gtreqless 0$ (i.e. $D'_c \gtreqless O'_c$) at that price.

In the same way we can obtain the equation

$$F_d(p''_b, p''_c, p''_d \ldots) = 0$$

and so forth.

130. After these operations have been effected, we shall have

$$F_b(p''_b, p''_c, p''_d \ldots) \gtreqless 0.$$

It remains to be shown that this inequality[1] is closer to equality than the inequality

$$F_b(p'_b, p'_c, p'_d \ldots) \gtreqless 0$$

with which we started. This will appear probable if we remember that the change from p'_b to p''_b, which reduced the above inequality to an equality, exerted a direct influence that was invariably in the direction of equality at least so far as the demand for (B) was concerned; while the [consequent] changes from p'_c to p''_c, p'_d to p''_d, ..., which moved the foregoing inequality farther away from equality, exerted indirect influences, some in the direction of equality and some in the opposite direction, at least so far as the demand for (B) was concerned, so that up to a certain point they cancelled each other out. Hence, the new system of prices $p''_b, p''_c, p''_d \ldots$ is closer to equilibrium than the old system of prices $p'_b, p'_c, p'_d \ldots$; and it is only necessary to continue this process along the same lines for the system to move closer and closer to equilibrium.

We are now in a position to formulate the law of the establishment of equilibrium prices in the case of the exchange of several commodities for one another through the medium of a *numéraire*: *Given several commodities, which are exchanged for one another through the medium of a* numéraire, *for the market to be in a state of equilibrium or for the price of each and every commodity in terms of the* numéraire *to be stationary, it is necessary and sufficient that at these prices the effective demand for each commodity equal its effective offer. When this equality is absent, the attainment of equilibrium prices requires a rise in the prices of those commodities the effective demand for which is greater than the effective offer, and a fall in the prices of those commodities the effective offer of which is greater than the effective demand.*

Lesson 13

THE LAW OF THE VARIATION OF COMMODITY PRICES

131. It can clearly be seen from the foregoing discussion that in the case of several, as in the case of two commodities, the necessary and sufficient data for the establishment of current or equilibrium prices are: (1) the traders' utility or want equations for commodities, which can generally be represented by curves, and (2) the initial quantities of the commodities in their possession. From these constituent elements we can always deduce mathematically: (1) the demand or offer equations of each individual and of all individuals taken together, and (2) the current or equilibrium prices. Nevertheless, besides the two conditions of maximum satisfaction and consistency of the prices of any two commodities with equality between their aggregate demand and offer for each other, we must also have the condition of general equilibrium of prices.

Thus: *The exchange of several commodities for one another in a market ruled by free competition is an operation by which all holders of one, several or all of the commodities exchanged can obtain*[a] *the greatest possible satisfaction of their wants consistent with the twofold condition*: (1) *that any two commodities be exchanged for each other in one and the same ratio for all parties and* (2) *that the two ratios in which these commodities are exchanged for any third commodity be proportional to the ratio in which they are exchanged for each other.*

132.[b] If prices are cried in terms of a *numéraire*, the condition of general equilibrium is fulfilled *ipso facto*. Otherwise arbitrage transactions are required for the attainment of general equilibrium. We must now inquire into the precise result of such transactions.

Let party (1) be a holder of (A), party (2) a holder of (B) and party (3) a holder of (C). Let $r_{a,1}$, $r_{b,1}$, $r_{c,1}$, $r_{d,1} \cdots r_{a,2}$, $r_{b,2}$, $r_{c,2}$, $r_{d,2} \cdots r_{a,3}$, $r_{b,3}$, $r_{c,3}$, $r_{d,3} \cdots$ be the *raretés* of (A), (B), (C), (D)... for these three parties. Moreover, for the time being, let these *raretés* be variables corresponding to variable prices. If we assume the possibility of arbitrage to be excluded, we may express the condition of maximum satisfaction as follows:

$$p_{b,a} = \frac{r_{b,1}}{r_{a,1}}, \qquad p_{c,a} = \frac{r_{c,1}}{r_{a,1}}, \qquad p_{d,a} = \frac{r_{d,1}}{r_{a,1}} \cdots$$

$$p_{a,b} = \frac{r_{a,2}}{r_{b,2}}, \qquad p_{c,b} = \frac{r_{c,2}}{r_{b,2}}, \qquad p_{d,b} = \frac{r_{d,2}}{r_{b,2}} \cdots$$

$$p_{a,c} = \frac{r_{a,3}}{r_{c,3}}, \qquad p_{b,c} = \frac{r_{b,3}}{r_{c,3}}, \qquad p_{d,c} = \frac{r_{d,3}}{r_{c,3}} \cdots$$

173

174   ELEMENTS OF PURE ECONOMICS

Now let us suppose arbitrage to become possible and let us still think in terms of three commodities (A), (B), and (C) and three parties (1), (2), and (3). By virtue of the reciprocal relationship between prices, we already had prior to arbitrage

$$\frac{r_{b,1}}{r_{a,1}}=p_{b,a}=\frac{1}{p_{a,b}}=\frac{r_{b,2}}{r_{a,2}},$$

$$\frac{r_{c,1}}{r_{a,1}}=p_{c,a}=\frac{1}{p_{a,c}}=\frac{r_{c,3}}{r_{a,3}},$$

$$\frac{r_{c,2}}{r_{b,2}}=p_{c,b}=\frac{1}{p_{b,c}}=\frac{r_{c,3}}{r_{b,3}}.$$

And now, as a result of arbitrage operations, we have in general equilibrium

$$\frac{r_{b,2}}{r_{a,2}}=p_{b,a}=\frac{p_{b,c}}{p_{a,c}}=\frac{r_{b,3}}{r_{a,3}},$$

$$\frac{r_{c,1}}{r_{a,1}}=p_{c,a}=\frac{p_{c,b}}{p_{a,b}}=\frac{r_{c,2}}{r_{a,2}},$$

$$\frac{r_{c,2}}{r_{b,2}}=p_{c,b}=\frac{p_{c,a}}{p_{b,a}}=\frac{r_{c,1}}{r_{b,1}}.$$

Once we realize that the above argument relative to three commodities (A), (B), and (C) and three parties (1), (2), and (3) can be generalized and applied to any number of the commodities and to any number of parties to the exchange, we conclude that: *When the market is in a state of general equilibrium, and the ratio of the* raretés *of any two commodities is equal to the price of one of them in terms of the other, that ratio will be the same for all holders of these two commodities.*

133. If we let v_a, v_b, v_c, v_d... represent the values in exchange of the commodities (A), (B), (C), (D)... and $r_{a,1}, r_{b,1}, r_{c,1}, r_{d,1}... r_{a,2}, r_{b,2}, r_{c,2}, r_{d,2}... r_{a,3}, r_{b,3}, r_{c,3}, r_{d,3}...$ represent the *raretés* of these commodities for parties (1), (2), (3)..., then, when the trading is completed, we have

$$p_b=\frac{r_{b,1}}{r_{a,1}}=\frac{r_{b,2}}{r_{a,2}}=\frac{r_{b,3}}{r_{a,3}}=...$$

$$p_c=\frac{r_{c,1}}{r_{a,1}}=\frac{r_{c,2}}{r_{a,2}}=\frac{r_{c,3}}{r_{a,3}}=...$$

$$p_d=\frac{r_{d,1}}{r_{a,1}}=\frac{r_{d,2}}{r_{a,2}}=\frac{r_{d,3}}{r_{a,3}}=...$$

. . . .

which can also be written in the form:

$$v_a \quad :v_b \quad :v_c \quad : \quad v_d :\ldots$$
$$::r_{a,1}:r_{b,1}:r_{c,1}:r_{d,1}:\ldots$$
$$::r_{a,2}:r_{b,2}:r_{c,2}:r_{d,2}:\ldots$$
$$::r_{a,3}:r_{b,3}:r_{c,3}:r_{d,3}:\ldots$$
$$:: \quad . \quad . \quad . \quad . \quad . \quad .$$

Up to this point we have been writing and solving equations of exchange on the assumption that the commodities in question can be consumed in infinitely small quantities and that their want or utility curves are continuous. We must, however, also consider the case of those commodities which are naturally consumed in whole units and which have want or utility curves that are discontinuous. This occurs very frequently, in the case of furniture, clothing, etc.[c] There is always an appreciable difference between the intensity of utility of a first bed, a first suit of clothes, a first hat, or a first pair of shoes and that of a second unit of the same commodity; or between the intensity of utility of a second unit and that of a third unit, and so on. In some cases this difference is considerable. For example, a cripple's first pair of crutches, a near-sighted person's first pair of glasses, or a professional musician's first violin is practically indispensable; a second pair of crutches, a second pair of glasses or a second violin is, in a sense, superfluous.[d] In all such cases it would be necessary to adopt the same procedure for several commodities as for two,[11] and insert in our table of *raretés* appropriately adjusted terms underlined to indicate that they are roughly equal in each instance to the average of the intensities of the last want satisfied and the first want unsatisfied.

Here again, it is possible also that one or more of the *r* terms may be missing among the *raretés* of a given trader. This will occur whenever the trader in question neither has nor wants to buy a commodity at the current price or whenever he has the commodity but offers all he has of it for sale. The rich are those whose last wants satisfied are numerous and of slight intensity; and the poor are those whose last wants satisfied are, on the contrary, few and of great intensity. In this connection, also, we may have occasion to follow the same procedure for several commodities as for two[11] and insert in the above tables of *raretés* certain terms placed in parentheses to indicate that they are obtained by multiplying in each instance the price of a commodity that remains unconsumed by the *rareté* of some other commodity in terms of which the price is expressed.[e]

Subject to these two reservations, we may enunciate the following proposition: *Values in exchange are proportional to the* raretés.

134.[1] On the one hand, let (A), (B), and (D) be commodities
which can be consumed in infinitely small quantities; and, in conse-
quence, let $\alpha_{r,1}\alpha_{q,1}$, $\alpha_{r,2}\alpha_{q,2}$, $\alpha_{r,3}\alpha_{q,3}$, $\beta_{r,1}\beta_{q,1}$, $\beta_{r,2}\beta_{q,2}$, $\beta_{r,3}\beta_{q,3}$,
$\delta_{r,1}\delta_{q,1}$, $\delta_{r,2}\delta_{q,2}$, $\delta_{r,3}\delta_{q,3}$, of Fig. 17 be the corresponding want or
utility curves of these commodities for parties (1), (2) and (3). On
the other hand, let (C) be a commodity which is naturally consumed
in whole units, so that its corresponding want or utility curves
$\gamma_{r,1}\gamma_{q,1}$, $\gamma_{r,2}\gamma_{q,2}$, $\gamma_{r,3}\gamma_{q,3}$ for parties (1), (2) and (3) are
discontinuous. Let 2, 2·5 and 0·5 be the respective prices of (B),
(C) and (D) in terms of (A).

In the example, illustrated by Fig. 17, party (1) is a rich man
who consumes 7 units of (A), 8 of (B), 7 of (C) and 6 of (D), thus
bringing the *raretés* of these commodities for him to the low levels

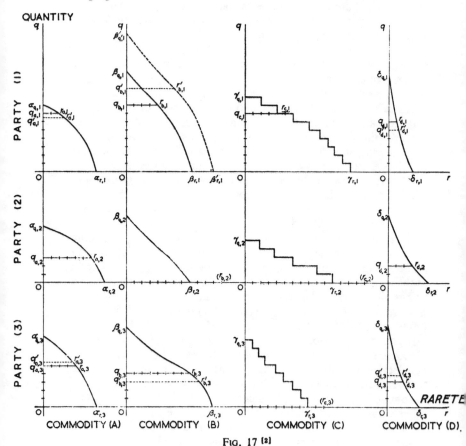

FIG. 17 [2]

of 2, 4, 6 and 1 respectively. He enjoys a rather large sum total of effective utility, represented by the sum of the areas $Oq_{a,1}r_{a,1}\alpha_{r,1}$, $Oq_{b,1}r_{b,1}\beta_{r,1}$, $Oq_{c,1}r_{c,1}\gamma_{r,1}$, and $Oq_{d,1}r_{d,1}\delta_{r,1}$. The *raretés* of (A), (B) and (D), i.e. 2, 4, and 1, are exactly proportional to the prices 1, 2 and 0·5 [in terms of (A)]. The *rareté* of (C), 6, has to be replaced by an underlined number $\underline{5}=2\times2{\cdot}5$,[3] which is half-way between intensity 6 of the last want satisfied and intensity 4 of the first want not satisfied by (C). Party (2) is a poor man who consumes 3 units of (A) and 2 of (D), so that the *raretés* of these commodities for him will be at the high level of 6 and 3 respectively. He enjoys a rather small sum total of effective utility represented by the sum of the areas $Oq_{a,2}r_{a,2}\alpha_{r,2}$ and $Oq_{d,2}r_{d,2}\delta_{r,2}$. But he goes without (B) and (C), because the numbers $12=6\times2$,[4] and $15=6\times2{\cdot}5$,[5] which ought to have appeared in his particular row of *raretés* are larger than the intensities 8 and 11 of the first wants that could be satisfied by (B) and (C) respectively [as shown by the lengths $O\beta_{r,2}$ and $O\gamma_{r,2}$ of Fig. 17]. Finally, party (3) is a man of moderate circumstances who consumes 5 units of (A), 4 of (B) and 3 of (D), so that the *raretés* of these commodities for him will be the average *raretés*[6] 4, 8 and 2 respectively. He enjoys a sum total of effective utility represented by the sum of the areas $Oq_{a,3}r_{a,3}\alpha_{r,3}$, $Oq_{b,3}r_{b,3}\beta_{r,3}$, and $Oq_{d,3}r_{d,3}\delta_{r,3}$; but he goes without (C), because the number $10=4\times2{\cdot}5$,[7] which ought to have appeared in his row of *raretés* is larger than the intensity 8 of the first want that could be satisfied by this commodity [as shown by the length $O\gamma_{r,3}$ of Fig. 17]. After placing in parentheses these proportionately adjusted numbers which correspond to the virtual rather than the effective *raretés*, we have the following table:

$$
\begin{array}{llll}
1 & :\ 2 & :\ 2{\cdot}5 & :\ 0{\cdot}5 \\
::\ 2 & :\ 4 & :\ 5 & :\ 1 \\
::\ 6 & :\ (12) & :\ (15) & :\ 3 \\
::\ 4 & :\ 8 & :\ (10) & :\ 2.
\end{array}
$$

135.[9] We know that the ratio of the average *raretés* should be the same as the ratio of the individual *raretés* to one another. In computing these averages we must be sure to include the proportionately adjusted numbers which are either underlined or in parentheses. Under these conditions, we may designate the average *raretés* of (A), (B), (C), (D)... by R_a, R_b, R_c, R_d... and replace the equations

$$
p_b = \frac{v_b}{v_a}, \qquad p_c = \frac{v_c}{v_a}, \qquad p_u = \frac{v_d}{v_a} \ldots
$$

by

$$
p_b = \frac{R_b}{R_a}, \qquad p_c = \frac{R_c}{R_a}, \qquad p_d = \frac{R_d}{R_a} \ldots,
$$

which are of crucial significance for the solution of the principal problems of economics.[h]

136. The phenomenon of value in exchange, which is so complex, particularly where several commodities are involved, at last appears in its true light. What are v_a, v_b, v_c, v_d...? They are really nothing but indeterminate, arbitrary terms that have meaning only in their proportionate relationship to one another. And this relationship corresponds exactly to the proportions which the *raretés* of all commodities bear to one another and which are common to all parties and the same for all when the market is in a state of general equilibrium. Hence, only the ratios between pairs of $v_a, v_b, v_c, v_d...$, which are equal to the ratios between corresponding pairs of *raretés* for any party, can be evaluated numerically.[i] Thus value in exchange remains essentially a relative phenomenon which is always caused by *rareté*, the one and only absolute phenomenon.[1][j] Still the fact remains that since there can be no more than m *raretés* for each trader in a market of m commodities, there are at most only m indeterminate v terms expressing the values in exchange of the m commodities when the market is in a state of general equilibrium. These terms, taken two at a time, yield $m(m-1)$ prices of the m commodities in terms of one another. This makes it possible, under certain circumstances, to insert the arbitrary terms themselves, instead of their ratios, in our calculations.[k] One might even be tempted to go a little further and deduce from this the proposition that in a state of general equilibrium *each commodity has only one value in exchange in relation to all the other commodities on the market*.[l] This way of putting it, however, is perhaps[m] too likely to be construed as if absolute value were meant, and, therefore, it is preferable to describe the phenomenon in question in terms of the theorem of general equilibrium (§111) or in terms of the analytical definition of exchange (§131).

137. Since the utilities and the quantities possessed are, as we have already seen,[8] the primary causes and conditions of the establishment of prices, it follows that they are also the primary causes and conditions of variations in these prices.

Let us suppose equilibrium to be established so that the several traders possess the requisite quantities of each of (A), (B), (C), (D)..., which will yield them maximum satisfaction at the prices p_b, p_c, p_d... of (B), (C), (D), in terms of (A). Moreover, let us restrict our use of the expressions *increase* and *decrease in utility*, as we did before,[9] to shifts in the want curve which result in an

---

[1] This distinction between value in exchange, which is *relative* and *objective*, and *rareté*, which is *absolute* and *subjective*, is a rigorous expression of the difference between *value in exchange* and *value in use*. [This note was added in ed. 4.]

increase or a decrease in the *rareté* or in the intensity of the last want
satisfied after the completion of exchange. With this in mind, let us
suppose an increase in the utility of (B), in other words, a shift in the
want curve of (B) resulting in an increase in the *rareté* of (B) for
certain parties. These parties will no longer enjoy maximum satisfaction [by maintaining the *status quo*]. They will, however, find it to
their advantage to demand (B) by offering some of their (A), (C),
(D)... at the prices p_b, p_c, p_d.... Inasmuch as the offer was equal to
the demand for each and every one of the commodities (A), (B),
(C), (D)... at the prices p_b, p_c, p_d... [before the increase in the utility
of (B) for some of the traders], there will now be an excess of demand
over offer in the case of (B) and an excess of offer over demand in the
cases of (A), (C), (D)... at these same prices. Hence there will be a
rise in p_b. It follows also that the other traders [for whom the utility
of (B) had not increased] will no longer enjoy maximum satisfaction
[from the previously determined quantities of (A), (B), (C), (D)...
which they consumed]. They will find it to their advantage, when the
price of (B) in terms of (A) becomes greater than p_b, to offer some of
their (B) and demand (A), (C), (D)... in exchange. Equilibrium will
be re-established when the demand and offer for all the commodities
(A), (B), (C), (D)... become equal again. Thus an increase in the
utility of (B) for some individuals will result in an increase in the
price of (B). It may also result in a change in the prices of (C),
(D).... These secondary effects, however, will be less appreciable
than the primary effect if there are a great many commodities other
than (B) on the market and if, in consequence, the quantity of each
commodity exchanged for (B) is very small. Besides, there is no way
of knowing whether the prices of (C), (D)... will rise or fall; nor can
we even know that they will change at all. This is clearly seen when
we consider the situation of the *raretés* after the establishment of
a new equilibrium on the completion of the secondary exchanges.[10]
As a result of these operations, the ratios of the *raretés* of (B) to the
raretés of (A) will necessarily rise for all parties in the market: not
only for those whose utility curve of (B) remained unchanged, and
who resold part of their (B) and bought back some (A), (C), (D)...
[as p_b rose], thus increasing their *raretés* of (B) and decreasing their
raretés of (A); but also for those whose utility curve of (B) shifted
upwards in the first instance so that they bought back some (B) and
resold part of their (A), (C), (D)... thus bringing about an increase
in their *raretés* of (A) accompanied by a still greater increase in their
raretés of (B). So far as the ratios of the *raretés* (C), (D)... to those of
(A) are concerned, some will become larger, some smaller, and still
others will remain constant. The effect on the prices of (C), (D)... will
be that some will rise, others fall and still others remain unchanged.

We observe, in short, that the *raretés* of (B) must increase for all
parties, so that, the average *rareté* of (B) will have to increase. The
raretés of (A), (C), (D)..., on the other hand, will increase for some
parties and decrease for others, so that their average *raretés* will not
change much. We may, if we wish, represent these phenomena
graphically and consider a single party in each category. For
example, in Fig. 17, when party (1) finds that the utility of (B) has
risen for him, he buys back some (B) and resells part of his (A) and
(D). Party (2) does nothing. Party (3) resells part of his (B) and
buys back some (A) and (D). These are the consequences of an
increase in the utility of (B). A fall in the utility of (B) for party (1)
would obviously have the converse effect, i.e. there would be a fall
in the price of (B) and not much change in the prices of (C), (D)....[n]

A glance at the utility curves is sufficient to show that an increase
in the quantity possessed will result in a decrease in *rareté*, and that
a decrease in the quantity possessed will result in an increase in
rareté.[9] Moreover, we have just seen that *rareté* and price move in
the same direction, increasing and decreasing together. The effects
of variations in the quantity possessed are, therefore, exactly the
opposite of the effects of variations in utility. We may now state the
law we are seeking in the following terms: *Given a state of general
equilibrium in a market for several commodities where exchanges take
place with the aid of a* numéraire, *if the utility of one of these commodities increases or decreases for one or more of the parties, everything
else remaining equal, the price of this commodity in terms of the*
numéraire *will increase or decrease.*

*If the quantity of one of the commodities in the hands of one or more
holders increases or decreases, all other things remaining equal, the
price of this commodity will decrease or increase.*

It should be noted that although any change in prices necessarily
implies a change in the determinants of the prices concerned, it does
not follow that stability of prices necessarily implies stability of their
determinants. In fact, we are prepared to enunciate, without further
proof, the following double proposition:

*Given several commodities, if both the utility and the quantity of one
of these commodities in the hands of one or more parties or holders
vary in such a way that the* raretés *remain the same, the price of this
commodity will not change.*

*If the utility and the quantity of all the commodities in the hands of
one or more parties or holders vary in such a way that the ratios of the*
raretés *remain the same, none of the prices will change.*

138. Such is the *law of the variation of equilibrium prices*. When it
is combined with the *law of the establishment of equilibrium prices*
(§130), we have the scientific formulation of what is known in

economics as the LAW OF SUPPLY AND DEMAND. This fundamental law has hitherto been stated either erroneously or in a form devoid of meaning.[11] For example, sometimes it is said: "The price of things is determined by the ratio between supply and demand," which is supposed to explain the establishment of prices; and sometimes: "The price of things varies directly with demand and inversely with supply," which is supposed to explain variations in prices. Now, in the first place, in order to give any meaning at all to these two expressions, which are really identical, it would be necessary to define supply and demand. And, in the second place, however we define these terms, whether we take supply to mean effective offer, or quantity possessed, or quantity in existence; whether we regard demand as tantamount to effective demand, or to extensive utility, or intensive utility, or both extensive and intensive utility, or even virtual[o] utility, so long as we assign to the word ratio its mathematical significance of a quotient, surely price is no more the ratio of demand to supply than it is the ratio of supply to demand, and price no more varies directly with demand and inversely with supply than it varies directly with supply and inversely with demand. I venture, therefore, to assert that, up to the present, this fundamental law of economics has neither been demonstrated nor even correctly[p] formulated. And I go so far as to maintain that it is impossible either to formulate or to demonstrate the law of supply and demand or the two laws of which it is composed, without defining effective demand and effective offer, and showing their relationship to price, or without defining *rareté* and showing its relationship to price too. We can do this only by recourse to the language, the method and the principles of mathematics.[q] Hence we conclude that the use of mathematics is not only possible but necessary and indispensable in the formulation of pure economics. I believe, moreover, that no reader who has followed me up to this point can entertain the slightest doubt as to the validity of this conclusion.

THE THEOREM OF EQUIVALENT REDISTRIBUTIONS OF COMMODITY HOLDINGS. CONCERNING A STANDARD OF MEASURE AND A MEDIUM OF EXCHANGE

139. With parties (1), (2), (3)... possessing respectively the quantities $q_{a,1}, q_{b,1}, q_{c,1}, q_{d,1} \cdots, q_{a,2}, q_{b,2}, q_{c,2}, q_{d,2} \cdots, q_{a,3}, q_{b,3}, q_{c,3}, q_{d,3} \cdots$ of commodities (A), (B), (C), (D)..., the total amounts of these commodities in existence are

$$Q_a = q_{a,1} + q_{a,2} + q_{a,3} + \cdots$$
$$Q_b = q_{b,1} + q_{b,2} + q_{b,3} + \cdots$$
$$Q_c = q_{c,1} + q_{c,2} + q_{c,3} + \cdots$$
$$Q_d = q_{d,1} + q_{d,2} + q_{d,3} + \cdots$$

. . . .

Given the above distribution of ownership and given certain conditions of virtual utility determined by the want or utility equations, these commodities will be exchanged for one another at general equilibrium prices $p_b, p_c, p_d \cdots$[a]

Now let us suppose a change in the distribution of these same commodities (A), (B), (C), (D)... among the same parties (1), (2), (3)..., such that the sum of the new quantities possessed by each party, $q'_{a,1}, q'_{b,1}, q'_{c,1}, q'_{d,1} \cdots q'_{a,2}, q'_{b,2}, q'_{c,2}, q'_{d,2} \cdots q'_{a,3}, q'_{b,3}, q'_{c,3}, q'_{d,3} \cdots$, is the same in value as the sum of the quantities originally possessed, so that we have[b]

$$q_{a,1} + q_{b,1}p_b + q_{c,1}p_c + q_{d,1}p_d + \cdots$$
$$= q'_{a,1} + q'_{b,1}p_b + q'_{c,1}p_c + q'_{d,1}p_d + \cdots$$
$$q_{a,2} + q_{b,2}p_b + q_{c,2}p_c + q_{d,2}p_d + \cdots$$
$$= q'_{a,2} + q'_{b,2}p_b + q'_{c,2}p_c + q'_{d,2}p_d + \cdots \quad ..(1)$$
$$q_{a,3} + q_{b,3}p_b + q_{c,3}p_c + q_{d,3}p_d + \cdots$$
$$= q'_{a,3} + q'_{b,3}p_b + q'_{c,3}p_c + q'_{d,3}p_d + \cdots$$

. . . .

Let us assume, also, that the total existing quantities of (A), (B), (C), (D)... are the same under the new distribution of ownership as under the old, so that

$$Q_a = q'_{a,1} + q'_{a,2} + q'_{a,3} + \cdots$$
$$Q_b = q'_{b,1} + q'_{b,2} + q'_{b,3} + \cdots \quad ..(2)$$
$$Q_c = q'_{c,1} + q'_{c,2} + q'_{c,3} + \cdots$$
$$Q_d = q'_{d,1} + q'_{d,2} + q'_{d,3} + \cdots$$

. . . .

The point I wish to make is that, under these changed conditions of distribution of ownership, so long as the original conditions of virtual utility persist, the old prices p_b, p_c, p_d...[a] will still be the equilibrium prices both in theory and in practice.

140. Let us fix our attention on party (1), and let us suppose that, at the above-mentioned prices, he buys such quantities x'_1, y'_1, z'_1, w'_1... of commodities (A), (B), (C), (D)... respectively, that he ends up with

$$q'_{a,1}+x'_1=q_{a,1}+x_1,$$
$$q'_{b,1}+y'_1=q_{b,1}+y_1, \qquad ..(3)$$
$$q'_{c,1}+z'_1=q_{c,1}+z_1,$$
$$q'_{d,1}+w'_1=q_{d,1}+w_1,$$
$$\cdot \quad \cdot \quad \cdot \quad \cdot \quad \cdot \quad \cdot \quad \cdot$$

Party (1) will then have attained maximum satisfaction of his wants, the following system of equations having evidently been satisfied:[c]

$$\phi_{b,1}(q'_{b,1}+y'_1)=p_b\phi_{a,1}(q'_{a,1}+x'_1),$$
$$\phi_{c,1}(q'_{c,1}+z'_1)=p_c\phi_{a,1}(q'_{a,1}+x'_1),$$
$$\phi_{d,1}(q'_{d,1}+w'_1)=p_d\phi_{a,1}(q'_{a,1}+x'_1),$$
$$\cdot \quad \cdot \quad \cdot \quad \cdot \quad \cdot \quad \cdot \quad \cdot \quad \cdot \quad \cdot \quad \cdot$$

Parties (2), (3)... will also achieve maximum satisfaction of their wants if, at the prices indicated above, they buy such quantities x'_2, y'_2, z'_2, w'_2... x'_3, y'_3, z'_3, w'_3... of commodities (A), (B), (C), (D)... that they end up with

$$q'_{a,2}+x'_2=q_{a,2}+x_2,$$
$$q'_{b,2}+y'_2=q_{b,2}+y_2, \qquad ..(3)$$
$$q'_{c,2}+z'_2=q_{c,2}+z_2,$$
$$q'_{d,2}+w'_2=q_{d,2}+w_2,$$
$$\cdot \quad \cdot \quad \cdot \quad \cdot \quad \cdot \quad \cdot \quad \cdot$$

$$q'_{a,3}+x'_3=q_{a,3}+x_3,$$
$$q'_{b,3}+y'_3=q_{b,3}+y_3, \qquad ..(3)$$
$$q'_{c,3}+z'_3=q_{c,3}+z_3,$$
$$q'_{d,3}+w'_3=q_{d,3}+w_3,$$
$$\cdot \quad \cdot \quad \cdot \quad \cdot \quad \cdot \quad \cdot \quad \cdot$$

All that remains to be shown is: (1) that, under the stipulated conditions, these parties can demand or offer quantities of this sort, and (2) that, under these same conditions, the total effective demand for each commodity is equal to its total effective offer.

141.[d] From system of equations (1) we immediately obtain

$$q_{a,1}-q'_{a,1}+(q_{b,1}-q'_{b,1})p_b+(q_{c,1}-q'_{c,1})p_c$$
$$+(q_{d,1}-q'_{d,1})p_d+...=0,$$

which, according to system (3), can be rewritten[1]

$$x'_1 - x_1 + (y'_1 - y_1)p_b + (z'_1 - z_1)p_c$$
$$+ (w'_1 - w_1)p_d + \ldots = 0.$$

Since we already have[2]

$$x_1 + y_1 p_b + z_1 p_c + w_1 p_d + \ldots = 0,$$

it follows that:

$$x'_1 + y'_1 p_b + z'_1 p_c + w'_1 p_d + \ldots = 0.$$

For the same reason

$$x'_2 + y'_2 p_b + z'_2 p_c + w'_2 p_d + \ldots = 0,$$
$$x'_3 + y'_3 p_b + z'_3 p_c + w'_3 p_d + \ldots = 0,$$
$$\cdots \cdots \cdots \cdots \cdots \cdots$$

Hence the sum total of commodities (A), (B), (C), (D)... demanded by parties (1), (2), (3)... under the conditions defined above is equal in value to the sum total of these commodities offered by these parties.

142. If, now, we add the appropriate equations [relating to commodity (A)] in system (3), we obtain

$$x'_1 + x'_2 + x'_3 + \ldots = q_{a,1} + q_{a,2} + q_{a,3} + \ldots$$
$$- (q'_{a,1} + q'_{a,2} + q'_{a,3} + \ldots) + x_1 + x_2 + x_3 + \ldots.$$

Since we already know that[3]

$$X = x_1 + x_2 + x_3 + \ldots = 0,$$

and also that[4]

$$q'_{a,1} + q'_{a,2} + q'_{a,3} + \ldots = q_{a,1} + q_{a,2} + q_{a,3} + \ldots$$

it follows that[5]

$$X' = x'_1 + x'_2 + x'_3 + \ldots = 0.$$

Similarly,

$$Y' = y'_1 + y'_2 + y'_3 + \ldots = 0,$$
$$Z' = z'_1 + z'_2 + z'_3 + \ldots = 0,$$
$$W' = w'_1 + w'_2 + w'_3 + \ldots = 0,$$
$$\cdots \cdots \cdots \cdots \cdots \cdots$$

Consequently, for each and every commodity the total effective demand equals the total effective offer.

143. Theoretically, then p_b, p_c, p_d... are as much equilibrium prices after the change in distribution of ownership as they were before. Moreover, since the mechanism of competition in the market is nothing but a device for reaching in practice these mathematically

derived prices, it follows that: *Given several commodities in a market in a state of general equilibrium, the current prices of these commodities will remain unchanged no matter in what way the ownership of the respective quantities of these commodities are redistributed among the parties to the exchange, provided, however, that the value of the sum of the quantities possessed by each of these parties remains the same.*

144. All through this discussion we have supposed Q_a, Q_b, Q_c, Q_d... to be invariable. Consequently, should the quantity of commodities (A), (B), (C), (D)... held by any one party, say party (1), increase or decrease within the limits set by the condition that the value of the commodities he possesses always remain the same, then it is evident that the quantity of these commodities held by one or more other parties, say party (2) or party (3), must decrease or increase correspondingly, within the same limits, if the quantity of each commodity in the market is to remain constant. We can be sure that, provided there are large quantities of every commodity in the market and quite a large number of traders, even in the absence of compensating changes in the quantities held by other traders, a change in the quantities of the various commodities held by any one trader, subject to the condition of constancy of value of his aggregate holdings, would have no appreciable influence on prices and could be considered as changing neither the particular situation of the party in question nor the general situation of the market. Here we have an example of the law of large numbers from which it is possible to draw far-reaching conclusions in certain cases. But in the present case we prefer to remain within the bounds prescribed by mathematical rigour. Within these bounds the only way we can affirm that there will be absolutely no change in prices is by assuming both conditions to be satisfied: that of constant value of the quantities possessed by each holder and that of constancy of the total existing quantities in the market.[e]

145. The theorem of general equilibrium in the market may be stated in the following terms:

When the market is in a state of general equilibrium, the $m(m-1)$ *prices which govern the exchange between all possible pairs drawn from* m *commodities are implicitly determined by the* $m-1$ *prices which govern the exchange between any* $m-1$ *of these commodities and the* m*th.*

Thus the situation of a market in a state of general equilibrium can be completely defined by relating the values of all the commodities to the value of any particular one of them. That particular commodity is called the *numéraire* [or *standard commodity*];[6] and a unit quantity of this commodity is called a *standard* ['*étalon*']. If,

now, we suppose the values of (A), (B), (C), (D)... all to be related
to the value of (A), we obtain the following series of prices:

$$p_{a,a}=1, \qquad p_{b,a}=\mu, \qquad p_{c,a}=\pi, \qquad p_{d,a}=\varrho.$$

If, instead of relating these values to the values of (A), we were to
relate them to the value of (B), we should have the following series
of prices:

$$p_{a,b}=\frac{1}{\mu}, \qquad p_{b,b}=\frac{\mu}{\mu}, \qquad p_{c,b}=\frac{\pi}{\mu}, \qquad p_{d,b}=\frac{\varrho}{\mu}.$$

Thus: *To shift from one* numéraire *to another, it is only necessary
to divide the prices expressed in terms of the old* numéraire *by the price
of the new* numéraire *in terms of the old.*

146. In the above system, let (A) be silver, and let a half-decagram
0·900 fine be the unit quantity of silver. Let (B) be wheat, and let
a hectolitre be the unit quantity of wheat. To express the fact that,
in a market in a state of general equilibrium, a hectolitre of wheat is
currently exchanged for 24 half-decagrams of silver 0·900 fine, we
write the equation

$$p_{b,a}=24.$$

This should be read as follows: "The price of wheat in terms of silver
is 24"; or, in terms of units of quantity: "The price of a hectolitre of
wheat is 24 half-decagrams of silver 0·900 fine"; or finally: "Wheat
is worth 24 half-decagrams of silver 0·900 fine per hectolitre." There
is a difference between this statement and the one derived from
current usage which we cited earlier in our discussion (§29): "Wheat
is worth 24 francs a hectolitre." The difference is that the word
francs took the place of the expression *half-decagrams of silver 0·900
fine.* This needs to be carefully considered.

The word *franc*, in the minds of most people, is analogous to the
words *metre, gramme, litre,* etc. Now, the word *metre* expresses two
things: on the one hand, the length of a certain fraction of the earth's
meridian, and, on the other hand, a fixed and invariable unit of
length. Likewise, the word *gramme* expresses two things: the weight
of a certain quantity of distilled water at maximum density and a
fixed and invariable unit of *weight.* The same can be said of the word
litre as regards *volume.* And, in the eyes of the man in the street, the
same is true of the franc. This word means two things to him: first,
the value of a certain quantity of silver of a certain fineness and
second, a fixed and invariable unit of *value.*

According to this view we must distinguish between two statements: first that the word *franc* stands for the value of a half-
decagram of silver 0·900 fine, and second that this value, once

adopted as a unit, is fixed and invariable. This second statement is an egregious error into which no economist would fall. Anyone who has the slightest acquaintance with economics will agree that there is an essential difference between a *metre* and a *franc*, since the metre is a fixed and invariable unit of length, whereas the franc is a unit of value which, far from being fixed and invariable, differs from place to place and varies from one moment to the next, for reasons that are more or less generally agreed upon. There is no need to labour this point.

Having disposed of the second statement, we return to the first, namely that the franc is the value of a half-decagram of silver 0·900 fine, in the same sense that the metre is the length of the ten-millionth part of a quarter of the earth's meridian. The economists who have taken this point of view say that, though the franc is variable, it is still a measuring rod. If all lengths without exception were in a state of continual variation in consequence of the contraction and expansion of all bodies, they could be measured only under specified conditions, but under such conditions these lengths could still be measured. Certainly, all values are in a continual process of change, as we well know. This only means that we cannot make any comparisons between values from place to place or from time to time, but that does not preclude us from comparing them with one another and measuring them at a given place and at a given moment. These are the conditions [we are told] under which we measure values.

In such a system, if we let (A) represent silver, measured quantitatively in units of a half-decagram 0·900 fine and if we let (B) represent wheat measured quantitatively in units of a hectolitre, it is said that we can write the equation

$$v_a = 1 \text{ franc};$$

and then, to express the fact that 1 hectolitre of wheat is currently exchanged in the market for 24 half-decagrams of silver 0·900 fine, we can write

$$v_b = 24 \text{ francs},$$

which is read: "Wheat is worth 24 francs a hectolitre."

The second statement is just as erroneous as the first, for there is no analogy in either case between value on the one hand and length, weight or volume on the other. When I measure any given length, for example the length of a façade, I have to take three things into account: the length of the façade, the length of a ten-millionth part of a quarter of the earth's meridian and the ratio of the first length to the second, which is the measure of the façade. For the analogy

between value and length to hold, and for it to be possible to
measure a given value, say the value of a hectolitre of wheat at a
given moment and given place, as length is measured, it would
again be necessary to refer to three things: the value of a hectolitre
of wheat, the value of a half-decagram of silver 0·900 fine and the
ratio of the first value to the second, which would be the measure
[required]. But, of these three things, two are non-existent, the first
and the second. Only the third exists. Our analysis has demonstrated
perfectly that value is essentially relative. To be sure, behind relative
value, there is something absolute, namely the intensities of the last
wants satisfied or the *raretés*. These *raretés*, which are indeed absolute
and not relative, are nevertheless subjective or personal and not physical or objective. They are in us and not in things. It is therefore
impossible to substitute them for values in exchange. Hence there
is no such thing as *the* rareté *or the value of a half-decagram of silver
0·900 fine*; and the word *franc* [denoting a standard of value] is the
name of a thing which does not exist. Our science should never lose
sight of this truth which was clearly perceived by J. B. Say.[7]

147. It does not follow that we cannot measure value or wealth.
All that follows is that our standard of measure must be a certain
quantity of a given commodity and not the value of this quantity of
the given commodity.

Let (A) again represent the *numéraire* and let some quantitative
unit of (A) be the standard. So far as values are concerned, they are
self-measured, since the ratios of these values are found immediately in the inverse ratios of the quantities of the commodities
exchanged. Thus the ratios of the values of (B), (C), (D)... to the
value of (A) are seen at once in the number of units of (A) exchanged
for 1 unit of (B), 1 unit of (C), 1 unit of (D)..., that is, in the prices
of (B), (C), (D)... in terms of (A).

This being so, let $Q_{a,1}$ be the quantity of (A) which is equal in
value to the sum total of the quantities of (A), (B), (C), (D)... in the
possession of party (1); so that, if we designate the prices of (B), (C),
(D)... in terms of (A) by p_b, p_c, p_d..., we have

$$Q_{a,1} = q_{a,1} + q_{b,1}p_b + q_{c,1}p_c + q_{d,1}p_d + \cdots.$$

In accordance with the theorem of equivalent distributions of commodity holdings, we could allow $q_{a,1}, q_{b,1}, q_{c,1}, q_{d,1}$... to vary as we
please. Provided that the new quantities possessed by our individual
continue to satisfy the above equation (and provided that the total
quantities of the various commodities remain constant), party (1)
will always be able to obtain on the market, at the prices p_b, p_c,
p_d...,[7] the same quantities of (A), (B), (C), (D)... which will

afford him maximum satisfaction at these prices. Our $Q_{a,1}$ which represents not only all the above-mentioned quantities of the different commodities but also the quantities of maximum satisfaction is, therefore, a quantitative expression of the wealth which party (1) possesses.

In the same way, let

$$Q_{a,2}=q_{a,2}+q_{b,2}p_b+q_{c,2}p_c+q_{d,2}p_d+\cdots$$
$$Q_{a,3}=q_{a,3}+q_{b,3}p_b+q_{c,3}p_c+q_{d,3}p_d+\cdots$$
. . . .

where $Q_{a,2}$, $Q_{a,3}\cdots$ are respectively the quantities of wealth which parties (2), (3)... possess. These quantities are comparable with $Q_{a,1}$ and with one another, because they are made up of units that are homogeneous.

Let $Q_a, Q_b, Q_c, Q_d\cdots$ represent the total existing quantities of (A), (B), (C), (D)... in the market, and let

$$\mathbf{Q}_a=Q_{a,1}+Q_{a,2}+Q_{a,3}+\cdots$$
$$=Q_a+Q_bp_b+Q_cp_c+Q_dp_d+\cdots.$$

$\mathbf{Q}_a$ will then represent the total existing quantity of wealth in the market; and this quantity will be commensurable both with $Q_{a,1}$, $Q_{a,2}$, $Q_{a,3}\cdots$ and with $Q_a, Q_bp_b, Q_cp_c, Q_dp_d\cdots$.

148. This shows the true role of the standard of measure of value and wealth. In general, however, the commodity which serves as the *numéraire* serves also as money and acts as a medium of exchange. The standard of measure of value thus becomes the monetary standard. The two functions are, nevertheless, distinct, even when they are found in the same commodity. Having already explained the first of these functions [i.e. the *numéraire* function], we must now turn our attention to the second [i.e. the monetary function].

Let the commodity which is to be used as a medium of exchange again be (A). And let $p_b=\mu$, $p_c=\pi$, $p_d=\varrho\cdots$ as before. Corresponding to these general equilibrium prices, we have, by virtue of the condition of maximum satisfaction, the following quantities effectively demanded, equal [in each case] to the quantities effectively offered: $M, P, R\cdots$ of (A) [exchanged for (B), (C), (D)... respectively]; $N, F, H\cdots$ of (B) [exchanged for (A), (C), (D)... respectively]; Q, $G, K\cdots$ of (C) [exchanged for (A), (B), (D)... respectively]; S, J, $L\cdots$ of (D) [exchanged for (A), (B), (C)... respectively]; and so forth.[8] [9] Now, if all exchanges are direct, they will take place according to the following equations:

$$Nv_b=Mv_a, \qquad Qv_c=Pv_a, \qquad Sv_d=Rv_a\ldots$$
$$Gv_c=Fv_b, \qquad Jv_d=Hv_b, \qquad Lv_d=Kv_c\ldots.$$

149. If, on the other hand, money intervenes in these exchanges—which is a hypothesis closer to actuality—the result is different. Let (A) be silver, (B) wheat, (C) coffee, etc. In the real world, the producer of wheat sells his wheat for silver, and the producer of coffee does the same. With this silver the first producer will buy coffee and the second wheat. This, at any rate, is what we shall now suppose them to do. Holders of (A) set up as middlemen, because they have the commodity which serves as money. They are the ones to whom the holders of (B) sell all the (B) they are willing to sell at the price μ, in order to buy what (C) they want at the price π, what (D) they want at the price $\varrho\ldots$. These transactions can be expressed by the equations[9]

$$(N+F+H+\ldots)v_b=(M+F\mu+H\mu+\ldots)v_a,$$
$$(F\mu=G\pi)v_a=Gv_c, \qquad (H\mu=J\varrho)v_a=Jv_d\ldots.$$

The holders of (C), the holders of (D)... perform analogous transactions which can be expressed by the equations

$$(Q+G+K+\ldots)v_c=(P+G\pi+K\pi+\ldots)v_a,$$
$$(G\pi=F\mu)v_a=Fv_b, \qquad (K\pi=L\varrho)v_a=Lv_d\ldots$$
$$(S+J+L+\ldots)v_d=(R+J\varrho+L\varrho+\ldots)v_a,$$
$$(J\varrho=H\mu)v_a=Hv_b, \qquad (L\varrho=K\pi)v_a=Kv_c\ldots.$$

150. We are assuming at this stage of our argument that the buying and reselling of (A) as a medium of exchange take place in a way that does not exert any influence on the price of commodity (A). In the real world the matter presents itself quite differently. Every trader keeps available a stock of money for eventual exchange; and, this being the case, the use of a commodity as money does affect its value in ways that we shall study later on.[10] But, until we reach this aspect of our problem, we may note, provisionally at least, that there is a perfect analogy between the intervention of money and the intervention of a *numéraire*. Just as we can start with the two equations

$$\frac{v_b}{v_a}=\mu \qquad \text{and} \qquad \frac{v_c}{v_a}=\pi$$

and derive

$$\frac{v_c}{v_b}=\frac{\pi}{\mu};$$

so we can start with the two equations

$$(F\mu = G\pi)v_a = Gv_c \qquad \text{and} \qquad (G\pi = F\mu)v_a = Fv_b,$$

and derive

$$Gv_c = Fv_b.$$

Consequently, just as we can pass from indirect to direct prices at will simply by abstracting from the *numéraire*, so we can pass from indirect to direct exchange, whenever it suits us, simply by abstracting from money.[h]

PURCHASE AND SALES CURVES. COMMODITY
PRICE CURVES

151. It follows from our solution of equations of exchange (§§ 127–130), that[a] the designation of a commodity as *numéraire* simplifies the determination of current general equilibrium prices by making it possible, up to a certain point, to identify the case of the exchange of several commodities with that of the exchange of two commodities for each other. We must call attention once again to this simplifying device, which is so important, not only for pure and applied theory, but also for practice. It is all the more important to stress this point because the assumption of the use of a *numéraire* brings us closer to the world of reality.

Now, let commodity (A) be the *numéraire*. Then, on the one side, let P', Q', R', S', K', L'... be the quantities of commodities (A), (C), (D)... effectively demanded and equal to the quantities effectively offered, when they are exchanged or about to be exchanged for one another at prices determined by general equilibrium $p_c=\pi$, $p_d=\varrho$... of (C), (D)... in terms of (A). On the other side, let commodity (B) become available in the market for exchange against commodities (A), (C), (D)....[b]

With this in mind, let us consider one of the various holders of (B). If, at any price of (B) in terms of (A), say p_b, which will always correspond to a price of (A) in terms of (B) equal to $\frac{1}{p_b}$, our holder of (B) offers a quantity o_b of (B), he will receive in return a quantity $d_a=o_b p_b$ of (A). Moreover, since he is presumed to know the prices of (C), (D)... in terms of (A), he will have all the information necessary for deciding how to allocate this quantity of (A) among (A), (C), (D).... We are saying, then, that he knows the already determined prices π, ϱ..., but does not know p_b which still remains to be determined. Nevertheless, he can hypothetically assign all possible values to this unknown price and express his propensity to trade at each of these hypothetical prices by a curve portraying his offer of (B) as a function of p_b, or, alternatively, by a demand curve for (A), $a_d a_p$, drawn as a function of $\frac{1}{p_b}$ [c] (Fig. 18).

This is the way things really happen. When a new commodity is introduced into the market, its holders regulate their offer according to the price by deciding how much of this commodity they are willing to give up and how much of the other commodities they wish to acquire.

Let us consider, in like manner, a holder of (A), (C), (D).... If, at a price p_b of (B) in terms of (A), this holder demands a quantity d_b of (B), he will have to give up in exchange a quantity of (A), (C),

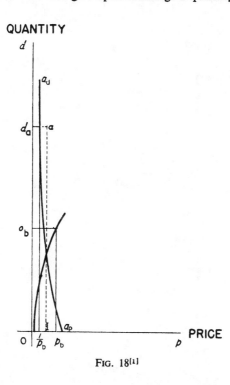

FIG. 18[1]

(D)... equal in value to $o_a = d_b p_b$. Since he is presumed to know also the prices of (C), (D)... in terms of (A), he will have all the information necessary for deciding how to make up this quantity o_a of (A) out of (A), (C), (D).... In other words, he knows the already determined prices π, ϱ..., but does not know p_b which remains to be determined. Nevertheless he can assign hypothetically all possible values to this unknown price, and express his propensity to trade at each of these hypothetical prices by a demand curve for (B), $b_d b_{\mathscr{P}}$, drawn as a function of p_b (Fig. 19).

Again, this is the way things actually happen in the real world. When a new commodity is introduced into the market, the holders of the other commodities regulate their demand for it according to its price, by deciding how much of the new commodity they wish to acquire and how much of the other commodities they are willing to give up.

We have not mentioned the case where a party holds both (B) and (A), (C), (D).... This case, however, is also covered by the theory of

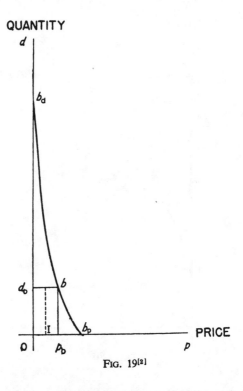

FIG. 19[2]

the exchange of two commodities for each other. Such a party would have to construct two curves: one curve showing the demand for (A) or alternatively the offer of (B) at certain prices, and another curve showing the demand for (B) or alternatively the offer of (A) at reciprocals of these prices (§94). These two curves would take their place alongside the preceding curves.

By adding these individual demand curves [vertically], we obtain the total demand curves A_dA_p and B_dB_p (Fig. 20). We can derive the offer curve of (B), NP, either from the demand curve for (A), A_dA_p, or, more directly, by adding [vertically] the individual offer curves of (B). The constantly falling curve B_dB_p is the demand curve for (B) in exchange for the *numéraire* and can be called a *purchase curve*; while the curve *NP*, which first rises from zero and then falls to zero (at infinity) is the offer curve of (B) in exchange for the *numéraire* and can be called a *sales curve*. The intersection of these two curves at the point *B* determines the price $p_b = \mu$.

152. But will this first result be final? Now we are confronted with a question which did not arise in connection with the exchange of

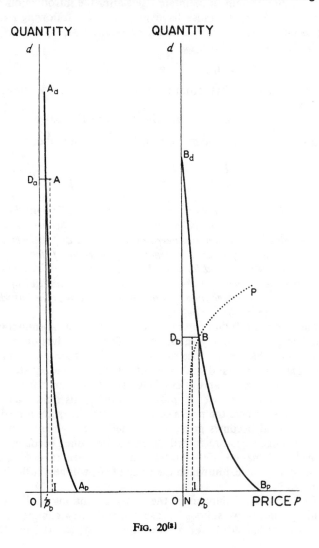

FIG. 20[a]

two commodities for each other. When the market was in general equilibrium before (B) made its appearance, the following relations held between the prices π, ϱ... and the quantities P', Q', R', S', K', L'... exchanged at these prices:

$$P' = Q'\pi \qquad R' = S'\varrho, \qquad K'\pi = L'\varrho....$$

For this equilibrium to maintain itself after the introduction of (B) into the market, we must have not only the following relations between the prices μ, π, ϱ... and the quantities M, N, P, Q, R, S, F, G, H, J, K, L... (§148):

$$M = N\mu, \qquad F\mu = G\pi, \qquad H\mu = J\varrho...,$$

which we have, in fact, from the way μ is determined, but also the relations

$$P = Q\pi, \qquad R = S\varrho, \qquad K\pi = L\varrho....$$

Combining this last system with the first, we easily obtain

$$\frac{P}{Q} = \frac{P'}{Q'}, \qquad \frac{R}{S} = \frac{R'}{S'}, \qquad \frac{K}{L} = \frac{K'}{L'}....$$

Thus: *If a new commodity makes its appearance in a market which is already in general equilibrium and if the price of this new commodity is determined by the equality between its demand and its offer against the* numéraire, *then for the general equilibrium of the market to continue undisturbed and for the price of the new commodity to remain final, it is necessary that the ratios between the quantities of the old commodities exchanged for each other be the same after the introduction of the new commodity as before.*[d]

The complete fulfilment of these conditions in absolutely every detail is no more likely in the case of the introduction of a new commodity than in the case of a rise in price of an old commodity. For, once the demand and offer of (B) have been equated at the price μ, the demand and offer of (A), (C), (D)... are thrown out of equilibrium at the prices π, ϱ.... This brings us right back to the general case, where the prices of some commodities are forced up as their demand becomes greater than their offer, while the prices of other commodities are forced down as their offer becomes greater than their demand (§130). In this way a new general equilibrium is [ultimately] reached in which the price of (B) will be a little different from μ.

The complete fulfilment of the above conditions is all the more unlikely since, if we suppose a case where the new commodity (B) is an excellent substitute for an old commodity, say (C) or (D), the price of the latter commodity will be brought down considerably by the appearance of (B) on the market. This is a common occurrence. If, however, we leave this special case aside and assume that (B) is a commodity *sui generis*, or if we take into consideration only those of the old commodities with which (B) does not enter into direct competition, we readily see that, provided that these commodities are of many different kinds and large in quantity, the price μ, determined by the intersection of the above-mentioned purchase and sales curves of (B), or a price very close to μ, will be the final price. What effectively happens in a case of this kind is that the amounts of (A), (C), (D)... set aside to be offered in exchange for (B) will represent such small fractions of each of the many commodities offered— fractions which will be all the smaller the larger the quantity of each kind of commodity—that they cannot affect to any appreciable extent the original ratios between the quantity of any one commodity and the quantities of the others for which it is exchanged.

153. There is a special case of the problem under discussion which is extremely simple and which deserves particular consideration. This is the case where all the holders of the new commodity, whether they be holders of that commodity alone or holders of other commodities as well, offer all they have of the new commodity, i.e. its total existing quantity, unconditionally at whatever price they can get. The bidding in such a case takes the form of an auction, provided we suppose that the entire quantity of this commodity is offered for sale at once. The current price is then determined mathematically, as is shown in Fig. 21, by the intersection at π_b of the purchase curve $B_d B_p$ with a straight line $Q_b \pi_b$ drawn parallel to the price axis through Q_b which measures the total existing quantity of (B) by its distance $O Q_b$ from the origin. This straight line turns out to be the sales curve. Cases of this kind, which are so simple, occur quite frequently in the real world, because most commodities are produced, and generally the producers offer all or nearly all their output for sale, retaining only an insignificant portion for their own use. Under these conditions the purchase curve acquires a new and truly remarkable significance: it becomes a *price curve*, where price is a function of the total existing quantity since the prices of the commodity shown by the abscissas of the curve are functions of the total existing quantities represented by the ordinates.

154. Instead of first supposing an initial equilibrium to be established for (A), (C), (D)... and then bringing (B) into the system in order to determine p_b, we might just as well have started by supposing an initial equilibrium to be established for (A), (B), (D)... and then allowed (C) to be brought in in order to determine p_c, or we might have presupposed an initial equilibrium for (A), (B), (C)... and then

introduced (D) in order to determine p_d... and so forth. It follows that each commodity may be regarded as having a purchase curve which can also be interpreted as a price curve provided, in the first place, that its offer is equal to the total existing quantity and, in the

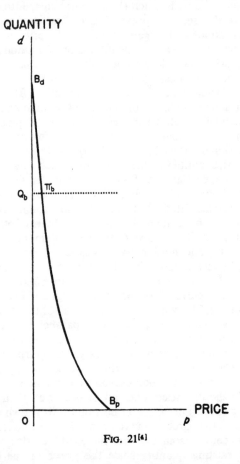

FIG. 21[a]

second place, that we abstract, by virtue of the law of large numbers, from variations in the ratios of the quantities exchanged resulting from the introduction of the commodity in question. The typical equation of this curve considered as a purchase curve is $D=F(p)$; but when the same curve is considered as a price curve the type equation is $Q=F(p)$, or, if solved for price,

$$p = \mathscr{F}(Q).$$

This is precisely the equation which Cournot posits *a priori* in his *Recherches sur les principes mathématiques de la théorie des richesses* (1838), and which he calls an equation *of demand* or *of sales* ['*débit*'].[5] It has a wide range of useful application.

155.[6] The connection between purchase and sales curves, on the one hand, and equations of exchange, on the other, can be shown in the following way.

Let (A) be the *numéraire*. Then, on the one side, let (A), (C), (D)... be commodities that are exchanged or about to be exchanged for one another at the predetermined general equilibrium prices $p_c=\pi$, $p_d=\varrho$... of (C), (D)... in terms of (A). On the other side, let (B) be the commodity which is introduced into the market and exchanged against commodities (A), (C), (D)....

Theoretically, the appearance of (B) on the market should make it necessary to set up a new system of exchange equations (§123) containing a new unknown p_b and an additional equation

$$F_b(p_b, p_c, p_d...)=0.$$

Denoting, as we did before (§§127 and 128), the sum of the positive y's, or D_b, by the function Δ_b and the sum of the negative y's taken positively, or O_b, by the function Ω_b, we may rewrite the above equation as follows:

$$\Delta_b(p_b, p_c, p_d...)=\Omega_b(p_b, p_c, p_d...).$$

But if we disregard all variations in the prices and in the effective demands and offers which had already been determined before (B) was introduced and consider them as constants, then the left-hand side of this equation

$$\Delta_b(p_b, \pi, \varrho...)$$

becomes a decreasing function of a single variable p_b. This function can be represented geometrically by a purchase curve like B_dB_p (Fig. 20). Similarly, the right-hand side of the equation

$$\Omega_b(p_b, \pi, \varrho...)$$

becomes a function of the same variable, p_b, which first increases from zero and then returns to zero again (at infinity). This function can be represented by a sales curve like NP of the same figure. The intersection of the two curves B_dB_p and NP at B will determine the price $p_b=\mu$, at least approximately.

We shall later show the connection between price curves and production equations in the same way.

156.[7] Before leaving this subject, however, we have one more comment of interest to make concerning a point we raised earlier.

When the number of commodities in the market is very large, the sales curve of each commodity, even when it does not actually coincide in whole or in part with the parallel of the total existing quantity, will evidently run close to this parallel for most prices, at least in the interval between very low and very high prices. Hence, multiple current equilibrium prices, which, as we have seen in §68, were perfectly possible in the case of the exchange of two commodities for each other, are, in general, not possible in the case of the exchange of several commodities for one another.[g]

Lesson 16

EXPOSITION AND REFUTATION OF ADAM SMITH'S AND J. B. SAY'S DOCTRINES OF THE ORIGIN OF VALUE IN EXCHANGE

157. The science of economics offers three major solutions to the problem of the origin of value. The first, that of Adam Smith, Ricardo and McCulloch, is the English solution, which traces the origin of value to *labour*. This solution is too narrow, because it fails to attribute value to things which, in fact, do have value. The second solution, that of Condillac and J. B. Say, is the French solution, which traces the origin of value to *utility*. This solution is too broad, because it attributes value to things which, in fact, have no value. Finally, the third solution, that of Burlamaqui and my father, A. A. Walras, traces the origin of value to *scarcity* ['*rareté*']. This is the correct solution.

158. Adam Smith formulated his doctrine in the following terms in Book I, Chapter V of the *Wealth of Nations*:

> The real price of everything, what everything really costs to the man who wants to acquire it, is the toil and trouble of acquiring it. What everything is really worth to the man who has acquired it, and who wants to dispose of it or exchange it for something else, is the toil and trouble which it can save to himself, and which it can impose upon other people. What is bought with money or with goods is purchased just as much by labour as what we acquire by the toil of our own body. That money or those goods indeed save us this toil. They contain the value of a certain quantity of labour which we exchange for what is supposed at the time to contain the value of an equal quantity. Labour was the first price, the original purchase-money that was paid for all things. It was not by gold or by silver, but by labour, that all the wealth of the world was originally purchased; and its value, to those who possess it, and who want to exchange it for some new productions, is precisely equal to the quantity of labour which it can enable them to purchase or command.[1]

More often than not, this theory has been inadequately criticized. The essence of the theory lies in the assertion that all things which have value and are exchangeable are labour in one form or another, so that labour alone constitutes the whole of social wealth. The critics of Adam Smith point out that there are certain things not derived from labour which have value, are exchangeable and constitute social wealth. This is a shallow criticism. Whether labour is all or only a part of social wealth is beside the point. In either case why is labour worth anything? Why is it exchangeable? That is the question before us. Adam Smith neither asked it nor answered it.

201

Surely, if labour has value and is exchangeable, it is because it is both useful and limited in quantity, that is to say because it is scarce (§101). Value, thus, comes from scarcity. Things other than labour, provided they are scarce, have value and are exchangeable just like labour itself. So the theory which traces the origin of value to labour is a theory that is devoid of meaning rather than too narrow, an assertion that is gratuitous rather than inacceptable.

159. Turning to the second solution, we shall give it in J. B. Say's own words taken from Chapter II of his *Catéchisme*:

Why does the utility of a thing make it have value?
Because its utility makes the thing desirable and incites men to make sacrifices in order to possess it. No one will give anything in exchange for something that is good for nothing; but everyone will give a certain quantity of the things he already possesses (say a certain number of coins) in order to obtain the thing he wants. This is what makes it have value.[a]

Here at least an attempt is made to formulate a proof, albeit a poor one. "The utility of a thing makes it desirable." Certainly! "It prompts men to make sacrifices in order to possess that thing." Ah, that depends, for it will only prompt men to make sacrifices, if they cannot get the thing in any other way. "No one will give anything in exchange for a thing that is good for nothing." True enough! "Everyone will give a certain quantity of the things he already possesses in order to obtain the thing he wants." On one condition: namely, that he cannot get it without giving something in exchange. Utility, therefore, is not sufficient to create value. Besides being useful, a thing must be scarce, i.e. it must not exist in unlimited quantities. This reasoning is confirmed by facts. The air we breathe, the wind that fills the sails at sea or turns windmills on land, the sun that gives us light and heat and ripens our harvests, water and steam from heated water, these and many other forces of nature are not only useful, but indispensable. And yet they have no value. Why? Because they are unlimited in quantity and everyone can obtain all he wants of them, whenever they are present at all, without giving up anything or making any sacrifice in return.

Condillac and J. B. Say both met with this objection in the course of their studies; and each dealt with it in his own way. Condillac regarded air, light and water as very useful things; and then he tried to prove that they really cost us something. What do they cost? The trouble of taking them. Condillac argues that the act of breathing, the act of opening one's eyes to see the light, or the act of stooping to take the water from a river are the sacrifices by which we pay for these goods.[3] This puerile argument has been cited more often than one would think possible, but that does not make it a better argument. Surely, if we are going to call these actions economic sacrifices, we shall have to find another word for the sacrifice associated with value properly so called. When I go to the butcher's for meat or to the tailor's for a suit of clothes, I make an effort or a sacrifice in the act of taking these things away, but I also make another sacrifice of a very special kind which consists in taking out of my pocket a certain sum of money which goes to the merchant.

J. B. Say attacks the problem in a different way. He tells us that air, sunlight and the waters of streams and rivers are useful and therefore have value. They are, indeed, so useful, so necessary and so indispensable that their value is immense—in fact, infinite. And that is exactly why we get them for nothing. We do not pay for them, because we could never pay the price. The explanation is ingenious, but unfortunately for the argument, there are times when we do pay for air, light and water—when, for example, they are scarce.

160. The above are two well-known, characteristic passages of Adam Smith and J. B. Say; but it must be admitted that, in reality, these authors barely skimmed the surface of the problem of the origin of value in exchange and that neither Adam Smith nor J. B. Say remained within the bounds of these inadequate theories. Only a few lines below the ones we have quoted, J. B. Say turns his utility theory into a labour theory, and elsewhere he seems to come round to a scarcity theory. As for Adam Smith, he fortunately contradicted himself by admitting land as well as labour into the category of social wealth. Bastiat alone undertook to systematize the English theory; he accepted, and tried to persuade others to accept, consequences diametrically opposed to the facts of real life.

161. We now come to the last of our theories, that of scarcity. An excellent statement of this theory is found in Part III, Chapter XI, of Burlamaqui's *Eléments du droit naturel* where we find the following passage:

One of the foundations of inherent and intrinsic price is the capacity which things have to serve our wants, our convenience and our pleasures of life; in other words, it is the *utility* of these things. Another foundation is their *scarcity*.

When I speak of utility I mean not only real utility, but also utility that is only arbitrary or imaginary, like the utility of precious stones. It is common knowledge that a thing that is absolutely useless has no price.

But utility alone, be it ever so real, does not suffice to give a price to things In addition, their *scarcity* must be considered—that is to say, the difficulty of procuring them, so that no one can easily get as much as he wants of them.

Need alone is very far from determining the price of a thing. Everyday experience shows us that those things which are the most necessary to human life are the cheapest—ordinary water, for example.

Scarcity alone is not sufficient to give price to things either. They must be of some use as well.

As these elements, which are the true foundations of the price of things, are

ELEMENTS OF PURE ECONOMICS

now combined in one way and now in another, they also cause the price to
rise or fall.

If a thing goes out of fashion, or if fewer people care for it, it will become
cheap, however dear it may have been in the past. On the other hand, as soon
as an ordinary, commonplace thing, which may have cost little or nothing,
becomes scarce, it immediately begins to rise in price, and sometimes becomes
very dear. This is true of water in arid regions or in certain eventualities, as during
a siege or in the course of a long sea voyage, etc.

To resume, all the special circumstances which cause a thing to have a high
price can be brought under the heading of scarcity. Such special circumstances
are, for example, the difficulty of making the thing, or its peculiar intricacy, or
the unique reputation of the artisan who made it.

The same explanation is applicable to what is called *sentimental* or *affective
price* which manifests itself whenever anyone, for reasons of his own, esteems
one of his possessions at a higher price than is ordinarily paid for it, if, for
example, the possession had been instrumental in saving him from great
danger or if it was a souvenir of some exceptional event or a mark of honour,
etc.[4]

This is the doctrine of scarcity. Abbé Genovesi[5] taught it at
Naples towards the middle of the eighteenth century, Nassau W.
Senior[6] taught it at Oxford about 1830. But actually it was my
father who made it an integral part of economics. He presented it
in a special way with all the necessary developments[a] in his book
entitled *De la nature de la richesse et de l'origine de la valeur*, [Paris,
Johanneau] (1831).[1] No one could have utilized the resources of
ordinary logic to better advantage than he did in this book. To
carry the theory any further, it would have been necessary to apply
the methods of mathematical analysis, as I have done.[b]

162.[c] I am not the only one to have used mathematics for this
purpose. Others have done it before me. The first was a German,
Hermann Heinrich Gossen, in a book entitled *Entwickelung der
Gesetze des menschlichen Verkehrs und der daraus fliessenden Regeln
für menschliches Handeln*, published in 1854; and he was followed by
an Englishman, William Stanley Jevons, in a work entitled *Theory of
Political Economy*, the first edition of which appeared in 1871 and the
second in 1879. First Gossen and later Jevons, who knew nothing of
Gossen's work, originated the negatively inclined utility or want
curves. By the use of mathematics, Gossen, on his side, derived the
condition of maximum utility from these curves, while Jevons derived
the equations of exchange.

Gossen stated the condition of maximum utility in the following
terms: "*Upon completion of the process of exchange, the two commodities must be so divided between the two trading parties that the last*

---

[1] See especially: Chapter III, p. 41; Chapter XVI, p. 234; Chapter XVIII, p. 279.
[The passages referred to are found on pp. 95–96, 236–237 and 267 of the new edition
of Auguste Walras's *De la nature de la richesse et de l'origine de la valeur*, Paris,
Alcan, 1938, annotated by Professor Gaston Leduc and published in the Collection
des principaux économistes, edited by Gaëtan Pirou and François Simiand.]

atom of each commodity changing hands has the same value for one party as for the other."[7] In order to express this statement in terms of our own formulae, we shall call the two commodities (A) and (B), and the two parties (1) and (2). Let $r=\phi_{a,1}(q)$ and $r=\phi_{b,1}(q)$ be the equations of the utility curves of commodities (A) and (B) for party (1). Let $r=\phi_{a,2}(q)$ and $r=\phi_{b,2}(q)$ be the corresponding equations for party (2). Let q_a be the initial quantity of (A) held by party (1) and q_b be the initial quantity of (B) held by party (2); and let d_a and d_b be the quantities of (A) and (B) to be exchanged. Now, Gossen's principle can be expressed by the following equations:

$$\phi_{a,1}(q_a-d_a)=\phi_{a,2}(d_a),$$
$$\phi_{b,1}(d_b)=\phi_{b,2}(q_b-d_b),$$

which determine d_a and d_b for parties (1) and (2). It is obvious that the maximum utility arrived at in this way is not the relative maximum utility of free competition, nor is it compatible with the condition that all parties buy and sell the two commodities freely at a common and uniform rate of exchange. It is rather an absolute maximum which takes no account of the twofold condition of uniformity of price throughout the market[d] and of equality between effective offer and demand at that price. It consequently does away with private property.[1]

163.[e] Jevons, on the other hand, formulated his equations of exchange as follows: "*The ratio of exchange of any two commodities will be the reciprocal of the ratio of the final degrees of utility of the quantities of commodity available for consumption after the exchange is completed.*" (Ed. 2, p. 103.)[8] Letting (A) and (B) be the two commodities, (1) and (2) the two parties, ϕ_1 and ψ_1 the symbols of the utility functions of (A) and (B) for party (1), ϕ_2 and ψ_2 the corresponding symbols for party (2), a the initial quantity of (A) in the possession of party (1), and b the initial quantity of (B) in the possession of party (2), and x and y the quantities of (A) and (B) to be exchanged, Jevons translated his principle into the two equations

$$\frac{\phi_1(a-x)}{\psi_1 y}=\frac{y}{x}=\frac{\phi_2 x}{\psi_2(b-y)}.$$

In our system of notation these equations would read

$$\frac{\phi_{a,1}(q_a-d_a)}{\phi_{b,1}(d_b)}=\frac{d_b}{d_a}=\frac{\phi_{a,2}(d_a)}{\phi_{b,2}(q_b-d_b)},$$

from which d_a and d_b could be determined. This formulation differs from our own in two respects. In the first place, where we refer to

[1] See my *Etudes d'économie sociale* [pp. 209–213]. Théorie de la propriété, §4. [This footnote appears first in ed. 4.]

prices which we define as the reciprocals of the ratios of the quantities of the commodities exchanged, Jevons referred to *ratios of exchange* which he defined as the direct ratios of these quantities, which are always given by the relation between the two terms, d_a and d_b, of these ratios.[9] In the second place, Jevons considered his problem as completely solved once it had been solved for two parties. He simply reserved the right to consider each of these parties (*"trading bodies"*) as made up of a group of individuals, such as, all the inhabitants of a continent or all the manufacturers in a certain kind of industry of a given country (p. 95).[10] He admitted, however, that in making such a supposition, he left the world of reality for a world of *"fictitious means"* (p. 97).[11] We, on the other hand, wish to remain within the world of reality; and consequently we can only regard Jevons's formula as valid for the limited case of exchange between two individuals only. For this limited case, Jevons's formula is identical with our own, except that he used quantities exchanged where we use prices. There is still to be considered the general case in which any number of individuals enter into mutual exchange relations, first on the supposition that only two commodities are being exchanged for each other and then on the supposition that any number of commodities are being exchanged for one another. Jevons was precluded from doing this,[f] because he clung to the useless idea of considering quantities exchanged instead of prices as the unknowns of the problem.[g]

164.[h] Just about the time that Jevons published the first edition of his *Theory of Political Economy* (1871-1872), Professor Carl Menger of the University of Vienna published his *Grundsätze der Volkswirtschaftslehre*. This was a third book, antedating my own, in which the foundations of the new theory of exchange were laid in an independent and original manner. Professor Menger developed a utility theory along the same lines as we have done. Starting with the law that wants diminish as the quantity consumed increases, he worked from this postulate towards the derivation of the theory of exchange. He employed the deductive method, but was opposed to the mathematical method, although he did use, if not functions or curves, at least arithmetical tables to express either utility or demand. This makes it impossible for me to comment upon his theory in a few lines as I have upon the theories of Gossen and Jevons. I shall only say of Carl Menger, as of his disciples, von Wieser and von Böhm-Bawerk,[i] that, in my opinion, their refusal to make undisguised use of the method and language of mathematics in treating an essentially mathematical subject deprives them of a tool that is not merely useful, but indispensable. Nevertheless, I must concede that in spite of their imperfect method and language, these authors subjected[j] the problem of exchange to very close analysis. At least, they definitely succeeded in bringing the theory of *rareté*, which they called *Grenznutzen* (final utility), sharply to the attention of economists.[k] This theory, as it is now being developed in our science, appears to be very fruitful. From it I have derived an abstract theory of the prices of commodities in terms of a *numéraire*.[l] In the following pages, I propose to deduce: (1) the theory of the simultaneous determination of the prices of products and the prices of land-services, personal services and capital-services; (2) the theory of the determination of the rate of net income and the consequent prices of landed capital, personal capital and capital proper;[m] and (3) the theory of the determination of prices in terms of money. All these theories are, admittedly, abstract; but when they are progressively enfolded in one another by a process of systematic synthesis, they take us right into the midst of reality.[1]

---

[1] So that there may be no misunderstanding, I feel I must repeat that the last three sections of this Lesson first appeared in the second edition of my book. In the first edition, dated 1874, I did not refer to the three above-mentioned works which had been published before mine, simply because I had absolutely no knowledge of their existence at that time. [This footnote was first inserted at this point in ed. 4. See Collation Note [c] of Lesson 16.]

PART IV
Theory of Production

Lesson 17

CAPITAL AND INCOME
THE THREE SERVICES

165.[a] Any order of phenomena, however complicated, may be studied scientifically provided the rule of proceeding from the simple to the complex is always observed. In formulating our mathematical theory of exchange, we began with the exchange in kind of two commodities for each other and then passed to the exchange of several commodities for one another through the medium of a *numéraire*. Thus far, however, we have left out of consideration the fact that commodities are *products* which result from the combination of productive factors such as land, men and capital goods. We have now reached the point where we must take this fact into account. Having studied the problem of the mathematical determination of the prices of products, we are ready to pose and examine the problem of the mathematical determination of the prices of productive services. Our solution of the problem of exchange led to a scientific formulation of the *law of offer and demand*. Our solution of the problem of production brings us to a scientific formulation of the *law of the cost of production or of cost price*.[1] Though, in the end, I shall do no more than rediscover two well-known fundamental laws of economics, I shall do so with this difference, that instead of presenting them as conflicting and mutually contradictory in the determination of prices, I shall assign to each its proper role by showing how the determination of the price of products is founded on the first of these laws, while the determination of the price of productive services is founded on the second. It is a truth long acknowledged by economists—and I hope I may be believed when I say that this point has not completely escaped me—that under certain normal and ideal conditions, the selling prices of commodities are equal to their costs of production. Under these normal or ideal conditions, which are really conditions of equilibrium in exchange and production, a bottle of wine which sells for 5 francs will have a cost of production amounting to 2 francs in rent, 2 francs in wages and 1 franc in interest charges. Granting this, it still remains to be seen whether it was because 2 francs were paid out in rent, 2 francs in wages and 1 franc in interest that this bottle of wine sells for 5 francs, or whether it is because the bottle sells for 5 francs that 2 francs were paid out in rent, 2 francs in wages and 1 franc in interest. In other words, we still have to inquire whether the prices of productive services determine the

211

prices of products, as it is often claimed, or whether the prices of products, having already been determined, as we have seen, by the operation of the law of offer and demand, determine, in their turn, the prices of the productive services by the operation of the law of the cost of production or of cost price. This is the question we shall now examine.

166. The elementary factors of production are three in number. In listing these factors, most authors employ the terms: *land, labour* and *capital*. But these terms are not sufficiently rigorous to serve as a foundation for rational deduction. *Labour* is the service of human faculties or of *persons*. We must rank labour, therefore, not with land and capital, but with *land-services* ['*rente*'] rendered by *land*, and with *capital-services* ['*profit*'] rendered by *capital goods*.[2] Since I shall be using these terms in a very precise sense, I must define them with meticulous care. To this end, I shall begin by framing a definition of capital and income which is more restricted than the usual definition and even narrower than the one I shall be using myself later on, after giving the reader due notice of the change.

167. I define *fixed capital*, i.e. *capital* in general, just as my father did in his *Théorie de la richesse sociale* (1849), as all durable goods, all forms of social wealth which are not used up at all or are used up only after a lapse of time, i.e. every utility limited in quantity which outlasts its first use, or which, in a word, can be used more than once, like a house or a piece of furniture. And I mean by *circulating capital* or *income* all non-durable goods,[3] all forms of social wealth which are used up immediately, i.e. every scarce thing which does not outlast its first use, or which, in short, can be used only once, like bread or meat. Income comprises not only articles of private consumption but also the raw materials of agriculture and industry, like seeds, textile fibres, etc. The durability of which we speak in this context is not material durability, but durability in use or economic durability. Though textile fibres still continue to exist materially in the cloth, they cease to have existence as raw materials and cannot be used again as such once the cloth has been made. On the other hand, buildings and machines are items of capital, not of income. I should add that while certain kinds of social wealth are capital by their very nature and other kinds are intrinsically income, a large number of varieties of wealth can be either capital or income depending upon what use is made of them or what service they perform. Trees, for example, are capital when they bear fruit, but are income when they are cut down for fuel or lumber. Animals, too, are capital when they work or give milk or eggs, but are income when they are slaughtered for food. In fact, every kind of social wealth, whether from its intrinsic nature or from the use to which it is put, can serve either

more than once or only once, and is classified, accordingly, either as capital or as income.[4]

When we speak of people consuming their capital, we mean that they first exchange their capital for income and then consume this income. Similarly, the formation of capital out of income signifies a previous exchange of income for capital.

Capital should not be confused with stocks which are aggregates of income accumulated in advance for eventual consumption. Wine in the cellar, wood in the shed and raw materials in the store-room are stocks. Stones and minerals in quarries and mines are also accumulations of income, not of capital.

168. Since we have already defined social wealth as the sum total of all things, material or immaterial, which are scarce, that is to say, which are both useful and limited in quantity (§21), it is hardly necessary to add that the capital and income which make up this social wealth, may themselves be either material or immaterial. The question of materiality or immateriality is unimportant in either case. We shall see presently how capital gives rise to income; and in that connection it will be shown that material capital may very well engender immaterial income or immaterial capital engender material income. I mention this fact now because it helps in making clear the distinction between capital and income.

169. It is of the essence of capital to give rise to income; and it is of the essence of income to originate, directly or indirectly, in capital. How does this happen? Since capital, by definition, outlasts its first use and consequently affords a series of successive uses, the flow of uses evidently constitutes a flow of income. A field will grow a crop for us year after year; a dwelling-house will protect us against the inclemencies of the weather in summer as in winter. Fertility is the annual income of the soil; shelter the annual income of the house. A worker toils in the factory day after day; and a lawyer or a doctor has his consulting hours day in day out. Labour is the daily income of the worker; consultations the daily income of the professional man. Machines, instruments, tools, furniture and clothing engender incomes in the same way. Many authors are still confused and obscure in their writings because they fail to consider the income of capital separately from the capital itself.

In order to bring out the distinction between capital and income, we shall designate all those incomes which consist in the uses made of capital by the name of *services*. These services fall into two groups. The first group comprises those services that are utilized in their original form in private and public consumption. Such services are the shelter of a house, the consultations of the lawyer or doctor, and the use made of furniture and clothes. These we shall call *consumers' services*. The second group comprises those services which are transformed by means of agriculture, industry or commerce into income or capital, that is to say, into *products*. Such services are the fertility of the soil, the labour of the workman, or the use of machines, instruments and tools. These we shall call *productive services*. When we come to the theory of circulation, attention will have to be drawn to the fact that stores of income goods, while being held for the eventual performance of their single act of *use service*, perform in the meantime a *service of availability*,[5] which may be either a directly consumable service or a productive service.[b] Our distinction between consumers' services and productive services corresponds to the distinction made by most authors between *unproductive* and *reproductive* consumption.[c] Our special concern is with the study of the transformation of productive services into products.[d]

170. By means of our definition of capital and income we can proceed immediately to divide the whole of social wealth into four main categories, three of which are categories of capital, and the fourth of income.

Into the first category we shall put land of all kinds: land laid out as parks and pleasure grounds, both public and private; forest lands; agricultural land growing fruit, vegetables, cereals, fodder and other foodstuffs for man and beast; the ground beneath homes, public buildings, offices, factories, workshops or stores; land used for roads, highways, public squares, canals, railways, and all means of communication. All this land is truly capital. The garden and the park, stripped and stark through the winter, will have leaves and blossoms again in the summer; the land that brought forth this autumn's harvest will, in due season, bring forth the next; ground beneath a house or factory this year will be there the following year; and we shall walk along the familiar streets and roads in the year to come as we did in the year that has passed. Thus the land outlasts the first use that is made of it, and the succession of its uses constitutes its income. The enjoyment of a walk or of the view is the income of a park or garden; the fertility of the soil is the income from land; the suitability of the site for construction is the income from building land, and facilitation of movement is the income from streets and roads. This gives us our first category of capital, namely *landed capital* or *land*, capable of yielding *land-income* or *land-services*, which we shall also call "*rentes*".[2]

171. Our second category of social wealth is comprised of persons: those who do nothing but travel and seek amusement; those who serve other persons: coachmen, cooks, man-servants, maid-servants; public officials in the service of the State, such as administrators,

judges and military men; male and female workers in agriculture, industry and commerce; men engaged in the liberal professions, for example, lawyers, doctors and artists. All these persons are really capital. The idler who has wasted today will waste tomorrow; the blacksmith who has just finished this day's work will finish many more; the lawyer who leaves the courtroom will come back to plead again. Thus, persons still exist after rendering their first service, and the series of services they render constitutes their incomes. The pleasure enjoyed by the idler,[6] the job done by the worker and the plea made by the lawyer constitute the incomes of these people. This gives us our second category of capital; namely *personal capital* or *persons*, capable of yielding *personal incomes* or *services of persons*, which we shall also call *labour* ['*travaux*'].

172. We now come to our third category of social wealth composed of all the remaining assets which are capital assets without being land or persons: dwelling-houses in either town or country, and public buildings; business houses, factories, workshops, stores, constructions of all kinds, considered, of course, apart from the ground on which they stand; trees and plants of all sorts; animals; furniture, clothes, pictures, statues, carriages, jewels; machines, instruments, tools. We regard all these things not as income, but as capital productive of income. The house that now shelters me can do so for a long time to come; my paintings and jewels are always at my disposal; the train that comes from a neighbouring town today, bringing passengers and goods, will return tomorrow along the same tracks, with other passengers and other goods. The shelter of a house, the decorative effect of paintings and jewels, the transportation furnished by trains are the incomes from the capital goods in question. Thus we have a third category of capital, namely *capital proper*,[7] capable of yielding *capital-income* or *capital-services*, which we shall also call "*profits*".[8]

173. With the whole of capital accounted for in our first three categories of social wealth, the only thing left for the fourth is income which consists of: (1) *consumers' goods* such as wheat, flour, bread, meat, wine, beer, vegetables, fruit, illuminants and fuel directly consumed; and (2) *raw materials* such as fertilizers, seeds, metals, lumber, textiles, cloth, illuminants and fuel used in production—in fact, all things destined to disappear as raw materials only to reappear again as products.

174. We see that land, persons and capital proper constitute capital; while the services of land (i.e. land-services), the services of persons (i.e. labour) and the services of capital proper (i.e. capital-services) constitute income. In the interest of precision and exactness, we must view the elementary factors of production as consisting

of three kinds of capital and [their respective] services, viz. landed capital (i.e. land) and land-services; personal capital (i.e. persons) and services of persons (i.e. labour); and capital proper (i.e. capital goods) and capital-services. In this corrected form, the currently accepted classification of the factors of production can be admitted as being founded on the nature of things.[8]

Land is *natural* capital, which is not artificially produced; it is also *imperishable* capital which cannot be destroyed by use or accident. There are, however, certain kinds of landed capital which have been artificially produced by carrying soil to rocky declivities, by fertilizing waste lands and by draining marshes. Some landed capital, too, is subject to destruction by earthquake, flood or erosion. But such cases are small in number, so that, apart from a few exceptions, we may consider landed capital to be original and indestructible. Each of these two characteristics has an importance of its own; but it is their co-existence which is the distinguishing mark of landed capital. Since the quantity of land, while not absolutely fixed, is subject to very little change, the result is that what land there is may be exceedingly abundant in a primitive society, but quite insufficient in an advanced society in relation to the population and the quantity of capital proper. It follows, therefore, that in a primitive society land cannot have, and, in fact, as we shall see, does not have any scarcity or value, while in an advanced society its scarcity is great and its value extremely high.

175. Persons, like land, are *natural* capital, but they are *perishable*, that is to say, destructible by use or accident. They disappear, but they reappear, as each generation reproduces itself. Thus the number of people, far from being constant, is susceptible of indefinite increase under certain conditions. This part of our discussion calls for a special observation. In speaking of persons as natural capital and as reproducing themselves by procreation, we are not overlooking the principle of social ethics which is gaining ever wider acceptance: that persons should not be bought and sold like things, nor bred in barn-yards or stud-farms like cattle or horses. It might be thought beside the mark, therefore, to include persons in a theory of the determination of prices. On the other hand, although personal capital is not subject to purchase and sale, labour or personal services are offered and demanded every day on the market, so that personal capital can, and often should, at least be evaluated. Moreover, we should frankly recognize that, in the pure theory of economics at any rate, it is perfectly proper to abstract completely from considerations of justice and practical expediency, and to regard personal capital, like land and capital proper, exclusively from the point of view of value in exchange. We shall therefore continue to speak of the price

of labour, and even of the price of persons, quite apart from any argument either for or against slavery.

176. Capital proper consists of *artificial* or *produced* capital and is *perishable*. It is, perhaps, possible to cite a few examples of capital assets, other than land and persons, which are natural assets, like certain kinds of trees or animals; but it would be hard to find any that are indestructible. Capital assets are destroyed and vanish, like persons; and, like persons, they reappear, not, however, as a result of natural reproduction, but as a result of economic production. Their quantity, like that of persons, is, therefore, susceptible of an indefinite increase under given conditions. Again this calls for a special observation. Capital goods are always combined with land in production, particularly in agriculture. It should be clearly understood, however, that when we speak of land, we consider it apart from such things as dwellings or office buildings, enclosing or supporting walls, irrigation or drainage systems, in short, apart from all capital proper. *A fortiori* we consider it exclusive, also, of fertilizers, seeds and standing crops, that is, exclusive of all the income goods that are combined with land. We mean, therefore, by land-services only the services rendered by land so defined, for the services rendered by capital proper combined with land are called capital-services.

The characteristics of social wealth which we have just described not only explain but justify the distinction between land, persons and capital proper. It should be noted, however, that the significance of this discussion will be seen principally in [the theory of] social economics and in the later parts of the pure theory of economics which deal with capital formation and economic progress. All this reasoning is based on one fundamental proposition: that landed capital, personal capital and capital goods are capital and not income.

177. Having said this, we have still to inquire why and how it is that the services of land (or land-services), the services of personal faculties (or labour), and the services of capital proper (or capital-services) have current prices which are mathematically determinable quantities in an economy governed by free competition in production as in exchange. Strictly speaking, we have to formulate a system of equations of which rent, wages and interest charges are the roots.[e]

THE ELEMENTS AND MECHANISM
OF PRODUCTION

178. Just as we found it necessary to begin our study of the problem of the mathematical determination of the prices of products by working out a precise description of the mechanism of free competition in the domain of exchange, so now, as we come to the problem of the mathematical definition of the prices of productive services, we must look into the facts revealed by experience in order to formulate as exact an idea as possible of the mechanism of free competition in the domain of production. If, for purposes of this analysis, we imagine the process of economic production in a given country to be momentarily arrested, we shall be in a position to apply our distinction between consumers' services and productive services (§169) to the items of capital and income listed in §§170–173 and thus classify the elements involved in the productive process under the following thirteen headings.

With respect to capital, we have:

(1), (2) and (3): *landed capital, personal capital* and *capital goods proper* productive of consumers' services, that is to say, of income directly consumed either by the original holders of these different types of capital or by purchasers of the income derived from them, whether these purchasers be individuals, corporate bodies or the State. Examples of landed capital of this type are parks, gardens, sites for dwelling-houses or public buildings, streets, roads, public squares, etc. Examples of personal capital of this type are idle folk, servants, public officials, etc. Examples of capital goods proper of this type are dwelling-houses, public buildings, trees, animals kept for pleasure, decorative plants, furniture, clothes, art objects, luxury goods, etc.

(4), (5) and (6): *landed capital, personal capital* and *capital goods proper* yielding productive services, that is to say, items of income transformable into products through agriculture, industry or trade. Examples of such landed capital are farm land, sites for office buildings, factories, workshops and warehouses; examples of personal capital of this type are wage-earners, professional men, etc.; and examples of such capital goods proper are office buildings, factories, workshops, warehouses, fruit-bearing trees and crop plants, work animals, machines, instruments and tools.

(7): *new capital goods*, unproductive of income for the moment,

218

while their producers are holding them for sale in the form of such products as newly constructed buildings and houses built for sale; or plants, animals, furniture, clothes, art objects, luxury goods, machines, instruments, and tools which have been put into stock or on display.

With respect to income, we have:

(8) stocks of *income goods* consisting of *consumers' goods*, like bread, meat, wine, vegetables, fruit, oils, and firewood in the homes of consumers.

(9): stocks of *income goods* consisting of *raw materials*, like fertilizers, seeds, crude metals, lumber, textile fibres, cloth in bolts and industrial fuels held in the bins and store-rooms of producers.

(10): *new income goods* consisting of *consumers' goods* and *raw materials* held for sale by their producers, like bread at the baker's, meat at the butcher's, or metals, lumber, textile fibres, bolts of cloth which have been put into stock or placed on display by their producers.

Finally, with respect to money, we have:

(11), (12) and (13): *cash* holdings of consumers; *cash* holdings of producers, and *money savings*.

It is readily seen that we obtain our first six headings by subdividing each of our three kinds of capital into capital yielding consumers' services and capital yielding productive services; we obtain our seventh heading by segregating that part of capital proper which is not [for the moment] yielding any income; and we obtain our eighth, ninth, and tenth headings, on the one hand, and our eleventh, twelfth, and thirteenth headings, on the other, by making similar subdivisions of income goods and money respectively. We place money in a separate category, apart from capital and income, because of the mixed role it plays in production. From the social point of view, money is capital, since it is used in society more than once for making payments; from the individual point of view, money is income, for no individual can use it more than once, since he no longer has it after making a payment.

179. Up to this point we have been proceeding on the supposition that the process of economic production was momentarily arrested. Now let us suppose it is set in motion again.

Among the items classified under the first six headings, land will neither be used up nor destroyed in the process of economic production, since it is permanent by its very nature; men, of course, will die and new generations will be born, not as the result of productive activity in agriculture, industry or trade, but still, as we shall see, in a measure not unrelated to economic production; capital proper which is impermanent, will be worn out in use or destroyed by

accident only to be replaced by the new capital goods classified
under the seventh heading. In this way, the quantity of capital
goods proper is both reduced and restored in the course of the same
general process of production. In order to simplify our problem, we
may provisionally[1] skip over our seventh category by supposing
that the new capital goods pass, immediately upon being produced,
into the third and sixth categories.

The items classified under the eighth and ninth headings, viz. consumers' goods and raw materials which are directly consumable
income goods, will be consumed only to be replaced by the new
income goods classified under the tenth heading. And so the
quantity of income goods is both reduced and restored in the course
of the same general process of production. Once again we can ignore
one of the categories, the tenth, by supposing that new income
goods pass, immediately upon being produced, into the eighth and
ninth categories. We may even leave out the eighth and ninth
categories if we suppose that consumers' goods and raw materials
are consumed as soon as they are produced and are not stocked in
advance.

Money will intervene in exchanges. At every moment, part of the
money in circulation is absorbed by savings and part of the money
savings is thrown back into circulation by credit. If we choose to
leave savings entirely out of consideration, we can also disregard
money savings. As will be seen presently, [in our study of the
operation of the mechanism of production] we can abstract from
money in circulation as well.

180. In summary, what will be used up [in the course of the
productive process] are, on the one hand, certain consumers' services
which will immediately be reproduced by the landed capital, personal
capital and capital proper classified under headings (1), (2) and (3),
and, on the other hand, certain income goods, unfinished consumers'
goods and raw materials which will immediately be reproduced by
the landed capital, personal capital and capital proper classified
under headings (4), (5) and (6). Income, by definition, does not
outlast its first use. The very instant it renders a service, it passes out
of existence; technically speaking, it is *consumed*. Bread and meat
are eaten; wine is drunk; oil and wood are burned; fertilizers and
seeds are put in the soil; metals, lumber and textile fibres are worked
up, fuels are consumed. But no sooner do these income goods
disappear than they reappear again as a result of the working of
capital. Capital goods, by definition, do outlast their first use. As
they render the successive services for which they are suited, capital
goods serve their purpose; technically speaking, they *produce*. Farm
land will be cultivated, building sites will support factories; workmen

will toil in these factories and use their machines, instruments and tools. In short, landed capital, personal capital and capital proper will render their respective services; and from a combination of these services agriculture, industry and trade will create new income goods to replace the income goods consumed.

181. This, however, does not tell the whole story. Besides the consumers' goods and the raw materials which are consumed instantaneously, there are various kinds of capital goods proper which are consumed slowly. Houses and buildings depreciate, furniture, clothes, art objects and luxury goods wear out in time. The same is true of factories, machines, instruments and tools. All these capital goods are used up more or less rapidly. They are also subject to sudden destruction by unforeseeable accidents. Consequently, it is not enough for the landed capital, personal capital and capital proper under headings (4), (5) and (6) to produce new income; our three categories of capital must also produce new capital goods proper to replace the capital goods worn out in use and destroyed by accident, and even to increase, if possible, the existing quantity of capital proper. Here we have one of the indices of economic progress. Imagine that we arrest the process of production again after a certain interval of time [and make an inventory], as we did before; and imagine that we find an enlarged quantity of capital goods proper. That would be a sign of a progressive state. One of the characteristic traits of economic progress is an increase in the quantity of capital goods proper. Since we shall make a special study of the production of new capital goods in Part V, we may defer our examination of economic progress until then and confine ourselves, for the present, to a discussion of the production of new income in the form of consumers' goods and raw materials.[a]

182. No one category of productive capital ever functions by itself in the production of consumable income and capital goods, but always in combination with other categories. Even in agriculture, where landed capital plays the preponderant role, the products are composed not merely of land-services, but also of labour and capital-services. And in industry, where capital proper is the most important factor, land-services also enter into the composition of the products along with labour and capital-services. There is perhaps not a single exception to the rule that the production of every conceivable thing requires some land (if only to afford standing room for the workman) as well as personal faculties, and some sort of tool which is capital. The co-operation of land, man and capital is, therefore, the very essence of economic production; and this calls now for a careful and detailed description. In this connection, the distinction between capital and income, which we have already

found so useful in classifying the factors of production (§178), will also prove useful in giving a summary account of the mechanism of production.

183. The very fact that income does not outlast the first use which is made of it, means that it can only be *sold* or *given away*. It cannot be hired out—at least in kind. How can bread or meat be hired out? A capital good, on the other hand, by virtue of the fact that it does outlast the first use which is made of it, can be *hired out*, either for a consideration or free of charge. For example, a house or a piece of furniture can be rented. And what is the reason for such a transaction? To procure the use or service for the renter. *The hiring out of a capital good is the alienation of the service of that capital good.* This definition is based entirely on the distinction between capital and income and is fundamental, for without it both the theory of production and the theory of credit would be impossible. The hiring out of a capital good for a consideration constitutes the sale of its service, and, when the hiring out is done gratuitously, it constitutes a free gift of its service. In fact, it is by being hired for a consideration that items of landed capital, personal capital and capital proper classified under headings (4), (5) and (6) are brought together for production.

184. Let us call the holder of land, whoever he may be, a *land-owner*, the holder of personal faculties a *worker* and the holder of capital proper a *capitalist*. In addition, let us designate by the term *entrepreneur* a fourth person, entirely distinct from those just mentioned, whose role it is to lease land from the land-owner, hire personal faculties from the labourer, and borrow capital from the capitalist, in order to combine the three productive services in agriculture, industry or trade. It is undoubtedly true that, in real life, the same person may assume two, three, or even all four of the above-defined roles. In fact, the different ways in which these roles may be combined give rise to different types of enterprise. However that may be, the roles themselves, even when performed by the same individual, still remain distinct. From the scientific point of view, we must keep these roles separate and avoid both the error of the English economists who identify the entrepreneur with the capitalist and the error of a certain number of French economists who look upon the entrepreneur as a worker charged with the special task of managing a firm.

185. This being granted, it follows from our initial conception of the role of the entrepreneur that we must think in terms of two distinct markets.

The first is the *services market*.[b] Here land-owners, workers and capitalists appear as sellers, and entrepreneurs as buyers of the various productive services, i.e. land-services, labour and capital-services. In this same market, alongside the entrepreneurs buying land-services, labour and capital-services for productive purposes, are also found land-owners, labourers, and capitalists buying services for purposes of consumption. We shall discuss these latter purchases in due course; but for the present we shall be concerned principally with the purchase of services for purposes of production.[6] Such productive services are exchanged with the aid of a *numéraire* and in accordance with the mechanism of free competition (§42). For every service a price is cried in terms of the *numéraire*. If at this price effective demand exceeds effective offer, the entrepreneurs will bid against one another and the price will rise. If the effective offer exceeds effective demand, the land-owners, workers and capitalists will underbid one another, and the price will fall. The current price of each service is the one at which effective demand and effective offer are equal.

The current contract price of land-services[2] in terms of *numéraire*, reached in the above manner, will be called *rent* ['*fermage*'].

The current contract price of labour in terms of *numéraire* will be called *wages*.

The current contract price of capital-services in terms of *numéraire* will be called the *interest charge* [l'*intérêt*]. [3]

Thus, thanks to the distinction we have drawn between capital and income and thanks to our definition of the entrepreneur, we have immediately the concepts of productive services, of a market for these services, of effective offer and demand on this market and finally of a current price resulting from this offer and demand. Later on, we shall discuss the fruitless efforts made by French and English economists to determine rent, wages and interest, that is to say, the price of productive services, without reference to any market for these services.[4]

186. The second market is the *products market*. Here the entrepreneurs appear as sellers, and the land-owners, labourers and capitalists as buyers of products. These products are exchanged, like services, with the aid of a *numéraire* and in accordance with the mechanism of free competition. For every product a price is cried in terms of the *numéraire*. If at this price effective demand exceeds effective offer, the land-owners, labourers and capitalists will bid against one another and the price will rise. If effective offer exceeds effective demand, the entrepreneurs will underbid each other, and the price will fall. The current price of each product is the one at which effective demand equals effective offer.

Thus we have, in this connection also, a market, offer and demand, and a current price for products.

187. It should be noted that these conceptions are in exact conformity with the facts as revealed by observation and experience.
Thanks to the intervention of money, the two markets, one for services and the other for products, are as completely distinct from each
other in the real world as they are in our scientific analysis. In each
of these markets purchases and sales take place according to the
mechanism of competitive bidding. When you go to a shoe manufacturer to buy a pair of shoes he acts as an entrepreneur delivering
the product and receiving the money. The transaction takes place
on the market for products. If more products are demanded than
supplied,[5] another consumer will outbid you; if more products are
supplied than demanded another producer will underbid your shoe
manufacturer. Behind the scenes a workman sets his price for making
a pair of shoes; and the manufacturer again acts as an entrepreneur,
purchasing the productive service and paying out money for it. This
transaction takes place on the market for services. If more labour is
demanded than offered another entrepreneur will outbid your shoe
manufacturer; and if more labour is offered than demanded another
workman will offer his services at a lower price. Although these two
markets are distinct, they are, nevertheless, closely related to each
other, for it is with the money the land-owners, labourers and
capitalists receive in the market for their productive services that they
go as consumers to the other market to buy products; and, on the
other hand, it is with the money the entrepreneurs receive in the
market for their products that they go as producers to the services
market to buy productive services.

188. Equilibrium in production, which implies equilibrium in
exchange, can now be easily defined. First, it is a state in which the
effective demand and offer of productive services are equal and
there is a stationary current price in the market for these services.
Secondly, it is a state in which the effective demand and supply of
products are also equal and there is a stationary current price in
the products market. Finally, it is a state in which the selling prices
of products equal the costs of the productive services that enter into
them. The first two conditions relate to equilibrium in exchange; the
third to equilibrium in production.

Equilibrium in production, like equilibrium in exchange, is an
ideal and not a real state. It never happens in the real world that the
selling price of any given product is absolutely equal to the cost of
the productive services that enter into that product, or that the
effective demand and supply of services or products are absolutely
equal. Yet equilibrium is the normal state, in the sense that it is the
state towards which things spontaneously tend under a régime of free
competition in exchange and in production. In fact, under free

competition, if the selling price of a product exceeds the cost of the productive services for certain firms and a *profit* results, entrepreneurs will flow towards this branch of production or expand their output, so that the quantity of the product [on the market] will increase, its price will fall, and the difference between price and cost will be reduced; and, if [on the contrary], the cost of the productive services exceeds the selling price for certain firms, so that a *loss* results, entrepreneurs will leave this branch of production or curtail their output, so that the quantity of the product [on the market] will decrease, its price will rise and the difference between price and cost will again be reduced. It is to be observed, however, that although the multiplicity of firms conduces to equilibrium in production, such multiplicity is not absolutely necessary in order to bring about this equilibrium, for, theoretically, one entrepreneur alone might do so, if he bought his services and sold his products by auction, and if, in addition, he always decreased his output in case of loss and always increased it in case of a profit.[d] That is not all, for we now see that the desire to avoid losses and to make profits is the mainspring of the entrepreneur's actions in demanding productive services and offering products for sale, just as we saw earlier that the desire to obtain maximum satisfaction was the mainspring of the actions of land-owners, labourers and capitalists in offering productive services and in demanding products. One final observation: as we have shown in §179, with exchange and production in a state of equilibrium we may abstract, if not from *numéraire*, at least from money, provided that the land-owners, labourers and capitalists receive from the entrepreneurs a certain quantity of products in the form of rent, wages and interest in exchange for a certain quantity of productive services in the form of land-services, labour and capital-services. Assuming equilibrium, we may even go so far as to abstract from entrepreneurs and simply consider the productive services as being, in a certain sense, exchanged directly for one another, instead of being exchanged first against products, and then against productive services. It was Bastiat's idea that, in final analysis, services are exchanged against services, but he meant only personal services, while we have in mind the services of land, persons and capital goods.

Thus, in a state of equilibrium in production, entrepreneurs make neither profit nor loss ['les entrepreneurs ne font ni bénéfice ni perte'].[6] They make their living not as entrepreneurs, but as land-owners, labourers or capitalists in their own or other businesses. In my opinion, rational bookkeeping requires that an entrepreneur who owns the land which he works or occupies, who participates in the management of his firm and who has his own funds invested in the business, ought to charge to business expense and credit to his own account [the corresponding] rent, wages and interest charges calculated according to the going market prices of productive services. In this way he earns his living without necessarily making any profits or suffering any losses as an entrepreneur. Surely, it must be evident that, if he gets a higher or lower price for his productive services in his own business than he can get elsewhere, then the difference represents a profit or a loss.[6]

Lesson 19

THE ENTREPRENEUR. BUSINESS ACCOUNTING AND INVENTORY[1]

189. The entrepreneur is, as we have seen, a person (natural or corporate) who buys raw materials from other entrepreneurs, then leases land from land-owners on payment of a rent, hires the personal faculties of workers on payment of wages, borrows capital from capitalists on payment of interest charges and, finally, having applied certain productive services to the raw materials, sells the resulting product on his own account. The agricultural entrepreneur buys seed, fertilizers and unfattened livestock, then leases land and farm buildings, rents farm implements, employs farm labourers, harvesters and cattle-hands, and finally sells his crops and fattened livestock. The industrial entrepreneur buys textile fibres or crude metals, then leases factories and workshops, rents machines and tools, employs spinners or metal workers and mechanics, and finally sells his manufactured products, such as fabrics or metal wares. The commercial entrepreneur buys merchandise wholesale, then leases warehouses and shops, employs clerks and travelling salesmen, and finally sells his merchandise retail. Whenever entrepreneurs, of whatever category, sell their products or merchandise at a price higher than the cost of the raw materials, rent, wages and interest charges, they make a profit; and whenever they sell their products or merchandise at a lower price, they incur a loss. This is the alternative that the entrepreneur characteristically faces in the performance of his function.

190. The foregoing definition, when considered in relation to our table of elements of production (§178), explains the table and shows the reason for it. The capital goods classified under the first, second and third headings, i.e. the capital goods that yield directly consumable services, are those found in the possession of land-owners, workers and capitalists in their capacity as consumers. The capital goods classified under the fourth, fifth and sixth headings, i.e. the capital goods that yield productive services, are those found in the possession of entrepreneurs. In this way it is always possible to tell whether a service is a directly consumable service or a productive service. For example, the land-services of public parks, the labour of public officials and the capital-services of public edifices are not productive services but directly consumable services, because the State is not an entrepreneur trying to sell products at a price at least

227

equal to their cost of production, but a consumer, acting through the power of taxation in the place of land-owners, workers and capitalists, and purchasing services and products in their stead.

Similarly, among the items of income, those classified under the eighth heading are found in the hands of consumers; and those classified under the ninth heading in the possession of entrepreneurs. This, however, calls for a very important comment.

Landed capital and personal capital are hired in kind. The land-owner lets his land and the worker hires out his personal faculties for a year, a month, or a day, and at the end of the contracted period they regain possession of what was let or hired out. Capital goods, proper, apart from buildings and a few special kinds of furnishings and machines, are hired out not in kind, but in money. The capitalist accumulates his capital by successive savings and lends money to the entrepreneur for a given period; the entrepreneur converts this money into capital proper and at the expiration of the contract he returns the money to the capitalist. This operation constitutes *credit*. The result is that the income goods consisting of raw materials classified under the ninth heading and the capital goods classified under the sixth heading can be considered as forming part of the capital which the entrepreneur borrows. Capital goods proper are usually called *fixed capital*,[2] which consists of the sum total of all those things that are used more than once in production. The term *circulating* or *working capital* is used to designate raw materials along with the capital goods classified under the seventh heading and the new income goods classified under the tenth heading. It consists of the sum total of all those things that are not used more than once in production.

The cash classified under the eleventh heading is held by consumers, while cash classified under the twelfth heading forms part of the working capital of entrepreneurs. The savings classified under the thirteenth heading are held by consumers and represent exactly the excess of income over consumption.

191. The profit and loss position of an entrepreneur can be computed at any moment from the statement of account shown in his books after taking into consideration his inventory of raw materials and finished goods. Hence this is a suitable place to discuss the methods of bookkeeping and of making inventories in business. These methods, which are derived from everyday experience, will be found to be completely in harmony with our earlier concepts, thus proving that our theory of production is indeed founded on reality. I shall first explain briefly the principles of double entry bookkeeping.

192. As an entrepreneur I begin with a till into which I put money

whenever I receive it, and from which I take cash whenever I need any for my expenses. There is thus a double flow of money to and from this till: one of money received and the other of money paid out. It is clear, moreover, that the quantity of money in this till at any given moment is always equal to the difference between the quantity of money put in and the quantity of money paid out. Granting this, if I take a blank page in an account book and head it *Cash*; if I enter in a column on one side of the page, on the left for example, the various amounts that I have successively put into my till; if I enter in a like column on the other side of the page, the right side in this case, the various amounts that I have successively taken out, then the difference between the total on the left and the total on the right must always represent exactly the cash on hand. These two totals may be equal and their difference zero—which happens when the till is empty; but the right-hand total can never be greater than the left. The two columns taken together make up what is called the *Cash Account*. The total on the left is usually called the *debit* ['*doit* ou *débit*'], while that on the right is called the *credit* ['*avoir* ou *crédit*'] of the Cash Account. The difference between the two, which may be positive or zero but never negative, is called the *balance* of the Cash Account.

193. Up to this point we have not encountered anything resembling double entry bookkeeping; but we are coming to that now.

The money which enters my till comes either from capitalists who have lent it to me or from consumers who have bought products from me, and the money which leaves my till will be converted either into fixed capital or working capital. Now, I am supposing that whenever I enter on the debit side of my Cash Account an amount put into my till I always wish to record where it comes from and that similarly, whenever I enter on the credit side of my Cash Account an amount taken out of my till, I always wish to record where it is going. Let us see how I do this. For instance, the first money that I am going to put into my till is a sum lent to me by my friend named Martin to whom I promise repayment in instalments over a period of two or three years. How shall I indicate that this sum comes from Martin? Very simply. Immediately following the entry to the debit of Cash, I write these words: *To Capitalist* or *To Martin*. But if I am going to do this properly, I cannot stop there. I take another blank page in my account book and I write at the top: *Capitalist* or *Martin*; and then, after entering the amount on the debit or left side of the page of the Cash Account, I enter the same amount on the credit or right side of the page of Capitalist's or Martin's account; and to the left of the amount so credited I write the words: *By Cash*. So much for this step. But, as might even now be surmised, there is another step to be taken when, instead of putting money into the till, I take it out to pay an instalment on what I owe to my capitalist Martin. I enter this sum to the credit of my Cash Account with the notation: *By Capitalist* or *By Martin*, and at the same time I write it to the debit of Martin's account with the notation: *To Cash*. Consequently, just as the debit balance of the *Cash Account* at all times furnishes information concerning the cash I have on hand, so also the credit balance of Martin's account always keeps me informed on another matter which I must constantly keep in view, namely the amount of money which I still owe to my capitalist Martin.

It is the same for all other sums that I withdraw from or put into my till. If, for example, I take out cash in order to install a machine in my workshop, that machine becomes part of what I have called fixed capital, the amount of which I must be in a position to ascertain rapidly at all times; therefore, I open an account: *Fixed Assets*,[2] and simultaneously enter the sum withdrawn to the credit of Cash with the notation: *By Fixed Assets* and to the debit of Fixed Assets with the notation: *To Cash*. I deal in the same way with items of working capital.[a] If I take money out of the till to buy raw materials or merchandise wholesale, or to pay my rent or my workers, that is, generally speaking, to pay rent, wages and interest charges, I enter the sum withdrawn simultaneously to the credit of Cash and to the debit of *Working Capital*. And if I put into my till any proceeds from the sale of my products, I enter the sum so received to the debit of the Cash Account and to the credit of the Working Capital Account. In current accounting practice, the Working Capital Account has been replaced by two others: a *Merchandise Account* which is charged with raw materials and merchandise purchased wholesale, and a *General Expenses Account* which is charged with rent, wages and interest charges. This or any other subdivision may be made as convenience dictates, but, as we shall see presently, all these special accounts which replace the general Working Capital Account, will have to be combined when the inventory is made.

This is double entry bookkeeping. Its cardinal principle *is never to enter a sum to the debit or credit of an account without simultaneously entering the amount to the credit or debit of some other account*. It follows that the total of the debit balances, or *assets*, is always equal to the total of the credit balances, or *liabilities*. The book which contains entries made primarily in the order of accounts and secondarily in the order of dates is called the *Ledger* ['*Grand-livre*']. It is accompanied by another record containing the same entries primarily in the order of dates and secondarily in the order of accounts, known as the *Journal*.

194. There are thus four accounts essential to every business: a Cash Account, which is sometimes debited and sometimes credited; a Capitalist Account [liability] which may be divided into as many sub-accounts as there are capitalists investing money in the business; a Fixed Assets Account which is generally debited; and a Working Capital Account, which is sometimes debited and sometimes credited. The debit side of the Fixed Assets Account represents the money value of the fixed capital; and the debit side of the Working Capital Account represents the money value of the unrealized circulating capital. A question very much to the fore these days is whether double entry bookkeeping which we have described above is or is not as suitable for use in agriculture as it is in industry, commerce and banking. The real issue is whether or not agriculture is an industry which consists in applying land-services, labour and capital-services to raw materials in order to obtain products. If so, and this most certainly is the case, then unquestionably double entry book-keeping can be used in agricultural enterprises just as well as in industrial, commercial and financial enterprises. And if people have not succeeded up to now in making use of double entry book-keeping in agriculture, it is only because they do not know how to open the various accounts on a rational basis. We have here a striking example of the way in which theory and practice owe it to each other to be of mutual assistance, for surely, industrial practice, when translated into accounting terms, can help enormously in the formulation of a theory of production; and this theory, once elaborated, can be equally helpful in explaining agricultural practice in terms of accounting.[b]

195. We now have to explain the method of making business inventories and to show how an entrepreneur's profit or loss position is established. The best way of going about this will be to take an example which conforms to the usages and terminology of modern accounting.

Suppose, then, that I am an entrepreneur in the business of cabinet making. I started with 3,000 francs that I had saved up myself and 7,000 francs lent to me by relatives and friends who were interested and had confidence in me. These persons and I signed a private deed according to which they agreed to let me have their 7,000 francs for ten years while I agreed to pay them 5 per cent interest per annum. They have thus become [so to speak] my *"silent partners"* ['*commanditaires*']; and I, for my part, am my own "silent partner" ['commanditaire'] and ought to pay myself 5 per cent on my 3,000 francs.[3] When I put the 10,000 francs into my till, I entered that amount both to the debit of my Cash Account and to the credit of my *Capitalist* Account ['compte *Commandite*']. If the "silent partners" were not obliged to pay the whole sum at once or if they did not all pay at the same time, I should have had to open separate accounts A, B, C, etc.

Having done this, I rented a plot of ground at 500 francs a year and on it I had a workshop built which I equipped with machines, work-benches and lathes. The total cost of the workshop and equipment was 5,000 francs which I paid out in cash. Upon withdrawing these 5,000 francs from my till, I credited Cash 5,000 francs and debited my *Fixed Assets* Account 5,000 francs.

Then I bought lumber, cloth, etc., for 2,000 francs, and, consequently, credited this amount to Cash, while debiting it to *Merchandise*.

In addition, I paid out 500 francs for interest on the capital invested, 500 francs for the lease of my land and 2,000 francs for wages. I credited Cash 3,000 francs and debited *General Expenses* 3,000 francs.

Now, in return for all these disbursements, I had pieces of woodwork and furniture which I made to order and delivered. I received for them a cash payment of 6,000 francs, which I put into my till, debiting Cash 6,000 francs and crediting Merchandise the same amount.

196. Having reached this point, I make my inventory. In order to simplify the problem as much as possible, I assume that I have no merchandise left in stock, neither raw materials nor products. Although I have no more merchandise, still the Merchandise Account is not balanced. It is debited with 2,000 francs to Cash, and credited with 6,000 francs by Cash. The difference is 4,000 francs. Whence this difference? The answer is clear. This difference results from the fact that I sold my merchandise for more than I paid for it. In fact, that is what I set out to do. I bought lumber, cloth and other raw materials, and I sold pieces of wood-work, furniture and other manufactured products. Surely, it is not only the outlay on raw materials that I must get back from the sales of my finished goods; it is also essential that I recover the labour cost as well as my overhead expenses and have a certain profit left over besides. Hence, the above-mentioned difference of 4,000 francs covers my general expenses amounting to 3,000 francs and leaves me with a profit of 1,000 francs. And consequently, I first close the General Expenses Account to Merchandise, and then I close the Merchandise Account, which must be balanced since there is no merchandise left in stock, by crediting 1,000 francs to a *Profit and Loss* Account which appears among the liabilities. If I had sustained a loss, this Profit and Loss Account would appear among the assets as a debit balance.

197. Once this has been done, my accounts should balance as follows.

The Cash Account has received 16,000 francs and has provided 10,000 francs. It has a debit balance of 6,000 francs.

The Capitalist Account has provided 10,000 francs. It has a credit balance of 10,000 francs.

The Fixed Assets Account has been debited with 5,000 francs, and has a debit balance of 5,000 francs.

The Merchandise Account has been debited with 6,000 francs and credited with a like amount. It shows no balance.

The General Expenses Account has received debits of 3,000 francs and has credits of 3,000 francs. It is balanced.

The Profit and Loss Account shows a profit, i.e. a credit balance, of 1,000 francs.

Thus to summarize, my Balance Sheet stands as follows:

ASSETS (composed of all accounts with a debit balance)

		Francs
Cash	. . . . .	6,000
Fixed Assets	. . . .	5,000
Total	. .	11,000

LIABILITIES (composed of all accounts with a credit balance)

		Francs
Capitalist	. . . .	10,000
Profit and Loss	. . .	1,000
Same Total	.	11,000

I have made a Profit of 1,000 francs and begin the new accounting period with a capital of 11,000 francs instead of 10,000 francs, i.e. with 5,000 francs in fixed capital and 6,000 francs in working capital.

198. We have made things as simple as possible. In practice, however, there are certain complications of normal and not exceptional character to which we must now call attention.

(1) The entries are neither found nor made in the aggregate, but always piecemeal. When I pay out 5,000 francs for fixed capital, or 2,000 francs for merchandise, or 3,000 francs for general expenses and when I receive 6,000 francs for merchandise sold, these things are not done in a single transaction, but in a series of transactions.

(2) I do not necessarily sell for cash, but on credit. And when I sell on credit to customers L, M and N, instead of crediting the Merchandise Account and debiting Cash, I credit Merchandise and

debit Messrs. L, M and N; and later, when they pay, I credit the accounts of L, M and N and debit Cash. I therefore normally have a certain number of *Customers'* Debtor Accounts.

(3) That is not all. My customers L, M and N, after enjoying credit on my books for a certain time, do not usually settle their accounts in cash, but either in promissory notes which they make payable to me, or in bills of exchange which I draw on them and which they accept. When I receive these documents, instead of crediting L, M and N's accounts with offsetting debits to Cash, I credit their accounts and debit a *Bills Receivable* Account; and later when I make the collections I credit the Bills Receivable Account by debiting Cash. I have therefore under normal conditions a Bills Receivable Account or *Portfolio* Account with a debit balance ['Portefeuille débiteur']. This account is analogous to the Cash Account, inasmuch as the difference between the debit and the credit sides always corresponds exactly to the sum of notes or bills of exchange in my portfolio.

(4) There is still more to this. Ordinarily, I do not collect my bills, but I negotiate them with a banker who discounts them before maturity. When I negotiate bills in this way, instead of crediting Bills Receivable and debiting Cash, I credit Bills Receivable with an offsetting debit to my *Bank* Account, and later credit my Bank Account against debits of my Cash Account when my banker remits the funds. The discount, which is really interest, is naturally carried to the debit of General Expenses.

(5) Moreover, I do not usually buy for cash, but on credit. And when I buy on credit from suppliers X, Y and Z, instead of debiting the Merchandise Account and crediting Cash, I debit Merchandise and credit X, Y and Z's accounts; and then later I debit these accounts and credit Cash when I pay X, Y and Z. Therefore, under normal conditions I have a certain number of *Suppliers'* Creditor Accounts.

(6) Here again, after a certain period of book credit, I pay the bills of my suppliers X, Y and Z not in cash, but either in promissory notes which I make payable to them or in bills of exchange which they draw on me and which I accept. And then, when I deliver these documents to my creditors, instead of debiting X, Y and Z's accounts with offsetting credits to Cash, I debit their accounts and credit a *Bills Payable* Account, leaving it until later to debit the Bills Payable Account with credits to Cash when I pay these notes and bills. Thus, in the normal course of events, I also have a credit account under Bills Payable.

(7) Finally, I never let myself run completely out of stock, whether of raw materials or products, at my inventory dates. If I did, it would mean that at the end of each accounting period I should be

interrupting the operation of my business, which would be entirely useless, if not wasteful. Consequently, as I sell furniture I constantly replenish my stock of lumber and cloth. This is the merchandise of which I make an inventory. I always close my General Expenses Account by debiting to Merchandise; but instead of closing my Merchandise Account, I simply transfer a portion of the account to the Profit and Loss Account in such a way as to leave the Merchandise Account with a debit balance exactly equal to the inventoried merchandise. This is how I do it. Let M_d and M_c be respectively the amounts carried to the debit and credit of the Merchandise Account; let F be the debit balance of the General Expenses Account and I the money value of the Inventory. When I make a profit I must add to M_d+F on the debit side of my Merchandise Account a sum P such that

$$(M_d+F+P)-M_c=I,$$

for then the Merchandise Account must always have a debit balance of I and the Profit and Loss Account a credit balance of P. In case of a loss, I must add to M_c of the Merchandise Account an amount P such that

$$(M_d+F)-(M_c+P)=I,$$

for the Merchandise Account must always have a debit balance of I, and the Profit and Loss Account a debit balance of P. Both summations are given by a single equation

$$M_d+F-I\pm P=M_c,$$

which equation may be directly deduced from the fact that the money value of the raw materials bought plus disbursements for the general expenses, less [the money value of] the unused raw materials and the products in stock, plus or minus the profit or loss, is equal to the money value of the products sold.

According to this, the Customers' Debtor Accounts, the Bills Receivable, the Bank Account and the Merchandise Inventory are added to Cash and to Fixed Assets to make up the Assets; while the Suppliers' Creditor Accounts and the Bills Payable Account are added to the Capitalist Account and the Profit and Loss Account to make up the Liabilities. These additional items give us the ordinary balance sheet of an industrial enterprise. Balance sheets of agricultural, commercial and financial enterprises can be established along exactly analogous lines.

199. We have seen how, in principle, an entrepreneur can find out at any moment from an inventory whether he is making a profit or a loss. Having established our definitions both in theory and in

practice, we now are going to suppose that our entrepreneurs make neither profit nor loss; and we shall leave out of consideration, as we have said in §179, not only the entrepreneurs' working capital in the form of raw materials, new capital goods, new income goods and cash on hand, but also the consumers' working capital in the form of accumulations of income goods, cash and money savings. And then we shall show how current prices of products and of services are mathematically determined in a state of equilibrium.[e]

Lesson 20

PRODUCTION EQUATIONS

200. Now let us take up the services[a] classified under the first six headings in §178, for, after we have made all the aforementioned simplifications, these services still remain the essential data of our problem. Let us designate these services, which are to be made available over a certain period of time,[b] by the letters (T), (T′) (T″)... corresponding to different kinds of land, (P), (P′), (P″)... corresponding to different kinds of persons, (K), (K′), (K″)... corresponding to different kinds of capital goods. We shall suppose the quantities of the services to be measured in the following two types of units: (1) in units of natural or artificial capital, like a hectare of land, an individual person, or a piece of capital proper; and (2) in time units, like a day. Thus we have a certain quantity of land-service per day from a hectare of such and such a piece of land; a certain quantity of labour per day from such and such a person; a certain quantity of capital-service per day from such and such a capital good. Let the kinds of these services be *n* in number.

By means of the services just defined, it is possible to manufacture the products (A), (B), (C), (D)... for consumption during the same period of time.[c] This production can take place either directly or via a preliminary elaboration of raw materials; in other words, it is the result either of a combination of nothing but land-services, labour and capital-services or of an application of these services to raw materials. It will be seen, however, that the second case is reducible to the first. Let the kinds of products thus manufactured be *m* in number.

201. Final products possess a utility for each individual which we may express by a want or utility equation of the familiar form $r=\phi(q)$ (§75). In addition, the services themselves have a direct utility for each individual. Not only may anyone, at will, either hire out or keep for himself all or part of the services of his own land, personal faculties and capital, but he may, if he so desires, acquire these services not as an entrepreneur in order to convert them into products, but as a consumer in order to use them directly, that is to say, in order to use them as consumers' services and not as productive services. This is what we had in mind when we made a separate category of the services classified under the first three headings in §178 and distinguished them from those classified under the fourth, fifth and sixth headings. Services, then, are also commodities the

237

utility of which can be expressed for each individual by a want or utility equation of the form $r = \phi(q)$.

So much being understood, let us single out an individual who has at his disposal q_t of (T), q_p of (P), q_k of (K).... And let $r = \phi_t(q)$, $r = \phi_p(q)$, $r = \phi_k(q)$... $r = \phi_a(q)$, $r = \phi_b(q)$, $r = \phi_c(q)$, $r = \phi_d(q)$... be this individual's want or utility equations for the services (T), (P), (K)... and the products (A), (B), (C), (D)... during a certain period of time. Let $p_t, p_p, p_k ... p_b, p_c, p_d ...$ be the current prices of the services and products in terms of (A). Let $o_t, o_p, o_k ...$ be the quantities of the services which our individual effectively offers at these prices. These quantities can be either positive when they represent quantities offered or negative when they represent quantities demanded. And finally let $d_a, d_b, d_c, d_d ...$ be the quantities of the products which our individual effectively demands at these same equilibrium prices. Until we come to Part V, we shall abstract from depreciation of existing capital proper, and also from saving for the purpose of creating new capital goods. We may, then, start with the following equation relating the above quantities and prices:

$$o_t p_t + o_p p_p + o_k p_k + ... = d_a + d_b p_b + d_c p_c + d_d p_d + ...$$

From the condition of maximum satisfaction (§80), which obviously determines the positive or negative offer of services and the demand for products, we have, in addition, the following equations relating the same quantities and prices:[1]

$$\phi_t(q_t - o_t) = p_t \phi_a(d_a),$$
$$\phi_p(q_p - o_p) = p_p \phi_a(d_a),$$
$$\phi_k(q_k - o_k) = p_k \phi_a(d_a),$$
. . . .
$$\phi_b(d_b) = p_b \phi_a(d_a),$$
$$\phi_c(d_c) = p_c \phi_a(d_a),$$
$$\phi_d(d_d) = p_d \phi_a(d_a),$$
. . . .

constituting in all $n + m - 1$ equations, which together with the preceding equation give us a system of $n + m$ equations. We can suppose that $n + m - 1$ of the unknowns $o_t, o_p, o_k ... d_a, d_b, d_c, d_d ...$ are eliminated one after another from these equations so that we are left with only one equation expressing the $(n + m)$th unknown as a function of the prices $p_t, p_p, p_k ... p_b, p_c, p_d ....$[2] We should then have the following equations of offer (or demand) of (T), (P), (K)...

$$o_t = f_t(p_t, p_p, p_k ... p_b, p_c, p_d ...),$$
$$o_p = f_p(p_t, p_p, p_k ... p_b, p_c, p_d ...),$$
$$o_k = f_k(p_t, p_p, p_k ... p_b, p_c, p_d ...),$$
. . . .

and the following equations of demand for (B), (C), (D)...

$$d_b = f_b(p_t, p_p, p_k \cdots p_b, p_c, p_d \cdots),$$
$$d_c = f_c(p_t, p_p, p_k \cdots p_b, p_c, p_d \cdots),$$
$$d_d = f_d(p_t, p_p, p_k \cdots p_b, p_c, p_d \cdots),$$

. . . .

The demand for (A) is given by the equation

$$d_a = o_t p_t + o_p p_p + o_k p_k + \ldots - (d_b p_b + d_c p_c + d_d p_d + \ldots).$$

202. In the same way, we could derive for all the other holders of services their individual offer and demand equations for services and their individual demand equations for products. Now, let $O_t, O_p, O_k \ldots$ designate the sum total of the several offers of services, i.e. the excess of the positive $o_t, o_p, o_k \ldots$'s over the negative $o_t, o_p, o_k \ldots$'s;[d] let $D_a, D_b, D_c, D_d \ldots$ designate the sum total of the several demands for products; and let $F_t, F_p, F_k \ldots F_b, F_c, F_d \ldots$ designate the sums of the several functions $f_t, f_p, f_k \ldots f_b, f_c, f_d \ldots$. Provided that suitable restrictions, like those indicated in the theory of exchange (§§119–121), are placed on the functions in cases where offer equals quantity possessed, we have, at once, the following system of n equations of total offer of services:[e]

$$O_t = F_t(p_t, p_p, p_k \cdots p_b, p_c, p_d \cdots),$$
$$O_p = F_p(p_t, p_p, p_k \cdots p_b, p_c, p_d \cdots), \qquad ..(1)$$
$$O_k = F_k(p_t, p_p, p_k \cdots p_b, p_c, p_d \cdots),$$

. . . .

and the following system of m equations of total demand for the products:

$$D_b = F_b(p_t, p_p, p_k \cdots p_b, p_c, p_d \cdots),$$
$$D_c = F_c(p_t, p_p, p_k \cdots p_b, p_c, p_d \cdots), \qquad ..(2)$$
$$D_d = F_d(p_t, p_p, p_k \cdots p_b, p_c, p_d \cdots),$$

. . . .

$$D_a = O_t p_t + O_p p_p + O_k p_k + \ldots - (D_b p_b + D_c p_c + D_d p_d + \ldots);$$

in all $n+m$ equations required for the determination of our unknowns.

203. Furthermore, let $a_t, a_p, a_k \ldots b_t, b_p, b_k \ldots c_t, c_p, c_k \ldots d_t, d_p, d_k \ldots$ designate the *coefficients of production*, that is to say, the quantities of each of the productive services (T), (P), (K)... which enter into the production of one unit of each of the products (A), (B), (C), (D).... For determining the unknown quantities we now have the following two systems:

$$a_t D_a + b_t D_b + c_t D_c + d_t D_a + \ldots = O_t,$$
$$a_p D_a + b_p D_b + c_p D_c + d_p D_a + \ldots = O_p, \qquad ..(3)$$
$$a_k D_a + b_k D_b + c_k D_c + d_k D_a + \ldots = O_k,$$

. . . .

the first system, consisting of n equations expressing the fact that *the quantities of productive services used are equal to the quantities effectively offered*; and

$$a_t p_t + a_p p_p + a_k p_k + \ldots = 1,$$
$$b_t p_t + b_p p_p + b_k p_k + \ldots = p_b,$$
$$c_t p_t + c_p p_p + c_k p_k + \ldots = p_c, \qquad ..(4)$$
$$d_t p_t + d_p p_p + d_k p_k + \ldots = p_d,$$

. . . .

the second, consisting of m equations expressing the fact that *the selling prices of the products are equal to the cost of the productive services* employed in their manufacture.

204. We are evidently assuming the coefficients a_t, a_p, $a_k \ldots b_t$, b_p, $b_k \ldots c_t$, c_p, $c_k \ldots d_t$, d_p, $d_k \ldots$ to be determined a priori.[3] In reality they are not determined in this way, for in the making of a product, it is possible to employ more or less of some productive services, say land-services, provided that correspondingly less or more of other productive services, say labour or capital services, are employed. The respective quantities of each of the productive services which thus enter into the making of a single unit of each of the products are determined, along with the prices of the productive services, by the condition that the cost of production of the products be a minimum. We shall later express this condition by a system of as many equations as there are coefficients of production to be determined.[1] For the present, we shall neglect this condition in the interest of greater simplicity, and we shall suppose, instead, that the above coefficients figure among the knowns rather than the unknowns of the problem.

In making this assumption, we are neglecting another matter, namely that of the distinction between fixed and variable costs in business. But since we are assuming that entrepreneurs make neither profit nor loss, we may as well assume that they are also manufacturing equal quantities of products, in which case costs of all kinds may be considered as variable ['proportionnels'].[4]

205. We shall now proceed, as we have already indicated [in §200], to reduce the case of the application of raw materials to the case of the direct combination of productive services alone. Indeed, we must proceed in this manner, because raw materials are themselves products which are obtained either by the exclusive

application of productive services alone or by the application of these services to other raw materials, which were in turn obtained by similar applications to still prior raw materials, and so on.

For example, if a unit of the product (B) is obtained by the application of quantities β_t of (T), β_p of (P), β_k of (K)... to a quantity β_m of the raw material (M), then the cost of production of (B), p_b, is given by the equation

$$p_b = \beta_t p_t + \beta_p p_p + \beta_k p_k + \ldots + \beta_m p_m,$$

where p_m is the cost of production of (M). But since the raw material (M) is itself a product, a unit of which is obtained by combining m_t of (T), m_p of (P), m_k of (K)... with one another, the cost of production of (M), p_m, is given by the equation

$$p_m = m_t p_t + m_p p_p + m_k p_k + \ldots.$$

Substituting this value of p_m in the preceding equation, we have

$$p_b = (\beta_t + \beta_m m_t) p_t + (\beta_p + \beta_m m_p) p_p + (\beta_k + \beta_m m_k) p_k + \ldots,$$

which reduces to the second equation of system (4) if we set

$$\beta_t + \beta_m m_t = b_t, \quad \beta_p + \beta_m m_p = b_p, \quad \beta_k + \beta_m m_k = b_k \ldots.$$

We see at once what would need to be done if the raw material (M) had been obtained, not by a combination of productive services alone, but by the application of productive services to some other raw material.

206. We have thus, in all, $2m+2n$ equations. But these $2m+2n$ reduce to $2m+2n-1$ equations. For example, if we multiply both sides of the n equations of system (3) in succession by $p_t, p_p, p_k \ldots$ respectively, and if we multiply both sides of the m equations of system (4) in succession by $D_a, D_b, D_c, D_d \ldots$ respectively, and then add the equations of each system separately, we obtain two equations, the left-hand sides of which are identical, so that the right-hand sides are equal and we have the equation

$$O_t p_t + O_p p_p + O_k p_k + \ldots = D_a + D_b p_b + D_c p_c + D_d p_d + \ldots$$

which is none other than the mth equation of system (2). We can either eliminate this equation or, if we wish, retain it, provided we eliminate some other equation, say the first of system (4). At all events, in a state of general equilibrium, there will remain $2m+2n-1$ equations to determine $2m+2n-1$ unknowns which are: (1) the n total quantities of services offered, (2) the n prices of these services, (3) the m total quantities of the products demanded and (4) the $m-1$ prices of these products in terms of the mth. It still remains to be shown that, for equilibrium in production as for equilibrium in exchange, this problem to which we have given a theoretical solution

is the same problem which is solved in practice in the market
by the mechanism of free competition.[g]

207. We propose to establish equilibrium in production *ab ovo*,[5]
just as we established equilibrium in exchange, that is to say, by
assuming the data of the problem to be any data whatsoever and yet
invariable over a certain period of time, except that we may later
suppose them to change in order to study the effects of such changes.
But the process of groping ['tâtonnement'] in production entails a
complication which was not present in the case of exchange.

In exchange, [the total existing quantities of] commodities do not
undergo any change. When a price is cried, and the effective demand
and offer corresponding to this price are not equal, another price is
cried for which there is another corresponding effective demand and
offer. In production, productive services are transformed into
products. After certain prices for services have been cried and
certain quantities of products have been manufactured, if these
prices and quantities are not the equilibrium prices and quantities,
it will be necessary not only to cry new prices but also to manufacture
revised quantities of products.[h] In order to work out as rigorous
a description of the process of groping [towards equilibrium] in
production as we did in exchange [§§125–130] and yet take
this additional circumstance into account, we have only to imagine,
on the one hand, that entrepreneurs use *tickets* ['*bons*'][6] to represent the successive quantities of *products* which are first determined
at random and then increased or decreased according as there is an
excess of selling price over cost of production or vice versa, until
selling price and cost are equal; and, on the other hand, that land-
owners, workers and capitalists also use *tickets* to represent the
successive quantities of *services* [which they offer] at prices first cried
at random and then raised or lowered according as there is an excess
of demand over offer or vice versa, until the two become equal.[i]

There is still another complication. Once the equilibrium has been
established in principle, exchange can take place immediately. Production, however, requires a certain lapse of time. We shall resolve
the second difficulty purely and simply by ignoring the time element
at this point. And later on, in Part VI, we shall bring in *circulating
capital* and *money* and thereby make it possible for productive
services to be transformed into products instantaneously, provided
that the consumers pay the interest charges on the capital required
for this sort of transformation.

Thus, equilibrium in production will first be established *in principle*.
Then it will be established *effectively* through the reciprocal exchange
between services employed and products manufactured *within a given
period of time* during which *no change in the data is allowed*.

SOLUTION OF THE EQUATIONS OF PRODUCTION. THE LAW OF THE ESTABLISHMENT OF THE PRICES OF PRODUCTS AND SERVICES

208. Let us suppose that we come to a market where the n prices p'_t, p'_p, p'_k... of services and the m quantities of products to be manufactured $\Omega_a, \Omega_b, \Omega_c, \Omega_d$... represented by tickets [§207] are determined at random. To make the following operations easier to grasp, we shall assume, in the first place, that entrepreneurs sell certain quantities of products (A), (B), (C), (D)... to consumers from whom, in turn, they purchase productive services (T), (P), (K)... not in the same amounts but in amounts having the same value, so that $\Omega_a, \Omega_b, \Omega_c, \Omega_d$... are determined in such a way that entrepreneurs make neither profit nor loss. We shall assume, in the second place, that the quantities of productive services purchased by entrepreneurs have not only the same value as the quantities sold by consumers, but are the same in amount, so that p'_t, p'_p, p'_k... are determined in such a way that the effective demand and offer of services are equal. We can now see how this procedure makes it possible to abstract, if not from *numéraire*, at least from money.[a]

It may perhaps be useful to point out that, under the conditions we have laid down, we are assuming for the time being that capital proper is lent in kind. We have already explained in §190, however, that actually, in the real world, capital is lent in cash, because the capitalist accumulates it in that form by saving. Later on we shall consider both the creation and the lending of capital in the form of money.

209. Once the prices p'_t, p'_p, p'_k... of (T), (P), (K)... have been determined, as we have said, at random, certain [unit] *costs of production* p'_a, p'_b, p'_c, p'_d... result for the entrepreneurs, according to equations

$$p'_a = a_t p'_t + a_p p'_p + a_k p'_k + \ldots$$
$$p'_b = b_t p'_t + b_p p'_p + b_k p'_k + \ldots$$
$$p'_c = c_t p'_t + c_p p'_p + c_k p'_k + \ldots$$
$$p'_d = d_t p'_t + d_p p'_p + d_k p'_k + \ldots$$
$$\cdots \cdots \cdots \cdots \cdots \cdots$$

It will no doubt be observed that we were perfectly free to determine p'_t, p'_p, p'_k ... in such a way that $p'_a = 1$. We shall make use of this freedom in the proper place [§§ 218–219], and still later [§259]

243

show that the cost of production of the commodity serving as numéraire tends automatically to equal unity under free competition.[b] For the moment, we shall reason as if the cost of production of (A) could be larger or smaller than its selling price, or equal to it.

Furthermore, the quantities Ω_a, Ω_b, Ω_c, Ω_d... of (A), (B), (C), (D)... which are also determined at random, require for their production certain quantities Δ_t, Δ_p, Δ_k... of (T), (P), (K)..., according to equations

$$\Delta_t = a_t \Omega_a + b_t \Omega_b + c_t \Omega_c + d_t \Omega_d + \ldots$$
$$\Delta_p = a_p \Omega_a + b_p \Omega_b + c_p \Omega_c + d_p \Omega_d + \ldots$$
$$\Delta_k = a_k \Omega_a + b_k \Omega_b + c_k \Omega_c + d_k \Omega_d + \ldots$$
$$\cdot \; \cdot \; \cdot \; \cdot \; \cdot \; \cdot \; \cdot \; \cdot \; \cdot \; \cdot \; \cdot \; \cdot$$

These quantities Ω_a, Ω_b, Ω_c, Ω_d... will be sold by the entrepreneurs in accordance with the mechanism of free competition.[c] First, let us examine the conditions of sale of the products (B), (C), (D).... After that, we shall turn to the conditions of sale of the product (A) which serves as the numéraire.

210. The quantities Ω_b, Ω_c, Ω_d... of (B), (C), (D)... will be sold at certain selling prices π_b, π_c, π_d... according to equations

$$\Omega_b = F_b(p'_t, p'_p, p'_k \ldots \pi_b, \pi_c, \pi_d \ldots),$$
$$\Omega_c = F_c(p'_t, p'_p, p'_k \ldots \pi_b, \pi_c, \pi_d \ldots),$$
$$\Omega_d = F_d(p'_t, p'_p, p'_k \ldots \pi_b, \pi_c, \pi_d \ldots),$$
$$\cdot \; \cdot \; \cdot \; \cdot \; \cdot \; \cdot \; \cdot \; \cdot \; \cdot \; \cdot \; \cdot \; \cdot$$

In fact, the market being ruled by free competition, the products will sell in conformity with the following three conditions: (1) that of the maximum satisfaction of wants, (2) that of a uniform price for each product and for each service and (3) that of general equilibrium (§124). Now, the above system of $m-1$ equations involving $m-1$ unknowns fulfils these three conditions perfectly.

Since the selling prices π_b, π_c, π_d... are, in general, different from the costs of production p'_b, p'_c, p'_d..., the entrepreneurs manufacturing (B), (C), (D)... will consequently make profits or losses, as shown by the differences

$$\Omega_b(\pi_b - p'_b), \qquad \Omega_c(\pi_c - p'_c), \qquad \Omega_d(\pi_d - p'_d) \ldots.$$

Obviously, if Ω_b, Ω_c, Ω_d... are functions of π_b, π_c, π_d..., these latter magnitudes are, ipso facto, functions of the former; and, therefore, by making appropriate adjustments in the quantities to be manufactured of (B), (C), (D)... we shall bring the selling prices of these products into equality with their costs of production.[d]

211. Although we do not know [the specific form of] the functions F_b, F_c, F_d..., still it follows from the very nature of exchange that F_b

will be either an increasing or decreasing function according as the
value of p_b falls or rises, F_c will be either an increasing or decreasing
function according as the value of p_c falls or rises, and so forth. Thus,
if we suppose, for example, that $\pi_b > p'_b$, we can decrease π_b by
increasing Ω_b; and conversely, if we suppose that $\pi_b < p'_b$, we can
increase π_b by decreasing Ω_b. In the same way, when $\pi_c \gtrless p'_c$,
$\pi_d \gtrless p'_d \ldots$, we can decrease or increase π_c, $\pi_d \ldots$ by increasing or
decreasing Ω_c, $\Omega_d \ldots$.

Let Ω'_b, Ω'_c, $\Omega'_d \ldots$ be the quantities of (B), (C), (D)... to be
manufactured for which we have the following equations:

$$\Omega'_b = F_b(p'_t, p'_p, p'_k \ldots p'_b, \pi_c, \pi_d \ldots),$$
$$\Omega'_c = F_c(p'_t, p'_p, p'_k \ldots \pi_b, p'_c, \pi_d \ldots),$$
$$\Omega'_d = F_d(p'_t, p'_p, p'_k \ldots \pi_b, \pi_c, p'_d \ldots),$$

$$\cdot \quad \cdot \quad \cdot \quad \cdot \quad \cdot \quad \cdot \quad \cdot \quad \cdot \quad \cdot \quad \cdot \quad \cdot \quad \cdot$$

When, in the process of groping, these quantities are substituted
for Ω_b, Ω_c, $\Omega_d \ldots$ they will sell, in accordance with the mechanism
of free competition, at prices π'_b, π'_c, $\pi'_d \ldots$, in conformity with the
equations

$$\Omega'_b = F_b(p'_t, p'_p, p'_k \ldots \pi'_b, \pi'_c, \pi'_d \ldots),$$
$$\Omega'_c = F_c(p'_t, p'_p, p'_k \ldots \pi'_b, \pi'_c, \pi'_d \ldots),$$
$$\Omega'_d = F_d(p'_t, p'_p, p'_k \ldots \pi'_b, \pi'_c, \pi'_d \ldots),$$

$$\cdot \quad \cdot \quad \cdot \quad \cdot \quad \cdot \quad \cdot \quad \cdot \quad \cdot \quad \cdot \quad \cdot \quad \cdot \quad \cdot$$

What we must now prove is that π'_b, π'_c, $\pi'_d \ldots$ are closer to equality
with p'_b, p'_c, $p'_d \ldots$ than were π_b, π_c, $\pi_d \ldots$.

212. One of the assumptions underlying the particular process of
groping that we are now considering is that the prices of the services
are fixed and invariable. Hence each party to the exchange has the
same income ['revenu'] in terms of *numéraire*[1]

$$\mathbf{r} = q_t p'_t + q_p p'_p + q_k p'_k + \ldots$$

and he distributes this income over the services and products which
he consumes according to the equation

$$(q_t - o_t)p'_t + (q_p - o_p)p'_p + (q_k - o_k)p'_k + \ldots$$
$$+ d_a + d_b p_b + d_c p_c + d_d p_d + \ldots = \mathbf{r}.$$

Certain prices of (B), (C), (D)... having once been established
on the basis of the quantities manufactured of these commodities, if
the quantity produced of one of these commodities, say (B), should increase or decrease, the first thing that would have to be done in order
to restore equilibrium anew, would be to bring about an expansion
or a contraction of the demand for (B) by all parties to the exchange
until the *rareté* of (B) was decreased or increased in the same proportion for all alike, while the price of (B) fell or rose proportionately.

This adjustment is what might be called a consequence of the first order, which is of prime importance so far as the price of (B) is concerned. The same adjustment might even restore equilibrium [in the market as a whole], if the total amount $d_b p_b$ spent by each and every party on the consumption of (B) remained unchanged.[2] But since each individual's outlay on (B) would undoubtedly change in every case, increasing for some parties while decreasing for others, whether the quantity of (B) manufactured expanded or contracted, it follows that those parties whose outlay on (B) increased would have to sell a quantity of various [other] commodities, which would tend to depress [their] prices, while those parties whose outlay on (B) decreased would have to buy a quantity of various [other] commodities, which would tend to raise [their] prices. This would be a consequence of the second order, which, so far as the prices of (B), (C), (D)... are concerned, turns out to be of minor importance for the following three reasons: (1) that the change in the total amount $d_b p_b$ to be spent on the consumption of (B) is limited by the fact that the two factors d_b and p_b vary in opposite directions; (2) that this change in outlay on (B) which entails the purchase and sale of all commodities, can, therefore, only entail the purchase and sale of an extremely small quantity of any one of them; and (3) that the effects of these purchases and sales cancel each other out.

What has just been said of the consequences of a change in the quantity manufactured of (B) applies also to the consequences of changes in the quantities manufactured of (C), (D).... Hence, we may be sure that the [primary] change in the quantity manufactured of any given product has a direct effect on the selling price of that product, which is all in one direction, whereas [the consequent] changes in the quantities manufactured of other products, if we suppose all these changes to take place in the same direction, will only have indirect effects on the selling price of the first product, some in one direction and some in another, thus cancelling each other out, more or less. The [resulting] system of new quantities of manufactured products and of new selling prices is thus closer to equilibrium than the old one; and we have only to continue the process of groping to approach still more closely to equilibrium.[6]

The quantities D'_b, D'_c, D'_d... of (B), (C), (D)... which have been thus determined[f] require for their production certain quantities D'_t, D'_p, D'_k... of (T), (P), (K)..., according to the equations[3]

$$D'_t = a_t \Omega_a + b_t D'_b + c_t D'_c + d_t D'_d + \dots$$
$$D'_p = a_p \Omega_a + b_p D'_b + c_p D'_c + d_p D'_d + \dots$$
$$D'_k = a_k \Omega_a + b_k D'_b + c_k D'_c + d_k D'_d + \dots$$
$$\cdot \quad \cdot \quad \cdot \quad \cdot \quad \cdot \quad \cdot \quad \cdot \quad \cdot \quad \cdot \quad \cdot \quad \cdot \quad \cdot \quad \cdot$$

and will sell at certain prices $p'_b, p'_c, p'_d...$ respectively, according to the equations

$$D'_b=F_b(p'_t, p'_p, p'_k...p'_b, p'_c, p'_d...),$$
$$D'_c=F_c(p'_t, p'_p, p'_k...p'_b, p'_c, p'_d...),$$
$$D'_d=F_d(p'_t, p'_p, p'_k...p'_b, p'_c, p'_d...),$$

. . . .

at which the entrepreneurs manufacturing (B), (C), (D)... make neither profit nor loss.

This is precisely the sort of groping which takes place spontaneously in the products market under conditions of free competition, as entrepreneurs increase or decrease their output according as they make profits or losses (§188).

213. At the selling prices $p'_b, p'_c, p'_d...$ equal to cost of production, certain quantities $O'_t, O'_p, O'_k...$ of (T), (P), (K)... effectively offered in the form of tickets[g] will correspond in the market of a given country to the quantities $D'_b, D'_c, D'_d...$ of (B), (C), (D)... effectively demanded, according to the equations of total offer of services

$$O'_t=F_t(p'_t, p'_p, p'_k...p'_b, p'_c, p'_d...),$$
$$O'_p=F_p(p'_t, p'_p, p'_k...p'_b, p'_c, p'_d...),$$
$$O'_k=F_k(p'_t, p'_p, p'_k...p'_b, p'_c, p'_d...),$$

. . . .

These equations, together with the equations of total demand for products, form a system of equations of exchange which satisfy the three conditions of maximum satisfaction, uniformity of prices, and general equilibrium.

It follows also that there is an effective demand for a quantity D'_a of (A) determined by the equation

$$D'_a=O'_tp'_t+O'_pp'_p+O'_kp'_k+...-(D'_bp'_b+D'_cp'_c+D'_dp'_d+...).$$

From the two systems of equations previously derived, the first giving the costs of production of the products as functions of the prices of the productive services (§209) and the second giving the quantities demanded of the productive services as functions of the quantities of products manufactured (§212), we can obtain another equation by first multiplying both sides of each of the m equations of the first system in succession by $\Omega_a, D'_b, D'_c, D'_d...$ respectively,[h] then multiplying both sides of each of the n equations of the second system in succession by $p'_t, p'_p, p'_k...$ respectively, and finally adding together each of the two resulting systems. We observe that the right-hand sides of the two sums are identical, so that we have [upon equating the two left-hand sides and transposing]

$$\Omega_ap'_a=D'_tp'_t+D'_pp'_p+D'_kp'_k+...$$
$$-(D'_bp'_b+D'_cp'_c+D'_dp'_d+...).$$

We have also[4]

$$D'_a - \Omega_a p'_a = (O'_t - D'_t)p'_t + (O'_p - D'_p)p'_p + (O'_k - D'_k)p'_k \cdots$$

Up to this point, the quantity produced of the *numéraire* (A) has been determined solely at random; it ought to be determined, like the other commodities, in such a way that the entrepreneurs [manufacturing (A)] make neither profit nor loss.[i] Obviously, this requires that the cost of production of the *numéraire* equal its selling price. This will be true if we take care to posit at the start that

$$p'_a = a_t p'_t + a_p p'_p + a_k p'_k + \ldots = 1.$$

Where this equation is not satisfied, no equilibrium is possible. When it is assumed that this equation is satisfied, equilibrium will exist provided that $D'_b, D'_c, D'_d \ldots$ have been determined as indicated above. In fact, the quantities of productive services which entrepreneurs owe[5] will have the same value as the quantities owed to them for their products, for, as long as p'_a is equal to 1, the entrepreneurs manufacturing (A), like those manufacturing (B), (C), (D)..., will make neither profit nor loss. Thus we shall have

$$(O'_t - D'_t)p'_t + (O'_p - D'_p)p'_p + (O'_k - D'_k)p'_k + \ldots = 0:$$

and, in consequence, also[6]

$$D'_a = \Omega_a p'_a = \Omega_a.$$

It turns out that when the prices of the services are so determined that the cost of production of the *numéraire* equals unity, all that is needed in order to obtain the partial equilibrium under consideration, is to determine $D'_b, D'_c, D'_d \ldots$ in the manner described above, so that the entrepreneurs manufacturing (B), (C), (D)... make neither profit nor loss. The quantity D'_a demanded of (A) will naturally be the random quantity manufactured Ω_a.[j] Consequently, when producers sell products in the form of tickets worth $D'_a + D'_b p'_b + D'_c p'_c + D'_d p'_d + \ldots$ in order to buy services worth $D'_t p'_t + D'_p p'_p + D'_k p'_k + \ldots$ and when consumers sell services in the form of tickets worth $O'_t p'_t + O'_p p'_p + O'_k p'_k + \ldots$ in order to buy products worth $D'_a + D'_b p'_b + D'_c p'_c + D'_d p'_d + \ldots$, all the production equations will be satisfied except those of system (3)[7] which equate the quantities of productive services employed to the quantities offered.

214. This last system must be satisfied like the others. The quantities bought and the quantities sold of productive services must not only be equal in value, but they must also be equal in amount, since it is these very quantities that necessarily enter into the making of the products. Now, the time has come to close the circle of

production, as it were, by bringing about an equality between the demand and offer of services.[k]

This equality would be realized if $D'_t=O'_t$, $D'_p=O'_p$, $D'_k=O'_k$.... In that case, brokers in various markets would remit to producers tickets representing services in return for tickets representing products and they would remit to consumers tickets representing products in return for tickets representing services; and in this way the exchange of services for products and of services for services would take place. But generally $D'_t \gtrless O'_t$, $D'_p \gtrless O'_p$, $D'_k \gtrless O'_k$.... In that case the process of groping comes into play again through appropriate adjustments in the price of services.[l] We observe that, since p'_t, p'_p, p'_k... are essentially positive, when we set $p'_a=1$ and find that $\Omega_a=D'_a$, then, if some of the differences $O'_t-D'_t$, $O'_p-D'_p$, $O'_k-D'_k$... are positive, others will be negative.

215. The function O'_t can be written in the form $U-u$, where the function U represents the sum of the positive o_t's, i.e. the quantities of service (T) effectively offered, and the function u represents the sum of the negative o_t's, i.e. the quantities of this service effectively demanded not by entrepreneurs for the production of (A), (B), (C), (D)... but by consumers for use as a commodity, that is to say, not as a productive service but as a consumers' service. Thus the inequality $D'_t \gtrless O'_t$ can be written in the form

$$a_t D'_a + b_t D'_b + c_t D'_c + d_t D'_d + \ldots + u \gtrless U.$$

Let us suppose that D'_a does not vary, that is to say that entrepreneurs manufacturing (A) always produce the same quantity of (A), whatever the variations in p_t, p_p, p_k... and consequently whatever the variations in the cost of production p_a. On the left-hand side of the above inequality we still have the variables $b_t D'_b$, $c_t D'_c$, $d_t D'_d$...[8] which are decreasing functions of the prices p_b, p_c, p_d... and consequently of the price p_t, while costs of production are increasing functions of p_t. The variable u taken by itself is also a decreasing function of p_t. Thus, as p_t increases from zero to infinity while p'_p, p'_k... remain constant, D'_t+u will diminish from a certain determined value to zero.[9]

As for U, the single term of the right-hand side of the above inequality, it is zero when p_t is zero and even for some positive values of p_t. This is the case whenever the values of the several products in terms of the service (T) are so high that the proprietors of this service will not demand any of these products at all. As the price p_t increases, the function U at first increases. The products then become cheaper in terms of the service (T), and the demand for products makes its appearance concomitantly with the associated offer of the service (T). But this offer does not increase indefinitely. It passes through at

250 ELEMENTS OF PURE ECONOMICS

least one maximum which cannot be greater than the total quantity possessed Q_i; and then it decreases, returning to zero again, if the price of (T) becomes infinite, that is to say, if (A), (B), (C), (D)... all become free goods.[10] Thus, as p_t increases from zero to infinity, U starts at zero, increases and decreases until it becomes zero again.[11]

216. Under these conditions, provided only that [the total effective demand for (T)] D'_t+u does not fall to zero before U starts to rise above zero, in which case there will be no solution at all, there will be a certain value of p_t, greater or less than p'_t according as $D'_t+u \gtrless U$, at which the effective demand and offer of (T) are equal. Letting p''_t be this value; letting π''_b, π''_c, π''_d...[m] be the selling prices of (B), (C), (D)... equal to their [new] costs of production obtained in the manner described above; and letting Ω''_t be the corresponding offer of (T) equal to the demand for it, we then have

$$\Omega''_t = F_t(p''_t, p'_p, p'_k \dots \pi''_b, \pi''_c, \pi''_d \dots).$$

In consequence of this operation on the offer of (T),

$$O'_p = F_p(p'_t, p'_p, p'_k \dots p'_b, p'_c, p'_d \dots)$$

becomes

$$\Omega''_p = F_p(p''_t, p'_p, p'_k \dots \pi''_b, \pi''_c, \pi''_d \dots).$$

This [new] offer of the service (P) will be greater or less than the demand for it. But there is a certain value of p_p which equates the effective demand and offer of (P) and which can be found in the same way that p''_t was found. Letting p'''_p be this value; letting π'''_b, π'''_c, π'''_d... be the selling prices of (B), (C), (D)... equal to their [revised] costs of production obtained in the manner described above (§§211 and 212); and letting Ω'''_p be the corresponding offer of (P) equal to the demand for it, we then have

$$\Omega'''_p = F_p(p''_t, p''_p, p'_k \dots \pi'''_b, \pi'''_c, \pi'''_d \dots).$$

Similarly we could obtain

$$\Omega^{IV}_k = F_k(p''_t, p''_p, p''_k \dots \pi^{IV}_b, \pi^{IV}_c, \pi^{IV}_d \dots),$$

and so forth.

217. Once all these operations have been effected, we have

$$O''_t = F_t(p''_t, p''_p, p''_k \dots p''_b, p''_c, p''_d \dots).$$

We now have to prove that this offer O''_t is closer to equality with the [new] demand D''_t than the offer O'_t was with the [old] demand D'_t. This will appear probable if we remember that the change from p'_t to p''_t which brought the offer and the demand for (T) into equality with each other, exerted a direct influence that was invariably in the direction of equality, at least so far as the demand for (T) was concerned, while the [consequent] changes from p'_p, p'_k to p''_p, p''_k...., which tended to destroy the equality between the offer and demand for (T), exerted indirect influences, some in the direction of equality and some in the opposite direction at least so far as the demand for (T) was concerned, so that up to a certain point they cancelled each other out. The new system of prices p''_t, p''_p, p''_k... is therefore closer to equilibrium than the old system of prices p'_t, p'_p, p'_k..., and it is only necessary to continue the process along the same lines for the system to move closer and closer to equilibrium.

This groping takes place naturally in the services market under a system of free competition, since, under such a system, the price of services rises when demand exceeds offer and falls when offer exceeds demand.

218. If we suppose equilibrium to have been reached, we then have, on the one hand, the following prices of products:

$$p''_a = a_t p''_t + a_p p''_p + a_k p''_k + \ldots$$
$$p''_b = b_t p''_t + b_p p''_p + b_k p''_k + \ldots$$
$$p''_c = c_t p''_t + c_p p''_p + c_k p''_k + \ldots$$
$$p''_d = d_t p''_t + d_p p''_p + d_k p''_k + \ldots$$

. . . .

and, on the other hand, the following quantities demanded of productive services:

$$D''_t = a_t D'_a + b_t D''_b + c_t D''_c + d_t D''_d + \ldots$$
$$D''_p = a_p D'_a + b_p D''_b + c_p D''_c + d_p D''_d + \ldots$$
$$D''_k = a_k D'_a + b_k D''_b + c_k D''_c + d_k D''_d + \ldots$$

. . . .

where D''_b, D''_c, D''_d... are the quantities that satisfy the equations of demand for the final products (B), (C), (D)... and $D''_t = O''_t$, $D''_p = O''_p$, $D''_k = O''_k$... are the quantities that satisfy the equations of offer of the services (T), (P), (K)... in which p''_t, p''_p, p''_k... p''_b, p''_c, p''_d... are independent variables. From the above two systems we obtain the equation[12]

$$D'_a p''_a = D''_t p''_t + D''_p p''_p + D''_k p''_k + \ldots$$
$$- (D''_b p''_b + D''_c p''_c + D''_d p''_d + \ldots).$$

A quantity D''_a of (A) is, therefore, demanded according to the equation

$$D''_a = O''_t p''_t + O''_p p''_p + O''_k p''_k + \ldots$$
$$- (D''_b p''_b + D''_c p''_c + D''_d p''_d + \ldots).$$

Since $D''_t=O''_t$, $D''_p=O''_p$, $D''_k=O''_k\ldots$, we have

$$D''_a=D'_a p''_a.$$

It is seen from the preceding discussion that all but one of the equations are satisfied. The remaining equation is either the equation of cost of production of the *numéraire* which entails equality between its supply and its demand, or the equation of demand for the *numéraire* which entails equality between its selling price and its cost of production, i.e. unity. Thus, if perchance $p''_a=1$, we should also have $D'_a=D''_a$; or, alternatively, if it happened that $D'_a=D''_a$, then $p''_a=1$, and the problem would be completely solved. But, in general, after the adjustments in p'_t, p'_p, $p'_k\ldots$ and after their change to p''_t, p''_p, $p''_k\ldots$ in the manner described above, we have

$$p''_a \gtrless 1;$$

and consequently

$$D''_a \gtrless D'_a.$$

219. In order to complete the solution of the system of equations of production we should have to recommence the whole process of groping by determining p'''_t, p'''_p, $p'''_k\ldots$ in accordance with the equation

$$a_t p'''_t + a_p p'''_p + a_k p'''_k + \ldots = p'''_a = 1.$$

This is done by making $p'''_t \lessgtr p''_t$, $p'''_p \lessgtr p''_p$, $p'''_k \lessgtr p''_k\ldots$ according as $p''_a \gtrless 1$.

Taking this as our new point of departure, we should arrive, in the course of the first phase of the groping process at a determination of D'''_a in the products market, according to the equation

$$D'''_a=O'''_t p'''_t + O'''_p p'''_p + O'''_k p'''_k + \ldots \\ -(D'''_b p'''_b + D'''_c p'''_c + D'''_d p'''_d + \ldots);$$

and then, at the end of the second phase, we should arrive at a determination of D^{IV}_a in the services market, according to the equation

$$D^{IV}_a = D'''_a p^{IV}_a.$$

We now have to prove that p^{IV}_a is closer to unity than p''_a. This will appear probable if we remember that, when, for example, $p''_a>1$, we found that $p'''_b<p''_b$, $p'''_c<p''_c$, $p'''_d<p''_d\ldots$ with the consequence that $D'''_b>D''_b$, $D'''_c>D''_c$, $D'''_d>D''_d\ldots$, and $D'''_a<D''_a$. Thus $p'''_a=1$ became p^{IV}_a as a result of being simultaneously forced up by the increase in demand for (B), (C), (D)… and forced down by the decrease in demand for (A). Had p''_a been <1, p'''_a would have become p^{IV}_a as a result of being simultaneously forced down by the decrease in demand for (B), (C), (D)... and forced up by the increase in demand for (A). In either case, since these movements are opposite in direction, their resulting pull on p_a away from unity is probably not as strong as the pull towards unity resulting from the decrease or increase in p_t, p_p, p_k.... The same process of adjustment need only be continued to bring p_a closer and closer to unity. If we suppose this goal to be reached with $p^{IV}{}_a=1$, we shall also have $D'''{}_a=D^{IV}{}_a$, and then the problem will be completely solved.

Actually the groping which we have just described takes place of itself under a system of free competition. In fact, when

$$D''{}_a=D'{}_a p''{}_a,$$

the cost to manufacturers of (A) is $D'{}_a p''{}_a$. If, in that case, they sell the quantity $D''{}_a$ of (A) demanded at the price 1, their profit will be $D'{}_a-D''{}_a=D'{}_a(1-p''{}_a)$. This difference will be a true profit if $p''{}_a<1$ and $D'{}_a>D''{}_a$. But then the manufacturers of (A) will expand their production thereby forcing up $p''{}_t, p''{}_p, p''{}_k...$, and consequently $p''{}_a$ which will then approach unity. The difference would be a loss if $p''{}_a>1$ and $D'{}_a<D''{}_a$. The loss sustained by the manufacturers in that case would be $D''{}_a-D'{}_a$. But then they would contract their production, thereby forcing down $p''{}_t, p''{}_p, p''{}_k...$ and consequently $p''{}_a$ which would again approach unity. It is to be observed that the manufacturers of (A) can avoid the latter contingency by producing only when the cost of production of the numéraire is less than or equal to unity and by not producing at all, since they face certain loss, whenever the cost of production is greater than the selling price (i.e. greater than unity). In short, the manufacturers of (A) are like the manufacturers of (B), (C), (D)..., in that they have only to expand their output, as they do in fact, whenever the selling price exceeds cost of production, and to curtail their output whenever cost of production exceeds selling price. In the first case the prices of services are forced up and in the second they are forced down in the services market. In both cases the tendency is towards the establishment of equilibrium.

220. On drawing together all the different parts of this demonstration, we are in a position to formulate the law of the establishment of current or equilibrium prices in production[n] as follows: *Given several services by means of which various products can be manufactured and assuming that these services are exchanged for their products through the medium of a* numéraire, *for the market to be in equilibrium, or for the prices of all the services and all the products in terms of the* numéraire *to be stationary, it is necessary and sufficient* (1) *that the effective demand for each service and each product be equal to its effective supply at these prices*; *and* (2) *that the selling prices of*

the products be equal to the cost of the services employed in making them. If this twofold equality does not exist, in order to achieve the first it is necessary to raise the prices of those services or products the effective demand for which is greater than the effective supply and to lower the price of those services or products the effective supply of which is greater than the effective demand; and, in order to achieve the second, it is necessary to increase the output of those products the selling price of which is greater than the cost of production and to decrease the output of those products of which the cost of production is greater than the selling price.

This is the *law of the establishment of equilibrium prices* in production.[n] By joining it with a suitably generalized form of the *law of the variation of equilibrium prices*, which we shall do in the next Lesson, we shall have the scientific formulation of the double LAW OF SUPPLY AND DEMAND, AND OF COST OF PRODUCTION.[o]

THE PRINCIPLE OF FREE COMPETITION. THE LAW OF THE VARIATION OF PRICES OF PRODUCTS AND SERVICES. PURCHASE AND SALES CURVES OF SERVICES; PRICE CURVES OF PRODUCTS

221. It follows from the proof we have just given in Lesson 21 that free competition in production provides a practical solution of the equations set out in Lesson 20, since free competition consists, on the one hand, in allowing entrepreneurs freedom to expand output in case of a profit and to restrict output in case of a loss; and, on the other hand, in allowing land-owners, workers and capitalists, as well as entrepreneurs, freedom to buy or sell services and products by bidding against one another. If, therefore, we refer back to the equations of Lesson 20 and to the conditions on which they rest, we see that:

Production in a market ruled by free competition is an operation by which services can be combined and converted into products of such a nature and in such quantities as will give the greatest possible satisfaction of wants within the limits of the double condition, that each service and each product have only one price in the market, namely the price at which the quantity supplied equals the quantity demanded, and that the selling price of the products be equal to the cost of the services employed in making them.[a]

222. We have, perhaps, at last reached the place where we can see the importance of a scientific formulation of pure economics. From the viewpoint of pure science, all that we needed to do, and all that we actually have done up to the present, was to treat free competition as a datum, or rather as an hypothesis, for it did not matter whether or not we observed it in the real world, since, strictly speaking, it was sufficient that we should be able to form a conception of it. It was in this light that we studied the nature, causes and consequences of free competition. We now know that these consequences may be summed up as the attainment, within certain limits, of maximum utility. Hence free competition becomes a principle or a rule of practical significance, so that it only remains to extend the detailed application of this rule to agriculture, industry and trade.[b] Thus the conclusions of pure science bring us to the very threshold of applied science. We can now see how certain objections to our method fall

to the ground of their own weight. We are told, in the first place:[c] "One of the elements of the determination of prices under free competition is free will which entails decisions that are unpredictable." Actually, we have never attempted to predict decisions made under conditions of perfect freedom; we have only tried to express the effects of such decisions in terms of mathematics. In our theory each trader may be assumed to determine his own utility or want curves as he pleases. Once these curves have been determined, we show how prices result from them under a hypothetical régime of absolutely free competition. "Precisely," we are told, "absolutely free competition is only an hypothesis. In reality, the working of free competition is obstructed by an infinite number of disturbing factors. It is, therefore, pointless, apart from the gratification of idle curiosity, to study free competition by itself, uninfluenced by perturbations which defy mathematical computation." The futility of this objection is obvious. Even supposing that the future development of our science will never allow these disturbing factors to be incorporated into our equations of exchange—certainly a useless prognostic, if not a rash one—nevertheless, the equations we have developed do show freedom of production to be the superior general rule. Freedom procures, within certain limits, the maximum of utility; and, since the factors which interfere with freedom are obstacles to the attainment of this maximum, they should, without exception, be eliminated as completely as possible.[d]

223. Of course, economists have been saying all along that they advocate *laisser-faire, laisser-passer*. Unfortunately, it must be said that up to the present economists have been less concerned with establishing proofs for their arguments in favour of *laisser-faire, laisser-passer* than they have been with using them as weapons against the socialists, new and old, who for their part are equally negligent in establishing proofs for their arguments in favour of State intervention. I am well aware that in saying this I shall outrage a few susceptibilities. Nevertheless, I should like to ask: how could these economists prove that the results of free competition were beneficial and advantageous if they did not know just what these results were? And how could they know these results when they had neither framed definitions nor formulated relevant laws to prove their point? My own argument has so far been *a priori*. But now, let us turn to some *a posteriori* reasons. Once a principle has been scientifically established, the first thing that one can do is to distinguish immediately between the cases to which the principle applies and those to which it does not apply. Conversely, the fact that economists have often extended the principle of free competition beyond the limits of its true applicability is

proof positive that the principle has not been demonstrated. For example, in the theory we are developing in this book, the first foundation on which our proof of the principle of free competition rests is the individual consumer's appreciation of the utility of final products and services. Our proof implies a fundamental distinction between individual wants, i.e. private utility which the individual is capable of estimating, and social wants or public utility which is estimated in an entirely different way. Therefore, the principle of free competition, which is applicable to the production of things for private demand, is not applicable to the production of things where public interest is involved. Are there not economists, however, who have fallen into the error of advocating that public services be brought within the fold of free competition by turning these services over to private industry? Take another example. A second foundation on which our proof rests is the equalization of the selling prices of products with their costs of production. Our proof, consequently, presupposes that it is possible for entrepreneurs to enter profitable businesses and to withdraw from those operating at a loss. Hence, the principle of free competition is not generally applicable to the production of things which are within the province of natural and necessary monopolies. Are there not economists, however, who go on tirelessly advocating free competition for monopolized industries? Let us make one last observation to close the argument, and this is an observation of fundamental importance. Though our description of free competition emphasizes the problem of utility, it leaves the question of justice entirely to one side, since our sole object has been to show how a certain distribution of services gives rise to a certain distribution of products. The question of the [original] distribution of services remains open, however. And yet, are there not economists who, not content with exaggerating the applicability of *laisser-faire, laisser-passer* to industry, even extend it to the completely extraneous question of property? Such are the pitfalls into which a science stumbles when treated as literature. Some authors mingle the true and the false indiscriminately in their positive assertions, whereupon others come in who reject the true along with the false no less indiscriminately. Meanwhile public opinion, whichever side it takes, is baffled, for it is pulled this way and that by adversaries who are both right and wrong at one and the same time.

224. If we let v_t, v_p, v_k... designate the values in exchange of the services (T), (P), (K)..., so that the ratios of these values to v_a, the value in exchange of the product (A), constitute the prices of these services; and if we let $r_{t,1}$, $r_{p,1}$, $r_{k,1}$... $r_{t,2}$, $r_{p,2}$, $r_{k,2}$... $r_{t,3}$, $r_{p,3}$, $r_{k,3}$... designate the *raretés* of these services or the intensities of the

last wants satisfied by them after the exchange in which individuals (1), (2), (3)... retain or acquire services for direct consumption, then we can complete the table of general equilibrium (§133) as follows:

$$v_a \quad : v_b \quad : v_c \quad : v_d \quad : \ldots : v_t \quad : v_p \quad : v_k \quad : \ldots$$
$$:: r_{a,1} : r_{b,1} : r_{c,1} : r_{d,1} : \ldots : r_{t,1} : r_{p,1} : r_{k,1} : \ldots$$
$$:: r_{a,2} : r_{b,2} : r_{c,2} : r_{d,2} : \ldots : r_{t,2} : r_{p,2} : r_{k,2} : \ldots$$
$$:: r_{a,3} : r_{b,3} : r_{c,3} : r_{d,3} : \ldots : r_{t,3} : r_{p,3} : r_{k,3} : \ldots$$
$$:: \quad . \quad . \quad . \quad . \quad . \quad . \quad . \quad . \quad . \quad . \quad . \quad . \quad . \quad .$$

The land-services, labour and capital-services that are directly consumed are capable of being consumed either in infinitely small quantities as measured in time, or in quantities corresponding to conventional units of land, persons and capital goods. There may be occasion, therefore, to insert in the appropriate places of our table of *raretés* some terms that are underlined to represent *raretés* that lie between the intensities of the last wants satisfied and the first wants unsatisfied. Moreover, in the case of services as in the case of products, it is always possible to include in our table of *raretés* those proportional terms which we place in parenthesis to represent *raretés* higher than the intensities of such first wants as might have been satisfied.[1] Subject to these two reservations,[e] we may extend to services the proposition which we have already established for products, namely that: *Values in exchange are proportional to* raretés.

225.[f] Let (T), (P) and (K) be respectively the services of land, persons and capital goods which can be consumed in infinitely small quantities, and let $\tau_{r,1}\,\tau_{q,1}$, $\tau_{r,2}\,\tau_{q,2}$, $\tau_{r,3}\,\tau_{q,3}$, $\pi_{r,1}\pi_{q,1}$, $\pi_{r,2}\pi_{q,2}$, $\pi_{r,3}\,\pi_{q,3}$, $\varkappa_{r,1}\,\varkappa_{q,1}$, $\varkappa_{r,2}\,\varkappa_{q,2}$, and $\varkappa_{r,3}\,\varkappa_{q,3}$ (Fig. 22) be the continuous utility or want curves of these services for parties (1), (2) and (3). Let 0·75, 2·16 and 1·50 be the prices of (T), (P) and (K) in terms of (A). In this hypothetical case, party (1) and party (3) consume all three services, the former in quantities 7, 9 and 5 respectively, which have for him the corresponding *raretés* 1·50, 4·33 and 3; the latter in quantities 3, 1 and 2 respectively, which have for him the corresponding *raretés* 3, 8·66 and 6. As for party (2), he consumes a quantity 1 of the land-services (T), which has for him a *rareté* of 4·50; but he goes without labour (P) and capital-services (K), because the numbers 13 and 9 which should have appeared in his particular row of *raretés* exceed the intensities 9 and 6 of the first wants which these services might have satisfied.

We now have the following table of equilibrium:[2]

$$0{\cdot}75 : 2{\cdot}16 : 1{\cdot}50$$
$$:: 1{\cdot}50 : 4{\cdot}33 : 3$$
$$:: 4{\cdot}50 : (13): (9)$$
$$:: 3 \quad : 8{\cdot}66 : 6.$$

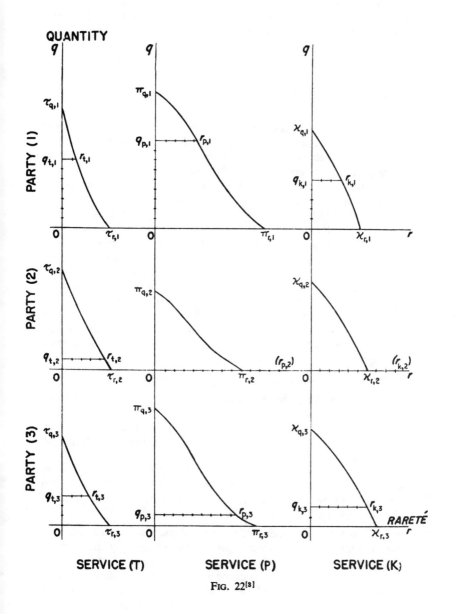

QUANTITY

PARTY (1)

PARTY (2)

PARTY (3)

SERVICE (T)   SERVICE (P)   SERVICE (K)

RARETÉ

FIG. 22[3]

226.[a] If we let R_t, R_p, R_k... be the average *raretés* of (T), ($\dot{P}$), (K)..., in the computation of which both the underlined terms and those in parentheses are taken into account, we may posit[4]

$$p_t = \frac{R_t}{R_a}, \qquad p_p = \frac{R_p}{R_a}, \qquad p_k = \frac{R_k}{R_a} \dots.$$

227. We may also generalize the law of the variation of prices (§137) in the following terms:

Given several products or services and given a state of general equilibrium in a market where exchange is effected with the aid of a numéraire, *if, all other things remaining equal, the utility of one of these products or services increases or decreases for one or more of the parties to the exchange, the price of this product or service in terms of the* numéraire *will increase or decrease.*

If, all other things being equal, the quantity of one of these products or services in the hands of one or more holders increases or decreases, the price of this product or service will decrease or increase.

Given several products or services, if both the utility and the quantity of one of these products or services in the hands of one or more parties or holders vary in such a way that the raretés *remain the same, the price of this product or service will not change.*

If the utilities and the quantities of all the products or services in the hands of one or more of the parties or holders vary in such a way that the ratios of the raretés *remain the same, the prices of these products or services will not change.*

To which we may add two more propositions:

If, all other things being equal, the quantity of a service owned by one or more individuals increases or decreases (its effective offer then increasing or decreasing so that its price falls or rises), *the prices of those products in the production of which this service is employed will fall or rise.*

If, all other things being equal, the utility of a product increases or decreases for one or more consumers (its effective demand then increasing or decreasing so that its price rises or falls), *the prices of the services employed in its production will rise or fall.*[h]

228. In §151 of Lesson 15, we defined *purchase curves* and *sales curves*, that is to say curves representing respectively the demand against *numéraire* and the offer against *numéraire* of commodities which were each in turn considered as the last to be introduced into an exchange market already in general equilibrium. Then in §153 we transformed the purchase curves into *price curves* by making the assumption that offer was equal to quantity possessed. We shall now

take up this idea again and extend it to include services as well as products.

229. Let (A) be the *numéraire*. And let us suppose that the services (P), (K)... and the products (A), (B), (C), (D)... are being exchanged or are about to be exchanged for one another at the given general equilibrium prices p'_p, p'_k... p'_b, p'_c, p'_d..., when a new

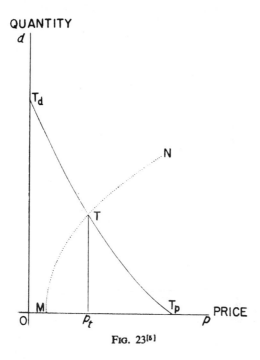

FIG. 23[5]

service (T) is discovered, duly appropriated and introduced into the market, so that it becomes an integral part of the mechanism of exchange and production.

Theoretically, this appearance of (T) would necessitate a revision of all four systems of the production equations (§§202 and 203), because it entails the introduction of two new unknowns p_t and O_t, and of two additional equations: one an equation of demand for (T),

$$a_t D_a + b_t D_b + c_t D_c + d_t D_d + \ldots = O_t,$$

and the other an equation of offer of (T),

$$O_t = F_t(p_t, p_p, p_k \ldots p_b, p_o, p_d \ldots).$$

If we let U and u represent the sums of the positive and negative o_i's respectively, as we did in §215, these two equations reduce to a single equation

$$a_i D_a + b_i D_b + c_i D_c + d_i D_d + \ldots + u = U.$$

But if we abstract from all changes in the other prices and in the other effective demands and offers, which are thus considered as

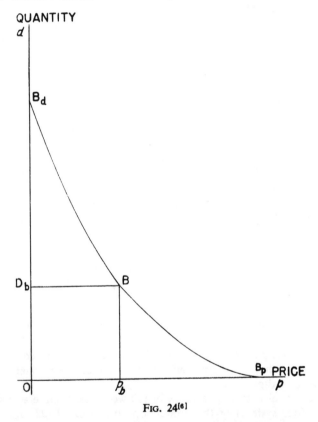

FIG. 24[6]

constants, then the left-hand side of this equation becomes a decreasing function of the single variable p_i and can be represented geometrically by the *purchase curve* $T_d T_p$ (Fig. 23); while the right-hand side becomes a different sort of function of the same variable p_i, since it first rises from zero and then falls to zero again (at $p_i = \infty$) as shown in the *sales curve MN*. The intersection of these two curves at the point T determines the price p_i.[4]

230. As before, we suppose (A) to be the *numéraire*. Let us imagine, now, that the services (T), (P), (K)... and the products (A), (C), (D)... are being exchanged or are about to be exchanged for one another at the given general equilibrium prices p'_t, p'_p, p'_k... p'_c, p'_d..., when a new product (B) is made available by manufacturers and developed commercially for the first time, so that it is introduced into the market and becomes an integral part of the mechanism of exchange and production.

Theoretically, this appearance of (B) would necessitate a revision of all four systems of production equations, because it entails the introduction of two new unknowns p_b and D_b, and of two additional equations: one an equation of demand for (B),

$$D_b = F_b(p_t, p_p, p_k \ldots p_b, p_c, p_d \ldots),$$

and the other an equation of cost of production of (B),

$$b_t p_t + b_p p_p + b_k p_k + \ldots = p_b.$$

But if we abstract from all changes in the other prices and in the other effective demands and supplies, which are thus considered as constants, then D_b becomes a decreasing function of the single variable p_b and can be represented geometrically by a *price curve* $B_d B_p$ (Fig. 24). The ordinate of the point B, corresponding to the abscissa p_b, represents the demand D_b. Thus we get back to the same geometrical formulation which we gave earlier.[j][7]

PART V

Theory of Capital Formation ['*Capitalisation*'[1]] *and Credit* [a]

Lesson 23

GROSS AND NET INCOME. THE RATE OF NET INCOME. THE EXCESS OF INCOME OVER CONSUMPTION

231. The existence of different kinds of income (T), (T'), (T'')... (P), (P'), (P'')... (K), (K'), (K'')... from land, persons and capital proper presupposes the existence of landed capital, personal capital and capital goods of corresponding categories. In the preceding pages we have determined the prices of various types of income, but we have not yet determined the prices of the capital goods yielding these incomes in the form of uses and services. The determination of the prices of capital goods is the third major problem of the mathematical theory of social wealth. It is with this problem that Part V is now concerned.

From our point of view, there can be no prices other than market prices. Consequently, just as we previously contemplated a products market and a services market to determine the prices of products and the prices of services,[a] so now we must contemplate a market which we shall call a *capital goods market*, where capital goods are bought and sold. Consumers' goods are demanded because of their utility; services are demanded not only because of their utility but also because of the prices obtained for the products they help to produce. But why are capital goods demanded? They are demanded because of the land-services, labour and capital-services they render, or better, because of the rent, wages and interest which these services yield. Undoubtedly, it is possible to buy a capital good for the consumption as well as for the sale of its services; but the latter purpose must be considered as the more important one in the acquisition of capital, for otherwise it would be sufficient to purchase the service or to hire the capital good. A man who buys a house for his own use must be resolved by us into two individuals, one making an investment and the other consuming directly the services of his capital. We have already discussed the latter individual; we shall now be concerned with the former.

232. The price of a capital good depends essentially on the price of its services, that is to say, on its *income*. We are now enlarging, to some extent, the meaning of the word *income* to include the price of the service as well as the service itself.[1] This price is made up of three distinct elements.

In the first place, all existing capital goods are not used up with the

267

same rapidity. Hence different capital goods, though yielding the same income, will sell more or less dearly according to their respective rates of wear and tear.

In the second place, all capital goods are not equally subject to sudden and unforeseen destruction by accident. Hence different capital goods, though yielding the same income, will sell more or less dearly according to the probability of accidental destruction.

Nothing could be simpler than to take these two circumstances into account mathematically.

As for the first element, we need only suppose that whatever sum is necessary for maintaining the capital good intact or for replacing it when it is worn out is deducted from its annual [gross] income and reckoned as proportional to the price of the capital good. This is called the *depreciation* ('*amortissement*') of capital. The amount set aside for this purpose, i.e. the *depreciation charge*, will vary with different capital goods; but once this charge has been levied, all capital goods become rigorously identical with respect to impairment through use, since they all become, as it were, permanent.

The same is true of the second element. We need only suppose that whatever sum is required as a contribution to the restoration of all similar capital goods annually destroyed by accident is [also] deducted from the annual [gross] income of the capital good in question and reckoned as proportional to the price of that capital good. This is called the *insurance* of capital. The amount deducted for this purpose, i.e. the *insurance premium*, will also vary with different capital goods; but once this charge has been levied, all capital goods become rigorously identical with respect to accidental loss, since they all become, as it were, indestructible.

Let P be the price of a capital good. Let p be its *gross* income, that is, the price of its service inclusive of both the depreciation charge and the insurance premium. Let μP be the portion of this income representing the depreciation charge and νP the portion representing the insurance premium. What remains of the gross income after both charges have been deducted, $\pi = p - (\mu + \nu)P$, is the *net* income.[b]

233. We are now able to explain the differences in gross incomes derived from [various] capital goods having the same value, or conversely the differences in values of [various] capital goods yielding the same gross incomes. It is, however, readily seen that the values of capital goods are rigorously proportional to their net incomes.[c] At least this would have to be so under certain normal and ideal conditions when the market for capital goods is in equilibrium. Under equilibrium conditions the ratio $\dfrac{p - (\mu + \nu)P}{P}$, or the rate of net

income, is the same for all capital goods. Let i be this [common] ratio.[2] When we determine i, we also determine the prices of all landed capital, personal capital and capital goods proper by virtue of the equation

$$p-(\mu+\nu)P=iP$$

or[3]

$$P= \frac{p}{i+\mu+\nu}.$$

234. All the foregoing relations we have established so far are not sufficient for this determination of i and the prices of capital goods. Up to this point we have assumed that the quantities of land, personal faculties and capital proper are given, and that land-owners, workers and capitalists exchange all the services of their capital goods for consumers' goods and services, except for that fraction of the services of their capital goods which they consume directly. Under such circumstances, there could be no purchase or sale of capital goods, for these goods could only be exchanged for one another in ratios proportional to their net incomes; and such transactions, being theoretically without rational motive, could not give rise to any prices of capital goods in terms of *numéraire*.[d] If there is to be a demand for, a supply of, and prices of capital goods, we must suppose that there are land-owners, workers and capitalists who purchase consumers' goods and services in amounts that either fall short of or exceed their incomes, thus leaving them either a surplus with which to buy capital goods or a deficit which compels them to sell their capital goods. According as the excess of income over consumption in the aggregate is greater or less than the excess of consumption over income in the aggregate, an economy is either progressive or retrogressive; but in either case the economy may still be stationary if the propensities to save and the propensities to consume are assumed to be fixed over a given interval of time (§§74 and 201). In the case of a progressive economy, which is the only case we shall consider, we must suppose that there are some entrepreneurs who are engaged in manufacturing new capital goods instead of consumers' goods. With these additional data, we have all the elements necessary for the solution of our problem. New capital goods are exchanged against the excess of income over consumption; and the condition of equality between the value of the new capital goods and the value of the excess gives us the equation required for the determination of the rate of net income and consequently for the determination of the prices of capital goods. Moreover, new capital goods are products; and the condition of equality between their selling price and their cost of production gives us the

equations required for the determination of the quantities manufactured. Once again we have to describe this equilibrium mathematically and then show how it is automatically realized in the market. Before turning to that, however, we must call attention to an important fact to which we have already referred in §208 where we postponed its consideration until this point.

235. In reality, only land and personal faculties are always hired in kind; capital proper is usually hired in the form of money in the market for services. The capitalist accumulates his savings in money and lends this money to the entrepreneur who, at the expiration of the loan, repays the money. This operation is known as *credit*. Hence, the demand for new capital goods comes from entrepreneurs who manufacture products and not from capitalists who create savings. Clearly, from the theoretical point of view it is immaterial to the capitalist and to the entrepreneur whether what the one lends and the other borrows is the capital good itself, new or old, or the price of this capital good in the form of money.[e] It is only from the point of view of practical convenience that the latter arrangement is distinctly preferable to the former. We must remember, however, that the *capital goods market*, i.e. the market where capital goods are bought and sold, should not be confused with the *money market* ['*marché du capital*'], i.e. the market where *money capital* is borrowed and lent, which is merely an annex to the service market. In the course of our demonstration we shall find that these two markets appear quite distinct from each other. It should be noted that so long as we are abstracting from money, we shall have to speak not of money capital but of *numéraire*-capital,[4][f] and that if we happen to use the word *capital* alone, as a great many authors do, we shall attach a special meaning to this word.

236. Except in rare instances, which could easily have been taken into account but for the fact that they would needlessly complicate our formulae, land is a natural capital good and is not artificial or produced. So far as land is concerned, then, there is no action of price on quantity or reaction of quantity on price. Furthermore, with rare exceptions which we shall regard in the same light as those previously mentioned, land is an indestructible capital good which cannot be used up or destroyed by accident. There is no occasion to deduct either a depreciation charge or an insurance premium from its income. From these two observations it follows that the aggregate quantity of land is always a given and not an unknown element of our problem and that the price of land is equal, purely and simply, to the quotient of its gross income divided by the rate of net income once that rate has been determined. This is shown in the equation

$$P_t = \frac{p_t}{i}.$$

237. Personal faculties are also natural capital goods. Their quantity does not depend on fluctuations in industrial productivity, but on changes in population. On the other hand, personal faculties are subject to wear and tear and to destruction by accident. As for their depreciation and insurance, we can think of them as being provided for by procreation and by the maintenance, rearing and education of the wives and children of workers.[5] Hence the quantity of personal faculties, like the quantity of land, is always a given and not an unknown element of our problem; and the prices of personal faculties, if we should ever want such prices, are equal to the quotients of their net incomes divided by the rate of net income, as shown in the equation $P_p = \dfrac{\pi_p}{i}$.

238. Capital goods proper are artificial capital goods; they are products and their prices are subject to the law of cost of production. If their selling price is greater than their cost of production, the quantity produced will increase and their selling price will fall; if their selling price is lower than their cost of production the quantity produced will diminish and their selling price will rise. In equilibrium their selling price and their cost of production are equal. Now let there be l different kinds (K), (K'), (K'')... of capital goods proper, which are either already in existence or about to be produced. Let $P_k, P_{k'}, P_{k''}$... be their respective prices. If p_t... p_p... $p_k, p_{k'}, p_{k''}$... are respectively the prices of services[6] of the types (T)... (P)... (K), (K'), (K'')... and if k_t... k_p... $k_k, k_{k'}, k_{k''}$... k'_t... k'_p... $k'_k, k'_{k'}, k'_{k''}$... k''_t... k''_p... $k''_k, k''_{k'}, k''_{k''}$... are respectively the quantities of these various services which enter into the production of a single unit of (K), (K'), (K'')..., we shall have the following l equations:

$$k_t p_t + \ldots + k_p p_p + \ldots + k_k p_k + k_{k'} p_{k'} + k_{k''} p_{k''} + \ldots = P_k,$$
$$k'_t p_t + \ldots + k'_p p_p + \ldots + k'_k p_k + k'_{k'} p_{k'} + k'_{k''} p_{k''} + \ldots = P_{k'},$$
$$k''_t p_t + \ldots + k''_p p_p + \ldots + k''_k p_k + k''_{k'} p_{k'} + k''_{k''} p_{k''} + \ldots = P_{k''},$$

. . . .

Moreover, capital goods proper are subject to wear and tear and to accidental destruction. Hence the need to deduct depreciation charges and insurance premiums from their incomes. If we let $\mu_k P_k, \mu_{k'} P_{k'}, \mu_{k''} P_{k''}$... and $\nu_k P_k, \nu_{k'} P_{k'}, \nu_{k''} P_{k''}$... be the portions representing respectively the depreciation charges and the insurance premiums to be deducted from the gross incomes $p_k, p_{k'}, p_{k''}$... of the capital goods (K), (K'), (K'')..., the prices of these capital goods will be equal either to the quotients of their net incomes divided by the rate of net income or to the quotients of their gross incomes divided by the sum of the following three rates: the rate of net income, the rate of depreciation and the insurance rate, in accordance with the following l equations:

$$P_k = \frac{\pi_k}{i} = \frac{p_k}{i+\mu_k+\nu_k},$$

$$P_{k'} = \frac{\pi_{k'}}{i} = \frac{p_{k'}}{i+\mu_{k'}+\nu_{k'}},$$

$$P_{k''} = \frac{\pi_{k''}}{i} = \frac{p_{k''}}{i+\mu_{k''}+\nu_{k''}},$$

. . . .

239. Let us now imagine an individual owner of q_t of (T)... q_p of (P)... q_k of (K), $q_{k'}$ of (K'), $q_{k''}$ of (K'').... At the prices p_t... p_p... p_k, $p_{k'}$, $p_{k''}$... for services, and at the prices P_t... P_p... P_k, $P_{k'}$, $P_{k''}$... for capital goods, his income will be worth

$$q_t p_t + \ldots + q_p p_p + \ldots + q_k p_k + q_{k'} p_{k'} + q_{k''} p_{k''} + \ldots$$

and his capital will be worth

$$q_t P_t + \ldots + q_p P_p + \ldots + q_k P_k + q_{k'} P_{k'} + q_{k''} P_{k''} + \ldots.$$

The words *capital* and *income* are here used to mean the "amount of an individual's capital goods and services expressed in terms of a *numéraire*".

If this individual sells certain quantities, positive or negative, of services (T)... (P)... (K), (K'), (K'')..., worth

$$o_t p_t \ldots o_p p_p \ldots o_k p_k, o_{k'} p_{k'}, o_{k''} p_{k''} \ldots$$

the several quantities left for his consumption will be worth

$$(q_t-o_t)p_t \ldots (q_p-o_p)p_p \ldots$$
$$(q_k-o_k)p_k, (q_{k'}-o_{k'})p_{k'}, (q_{k''}-o_{k''})p_{k''} \ldots.$$

Besides that, he will consume certain quantities of commodities (A), (B), (C), (D)..., worth

$$d_a, d_b p_b, d_c p_c, d_d p_d \ldots.$$

240. It is possible that our individual may demand (A), (B), (C), (D)... for a value exactly equal to the value of the services he offers, in accordance with the equation

$$o_t p_t + \ldots + o_p p_p + \ldots + o_k p_k + o_{k'} p_{k'} + o_{k''} p_{k''} + \ldots$$
$$= d_a + d_b p_b + d_c p_c + d_d p_d + \ldots.$$

But it is also possible that the value of the productive services offered may exceed the value of the products demanded, so that there will be an *excess* ['*éxcédent*']:[7]

$$\mathbf{e}=o_t p_t+\ldots+o_p p_p+\ldots+o_k p_k+o_{k'}p_{k'}+o_{k''}p_{k''}+\ldots$$
$$-(d_a+d_b p_b+d_c p_c+d_d p_d+\ldots).$$

If we add to and subtract from the right-hand side of the previous equation the right- and left-hand sides of[8] $\mathbf{r}=q_t p_t+\ldots+q_p p_p+\ldots+q_k p_k+q_{k'}p_{k'}+q_{k''}p_{k''}+\ldots$ respectively, we obtain

$$\mathbf{e}=\mathbf{r}-[(q_t-o_t)p_t+\ldots+(q_p-o_p)p_p+\ldots$$
$$+(q_k-o_k)p_k+(q_{k'}-o_{k'})p_{k'}+(q_{k''}-o_{k''})p_{k''}+\ldots$$
$$+d_a+d_b p_b+d_c p_c+d_d p_d+\ldots].$$

Thus: *The excess of the value of the services offered over the value of the consumers' goods demanded is the same thing as the excess of income over consumption.*

This excess can be negative, that is to say, it can turn into an excess of consumption over income. We must then suppose that our individual sells not only all the services he owns, except those which he consumes himself, but also a part of his capital goods. This is called "eating into one's capital". It may even happen that this negative excess is greater than the total value of the individual's capital goods,

$$q_t P_t+\ldots+q_p P_p+\ldots+q_k P_k+q_{k'}P_{k'}+q_{k''}P_{k''}+\ldots.$$

In that case our individual squanders other people's property as well as his own.[9]

241. Given these definitions, we are confronted with three possibilities:

(1) that of a positive excess which is just equal to the amount needed to cover the depreciation and insurance of the capital goods of the types (K), (K'), (K'').... We then have

$$\mathbf{e}=q_k P_k(\mu_k+\nu_k)+q_{k'}P_{k'}(\mu_{k'}+\nu_{k'})+q_{k''}P_{k''}(\mu_{k''}+\nu_{k''})+\ldots.$$

In this case our individual merely holds constant the quantity of the capital goods proper he owns, without increase or decrease.

(2) that of an excess positive, zero or negative, which is less than the amount needed to cover depreciation and insurance. Then we have

$$\mathbf{e}<q_k P_k(\mu_k+\nu_k)+q_{k'}P_{k'}(\mu_{k'}+\nu_{k'})+q_{k''}P_{k''}(\mu_{k''}+\nu_{k''})+\ldots.$$

In this case our individual really consumes a part of his capital goods proper, which, for want of adequate provision for depreciation and insurance, will not remain in his possession intact or quantitatively the same next year, because they will be partly used up and partly destroyed by accident.

(3) and finally, that of a positive excess which is larger than the amount needed to cover depreciation and insurance. In such a case we have

$$e > q_k P_k(\mu_k + \nu_k) + q_{k'} P_{k'}(\mu_{k'} + \nu_{k'}) + q_{k''} P_{k''}(\mu_{k''} + \nu_{k''}) + \ldots$$

and our individual will then increase the quantity of his capital goods by calling upon producers to supply new capital goods instead of consumers' goods. He *saves*.

Thus: *Savings are the positive difference between the excess of income over consumption and the amount necessary to cover the depreciation and insurance of capital goods proper.*

Whether the individual in question merely provides for the depreciation and insurance of his capital goods proper, or eats into his capital in whole or in part, or actually saves, in every case he will have to call upon production for more or less consumers' goods in preference to new capital goods or for more or less new capital goods in preference to consumers' goods. Hence we regard the positive, zero or negative excess of income over consumption as an element which may appropriately be introduced at this point into the system of production equations, in order to deduce from these equations the system of equations of capital formation ['capitalisation']. It will be understood that the excess does not constitute true saving unless it is both positive and greater than the sum needed to cover the depreciation and insurance of existing capital goods proper.

242.[h] In order to effect the introduction of this new element rationally, we need only imagine a commodity (E) consisting of *perpetual net income* of which both the price $p_e = \dfrac{1}{i}$ and the quantity demanded d_e are expressed in units of *numéraire*.[9] i is the *rate of perpetual net income*. If the net income were not perpetual, its price would be $p_{e'} < \dfrac{1}{i}$, which would [still] be a function of i.

A fairly exact counterpart of the ideal commodity (E) is to be found in the perpetual net income whose variable rate i, once it has been determined for a certain period of time, serves as a basis for the computation of life insurance rates. Insurance companies are intermediaries between those who create savings, positive or negative, and the market for capital goods. Thus insurance companies require net income in order to pay *death benefits* and *endowments* to some; while they supply net income by paying *annuities* to others. If, all things considered, their reserves increase, the country is producing new capital goods; in the contrary case it is consuming existing capital goods.

In speaking here of the price of (E), I am simply reviving the old concept of *number of years' purchase* (twenty years' purchase, twenty-five years' purchase),[10] which is the reciprocal of the more recent concept of *rate* (5 per cent$=\frac{1}{20}$, 4 per cent$=\frac{1}{25}$). I find it helpful to use these two concepts concurrently in developing a scientific theory of capital formation. Now, in the light of these definitions, we may regard every member of an exchange economy as having, over a given period of time, a certain want for (E), that can be expressed by a function $r=\phi_e(q)$ which decreases as q increases, and as possessing a certain quantity of (E),

$$q_e=q_t p_t+\ldots+q_p \pi_p+\ldots+q_k \pi_k+q_{k'} \pi_{k'}+q_{k''} \pi_{k''}+\ldots$$

which, within certain limits, can be increased by demand, or decreased by offer, so that

$$\phi_e(q_e+d_e)=p_e\phi_a(d_a)$$

is the condition of maximum satisfaction (§80). This condition combined with the equation of exchange

$$o_t p_t+\ldots+o_p p_p+\ldots+o_k p_k+o_{k'}p_{k'}+o_{k''}p_{k''}+\ldots$$
$$=d_a+d_b p_b+d_c p_c+d_d p_d+\ldots+d_e p_e$$

and with the other equations of maximum satisfaction, gives us the following [individual] demand for net income (§201):

$$d_e=f_e(p_t\ldots p_p\ldots p_k, p_{k'}, p_{k''}\ldots p_b, p_c, p_d\ldots p_e).$$

The sum total of all individual demands for net income will be

$$D_e=F_e(p_t\ldots p_p\ldots p_k, p_{k'}, p_{k''}\ldots p_b, p_c, p_d\ldots p_e).$$

This sum, D_e, is positive and equal to E_d for $p_e=0$; and then it decreases as p_e increases while all other prices of services and products are assumed to be determined and constant, until it falls to zero for $p_e=E_p$; after which [as p_e increases still further], it becomes negative, first increasing and then decreasing (in absolute value) until it returns to zero again at $p_e=\infty$.[11] Moreover, the algebraic sum of the individual excesses of income over consumption will be[12]

$$E=D_e p_e=F_e(p_t\ldots p_p\ldots p_k, p_{k'}, p_{k''}\ldots p_b, p_c, p_d\ldots p_e)p_e$$
$$=F_e(p_t\ldots p_p\ldots p_k, p_{k'}, p_{k''}\ldots p_b, p_c, p_d\ldots i)$$

which is subtracted from income and added to capital ['au fonds'], thus constituting *positive savings*. As $\frac{1}{i}$ increases from zero to E_p, or alternatively as i decreases from ∞ to $\frac{1}{E_p}$, E first increases from zero and then decreases to zero again.[i] Since we have chosen to put the offers of services on the left-hand side of the equation of exchange when they are considered as positive quantities, and to put the demands for products on the right-hand side when they too are considered as positive quantities, we shall add the demand for new capital goods to the latter items and *always assume it to be positive*. In making this assumption we are restricting ourselves to a study of the production of new capital goods in a progressive society; and we are neglecting the study of consumption of existing capital goods in a retrogressive society.

If we let $D_k, D_{k'}, D_{k''}$... designate the respective quantities of new capital goods (K), (K'), (K'')... produced, we have the equation

$$D_k P_k + D_{k'} P_{k'} + D_{k''} P_{k''} + \ldots = E.$$

243. Now we have in all $2l+2$ equations (§§238 and 242) to determine: the l quantities produced of new capital goods proper; the l prices of these capital goods, which, from the way they are determined are necessarily the same as the prices of existing capital goods proper; the aggregate excess of income over consumption to be converted into capital goods; and, lastly, the rate of net income; so that there are as many equations as unknowns.[1] It is evident at a glance that the $2l+2$ equations reduce to $l+1$ equations simply by eliminating $P_k, P_{k'}, P_{k''}$... and E. We should then have l equations expressing the equality between cost of production and selling price of the new capital goods to determine the l quantities of these new capital goods $D_k, D_{k'}, D_{k''}$... to be manufactured; and one equation expressing equality between the value of the new capital goods and the excess of income over consumption to determine the rate of net income i. If we also eliminated i, we should have l equations describing the distribution of the excess of aggregate income over consumption among the l varieties of capital formation as one in which the ratio of the net income to the cost of production would be the same for all capital goods.[k] I shall show later on[13] that, subject to a certain reservation, this condition of equality of ratios of net income to prices of new capital goods constitutes the condition of maximum effective utility which an economy derives from the services of these new capital goods in distributing its excess of income over consumption among the different branches of capital formation, for if the above condition of equality of ratios is not fulfilled with respect to any two capital goods, it will be advantageous to produce less of the capital good for which the ratio is smaller and more of the capital good for which this ratio is larger. That being so, we might have proceeded with the aid of the above equations to determine the $l+1$ unknowns from which we could then have deduced the prices of the new capital goods and the aggregate value of savings,

provided, however, that we neglected the resulting changes in the quantities of products to be manufactured and in the prices of products and services attributable to saving and capital formation. But our aim is to gain a comprehension of the economic mechanism as a whole. Consequently, in spite of the complexity of the notations (which is, after all, a minor, though unavoidable, inconvenience), we propose to combine into one system both the $2m+2n-1$ production equations and the $2l+2$ equations of capital formation and credit.

Lesson 24

EQUATIONS OF
CAPITAL FORMATION AND CREDIT

244.[a] We shall now start with a given individual's equation of exchange of services against consumers' goods and services and net income (§242):

$$o_t p_t + \ldots + o_p p_p + \ldots + o_k p_k + o_{k'} p_{k'} + o_{k''} p_{k''} + \ldots$$
$$= d_a + d_b p_b + d_c p_c + d_d p_d + \ldots + d_e p_e.$$

In addition, since the condition of maximum satisfaction (§80) always determines [the individual's] offer of services as well as his demand for consumers' goods and net income, we have also the following equations relating the quantities offered, the quantities demanded and the prices:

$$\phi_t(q_t - o_t) = p_t \phi_a(d_a),$$
$$\cdot \quad \cdot \quad \cdot \quad \cdot \quad \cdot \quad \cdot \quad \cdot$$
$$\phi_p(q_p - o_p) = p_p \phi_a(d_a),$$
$$\cdot \quad \cdot \quad \cdot \quad \cdot \quad \cdot \quad \cdot \quad \cdot \quad \cdot$$
$$\phi_k(q_k - o_k) = p_k \phi_a(d_a),$$
$$\phi_{k'}(q_{k'} - o_{k'}) = p_{k'} \phi_a(d_a),$$
$$\phi_{k''}(q_{k''} - o_{k''}) = p_{k''} \phi_a(d_a),$$
$$\cdot \quad \cdot \quad \cdot \quad \cdot \quad \cdot \quad \cdot \quad \cdot \quad \cdot$$
$$\phi_b(d_b) = p_b \phi_a(d_a),$$
$$\phi_c(d_c) = p_c \phi_a(d_a),$$
$$\phi_d(d_d) = p_d \phi_a(d_a),$$
$$\cdot \quad \cdot \quad \cdot \quad \cdot \quad \cdot \quad \cdot$$
$$\phi_e(q_e + d_e) = p_e \phi_a(d_a),$$

in all $n+m$ equations. These, together with the immediately preceding equation, form a system of $n+m+1$ equations from which we may suppose it possible to derive, by successive eliminations, first, the n equations of positive or negative offer of (T)... (P)... (K), (K'), (K'')...

$$o_t = f_t(p_t \ldots p_p \ldots p_k, p_{k'}, p_{k''} \ldots p_b, p_c, p_d \ldots p_e),$$
$$\cdot \quad \cdot \quad \cdot \quad \cdot \quad \cdot \quad \cdot \quad \cdot \quad \cdot \quad \cdot \quad \cdot \quad \cdot \quad \cdot$$
$$o_p = f_p(p_t \ldots p_p \ldots p_k, p_{k'}, p_{k''} \ldots p_b, p_c, p_d \ldots p_e),$$
$$\cdot \quad \cdot \quad \cdot \quad \cdot \quad \cdot \quad \cdot \quad \cdot \quad \cdot \quad \cdot \quad \cdot \quad \cdot \quad \cdot$$

278

$$o_k = f_k\ (p_t \dots p_p \dots p_k,\ p_{k'},\ p_{k''} \dots p_b,\ p_c,\ p_d \dots p_e),$$
$$o_{k'} = f_{k'}\ (p_t \dots p_p \dots p_k,\ p_{k'},\ p_{k''} \dots p_b,\ p_c,\ p_d \dots p_e),$$
$$o_{k''} = f_{k''}(p_t \dots p_p \dots p_k,\ p_{k'},\ p_{k''} \dots p_b,\ p_c,\ p_d \dots p_e),$$

. . . .

and secondly the m equations of demand for (B), (C), (D)... (E)

$$d_b = f_b(p_t \dots p_p \dots p_k,\ p_{k'},\ p_{k''} \dots p_b,\ p_c,\ p_d \dots p_e),$$
$$d_c = f_c(p_t \dots p_p \dots p_k,\ p_{k'},\ p_{k''} \dots p_b,\ p_c,\ p_d \dots p_e),$$
$$d_d = f_d(p_t \dots p_p \dots p_k,\ p_{k'},\ p_{k''} \dots p_b,\ p_c,\ p_d \dots p_e),$$

. . . .

$$d_e = f_e(p_t \dots p_p \dots p_k,\ p_{k'},\ p_{k''} \dots p_b,\ p_c,\ p_d \dots p_e).$$

The demand for (A) is given without elimination by the equation of exchange

$$d_a = o_t p_t + \dots + o_p p_p + \dots + o_k p_k + o_{k'} p_{k'} + o_{k''} p_{k''} + \dots$$
$$- (d_b p_b + d_c p_c + d_d p_d + \dots + d_e p_e).$$

245. We could obtain the equations of individual demand or offer of services and individual demand for products and net income in the same way for all the other holders of services. Finally, retaining our usual notation, we have the following system of equations of aggregate offer of services:

$$O_t = F_t\ (p_t \dots p_p \dots p_k,\ p_{k'},\ p_{k''} \dots p_b,\ p_c,\ p_d \dots p_e),$$

. . . .

$$O_p = F_p(p_t \dots p_p \dots p_k,\ p_{k'},\ p_{k''} \dots p_b,\ p_c,\ p_d \dots p_e), \quad ..(1)$$

. . . .

$$O_k = F_k\ (p_t \dots p_p \dots p_k,\ p_{k'},\ p_{k''} \dots p_b,\ p_c,\ p_d \dots p_e),$$
$$O_{k'} = F_{k'}\ (p_t \dots p_p \dots p_k,\ p_{k'},\ p_{k''} \dots p_b,\ p_c,\ p_d \dots p_e),$$
$$O_{k''} = F_{k''}(p_t \dots p_p \dots p_k,\ p_{k'},\ p_{k''} \dots p_b,\ p_c,\ p_d \dots p_e),$$

. . . .

and also as the following system of m equations of the aggregate demand for products:

$$D_b = F_b(p_t \dots p_p \dots p_k,\ p_{k'},\ p_{k''} \dots p_b,\ p_c,\ p_d \dots p_e),$$
$$D_c = F_c(p_t \dots p_p \dots p_k,\ p_{k'},\ p_{k''} \dots p_b,\ p_c,\ p_d \dots p_e),$$
$$D_d = F_d(p_t \dots p_p \dots p_k,\ p_{k'},\ p_{k''} \dots p_b,\ p_c,\ p_d \dots p_e), \quad ..(2)$$

. . . .

$$D_a = O_t p_t + \dots + O_p p_p + \dots + O_k p_k + O_{k'} p_{k'} + O_{k''} p_{k''} + \dots$$
$$- (D_b p_b + D_c p_c + D_d p_d + \dots + E).$$

246. We shall give a separate place to the equation

$$E = D_e p_e = F_e(p_t \dots p_p \dots p_k,\ p_{k'},\ p_{k''} \dots p_b,\ p_c,\ p_d \dots p_e)p_e \quad ..(3)$$
$$= F_e(p_t \dots p_p \dots p_k,\ p_{k'},\ p_{k''} \dots p_b,\ p_c,\ p_d \dots i)$$

that is, 1 equation expressing the aggregate excess of income over consumption, derived in the manner indicated above in §242.

247. If we let a_t, b_t, c_t, d_t... k_t, k'_t, k''_t... a_p, b_p, c_p, d_p... k_p, k'_p, k''_p... a_k, b_k, c_k, d_k... k_k, k'_k, k''_k... $a_{k'}$, $b_{k'}$, $c_{k'}$, $d_{k'}$... $k_{k'}$, $k'_{k'}$, $k''_{k'}$... $a_{k''}$, $b_{k''}$, $c_{k''}$, $d_{k''}$... $k_{k''}$, $k'_{k''}$, $k''_{k''}$... represent the respective quantities (still assumed to be constant) of the productive services (T)... (P)... (K), (K'), (K'')... which enter into the manufacture of a single unit of each of the consumers' goods (A), (B), (C), (D)... and of each type of capital goods (K), (K'), (K'')..., we have the following three systems of equations, first:

$$a_t D_a + b_t D_b + c_t D_c + d_t D_d + ...$$
$$+ k_t D_k + k'_t D_{k'} + k''_t D_{k''} + ... = O_t,$$

$$\cdots \cdots \cdots \cdots \cdots$$

$$a_p D_a + b_p D_b + c_p D_c + d_p D_d + ...$$
$$+ k_p D_k + k'_p D_{k'} + k''_p D_{k''} + ... = O_p,$$

$$\cdots \cdots \cdots \cdots \cdots$$

$$a_k D_a + b_k D_b + c_k D_c + d_k D_d + ...$$
$$+ k_k D_k + k'_k D_{k'} + k''_k D_{k''} + ... = O_k, \qquad ..(4)$$
$$a_{k'} D_a + b_{k'} D_b + c_{k'} D_c + d_{k'} D_d + ...$$
$$+ k_{k'} D_k + k'_{k'} D_{k'} + k''_{k'} D_{k''} + ... = O_{k'},$$
$$a_{k''} D_a + b_{k''} D_b + c_{k''} D_c + d_{k''} D_d + ...$$
$$+ k_{k''} D_k + k'_{k''} D_{k'} + k''_{k''} D_{k''} + ... = O_{k''},$$

$$\cdots \cdots \cdots \cdots \cdots$$

comprising *n* equations, which express *equality between the quantities of productive services employed and the quantities effectively offered*; secondly:

$$a_t p_t + ... + a_p p_p + ... + a_k p_k + a_{k'} p_{k'} + a_{k''} p_{k''} + ... = 1,$$
$$b_t p_t + ... + b_p p_p + ... + b_k p_k + b_{k'} p_{k'} + b_{k''} p_{k''} + ... = p_b,$$
$$c_t p_t + ... + c_p p_p + ... + c_k p_k + c_{k'} p_{k'} + c_{k''} p_{k''} + ... = p_c, \qquad ..(5)$$
$$d_t p_t + ... + d_p p_p + ... + d_k p_k + d_{k'} p_{k'} + d_{k''} p_{k''} + ... = p_d,$$

$$\cdots \cdots \cdots \cdots \cdots$$

comprising *m* equations, which express *equality between the selling prices of the consumers' goods and their costs of production*; and thirdly:

$$k_t p_t + ... + k_p p_p + ... + k_k p_k + k_{k'} p_{k'} + k_{k''} p_{k''} + ... = P_k,$$
$$k'_t p_t + ... + k'_p p_p + ... + k'_k p_k + k'_{k'} p_{k'} + k'_{k''} p_{k''} + ... = P_{k'},$$
$$\qquad\qquad ..(6)$$
$$k''_t p_t + ... + k''_p p_p + ... + k''_k p_k + k''_{k'} p_{k'} + k''_{k''} p_{k''} + ... = P_{k''},$$

$$\cdots \cdots \cdots \cdots \cdots$$

comprising *l* equations, which express *equality between the selling prices of new capital goods and their costs of production* (§238).

248. In addition, we have the equation which indicates that the new capital goods proper and the aggregate excess of income over consumption are equal in value [in terms of *numéraire*]

$$D_k P_k + D_{k'} P_{k'} + D_{k''} P_{k''} + \ldots = E, \qquad ..(7)$$

that is, 1 equation of exchange of the total excess against new capital goods (§242).

249. And finally, we have the equations

$$P_k = \frac{p_k}{i + \mu_k + \nu_k},$$

$$P_{k'} = \frac{p_{k'}}{i + \mu_{k'} + \nu_{k'}}, \qquad ..(8)$$

$$P_{k''} = \frac{p_{k''}}{i + \mu_{k''} + \nu_{k''}},$$

$$\cdot \quad \cdot \quad \cdot \quad \cdot \quad \cdot \quad \cdot \quad \cdot$$

which give us a system of *l* equations, expressing the *uniformity of the rate of net income* for all capital goods proper (§238).

250. To sum up, we have in all $2n+2m+2l+2$ equations. But these $2n+2m+2l+2$ equations reduce to $2n+2m+2l+1$.[b] If, for example, we multiply both sides of each of the *n* equations of system (4) in succession by $p_t \ldots p_p \ldots p_k, p_{k'}, p_{k''} \ldots$ respectively, and both sides of each of the $m+l$ equations of systems (5) and (6) in succession by $D_a, D_b, D_c, D_d \ldots D_k, D_{k'}, D_{k''} \ldots$ respectively and then add separately the equations of the two resulting systems, the two sums we obtain give us two equations of which the left-hand sides are identical. Equating, then, the two right-hand sides, we have

$$O_t p_t + \ldots + O_p p_p + \ldots + O_k p_k + O_{k'} p_{k'} + O_{k''} p_{k''} + \ldots$$
$$= D_a + D_b p_b + D_c p_c + D_d p_d + \ldots$$
$$+ D_k P_k + D_{k'} P_{k'} + D_{k''} P_{k''} + \ldots.$$

From the *m*th equation of system (2) we have

$$O_t p_t + \ldots + O_p p_p + \ldots + O_k p_k + O_{k'} p_{k'} + O_{k''} p_{k''} + \ldots$$
$$= D_a + D_b p_b + D_c p_c + D_d p_d + \ldots + E.$$

It follows that

$$D_k P_k + D_{k'} P_{k'} + D_{k''} P_{k''} + \ldots = E,$$

which is none other than equation (7). We have, therefore, the choice either of retaining the preceding equation and eliminating alternatively the *m*th equation of system (2) or the first equation of system (5), or else of retaining the latter equations and eliminating the former. Whichever we do, there will remain $2n+2m+2l+1$ equations to determine exactly $2n+2m+2l+1$ unknowns which are: (1) the n total quantities of services offered, (2) the n prices of these services, (3) the m total quantities of final products demanded, (4) the $m-1$ prices of $m-1$ of these products in terms of the mth, (5) the value of the aggregate excess of income over consumption, (6) the l quantities of new capital goods manufactured, (7) the l prices of these capital goods and (8) the price or rate of net income.[c] But it remains to be shown that the above problem which we have so far stated theoretically is the same problem which in practice is solved in the market by the mechanism of free competition.[d]

251. Again our problem is to reach equilibrium in capital formation *ab ovo* in precisely the same way that we reached equilibrium earlier, first in exchange and then in production.[1] In other words, we propose to start by assuming the arbitrary data of our problem to be constant over a certain period of time,[e] and subsequently we shall suppose them to change in order to study the effects of such changes. Capital formation consists, moreover, in the transformation of services into new capital goods, just as production consists in the transformation of services into consumers' goods. After a certain rate of net income and certain prices of services have been cried and after certain quantities of consumers' goods and new capital goods have been manufactured, if this rate, these prices and these quantities do not satisfy the conditions of general equilibrium, it will be necessary not only to cry a new rate and new prices, but also to manufacture revised quantities of consumers' goods and new capital goods.[f] We shall solve this first difficulty by imagining that the entrepreneurs manufacturing new capital goods use *tickets* to represent the successive quantities of these *products* which are first determined at random and then increased or decreased according as there is an excess of selling price over cost or vice versa, until selling price and cost become equal; and by imagining, at the same time, that land-owners, workers and capitalists also use *tickets* to represent the successive quantities of *services* which are offered and demanded at prices first cried at random and then raised or lowered according as the amount of new capital goods demanded is greater or less, in terms of *numéraire*, than the amount offered, until the two amounts are equal. We shall resolve the further difficulty apropos of the lapse of time required in the production of new capital goods in the same way that we resolved it in the case of final products, by assuming production to be instantaneous.

Thus equilibrium in capital formation will first be established *in principle*. Then it will be established *effectively* by the reciprocal exchange between savings to be accumulated and new capital goods to be supplied *within a given period of time*, during which *no change in the data is allowed*. Although the economy is becoming *progressive*, it remains [for the time being] *static* because of the fact that the new capital goods play no part in the economy until later in a period subsequent to the one under consideration.

SOLUTION OF THE EQUATIONS OF CAPITAL FORMATION AND CREDIT. LAW OF THE ESTABLISHMENT OF THE RATE OF NET INCOME

252.[a] Let us suppose that we come to a market, where a certain price of net income $p'_e = \frac{1}{i}$, plus l quantities of new capital goods $D'_k, D'_{k'}, D'_{k''}...$ to be manufactured, plus n prices of services, plus m quantities of final products to be manufactured, are all determined at random. From the solution we have already given to the problem of production, we know how the process of groping, which is precisely the process employed by the mechanism of free competition, can operate to adjust the prices of productive services towards such values as $p'_t... p'_p... p'_k, p'_{k'}, p'_{k''}...$ which, in turn, determine the m values of the costs of production of final products according to the equations

$$\begin{aligned} p'_a &= a_t p'_t + ... + a_p p'_p + ... + a_k p'_k + a_{k'} p'_{k'} + a_{k''} p'_{k''} + ... \\ p'_b &= b_t p'_t + ... + b_p p'_p + ... + b_k p'_k + b_{k'} p'_{k'} + b_{k''} p'_{k''} + ... \\ p'_c &= c_t p'_t + ... + c_p p'_p + ... + c_k p'_k + c_{k'} p'_{k'} + c_{k''} p'_{k''} + ... \\ p'_d &= d_t p'_t + ... + d_p p'_p + ... + d_k p'_k + d_{k'} p'_{k'} + d_{k''} p'_{k''} + ... \end{aligned} \quad ..[\alpha]$$

. . . .

so that, given these n prices of services and m prices of final products, we have:[b]

(1) n quantities of services offered

$$O'_t = F_t(p'_t... p'_p... p'_k, p'_{k'}, p'_{k''}... p'_b, p'_c, p'_d...p'_e),$$

. . . .

$$O'_p = F_p(p'_t... p'_p... p'_k, p'_{k'}, p'_{k''}... p'_b, p'_c, p'_d... p'_e),$$

. . . .

$$O'_k = F_k(p'_t... p'_p... p'_k, p'_{k'}, p'_{k''}... p'_b, p'_c, p'_d... p'_e),$$
$$O'_{k'} = F_{k'}(p'_t... p'_p... p'_k, p'_{k'}, p'_{k''}... p'_b, p'_c, p'_d... p'_e),$$
$$O'_{k''} = F_{k''}(p'_t... p'_p... p'_k, p'_{k'}, p'_{k''}... p'_b, p'_c, p'_d... p'_e),$$

. . . .

(2) $m-1$ quantities of final products (B), (C), (D)... demanded

$$D'_b = F_b(p'_t... p'_p... p'_k, p'_{k'}, p'_{k''}... p'_b, p'_c, p'_d... p'_e),$$
$$D'_c = F_c(p'_t... p'_p... p'_k, p'_{k'}, p'_{k''}... p'_b, p'_c, p'_d... p'_e),$$
$$D'_d = F_d(p'_t... p'_p... p'_k, p'_{k'}, p'_{k''}... p'_b, p'_c, p'_d... p'_e),$$

. . . .

and (3) an aggregate excess of income over consumption

$$E' = F_e(p'_t \ldots p'_p \ldots p'_k, p'_{k'}, p'_{k''} \ldots p'_b, p'_c, p'_d \ldots i').$$

The above quantities and the above excess of income over consumption when combined with the quantities $D'_k, D'_{k'}, D'_{k''} \ldots$ [1] of new capital goods and Ω_a of (A) [2] to be manufactured which are determined at random, will satisfy the equations [c]

$$a_t\Omega_a + b_tD'_b + c_tD'_c + d_tD'_d + \ldots$$
$$+ k_tD'_k + k'_tD'_{k'} + k''_tD'_{k''} + \ldots \qquad = O'_t,$$

$$a_p\Omega_a + b_pD'_b + c_pD'_c + d_pD'_d + \ldots$$
$$+ k_pD'_k + k'_pD'_{k'} + k''_pD'_{k''} + \ldots \qquad = O'_p,$$

$$\qquad \qquad \qquad \qquad \qquad \qquad \qquad \qquad \ldots [\beta]$$

$$a_k\Omega_a + b_kD'_b + c_kD'_c + d_kD'_d + \ldots$$
$$+ k_kD'_k + k'_kD'_{k'} + k''_kD'_{k''} + \ldots \qquad = O'_k,$$

$$a_{k'}\Omega_a + b_{k'}D'_b + c_{k'}D'_c + d_{k'}D'_d + \ldots$$
$$+ k_{k'}D'_k + k'_{k'}D'_{k'} + k''_{k'}D'_{k''} + \ldots \qquad = O'_{k'},$$

$$a_{k''}\Omega_a + b_{k''}D'_b + c_{k''}D'_c + d_{k''}D'_d + \ldots$$
$$+ k_{k''}D'_k + k'_{k''}D'_{k'} + k''_{k''}D'_{k''} + \ldots = O'_{k''},$$

The values $p'_t \ldots p'_p \ldots p'_k, p'_{k'}, p'_{k''} \ldots$ assigned to the prices of services not only determine the m values of costs of production of final products, but they also determine the l values of costs of production of new capital goods

$$P'_k = k_tp'_t + \ldots + k_pp'_p + \ldots + k_kp'_k + k_{k'}p'_{k'} + k_{k''}p'_{k''} + \ldots$$
$$P'_{k'} = k'_tp'_t + \ldots + k'_pp'_p + \ldots + k'_kp'_k + k'_{k'}p'_{k'} + k'_{k''}p'_{k''} + \ldots$$
$$\qquad \qquad \qquad \qquad \qquad \qquad \qquad \ldots [\gamma]$$
$$P'_{k''} = k''_tp'_t + \ldots + k''_pp'_p + \ldots + k''_kp'_k + k''_{k'}p'_{k'} + k''_{k''}p'_{k''} + \ldots$$

If, on the one hand, we multiply in succession [each of] the $m+l$ equations defining the m costs of production [d] of final products [system [α]] and the l costs of production of new capital goods [system [γ]] by $\Omega_a, D'_b, D'_c, D'_d \ldots D'_k, D'_{k'}, D'_{k''} \ldots$ respectively, and if, on the other hand, we multiply in succession [each of] the n equations expressing equality between the total demand and offer of services [system [β]] by $p'_t \ldots p'_p \ldots p'_k, p'_{k'}, p'_{k''} \ldots$ respectively, and then add separately the two systems of equations thus derived, we observe that the right-hand side of the first sum is identical with the left-hand side of the second sum, and we obtain the equation [3]

$$\Omega_aP'_a + D'_bp'_b + D'_cp'_c + D'_dp'_d + \ldots$$
$$+ D'_kP'_k + D'_{k'}P'_{k'} + D'_{k''}P'_{k''} + \ldots$$
$$= O'_tp'_t + \ldots + O'_pp'_p + \ldots + O'_kp'_k + O'_{k'}p'_{k'} + O'_{k''}p'_{k''} + \ldots$$

Then it follows[4] that a quantity D'_a of (A) is demanded according to the equation

$$D'_a + D'_b p'_b + D'_c p'_c + D'_d p'_d + \ldots + E'$$
$$= O'_t p'_t + \ldots + O'_p p'_p + \ldots + O'_k p'_k + O'_{k'} p'_{k'} + O'_{k''} p'_{k''} + \ldots.$$

It follows also that

$$\Omega_a p'_a + D'_k P'_k + D'_{k'} P'_{k'} + D'_{k''} P'_{k''} + \ldots = D'_a + E',$$

which tells us that in this state of what we may call preliminary equilibrium, the aggregate cost of production of the *numéraire* and new capital goods is necessarily equal to the demand for the *numéraire* plus the excess of income over consumption. Thus, up to this point, we have satisfied all the equations of systems (1), (2), (3), (4), (5) and (6) of the previous Lesson except the mth equation of system (2) and the first equation of system (5); so that all that remains to be satisfied are the mth equation of system (2), the first equation of system (5) as well as the equations of system (7) and (8).[5] Consequently, if perchance

$$D'_k P'_k + D'_{k'} P'_{k'} + D'_{k''} P'_{k''} + \ldots = E'$$

and if

$$P'_k = \frac{p'_k}{i' + \mu_k + \nu_k},$$

$$P'_{k'} = \frac{p'_{k'}}{i' + \mu_{k'} + \nu_{k'}},$$

$$P'_{k''} = \frac{p'_{k''}}{i' + \mu_{k''} + \nu_{k''}},$$

$$\cdots \cdots \cdots \cdots$$

then

$$\Omega_a p'_a = D'_a,$$

so that a final groping towards the adjustments in production which would simultaneously equate the cost of production of the *numéraire* to unity and its effective supply to its effective demand is all that remains to be done to complete the solution of the problem. Generally, however, the situation that confronts us is one in which

$$D'_k P'_k + D'_{k'} P'_{k'} + D'_{k''} P'_{k''} + \ldots \gtrless E'$$

and

$$P'_k \gtrless \frac{p'_k}{i' + \mu_k + \nu_k},$$

$$P'_{k'} \gtrless \frac{p'_{k'}}{i' + \mu_{k'} + \nu_{k'}},$$

$$P'_{k''} \gtrless \frac{p'_{k''}}{i' + \mu_{k''} + \nu_{k''}},$$

$$\cdots \cdots \cdots \cdots$$

and hence these inequalities will first have to be converted into equalities by groping towards appropriate adjustments in the quantities i', D'_k, $D'_{k'}$, $D'_{k''}$... hitherto determined at random. This is the problem we have now to consider.

253. Let us first examine the inequality

$$D'_k \frac{p'_k}{i'+\mu_k+\nu_k} + D'_{k'} \frac{p'_{k'}}{i'+\mu_{k'}+\nu_{k'}} + D'_{k''} \frac{p'_{k''}}{i'+\mu_{k''}+\nu_{k''}} + \dots$$
$$\geqq F_e(p'_t \dots p'_p \dots p'_k, p'_{k'}, p'_{k''} \dots p'_b, p'_c, p'_d \dots i');$$

and let us try to convert it into an equality. The left-hand side is a decreasing function of i. We know from the facts underlying the function F_e that the right-hand side is a function of i which first increases from zero [as i increases] and then decreases to zero again (at $i=\infty$) (§242).[1] This being the case, we see at once that, in order to make an equality of this inequality, i' will have to fall or rise according as the left-hand side is less than or greater than the right-hand side for the initial value i'.

Let i'' be the rate at which

$$D'_k \frac{p'_k}{i''+\mu_k+\nu_k} + D'_{k'} \frac{p'_{k'}}{i''+\mu_{k'}+\nu_{k'}} + D'_{k''} \frac{p'_{k''}}{i''+\mu_{k''}+\nu_{k''}} + \dots$$
$$= F_e(p'_t \dots p'_p \dots p'_k, p'_{k'}, p'_{k''} \dots p'_b, p'_c, p'_d \dots i'').$$

If i'' is substituted [throughout] for i' in the process of groping, the end result of the operation at this stage will be the following inequality:

$$D'_k \frac{p''_k}{i''+\mu_k+\nu_k} + D'_{k'} \frac{p''_{k'}}{i''+\mu_{k'}+\nu_{k'}} + D'_{k''} \frac{p''_{k''}}{i''+\mu_{k''}+\nu_{k''}} + \dots$$
$$\geqq F_e(p''_t \dots p''_p \dots p''_k, p''_{k'}, p''_{k''} \dots p''_b, p''_c, p''_d \dots i'').$$

Now we must prove that the two sides of this inequality are closer to equality than the two sides of the preceding inequality.

254. It is assumed in the particular stage of the groping process which we are now describing that the quantities to be manufactured of the *numéraire* (A) and of the new capital goods (K), (K'), (K'')... are fixed and do not change. Consequently, the quantity of the productive service (T) devoted to these branches of manufacture must always be

$$a_t\Omega_a + K'_t = a_t\Omega_a + k_t D'_k + k'_t D'_{k'} + k''_t D'_{k''} + \dots$$

where K'_t is the quantity of (T) employed in the manufacture of new capital goods. The rest of (T) must be divided between one part that is directly consumed in the form of services and another part that is employed in the manufacture of final products, according to the formula

$$b_t D_b + c_t D_c + d_t D_d + \ldots + S_t = Q_t - (a_t \Omega_a + K'_t),$$

where Q_t is the total quantity of the service (T) and S_t is the quantity consumed directly. The same holds for all other services.

Once i'' has been substituted [throughout] for i' in the process of groping, the total value of new capital goods and the total excess of income over consumption will be brought into equality with each other through changes in these two quantities which may be considered as a first order effect of the variation in the rate of net income. But there is a second order effect to be studied. With every [first order] increase (or decrease) in the excess of income over consumption, so long as the prices are $p'_t \ldots p'_p \ldots p'_k, p'_{k'}$, $p'_{k''} \ldots p'_b, p'_c, p'_d \ldots$, the total value of consumption [in terms of the *numéraire*] will tend initially to decrease (or increase); and, since the total quantity of the services used in direct consumption and in production remains constant [by hypothesis], all prices will fall (or rise), for these prices will be equal to the ratios of the nearly constant *raretés* of the commodities (T) . . . (P) . . . (K), (K'), (K'') . . . (B), (C), (D) . . . already bought ['obtenues'] to the increased (or decreased) *raretés* of commodity (A) demanded. It remains to be seen what will be the effect of this fall (or rise) in prices on the changed total value of new capital goods and on the changed aggregate excess of income over consumption. The first of these two quantities will decrease with a fall (or increase with a rise) in prices, since it is an increasing function of these prices $p_k, p_{k'}, p_{k''} \ldots$. The second will likewise decrease with a fall (or increase with a rise) in prices, because the aggregate value of income decreases (or increases) as prices fall (or rise), and consequently both the total value of consumption and the total value of capital formation must decrease (or increase) together. Since the total value of new capital goods and the excess of income over consumption both move in the same direction when prices fall (or rise), it follows that the tendency of the change in prices from $p'_t \ldots$ $p'_p \ldots p'_k, p'_{k'}, p'_{k''} \ldots p'_b, p'_c, p'_d$ to $p''_t \ldots p''_p \ldots p''_k, p''_{k'}$, $p''_{k''} \ldots p''_b, p''_c, p''_d \ldots$ to destroy the equality between these two quantities will be weaker than the tendency of the shift in the rate of net income from i' to i'' to bring the total value of new capital goods and the excess of income over consumption into equality with each other. Thus the system involving the new rate of net income and the new prices will be closer to equilibrium than the old system; and it is only necessary to continue the process of groping for the system to move still more closely to equilibrium.

In this way we obtain the equality

$$D'_k = \frac{p'''_k}{i'''+\mu_k+\nu_k} + D'_{k'}\frac{p'''_{k'}}{i'''+\mu_{k'}+\nu_{k'}} + D'_{k''}\frac{p'''_{k''}}{i'''+\mu_{k''}+\nu_{k''}} + \ldots$$
$$= F_e(p'''_t \cdots p'''_p \cdots p'''_k, \, p'''_{k'} \, p'''_{k''} \cdots p'''_b, \, p'''_c, \, p'''_d \cdots i'''),$$

so that equation (7) would be satisfied in consequence.[g]

The particular groping which we have just described actually takes place in the stock exchange, which is the market for new capital goods, where the prices of these goods rise (or fall) through a fall (or rise) in the rate of net income, according as the demand for new capital in terms of the *numéraire* is greater (or less) than the supply.[h]

255. Instead of supposing, as we have done hitherto, that the creators of excesses of income over consumption go in person to the market of capital goods to buy new capital goods which they then rent in the market for services to entrepreneurs engaged in industry, let us now suppose that savers lend all or part [i] of the value of these capital goods in *numéraire* to the manufacturers who go in place of the savers to the market for capital goods and buy the new capital goods they want directly. Nothing will be changed in the latter market except that the demand for new capital goods will come from the entrepreneurs and not from the creators of excesses of income over consumption. Consequently, the rate of net income will be determined in that market in exactly the same way as we have already described. On the other hand, the market for services will be wholly or partly[i] replaced so far as the renting of new capital goods is concerned, by a *market for numéraire-capital*, where the unit price of the hire of *numéraire*-capital, which goes under the name of *rate of interest*, will be determined. But it is evident that this rate of interest, when determined by the operations of bidding and by the law of offer and demand, always tends to coincide with a rate of net income like the one we have just defined.[j] In fact, if this rate of interest were higher than the rate of net income, it would be to the advantage of the creators of excesses of income over consumption to lend their capital in the form of *numéraire* in the market for *numéraire*-capital rather than lend it in kind in the market for services, so that they would shift from the latter market to the former; whereas the entrepreneurs, on their side, rather than borrow capital in the form of *numéraire* in the market for *numéraire*-capital would find it to their advantage to borrow capital in kind in the market for services so that they would shift, on the contrary, from the former market to the latter. Thus as the effective offer of *numéraire*-capital increases and the effective demand for it decreases, the rate of interest will fall. On the other hand, if the rate of interest were lower

than the rate of net income, the consequences would be exactly the
reverse, with the result that, as the effective supply of *numéraire*-
capital decreased and the effective demand for it increased, the rate
of interest would rise. Thus the rate of interest, which is the ratio of
net profit to the price of securities, manifests itself, to be sure, in
the market for *numéraire*-capital, that is to say in the banking
system, though actually it is determined in the capital goods market
that is to say in the stock exchange, as a rate of net income which
is the common ratio of the net price of services to the price of landed
capital, personal capital as well as capital proper. It is clearly seen
now that the key to the whole theory of capital is to be found in
thus eliminating capital loans *in the form of numéraire* so that
attention is directed exclusively to the lending of capital *in kind*. The
market for *numéraire*-capital, however useful in practice, being
nothing but a superfoetation in theory,[k] we shall leave it on one
side and return to the market for capital goods in order to find out
how the equilibrium price of new capital goods is determined.

256. At the point we have now reached in our discussion of the
latter market, the prices of the services are p'''_k, $p'''_{k'}$, $p'''_{k''}$... and
consequently the prices of the new capital goods (K), (K'), (K'')...
will be

$$\Pi_k = \frac{p'''_k}{i''' + \mu_k + \nu_k},$$

$$\Pi_{k'} = \frac{p'''_{k'}}{i''' + \mu_{k'} + \nu_{k'}},$$

$$\Pi_{k''} = \frac{p'''_{k''}}{i''' + \mu_{k''} + \nu_{k''}},$$

. . . .

Thus Π_k, $\Pi_{k'}$, $\Pi_{k''}$... are the selling prices of the new capital
goods, while P'''_k, $P'''_{k'}$, $P'''_{k''}$... are their costs of production.
Furthermore, since these selling prices and cost prices are, in general,
not equal, the entrepreneurs manufacturing new capital goods will
make profits or losses shown by the differences

$$D'_k(\Pi_k - P'''_k), \quad D'_{k'}(\Pi_{k'} - P'''_{k'}), \quad D'_{k''}(\Pi_{k''} - P'''_{k''})....$$

It is not immediately apparent, as it was in the case of the inequality between the selling prices and the costs of production of
consumers' goods,[5] how changes in the quantities D'_k, $D'_{k'}$,
$D'_{k''}$..., can bring Π_k and P'''_k, $\Pi_{k'}$ and $P'''_{k'}$, $\Pi_{k''}$ and $P'''_{k''}$...
into equality with each other. This is because it is not obvious at
first glance that these selling prices and costs of production are

functions of the quantities manufactured of new capital goods. It is, however, not difficult to show this relationship.

Let us refer back to the various systems of equations of capital formation which were set forth in the preceding Lesson. If we suppose that the values of p_b, p_c, p_d... given by the equations of system (5) are substituted into the equations of systems (1) and (2),[1] and that the new values of O_t... O_p... O_k, O_k', O_k''... and of D_a, D_b, D_c, D_d... given by the now modified equations of systems (1) and (2) are substituted into the equations of system (4), then this last system will be made up of n equations involving $n+l+1$ unknowns, namely, the n prices of the productive services p_t... p_p... p_k, p_k', p_k''..., the l quantities D_k, D_k', D_k''... of the new capital goods to be manufactured and the price of net income p_e. If we consider the last $l+1$ quantities of this list as known and only the first n quantities as unknown,[m] and if we suppose $n-1$ of these unknowns to be successively eliminated, we shall have n equations expressing the prices of services as functions of the quantities of new capital goods to be manufactured and the price of net income

$$p_t = \mathscr{F}_t(D_k, D_k', D_k''... p_e),$$

$$\cdot \quad \cdot \quad \cdot \quad \cdot \quad \cdot \quad \cdot \quad \cdot \quad \cdot$$

$$p_p = \mathscr{F}_p(D_k, D_k', D_k''... p_e),$$

$$\cdot \quad \cdot \quad \cdot \quad \cdot \quad \cdot \quad \cdot \quad \cdot \quad \cdot$$

$$p_k = \mathscr{F}_k(D_k, D_k', D_k''... p_e),$$

$$p_k' = \mathscr{F}_k'(D_k, D_k', D_k''... p_e),$$

$$p_k'' = \mathscr{F}_k''(D_k, D_k', D_k''... p_e),$$

$$\cdot \quad \cdot \quad \cdot \quad \cdot \quad \cdot \quad \cdot \quad \cdot \quad \cdot$$

If, furthermore, we suppose that the values of p_t... p_p... p_k, p_k', p_k''... given by these equations are substituted into the equations of systems (6) and (8), we shall finally have two systems of l equations each, the first giving the costs of production and the second giving the selling prices of new capital goods as functions of the quantities to be manufactured of these new capital goods and the price or rate of net income.

257. We do not know the equations which, as we have already said, would give us p_t... p_p... p_k, p_k', p_k''... as functions of D_k, D_k', D_k''... and p_e. But it follows quite explicitly from the laws of the variation of the prices of services which we have established that, given the inequalities[n]

$$k_t p'''_t + ... + k_p p'''_p + ... + k_k p'''_k + k_k' p'''_k' + k_k'' p'''_k'' + ...$$
$$\geq \frac{p'''_k}{i''' + \mu_k + \nu_k},$$

$$k'_t p'''_t + \ldots + k'_p p'''_p + \ldots + k'_k p'''_k + k'_{k'} p'''_{k'} + k'_{k''} p'''_{k''} + \ldots$$
$$\lessgtr \frac{p'''_{k'}}{i''' + \mu_{k'} + \nu_{k'}},$$

$$k''_t p'''_t + \ldots + k''_p p'''_p + \ldots + k''_k p'''_k + k''_{k'} p'''_{k'} + k''_{k''} p'''_{k''} + \ldots$$
$$\lessgtr \frac{p'''_{k''}}{i''' + \mu_{k''} + \nu_{k''}},$$

. . . .

if we increase indefinitely the prices of all the productive services which are used in the manufacture of a capital good, and consequently raise its cost of production, we cause the offer of these services, and therefore the quantity manufactured of this capital good, first to increase from zero and then to fall to zero again (at infinity). In other words, the quantity manufactured of a capital good is a function which first increases from zero and then decreases to zero (at infinity) as the cost of production, expressed by the left member of each inequality, increases. It is precisely this law of variation of the quantity manufactured as a function of the cost of production which enables us to bring the cost of production and the selling prices of new capital goods into equality with each other.

As we saw above in §252, a state of preliminary equilibrium in capital formation necessarily implied that

$$\Omega_a p'_a + D'_k P'_k + D'_{k'} P'_{k'} + D'_{k''} P'_{k''} + \ldots = D'_a + E'.$$

Then, when i' was replaced by i''' in the course of the process of groping, we obtained the equality

$$D'_k \Pi_k + D'_{k'} \Pi_{k'} + D'_{k''} \Pi_{k''} + \ldots = E'''$$

and also

$$\Omega_a p'''_a + D'_k P'''_k + D'_{k'} P'''_{k'} + D'_{k''} P'''_{k''} + \ldots = D'''_a + E'''.$$

Consequently, under our assumptions, we have the following formula to express equality between aggregate profits and aggregate losses in all the firms manufacturing capital goods and *numéraire*:

$$D'_k(P'''_k - \Pi_k) + D'_{k'}(P'''_{k'} - \Pi_{k'}) + D'_{k''}(P'''_{k''} - \Pi_{k''}) + \ldots$$
$$+ \Omega_a p'''_a - D'''_a = 0.$$

The entrepreneurs producing (K), (K'), (K'')... and those producing (A) are all in the same situation. They all know their costs of production P'''_k, $P'''_{k'}$, $P'''_{k''} \ldots p'''_a$ and their selling prices Π_k, $\Pi_{k'}, \Pi_{k''} \ldots 1$; and so they know in advance whether they will make a profit or a loss. If it is a loss, they ought to abstain completely from producing and retire all the *tickets* they have issued to represent either *new capital goods* or the *product which serves as numéraire*. In this way, they will certainly force the prices of productive services down and consequently lower the costs of production, which will then fall to meet the selling prices. If, on the other hand, the entrepreneurs make a profit, they ought to produce and issue *tickets*. In this way they will certainly force the prices of productive services up (without, however, necessarily increasing the quantities manufactured in every case), and consequently raise the costs of production which will rise to meet the selling prices.

258. Let Δ_k be the quantity of the capital good (K) to be manufactured which, when substituted for D'_k in the process of groping, renders the two sides of the first inequality [in §257] equal; let $\Delta_{k'}=0$ for the moment, on the assumption that the cost of production of the capital good (K') is greater than its selling price; and let $\Delta_{k''}$ be the quantity of the capital good (K'') to be manufactured which, when substituted by groping for $D'_{k''}$, renders the two sides of the third inequality equal. . . . These quantities $\Delta_k, 0, \Delta_{k''}$ will certainly not be the equilibrium quantities; but they will be very close to being so. It is immediately seen that for any capital good, let us say (K): (1) the substitution of Δ_k for D'_k of (K) must raise its cost of production appreciably, (2) the substitution of 0 for $D'_{k'}$ of (K') and for all the other quantities of capital goods which are discontinued cannot lower the cost of production of (K) at all significantly, (3) the substitution of $\Delta_{k''}$ for $D'_{k''}$ of (K'') and similar substitutions of quantities of capital goods which will continue to be manufactured cannot increase the cost of production of (K) very much, and (4) all these substitutions can hardly change the rate of net income and consequently can hardly affect the selling price in any significant degree.[o] Under these circumstances, it is probable that the effect of changes in the output of any new capital good making for equality between the cost of production of that capital good and its selling price will be stronger than the contrary effect of interrelated changes in the output of other capital goods[p] tending towards the undoing of that equality. The new system of revised quantities manufactured and of revised costs of production and selling prices of new capital goods is thus nearer equilibrium than the original system; and it is only necessary to continue the process of groping for the system to move closer and closer to equilibrium.

When the results of this particular stage of groping are combined with the results of the groping previously described, the quantities $D''_k, D''_{k''}\ldots$ determined in this way are such that we have

$$k_t p^{IV}_t + \ldots + k_p p^{IV}_p + \ldots + k_k p^{IV}_k + k_{k'} p^{IV}_{k'} + k_{k''} p^{IV}_{k''} + \ldots$$
$$= \frac{p^{IV}_k}{i^{IV} + \mu_k + \nu_k},$$

$$k''_t p^{IV}_t + \ldots + k''_p p^{IV}_p + \ldots + k''_k p^{IV}_k + k''_{k'} p^{IV}_{k'} + k''_{k''} p^{IV}_{k''} + \ldots$$

$$= \frac{p^{IV}_{k''}}{i^{IV} + \mu_{k''} + \nu_{k''}},$$

. . . .

and all the remaining equations of system (8) will be satisfied[q] after the exclusion of those new capital goods which it was not worth while to produce.

This is precisely the sort of groping which actually takes place of its own accord in the real market for products under conditions of free competition, when entrepreneurs manufacturing new capital goods, like the entrepreneurs manufacturing consumers' goods,[6] increase or decrease their output according as they make profits or incur losses.

259. If we call the cost of production of (A) and the effective demand for (A) which result at the conclusion of this stage of groping p^{IV}_a and D^{IV}_a respectively, we have [r]

$$\Omega_a p^{IV}_a = D^{IV}_a;$$

and it remains only to continue the process of groping described in §219 to bring about a simultaneous equality between the cost of production of (A) and unity, and between its effective supply and effective demand.

260. On drawing together all the different parts of our demonstration, we may formulate the law of the establishment of equilibrium prices of new capital goods through the determination of the rate of net income as follows: *Let there be given several services, from the prices of which it is possible to deduct an excess of income over consumption to be transformed into new capital goods proper, and which can be exchanged against various consumers' goods and various new capital goods through the medium of a numéraire. Then for the market for capital goods to be in equilibrium, or for the prices of all new capital goods in terms of* numéraire[8] *to be stationary, it is necessary and sufficient: (1) that at selling prices equal to the ratio of net incomes to the current rate of net income, the effective demand for these new capital goods be equal in terms of* numéraire *to their effective supply; and (2) that the selling prices and the costs of production of the new capital goods be equal. When these two equalities do not exist, in order to achieve the first equality, it is necessary to raise[t] the selling prices by lowering the rate of net income in case effective demand is greater than effective supply or to lower[t] the selling prices by raising the rate of net income, in case effective supply is greater than effective demand; and, in order to achieve the second equality, it is necessary to increase the output of those new capital goods the selling price*

of which is greater than their cost of production and to decrease the output of those new capital goods of which the cost of production is greater than the selling price. Since new capital goods proper are really products and since the condition of equality between their selling price and cost of production falls under the principle of cost of production (§220), the prime result of this study resolves itself into the determination of the rate of net income in the market for capital goods, in conformity with the law of equality between supply and demand of new capital goods in terms of *numéraire*.[u]

THEOREM OF MAXIMUM UTILITY OF NEW CAPITAL GOODS YIELDING CONSUMERS' SERVICES[a]

261. In §243, I promised to show that, subject to a certain constraint, the condition of equality of ratios between the net incomes and the prices of new capital goods was the condition of the maximum effective utility obtainable from the services of these capital goods on which the social excess of income over consumption was spent, just as the condition of equality of ratios between the *raretés* and the prices of [consumers'] goods and services was the condition of the maximum effective utility obtainable from these goods and services on which the individual incomes were spent. The time has now come to give the promised demonstration.

Let $\delta_t \ldots \delta_p \ldots \delta_k,\ \delta_{k'},\ \delta_{k''} \ldots \delta_a,\ \delta_b,\ \delta_c,\ \delta_d \ldots$ represent the quantities of [consumers'] services (T)... (P)... (K), (K'), (K'')... and [consumers'] goods (A), (B), (C), (D)... which a party to the exchange retains or purchases when the prices of these services and goods are $p_t \ldots p_p \ldots p_k, p_{k'}, p_{k''} \ldots p_b, p_c, p_d \ldots$ in terms of (A), so that we have

$$\delta_t p_t + \ldots + \delta_p p_p + \ldots + \delta_k p_k + \delta_{k'} p_{k'} + \delta_{k''} p_{k''} + \ldots$$
$$+ \delta_a + \delta_b p_b + \delta_c p_c + \delta_d p_d + \ldots = s, \qquad ..(1)$$

where s is the income which our individual distributes among n different kinds of [consumers'] services and m different kinds of consumers' goods that serve his wants.

Moreover, using the notation of §75, we may let

$$u = \Phi_t(q) \ldots \quad u = \Phi_p(q) \ldots \quad u = \Phi_k(q), \quad u = \Phi_{k'}(q), \quad u = \Phi_{k''}(q) \ldots$$
$$u = \Phi_a(q), \quad u = \Phi_b(q), \quad u = \Phi_c(q), \quad u = \Phi_d(q) \ldots$$

be the equations expressing the several effective utilities of (T)... (P)... (K), (K'), (K'')..., and (A), (B), (C), (D)... for our individual as functions of the quantities consumed,[b] so that

$$\Phi_t(\delta_t) + \ldots + \Phi_p(\delta_p) + \ldots + \Phi_k(\delta_k) + \Phi_{k'}(\delta_{k'}) + \Phi_{k''}(\delta_{k''}) + \ldots$$
$$+ \Phi_a(\delta_a) + \Phi_b(\delta_b) + \Phi_c(\delta_c) + \Phi_d(\delta_d) + \ldots$$

represents the total effective utility to be maximized of the quantities of goods and services retained or purchased. Since the derivatives of the Φ functions are essentially decreasing, the maximum sought will be attained by our individual, when the algebraic sum of pairs[1] of

differential increments of utility with respect to the quantities consumed of each of the commodities is zero. For if we suppose any
two of these increments to be unequal and opposite in sign, it will be
advantageous to demand more of the commodity having the larger
differential increment and less of the commodity having the smaller
differential increment, and also to offer more of the commodity
having the smaller differential increment and less of the commodity
having the larger differential increment. The condition of maximum
satisfaction of wants can therefore be expressed by the following
system of equations:

$$\Phi'_a(\delta_a)d\delta_a + \Phi'_t(\delta_t)\,d\delta_t = 0$$
$$\cdot\ \cdot\ \cdot\ \cdot\ \cdot\ \cdot\ \cdot\ \cdot\ \cdot$$
$$\Phi'_a(\delta_a)d\delta_a + \Phi'_p(\delta_p)\,d\delta_p = 0$$
$$\cdot\ \cdot\ \cdot\ \cdot\ \cdot\ \cdot\ \cdot\ \cdot\ \cdot$$
$$\Phi'_a(\delta_a)d\delta_a + \Phi'_k(\delta_k)d\delta_k = 0,$$
$$\Phi'_a(\delta_a)d\delta_a + \Phi'_{k'}(\delta_{k'})d\delta_{k'} = 0,$$
$$\Phi'_a(\delta_a)d\delta_a + \Phi'_{k''}(\delta_{k''})d\delta_{k''} = 0$$
$$\cdot\ \cdot\ \cdot\ \cdot\ \cdot\ \cdot\ \cdot\ \cdot\ \cdot$$
$$\Phi'_a(\delta_a)\,d\delta_a + \Phi'_b(\delta_b)\,d\delta_b = 0,$$
$$\Phi'_a(\delta_a)\,d\delta_a + \Phi'_c(\delta_c)\,d\delta_c = 0,$$
$$\Phi'_a(\delta_a)\,d\delta_a + \Phi'_d(\delta_d)\,d\delta_d = 0$$
$$\cdot\ \cdot\ \cdot\ \cdot\ \cdot\ \cdot\ \cdot\ \cdot\ \cdot$$

..[δ]

On the one hand, the derivatives of effective utility with respect to
the quantities consumed are none other than the *raretés*; and, on the
other hand, from the point of view of the problem the individual
faces in distributing a given income among his various wants, the
algebraic sums of pairs[1] of commodity prices, each multiplied by
the differential increments of the quantities consumed, are equal to
zero by virtue of equation (1),[2] as shown by the equations

$$d\delta_a + p_t\,d\delta_t = 0$$
$$\cdot\ \cdot\ \cdot\ \cdot\ \cdot\ \cdot$$
$$d\delta_a + p_p\,d\delta_p = 0$$
$$\cdot\ \cdot\ \cdot\ \cdot\ \cdot\ \cdot$$
$$d\delta_a + p_k\,d\delta_k = 0,$$
$$d\delta_a + p_{k'}\,d\delta_{k'} = 0,$$
$$d\delta_a + p_{k''}d\delta_{k''} = 0$$
$$\cdot\ \cdot\ \cdot\ \cdot\ \cdot\ \cdot$$
$$d\delta_a + p_b\,d\delta_b = 0,$$
$$d\delta_a + p_c\,d\delta_c = 0,$$
$$d\delta_a + p_d\,d\delta_d = 0$$
$$\cdot\ \cdot\ \cdot\ \cdot\ \cdot\ \cdot$$

..[ε]

The preceding system of equations can, therefore, be replaced by[3]

$$\frac{r_t}{p_t} = \ldots = \frac{r_p}{p_p} = \ldots = \frac{r_k}{p_k} = \frac{r_{k'}}{p_{k'}} = \frac{r_{k''}}{p_{k''}} = \ldots$$

$$= \frac{r_a}{1} = \frac{r_b}{p_b} = \frac{r_c}{p_c} = \frac{r_d}{p_d} = \ldots .$$

262. So much being understood, we shall begin now by supposing that all capital-services derived from new capital goods are employed as consumers' services and none as productive services; and we shall let

$$D_k = \delta_{k,1} + \delta_{k,2} + \delta_{k,3} + \ldots$$
$$D_{k'} = \delta_{k',1} + \delta_{k',2} + \delta_{k',3} + \ldots$$
$$D_{k''} = \delta_{k'',1} + \delta_{k'',2} + \delta_{k'',3} + \ldots$$

. . . .

define at one and the same time the *quantities of new capital-services* of the types (K), (K'), (K'')... *consumed* by parties (1), (2), (3)... respectively at the prices p_k, $p_{k'}$, $p_{k''}$... of these capital-services in terms of (A), and the *quantities of new capital goods* of the types (K), (K'), (K'')... *manufactured* either to be retained by their proprietors or else to be rented to consumers. Also, let P_k, $P_{k'}$, $P_{k''}$... be the prices of the new capital goods, so that we have

$$D_k P_k + D_{k'} P_{k'} + D_{k''} P_{k''} + \ldots = E, \qquad ..(2)$$

where E represents the aggregate excess of income over consumption which is to be distributed by the economy among the l different kinds of new capital goods.

Moreover, let

$$u = \Phi_{k,1}(q), \qquad u = \Phi_{k',1}(q), \qquad u = \Phi_{k'',1}(q) \ldots$$

be the equations expressing the several effective utilities of the capital-services (K), (K'), (K'')... for party (1) either as functions of the *quantities of the capital-services consumed or* as functions of *the quantities of the capital goods produced.*[c] Consequently

$$\Phi_{k,1}(\delta_{k,1}) + \Phi_{k',1}(\delta_{k',1}) + \Phi_{k'',1}(\delta_{k'',1}) + \ldots$$

represents the total effective utilities to be maximized of either the quantities of capital-services consumed or, alternatively, the quantities of capital goods manufactured. Since the derivatives of the Φ functions are essentially decreasing, the maximum sought will be attained by our individual when the algebraic sums of pairs[4] of differential increments of utility with respect to the quantities manufactured of each of the new capital goods are zero. For if we suppose any two of these increments to be unequal and opposite in sign, it will be advantageous to manufacture less of the capital good having the smaller differential increment and more of the capital good having the larger differential increment. The condition of maximum utility of new capital goods for party (1) can therefore be expressed by the following system of equations:

$$\Phi'_{k,1}(\delta_{k,1})d\delta_{k,1} + \Phi'_{k',1}(\delta_{k',1})d\delta_{k',1} = 0,$$
$$\Phi'_{k,1}(\delta_{k,1})d\delta_{k,1} + \Phi'_{k'',1}(\delta_{k'',1})d\delta_{k'',1} = 0 \qquad ..[\zeta]$$
$$\cdots \cdots \cdots \cdots \cdots \cdots \cdots$$

On the one hand, the derivatives of the effective utility functions with respect to the quantities manufactured of each of the corresponding new capital goods, or the derivatives of these functions with respect to the quantities consumed of each of the corresponding capital-services, are none other than the *raretés* which are directly proportional to the prices p_k, $p_{k'}$, $p_{k''}$... of the capital-services, as shown by the equations

$$\frac{r_{k,1}}{p_k} = \frac{r_{k',1}}{p_{k'}} = \frac{r_{k'',1}}{p_{k''}} = \cdots$$

On the other hand, from the point of view of the problem here considered, which an economy faces in distributing a given excess of income over consumption among the different varieties of capital goods to be produced,[d] the algebraic sums of pairs[4] of prices P_k, $P_{k'}$, $P_{k''}$... of the various capital goods, each multiplied by the differential increments of the quantities manufactured of these goods, are equal to zero by virtue of equation (2), as shown by the equations

$$P_k d\delta_{k,1} + P_{k'} d\delta_{k',1} = 0,$$
$$P_k d\delta_{k,1} + P_{k''} d\delta_{k'',1} = 0 \qquad ..[\eta]$$
$$\cdots \cdots \cdots \cdots \cdots$$

The preceding system of equations can, therefore, be replaced by[5]

$$\frac{p_k}{P_k} = \frac{p_{k'}}{P_{k'}} = \frac{p_{k''}}{P_{k''}} = \cdots$$

which expresses, likewise, the condition of maximum effective utility of new capital goods for the other parties (2), (3)....

In this demonstration nothing has been said about the duration of the use of the service, nor is there any need to do so. According as the length of time is a year, a month or a day, the ratio $\frac{p}{P}$ will represent the annual, monthly or daily rate of gross income. We shall understand the annual rate to be meant here.

Nor has any account been taken of the depreciation and insurance of capital goods; in other words, our proof was developed on the assumption either that these capital goods were infinitely durable and indestructible, or that their depreciation and insurance were covered gratuitously at the expense of the owners. If we now wish to interject the condition that depreciation and insurance must be covered at the expense of the consumers of the services, then, while still leaving the maximum satisfaction of wants to be determined by the proportionality of the *raretés* of capital-services to their prices, we shall be obliged to increase the cost of production of each item of capital by whatever amount is required to yield enough at the particular rate of net income of the capital goods in question, to provide for its depreciation and insurance.[e] We shall then find that the algebraic sums of pairs of the expressions[4]

$$P_k+\frac{\mu_k+\nu_k}{i_k}P_k, \qquad P_{k'}+\frac{\mu_{k'}+\nu_{k'}}{i_{k'}}P_{k'}, \qquad P_{k''}+\frac{\mu_{k''}+\nu_{k''}}{i_{k''}}P_{k''}...$$

or of the expressions[6]

$$\frac{p_k}{\pi_k}P_k, \qquad \frac{p_{k'}}{\pi_{k'}}P_{k'}, \qquad \frac{p_{k''}}{\pi_{k''}}P_{k''}...$$

each multiplied by the differential increments of the quantities manufactured of the various capital goods are equal to zero, as shown by the equations

$$\frac{p_k}{\pi_k}P_kd\delta_{k,1}+\frac{p_{k'}}{\pi_{k'}}P_{k'}d\delta_{k',1}=0,$$
$$\frac{p_k}{\pi_k}P_kd\delta_{k,1}+\frac{p_{k''}}{\pi_{k''}}P_{k''}d\delta_{k'',1}=0,$$

. . [θ]

. . . .

And we shall finally obtain[7]

$$\frac{\pi_k}{P_k}=\frac{\pi_{k'}}{P_{k'}}=\frac{\pi_{k''}}{P_{k''}}=...$$

as the condition of maximum utility of new capital goods.

Lesson 27

THEOREM OF MAXIMUM UTILITY OF NEW CAPITAL GOODS YIELDING PRODUCTIVE SERVICES

263.[a] In the present Lesson we shall suppose that the new capital goods are destined to yield productive capital-services, in other words, capital-services that are not consumed directly, but indirectly in the production of consumers' goods. Our problem is to define the condition of maximum effective utility of new capital goods in this case.

We shall, therefore, let

$$\Delta_a = \delta_{a,1} + \delta_{a,2} + \delta_{a,3} + \dots$$
$$\Delta_b = \delta_{b,1} + \delta_{b,2} + \delta_{b,3} + \dots$$
$$\Delta_c = \delta_{c,1} + \delta_{c,2} + \delta_{c,3} + \dots$$
$$\Delta_d = \delta_{d,1} + \delta_{d,2} + \delta_{d,3} + \dots$$
$$\cdot \quad \cdot \quad \cdot \quad \cdot \quad \cdot \quad \cdot \quad \cdot \quad \cdot \quad \cdot$$

represent the quantities of the final products (A), (B), (C), (D)... consumed respectively by parties (1), (2), (3)... at the prices p_b, p_c, p_d... of (B), (C), (D)... in terms of (A). As before (§247), let a_t... a_p... a_k, $a_{k'}$, $a_{k''}$... b_t... b_p... b_k, $b_{k'}$, $b_{k''}$... c_t... c_p... c_k, $c_{k'}$, $c_{k''}$... d_t... d_p... d_k, $d_{k'}$, $d_{k''}$... be the coefficients of production, i.e. the respective quantities of the services (T)... (P)... (K), (K'), (K'')... which enter into the manufacture of [a single unit of] each of the final products (A), (B), (C), (D).... Consequently the equations

$$D_k = a_k \Delta_a + b_k \Delta_b + c_k \Delta_c + d_k \Delta_d + \dots$$
$$D_{k'} = a_{k'} \Delta_a + b_{k'} \Delta_b + c_{k'} \Delta_c + d_{k'} \Delta_d + \dots$$
$$D_{k''} = a_{k''} \Delta_a + b_{k''} \Delta_b + c_{k''} \Delta_c + d_{k''} \Delta_d + \dots$$
$$\cdot \quad \cdot \quad \cdot \quad \cdot \quad \cdot \quad \cdot \quad \cdot \quad \cdot \quad \cdot \quad \cdot \quad \cdot \quad \cdot \quad \cdot$$

define at one and the same time the *quantities of new*[b] *capital-services* (K), (K'), (K'')... *employed* in the manufacture of (A), (B), (C), (D)... respectively and the *quantities of new capital goods* (K), (K'), (K'')... *manufactured* and rented to the producers of these final products. If, once more, we let P_k, $P_{k'}$, $P_{k''}$... be the prices of these capital goods, we have

$$D_k P_k + D_{k'} P_{k'} + D_{k''} P_{k''} + \dots = E, \qquad \qquad ..(2)$$

where E is again the aggregate excess of income over consumption which is to be distributed by the economy among l different kinds of new capital goods.

Moreover, let

$$u = \Phi_{a,1}(q), \qquad u = \Phi_{b,1}(q), \qquad u = \Phi_{c,1}(q), \qquad u = \Phi_{d,1}(q) \ldots$$

be equations expressing the several effective utilities of the consumers' goods (A), (B), (C), (D)... for party (1) as functions of the quantities he consumes of these products, where the quantities so consumed are equal to the quotients obtained by dividing the coefficients of production either into the *quantities of productive services employed* [in their production], or, alternatively, into the *quantities manufactured of productive capital goods* [so used].[c] Consequently the sum

$$\Phi_{a,1}(\delta_{a,1}) + \Phi_{b,1}(\delta_{b,1}) + \Phi_{c,1}(\delta_{c,1}) + \Phi_{d,1}(\delta_{d,1}) + \ldots$$

represents the total effective utility of these final products to be maximized by the [appropriate] distribution of savings among different varieties of new capital goods. Since the derivatives of the Φ functions are essentially decreasing, the maximum effective utility of new capital goods will be attained by the individual in question when pairs[1] of sums of partial differential increments of utility[d] with respect to the quantities manufactured of each of the new capital goods are equal and opposite in sign.[2][e] For if we suppose any two of these sums to be unequal and opposite in sign,[f] it will be advantageous to manufacture less of that capital good with respect to which the sum of partial differential increments [of effective utility] is smaller and to manufacture more of the other capital good with respect to which the sum of the partial differential increments is larger. The only difficulty we encounter at this point is that the differential increments of utility with respect to the quantities manufactured of each new capital good do not appear separately and distinct from one another, but are found commingled in the sum of the differential increments of utility with respect to the quantities consumed of final products

$$\Phi'_{a,1}(\delta_{a,1})d\delta_{a,1} + \Phi'_{b,1}(d_{b,1})d\delta_{b,1} + \Phi'_{c,1}(d_{c,1})d\delta_{c,1}$$
$$+ \Phi'_{d,1}(\delta_{d,1})d\delta_{d,1} + \ldots$$

from which we have to separate them.

Now, on the one hand, since the derivatives of the effective utility functions with respect to the quantities consumed of final products are none other than the *raretés* which are directly proportional to the selling prices 1, p_b, p_c, p_d... of these products, according to the equations

$$\frac{r_{a,1}}{1} = \frac{r_{b,1}}{p_b} = \frac{r_{c,1}}{p_c} = \frac{r_{d,1}}{p_d} = \ldots$$

and since these selling prices of the final products are equal to their costs of production, according to the equations

$$1=a_t p_t+\ldots+a_p p_p+\ldots+a_k p_k+a_{k'} p_{k'}+a_{k''} p_{k''}+\ldots$$
$$p_b=b_t p_t+\ldots+b_p p_p+\ldots+b_k p_k+b_{k'} p_{k'}+b_{k''} p_{k''}+\ldots$$
$$p_c=c_t p_t+\ldots+c_p p_p+\ldots+c_k p_k+c_{k'} p_{k'}+c_{k''} p_{k''}+\ldots$$
$$p_d=d_t p_t+\ldots+d_p p_p+\ldots+d_k p_k+d_{k'} p_{k'}+d_{k''} p_{k''}+\ldots$$

. . . .

it follows that all the derivatives in question can be resolved into parts which are directly proportional to the [various] costs of production, such as rent, wages, and interest, and, in particular, to the coefficients of production multiplied by the corresponding prices p_k, $p_{k'}$, $p_{k''}$... of the capital-services. On the other hand, the differentials of the quantities consumed of final products can be successively replaced by the quotients obtained by dividing the coefficients of production into the differentials of the quantities of capital-services employed in the making of these products (or, alternatively, into the differentials of the quantities manufactured of each of the new capital goods so used) according to the equations

$$d\delta_{a,1}=\frac{d\delta_{k,1,a}}{a_k}=\frac{d\delta_{k',1,a}}{a_{k'}}=\frac{d\delta_{k'',1,a}}{a_{k''}}=\ldots$$

$$d\delta_{b,1}=\frac{d\delta_{k,1,b}}{b_k}=\frac{d\delta_{k',1,b}}{b_{k'}}=\frac{d\delta_{k'',1,b}}{b_{k''}}=\ldots$$

$$d\delta_{c,1}=\frac{d\delta_{k,1,c}}{c_k}=\frac{d\delta_{k',1,c}}{c_{k'}}=\frac{d\delta_{k'',1,c}}{c_{k''}}=\ldots$$

$$d\delta_{d,1}=\frac{d\delta_{k,1,d}}{d_k}=\frac{d\delta_{k',1,d}}{d_{k'}}=\frac{d\delta_{k'',1,d}}{d_{k''}}=\ldots$$

. . . .

From the standpoint of the problem of how an economy distributes a certain excess of income over consumption among the different varieties of capital goods to be produced, these differentials of the quantities manufactured of each of the new capital goods are equal to one another, for any one [variety of] capital good, according to the equations [g]

$$d\delta_{k,1,a}=d\delta_{k,1,b}=d\delta_{k,1,c}=d\delta_{k,1,d}=\ldots=d\delta_{k,1},$$
$$d\delta_{k',1,a}=d\delta_{k',1,b}=d\delta_{k',1,c}=d\delta_{k',1,d}=\ldots=d\delta_{k',1},\qquad[\iota]$$
$$d\delta_{k'',1,a}=d\delta_{k'',1,b}=d\delta_{k'',1,c}=d\delta_{k'',1,d}=\ldots=d\delta_{k'',1}$$

. . . .

Hence finally, we have equality between pairs[1] of sums, opposite in sign, of the partial differential increments of utility, which is the condition of the maximum we are seeking and which can be expressed by the following system of equations:

$$\left(\frac{a_k p_k}{a_k} + \frac{b_k p_k}{b_k} + \frac{c_k p_k}{c_k} + \frac{d_k p_k}{d_k} + \ldots\right) d\delta_{k,1}$$
$$+\left(\frac{a_{k'} p_{k'}}{a_{k'}} + \frac{b_{k'} p_{k'}}{b_{k'}} + \frac{c_{k'} p_{k'}}{c_{k'}} + \frac{d_{k'} p_{k'}}{d_{k'}} + \ldots\right) d\delta_{k',1} = 0,$$

$$\left(\frac{a_k p_k}{a_k} + \frac{b_k p_k}{b_k} + \frac{c_k p_k}{c_k} + \frac{d_k p_k}{d_k} + \ldots\right) d\delta_{k,1}$$
$$+\left(\frac{a_{k''} p_{k''}}{a_{k''}} + \frac{b_{k''} p_{k''}}{b_{k''}} + \frac{c_{k''} p_{k''}}{c_{k''}} + \frac{d_{k''} p_{k''}}{d_{k''}} + \ldots\right) d\delta_{k'',1} = 0,$$

. . . .

Moreover, continuing along the same lines suggested by our present problem, we observe that, by virtue of equation (2), the algebraic sums of pairs[1] of the prices P_k, $P_{k'}$, $P_{k''}\ldots$ of the various new capital goods, each multiplied by the differentials of the quantities manufactured of the corresponding capital good, are always equal to zero, according to the equations

$$P_k d\delta_{k,1} + P_{k'} d\delta_{k',1} = 0,$$
$$P_k d\delta_{k,1} + P_{k''} d\delta_{k'',1} = 0$$

. . . .

The condition of maximum utility of new capital goods for the party in question can, therefore, be expressed by the system of equations

$$\frac{a_k p_k}{a_k P_k} + \frac{b_k p_k}{b_k P_k} + \frac{c_k p_k}{c_k P_k} + \frac{d_k p_k}{d_k P_k} + \ldots$$
$$= \frac{a_{k'} p_{k'}}{a_{k'} P_{k'}} + \frac{b_{k'} p_{k'}}{b_{k'} P_{k'}} + \frac{c_{k'} p_{k'}}{c_{k'} P_{k'}} + \frac{d_{k'} p_{k'}}{d_{k'} P_{k'}} + \ldots$$
$$= \frac{a_{k''} p_{k''}}{a_{k''} P_{k''}} + \frac{b_{k''} p_{k''}}{b_{k''} P_{k''}} + \frac{c_{k''} p_{k''}}{c_{k''} P_{k''}} + \frac{d_{k''} p_{k''}}{d_{k''} P_{k''}} + \ldots$$
$$= \quad . . . .$$

which would also express the condition of maximum effective utility of new capital goods for parties (2), (3).... This being so, the condition of maximum effective utility of services of new capital goods, in the case where these goods yield productive capital-services only, and no consumers' capital-services, is again expressed by the system of equations

$$\frac{p_k}{P_k} = \frac{p_{k'}}{P_{k'}} = \frac{p_{k''}}{P_{k''}} = \ldots.$$

Hence, it is certain that: *Whether the excess of income over consumption is transformed into capital goods yielding consumers' services or capital goods yielding productive services, the maximum effective utility of the services of these new capital goods is attained for the economy as a whole when the ratio of the price of the capital-service to the price of the capital good, i.e. the rate of gross income, is the same for all capital goods.*

264.[h] The system [(8) of §249] which figured among our equations of capital formation and credit [and which reduces to]

$$\frac{\pi_k}{P_k} = \frac{\pi_{k'}}{P_{k'}} = \frac{\pi_{k''}}{P_{k''}} = \cdots$$

differs from the immediately preceding system in §263 in that the net incomes of the former system are replaced by gross incomes in the latter.[3] Consequently, as can also be seen from our demonstration [in Lesson 25], free competition in the creation of new capital goods actually solves our equations of capital formation and credit by groping, and it follows that:

Capital formation in a market ruled by free competition is an operation by which the excess of income over consumption can be transformed into such types and quantities of new capital goods proper as are best suited to yield the greatest possible satisfaction of wants[i] both to the individual creators of savings and to the whole body of consumers of the services of new capital goods, within limits defined by the condition that the depreciation and insurance of capital goods proper be covered at the expense of consumers of the capital-services and not at the expense of the owners of the capital goods.

Maximum effective utility, on the one hand; uniformity of price, on the other hand—be it the price of a consumers' good on the final products market, or the price of a service on the services market, or the price of net income on the capital goods market[j]—these always constitute the double condition by which the universe of economic interests is automatically governed, just as the universe of astronomical movements is automatically governed by the double condition of gravitation which acts in direct proportion to the masses and in inverse proportion to the square of the distances. In one case as in the other, the whole science is contained in a formula two lines in length which serves to explain a countless multitude of particular phenomena.[k]

Furthermore, an important truth, which economists have proclaimed over and over again but have left unproven, is finally established in the face of the denials of socialists, namely, that under certain conditions and within certain limits the mechanism of free competition is a self-driven and self-regulating mechanism not only for transforming services into products but also for turning savings into capital goods proper. And so, in the case of capital formation and credit, as in the case of exchange and production, the conclusions drawn from pure economics become the point of departure for applied economics. In one case as in the other, these conclusions clearly point to the task which social economics has to perform. Free competition in exchange and production results in maximum utility from services and products, subject only to the condition that every service and every product have one and the same exchange ratio for all trading parties. Free competition in capital formation and credit results in maximum utility from capital goods, subject only to the condition that the ratio of net interest to capital is the same for all savers. Are these conditions of maximum utility just? That is for the ethical theory of the distribution of social wealth to say; only then can the economic theory of the production of social wealth boldly proceed to work out in detail the application of the principle of free competition to agriculture, industry, commerce, banking and speculation.[1]

Lesson 28

THE LAW OF THE VARIATION OF THE RATE OF NET INCOME. PURCHASE AND SALES CURVES OF NEW CAPITAL GOODS. THE LAW OF THE ESTABLISHMENT AND VARIATION OF PRICES OF CAPITAL GOODS

265.[a] If we let v_e designate the value in exchange of the net income (E), so that the ratio of this value to the value in exchange of (A) v_a constitutes the price $p_e = \frac{1}{i}$ of net income; and if we let $r_{e,1}, r_{e,2}, r_{e,3} \ldots$ designate the *raretés* of the net income for individuals (1), (2), (3)..., or the intensities of their last wants satisfied by it after the exchange, we could then include these quantities in the table of general equilibrium (§224). Thus if we let R_e be the average *rareté*[1] of net income, or the average intensity of the last want satisfied by it, we have:

$$p_e = \frac{1}{i} = \frac{R_e}{R_a}.$$

We can now enunciate the following law of the variation of the rate of net income:

If, all other things being equal, the utility of net income increases or decreases for one or more parties to the exchange when the market is in a state of general equilibrium, the rate of net income will decrease or increase.

If the quantity of net income increases or decreases for one or more holders, the rate of net income will increase or decrease.

If [both] the utility and the quantity of net income vary for one or more parties or holders in such a way that the raretés *remain unchanged, the rate of net income will not change.*

266. Theoretically, all the unknowns of an economic problem depend on all the equations of economic equilibrium. Nevertheless, even from the viewpoint of static theory, it is permissible to consider some of these unknowns as especially dependent on the equations which were introduced at the same time as the unknowns when the problem of their determination was first raised. It is all the more legitimate to do this when we pass from the static to the dynamic point of view, or, better still, when we pass from the realm of pure theory to that of applied theory or to actual practice, for then the

307

variations in the unknown quantities will be effects of either the first
or the second order, that is to say, effects which need or need not be
taken into consideration, according as they arise from variations in
the special or the general data.[2] Consequently, having already
formulated the law of the establishment of the rate of net income
from a consideration of the whole economic system, we can now
construct purchase and sales curves of new capital goods against
numéraire, by reverting to the $l+1$ specific equations of capital
formation (§§238, 242, 243) and rewriting them in the following
simplified form:

$$E = \frac{D_k \pi_k + D_{k'} \pi_{k'} + D_{k''} \pi_{k''} + \dots}{i},$$

$$P_k = \frac{\pi_k}{i}, \qquad P_{k'} = \frac{\pi_{k'}}{i}, \qquad P_{k''} = \frac{\pi_{k''}}{i} \dots$$

where the first of these equations determines i; and the remaining
l equations determine $D_k, D_{k'}, D_{k''} \dots$.

267. If we suppose that old fixed capital goods proper of the types
(K), (K'), (K'')... are already found in the economy in quantities
$Q_k, Q_{k'}, Q_{k''} \dots$ respectively and that their gross and net incomes are
paid for at prices determined by the system of production equations
and by the rates of depreciation and insurance, it is not at all certain
that the amount of savings E will be adequate for the manufacture
of new fixed capital goods proper in just such quantities as will
satisfy the last l equations of the above system. In an economy like
the one we have imagined, which establishes its economic equilibrium *ab ovo*, it is probable that there would be no equality of rates
of net income. Nor would such an equality be likely to exist in an
economy which had just been disrupted by a war, a revolution or
a business crisis. All we could be sure of, under these circumstances,
is: (1) that the utility of new capital goods would be maximized if
the first new capital goods to be manufactured were those yielding
the highest rate of net income, and (2) that this is precisely the order
in which new capital goods would be manufactured under a system
of free competition. On the other hand, in an economy in normal
operation which has only to maintain itself in equilibrium, we may
suppose the last l equations to be satisfied. Apart from that, the first
equation can always be satisfied, at least in a progressive economy.
And, if we neglect the fact that E is a function of other variables
besides i, and that net incomes are themselves functions of the rate
of net income, the solution of this first equation can be represented
by the intersection of two curves. One of the curves, which rises from
zero as i increases and then descends to zero again (at infinity), thus

tracing the course of the demand for net income D_e multiplied by $p_e = \frac{1}{i}$, is the demand curve for net income expressed in terms of the *numéraire*, and is also, therefore, the *purchase curve* of new capital goods; while the other curve, which decreases throughout its length as i increases, thus tracing the course of the supply of net income, $D_k \pi_k + D_{k'} \pi_{k'} + D_{k''} \pi_{k''} + \ldots$ multiplied by $\frac{1}{i} = p_e$, is the supply curve of net income in terms of the *numéraire*, and is also, therefore, the *sales curve* of new capital goods.

268. The rate of net income and the prices of new capital goods having once been determined, the prices of all existing capital goods of whatever category, be they capital goods proper, landed capital or personal capital, are determined *ipso facto*, for the net incomes from these goods are simply quantities of commodity (E) the price of which is determined, as it happens, by the equality between its offer and the demand for it based on the pursuit of maximum satisfaction in the light of the initial quantity possessed (§§ 242, 253 and 254).[b]

The prices of existing capital goods proper are equal to the prices of new capital goods proper and are established in the market for capital goods, according to the equations of system (8) [§248][c]

$$P_k = \frac{p_k}{i + \mu_k + \nu_k} \qquad P_{k'} = \frac{p_{k'}}{i + \mu_{k'} + \nu_{k'}} \qquad P_{k''} = \frac{p_{k''}}{i + \mu_{k''} + \nu_{k''}} \ \ldots$$

The prices of land and personal faculties are established in the same way, the former according to equations

$$P_t = \frac{p_t}{i}, \qquad P_{t'} = \frac{p_{t'}}{i}, \qquad P_{t''} = \frac{p_{t''}}{i} \ldots$$

and the latter according to equations

$$P_p = \frac{p_p}{i + \mu_p + \nu_p}, \qquad P_{p'} = \frac{p_{p'}}{i + \mu_{p'} + \nu_{p'}}, \qquad P_{p''} = \frac{p_{p''}}{i + \mu_{p''} + \nu_{p''}} \ \ldots$$

Thus, from a simple inspection of these three systems of equations, we can easily deduce the following laws of the establishment and variation of prices of capital goods:[d]

In the market for capital goods, the equilibrium prices of these goods in terms of the numéraire *are equal to the ratios of the prices of their net incomes to the rate of net income.*

If, all other things being equal, the price of the gross income of a capital good increases or decreases, the price of the capital good itself will increase or decrease.

If the rate of depreciation or the premium rate of insurance increases or decreases, the price of the capital good will decrease or increase.

If, all other things being equal, the rate of net income increases or decreases, the prices of all capital goods will decrease or increase.[e]

269. It should be noted, however, that the prices obtained in this way are, in a sense, nominal prices, that is to say, prices which are established without any exchange[f] other than that of the excesses (in *numéraire*) of income over consumption for new and existing capital goods which are offered for sale because of excesses of consumption over income. In the market for products, once the equilibrium prices have been determined, the exchange of services against products[g] takes place instantaneously; in the market for capital goods, however, there will not necessarily be any trading in existing capital goods[h] under our ideal assumptions of a rational system. Unquestionably, the prices under consideration are determined in terms of the *numéraire*; but, on looking more closely into the matter, we see that these prices reduce finally to a single price that is, the price in *numéraire* of a unit of net income. If the rate of net income is i, equal, let us say, to 3/100, 2·5/100, 2/100..., then a capital good yielding a net income of 1 will have a price in terms of the *numéraire* equal to $p_e = \frac{1}{i}$,[i] or 33·33, 40, 50.... But even when we grant all this, what reason is there to exchange net income against net income, to sell, for example, a house yielding 2,500 francs net in rentals for 100,000 francs, only to buy a piece of land for 100,000 francs yielding 2,500 francs in rent? Such an exchange of one capital good for another makes no more sense than the exchange of a commodity for itself. To understand why purchases and sales take place in the market for capital goods we have to fall back upon certain crucial facts of experience in the world of reality. Thus, we must remember that alongside of those who have an excess of income over consumption and who can buy capital goods there are others, as we noted above in §240, whose consumption exceeds their income and who must sell capital goods.[j] We must remember, also, that the net income from new capital goods is not known to the same extent as the income from existing capital goods; the net income from new capital goods may prove to be larger or smaller [than expected], in short, it is attended with more risk. The result is that the more prudent and circumspect savers do not convert their savings into new capital goods but into existing capital goods; and then the sellers of these existing capital goods invest the proceeds in new capital goods. Applied economics studies the role of these *speculators* whose business it is to *classify* capital.[k] In addition, we must remember that the price of capital goods varies not only by reason of past changes but also by reason of expected changes either in gross income or in rates of depreciation and insurance; and that,

especially with regard to future changes, expectations differ from individual to individual. It follows that numbers of people will sell the capital goods which, rightly or wrongly, they fear may be subject to a diminution in net income, and buy with the proceeds other capital goods which they hope, rightly or wrongly, will enjoy an increase in net income. Here we have another aspect of speculation to be studied along with the one previously mentioned. In any case, once the decision has been made on the basis of the rate of net income[1] to exchange capital goods, both new and old, the exchange takes place in conformity with the mechanism of free competition and the law of offer and demand.

270. Of the three systems of equations relating to the market for capital goods, there is one that is particularly important, namely, the system pertaining to capital goods proper. This is so, because the identity of gross and net income from land exempts the price of land from two causes of variation, viz. changes in the rate of depreciation and changes in the premium rate of insurance. Personal faculties are neither bought nor sold where slavery is inadmissible. Only in the case of capital goods proper are the gross incomes, depreciation rates and premium rates of insurance all subject to change, so that their prices are quite variable[m] and they are constantly being bought and sold for speculation. Thus, in discussing the market for capital goods, we must distinguish the market for capital goods proper from the market for landed capital and personal capital, just as we found it necessary before, in discussing the market for services, to distinguish the market for the hire of capital goods proper from the markets for the hire of land and personal faculties. This market for capital goods is, in fact, the same *stock exchange* we mentioned right at the beginning of our study of pure economics, when we wanted simply to describe the mechanism of free competition in exchange (§42); but then we left this market to one side, for the time being, while we explored the complexities of exchange,[n] production, capital formation and credit. Now, system of equations (8) makes it possible for us to discuss all the variations in price which take place in the stock exchange. For example, if we let capital (K) be a railway and p_k be the annual dividend [per share], the price per share of this railway P_k[o] will vary in proportion to the past and expected fluctuations in the dividend. If (K') is a capital good which has been lent to an industrial enterprise or to the State and if $v_{k'}$ is a premium corresponding to the risks of failure of the business or of the nation, the price of the industrial debenture or of the State bond $P_{k'}$ will vary in proportion to the past and expected fluctuations in these risks. Frequently these variations in price are purely nominal or, at least, they take place with very little trading in securities.

271. If the price P_k increases indefinitely, it tends more and more to exceed the ratio of its own net income to the current rate of net income, with the consequence that the demand for capital good (K) diminishes indefinitely. At the same time, the offer of this capital good increases indefinitely, since its owners, by exchanging it against other capital goods, would procure a larger and larger income. Exactly the reverse consequences would follow from an indefinite fall [in P_k]. And so it happens that on the stock exchange a rise (or fall) in price always brings about a decrease (or increase) in demand and an increase (or decrease) in offer—which, as we have seen in §§48, 59, 98, 128 and 215, is not the case in the markets for products and services.[p]

PART VI

Theory of Circulation and Money[a]

Lesson 29

THE MECHANISM AND
EQUATIONS OF CIRCULATION AND MONEY

272. In the course of establishing and solving the equations of production and capital formation in Lessons 20, 21, 24 and 25, we deliberately abstracted in §179 from the following seven categories of the elements of production enumerated in §178:

(7) *new capital goods* which producers hold for sale in the form of products;

(8) stocks of *income goods* consisting of *consumers' goods* in the homes of consumers;

(9) stocks of *income goods* consisting of *raw materials* held [for future use] by producers;

(10) new income goods consisting of *consumers' goods* and *raw materials* held for sale by the producers of these goods;

(11), (12) and (13) consumers' *cash* holdings; producers' cash holdings; and *money savings.*

The time has now come to introduce these elements in order to complete our general problem of economic equilibrium.

We can eliminate the seventh category. We need only assume that the *coefficient of production* a_k, which represents the part played by capital good (K) in the production of each unit of (A) manufactured, includes both the quantity of *productive services* and the quantity of *services of availability*[1] rendered by capital good (K) in the production of 1 unit of (A). In this way the capital goods under the seventh heading are comprised in the quantity of service (K) which is effectively demanded at the price p_k and which is equal to the quantity effectively offered O_k.

We can combine the ninth and tenth categories into one. We need only assume that the coefficient of production a_m, which represents the part played by raw material (M) in the production of each unit of (A) manufactured, includes the quantities of two sorts of services of availability: that rendered by the raw material while it is held *in stock* for future use and that rendered while it is placed *on display* for sale. In this way the raw materials under the ninth and tenth headings are comprised in the quantity of service (M) which is effectively demanded at the price $p_m{}'$ and which is equal to the total existing quantity Q_m.

Bearing these simplifications in mind, we shall now introduce

315

circulating capital and money into the system of economic equilibrium. But further explanation is required in order to make clear how we intend to formulate the problem of circulation at this point and link it with the problems of exchange, production and capital formation already treated, without abandoning the *static* point of view, but at the same time bringing ourselves as close as possible to the *dynamic* point of view.[2]

273. In the theories of production and capital formation, we represented the entrepreneurs as buying certain quantities of productive services to be placed at their disposal over a given period of time by land-owners, workers and capitalists to whom they sell, in accordance with the mechanism of free competition, certain quantities of products to be manufactured during the same period. Equilibrium was then achieved when the value of the services was just equal to the value of the products in terms of *numéraire*. In the theory of circulation we shall introduce the following additional conditions.

Once equilibrium has been achieved in principle, upon completion of the preliminary process of groping by means of *tickets*[3] the actual transfer of services will begin immediately and will continue in a given manner during the whole period of time considered. The payments for these services, evaluated in *numéraire*, will be made in money at fixed dates. The delivery of the products will also begin immediately and will continue in a given manner during the same period. And the payments for these products, evaluated in *numéraire*, will also be made in money at fixed dates. It is readily seen that the introduction of these conditions makes it necessary, first, so far as consumers are concerned, that they have on hand a fund of circulating or working capital consisting of:

(1) certain quantities of final products which are mathematically determined, under the above conditions, by the attainment of maximum satisfaction in accordance with each consumer's initial quantities of these products and his utility or want functions for their services of availability; and

(2) a certain quantity of cash on hand and savings which are mathematically determined by the same attainment of maximum satisfaction, under the same aforementioned conditions, in accordance with each consumer's initial quantity of money and not only his utility or want functions for the services of availability of consumers' goods and services but also his special utility or want functions for the services of availability of new capital goods *in the form of money* rather than in *kind*;

—and, secondly, so far as producers are concerned, that they have on hand a fund of circulating and working capital, consisting, in this case, of:

(1) certain quantities of raw materials held in stock for future use and certain quantities of finished products placed on display for sale, which are mathematically determined, under the given conditions, by the attainment of equality between selling price and cost of production, given the coefficients of production made up of raw materials and already manufactured products which are required for the production of future products; and

(2) a certain quantity of cash on hand which is mathematically determined, under identically the same conditions as above, by the same attainment of equality between selling price and cost of production, given the coefficients of production made up of raw materials and already manufactured products *in the form of money*, rather than *in kind*, which are required for the production of future products.

This conception is drawn from reality, but is here given rigorous expression for purposes of scientific analysis.

In a real operating economy, every consumer, whether land-owner, labourer or capitalist, has at every moment a fairly exact idea of: (1) what stocks of [final] products he ought to have for his convenience and (2) what cash balance he ought to have, not only in order to replenish these stocks and make current purchases of consumers' goods and services for daily consumption while waiting to receive rents, wages and interest payable at fixed future dates, but also in order to acquire new capital goods. There may be a small element of uncertainty which is due solely to the difficulty of fore-seeing possible changes in the data of the problem. If, however, we suppose these data constant for a given period of time and if we suppose the prices of goods and services and also the dates of their purchase and sale to be known for the whole period, there will be no occasion for uncertainty.

That is not all. *Capital* being defined as "the sum total of fixed and circulating capital goods *hired*, not in kind, but *in money*, by means of *credit*",[4] it follows that every day in the operation of an economy a certain fraction of this capital becomes due and is repaid by the entrepreneur-borrowers to the capitalist-lenders. This quantity of repaid capital, to which land-owners, workers and capitalists add a certain excess of income over consumption, or from which they subtract a certain excess of consumption over income, constitutes the day-to-day amount of savings available for lending in the form of money. The hypothesis of constant data during the period under consideration allows us to take into account not only the [ordinary] cash savings balance alongside the cash balance required for consumption, but also a [special] cash savings balance to be lent as new capital goods in the form of money alongside the cash savings balance required for the purchase of new capital goods to be hired out in kind.

Finally, in the operation of the economy, every entrepreneur engaged in agriculture, industry or trade has at all times a fairly exact idea of: (1) what stocks of raw materials and manufactured products he ought to have for his particular volume of production and sales; and (2) what cash balances he ought to have for the replenishment of these stocks and for the purchase of productive services while waiting to be paid for the products he has sold. Here again, there may be some uncertainty because of the possibility of changes in the data of the problem and because of the difficulty of foreseeing these changes. But if, as before, we remove this possibility of change for a given period of time, and if we suppose the prices of goods and services and also the dates of their purchase and sale to be known for the entire period, we eliminate all occasion for uncertainty.

Such is the mechanism of circulation as seen from the same *static* viewpoint from which we studied the mechanisms of exchange, production and capital formation. We propose to solve the problem of equilibrium of the mechanism of circulation in the same general way as we solved the problem of equilibrium of the other mechanisms previously considered. Thus, we shall imagine an economy establishing this equilibrium *ab ovo*[5] over a given period of time during which no changes take place in the data of the problem. We shall, accordingly, endow our land-owners, workers and capitalists, viewed as consumers, with random quantities of circulating capital and money, just as we endowed them before with random quantities of fixed assets in the form of landed capital, personal capital and capital proper. Furthermore, we shall suppose our entrepreneurs to borrow the circulating capital goods and the money they need for production, just as we previously supposed them to borrow the fixed capital goods they required. We shall describe equilibrium in principle, as before, first theoretically and mathematically, and then practically as it manifests itself in the market. Our economy will then be ready to function, and we shall be in a position, if we so desire, to pass from the static to the *dynamic* point of view. In order to make this transition we need only suppose the data of the problem, viz. the quantities possessed, the utility or want curves, etc., to vary as a function of *time*. The *fixed* equilibrium will then be transformed into a *variable* or *moving* equilibrium, which re-establishes itself automatically as soon as it is disturbed. In the theory of bimetallism we find an equilibrium of this kind.

274. Thanks to our hypothetical use of *tickets*, we are able to distinguish the following three phases quite clearly, particularly if we view them as successive:

(1) the phase of *preliminary gropings* towards the establishment of equilibrium in principle;

(2) the *static* phase in which equilibrium is effectively established *ab ovo* as regards the quantity of productive services and products made available during the period considered, under the stipulated conditions, and without any changes in the data of the problem;

(3) a *dynamic* phase in which equilibrium is constantly being disturbed by changes in the data and is constantly being re-established.

The *new capital goods*, both *fixed* and *circulating*, which are made available during the second phase at costs of production equal to selling prices determined by the ratio of the current prices of their services to the rate of net income, are not put to use until the third phase. This should be clearly understood from the above definitions and constitutes the first change in the data of our problem (§251).

If the economy were liquidated at the end of the second phase, the *old capital goods, both fixed and circulating*, would be returned *in kind* by the entrepreneurs to the capitalists, and the circulating capital goods would be returned in the form of *similar* goods.

If the economy continues in a state of dynamic equilibrium, we shall find it useful to assume that the *circulating* capital goods are borrowed by the entrepreneurs from the capitalists *in the form of money*, at the prices 1, $p_b \ldots p_m \ldots$, as *short-term loans* maturing immediately after the sale [of the products].

In this way we bring to completion our rational synthesis of economic equilibrium founded on the equations of exchange and maximum satisfaction.

275. Letting (A), (B), (C), (D)... (M)... (T), (P), (K)... be, as before, commodities of all sorts, i.e. final products, raw materials and productive fixed capital in the form of landed capital, personal capital and capital proper; we shall now let (A′), (B′)... (M)... be the same products and raw materials considered, however, as circulating capital goods, that is to say, as goods rendering a service of availability either in the larders and cupboards of consumers or in the storerooms and salesrooms of producers. Letting (A) or (A′) be the *numéraire*, as before, so that 1, $p_b, p_c, p_d \ldots p_m \ldots P_t, P_p, P_k \ldots$ are again the prices of commodities of all sorts in terms of (A), we shall now let $p_a{'}=i$, $p_b{'}=p_b i \ldots$, $p_m{'}=p_m i \ldots$ be the prices of the services of availability of (A′), (B′)... (M)..., just as $\pi_t=P_t i$, $\pi_p=P_p i$, $\pi_k=P_k i \ldots$ are the prices of the services of (T), (P), (K)....[1]

---

[1] We are ignoring the depreciation and insurance of circulating capital goods.

Let (U) be money which we shall first suppose to be an object without any utility of its own, but given in quantity, distinct from (A), having a price of its own p_u, and a price for its service of availability $p_u{'}=p_u i$. We reserve the right, however, later to identify (U) with (A), and then set $p_u=p_a=1$ and $p_u{'}=p_a{'}=i$.[6]

Let us next single out an individual holding $q_a{'}$ of (A'), $q_b{'}$ of (B')... q_m of (M)... and q_u of (U). And let $r=\phi_a{'}(q)$, $r=\phi_b{'}(q)$... be this individual's utility or want equations for the services (A'), (B').... The quantities $o_a{'}$, $o_b{'}$..., positive or negative, of these services which he effectively offers at the prices $p_a{'}$, $p_b{'}$... will be determined at one and the same time by the equation of exchange[7]

$$o_t p_t+o_p p_p+o_k p_k+...+o_a{'}p_a{'}+o_b{'}p_b{'}+...+q_m p_m{'}+...+o_u p_u{'}$$
$$=d_a+d_b p_b+d_c p_c+d_d p_d+...+d_e p_e$$

and by the equations of maximum satisfaction

$$\phi_a{'}(q_a{'}-o_a{'})=p_a{'}\phi_a(d_a),$$
$$\phi_b{'}(q_b{'}-o_b{'})=p_b{'}\phi_a(d_a),$$
$$.\quad.\quad.\quad.\quad.\quad.\quad.\quad.\quad.$$

from which we obtain the following quantities effectively offered:

$$o_a{'}=f_a{'}(p_t, p_p, p_k...p_b, p_c, p_d...p_a{'}, p_b{'}...p_m{'}...p_u{'}, p_e),$$
$$o_b{'}=f_b{'}(p_t, p_p, p_k...p_b, p_c, p_d...p_a{'}, p_b{'}...p_m{'}...p_u{'}, p_e),$$
$$.\quad.\quad.\quad.\quad.\quad.\quad.\quad.\quad.\quad.\quad.\quad.\quad.\quad.\quad.\quad.$$

In a similar manner, we could derive the quantities effectively offered by the other parties, so that among the equations (1) of capital formation (§245) we should have the following equations of total effective offer:

$$O_a{'}=F_a{'}(p_t, p_p, p_k...p_b, p_c, p_d...p_a{'}, p_b{'}...p_m{'}...p_u{'}, p_e),$$
$$O_b{'}=F_b{'}(p_t, p_p, p_k...p_b, p_c, p_d...p_a{'}, p_b{'}...p_m{'}...p_u{'}, p_e), \quad..(1)$$
$$.\quad.\quad.\quad.\quad.\quad.\quad.\quad.\quad.\quad.\quad.\quad.\quad.\quad.\quad.\quad.$$

So far as (M)... is concerned, inasmuch as consumers do not have any use for raw materials, the quantities they effectively offer will be equal to the total quantities they possess q_m... and, consequently, the total effective offer will equal the total existing quantities, Q_m....

Finally, as regards money, let $r=\phi_\alpha(q)$, $r=\phi_\beta(q)$... $r=\phi_\epsilon(q)$ be our individual's utility or want equations for the services of availability of products (A'), (B')... and perpetual net income (E'), not *in kind*, but *in money*. The quantities α, β... ϵ, positive or negative, of these services which he desires at the prices $p_a{'}$, $p_b{'}$... will be determined at one and the same time by the equation of exchange and by the following equations of maximum satisfaction:

$$\phi_\alpha(\alpha)=p_{a'}\phi_a(d_a),$$
$$\phi_\beta(\beta)=p_{b'}\phi_a(d_a),$$
$$\cdot\ \cdot\ \cdot\ \cdot\ \cdot\ \cdot$$
$$\phi_\epsilon(\varepsilon)=p_{a'}\phi_a(d_a),$$

from which we obtain, first, the quantities desired of the services (A'), (B') ... (E') [in the form of money]

$$\alpha=f_\alpha(p_t,\,p_p,\,p_k\cdots p_b,\,p_c,\,p_d\cdots p_{a'},\,p_{b'}\cdots p_{m'}\cdots p_{u'},\,p_e),$$
$$\beta=f_\beta(p_t,\,p_p,\,p_k\cdots p_b,\,p_c,\,p_d\cdots p_{a'},\,p_{b'}\cdots p_{m'}\cdots p_{u'},\,p_e),$$
$$\cdot\ \cdot\ \cdot\ \cdot\ \cdot\ \cdot\ \cdot\ \cdot\ \cdot\ \cdot\ \cdot\ \cdot$$
$$\varepsilon=f_\epsilon(p_t,\,p_p,\,p_k\cdots p_b,\,p_c,\,p_d\cdots p_{a'},\,p_{b'}\cdots p_{m'}\cdots p_{u'},\,p_e),$$

secondly, the value of these quantities expressed in terms of *numéraire*

$$\alpha p_{a'}+\beta p_{b'}+\ldots+\varepsilon p_{a'}$$

and finally the quantity of money effectively offered[8]

$$o_u=q_u-\frac{\alpha p_{a'}+\beta p_{b'}+\ldots+\varepsilon p_{a'}}{p_{u'}}.$$

In a similar manner we could derive the quantities effectively offered by the other parties and, consequently, the total effective offer of money[9]

$$O_u=Q_u-\frac{d_\alpha p_{a'}+d_\beta p_{b'}+\ldots+d_\epsilon p_{a'}}{p_{u'}}. \qquad ..(9)$$

The value of all or part of the final products and perpetual net income which the parties to the exchange wish to purchase, and which they desire to keep in their possession in the form of cash or money savings, constitutes their *desired cash-balance* ['*encaisse désirée*'].[10]

The equation of aggregate exchange of services for final products will then be

$$O_t p_t+O_p p_p+O_k p_k+\ldots+O_{a'}p_{a'}+O_{b'}p_{b'}+\ldots+Q_m p_{m'}+\ldots$$
$$+O_u p_{u'}=D_a+D_b p_b+D_c p_c+D_d p_d+\ldots+E.$$

276. Having considered the offer, we must now turn to the demand.

Letting D_a, D_b... be, as before, the quantities demanded of (A), (B)... in the form of final products and D_k... be the quantities demanded of (K)... in the form of new fixed capital goods, we shall now let $D_{a'}$, $D_{b'}$... D_m... be the quantities demanded of (A), (B)... (M)... in the form of new circulating capital goods. Moreover, we shall let $a_{a'}$, $a_{b'}$... a_m... $b_{a'}$, $b_{b'}$... b_m... $m_{a'}$, $m_{b'}$... m_m... $k_{a'}$, $k_{b'}$... k_m... be the coefficients of production made up of the services (A'), (B')... (M)... required for the production of (A), (B)... (M)... (K).... We shall have, therefore, among equations (4) of §247 certain equations which express equality between the demand and offer of the services (A'), (B')...

$$a_{a'}(D_a+D_{a'})+b_{a'}(D_b+D_{b'})+\ldots+m_{a'}D_m+\ldots+k_{a'}D_k+\ldots=O_{a'}$$
$$a_{b'}(D_a+D_{a'})+b_{b'}(D_b+D_{b'})+\ldots+m_{b'}D_m+\ldots+k_{b'}D_k+\ldots=O_{b'}$$
. . . .

and also certain equations which express equality between the demand and offer of the services (M)...

$$a_m(D_a+D_{a'})+b_m(D_b+D_{b'})+\ldots+m_mD_m+\ldots+k_mD_k+\ldots=Q_m$$
. . . .

Turning now to the service of money (U), if we let $\alpha_{a'}, \alpha_{b'}\ldots \alpha_m\ldots \alpha_k\ldots \beta_{a'}, \beta_{b'}\ldots \beta_m\ldots \beta_k\ldots \mu_{a'}, \mu_{b'}\ldots \mu_m\ldots \mu_k\ldots \varkappa_{a'}, \varkappa_{b'}\ldots \varkappa_m\ldots \varkappa_k\ldots$ be the coefficients of production made up of the services (A'), (B')... (M)... (K)... required *in money* and not *in kind* for the production of (A), (B)... (M)... (K)... respectively, we then have: first, the following quantities demanded of the services (A'), (B')... (M)... (K)... in the form of money:[11]

$$\alpha_{a'}(D_a+D_{a'})+\beta_{a'}(D_b+D_{b'})+\ldots+\mu_{a'}D_m+\ldots+\varkappa_{a'}D_k+\ldots=\delta_\alpha$$
$$\alpha_{b'}(D_a+D_{a'})+\beta_{b'}(D_b+D_{b'})+\ldots+\mu_{b'}D_m+\ldots+\varkappa_{b'}D_k+\ldots=\delta_\beta$$
. . . .
$$\alpha_m(D_a+D_{a'})+\beta_m(D_b+D_{b'})+\ldots+\mu_mD_m+\ldots+\varkappa_mD_k+\ldots=\delta_\mu$$
. . . .
$$\alpha_k(D_a+D_{a'})+\beta_k(D_b+D_{b'})+\ldots+\mu_kD_m+\ldots+\varkappa_kD_k+\ldots=\delta_\varkappa$$
. . . . ;

secondly, if we write[12]

$$a_u=\alpha_{a'}p_{a'}+\alpha_{b'}p_{b'}+\ldots+\alpha_mp_m'+\ldots+\alpha_kp_k+\ldots$$
. . . .
$$b_u=\beta_{a'}p_{a'}+\beta_{b'}p_{b'}+\ldots+\beta_mp_m'+\ldots+\beta_kp_k+\ldots$$
. . . .
$$m_u=\mu_{a'}p_{a'}+\mu_{b'}p_{b'}+\ldots+\mu_mp_m'+\ldots+\mu_kp_k+\ldots$$
. . . .
$$k_u=\varkappa_{a'}p_{a'}+\varkappa_{b'}p_{b'}+\ldots+\varkappa_mp_m'+\ldots+\varkappa_kp_k+\ldots$$
. . . . ,

the following total amount demanded of the service of money for productive purposes expressed in terms of *numéraire*:

$$a_u(D_a+D_{a'})+b_u(D_b+D_{b'})+\ldots+m_uD_m+\ldots+k_uD_k+\ldots$$
$$=\delta_\alpha p_{a'}+\delta_\beta p_{b'}+\ldots+\delta_\mu p_m'+\ldots+\delta_\varkappa p_k+\ldots;$$

and finally the equation[13]

$$\frac{\delta_\alpha p_{a'} + \delta_\beta p_{b'} + \ldots + \delta_\mu p_{m'} + \ldots + \delta_\kappa p_k + \ldots}{p_{u'}} = O_u \quad \ldots (10)$$

expressing equality between the demand and offer of the service of money (U).

The cost of production equations (5) and (6) in §247 then become

$$a_t p_t + a_p p_p + a_k p_k + \ldots + a_{a'} p_{a'} + a_{b'} p_{b'} + \ldots$$
$$+ a_m p_{m'} + \ldots + a_u p_{u'} = 1,$$

$$b_t p_t + b_p p_p + b_k p_k + \ldots + b_{a'} p_{a'} + b_{b'} p_{b'} + \ldots$$
$$+ b_m p_{m'} + \ldots + b_u p_{u'} = p_b$$

· · · · · · · · · · · · · ·

$$m_t p_t + m_p p_p + m_k p_k + \ldots + m_{a'} p_{a'} + m_{b'} p_{b'} + \ldots$$
$$+ m_m p_{m'} + \ldots + m_u p_{u'} = p_m$$

· · · · · · · · · · · · · ·

$$k_t p_t + k_p p_p + k_k p_k + \ldots + k_{a'} p_{a'} + k_{b'} p_{b'} + \ldots$$
$$+ k_m p_{m'} + \ldots + k_u p_{u'} = P_k$$

· · · · · · · · · · · · · ·

277. The equations of exchange (3) and (7) of the total excess of production over consumption in §§246 and 248 become[14]

$$D_k P_k + \ldots + D_{a'} + D_{b'} p_b + \ldots + D_m p_m + \ldots = E$$
$$= F_e(p_t, p_p, p_k \ldots p_b, p_c, p_d \ldots p_{a'}, p_{b'} \ldots p_{m'} \ldots p_{u'}, i);$$

and we have, therefore, among the equations of system (8) in §249 expressing equality in the rate of net income from all artificial capital goods the following equations relating to circulating capital goods:

$$1 = \frac{p_{a'}}{i}, \qquad p_b = \frac{p_{b'}}{i} \ldots \qquad p_m = \frac{p_{m'}}{i} \ldots \qquad p_u = \frac{p_{u'}}{i},$$

in all[15] $m+s+1$ equations, which, when added to the $m+1$ offer equations of the services of circulating capital goods (A'), (B')... and money (U), and to the $m+s+1$ demand equations of the services of circulating capital goods (A'), (B')..., raw materials (M)... and money (U), make up a total of $3m+2s+3$ equations for the determination of $3m+2s+3$ unknowns. These unknowns are the $m+1$ quantities exchanged of the services of circulating capital goods (A'), (B')... and money (U); the $m+s+1$ prices of the services of circulating capital goods (A'), (B')..., raw materials (M)... and money (U); the $m+s$ quantities manufactured of circulating capital goods and raw materials; and the price of money.

The $2m+s+2$ equations of demand and offer of the services (A'), (B')... (M) and (U) can be easily reduced by the elimination of $O_{a'}$, $O_{b'}$... and O_u, to $m+s+1$ equations expressing equality between their offer and demand at the current prices.[16] Of these $m+s+1$ equations, the m equations relating to (A'), (B')... are solved in precisely the same way as the equations relating to (T), (P), (K)... were solved in §§215, 216 and 217, by a rise or fall in price, according as the demand is greater or less than the offer, since demand in every case decreases continuously as price increases and offer first increases from zero and then decreases to zero again (at infinity). The s equations relating to (M)... are solved in like manner with due regard to its decreasing demand and constant offer. As for the equation relating to (U), we shall discuss that presently.

Of the $m+s+1$ equations expressing a uniform rate of net income, the $m+s$ equations relating to (A'), (B')... (M)... are solved in precisely the same way as the equations relating to the new capital goods (K), (K'), (K'')... were solved in §§256, 257 and 258, by an expansion or contraction in the quantity manufactured according as the selling price is greater or less than the cost of production, since the selling price is determined by the ratio of the net income to the rate of net income and the quantity manufactured increases from zero and then decreases to zero (at infinity) as the cost of production increases. The equation relating to (U) is completely solved as soon as the equation of circulation is solved.

Lesson 30

SOLUTION OF THE EQUATIONS OF CIRCULATION AND MONEY. THE LAW OF THE ESTABLISHMENT AND VARIATION OF THE PRICE OF MONEY. PRICE CURVE OF THE MONEY COMMODITY

278. Our next step is to pass from the theoretical solution which was formulated mathematically to the practical solution which is reached in the market.

To start with, let us suppose, as we have already done,[1] that (U) is money, but is neither a commodity nor anything that can serve as the *numéraire*. It is easy to imagine such a situation. It would be true, for example, of a country where money consisted of inconvertible *paper francs*, but where prices were quoted in *metallic francs* of gold or silver. In Austria and Italy at the present time,[2] for instance, money consists of inconvertible paper florins and liras; but under certain circumstances prices could be quoted in these countries in terms of gold or silver florins and liras. We say, then, that $p_b \ldots p_m \ldots P_k \ldots p_a', p_b' \ldots p_m' \ldots p_k \ldots p_u'$ are prices in terms of (A).

This very circumstance permits us to envisage the practical solution as a solution given by the theories of production and capital formation in so far as these theories relate to circulating capital goods. The circulating capital goods (A'), (B')... (M)... render their service of availability in exactly the same way as the fixed capital goods (K), (K'), (K")... render their use services. The prices $p_a', p_b' \ldots p_m' \ldots$ are determined in the same way as the prices $p_k, p_{k'}, p_{k''} \ldots$; and the prices $p_b \ldots p_m \ldots$ in the same way as the prices $P_k, P_{k'}, P_{k''} \ldots$. In fact, as we have seen in §§275, 276 and 277, the equations of capital formation in systems (2), (3), (5), (6) and (7) involve certain [additional] variables or terms relating to (A'), (B')... (M)... (U), while [in the expanded version] system (1) includes $m+s$ offer equations of (A'), (B')... (M)...; system (4) includes $m+s$ equations expressing equality between the demand and offer of (A'), (B')... (M)...; and system (8) includes $m+s+1$ equations expressing the equality of rates of net income from (A'), (B')... (M)... (U). Only the offer equation (9) of (U) and equation (10) expressing equality between the demand and offer of (U) remain outside [this solution]. Consequently, if a price p'_u is cried at random and is held fixed during the process of groping in production and capital formation, we come to the last equation from which the equality between the price of the *numéraire* and unity is deduced at the same time as the equality

325

between the demand and offer of the *numéraire*, so that there remains only to solve the equation

$$Q_u - \frac{d_\alpha p_a' + d_\beta p_b' + \ldots + d_\epsilon p_a}{p_u'} =$$

$$\frac{\delta_\alpha p_a' + \delta_\beta p_b' + \ldots + \delta_\mu p_m' + \ldots + \delta_\kappa p_k + \ldots}{p_u'}.$$

If we set[3]

$$d_\alpha p_a' + d_\beta p_b' + \ldots = D_\alpha,$$

$$\delta_\alpha p_a' + \delta_\beta p_b' + \ldots + \delta_\mu p_m' + \ldots + \delta_\kappa p_k + \ldots = \Delta_\alpha,$$

$$d_\epsilon p_a' = E_\alpha,$$

and

$$D_\alpha + \Delta_\alpha + E_\alpha = H_\alpha,$$

then the equation at the close of the preceding paragraph becomes

$$Q_u = \frac{H_\alpha}{p_u'}.$$

The three terms $\dfrac{D_\alpha}{p_u'}$, $\dfrac{\Delta_\alpha}{p_u'}$, $\dfrac{E_\alpha}{p_u'}$ represent respectively *cash* in the hands of consumers, *cash* in the hands of producers and *money savings*. But since there cannot be one p_u' for savings and another for cash in circulation, nor one p_u' for cash circulating in business transactions and another for cash circulating in current [private] transactions, one price common to both the service of money in circulation and the service of money in savings results from the single equation of monetary circulation given above. Hence, if perchance

$$Q_u p'_u' = H_\alpha,$$

the question would be completely settled. Generally, however, we find that

$$Q_u p'_u' \gtrless H_\alpha,$$

and the problem is to determine how equality between the demand and offer of money is reached by groping through adjustments in p'_u'.

On referring back to the various terms that enter into the composition of H_α, we perceive that they are not absolutely independent of p_u', since p_u' figures in the term $o_u p_u'$ of the equation of exchange which, together with the equations of maximum satisfaction, enables us to deduce the quantities α, $\beta \ldots \epsilon$ for any one party to the exchange and, consequently, the aggregate quantities d_α, $d_\beta \ldots d_\epsilon$ for all parties together. We must admit, however, that the dependence of these items on p_u' is very indirect and very weak.[4] That being the case, the equation of monetary circulation, when money is not a commodity, comes very close, in reality, to falling outside the system of equations of [general] economic equilibrium. If we first suppose [general] economic equilibrium to be established, then the equation of monetary circulation would be solved almost without any groping, simply by raising or lowering p_u' according as $Q_u \gtrless \dfrac{H_\alpha}{p'_u}$ at a price p'_u which had been cried at random. If, however, this increase or decrease in p_u' were to change H_α ever so slightly, it would only be necessary to continue the general process of adjustment by groping in order to be sure of reaching equilibrium. This is what actually takes place in the money market.

Thus: *The price of the service of money is established through its rise or fall according as the desired cash balance is greater or less than the quantity of money.*

There is, then, an equilibrium price p_u'; and, if i is the equilibrium rate of net income, the unit quantity of money will be worth $p_u = \dfrac{p_u'}{i}$.

Then also $\dfrac{p_u'}{i} = \dfrac{p_u}{1}$; so that, if there is an *agio*,[5] it is the same for the price of money as for the price of its service; that is to say, setting[6] $H_\alpha = H_\alpha i$, we have

$$Q_u = \frac{H_\alpha}{p_u}.$$

279. Having now seen how monetary equilibrium is established, we shall study its variations.

In this connection, we shall attribute conventional *raretés*[7] to such things as raw materials, productive services and the service of money which have no direct utility and hence no *raretés* of their own, these conventional *raretés* being proportional to the prices. Accordingly, let R_u', R_a', R_b'... R_m'... R_k'... be the *raretés* of the services (U), (A'), (B')... (M)... (K)....' From the equality between prices and the ratios of the *raretés* we have

$$Q_u \frac{R_u'}{R_a} = (d_\alpha + \delta_\alpha + d_\epsilon)\frac{R_a'}{R_a} + (d_\beta + \delta_\beta)\frac{R_b'}{R_a} + \dots$$
$$+ \delta_\mu \frac{R_m'}{R_a} + \dots + \delta_\kappa \frac{R_k'}{R_a}$$

or

$$Q_u R_u' = (d_\alpha + \delta_\alpha + d_\epsilon)R_a' + (d_\beta + \delta_\beta)R_b' + \dots$$
$$+ \delta_\mu R_m' + \dots + \delta_\kappa R_k' + \dots.$$

In other words, if we use the term *rectangular utility* to designate *quantity* multiplied by *average rareté*, the rectangular utility of the service of money is the sum of the rectangular utilities of the commodities and services of commodities which figure in the *desired cash balance*. Calling this sum H, we have

$$Q_u R_{u'} = H.$$

According as we take (A), (B)... as the *numéraire*, it follows rigorously that

$$Q_u \frac{R_{u'}}{R_a} = Q_u p_{u',a} = \frac{H}{R_a} = H_\alpha, \qquad Q_u \frac{R_{u'}}{R_b} = Q_u p_{u',b} = \frac{H}{R_b} = H_\beta \dots$$

Indeed, in the case of money which is not a commodity [like other commodities], it seems that, all other things being equal, the *raretés* (and consequently the value) of the service of money will vary in direct proportion to its utility, so long as its quantity remains the same, and in inverse proportion to its quantity so long as its utility remains the same. Here, however, we run into a minor difficulty. It is perfectly possible to imagine a change in utility without a change in quantity; but it is impossible to imagine a change in quantity without a change in utility, unless one assumes all the q_u's to vary in the same proportion.[8] If we assume this to be the case and $p_{u'}$ to vary in inverse proportion to quantity, then $q_u p_{u'}$, $(q_u - o_u)p_{u'}$, and $o_u p_{u'}$ will not vary at all, and the previously established equilibrium will remain unchanged in consequence of a change in $p_{u'}$ alone.[9] Aside from this special case, whenever the quantity $[Q_u]$ changes, the changes in the q_u's will entail a change in the $o_u p_{u'}$'s, and consequently in the α, β... ε's, the d_α, d_β... d_ε's and all the items of utility. Though this is perfectly true, we must nevertheless note in the general case that:

(1) the $q_u p_{u'}$'s constitute only a fraction of the income of the parties to the exchange and changes in the $q_u p_{u'}$'s are spread over all expenditures on reserve stocks, consumption goods, and savings;

(2) to the extent that the changes in the q_u's are not uniformly proportional, if the $q_u p_{u'}$'s, the $(q_u - o_u)p_{u'}$'s and the $o_u p_{u'}$'s increase or decrease for some parties, they will decrease or increase for other parties, so that the d_α, d_β... d_ε's and the δ_α, δ_β... δ_μ... δ_κ...'s will not be appreciably affected; and

(3) since the d_α, d_β... d_ε's and the δ_α, δ_β... δ_μ... δ_κ...'s on the one hand, and the $R_{a'}$, $R_{b'}$... $R_{m'}$... $R_{k'}$...'s, on the other, vary in opposite directions, it follows that, if these quantities change but little, their products, i.e. the rectangular utilities, will change still less with changes in the quantity of money. We may, therefore, enunciate with what amounts to almost rigorous exactness that: *The* rareté *or*

value of the service of money is directly proportional to its utility and inversely proportional to its quantity.

By virtue of the relation $p_u = \dfrac{p_u'}{i}$, the above proposition is no less applicable to the *rareté* or value of money itself than it is to the *rareté* or value of its service. In other words, setting $H=Hi$, $H_\alpha = H_\alpha i$, $H_\beta = H_\beta i \ldots$, we have

$$Q_u p_{u,a} = H_\alpha, \qquad Q_u p_{u,b} = H_\beta \ldots.$$

280. Nowadays it is no longer possible to use any kind of a capital good for money, as it is said cattle were once used. Landed capital, personal capital and capital proper are each made up of too many varieties, so that the definition of any one kind becomes excessively difficult. Moreover, there is no capital good which, after being divided into fractional parts, would retain a sufficient *rareté* or a high enough value for monetary use, since it would be practically impossible to divide any capital good without destroying it. Nor could a service, which is an immaterial thing, be used as money. The only thing that can be so used is a final product or a raw material. In fact, it seems that nature has conspired to bestow all the attributes of money, homogeneity, great scarcity, divisibility and immutability, upon two *precious metals*, gold and silver, which are final products and raw materials at one and the same time.[1] Hence it remains only to inquire how the price of a thing is established when it is both money and a final product or both money and a raw material.

We know that the price p_b' of the service of availability of a product (B') already in existence results from one equation

$$\Delta_{b'} = O_{b'},$$

in which $\Delta_{b'}$ is a monotonically decreasing function of p_b', and $O_{b'}$ is a function which first increases from zero and then returns to zero (at infinity) as p_b' increases (§276).

We know also from §276 that the price p_m' of the service of availability of a raw material (M) already in existence results from one equation

$$\Delta_{m'} = Q_m,$$

in which $\Delta_{m'}$ is a monotonically decreasing function of p_m', and Q_m is a constant quantity.

If we introduce into these equations a term representing the

[1] See my *Etudes d'économie politique appliquée*, "Théorie de la Monnaie", §11 [pp. 101–102].

demand for the monetary services [of (B') and (M)], the above equations become respectively:

$$\Delta_{b'} + \frac{H_\alpha}{p_{b'}} = O_{b'},$$

and

$$\Delta_{m'} + \frac{H_\alpha}{p_{m'}} = Q_m;$$

or alternatively,

$$\Delta_{b'} + \frac{H_\alpha}{p_b} = O_{b'},$$

and

$$\Delta_{m'} + \frac{H_\alpha}{p_m} = Q_m.$$

All of these equations, with or without the monetary term, are solved by a rise or fall in price according as demand exceeds offer or offer exceeds demand. The only difference [between the above equations and those of the preceding paragraph] is that the equilibrium price will obviously be higher after the introduction of the monetary term than it was before. Moreover, if we suppose the solution to be reached by a process of groping in two separate markets, we must admit that there will be some shifting of quantity from the commodity market to the money market, and vice versa, so long as the prices of the commodity in commodity use and in monetary use are not identical.

Thus: *The attribution of a monetary role to a commodity raises the price of the money commodity above what it would have been without the monetary attribute.*

The uniform and identical price of a money commodity or of its service in both its commodity and monetary roles is established by minting or melting according as its price as money is greater or less than its price as a commodity.

The law that the price of the money commodity varies *directly with its utility* and *inversely with its quantity* nearly always holds for the commodity in its monetary use, because, with the *quantities* and *raretés* of commodities varying in opposite directions, the *rectangular utility* of the fraction of the money commodity constituting the desired cash balance will be approximately the same after its designation as money as it was before. Hence H and H are always fairly constant. But the extent to which the law holds for the money commodity in its commodity use, and consequently for the money commodity [as a whole in both its uses], depends upon the extent to which the demand functions vary inversely with price and the offer functions are constant.[10]

281. The law that the value of money is directly proportional to its utility and inversely proportional to its quantity provides us with a simple expedient for passing from the case in which money is neither an ordinary commodity nor a *numéraire* to the case in which it is both.

This law, as we have already pointed out, is not absolutely rigorous. It is so, however, at least with respect to [variations in] quantity under the following conditions: (1) if we adopt the static point of view, as we have been doing, in the establishment of equilibrium *ab ovo*, under the supposition that consumers, whether land-owners, workers or capitalists, possess fixed and circulating capital goods which they lend to entrepreneurs engaged in production; and (2) if we let the quantity of money in the hands of capitalists vary proportionately. In that case, since the $o_u p_{u'}$ terms in the [individual] equations of exchange remain constant under the assumption that the value [of money] varies inversely with quantity, economic equilibrium will not be disturbed under this assumption.

Suppose, now, that what we have hitherto designated as (U) becomes (A'), and that the quantity Q_u and the price $p_{u'}$ of (U) are transformed into a quantity $Q''_{a'}$ and a price $p_{a'}$ of (A'), such that

$$Q''_{a'} p_{a'} = Q_u p_{u'}.$$

Then (A'), which is already *numéraire*, becomes money also. Its total quantity $Q_{a'}$ is made up of a quantity $Q'_{a'}$ of circulating capital and a quantity $Q''_{a'}$ of money. A price $p_{a'}$ for its service as circulating capital always results, as we have seen in §276, from one equation

$$\Delta_{a'} = O_{a'},$$

which can be rewritten in the form

$$Q'_{a'} = (Q'_{a'} - O_{a'}) + \Delta_{a'};$$

while the same price $p_{a'}$ for its service as money results from the equation (§278)

$$Q''_{a'} = \frac{H_\alpha}{p_{a'}},$$

so that

$$Q_{a'} = Q'_{a'} + Q''_{a'} = (Q'_{a'} - O_{a'}) + \Delta_{a'} + \frac{D_\alpha + \Delta_\alpha + E_\alpha}{p_{a'}}.$$

Thus: *In the case of a commodity that serves both as money and as* numéraire *the uniform and identical price of its service as circulating capital and as money is established by a rise or fall according as the demand is greater or less than the [total existing] quantity; and this price is maintained [the same in both uses] by minting or melting according as the price of its service as money is greater or less than the price of its service as circulating capital.*

Once a p_a' has been determined in this way, a special adjustment in capital formation must take place by the process of groping until

$$p^{IV}{}_a = \frac{p^{IV}{}_a'}{i^{IV}}, \qquad p^{IV}{}_b = \frac{p^{IV}{}_b'}{i^{IV}} \cdots p^{IV}{}_m = \frac{p^{IV}{}_m'}{i^{IV}} \cdots P^{IV}{}_k = \frac{p^{IV}{}_k}{i^{IV}} \cdots$$

as we have seen in §§256, 257 and 258. After that we should have

$$\Omega_a p^{IV}{}_a = D^{IV}{}_a + D^{IV}{}_a',$$

where $D^{IV}{}_a + D^{IV}{}_a'$ constitutes the total quantity of (A) to be manufactured (§259). One last adjustment by groping then remains to work itself out until equality is attained both between the cost of production of (A) and unity, and between its effective supply and its effective demand. Then $p_a' = p_a i = i$; and we have in conclusion

$$Q_{a'} = (Q'_{a'} - O_{a'}) + \Delta_{a'} + \frac{H_\alpha}{i}.$$

Since the role of (A') as circulating capital is generally overshadowed by its role as money, the crucial equation is

$$Q''_{a'} = \frac{H_\alpha}{i}.$$

From §278 we know that this equation can be replaced by the three equations

$$q'_{a'} = \frac{D_\alpha}{i}, \qquad q''_{a'} = \frac{\Delta_\alpha}{i} \qquad \text{and} \qquad q'''_{a'} = \frac{E_\alpha}{i}.$$

The last of these is by far the most important and can, in turn, be replaced by two equations

$$\chi'_{a'} = \frac{E'_\alpha}{j'} \qquad \text{and} \qquad \chi''_{a'} = \frac{E''_\alpha}{j''},$$

the first giving the *rate of interest j'* in the market for *fixed capital*, and the second giving the *discount rate j''* in the market for *circulating capital*.[11] Both j' and j'' oscillate around the *rate of net income i*, but they may deviate from it more or less, either temporarily or normally, for diverse reasons.[12]

282. Thus we obtain the following equation expressing, in the aggregate and in detail, the equality between the demand and supply

of (A') in the case where (A') is a commodity that serves both as money and as *numéraire*:

$$Q_{a'} = (Q'_{a'} - O_{a'}) + \Delta_{a'}$$
$$+ d_\alpha + d_\beta p_b + \ldots + \delta_\alpha + \delta_\beta p_b + \ldots + \delta_\mu p_m + \ldots + \delta_\kappa P_k + \ldots + \delta_\epsilon.$$

What is most remarkable, in the case of a commodity which serves both as money and as *numéraire*, is the manner in which all prices rise and fall in terms of (A) in response to an increase or decrease in the *rareté* or value of this commodity in its monetary use when there is a decrease or increase in its quantity. Let us suppose that, after equilibrium has once been established, the quantity $Q_{a'}$ increases or decreases with consequent increases or decreases in $Q'_{a'}$ and $Q''_{a'}$; and let us show how the increase or decrease in $Q''_{a'}$ in the money market would suffice, apart from other concomitant phenomena, to bring about a rise or a fall in all prices. By virtue of the equation

$$Q''_{a'} = \frac{H_\alpha}{i},$$

the rate of interest i will fall or rise in the money market [as $Q''_{a'}$ increases or decreases], with the result that consumers will increase or decrease their *desired cash balance*, since this cash balance is made up of quantities d_α, $d_\beta \ldots$ of (A'), (B')... which are decreasing functions of $p_{a'} = 1$, $p_{b'} = p_b i \ldots$ and consequently of i. But, so long as the quantity of products does not increase, these movements can only result in a rise or fall in the prices $p_b \ldots$ Entrepreneurs, on seeing this rise or fall in the prices of their products, will want to expand or contract their output, all the more so because the fall or rise in the rate of interest constitutes an additional cause of profit or loss to them. In the end, however, all they will succeed in doing is to raise or lower the prices of the productive services the quantity of which has remained fixed [*ex hypothesi*]. This rise or this fall will induce capitalists having more or less savings at their disposal to increase or decrease their demand for new capital goods; but since the aggregate quantity of capital goods still remains constant, the prices of these goods will merely rise or fall. Once the rise or fall in prices has permeated the entire system, the rate of interest will return to what it was [before the change in $Q''_{a'}$].

283. Under the foregoing assumption of a money commodity, the circumstance that the money commodity is at the same time *numéraire* makes it difficult to study the effects on prices of cumulating the commodity role with that of money, because, the price of the *numéraire* being always unity, or 1, the effects in question show themselves not as increases or decreases in the price of the money

commodity, but as decreases or increases in the prices of all [other] commodities. There is a very simple way of avoiding this difficulty, and that is by assuming that the money commodity is not the *numéraire* and then studying the effects of the cumulation of its two roles on its price in terms of some other commodity, say (B).

Suppose, now, that we take a raw material (A) for money, and suppose that its total existing quantity is Q_a of which one part Q'_a remains in commodity use, while another part Q''_a is monetized, so that its price in terms of (B) rises from p_a to P_a. This latter price will have to satisfy the equation[1]

$$Q''_a P_a = H.$$

Let us now draw two axes at right angles to each other, a horizontal *price axis* Op and a vertical *quantity axis* Oq as in Fig. 25.

The curve representing the price of the monetized (A) in terms of another commodity (B) as a function of the quantity of (A) monetized closely approximates an equilateral hyperbola $h''Hh'$ referred to its axes as asymptotes. The equation of this curve is

$$q = \frac{H}{p}.$$

It is a curve such that the product of its ordinates, representing quantities of (A) in monetary use, multiplied by its abscissas, representing the corresponding prices of the monetized (A) in terms of (B), is a constant and is equal in magnitude to H, the *desired cash balance* reckoned in terms of (B), which is assumed to be predetermined.

We know from §280, on the other hand, that the curve representing the price of the raw material (A) in terms of (B) as a function of the quantity of (A) in commodity use is a curve resembling $A_q A_p$ (Fig. 26). The equation of this curve is

$$q = F_a(p).$$

It is a curve such that, as the quantity of (A) [in commodity use as a raw material] decreases steadily from some finite quantity, represented by the length OA_q, to zero, the price of (A) [in this use]

---

[1] For the sake of typographical simplicity, I am retaining the notation H used in the two preceding editions [i.e. eds. 2 and 3], instead of introducing the notation H_β used above in §279 to designate the *desired cash balance* expressed in terms of the *numéraire* (B). It should be noted also that the two things we are combining here are the price of (A) in monetary use and the price of (A) as a raw material, which should not be confused with the price of the service of (A) as money and the price of the service of (A) as a raw material. [This note appears first in ed. 4.]

increases monotonically from zero to a price represented by the length OA_p, which may or may not be infinite.

From this it is easy to see that the curve portraying the price of (A) in terms of (B) as a function of the quantity of (A) in both its uses as a commodity and as money is a curve passing through the point G [Fig. 26]. The equation of this curve is

$$q = F_a(p) + \frac{H}{p}.$$

This curve can be derived graphically by superimposing the ordinates for all abscissas of the curve $h''Hh'$ [Fig. 25] on the ordinates of all

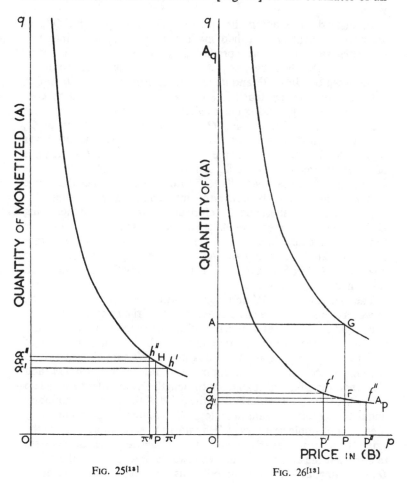

FIG. 25[13]

FIG. 26[13]

corresponding abscissas of the curve A_qA_p [Fig. 26]. Let us suppose such a curve to have been constructed, and let the length OA represent the total quantity of (A) Q_a. If, now, we draw a horizontal straight line from the point A until it meets the outer curve at the point G and then drop a perpendicular from G to P, the abscissa OP will represent the price P_a of (A) considered both as a commodity and as money when the quantity of (A) is Q_a. Moreover, the length $Oa=PF$ and the length $aA=FG=O\alpha$ of Fig. 25 represent respectively the quantities Q'_a of (A) in commodity use and Q''_a of (A) in monetary use, corresponding to the situation where there will be no conversion of (A) from commodity into monetary use or vice versa.

If, instead of dividing the quantity Q_a into Q'_a and Q''_a as we have done above, we had made a random division into two quantities so that one was represented by $Oa'>Oa$ and the other by $a'A=O\alpha'<O\alpha$, then the price of (A) in commodity use would be represented by $Op'<OP$ and its price in monetary use by $O\pi'>OP$, with the consequence that some of the commodity would be converted into money, making Oa' smaller and $O\alpha'$ larger, and therefore increasing Op' and decreasing $O\pi'$. If the random division of Q_a into two quantities had been such that one of these quantities was represented by $Oa''<Oa$ and the other by $a''A=O\alpha''>O\alpha$, the price of (A) in commodity use would be represented by $Op''>OP$ and its price in monetary use by $O\pi''<OP$ with the consequence that some of the money would be converted into commodity, making Oa'' larger and $O\alpha''$ smaller, and therefore decreasing Op'' and increasing $O\pi''$. Thus our curves give effectually a geometric solution of the problem of the determination of: (1) the price of the money commodity (A); (2) the quantity of (A) in commodity use; and (3) the quantity of (A) in monetary use. This is precisely the solution which is reached in the real world.

The two curves, $h''Hh'$ and A_qA_p, and the length OA, which are, as we have just seen, the basic determinants of the price of the money commodity and the respective quantities allocated to monetary and commodity uses, are also by that very fact the basic determinants of variations in this price and these quantities. We should need only to examine successively the effects of shifts in the curves $h''Hh'$ and A_qA_p and the effects of changes in the length OA in order to elucidate geometrically all the variations in the price of the money commodity and in the respective quantities allocated to monetary and commodity uses. For example, the curve $h''Hh'$ moves towards or away from the origin O according as the *desired cash balance* decreases or increases in size; and the curve A_qA_p moves towards or away from the origin O according as (A) in commodity use decreases or increases in utility. Furthermore, as these two curves move towards or away from the origin, the price of (A) decreases or increases. As for the length *OA*, it becomes longer or shorter with every increase or decrease in the quantity of (A). As this segment becomes longer or shorter, the price of (A) decreases or increases.

THE ESTABLISHMENT OF THE VALUE OF A BIMETALLIC STANDARD

284. The controversy between monometallists and bimetallists offers a striking example of the confusion of issues which befogs the argument simply for want of applying the only suitable method to the analysis of essentially quantitative phenomena. Given the will to do so, it is perfectly possible to demonstrate these fundamental questions with mathematical rigour.

In the preceding Lesson, I have shown that if only one commodity (A) is used as money, there are exactly three equations indicating

(1) that the sum of the quantities of (A) in both commodity and monetary uses is equal to the total quantity of (A);
(2) how the price of (A) in commodity use depends on the quantity of (A) in that use; and
(3) how the price of (A) in monetary use depends on the quantity of (A) in that use,

to determine the three unknowns, viz.

(1) the quantity of (A) remaining in commodity use;
(2) the quantity of (A) converted into money;
(3) the price common to (A) in both commodity and monetary uses expressed in terms of some other commodity.

If, now, two commodities (A) and (O) are used concurrently as money there would be no more than five equations indicating

(1) that the sum of the quantities of (A) in commodity and monetary uses is equal to the total quantity of (A);
(2) that the sum of the quantities of (O) in commodity and monetary uses is equal to the total quantity of (O);
(3) how the price of (A) in commodity use depends on the quantity of (A) so used;
(4) how the price of (O) in commodity use depends on the quantity of (O) so used;
(5) how the price of (A) in monetary use and the price of (O) in monetary use both depend on the quantity of (A) and the quantity of (O) in that use,

to determine the six unknowns, viz.

(1) the quantity of (A) in commodity use;
(2) the quantity of (A) in monetary use;
(3) the quantity of (O) in commodity use;
(4) the quantity of (O) in monetary use;
(5) the price of (A) in both commodity and monetary uses;
(6) the price of (O) in both commodity and monetary uses.

If three commodities were used concurrently as money, there would be only seven equations to determine nine unknowns.

If four commodities were so used, there would be only nine equations to determine twelve unknowns. And so on.

Thus, in the case of a single standard, the problem is completely determinate and is solved automatically in the market by the mechanism of free competition. All the legislator needs to do is: (1) to designate the commodity which is to serve as money, let us say (A); (2) to permit the conversion of money into commodity use whenever the value of (A) in commodity use is higher than the value of (A) in monetary use; and (3) to pledge himself to convert the commodity into money upon request, as soon as the value of (A) in money use rises above its value in commodity use.

In the case of a double standard, however, the problem is not completely determinate; so that the legislator can intervene, and either determine one of the six unknowns arbitrarily or introduce a sixth equation in one way or another. For example, he can arbitrarily either fix the quantity of (A) or the quantity of (O) in monetary use or else set the ratio between the two quantities. The last mentioned case would give us bimetallism *with a fixed quantity ratio*.[1] Another alternative open to the legislator is arbitrarily to fix the price of (A) or the price of (O) in monetary use or to set a given ratio between the two prices. The last mentioned case would give us bimetallism *with a fixed value ratio*. If the legislator exerts his arbitrary power on quantity, the value will be automatically determined in the market. If he exerts it on value, then the quantity will be automatically determined by the mechanism of free competition.

285. Let us suppose the legislator to decide on the latter course and to fix the ratio of the value of gold money to the value of silver money at 15½ to 1 by law, as the bimetallists wish; and let us see how the respective quantities of gold and silver in coin and in bullion will be determined in consequence. Whenever the ratio of the value of gold bullion to the value of silver bullion is *greater* than

[1] Mr. Alfred Marshall in an article entitled "On Remedies for Fluctuations in Prices", published in the *Contemporary Review* for March 1887, described a monetary system [symetallism], which is none other than bimetallism with a fixed quantity ratio. [This article was reprinted in the *Memorials of Alfred Marshall*, edited by A. C. Pigou, London, Macmillan, 1925, pp. 188–211.]

15½ to 1, not only will all newly mined gold be turned into jewellery and plate, but, in addition, part of the already existing gold coin will also be converted to commodity use; and at the same time, not only will all the newly mined silver be coined but, besides that, part of the silver already in commodity use will also be converted into silver coin. Thus the quantity of *gold coin will diminish* and the quantity of *silver coin will increase.* The quantity of *gold in commodity use will increase,* and the quantity of *silver in commodity use will decrease.* This will go on until the ratio of the value of gold bullion to the value of silver bullion falls back to 15½ to 1. When the bullion ratio is *less* than 15½ to 1, converse movements take place. The quantity of *gold coin will increase* and the quantity of *silver coin will decrease.* The quantity of *gold in commodity use will diminish,* and the quantity of *silver in commodity use will increase.* This will go on until the ratio of the value of gold bullion to the value of silver bullion rises again to 15½ to 1.

The foregoing explanation shows that the monometallists are mistaken when they assert without qualification that to promise an irrevocable 15½ to 1 ratio is to promise the impossible. Such irrevocability is possible, within certain limits, without any impairment of free competition. But the foregoing explanation also shows that the bimetallists, for their part, are equally mistaken when they imagine that it is enough to set the legal ratio of the value of gold coin to the value of silver coin at 15½ to 1 for this same ratio to be established immediately and for all time as the natural ratio between the value of gold bullion and the value of silver bullion. A commodity can be money as well as a commodity without thereby losing its identity as a commodity or ceasing to have its price determined in its commodity role by the law of supply and demand. Under exceptional circumstances this price may momentarily be either higher or lower than the mint price, and consequently it may be profitable for miners either to bring their metal to the mint or to sell it on the bullion market and profitable for money changers either to melt down their coins or to have their bullion ingots minted. This happens very frequently both under the single standard and under the double standard. It goes without saying that under the double standard the 15½ to 1 ratio imposed by the legislator on the metal in monetary use imposes itself on the bullion market, but not immediately or for all time. If the ratio of the value of gold bullion to the value of silver bullion is higher than 15½ to 1, it cannot be brought down otherwise than by the *demonetization of gold,* but only *so long as there is any gold left to demonetize.* When no more gold money is left, the ratio will remain firm at 16, 17, 18... to 1. If the ratio of the value of gold bullion to value of silver bullion is *less* than 15½ to 1, this bullion ratio cannot be raised otherwise than by *the demonetization of silver*, but only *so long as there is any silver left to demonetize*. When no more silver money is left, the ratio will remain firm at 15, 14, 13... to 1. Whether the bimetallists be right or wrong in asserting that the present fall in the value of silver is due to legislative action and not to natural causes, they cannot seriously mean that we are for ever guaranteed against natural causes having an effect on the value of silver. The essential point to bear in mind is that under a bimetallic system it is possible that there may be so great an increase in the quantity of silver as to entail the total demonetization of gold and consequently compel us to make our larger payments with cumbersome [silver] coins, or that there may be so great an increase in the quantity of gold as to entail the total demonetization of silver and consequently compel us to make our smaller payments with inconveniently tiny [gold] coins. In other words, a double standard system based on a legal ratio of $15\frac{1}{2}$ to 1, whether *local* or *universal*, is always, in final analysis, only an alternative standard system, in which the depreciated metal tends to drive the appreciated metal out of circulation.

This is the theory which we must now develop mathematically.

286. The geometric argument developed in Lesson 30 corresponds to the algebraic solution of the following three equations:

$$Q_a = Q'_a + Q''_a,$$
$$Q'_a = F_a(P_a),$$
$$Q''_a = \frac{H}{P_a};$$

by which the three unknowns, P_a, Q'_a and Q''_a, can be determined. In this case, then, there are exactly three equations to determine three unknowns.

Now let (A) and (O) be two commodities used concurrently as money. Let Q_a and Q_o be their respective total quantities, Q'_a and Q'_o their quantities remaining in the form of commodities, and Q''_a and Q''_o their quantities converted into monetary form. Let P_a and P_o be their respective prices in terms of some third commodity, say (B). To determine these six unknowns we have the following five equations:

$$Q_a = Q'_a + Q''_a, \qquad ..(1)$$
$$Q_o = Q'_o + Q''_o, \qquad ..(2)$$

stating that the total quantities of (A) and (O) are equal respectively to the sum of the quantities of (A) and the sum of the quantities of (O) in commodity and monetary uses;

$$Q'_a = F_a(P_a), \qquad ..(3)$$

$$Q'_o = F_o(P_o), \qquad ..(4)$$

indicating how the prices of (A) and (O) in commodity use are related respectively to the quantities of (A) and (O) in commodity use; and

$$Q''_a P_a + Q''_o P_o = H, \qquad ..(5)$$

which states that the sum of the quantities of (A) and (O) in monetary use constitutes the *desired cash balance*.

We can, if we wish, complete the determination of the problem by stipulating the equation

$$P_o = \omega P_a, \qquad ..(6)$$

which establishes a value ratio between P_a and P_o. This actually takes place whenever a State declares that 1 unit of (O) and ω units of (A) shall be equivalent to each other for all payments.[1]

287. Substituting into equations (4) and (5) the value of P_o given by equation (6),[11] and then substituting into equations (1) and (2) the values of Q'_a and Q'_o given by equation (3) and the modified equation (4), we obtain

$$Q_a = F_a(P_a) + Q''_a,$$

$$Q_o = F_o(\omega P_a) + Q''_o,$$

which may be written as

$$Q''_a = Q_a - F_a(P_a),$$

$$Q''_o = Q_o - F_o(\omega P_a).$$

Substituting these values of Q''_a and Q''_o into the modified equation (5), we obtain

$$\{Q_a - F_a(P_a)\}P_a + \{Q_o - F_o(\omega P_a)\}\omega P_a = H,$$

which may be written as

$$Q_a + \omega Q_o = F_a(P_a) + \frac{H}{P_a} + \omega F_o(\omega P_a).$$

---

[1] If we had assumed bimetallism with a fixed quantity ratio, our sixth equation would have read

$$Q''_a = \alpha Q''_o.$$

The mathematical theory of the system would then consist in the solution of these six equations, which would be exactly like the solution we shall develop for the case of bimetallism with a fixed value ratio.

This is an equation which can be solved for P_a algebraically or by very simple geometry.

Let[2] the curve passing through H in Fig. 25 (§283) be an equilateral hyperbola[3] referred to its axes as asymptotes, with the equation

$$q = \frac{H}{p} \; ;$$

and let the curve $A_q A_p$ [of Fig. 26 reproduced] in Fig. 27, with the equation

$$q = F_a(p),$$

be the curve of the price of (A) in commodity use, estimated in terms of (B), as a function of the quantity of (A). And, finally, in Fig. 28, let us again draw two axes at right angles to each other, a horizontal *price axis Op* and a vertical *quantity axis Oq*, within which we let the curve $O_q O_p$, with the equation

$$q = F_o(p),$$

be the curve of the price of (O) in commodity use, estimated in terms of (B), as a function of the quantity of (O). I shall now subject this last curve to the following transformation. Starting at the origin, O, I measure off on the horizontal axis certain abscissas with the lengths 1·5, 2, 2·5, 3... which are equal to $\frac{1}{\omega}$ times the original abscissas 15, 20, 25, 30... (ω in this figure being equal to 10). And on lines parallel to the vertical axis drawn through the extremities of the new abscissas, I measure off, from the horizontal axis, the ordinates of the points O'_q, s', s'', s'''... equal ω times the corresponding ordinates of the original points r, r', r'', r'''.... Thus I obtain the curve $O'_q O'_p$ the equation of which is

$$q = \omega F_o(\omega p).$$

The significance of this transformation becomes immediately apparent as soon as we perceive that in a system with a fixed value ratio between (A) and (O), 1 unit of (O) can take the place of ω units of (A), the price of (A) being $\frac{1}{\omega}$ times the price of (O). The curve $O'_q O'_p$, then becomes, as it were, the curve of the price of (O) in the form of (A).

These preliminary considerations make it possible to proceed to the following geometric solution of the equation

$$Q_a + \omega Q_o = F_a(P_a) + \frac{H}{P_a} + \omega F_o(\omega P_a).$$

I superimpose geometrically the ordinates of the curve passing through the point H in Fig. 25 on all the ordinates for corresponding abscissas of the curve $A_q A_p$, of Fig. 27, and I obtain in this manner the curve $\mu' K m''$ with the equation

$$q = F_a(p) + \frac{H}{p}.$$

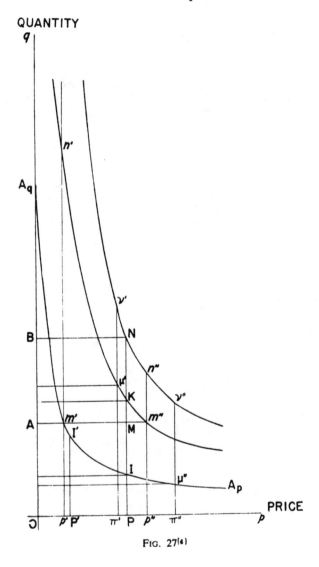

FIG. 27[4]

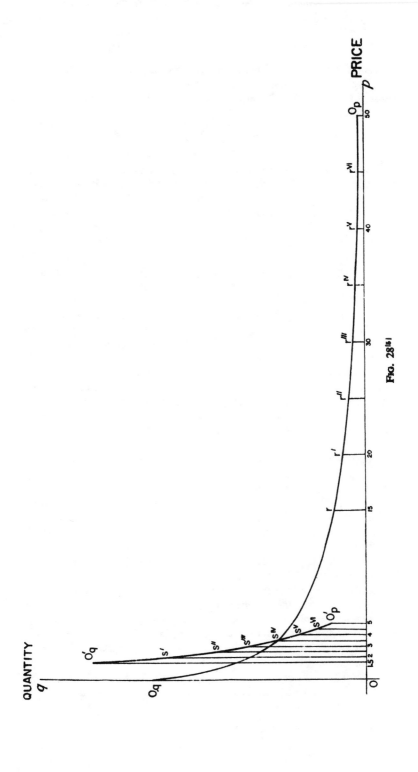

Fig. 28

I then superimpose geometrically the ordinates of the curve $O'_qO'_p$ of Fig. 28 on all the ordinates for corresponding abscissas of the curve $\mu'Km''$ of Fig. 27, and I obtain in this manner the curve $v'Nn''$ with the equation

$$q=F_a(p)+\frac{H}{p}+\omega F_o(\omega p).$$

Now let the length OA represent the total quantity Q_a of (A); and let the length AB represent ω times the total quantity of (O), i.e. ωQ_o. If from the point B we draw a horizontal straight line BN to the outermost curve, and from the point N we drop a perpendicular NP, the abscissa OP will represent the price P_a of (A) in both commodity and monetary uses corresponding to the quantity Q_a. Moreover, the segments PI and IM will represent respectively the quantities Q'_a of (A) in commodity use and Q''_a of (A) in monetary use, when there is no occasion for the conversion of (A) from commodity use to monetary use or vice versa. Referring now to Fig. 28 we find that the abscissa $50=\omega\times OP$ represents the price P_o of (O) in both commodity and monetary uses corresponding to the quantity Q_o of (O). Furthermore, the segments NK and KM of Fig. 27 represent respectively ω times the quantities Q'_o of (O) in commodity use and Q''_o of (O) in monetary use, when, as in the case of (A), there is no longer occasion for converting (O) in commodity use into (O) in monetary use or vice versa. We could show, exactly as we did in the case of the single standard, that if the division of Q_a into Q'_a and Q''_a and of Q_o into Q'_o and Q''_o had not been made in this manner, but had occurred at random and in different amounts, then there would have been conversions of (A) from commodity use into monetary use or vice versa, whichever was appropriate. For such a demonstration it would only be necessary to suppose that the three component segments of the length PN were different from PI, IK and KN and were differently situated between the Op axis and the three curves A_qA_p, $\mu'Km''$ and $v'Nn''$. I shall, however, not repeat this demonstration, not only for the sake of brevity but also in order to avoid complicating my figure which I propose to use again in another connection.

Thus: *In the case of two concomitant standards, as in the case of a single standard, the common and identical price (estimated in terms of any third commodity) of each of the two money commodities in both its commodity and monetary uses is established by minting or melting according as its price as money is greater or less than its price as a commodity.*

288. The three curves H, A_qA_p and O_qO_p of Figs. 25, 27 and 28, the two lengths OA and AB of Fig. 27, and the ratio ω to 1 are,

therefore, the basic determinants of the prices of the two money commodities as well as of the respective quantities of each of them allocated to commodity and monetary uses. For that very reason, they are also the basic determinants of variations in these prices and quantities. Here, again, we should need only to examine successively the effects of shifts in the curves H, A_qA_p and O_qO_p, as well as the effects of changes in the lengths OA and AB and in the ratio ω to 1, in order to elucidate all the variations in the prices of the two money commodities and in the respective quantities of each of them allocated to commodity and monetary uses. A comparison of the results of the foregoing analysis of the case of two concomitant standards with the results of a similar analysis of the case of a single standard should enable us, with full understanding, to draw conclusions regarding the respective merits of bimetallism and monometallism as systems for maintaining the value of the *numéraire* and money more steady in value. We shall do this in the following Lesson, but first we shall study the effects of changes in the lengths OA and AB corresponding to changes in the quantities Q_a and Q_o.

To begin with, let us suppose, that while Q_a, geometrically represented by OA, remains constant, Q_o, represented by $\dfrac{MN}{\omega}$, either increases to a quantity represented by $\dfrac{m'n'}{\omega}$ or decreases to a quantity represented by $\dfrac{m''n''}{\omega}$. Fig. 27 shows that in the first case the total quantity of silver, represented by $p'm'$, would be put to commodity use and the function of monetary circulation would be performed exclusively by gold; while in the second case the total quantity of gold represented by $\dfrac{m''n''}{\omega}$, would be put to commodity use and the function of monetary circulation would be performed exclusively by silver. The same figure also shows that if Q_o were either to increase in quantity above $\dfrac{m'n'}{\omega}$ or to decrease in quantity below $\dfrac{m''n''}{\omega}$, as long as the price of silver remained constant at either p' or p'' while the price of gold either fell below p' or rose above p'', the ratio of the value of gold in commodity use to the value of silver in commodity use would be less than ω to 1 in the first case and greater than ω to 1 in the second.

Now let us suppose that, while Q_o, geometrically represented by $\dfrac{MN}{\omega}=\dfrac{\mu'v'}{\omega}=\dfrac{\mu''v''}{\omega}$ remains constant, Q_a represented by PM, either increases to a quantity represented by $\pi'\mu'$ or decreases to a quantity represented by $\pi''\mu''$. From Fig. 27 it is seen that, in the first case the total quantity of gold represented by $\dfrac{\mu'\nu'}{\omega}$ will be reserved for commodity use and the function of monetary circulation will be performed exclusively by silver; while in the second case, the total quantity of silver represented by $\pi''\mu''$ will be reserved for commodity use and the function of monetary circulation will be performed exclusively by gold. It is seen, too, that if Q_a were either to increase in quantity above $\pi'\mu'$ or to decrease in quantity below $\pi''\mu''$, as long as the price of gold remained constant at π' or π'' while the price of silver fell below π' or rose above π'', the ratio of the value of gold in commodity use to the value of silver in commodity use would be greater than ω to 1 in the first case and less than ω to 1 in the second.

This, I believe, is sufficient to show how superficially the problems of monometallism and of bimetallism have been treated hitherto, and to suggest an appropriate method to those interested in making a more serious and adequate study of the question. It is absolutely necessary that the monometallists, on their side, give up harping on the stereotyped anti-bimetallist argument that "it is as difficult for the State to maintain a fixed ratio between the value of gold and that of silver as to maintain a fixed ratio between the value of wheat and that of rye".[1] It is very easy for the State to preserve a fixed ratio between the values of gold and silver in monetary use; and this ratio, once established, tends indirectly to become the ratio between the values of gold and silver bullion. At the same time, the bimetallists, on their side, must give up denying "that the money metal can change its value by changing its form", and must put an end to their insistence "that the values of a money metal in bullion, coin and jewellery are always equal".[2] This equality between the values of bullion and coin, far from being invariable, can only be maintained by the process of minting and melting, and ceases to exist when there is no more metal to demonetize.

289. The formulae employed in this theoretical discussion to clarify the principle of bimetallism could also be used to show the consequences of a practical application of this system. If we were to replace the above arbitrary and indeterminate functions or curves, in whole or in part, by statistically derived functions or curves having concrete coefficients, we could calculate approximately the real effects of a resumption of the coinage of silver on the basis of a given legal ratio between the values of gold and silver moneys. Let us imagine,

---

[1] M. Leroy-Beaulieu expressed this opinion in the *Journal des Economistes* for January 1874, p. 124. [This note appears first in ed. 4.]

[2] Mr. Cernuschi expressed this opinion in the *Journal des Economistes* for December 1876, p. 457.

now, that our geometrical figure holds true for a given country, and let us suppose that the quantity of silver in that country is increased after equilibrium has been established and that the natural and necessary effects of the legal ratio are prevented from being realized by a suspension of the coinage of silver. In this case, while the quantity of silver money will continue to be represented in Fig. 27 by IM and its price by OP, the quantity of silver in commodity use will be represented by $P'I'$ and its price by OP'. If, then, the coinage of silver is resumed, the effects of the legal ratio will show themselves in the addition of the length $P'I'$ to IN and in the position taken by the line $\pi'\nu'$, representing the sum of these segments, between the points P and P'. Clearly, under this arrangement the coinage of a certain amount of silver will be offset by the demonetization of a certain amount of gold and the rise in the price of silver bullion from OP' to $O\pi'$ will be accompanied not only by a fall in the price of silver money from OP to $O\pi'$ but also by a fall in the price of gold bullion and gold money from $\omega \times OP$ to $\omega \times O\pi'$. Had we chosen to consider concrete numbers as suitable to give a better grasp of the connection of these events, the following numbers would fit the situation described by the above curves for the country under consideration. In a state of equilibrium based on a legal ratio of $\omega = 10$ to 1, the total quantity of silver $OA = PM = 5$ milliard half-decagrams is divided between $PI = 2$ milliard half-decagrams in commodity use, and $IM = 3$ milliard half-decagrams in silver coin; and the total quantity of gold, $\dfrac{AB}{10} = \dfrac{MN}{10} = 433$ million half-decagrams, is divided between $\dfrac{MK}{10} = 100$ million half-decagrams in gold coin and $\dfrac{KN}{10} = 333$ million half-decagrams in commodity use. The price of silver in terms of wheat is 5 lb. a half-decagram; the price of gold in terms of wheat is 50 lb. a half-decagram. In other words, wheat is worth 0·20 francs per lb. If we suppose the total quantity of silver to be increased by 2 milliards and the coinage of silver to be suspended, the quantity of silver in commodity use will increase from 2 to 4 milliard half-decagrams, with the consequence that the price of silver in terms of wheat will fall from 5 to 1·66 lb. a half-decagram. It would then be possible to purchase 1 half-decagram of silver bullion with $0·33 = \dfrac{1·66}{5}$ of a half-decagram of silver coin. If the coinage of silver were then resumed, 2·166 milliards would remain in commodity use and 1·833 milliards would be coined; while, at the same time, the entire 100 million half-decagrams of gold coin would be melted down into bullion.

The price of silver bullion in terms of wheat would rise from 1·66 to 4·33 lb. a half-decagram, while the price of silver coin would fall from 5 to 4·33 lb. The price of gold bullion and gold coin in terms of wheat would both fall from 50 to 43·33 lb. a half-decagram. In other words, wheat would now be worth $\dfrac{1 \text{ franc}}{4 \cdot 33} = 0 \cdot 23$ francs per lb. It can be seen, then, that there would be a 15 per cent rise in the prices of all commodities.

Lesson 32

RELATIVE STABILITY OF THE VALUE OF THE BIMETALLIC STANDARD

290. In order to complete *The Mathematical Theory of Bimetallism*, we shall now discuss the bimetallic system from the point of view of the stability of the value of the monetary standard.

Assuming bimetallism, we shall designate by the term *silver franc* the unit quantity of silver, say 5 grammes or a half-decagram of silver 0·900 fine; but by the term *gold franc* we shall now designate, not the unit quantity of gold, i.e. 5 grammes or a half-decagram of gold 0·900 fine, as we have done hitherto, but the ωth part of this unit. In Fig. 28, where ω was assumed equal to 10, the gold franc, under our present definition, must be a half-gramme of gold. In that figure, the curve $O'_q O'_p$ with the equation $q = \omega F_o (\omega p)$, which was substituted for the curve $O_q O_p$ with the equation $q = F_o(p)$, was a curve expressing the price in wheat of a gold franc in the form of bullion as a function of its quantity.

For our present discussion, let us draw two axes at right angles, as in Fig. 29, the horizontal axis now being a *time axis Ot*, and the vertical axis a *price axis Op*. On the first axis let us mark off equal segments 0 to 1, 1 to 2..., each corresponding to a unit of time, or more exactly to equal time intervals between the price computations which we shall suppose to have been made from the mathematical data. On the second axis and on lines drawn parallel to it through points 1, 2..., we shall mark off segments corresponding to:

(1) the price in wheat of a silver franc in the form of bullion and coin, under the assumption that silver alone is money;

(2) the price in wheat of a gold franc in the form of bullion under the same hypothesis;

(3) the price in wheat of a gold franc in the form of both bullion and coin, under the assumption that gold alone is money;

(4) the price in wheat of a silver franc in the form of bullion under the same hypothesis [as in (3)]; and

(5) the price in wheat common to both the silver franc and the gold franc, assuming both gold and silver to be money.

From our earlier explanation and from Fig. 27, we see that at the very start [of the first period], immediately to the right of zero on the

351

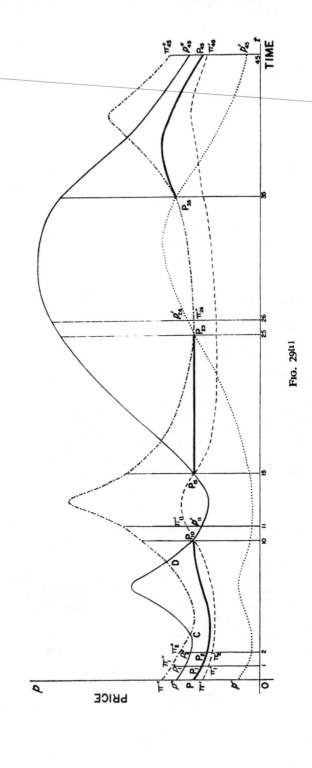

FIG. 29[11]

time axis, the first of the above enumerated quantities p'', geometrically represented by Op'', is the root of equation

$$Q_a = F_a(p'') + \frac{H}{p''} \, ;$$

the second of these quantities, π', represented by $O\pi'$, is the root of equation

$$\omega Q_o = \omega F_o(\omega\pi');$$

the third, π'', represented by $O\pi''$, is the root of equation

$$\omega Q_o = \frac{H}{\pi''} + \omega F_o(\omega\pi'');$$

the fourth, p', represented by Op', is the root of equation

$$Q_a = F_a(p');$$

and finally the fifth, P, represented by OP, is the root of equation

$$Q_a + \omega Q_o = F_a(P) + \frac{H}{P} + \omega F_o(\omega P).$$

Hence, beginning at the origin O of Fig. 29, we mark off the segments Op'', $O\pi'$, $O\pi''$, Op' and OP on the vertical axis Op.

Immediately after the first interval, the quantities Q_a, Q_o and H and the functions F_a and F_o having changed in the meantime, the above quantities would be p''_1, π'_1, π''_1, p'_1 and P_1, represented respectively by the segments 1 to p''_1, 1 to π'_1, 1 to π''_1, 1 to p'_1 and 1 to P_1, which we mark off on a line drawn parallel to the vertical axis and passing through point 1 on the horizontal axis.

Immediately after the second period, these quantities would become p''_2, π'_2, π''_2, p'_2 and P_2, represented by the segments 2 to p''_2, 2 to π'_2, 2 to π''_2, 2 to p'_2 and 2 to P_2 which we mark off on a line drawn parallel to the vertical axis and passing through point 2 on the horizontal axis.

And so on. In this way we obtain the following five curves:

(1) the curve $p''p''_1p''_2\ldots$ showing the variations in the price of a silver franc in the form of both bullion and coin under the hypothesis of a silver standard. Analytically it is derived from the equation

$$Q_a = F_a(p'') + \frac{H}{p''}$$

in which Q_a and H are independent variables, the function F_a changes, and p'' is a dependent variable instead of a predetermined value;

(2) the curve $\pi'\pi'_1\pi'_2...$ showing the variations in the price of a gold franc in the form of bullion again under the hypothesis of a silver standard. Analytically it is derived from the equation

$$\omega Q_o = \omega F_o(\omega\pi')$$

in which Q_o is an independent variable, the function F_o changes, and π' is a dependent variable instead of a predetermined value;

(3) the curve $\pi''\pi''_1\pi''_2...$ showing the variations in the price of a gold franc in the form of both bullion and coin under the hypothesis of a gold standard. It is derived from the equation

$$\omega Q_o = \frac{H}{\pi''} + \omega F_o(\omega\pi'')$$

in which Q_o and H are independent variables, F_o changes, and π'' is a dependent variable;

(4) the curve $p'p'_1p'_2...$ showing the variations in the price of a silver franc in the form of bullion again under the hypothesis of a gold standard. It is derived from the equation

$$Q_a = F_a(p')$$

in which Q_a is an independent variable, F_a changes, and p' is a dependent variable; and finally

(5) the curve $PF_1P_2...$ showing the variations in the price common to both the silver franc and the gold franc under the hypothesis of bimetallism. It is derived from the equation

$$Q_a + \omega Q_o = F_a(P) + \frac{H}{P} + \omega F_o(\omega P)$$

in which Q_a, Q_o and H are independent variables, F_a and F_o change, and P is a dependent variable.

A discussion of the first, third and fifth curves will give us the conclusion we are looking for concerning the respective advantages of monometallism and bimetallism as regards the stability of value of the monetary standard.

In order to simplify our diagram, we shall ignore variations in the quantity H as well as changes in the functions F_a and F_o; and we shall suppose only the quantities Q_a and ωQ_o to vary as delineated in Fig. 30 by the curves A and B respectively. The quantity of silver francs varies according to the curve AA_{45}; and that of the gold francs according to the curve BB_{45}. Our conclusions, however, will be entirely independent of this restriction.

291. To begin with, we note a striking similarity in Fig. 29 between curves $p''p''_1p''_2...$ and $p'p'_1p'_2...$ on the one hand, and between

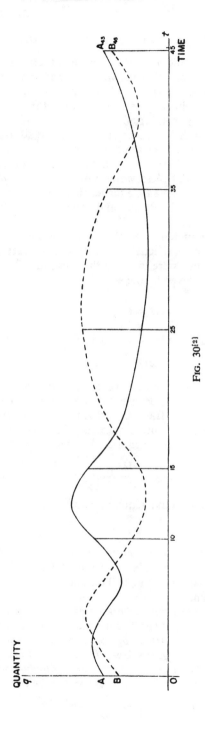

Fig. 30[2]

curves $\pi''\pi''_1\pi''_2\dots$ and $\pi'\pi'_1\pi'_2\dots$ on the other. This similarity is rational. The price of any metal which is used simultaneously as a commodity and as money is bound to be higher than the price of the same metal used exclusively as a commodity, for the attribution of a monetary role to a metal results in a diminution in the amount of this metal available for purposes of industry and adornment. Moreover, the adoption of a metal as money increases not only its price but also the amplitude of variations in this price without, in general, changing the nature of these variations. Thus curve $p''p''_1p''_2\dots$ is similar to, and at the same time higher than, curve $p'p'_1p'_2\dots$; just as curve $\pi''\pi''_1\pi''_2\dots$ is similar to, and at the same time higher than, curve $\pi'\pi'_1\pi'_2\dots$.

292. This being understood, let us return to our Fig. 30 and let us see why bimetallism is effective at the start of the curve. The reason is that, if silver alone were taken to the mint, the silver franc would acquire a value p'' given by the equation

$$Q_a = F_a(p'') + \frac{H}{p''},$$

and the gold franc would acquire a value π' given by the equation

$$\omega Q_o = \omega F_o(\omega\pi');$$

so that, as long as p'' is greater than π', it will pay to convert gold bullion into gold coin. Hence the silver franc in coin will fall relatively to the silver franc in bullion and silver money will be converted into bullion. Furthermore, if gold alone were taken to the mint, the gold franc would acquire a value π'' given by the equation

$$\omega Q_o = \frac{H}{\pi''} + \omega F_o(\omega\pi''),$$

and the silver franc would acquire a value p' given by the equation

$$Q_a = F_a(p');$$

so that, as long as π'' is greater than p', it will pay to convert silver bullion into silver coin. Hence the gold franc in coin will fall relatively to the gold franc in bullion and gold money will be converted into bullion.

Thus: *Bimetallism will only work on condition that the price of the silver franc in the form of both bullion and coin is higher than the price of the gold franc in the form of bullion alone and on condition that the price of the gold franc in the form of both bullion and coin is higher than the price of the silver franc in the form of bullion alone.* In other words, bimetallism is effective only as long as the curve $p''p''_1p''_2\dots$

THE STABILITY OF THE MONETARY STANDARD 357

in Fig. 29 lies above the curve $\pi'\pi'_1\pi'_2\ldots$ and the curve $\pi''\pi''_1\pi''_2\ldots$ in the same figure lies above the curve $p'p'_1p'_2\ldots$. This is what actually appears in the first 10 intervals of our diagram and also in the intervals from 15 to 25 and from 35 to 45.

293. The price P common to the silver franc and the gold franc in the form of both bullion and coin is the root of the following equation:

$$Q_a + \omega Q_o = F_a(P) + \frac{H}{P} + \omega F_o(\omega P);$$

besides which we have, on the one hand,

$$F_a(P) + \frac{H}{P} > Q_a > F_a(P),$$

and, on the other hand,

$$\frac{H}{P} + \omega F_o(\omega P) > \omega Q_o > \omega F_o(\omega P),$$

since the total quantities Q_a of silver and Q_o of gold are each made up in part of bullion to the amounts Q'_a and Q'_o, and in part of coin to the amounts Q''_a and Q''_o, so that evidently the first inequality implies the second and vice versa.

We already know that

$$Q_a = F_a(p') = F_a(p'') + \frac{H}{p''}$$

and that

$$\omega Q_o = \omega F_o(\omega\pi') = \frac{H}{\pi''} + \omega F_o(\omega\pi'').$$

We have then, on the one hand,

$$F_a(P) + \frac{H}{P} > F_a(p'') + \frac{H}{p''},$$

which implies that $p'' > P$; and we have, on the other hand,

$$F_a(p') > F_a(P),$$

which implies that $P > p'$. In addition, we have

$$\frac{H}{P} + \omega F_o(\omega P) > \frac{H}{\pi''} + \omega F_o(\omega\pi''),$$

which implies that $\pi'' > P$; and

$$\omega F_o(\omega\pi') > \omega F_o(\omega P),$$

which implies that $P > \pi'$.

Thus: *When bimetallism is effective, the price common to the gold franc and the silver franc in the form of both bullion and coin is: (1) simultaneously less than the bullion price of the silver franc and greater than the bullion price (i.e. the only price) of the gold franc under a monometallic silver standard; and (2) simultaneously less than the bullion price of the gold franc and greater than the bullion price (i.e. the only price) of the silver franc under a monometallic gold standard.* In other words [during the effective stage of bimetallism], the curve $PP_1P_2...$ of Fig. 29 is simultaneously below the two curves $p''p''_1p''_2...$ and $\pi''\pi''_1\pi''_2...$, and above the two curves $\pi'\pi'_1\pi'_2...$ and $p'p'_1p'_2....$ This too is seen in the intervals of our diagram previously mentioned [from 1 to 10, 15 to 25 and 35 to 45].

294. Let us refer again to Fig. 27 in order to see how bimetallism resolves itself into monometallism. It resolves itself into a monometallic silver standard whenever Q_a becomes equal to or greater than $\pi'\mu'$, or whenever ωQ_o becomes equal to or less than $m''n''$. It resolves itself into a monometallic gold standard whenever ωQ_o becomes equal to or greater than $m'n'$, or whenever Q_a becomes equal to or less than $\pi''\mu''$. In the first two cases [which result in the silver standard], the price p'' of the silver franc is given by the equation

$$Q_a = F_a(p'') + \frac{H}{p''},$$

and the price π' of the gold franc by the equation

$$\omega Q_o = \omega F_o(\omega\pi').$$

But so long as p'' remains equal to or less than π', there is nothing to be gained by transforming gold bullion into coin. In the latter two cases [which result in the gold standard], the price π'' of the gold franc is given by the equation

$$\omega Q_o = \frac{H}{\pi''} + \omega F_o(\omega\pi'')$$

and the price p' of the silver franc is given by the equation

$$Q_a = F_a(p').$$

But so long as π'' remains equal to or less than p', there is nothing to be gained by converting silver bullion into coin.

Thus: *Bimetallism resolves itself into a monometallic silver standard whenever the price of the gold franc in the form of bullion alone rises above the price of the silver franc in the form of both bullion and coin;* i.e. whenever the curve $\pi'\pi'_1\pi'_2...$ lies above the curve $p''p''_1p''_2..$

as is the case in Fig. 29 in the five intervals of time between 10 and 15. *Bimetallism resolves itself into a monometallic gold standard whenever the price of the silver franc in the form of bullion alone rises above the price of the gold franc in the form of both bullion and coin*; i.e. whenever the curve $p'p'_1p'_2$... lies above the curve $\pi''\pi''_1\pi''_2$... as is the case in Fig. 29 in the ten intervals of time between 25 and 35.

It is evident, furthermore, that *whenever bimetallism resolves itself into a monometallic silver or gold standard there ceases to be a single price common to the silver franc and the gold franc*. The curve PP_1P_2... breaks off.

295. Under circumstances corresponding to those illustrated in our Fig. 29, the transition from bimetallism to the silver standard during the period from 0 to 45 would cause the variations in the price of the *numéraire* and monetary standard in wheat to be represented by the curve PP_1P_2... $P_{10}p''_{11}$... P_{15}... $P_{25}\pi''_{26}$... P_{35}... P_{45} in place of the curve $p''p''_1p''_2$... p''_{45}. The passage from bimetallism to the gold standard would result in the replacement of curve $\pi''\pi''_1\pi''_2$... π''_{45} by the same curve. Surely the circumstances represented in this diagram have no relation to reality. They are all the more remote from the actual world because we have ignored certain factors, such as variations in the total amount of the *desired cash balance* and changes in the utility of the precious metals in their commodity role, which might have intensified or dampened the effects of variations in their quantities. It is, nevertheless, certain that the curve PP_1P_2... rises and falls with a smaller amplitude than either the curve $p''p''_1p''_2$... or the curve $\pi''\pi''_1\pi''_2$... because it always lies below these two curves and coincides with the lower one only when the upper curve tends to rise appreciably faster than the lower.[1(a)]

Thus: *The bimetallic standard preserves a certain relative stability of value in cases where the monometallic standards would have varied in opposite directions. It varies as much as these monometallic standards in cases where they would both have moved in the same direction.*

In short, bimetallism is as much at the mercy of chance as monometallism so far as the stability of value of the monetary standard is concerned; only bimetallism has a few more chances in its favour.

296. In their disputes over bimetallism economists have already given vague intimations of the curve $PP_{10}P_{15}P_{25}P_{35}P_{45}$. This is the curve which Jevons intended to present, and which he thought he had presented, in Chapter XII, called *The Battle of Standards*, of his book on *Money and the Mechanism of Exchange*. Bimetallists frequently cite this curve of Jevons's and confidently reproduce it.

[1] For a discussion of the price curve of the bimetallic standard, see my *Etudes d'économie politique appliquée* [pp. 112 ff.], Théorie de la monnaie, § 19. [This note appears first in ed. 4.]

360 ELEMENTS OF PURE ECONOMICS

There is, however, an important difference between my P curve, which is derived mathematically from the conditions determining the value of money, and Jevons's curve D which is given empirically. The P curve is at times separate and distinct from the p'' and π'' curves and lies below them, for example, between P and P_{10}, between P_{15} and P_{25} and between P_{35} and P_{45}. It is only under certain circumstances that it coincides with one or the other of these two curves. It coincides, for instance, with the p'' curve from P_{10} to P_{15} and with the π'' curve from P_{25} to P_{35}. Jevons's curve D always coincides with whichever of the two curves, p'' or π'', is the lower one. His curve would be the same as the curve $p''CDP_{10}p''_{11}\ldots$ in my Fig. 29. The behaviour of Jevons's curve follows from the assumption, quite explicitly stated in his text, that bimetallism is, in essence, a system with an alternative standard, in the sense that only one metal is ever left in circulation; sometimes it is gold, at other times silver. This is patently an error. We have proved *a priori*, and experience shows, that bimetallism can work. And when it does work, the single value common to the gold and silver franc is necessarily less than the value of the gold franc under a monometallic gold standard and less than the value of the silver franc under a monometallic silver standard. This example proves how important it is to proceed methodically in discussing quantitative relationships in which approximations, however close, cannot be tolerated.

The error once corrected, it still remains true, as Jevons has pointed out, that a compensatory action takes place under bimetallism. I need not repeat that this compensatory action is the result of a perpetual monetization and demonetization of metal, but I do wish to address one final remark to the bimetallists.

297. The moment we attempt to inject considerations of the degree of stability of the monetary standard into the applied theory of money, why should we be satisfied with an uncertain and imperfect stability? Why not aim at an assured and perfect stability? Let us see whether, subject to certain qualifications, wheat satisfies the conditions of a commodity with a fairly constant *rareté* and value. And let us see, further, whether the *rareté* and value of money ought to be constant or whether it would not be better for them to vary *pari passu* with the average *rareté* and value of social wealth. Would it not be better to replace wheat by some *multiple standard* which remains to be determined? In all such schemes the bimetallic P curve would be more nearly horizontal than either of the monometallic curves p'' or π''. We may ask, however, why be satisfied with the P curve? Why not try to obtain the desired horizontal curve directly by taking consciously planned measures to regulate the quantity of metal in circulation? This will result not from bimetallism, but from

a gold monometallism coupled with a silver billon which is distinct from the subsidiary coinage and which is alternatively issued and retired in such a way as to keep the multiple standard from fluctuating. The State in performing this operation would gain by the issue of this billon and lose by its withdrawal. The net loss or profit from this operation would be added to or deducted from the cost of minting and melting and would be the price the economy would have to pay for the stability or regularity of fluctuations of the value of the monetary standard. These questions of applied and practical economics will be treated elsewhere.[8][b] Here it is enough to have specified the most important points in the pure theory of money.

FIDUCIARY MONEY AND PAYMENTS
BY OFFSETS

298. It is a curious fact, certainly worth mentioning, that monetary theorists should hail the first advent of the use of money as such a wonderful advance, only to acclaim as a still greater advance any means of doing without money, once its use had been generally established. Indeed, the expedients for performing exchange operations without the intervention of metallic money are steadily growing in importance. We may list these expedients as follows:

299. *Book Credit*. Let X and Y be two merchants buying goods from each other on credit. On certain dates, say every six months, the sums that X owes Y and the sums that Y owes X are separately totalled to determine which of the two debits is the greater. Only the difference is payable in cash, but quite often this balance is carried over. Thus few and infrequent cash payments are needed to settle accounts arising from a large number of very substantial purchases and sales.

Here, then, is a certain volume of trade which takes place without the intervention of metallic money; but such transactions still presuppose the invention and the use of a *numéraire* and money, for even when precious metals are absent in fact, they are always present in principle. Without *numéraire* it would be impossible to keep debit and credit accounts; without money it would be impossible for each exchange transaction between X and Y to be considered as definitely settled [by means of book entries] apart from the actual remittance of cash, and for the cash involved in the mutual indebtedness to be considered by X and Y as left at each other's disposal while still remaining the property of the creditor. Furthermore, though the intervention of *numéraire* and money is not real, but virtual, without this intervention it would be impossible to find commensurable loan units, i.e. units of loaned money multiplied by units of time measuring the period of the loan, and hence it would be impossible to arrive at an exact accounting on settlement days of the difference between the credit extended by X to Y and that extended by Y to X.

300. *Commercial Paper*. It does not always happen, in fact it occurs very rarely, that two merchants have dealings with each other regularly enough and in large enough amounts for each to have an account with the other like the one described above. Hence, when X, for example, makes only a single purchase from Y, he will close

the transaction, either immediately or after an interval of book credit, in the following manner. If X and Y live in the same city, X will *make a promissory note* payable to Y in these terms: "So many months after date I promise to pay Y on order such and such a sum, value received in merchandise. Signed X." If X and Y live in different cities, Y will *draw a bill of exchange* on X in these terms: "So many months after date pay to my order such and such a sum, value received in merchandise. Signed Y." The bill of exchange will then be *accepted* by X in these terms: "Accepted. Signed X." It is true that at maturity X will have to lay out cash in discharge of his note or of Y's bill of exchange; but prior to maturity the following may take place. As soon as Y comes into possession of the promissory note or accepted bill of exchange, he may use it to square accounts with a third party, Z, by handing over the bill or note to Z, after endorsing it: "Pay to Z on order such and such a sum, value in account. Signed Y." Z may, in turn, use this same instrument in settling an account by endorsing it to a fourth party, W. And thus it is possible for a bill or note to serve as a means of payment in two, three, five, ten, or even twenty transactions between the date of writing and maturity. If X should fail to honour this instrument at maturity, it would be returned from endorser to endorser until it reached Y; but if X pays, the whole business is settled then and there, and as many as twenty transactions are closed by a single disbursement in cash.

Here again a *numéraire* and money must exist and must intervene virtually, if not actually. Each endorser is presumed to place his own cash at the disposal of X for as long a time as the endorser keeps the bill or note in his portfolio; and in remuneration for this service he receives a part of the interest paid in full by X.

301. *Bank Notes.* The free circulation of promissory notes and bills of exchange encounters various obstacles. For one thing, they are payable only at maturity, which opens the door to hazards of non-payment by the maker or the acceptor of the bill. For another, these instruments are negotiable only by endorsement, which not only puts each endorser under the obligation to compensate the holder in case of default but also exposes him to the risk of not being reimbursed himself. There are, however, institutions, called *banks of issue*, which perform the following operation. In return for notes and bills payable at some future date and negotiable only by endorsement, they issue sight bills called *bank notes*, which are negotiable without endorsement. The bank note is, in essence, a *draft at sight payable to bearer* which has been substituted for an instrument payable *to order at maturity*. And it is precisely because one can, in principle, convert bank notes at any moment into specie at the bank of issue

and because one can pass them without endorsement or liability, that they circulate much more readily than commercial paper. The fact that these notes are redeemable by all holders is the reason why they pass freely from hand to hand. Under normal circumstances the bank note remains in circulation at least until the maturity of the commercial paper for which it is a substitute. At due date the bank presents the bill or note for collection, receiving in payment either its own bank note, or else specie, which it holds until the bank note is returned from circulation and presented for redemption. The only thing required, therefore, is that the bank's bills and notes in the portfolio plus its cash in hand be equal in amount to the bank notes in circulation. In other words, with a given cash balance, a bank of issue may have notes in circulation amounting to two, three, four, or five times the value of that balance.[a] Clearly, then, if a bank's cash reserves are 100 millions and its notes in circulation 300 millions, two-thirds of the exchanges are indeed settled by bank notes, but by no means independently of *numéraire* and money though no specie is effectively employed in the transactions. Actually, the settlements are made by transfers of commercial paper without any real liquidation of indebtedness.

302. *Cheques.* Suppose that X, Y, Z and W open no mutual customers' accounts, make no promissory notes, draw no bills of exchange and do not even use bank notes in their business with one another. They will then proceed as follows. Each hands over to his banker a certain sum in money, commercial paper and bank notes to constitute his *balance on deposit*. The banker invests the money in securities, so that, in final analysis, all deposits, apart from cash reserves, are backed, like bank notes, by paper. X, Y, Z and W then make use of these deposits by means of *cheques*, which are orders drawn on the banker to pay for their purchases. If that ended the matter, the balances would soon be exhausted. But there is more to it, for X, Y, Z and W not only buy, but sell as well. And in payment for what they sell they receive cheques drawn either on their own bankers or on other bankers of the same city. Immediately on receipt, they deposit these cheques with their bankers, to be added to their balances. Then they can draw their own cheques on this addition to their balances just as they did on their original balances. This is not all. The city has an establishment called a *clearing house*, where all the bankers meet daily. There each banker turns over to the other bankers the cheques which he has against them, and receives, in turn, the cheques they have against him. Each, then, pays or receives the difference in cash, that is the difference between what he owes to others and what others owe to him. And so it is possible for the value of the cheques drawn to be far greater than that

of the original deposits. Cheques are in this way a very effective device for making purchases and sales without the actual use of metallic money, especially when there is a clearing house which is the capstone of the system. In the clearing houses of London and New York, business amounting to hundreds of millions of sterling or dollars is transacted with only a few thousand pounds or dollars actually changing hands in cash.[b] Thus we have two expedients for economizing metallic money which act with cumulative effect: (1) the offsetting of cheques in the clearing house, which, to all intents and purposes, is like offsetting orders to transfer cash; and (2) the use of cheques as orders to transfer securities in bankers' portfolios, securities which represent fixed or circulating capital and are of high or low grade depending upon the nature and character of the business done by the bankers.

303.[c] We pass no judgement on the facts; we simply note their existence and describe them. Gold and silver, by reason of their exceptional qualities, are real, liquid wealth. We can hide them in the ground or deposit them in a safe place, as we do in times of danger, with full assurance that they will always retain their value. Fixed and circulating capital goods, on the other hand, derive their value from the value of their services or uses; and in many cases this value can fall to zero. Hence debts settled by means of securities are not really discharged. Undoubtedly, the use of paper for transferring funds, in place of an equivalent amount of coin, releases additional precious metal for industry and ornament; but it still remains to be seen whether the pleasure that individuals get out of possessing impressive quantities of gold and silver plate and jewellery outweighs the inconvenience which the economy suffers from its inability to settle debts at any moment on however large or small a scale with complete security. An economy is not instituted to wind up in liquidation any more than a cart is set in motion simply for the sake of stopping; and yet, just as a cart must be able to stop or slow down, so perhaps an economy should always be able to liquidate more or less. Consequently those economists who display an excessive admiration for bank notes and cheques and those socialists who dream of *ametallism* and speak of metallic money as a "dead weight" are exactly like carters who throw away their drags and brakes as so much dead weight. In this connection, one further point should be added.

304.[d] The commercial paper and securities represented by bank notes or by cheques constitute the sum total of *fiduciary* or *paper money* as contrasted with *metallic* money. Already in §§281 and 283 we have given the equation of monetary circulation; and we must now complete this equation by inserting, alongside the symbol standing for the value of metallic money, the symbol F to represent the value of fiduciary money. It must be recognized that while the *desire for monetary cash balances* becomes weaker and weaker as the system of offsets develops through book-credit, orders to transfer cash, cheques, etc., at any given moment the size of this cash balance is determined by settlements which have to be made in cash after making due allowance for offsets.

By inserting the symbol F in our equation [§283], in the manner suggested above, we have generally

$$(Q''_a+F)P_a=H.$$

It now remains to be seen, and a moment's reflection will show, that when the quantity Q''_a of the money commodity, on the one hand, and prices in terms of money, on the other hand, increase or decrease proportionately, the term F will automatically increase or decrease in the same proportion and H will remain constant. If all the conditions necessary for the threefold equilibrium in production, capital formation and circulation are satisfied, then, as we have seen in §279, after a rise or fall in prices proportional to a given increase or decrease in the quantity of money, there is no reason why entrepreneurs and banks should not put the same quantity of capital into circulation for a proportionately greater or smaller nominal value of commercial paper and securities;[6] nor why people should not buy and sell the same quantity of commodities to be paid for by offsets for nominal values which may vary proportionately upwards or downwards;[7] nor again why the *desired cash balance* estimated in terms of (B) should vary at all. Hence, the theorem of the proportionality of prices to the quantity of money is not affected in any way by the existence of paper circulation and payments by offsets.[9]

This theorem, therefore, holds rigorously. It follows that if all bearers were simultaneously to demand the redemption of their bank notes and if, at the same time, all holders of cheque books were to request the complete withdrawal of their deposits at once, provided that these claims could be satisfied, the price P_a of money in terms of (B) would rise immediately from $\dfrac{H}{Q''_a+F}$ to $\dfrac{H}{Q''_a}$, entailing a fall in commodity prices in terms of money in precisely the inverse ratio.

305. The foregoing conclusions which embody the so-called *quantity theory*, i.e. *the law of inverse proportionality between the value and the quantity of money*, were arrived at by the deductive method. We shall see, in our study of applied economics,[1] how far-reaching are the consequences of this law which places the whole equilibrium of the market at the mercy of mine operators, issuers of bank notes

and drawers of cheques. Economists who challenge the quantity theory generally base their arguments on observation and history, thus arriving at their conclusions by the inductive method. They are, however, compelled to recognize that observation and history show striking instances of fluctuations in the value of money that are the inverse of fluctuations in its quantity. It has never been denied that in antiquity the rapid development of the argentiferous lead mines of Laurium raised the price of a medimnus of wheat from 1 to 3 drachmas in the interval between Solon and Aristophanes. It is no less incontestable that the discovery of America and of the silver mines of Potosi tripled all prices in Europe from the end of the fifteenth century to the middle of the seventeenth century. Everyone admits that the panning of gold-bearing sands in California raised prices by 38 per cent between 1851 and 1873. But the opponents of the quantity theory deny that these fluctuations were *inversely proportional*. In reply it can be easily shown: (1) that the quantity theory relates only to the quantity of money; (2) that the theory affirms a direct proportionality to utility at the same time as an inverse proportionality to quantity; and (3) that it assumes *all other things to remain constant*, a condition which is never satisfied in reality because of the length of time required for the phenomena in question to develop. In the case of an increase in the quantity of money resulting from the issue of paper money or other paper currency, the reactions take place more rapidly and the proportionality of the inverse movements becomes much more apparent. For example, the issue of 30 to 40 milliards in assignats in France from 1789 to 1796 lowered the value of the medium of exchange in the proportion of 100 to 2·5 or 3. This grandiose experiment cannot be repeated as often as would be necessary to convince the opponents of the quantity theory; and that is why it is particularly fortunate that economics is a science in which the process of reasoning makes up for the ambiguities and the deficiencies in our experience.

Lesson 34

FOREIGN EXCHANGE

306. Bank notes circulate almost exclusively within the country of issue, but bills of exchange circulate much more widely. Cities in all parts of Europe and as far away as the East Indies and America draw bills of exchange on Paris and London; and these bills pass through a great number of hands, in settlement of numerous and varied purchases and sales before they are presented for collection at the place on which they were drawn. Moreover, these bills constitute a very considerable part of the fiduciary money in circulation. The great banking and commercial centres, London, Paris, Amsterdam, Hamburg, Frankfort, Genoa, Trieste and New York, are bill markets. At each of these centres the bills of exchange against all other markets are quoted every day; and these quotations constitute what is called the *exchange rate* or the *exchange*. Thus in London exchange rates are quoted on Paris, Amsterdam, Hamburg and Genoa. In Paris we find the exchange rates quoted on London, Amsterdam, Frankfort and Trieste. We hear, for example, "To-day's rate of exchange of Paris on London is 25·15, on Amsterdam 208·25, on Frankfort 210, on Trieste 195·50." In other words, one pound sterling payable in London can be bought and sold in Paris for 25 francs 15 centimes, while 100 florins, payable at Amsterdam, Frankfort or Trieste, can be bought and sold in Paris for 208 francs 25 centimes, 210 francs or 195 francs 50 centimes respectively. Thus to quote a rate of exchange two terms are necessary, one "*certain*", which is unexpressed, e.g. one pound sterling or 100 florins, and the other "*uncertain*", which is mentioned in the quotation, e.g. 208 francs 25 centimes, 210 francs or 195 francs 50 centimes. In the above example, London, Amsterdam, Frankfort and Trieste "quote certain" and Paris "quotes uncertain".

307. Two elements enter into the establishment of these rates of exchange: one being the difference between the moneys and the other being the exchange proper. For example, a pound sterling contains as much pure gold as would be contained in 25 francs 22 centimes in coin. If, then, the rate of exchange of Paris on London were 25·22, the exchange rate would be *at par*, and a given quantity of gold would have the same value whether payable in London or in Paris. The difference between the rate 25·15 and parity 25·22 is the exchange proper. The case is simplified and the concept of exchange proper presents itself more clearly when the moneys are the same. When,

for instance, it is said that the rate of exchange of Paris on Brussels is 101 and on Genoa 95, this means that 100 francs payable in Brussels and 100 Italian lira payable in Genoa can be bought in Paris for 101 francs and 95 francs respectively. In that case the exchange on Brussels is above par and stands *at a premium*, while the exchange on Genoa is below par and stands *at a discount*.

The rate of exchange is generally, therefore, the price in one place of a sum payable at another place. What are the causes which make a sum payable at one place worth more or less in another place? This is the question we shall now consider. To answer it, let us first inquire into the conditions which make for trading in bills of exchange.

308. Usually the transfer of funds from one place to another is accomplished by remitting bills of exchange and not by transporting metallic moneys. For example, a merchant X in London sells commodities to a merchant Y in Paris, and at the same time another merchant Z in Paris sells other merchandise for, let us say, the same value to a merchant W in London. Under these circumstances, it is unnecessary for Y in Paris to send gold or silver to X in London and for W in London to send gold or silver to Z in Paris. Both payments can be made without any intervention of metallic money simply by drawing and remitting a bill of exchange. Let X of London draw on Y of Paris. If W in London buys the bill from X, X will be paid what Y owes him and W will have paid what he owes to Z. Now let W send this same bill to Z in Paris. When Z presents the bill to Y, who is also in Paris, for payment, then Z will be paid what W owes him and Y will have paid what he owes to X. And so the two debts will be paid back and extinguished.

309. This gives us the principle. Now let us turn to the application. For simplicity, let us take different markets using the same money. A number of merchants in Brussels have sold 101,000 francs worth of commodities to merchants in Paris. And at the same time a number of merchants in Paris have sold 100,000 francs worth of commodities to merchants in Brussels. From what we have just seen, there is no need for Paris to send 101,000 francs worth of gold or silver to Brussels and for Brussels to send 100,000 francs worth of gold or silver to Paris. Let the creditors in Brussels draw 101,000 francs worth of bills of exchange on Paris and sell them at any price on behalf of the debtors in Paris to the debtors in Brussels for 100,000 francs; or let the creditors in Paris draw 100,000 francs worth of bills of exchange on Brussels and sell them at any price on behalf of the debtors in Brussels to the debtors in Paris for 101,000 francs. Let the operation be performed partly in one way and partly in the other in appropriate proportions so that no debtor whether in Brussels or in Paris has anything to gain by buying a draft rather

than be drawn on. In every case, 101 francs payable in Paris will be worth 100 francs in Brussels and the Brussels rate on Paris will be $\frac{100}{101}$, quoted as 99·01; and 100 francs payable in Brussels will be worth 101 francs in Paris and the Paris rate on Brussels will be $\frac{101}{100}$, quoted as 101. The debtors in Paris will send 1,000 francs to Brussels, since their creditors are entitled to be paid in full, even if that entails the shipping of metallic money. These same debtors will have to bear the loss on exchange, while the debtors in Brussels benefit, in principle, by the corresponding exchange premium.

310. But, it might be argued, if Paris owed Brussels 200,000 francs while Brussels owed Paris only 100,000 francs, the Brussels quotation on Paris would be $\frac{100}{200}$ and the Paris quotation on Brussels would be $\frac{200}{100}$; in other words, 200 francs payable in Paris would be worth 100 francs in Brussels, and 100 francs payable in Brussels would be worth 200 francs in Paris. Nonsense! This conclusion is not only absurd, but impossible. There is a limit to the loss and premium on exchange; and this limit is the total cost, including insurance, of shipping 100 francs in specie from one of the two centres to the other. So long as the loss on exchange remains within this limit, the debtor will prefer to buy a draft or to let a bill be drawn on him rather than send specie. At the limit itself either procedure is indifferent to him. If the limit were exceeded, the debtor would prefer to send specie. Hence this limit cannot be exceeded.

311. Cournot devotes a special chapter to exchange in his *Researches into the Mathematical Principles of the Theory of Wealth.* I beg to refer the reader to this chapter for a fuller development of the theory and to confine myself here to a restatement of Cournot's general formula of exchange.

Let (1) and (2) be two centres of exchange; let $m_{1,2}$ be the total of the sums for which centre (1) is indebted to centre (2), and $m_{2,1}$ the total of the sums for which centre (2) is indebted to centre (1); let $c_{1,2}$ be the rate of exchange in place (1) on place (2), and $c_{2,1}$ be the rate of exchange in place (2) on place (1). Within the limits set by the cost of shipping specie, we have

$$c_{1,2} = \frac{m_{2,1}}{m_{1,2}}$$

and

$$c_{2,1} = \frac{m_{1,2}}{m_{2,1}}.$$

From these two equations it follows also that

$$c_{1,2}c_{2,1}=1.$$

Thus: *Rates of exchange are equal to the inverse ratios of the remittances to be made.*

They are reciprocals of each other.

Here again we come upon the same price ratios we discussed in §44, as was only to be expected, since exchange rates are, by definition, the prices in any one place of a unit or of a given quantity of money payable at various other places.

312.[a] The formula

$$c_{1,2}=\frac{m_{2,1}}{m_{1,2}},$$

is applicable to the case of two countries having the same kind of money, for instance gold money. In that case, a merchant who has a remittance to make from centre (2) to centre (1) and who has in his possession enough gold for this purpose, will buy a draft if

$$\frac{m_{2,1}}{m_{1,2}}<1+\gamma,$$

where γ represents the cost of shipping one unit of gold from (2) to (1). On the other hand, he will ship gold if

$$\frac{m_{2,1}}{m_{1,2}}>1+\gamma.$$

Thus there is a fixed limit to the rate of exchange, namely $1+\gamma$.

If the two countries do not have the same kind of money, the formula for the rate of exchange in centre (1) on centre (2) becomes

$$c_{1,2}=\frac{m_{2,1}}{m_{1,2}}p_{1,2},$$

where $p_{1,2}$ is the price of the monetary unit of centre (1) in terms of the money of centre (2). Usually the rate of exchange $c_{1,2}$ is quoted without any explicit reference to the values of the separate factors $\frac{m_{2,1}}{m_{1,2}}$ and $p_{1,2}$ which determine the rate. Both from the theoretical and practical points of view, however, it is important, in many cases, to distinguish between these two factors: one of which, the *exchange* proper, relates to the ratio of the respective debts and credits of the two centres, while the other, which may be called the *agio*, relates to the ratio between the values of the two moneys.

That being so, suppose centre (2) to have a money convertible into the money of centre (1), say silver money convertible into gold, and suppose a merchant at (2) to have silver in his till. Either he will buy a draft, if

$$\frac{m_{2,1}}{m_{1,2}} p_{1,2} < p_{1,2} + \gamma,$$

where γ represents the cost of shipping a unit of silver from (2) to (1); or he will ship silver if there is any tendency for

$$\frac{m_{2,1}}{m_{1,2}} p_{1,2} > p_{1,2} + \gamma.$$

We have now a variable limit to the ratio of exchange. Suppose, however, that centre (2) has a money which is not convertible into the money of centre (1), say an inconvertible paper currency, and suppose that a merchant of centre (2) has paper in his till which he cannot export under any circumstances. Whatever $\frac{m_{2,1}}{m_{1,2}}$ and $p_{1,2}$ may be, he must purchase either a draft or gold. In a case of this kind there is no limit at all to the rate of exchange.

313. Letting (1), (2), (3), (4)... be any number of centres of exchange; and letting $c_{2,1}$ and $c_{3,1}$ be the rates of exchange in places (2) and (3) on place (1) and $c_{3,2}$ be the rate of exchange in place (3) on place (2), it could be shown by a proof which is identically the same as the proof developed in §112 in the case of the exchange of several commodities for one another in a [free] market that general equilibrium among the exchange rates is impossible unless it is generally true that

$$c_{3,2} = \frac{c_{3,1}}{c_{2,1}}.$$

Thus: *In a state of general equilibrium, the rate of exchange in any one place on any other is equal to the ratio between the rates in each of the two places on any third.*

314. Whenever this state of general equilibrium is disturbed, it will be restored by arbitrage operations in bills of exchange exactly like the arbitrage operations in commodities which we imagined in §114. Bills of exchange are *par excellence* the most suitable commodity for arbitrage operations. At every commercial centre there are special bankers, called *cambists*, whose business it is to keep continual watch on the rates of exchange and to restore general equilibrium in foreign exchange by taking advantage of the possibility of any profit to be made by making indirect rather than direct purchases, or more accurately, by combining indirect purchases with direct sales or indirect sales with direct purchases. The intervention of these cambists has two very important consequences.

315. The first consequence is that the rate of exchange in a given place on any other place is not determined by the simple ratio of the indebtedness of this place to the reciprocal indebtedness of each of the other places, but depends in a more complex way on the ratio of the indebtedness of the given place to the reciprocal indebtedness of all the other places. In other words, all the rates of foreign exchange between a given country and foreign countries fluctuate together in the same direction and depend upon whether the total business done by the country in question with the outside world results in an aggregate excess of the value of exports over the value of imports or vice versa. Whenever a country sells more than it buys, the exchange rate of its paper tends to rise above parity; whenever it buys more than it sells, this rate tends to fall below parity. Under the old so-called *balance of trade system*, the exchange was said to be *for* or *against* a country, or it was said to be *favourable* or *unfavourable*. These expressions refer to the alleged advantages of importing, and the alleged disadvantages of exporting, precious metals. Opinion has undergone a notable change in this respect; and yet it is useful to know that, according as a country's exchange is favourable or unfavourable, money is imported or exported; which entails in the first case, a rise in prices and consequently an increase in imports and a decrease in exports, and in the second case a fall in prices and consequently a decrease in imports and an increase in exports, so that in either case equilibrium tends to re-establish itself automatically.[b]

316. The second consequence is that arbitraging in bills of exchange is of incalculable practical importance, because it makes possible the settlement of the great mass of international business in commodities and services with the smallest possible shipment of gold and silver. Not so long ago, international commitments and remittances originated, for the most part, in the importation and exportation of merchandise, i.e. of the products of agriculture, industry and trade. Today, however, a large number of other items enter into the composition of international indebtedness. The more important of these items have been enumerated by Mr. George J. Goschen in his *Theory of Foreign Exchanges*[1] as follows: the importation and exportation of debentures and shares, public and private; the payment and encashment of interest on these securities; the payment of profits, commissions and brokerage fees; expenditures of nationals travelling or residing abroad; etc., etc. In the case of England, for example, the annual excess in the value of imports over the value of exports in the narrow sense of the term runs into hundreds of millions, but the balance is restored by freights earned by her shipping companies, by commissions and brokerage fees charged

for the use of her commercial and banking facilities, and by the influx of income from her investments abroad. All this business is settled by trading in bills of exchange. Paris owes a balance to Brussels; but, at the same time, Amsterdam or Frankfort owes a balance to Paris; and the first balance is paid by means of the second. Thus the world market for bills of exchange serves as a vast *clearing house* where the transactions of all countries are liquidated by the mere payment of differences. And this result is obtained purely and simply by the automatic operation of the mechanism of free competition. The law of supply and demand regulates all these exchanges of commodities just as the law of universal gravitation regulates the movements of all celestial bodies. Thus the system of the economic universe reveals itself, at last, in all its grandeur and complexity: a system at once vast and simple, which, for sheer beauty, resembles the astronomic universe.[e]

Conditions and Consequences of Economic Progress. Critique of Systems of Pure Economics[a]

Lesson 35

THE CONTINUOUS MARKET[a]

317. [In the two preceding Parts] we have restored the items of social wealth classified under the seventh, eighth, ninth, tenth, eleventh, twelfth and thirteenth headings to their place among the elements of production; and we have shown how the respective quantities and prices of these classes of capital goods, income goods and money are determined. The way is now open to express the total capital of an economy mathematically.[b]

Let d_a, d_b... be the quantities of final products which consumers need to hold as reserves in kind; let d_α, d_β... be the quantities of consumers' goods and services they need to have on hand in the form of cash reserves; and let d_ϵ be the quantity of new capital goods evaluated in *numéraire* which consumers require in the form of money savings. Altogether these quantities make up a *fund of working or circulating capital for consumption*,

$$c = d_a + d_b p_b + ... + d_\alpha + d_\beta p_b + ... + d_\epsilon.$$

Furthermore, let δ_a, δ_b... δ_m... δ_k... be the quantities of newly produced final products, raw materials and new capital goods in stock and on display which producers need to have on reserve in kind; and let δ_α, δ_β... δ_μ... δ_κ... be the quantities of final products, raw materials, capital goods and productive services which these same producers require in the form of cash reserves. These quantities make up a *fund of working or circulating capital for production*,

$$\varkappa = \delta_a + \delta_b p_b + ... + \delta_m p_m + ... + \delta_k P_k + ...$$
$$+ \delta_\alpha + \delta_\beta p_b + ... + \delta_\mu p_m + ... + \delta_\kappa P_k + ...$$

These two revolving funds added together, $c + \varkappa$, constitute the economy's *circulating capital*, C'. Moreover, if we let Q_k, $Q_{k'}$, $Q_{k''}$... be the quantities of (K), (K'), (K'')... which consumers or producers require in the form of capital goods proper yielding consumers' services or productive services, the *fixed capital* will be

$$C = Q_k P_k + Q_{k'} P_{k'} + Q_{k''} P_{k''} + ...$$

The circulating and the fixed capital taken together, $C' + C$, constitute the economy's *total capital* K,[c] part of which is borrowed and lent in the market for *numéraire*-capital at the rate of interest i which is equal to the rate of net income (§255).

318. We notice at once, as is quite evident from the equations of production, capital formation and circulation, that every addition to the quantities D_a', D_b'... designed to increase new circulating capital entails a reduction in the quantities D_k, $D_{k'}$, $D_{k''}$... of new fixed capital, and conversely, every reduction in the quantity of new circulating capital makes an increase possible in the quantity of new fixed capital.

319. Granting all this and supposing that all the accessory facts which we have hitherto neglected are taken into account, let us drop the assumption of an indefinite period and imagine, instead, a determinate period of, let us say a day, or better a year, in order to allow for seasonal variations. Furthermore, to make our general system of economic phenomena readily understood, we shall, at the same time, discontinue using abstract symbols and replace them by concrete numbers.

We shall suppose the basic data of the economic problem (viz. the quantities possessed of capital goods, the utilities of consumers' goods and services, and the utility of additions to net income) to remain fixed, so as to give us something in economics analogous to what is called a *stable system* in mechanics. Moreover, we shall assume not only that the preliminary phase of groping has been completed with equilibrium established *in principle*, but also that the phase of static equilibrium has actually commenced, so that equilibrium is established *in fact*.[d]

Imagine now a country of some 25 or 30 million inhabitants, in which land has a total value of $T=80$ milliards, persons a total value of $P=50$ milliards, and fixed and circulating capital goods (i.e. capital proper and income goods) a total value of $K=60$ milliards. Assuming the rate of net income to be $i=\frac{2\cdot5}{100}$, land will yield an annual ground rent of $t=2$ milliards; persons a gross wage of $p=5$ milliards consisting of 1,250 millions in net income and 3,750 millions in depreciation and insurance charges which people devote to the support, upbringing and education of their families (§237); and capital goods proper a gross income of $k=3$ milliards consisting of 1,500 millions in net income and 1,500 millions in depreciation charges and insurance premiums which capitalists spend on the purchase of new capital goods proper, exclusive of those new capital goods, however, which these same capitalists as well as land-owners and workers can purchase with the proceeds of their savings properly so-called.[1]

We may imagine, furthermore, that the landed capital is divided between 32 milliards producing consumers' services and 48 milliards yielding productive services; that the personal capital is divided between 14 milliards producing consumers' services and 36 milliards yielding productive services; that the total capital is divided between 40 milliards in fixed capital and 20 milliards in circulating capital; that the fixed capital is divided between 12 milliards producing consumers' services and 28 milliards yielding productive services; and that the circulating capital is divided between 4 milliards in the hands of consumers (of which 2 milliards are in stocks of consumers' goods and the other 2 in cash and savings) and 16 milliards in the hands of entrepreneurs (of which 4 milliards are in new capital goods, another 4 milliards in stocks of raw materials, 6 milliards in new income goods and the remaining 2 milliards in money). Thus we revert to the thirteen categories of elements of production listed in §178.

320. It is easily seen that the value of circulating capital stands in a definite relationship to the aggregate value of annual production and consumption. Perhaps 100 milliards worth of business transactions, i.e. of exchanges, are required for an annual production and consumption of 10 milliards, since entrepreneurs not only sell to consumers, but also sell to other entrepreneurs who buy such things as raw materials and commodities at wholesale from one another. Now every entrepreneur has need of a definite amount of working capital for a given turnover. The proportion of working capital to annual turnover, however, is different for different kinds of production. In the case of certain agricultural products, like wine, the period of production is a year and hence the working capital must equal the annual turnover. There are other products handled by commercial enterprises, like fruit and vegetables, that are bought in the morning at wholesale and sold at retail in the course of the same day, thus necessitating a working capital fund of only one three-hundredths of the total annual turnover. We must take an average. If we suppose the aggregate annual turnover to be 100 milliards and the amount of working capital to be 20 milliards, we are assuming the average period of production to be one-fifth of a year.

321. It is important to bear in mind that the sum total $T+P+K$ =190 milliards represents without any exceptions the whole social wealth of the country in the form of capital goods and income goods, and that the terms t, p and k merely represent the proportions in which land, persons and capital goods, both fixed and circulating, are combined in the productive process, as well as the proportions in which land-owners, workers and capitalists share in the consumption of $t+p+k=10$ milliards of annual income. These 10 milliards of annual income are composed of: 3 milliards of land-services, labour-services and capital-services that are directly consumed either by the owners of the landed capital, personal capital and capital

goods proper or by purchasers of these services, where the owners and purchasers are either private individuals or the State; and 7 milliards of land-services, labour-services and capital-services which are transformed into products through agriculture, industry or trade. We may suppose, if we like, that out of the 10 milliards of aggregate annual income, 8 milliards are consumed and 2 milliards converted into capital: these latter 2 milliards, in turn, being divided between the [above mentioned] 1,500 millions for depreciation charges and insurance premiums on existing capital goods proper and 500 millions for the production of new capital goods proper.

322. Finally, in order to come still more closely to reality, we must drop the hypothesis of an annual market period and adopt in its place the hypothesis of a continuous market. Thus, we pass from the static to the dynamic state. For this purpose, we shall now suppose that the annual production and consumption, which we had hitherto represented as a constant magnitude for every moment of the year under consideration, change from instant to instant along with the basic data of the problem. The 2 milliards of consumers' goods in stock, the 4 milliards in new capital goods, the 4 milliards of raw materials in stock and the 6 milliards of new income goods are like so many shoots that are continually being pruned at one end while they are constantly growing at the other. Every hour, nay, every minute, portions of these different classes of circulating capital are disappearing and reappearing. Personal capital, capital goods proper and money also disappear and reappear, in a similar manner, but much more slowly. Only landed capital escapes this process of renewal. Such is the continuous market, which is perpetually tending towards equilibrium without ever actually attaining it, because the market has no other way of approaching equilibrium except by groping, and, before the goal is reached, it has to renew its efforts and start over again, all the basic data of the problem, e.g. the initial quantities possessed, the utilities of goods and services, the technical coefficients, the excess of income over consumption, the working capital requirements, etc., having changed in the meantime. Viewed in this way, the market is like a lake agitated by the wind, where the water is incessantly seeking its level without ever reaching it. But whereas there are days when the surface of a lake is almost smooth, there never is a day when the effective demand for products and services equals their effective supply and when the selling price of products equals the cost of the productive services used in making them. The diversion of productive services from enterprises that are losing money to profitable enterprises takes place in various ways, the most important being through credit operations, but at best these ways are slow. It can happen and frequently does happen in the real

world, that under some circumstances a selling price will remain for long periods of time above cost of production and continue to rise in spite of increases in output, while under other circumstances, a fall in price, following upon this rise, will suddenly bring the selling price below cost of production and force entrepreneurs to reverse their production policies. For, just as a lake is, at times, stirred to its very depths by a storm, so also the market is sometimes thrown into violent confusion by *crises*,[e] which are sudden and general disturbances of equilibrium. The more we know of the ideal conditions of equilibrium, the better we shall be able to control or prevent these crises.[f]

Lesson 36

THE MARGINAL PRODUCTIVITY THEOREM. EXPANDING OUTPUT. THE LAW OF GENERAL PRICE MOVEMENTS IN A PROGRESSIVE ECONOMY[a]

323. There is hardly any need to point out that the principle of the proportionality of the values of goods and services to their *raretés* when the market is in general equilibrium (§224) and the law of the variation of equilibrium prices when *raretés* vary by reason of changes in the utilities or in the initial quantities possessed (§227) hold just as true after the solution of the equations of capital formation and circulation as they did before. What does need to be discussed, however, in view of its extremely weighty consequences, is the fact already noted in our discussion of the equations of capital formation and circulation in §§236, 237 and 238, that the quantity of land cannot possibly increase though it is possible to increase the number of persons and the quantity of capital goods proper in an economy that saves and converts its savings into capital. We propose, now, to reduce the consequences of this fact to a certain number of laws that are essential to the completion of the theory of the determination of prices in terms of a *numéraire*. These are the *laws of the variation of prices in a progressive economy.*

324. Up to this point we have assumed that the coefficients of production figure as given elements and not as unknowns in the problem of production. These coefficients, $a_t, b_t, c_t, d_t \ldots k_t, k'_t, k''_t \ldots a_p, b_p, c_p, d_p \ldots k_p, k'_p, k''_p \ldots a_k, b_k, c_k, d_k \ldots k_k, k'_k, k''_k \ldots a_{k'}, b_{k'}, c_{k'}, d_{k'} \ldots k_{k'}, k'_{k'}, k''_{k'} \ldots a_{k''}, b_{k''}, c_{k''}, d_{k''} \ldots k_{k''}, k'_{k''}, k''_{k''} \ldots$ are the respective quantities of each of the productive services (T)... (P)... (K), (K'), (K'')... which enter into the manufacture of single units of each of the products (A), (B), (C), (D)... and each of the capital goods proper (K), (K'), (K'').... In §204 we explained why we decided to assume for the moment that these quantities were determined *a priori*, though, as we stated explicitly, they were not. In fact, they are not fixed either in their magnitudes or in their nature. This is a crucial circumstance of far-reaching importance.

If the respective quantities of a given type of land-service (T) required for the manufacture of single units of (A), (B), (C), (D)... (K), (K'), (K'')... were invariably fixed, then the multiplication of final products and new capital goods would be absolutely limited by the existing quantity Q_t of this type of land. If, for example, one-tenth of the annual land-service of a hectare of land were always required to grow a hectolitre of wheat, i.e. if a hectare of land could never, under any circumstances, produce more than 10 hectolitres of wheat per year, the quantity of wheat produced would be absolutely limited by the quantity of land suitable for growing wheat. But everyone knows that this is not the case. By adopting the system of rotation of crops in place of the three-field system, by using such fertilizers as guano, by introducing improved implements and machines such as grain drills and ploughs that go deeper or break the soil more effectively, a hectare of land can be made to yield a larger and larger number of hectolitres of wheat per annum. In general it is possible to employ smaller and smaller quantities of land-services per unit of output of consumers' goods and new capital goods provided that larger and larger quantities of the services of capital goods proper are used. Whence the possibility of indefinite progress.

Progress is, indeed, nothing but a diminution in the intensities of last wants satisfied, i.e. in the *raretés* of final products, in a country with an increasing population. Consequently, the possibility of progress depends on the possibility of the multiplication of products. If the multiplication of products were only possible within certain limits, there would be definite limits to the possibility of progress. Under these circumstances, *raretés* could only fall to a certain point so long as population remained the same; or population could only increase to a certain point so long as *raretés* remained the same; or *raretés* could only fall so far if population itself increased up to a certain point. If, however, there is no definite limit to the multiplication of products, there can be no definite limit to the possibility of progress. The indefinite multiplication of products can only take place to the extent that capital-services can be substituted more and more for land-services though never wholly replacing them. We have to distinguish between two cases. In one case, it is only the magnitudes of the coefficients of production that change as the coefficients representing the use of land-services decrease while those representing the use of capital-services increase. We shall call this *economic* progress. In the other case, a change takes place in the very nature of the coefficients of production as additional technical coefficients are introduced while others are abandoned. This we shall call *technical* progress. Since this distinction is fundamental, it is best to give it a precise mathematical formulation.

325.[1] Let b_t, b_p, b_k... be respectively the quantities of the productive services (T), (P), (K)... which are required in the

production of a unit of commodity (B). Consequently, the cost of
production per unit will be

$$p_b = b_t p_t + b_p p_p + b_k p_k + \ldots$$

To say, as we did, that in producing a good it is possible to utilize
more or less of some productive services, e.g. land-services, provided
that less or more of other productive services, e.g. capital-services or
labour, are utilized, implies that the coefficients of production b_t, b_p,
$b_k \ldots$ are variable and are related to one another by a *production
equation* [*équation de fabrication*] [b]

$$\phi(b_t, b_p, b_k \ldots) = 0$$

such that if any one coefficient, say b_t, decreases, one or more of the
others b_p, $b_k \ldots$ will increase. Moreover, to say, as we have already
said, that the respective quantities of each of the productive services
which enter into the manufacture of a unit of any product are determined, along with their prices, by the condition that the cost of
production be a minimum, implies that if the above implicit equation
is solved for each one of the variables in succession or is transformed
successively into the following explicit equations:

$$b_t = \theta(b_p, b_k \ldots), \qquad b_p = \psi(b_t, b_k \ldots), \qquad b_k = \chi(b_t, b_p \ldots) \ldots,$$

then the unknown quantities b_t, b_p, $b_k \ldots$ are determined by the
condition that

$$p_b = \theta(b_p, b_k \ldots)p_t + \psi(b_t, b_k \ldots)p_p + \chi(b_t, b_p \ldots)p_k + \ldots$$

be a minimum. This is the condition which we said it would be easy
to express by a system containing as many equations as there are
unknowns to be determined. [c]

326. [d] We can express this in another way. Let us insert a
predetermined quantity to be manufactured Q of the product (B)
into the cost of production equation, which can then be written in
the form

$$Qp_b = Qb_t p_t + Qb_p p_p + Qb_k p_k + \ldots$$

Or, if we set $Qb_t = T$, $Qb_p = P$, $Qb_k = K \ldots$, the above equation
becomes

$$Qp_b = Tp_t + Pp_p + Kp_k + \ldots \qquad \qquad ..(1)$$

Inserting Q now into the production equation, we have

$$Q = \phi(Qb_t, Qb_p, Qb_k \ldots),$$

or

$$Q = \phi(T, P, K \ldots). \qquad \qquad ..(2)$$

If any of the coefficients are fixed in quantity, they will not appear among the unknowns of the problem. We shall assume, for sim-plicity, that the coefficients which do appear in the equation of production are capable of varying by infinitely small quantities, as was the case of the quantities of commodities which figured in the utility equations.[6] When, therefore, we differentiate equations (1) and (2) to obtain the minimum cost of production, we have

$$\frac{\partial \phi}{\partial T}=\frac{p_t}{p_b}, \qquad \frac{\partial \phi}{\partial P}=\frac{p_p}{p_b}, \qquad \frac{\partial \phi}{\partial K}=\frac{p_k}{p_b} \dots, \qquad ..(3)$$

or,[7] eliminating p_b,

$$\frac{p_t}{\frac{\partial \phi}{\partial T}}=\frac{p_p}{\frac{\partial \phi}{\partial P}}=\frac{p_k}{\frac{\partial \phi}{\partial K}}= \dots . \qquad ..(4)$$

Thus: 1. *Free competition brings the cost of production down to a minimum.*

2. *In a state of equilibrium, when cost of production and selling price are equal, the prices of the services are proportional to their marginal productivities, i.e. to the partial derivatives of the production function.*

These two propositions taken together constitute the *theory of marginal productivity.* This is a cardinal theory in pure economics, because it introduces into the problem of production a system of n equations made up of equations (2) and (4) given above, which are equal in number to the coefficients of production that now appear as unknowns in these equations; and because it shows the underlying motive of the demand for services and the offer of products by entrepreneurs, just as *the theory of final utility* shows the underlying motive of the demand for products and offer of services by land-owners, workers and capitalists. I preferred, however, not to intro-duce the theory of marginal productivity into my general theory of economic equilibrium, for fear that the general theory, which was already complicated enough, might then be too difficult to grasp in its entirety.

This theory of marginal productivity, the germ of which is to be found in Chapters VI and VII of Jevons's *Theory of Political Economy,* has been broached by several American and Italian economists, especially by Wood, Hobson, Clark and Montemartini. But it is still an empirical theory unless tied to the production equation (§325) as we have just tied it, first by modifying the pro-duction equation to include the quantity of the product manufactured so that the coefficients of production may be considered as functions of this quantity, and then by differentiating the modified production equation and cost of production equation in order to derive the minimum cost of production of the product.[1][2]

327. It should, therefore, be clearly understood that every time the production function itself undergoes a change, we have a case of technical progress brought about by science and that every time the coefficients of production made up of land-services decrease while those made up of capital-services increase without any change in the production function, we have a case of economic progress resulting from saving. In reality, both kinds of progress may take place simultaneously when, for example, the production function changes at the same time as the land-service coefficients diminish while the capital-service coefficients increase. But in this discussion we shall abstract from technical progress and consider economic progress only; that is to say, we shall suppose the production function to be given and confine our attention to the conditions under which the land-service coefficients decrease as the capital-service coefficients increase.

The conditions of economic progress are self-evident. Since the quantity of land does not increase in a progressive state, we are faced with the problem of obtaining more products with the same, or very nearly the same, total quantity of land-services. Population, on the other hand, does increase, for such an increase is implicit in our definition of progress; and thus additional labour, naturally proportional to the additional future output, is assured. What else is needed? It is necessary that the quantity of capital goods be increased in order to furnish the required additional amounts of capital-services. Since we are assuming nothing but economic progress, the increase in capital-services would have to be considerable. In fact, it is not sufficient that this increase be proportional to the increase in future output, for not only would the additional capital-services have to compensate for the failure of land-services to increase

[1] I have already made use of the above equations (2) and (3) in my "Note sur la réfutation de la théorie anglaise du fermage de M. Wicksteed", which appeared first in the *Recueil publié par la Faculté de Droit de l'Université de Lausanne* (1896); and in ed. 4 of my *Eléments* where the present § 326 was added to take the place of Appendix III of ed. 3 which contained my "Note" of 1896. Both in this "Note" and in ed. 4 I mentioned Messrs Pareto and Barone as having related the theory of marginal productivity to the production equation. M. Pareto having declared this theory to be "erroneous" and the equations of system (3) to be "inadmissible" because "quantities which are not independent variables are there treated as if they were independent" (*L'Economie pure*, November 1901, p. 10), and having apparently converted M. Barone to his opinion, I am willing to assume full responsibility for the theory in question. At the same time, I should like to point out that, according to my view of the establishment of economic equilibrium, during the entire course of the process of groping in production, the quantity Q is always determined in a special way as it passes successively through the values Ω_b (§208), Ω'_b (§211)... D'_b (§212), D''_b (§218) and D'''_b (§219).... This quantity Q, like the prices of services, is a *given* and not an *unknown* of the problem of the determination of the coefficients of production; whence it follows, so it seems to me, that the variables $T = Qb_t$, $P = Qb_p$, $K = Qb_k$ ... are here just as independent as were b_t, b_p, b_k... [in §325]. (1902.)

proportionately, but it would also have to make possible an increase in output proportionately greater than the increase in population in order that there may be a fall in the *raretés*. Moreover, capital goods must evidently be created out of savings before their services can become available for use.

Consequently: *Progress, which consists in a diminution in the raretés of final products along with an increase in population, is possible, in spite of the failure of the quantity of land to increase, thanks to the increase in the quantity of capital goods proper, provided, however, that this increase in the quantity of capital goods proper precedes and is proportionately greater than the increase in population.*

328. At this point in our discussion we may turn to Malthus's much-debated theory of the relation of population to subsistence. The essence of this theory is found in the following well-known passages of Malthus's book.

It may safely be pronounced therefore, that population, when unchecked, goes on doubling itself every twenty-five years, or increases in a geometrical ratio. . . .

It may be fairly pronounced therefore, that, considering the present average state of the earth, the means of subsistence, under circumstances the most favourable to human industry, could not possibly be made to increase faster than in an arithmetical ratio. . . .

. . . the human species would increase as the numbers 1, 2, 4, 8, 16, 32, 64, 128, 256, and subsistence as 1, 2, 3, 4, 5, 6, 7, 8, 9. In two centuries the population would be to the means of subsistence as 256 to 9; in three centuries as 4096 to 13, and in two thousand years the difference would be almost incalculable.[1]

The first of these propositions comes close to being absolutely true. It is evident that, apart from considerations of subsistence, population tends to increase from one generation to the next, and, when subsistence is adequate, actually does increase according to a geometrical progression, the ratio of which is equal to half the number of children a woman can, on the average, leave behind her. Malthus supposes this number to be four, so that population doubles from generation to generation. This estimate is an understatement rather than an overstatement of reality, for the human race is subject to a law, now well established, that vegetable and animal species tend to perpetuate themselves by rapid and large increases. The conclusions which Darwin drew from this fact are debatable, but the fact itself is not.

The second proposition does not have anything like the same validity as the first. Malthus fails to distinguish between technical and economic progress. In either case it seems equally hazardous to assert that the quantity of means of subsistence increases in an arithmetical progression with a constant difference of one, whether

[1] T. R. Malthus, *An Essay on the Principle of Population*, Book I, Chapter I [in the second (1803) and subsequent editions].

this increase results from the introduction of wheat or potatoes, the invention of machinery, or the development of credit facilities, or whether it results from the expansion of capital.[v] Assertions of this kind are neither based on reason, nor founded on experience. It is much wiser, therefore, to confine oneself to stating that the progression according to which means of subsistence increases in consequence of economic and technical progress is less rapid than the progression which characterizes the tendency of population to increase.

329. An economy, in which nearly all the land is already under cultivation and in which the only way of producing any additional landed capital is by carrying soil to rocky slopes, fertilizing waste areas or draining swamps (§174), is after all like an individual who has a fixed income and a certain rate of consumption. If this individual keeps his consumption within his income and capitalizes what is left over, he will increase his income progressively and so be able to increase his consumption more and more rapidly; but if he pushes his consumption beyond his income all at once, he ruins himself. Similarly, if a community first takes care to expand its capital, it can then increase its population indefinitely; but if it does not first expand its capital, it is doomed to misery and famine. And it will always be this way, as long as human labour is not the only factor of production in agriculture and industry, and as long as the use of less land-services entails the use of more of the services of capital goods proper. As will be seen later, we shall not go so far as to infer from this that Malthus was right in disparaging social reforms; but at the same time we must acknowledge that Malthus brought to light a fundamental point in pure economics. The late Jules Duval exclaimed one day at the Société d'Economie Politique in Paris: "What! You rejoice at the birth of a calf and not at the birth of a man!" As I pointed out to him at the time, these two cases are very different, since one represents more food on the table and the other an extra mouth to feed. Surely, we must concede that they are not the same thing, even if we take exception to the practical conclusions Malthus drew from his theory.[h]

330. The question whether the prices of final products rise or fall in a progressive society has been the subject of much discussion without leading to any noteworthy definitive conclusion one way or the other. The question should be treated as follows. What must necessarily fall in a progressive society are the *raretés*. Prices, however, are the ratios of these *raretés* to the *raretés* of the commodity serving as the *numéraire*, and can remain constant, if we make the assumption, which we have no reason not to make, that the *raretés* of the commodity serving as the *numéraire* also diminish in the same

proportion. Prices will only fall if the *raretés* of the *numéraire* remain constant. Thus it is only under the assumption that the *raretés* of the product serving as the *numéraire* are constant, that it can be said that *the prices of products decline in a progressive society.* J. B. Say enunciated this proposition, while admitting he could not prove it.[3] On this point, as on many others, his remarkable insight stood him in good stead; the only thing he lacked was a more powerful method of investigation, for it is clear that the elucidation of this question rests *in toto* on a fully developed mathematical analysis of the establishment and variation of prices.

331. So much for the prices of products. Let us now pass to a consideration of the prices of services.

For the sake of clarity, we shall examine only the effects of progress and leave everything else constant as far as possible. Consequently, we shall suppose an economy like the one we have been considering up to this point, in which the number of individuals with given utility or want curves and with given stocks of capital goods (landed capital, personal capital and capital proper) is doubled, at a certain moment, as a result of progress. It is evident that if the foregoing economy were enlarged merely by the addition of a second economy identical in all respects to the first, neither the prices of services nor the prices of products would be affected. This follows mathematically from the production equations. But such an hypothesis runs counter to our empirical conception of progress. What we have to suppose, if we are going to remain within the bounds of this empirical conception, is that each individual in the original economy is replaced, at the end of a certain period of time, by two other individuals who will be part of the new economy and who, before the process of production and exchange gets under way, will each possess:

(1) the same utility or want curves;
(2) half the same land;
(3) the same personal faculties unchanged in amount; and
(4) such a proportionately greater quantity of the same capital goods proper as is necessary to enable entrepreneurs utilizing the original quantity of land and land-services and twice the amount of personal faculties and labour to produce at least twice as much of each of the products.

In this way, every member of the original economy will be replaced by two members of the new economy each having for direct consumption, after production and exchange are in full operation:

(1) half the same land-services;
(2) an unchanged amount of the same personal services;

(3) a quantity proportionately greater of the same services of capital goods proper; and

(4) at least an equal quantity of the same products as before.

332. Under these conditions, the market would not be in general equilibrium at the same prices in the new economy as it was in the old. It is obvious at a glance that of the two sets of ratios, the one relating the *raretés* of directly consumable land-services to the *raretés* of the *numéraire* will be much greater than the original prices (i.e. rents) of land-services, while the other ratio relating the *raretés* of directly consumable capital-services to the *raretés* of the *numéraire* will be much smaller than the original prices (i.e. interest charges) of capital-services. Immediately there will appear an effective demand for land-services and an effective offer of capital-services to be consumed directly; rents will rise and interest charges fall. So much is sure; but it is easy to show that if we suppose the rise in the price of land-services and the fall in the price of capital-services to take place quickly, general equilibrium will be re-established, if not at once, at least quite rapidly.

Rents having risen and interest charges having fallen, maximum satisfaction will be roughly realized as regards directly consumable land-services and capital-services. Maximum satisfaction will also be attained as regards directly consumable labour. Thus the prices of the services will be in equilibrium or very nearly so.

In production entrepreneurs will pay higher rents, but they will employ less land-services in the manufacture of their products. They will pay lower interest charges, but they will employ more capital-services. Thus costs of production will remain approximately the same as they were before and will be equal, or very nearly equal, to selling prices.

The land-owners, workers and capitalists, in their role as consumers, will sell less land-services, but they will sell them more dearly. They will sell more capital-services, but they will sell them less dearly. Thus they will have nearly the same income as before, and they will, on the whole, be able to buy at least the same quantity of the same products at approximately the same selling prices which will continue to be equal, more or less, to the costs of production.

Finally, since these selling prices must always be equal to the several ratios between the slightly lower *raretés* of the products and the slightly lower *raretés* of the *numéraire*, maximum satisfaction, or something very close to it, will be realized as regards products, and hence their prices will be in equilibrium or very nearly so.

This demonstration should be sufficient to enable us to conclude that: *In a progressive economy, the price of labour (wages) remaining substantially unchanged, the price of land-services (rent) will rise appreciably and the price of capital-services (the interest charge) will fall appreciably.*

333. Capital goods proper are products. Consequently, if we assume that the prices of their services (i.e. the interest charges) fall appreciably, while their own prices, equal to their costs of production, remain constant, it is seen that: *In a progressive economy the rate of net income will fall appreciably.*

334. The rate of net income is given by the ratio of the net interest charge to the price of capital proper. Once the rate of net income has been found, we can calculate the prices of personal faculties and the prices of land by dividing this rate into net wages and rents respectively. And since wages will remain fairly constant while rents definitely increase, it follows that: *In a progressive economy, the price of capital goods proper remaining constant, the price of personal faculties will rise in proportion to the fall in the rate of net income, and the price of land will rise both by reason of the fall in the rate of net income and by reason of the rise in rent.*

335. In the following lessons I shall show to what extent the triple theory of rent, wages and interest implicit in the foregoing discussion of the determination of the prices of services are in agreement with or differ from the current theories. Before doing that, however, I wish to make an observation which relates exclusively to the theory of rent, in order to point out how, in our theory, the value of land-services is seen to originate in an economy from the very same causes which make it increase, and is seen to increase for the same reasons that bring it into existence. This value is always proportional to the *raretés* of the land-services directly consumed, that is to say to the intensities of the last wants which these services satisfy. In an economy which has· just passed either from a hunting and fishing stage or from a pastoral stage to an agricultural stage, each individual finds all the land and land-services he wants, not only for tilling but also for his house and garden. The *raretés*, and consequently the values of land and its services, are zero. But in an economy which has reached an industrial and commercial stage, people live in very tall buildings and gardens tend to disappear. The *raretés* and consequently the values of land and its services rise considerably. Those economists who, like Carey and Bastiat, have tried to convince us that we do not pay for land-services when we buy agricultural and other products would have to prove that we have all the land we wish for our houses and gardens, not in the wilds of Africa or America, but here where we want to live. Such a proof has never been given and never will. The truth is that a progressive rise in the values of land and its services, which may take place without

392 ELEMENTS OF PURE ECONOMICS

necessarily bringing about an increase in the value of its products, is, along with the expansion of capital and population, the essential characteristic of economic progress. By clearly demonstrating this truth, pure economics sheds as much light on social economics, as in other respects, it sheds on applied economics.[4]

Lesson 37

CRITIQUE OF THE PHYSIOCRATIC DOCTRINE

336. Any picture such as we have sketched in Lesson 35 describing the economic life of a people in terms of concrete numbers is called an economic table ['tableau économique']. At least, there is one *Tableau économique*, analogous to our own, which is quite celebrated in the history of economic literature. This is Dr. Quesnay's, which was published at Versailles in 1758 as a résumé of the Physiocratic doctrine. An *Analyse du Tableau économique* is found in Du Pont de Nemours's volume entitled *Physiocratie*, published in 1768; and an *Explication du Tableau économique à Mme de * * ** by Abbé Baudeau is found in the *Ephémérides du citoyen* of the same year. Both were reproduced in the *Collection des principaux économistes*, published by Guillaumin.[1]

337. The *Analyse* begins as follows:

The nation is divided into three classes of citizens: a *productive* class, a *proprietary* class, and a *sterile* class.

The *productive class* is the class which renews the annual wealth of the nation by the cultivation of its territory; which makes advances to cover the expenses of agriculture; and which pays an annual revenue to the land-owners. Included among the responsibilities of this class are all the labour and all the expenses which are involved up to the first sale of the produce. It is from this sale that the value of the annual renewal of the wealth of the nation is known.

The *proprietary class* includes the sovereign, the land-owners and the tithe-owners. This class subsists on the revenue or the *net product* of agriculture, which the productive class pays to it every year after deducting from the annual output enough wealth to recoup its annual advances and to maintain its productive resources.

The *sterile class* is made up of all those citizens who are engaged in non-agricultural services and occupations and whose expenses are paid by the productive and the proprietary classes, the latter of which in turn draws its income from the former.

To give precision to their analysis, the Physiocrats devised a concrete case and imagined a kingdom 130 million acres in area with a population of 30 million souls.

[1] In 1894 Dr. Stephan Bauer found in the Archives Nationales at Paris among the papers of the elder Mirabeau a copy of the *Tableau économique* printed in 1759. The British Economic Association reproduced it in facsimile along with a bibliography of the *Tableau* and of recent works on the *Tableau* by Bauer, Hasbach, Knies, Lexis, Oncken, Schelle and Stern. [The *Analyse du tableau économique* is Dr. Quesnay's and not Du Pont de Nemours's. It was first published in the *Journal de l'agriculture, du commerce et des finances* for June 1766, and then republished in revised and augmented form in *Physiocratie ou constitution du gouvernement le plus avantageux au genre humain* (Yverdon, 1768) of which Du Pont was editor. *Vide* Auguste Oncken's *Œuvres économiques et philosophiques de F. Quesnay* (1888), p. 307, footnote, and *Physiocrates*, I, edited by Eugène Daire (1846) in the *Collection des principaux économistes*, vol. II, pp. 57–58.]

In this imaginary country the citizens of the productive or agricultural class possess a fund of their own in fixed capital, called *primitive advances*, worth 10 milliards and another fund of their own in working capital, called *annual advances*, worth 2 milliards. Thus endowed, this class draws annually from the soil 5 milliards worth of produce, 4 milliards of which consist of foodstuffs and 1 milliard of raw materials for industry. Two milliards worth of foodstuffs are turned over to the proprietary class as revenue, the remaining 2 milliards worth of foodstuffs being retained to restore the annual advances; and the 1 milliard worth of raw materials is given to the sterile class in exchange for 1 milliard worth of manufactured products to pay for the interest on, and the maintenance of, the primitive advances. The 3 milliards worth of agricultural and industrial products, which are in final analysis retained by the productive class, constitute the *returns* ['*reprises*'] of this class.

The proprietary class receives annually, as we have just seen, 2 milliards worth of foodstuffs as revenue from the productive class. It keeps 1 milliard worth for its own use and exchanges the other milliard worth with the sterile class for 1 milliard worth of manufactured goods.

The sterile class, that is to say the industrial class, possesses a fund of its own in working capital, called *advances*, consisting of 1 milliard worth of raw materials. It then fashions these materials into industrial products which are subsequently divided into three parts: one part worth 1 milliard, which, as we have noted before, it exchanges with the productive class against 1 milliard worth of raw materials, thus restoring its advances; another part also worth 1 milliard, which, as we have also seen, it exchanges with the proprietary class against 1 milliard worth of foodstuffs; and finally a third part, apparently worth 1 milliard again, about which the Physiocrats are not very clear, but which, it seems, the sterile class keeps for itself.

338. The most obvious and the most important criticism which comes to mind in connection with this economic table relates to the Physiocratic conception of the role of the sterile, i.e. the industrial and commercial, class. The Physiocrats tell us over and over again that, in calling this class *sterile*, they do not mean to say that it is *useless*, but only that it is *unproductive*, in the sense that it consumes all that it produces without leaving a net product. Even if, for the moment, we take it to be true that the industrial and commercial class have no residual net product with which to feed a proprietary class, the appellation is still faulty. This class which consumes all that it produces, also produces all that it consumes. Why conceal the facts of the case by saying that it neither produces nor consumes?

When we attempt to fathom the reason for this peculiar Physiocratic outlook, we perceive that the concept of wealth was inextricably bound up in their minds with the concept of materiality. The 4 milliards worth of foodstuffs and the 1 milliard worth of raw materials for industry constitute, as they saw it, all the wealth that is annually produced and consumed—produced in its entirety by the agricultural class, but consumed by all three classes in the following parts: of the foodstuffs, 2 milliards worth are consumed by the agricultural class, 1 milliard worth by the proprietary class, and 1 milliard worth by the industrial class; and of the raw materials, one-third of a milliard worth by each of the three classes. Starting in this way, they were obliged to consider the agricultural class as the productive class *par excellence*, which supports both the proprietary class and the industrial and commercial class. But it was precisely this point of departure that was wrong.

All things which have value and are exchanged, whether material or immaterial, are necessarily classified as social wealth. Consequently, since the Physiocrats themselves admit that the labour added by the industrial class to raw materials makes it possible for the raw materials bought for 1 milliard to sell for 3 milliards, surely we have the right to say that this so-called sterile class annually produces and consumes 2 milliards worth of social wealth, for, on the one hand, it produces 2 milliards worth of labour and, on the other hand, it consumes 1 milliard worth of agricultural products plus 1 milliard worth of manufactured products. Hence the total annual production in the country is in reality 7 milliards and not 5.

339. Now let us go further. Is it true that the industrial and commercial class produces no more than it consumes or that it consumes all that it produces, without leaving any net product for the support of a class of [landed] proprietors? It is not true at all. Industry and trade do not make the same use of land as agriculture, but they do, nevertheless, make a definite use of it. Industry and trade are not carried on in inter-stellar space. Standing-room must be found somewhere on solid ground. Just as agriculture yields land income capable of maintaining the class of rural land-owners, so industry and trade yield land income capable of maintaining the class of urban land-owners. Why, then, did the Physiocrats fail to recognize this income from urban land as a true net product of industry and trade? Evidently because it is immaterial income.

340. Thus we have established one point of similarity between the industrial and the agricultural classes. Now let us turn to another. Quesnay endows his productive class with two kinds of capital: initial capital in the form of primitive advances and working capital

in the form of annual advances; but to the sterile class he allows only advances in the form of raw materials. Why so? Is the loom less indispensable to the manufacturer than the plough to the tiller of the soil? Is the workshop less essential to the former than the barn to the latter? Certainly not. But the service of the plough is transformed into wheat which is a material thing; while the service of the loom makes for a change in form which is immaterial. And just because it is immaterial, its very existence is overlooked.

341. It is easily seen that if the idea of immaterial production and the consequences that follow from it are incorporated in the doctrine of the Physiocrats, their conception of the three classes—productive, proprietary and sterile—reduces to our conception of three classes, consisting of land-owners, workers and capitalists. We must, however, go further than this, and introduce entrepreneurs engaged in agriculture, industry and commerce as well as a market for products, a market for services, etc., in order to have a more complete and satisfactory system of pure economics.

Another very serious defect in the Physiocratic doctrine is this: it is a fact that nowhere in this doctrine is there to be found any theory of the prices of products or the prices of services. Neither Quesnay nor his disciples explain how the returns to the productive and sterile classes, and the net product which constitutes the returns to the proprietary class, are determined. In the *Tableau économique*, the determination remains completely arbitrary. While it is a mistake to reproach the Physiocrats for using concrete numbers in order to illustrate their theory, still they really did confuse the quantities that they were free to choose arbitrarily with the quantities that ought to have been deduced from the given numbers. In short, they failed to distinguish between the knowns and the unknowns of the problem. The *Tableau économique* contains no theory of the determination of rent, wages or interest. A complete treatise would have to include a detailed examination of all three, and would have to explore, in particular, the question whether the net product does or does not constitute interest charges on the original investments in the soil ['avances foncières']. Besides these criticisms, we might also have made others pointing to defects in the Physiocratic conception of working capital in the hands of the productive and sterile classes as well as to defects in their ideas of the circulation of wealth and the role of money. Despite the many faults with which we may reproach them, it is still true that the Physiocrats were not only the first, but the only school of economists in France who have shown originality in their pure theory. Mingled with their errors are found views of extraordinary profundity and accuracy,[a] two of which are of enduring value: the first, which lies at the very foundation of social economics, postulates that the support of the State should come from the price of land-services; and the second, which is fundamental to applied economics, declares that for the production of wealth free competition is the best general rule, subject to exceptions only when they can be justified.

EXPOSITION AND REFUTATION
OF THE ENGLISH THEORY OF THE
PRICE OF PRODUCTS

342. The efforts of the English School to develop a theory of rent, wages and interest were far more sustained and thorough than those of the various French schools that came into existence after the Physiocrats. We must turn, therefore, to a critical examination of the English theory. That is the purpose of this and the following two Lessons.

Ricardo, the founder of pure economics in England, tells us:

> There are some commodities the value of which is determined by their scarcity alone. No labour can increase the quantity of such goods, and therefore, their value cannot be lowered by an increased supply. Some rare statues and pictures, scarce books and coins, wines of a peculiar quality, which can be made only from grapes grown on a particular soil, of which there is a very limited quantity, are all of this description. Their value is wholly independent of the quantity of labour originally necessary to produce them, and varies with the varying wealth and inclinations of those who are desirous to possess them.
>
> These commodities, however, form a very small part of the mass of commodities daily exchanged in the market. By far the greatest part of those goods which are the objects of desire are procured by labour; and they may be multiplied, not in one country alone, but in many, almost without any assignable limit, if we are disposed to bestow the labour necessary to obtain them.[1]

The order and continuity of development and the enduring quality of the English doctrine are strikingly revealed in the following passage from John Stuart Mill, who repeats in almost exactly the same words what Ricardo had expressed nearly a half-century earlier.

> . . . There are things (he says) of which it is physically impossible to increase the quantity beyond certain narrow limits. Such are those wines which can be grown only in peculiar circumstances of soil, climate, and exposure. Such also are ancient sculptures; pictures by old masters; rare books or coins, or other articles of antiquarian curiosity. Among such may also be reckoned houses and building ground in a town of definite extent (such as Venice, or any fortified town where fortifications are necessary to security); the most desirable sites in any town whatever; houses and parks peculiarly favoured by natural beauty, in places where that advantage is uncommon. Potentially, all land whatever is a commodity of this class. . . .
>
> But there is another category (embracing the majority of all things that are bought and sold), in which the obstacle to attainment consists only in the labour

[1] Ricardo, *Principles of Political Economy and Taxation*, Chapter I [Gonner edition, London, George Bell and Sons, 1891, p. 6].

and expense requisite to produce the commodity. Without a certain labour and expense it cannot be had: but when any one is willing to incur these, there needs be no limit to the multiplication of the product.[1]

What this fundamental distinction evidently amounts to is a division of products into two categories: one consisting of a small number of products which cannot be increased in quantity, and the other of a large number of products which can be increased without limit. This being granted, the English economists left to one side the first category and confined their attention to the second; and then they declared that the selling prices of products of the latter category are determined by their costs of production. Had they simply divided products into two classes, those that cannot be increased in quantity and those that can, and then merely declared that the selling prices of the latter class of products tend, under free competition, to equal their costs of production, we should have no objection to raise. But when they assert that the products of the second class can be multiplied without limit, and that a certain value of their costs of production determines their selling prices, then we are faced with two fundamental errors which must be refuted.

343. There are no products that can be multiplied without limit. All things which form part of social wealth—land, personal faculties, capital goods proper and income goods of every kind—exist only in limited quantities.[a] Of these things, land and personal faculties are natural wealth, while capital goods proper and income goods are artificial wealth, because they are products by virtue of having passed through a productive process. In the production of some things, like fruit, wild animals, surface ores and mineral waters, land-services play the predominant part. In the production of other things like legal or medical services, professors' lectures, songs and dances, labour preponderates. In the production of most things, however, land-services, labour and capital-services are found together. It follows, therefore, that all things constituting social wealth consist of land or personal faculties or the products of the services of land and personal faculties. Now Mill admits that land exists in limited quantities only. If that is also true of human faculties, how can products be multiplied without limit?

344. Nor is there any one value of costs of production, which, having itself been determined, determines in turn the selling prices of products. The selling prices of products are determined in the market for products by reason of their utility and their quantity. There are no other conditions to consider, for these are the necessary and sufficient conditions. It does not matter whether the products

[1] John Stuart Mill, *Principles of Political Economy*, Book III, Chapter II, §2 [Ashley edition, London, Longmans, Green and Co., 1909, p. 444].

cost more or less to produce than their selling prices. If they cost more, so much the worse for the entrepreneur—it is his loss. If they cost less, so much the better for the entrepreneur—it is his gain. It is not the cost of the productive services that determines the selling price of the product, but rather the other way round. In fact, the prices of productive services are established in the market for services according to their offer by land-owners, workers and capitalists and their demand by entrepreneurs. On what does this demand depend? On the prices of the products. When the outlay on production is greater than the selling price, entrepreneurs reduce their demand for productive services and the prices of services decline. When the outlay on production is less than the selling price, entrepreneurs increase their demand for productive services and the prices of services rise. This is the way in which these phenomena are related. Any other conception of the relationship is erroneous.

345. Is it not possible for the prices of productive services to affect the prices of products? Of course it is, but only through their influence on the quantity of products. In order to study the reaction on the prices of products we must classify various possible cases according to the ease or difficulty with which the prices of productive services affect the quantity of products.

First, there is the case of productive services which have passed out of existence [after having produced], for example, Ricardo's "rare statues and pictures, scarce books and wines"; or Mill's "ancient sculptures, pictures by old masters, rare books or coins, or other articles of antiquarian curiosity". When productive services cease to exist, we cannot say that they have any value or that their value can have any effect on the quantity or the value of the products. The value of such products, as both Ricardo and Mill admit, is the result of the law of offer and demand alone.

346. Then there is the case of specific productive services. Ricardo, for example, speaks of "wines of a peculiar quality, which can be made only from grapes grown on a particular soil, of which there is a very limited quantity". Mill, too, speaks not only of "wines which can be grown only in peculiar circumstances of soil, climate and exposure"; but also of "houses and building ground in a town of definite extent (such as Venice, or any fortified town where fortifications are necessary to security); the most desirable sites in any town whatever; houses and parks peculiarly favoured by natural beauty in places where that advantage is uncommon". On looking more closely into this case, what do we find? These productive services are still in existence; they are not monopolized, that is to say, they are not all in the hands of a single owner; but they are specific to certain products. Other land may produce other fruit, but not

grapes, or if grapes, not the same kind of grapes. Other land may be used as sites for houses and parks, but not houses and parks with the same exposure. That is why these productive services need not fear competition. A rise in their prices cannot draw similar services into the productive process, because there are no similar services. If the prices of their products rise, the prices of the specific productive services will rise to the same extent, without affecting in turn either the prices or the quantities of their products. Had Ricardo and Mill been a little more methodical in their classification, they would have given examples of personal services which are no less specific than the land-services they mentioned, like the personal services of living artists, singers, eminent doctors and great surgeons. Let us turn, however, to the case they had in view.

347. This is the case of unspecialized productive services—which, admittedly, is the most frequent case. There are, in fact, certain productive services which have no speciality of their own; and these are the most numerous. We need only observe in this connection what takes place in cases a little different from those cited by Ricardo and Mill. Besides lands which produce grapes of an exceptional quality, there are lands which produce grapes of ordinary quality. Besides lands suited only for the production of grapes, there is wheat land, fodder land and market-garden land. Now wheat land can also produce barley, hops, clover and cole; and cabbage land can also produce lettuce. Nevertheless, we must be careful to note that however versatile a piece of land may be, there are definite limits to this versatility, and therefore there is always some specialization; for example, flat land with a dry, light soil is needed for wheat; and low land with a rich, damp soil is needed for forage crops. Particularly in the case of labour, specialization is perhaps the exception and non-specialization the rule. Apart from certain individuals naturally gifted with the voice of a great tenor, the limbs of an acrobat, the eye of a painter or the ear of a musician, the great mass of men are capable of performing a wide variety of tasks, just because they are not especially qualified for the performance of any one of them. A man educated to be a lawyer might often just as well have been a manager; and certainly a person trained as a carpenter could have been a locksmith. What do most men inquire into when they come to choose their occupation? Surely, it is the wages they can earn in it, in other words, the value of their productive services in that occupation. The unspecialized productive services, in contradistinction to specific services, have competition to fear. A rise in the prices of unspecialized services will attract to production other similar services which exist in more or less large quantities. If the prices of the products [of unspecialized services] rise, the prices of the productive

services will also rise, but only temporarily; for these will increase in quantity and hence the quantity of their products will also increase. The end result will be a slight rise in the price of both productive services in general and of products in general. Our reasoning would be the same [*mutatis mutandis*], if there had been a fall, instead of a rise in the price of unspecialized productive services.[b]

348. Thus, in reality, there is no absolute antithesis between the two cases distinguished by Ricardo and Mill. In one case as in the other, there is a natural tendency towards a concordance in movement between the prices of products and the prices of productive services. In both cases, a rise or fall in the prices of products entails a rise or a fall in the prices of productive services. The only difference is that in the case of specific productive services, a rise or a fall in the prices of productive services[c] remains definitive and does not react either on the quantity or on the prices of the products; whereas in the case of unspecialized productive services, a rise or a fall in the prices of these services is temporary, for though the immediate effect is to attract or repel similar services, the final outcome will be a general rise or fall in the prices of all unspecialized services and an equally general rise or fall, of smaller amplitude than the initial change, in the prices of all products which these services help to produce. What the initial rise or fall loses in intensity, it gains in extension. Neither in the case of specific productive services nor in the case of unspecialized services are the selling prices of the products determined by their costs of production. In neither case, moreover, is there anything like Ricardo's or Mill's "multiplication without limit". Coupled with Mill's definition of the first category [i.e. specific services] is the statement: "Potentially, all land whatever is a commodity of this class; . . ." That is certainly true; and it is also true that all human faculties can be put in the same class. What then is left in the second class? Nothing.[d]

349. "There is a third case", Mill then tells us, "intermediate between the two preceding. . . . There are commodities which can be multiplied to an indefinite extent by labour and expenditure, but not by a fixed amount of labour and expenditure. Only a limited quantity can be produced at a given cost: if more is wanted, it must be produced at a greater cost. To this class, as has been often repeated, agricultural produce belongs; and generally all the rude produce of the earth. . . ."[1] Here, without warning and apparently without realizing it himself, our author passes from the case of an increase in production at a given moment of time with a given quantity of productive services to the case of an increase of production from

<hr/>

[1] John Stuart Mill, *Principles of Political Economy*, Book III, Chapter II, §2 [*op. cit.*, p. 445].

one moment to the next by means of an increasing quantity of productive services. And now the fact that one of the productive services, that of land, cannot be increased in quantity leads Mill to constitute his third class of objects composed of "agricultural produce and generally all the rude produce of the earth". Proceeding in this way, our celebrated logician, in a manner quite characteristic of him as we shall see in another very remarkable example, confuses two very different questions, that of the establishment of the prices of products and that of the movement of these prices in a progressive society. We shall postpone following him any further along this line until we take up the theory of rent. For the moment, we simply maintain that the commodities of this third category can no more be multiplied without limit than can the commodities of the second category. And, furthermore, neither the commodities of the second category, nor those of the third, can be increased, even within finite limits, at a given moment of time and by means of a given quantity of productive services, in return for a fixed outlay of labour and money, or at least in return for a fixed outlay of money—which, let it be said in passing, is not at all the same thing as a fixed amount of labour.[e]

Lesson 39

EXPOSITION AND REFUTATION OF THE ENGLISH THEORY OF RENT

350. The theory of the price of land-services or rent developed by the English School is a theory which was first enunciated, it seems, at the end of the eighteenth century by Dr. Anderson,[1] restated by Sir Edward West[2] and Malthus[3] at the beginning of the nineteenth century, popularized by Ricardo whose name it bears, reformulated by James Mill[4] and McCulloch,[5] reproduced by John Stuart Mill, and is still professed by nearly all English economists. Ricardo gave it in the following terms:

Thus suppose land—No. 1, 2, 3—to yield, with an equal employment of capital and labour, a net produce of 100, 90, and 80 quarters of corn. In a new country, where there is an abundance of fertile land compared with the population, and where therefore it is only necessary to cultivate No. 1, the whole net produce will belong to the cultivator, and will be the profits of the stock which he advances. As soon as population had so far increased as to make it necessary to cultivate No. 2, from which ninety quarters only can be obtained after supporting the labourers, rent would commence on No. 1; for either there must be two rates of profit on agricultural capital, or ten quarters, or the value of ten quarters must be withdrawn from the produce of No. 1, for some other purpose. Whether the proprietor of the land, or any other person, cultivated No. 1, these ten quarters would equally constitute rent; for the cultivator of No. 2 would get the same result with his capital, whether he cultivated No. 1, paying ten quarters for rent, or continued to cultivate No. 2, paying no rent. In the same manner it might be shown that when No. 3 is brought into cultivation, the rent of No. 2 must be ten quarters, or the value of ten quarters, whilst the rent of No. 1 would rise to twenty quarters; for the cultivator of No. 3 would have the same profits whether he paid twenty quarters for the rent of No. 1, ten quarters for the rent of No. 2, or cultivated No. 3 free of all rent.[1]

John Stuart Mill reformulated this first part of Ricardo's demonstration in the following theorem: *The rent which any land will yield is the excess of its produce beyond what would be returned on the worst land in cultivation.*[2] Ricardo, however, immediately pursues the argument further as we shall now see.

351. It often, and indeed commonly happens, that before No. 2, 3, 4, or 5, or the inferior lands are cultivated, capital can be employed more productively on those lands already in cultivation. It may perhaps be found, that by doubling

[1] Ricardo, *Principles of Political Economy and Taxation*, Chapter II [*op. cit.*, §25, pp. 47–48].
[2] John Stuart Mill, *Principles of Political Economy*, Book II, Chapter XVI, §3. [*op. cit.*, p. 425. As Walras states it: '*La rente est égale à la différence de revenu de la terre qui la produit et de celui des plus mauvaises terres cultivées.*' Mill's sentence, which comes nearest to the above statement in the section cited, reads, "The rent, therefore, which any land will yield, is the excess of its produce beyond what would be returned to the same capital if employed on the worst land in cultivation."]

the original capital employed on No. 1, though the produce will not be doubled, will not be increased by 100 quarters, it may be increased by eighty-five quarters, and that this quantity exceeds what could be obtained by employing the same capital, on land No. 3.

In such case, capital will be preferably employed on the old land, and will equally create a rent; for rent is always the difference between the produce obtained by the employment of two equal quantities of capital and labour. If with a capital of £1,000, a tenant obtain 100 quarters of wheat from his land, and by the employment of a second capital of £1,000, he obtain a further return of eighty-five, his landlord would have the power at the expiration of his lease, of obliging him to pay fifteen quarters, or an equivalent value for additional rent; for there cannot be two rates of profit. If he is satisfied with a diminution of fifteen quarters in the return for his second £1,000, it is because no employment more profitable can be found for it. The common rate of profit would be in that proportion, and if the original tenant refused, some other person would be found willing to give all which exceeded that rate of profit to the owner of the land from which he derived it.

In this case, as well as in the other, the capital last employed pays no rent. For the greater productive powers of the first £1,000, fifteen quarters is paid for rent, for the employment of the second £1,000 no rent whatever is paid. If a third £1,000 be employed on the same land, with a return of seventy-five quarters, rent will then be paid for the second £1,000, and will be equal to the difference between the produce of these two, or ten quarters; and at the same time the rent of the first £1,000 will rise from fifteen to twenty-five quarters; while the last £1,000 will pay no rent whatever.[1]

This second part of Ricardo's demonstration was also reformulated by Mill in another theorem: *Rent is also measured by the excess of the return to a capital good above what the same capital good would yield if it were employed in as disadvantageous circumstances as possible.*[2]

352. This is a mathematical theory which must be expressed and discussed mathematically.[a]

Let us draw a system of co-ordinate axes (Fig. 31) consisting of a horizontal axis Ox and three vertical axes Oy. From each of the three origins on the horizontal axis, let us measure the segments Ox'_1, Ox'_2 and Ox'_3 corresponding to equal employments of capital on lands No. 1, 2 and 3 respectively. In the first part of his demonstration, Ricardo does not state expressly in what terms these employments of capital are evaluated or what their value is; but in the second part he explicitly supposes that they are evaluated in terms of money ['numéraire'] and that their value is £1,000 each.

---

[1] Ricardo, *Principles of Political Economy and Taxation*, Chapter II [*op. cit.*, §26, pp. 48–49].
[2] John Stuart Mill, *Principles of Political Economy*, Book II, Chapter XVI, §4. [*op. cit.*, pp. 427–428. As Walras states it: '*La rente est aussi la différence de revenu qui existe entre un capital et le capital employé dans les circonstances les plus défavorables.*' Mill's sentence which comes nearest to this statement in the section cited reads: "The rent of all land is measured by the excess of the return to the whole capital employed on it, above what is necessary to replace the capital with the ordinary rate of profit, or in other words, above what the same capital would yield were all employed in as disadvantageous circumstances as the least productive portion of it. . . ."]

Now, on the vertical axes let us mark off from the points O the lengths Ot_1, Ot_2 and Ot_3 such that, when we complete the rectangles which have these lengths for altitudes and the lengths Ox'_1, Ox'_2 and Ox'_3 respectively for bases, the areas of these rectangles $Ot_1y'_1x'_1$, $Ot_2y'_2x'_2$ and $Ot_3y'_3x'_3$ will be quantitatively proportional to the net yields of lands No. 1, 2 and 3. Ricardo supposes these net

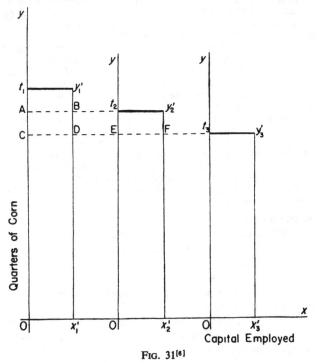

FIG. 31[6]

yields to be evaluated in [physical] units of product and equal to 100, 90 and 80 quarters respectively. This being understood, the first part of the demonstration amounts to saying that, since there cannot be two different rates of profit in agriculture, when it becomes necessary to cultivate land No. 2, a rent will be paid on land No. 1 amounting to the difference between the first two rectangles, i.e. to the area $At_1y'_1B$, which corresponds to 10 quarters. And when it becomes necessary to cultivate land No. 3, a rent will be paid both on land No. 1, amounting to the difference between the first rectangle and the third, i.e. to the area $Ct_1y'_1D$ which corresponds to 20 quarters, and on land No. 2, amounting to the difference between the second rectangle and the third, i.e. to the area $Et_2y'_2F$ which corresponds to 10 quarters; but no rent at all will be paid on land No. 3.

353. Now [in Fig. 32] measuring again from the point O, along the horizontal axis, let us mark off to the right of Ox'_1, the lengths $x'_1x''_1$ and $x''_1x'''_1$, to represent successive employments of £1,000 worth of capital on land No. 1. On the lines $x'_1y'_1$ and $x''_1y''_1$

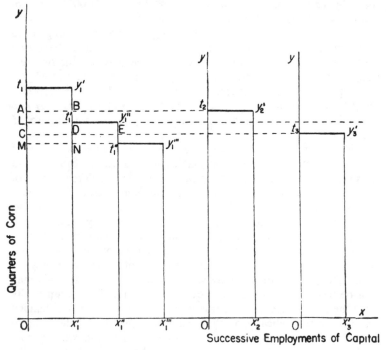

Successive Employments of Capital

FIG. 32[6]

drawn parallel to the vertical axis through the points x'_1 and x''_1, let us measure off from these points the lengths $x'_1t'_1$ and $x''_1t''_1$ such that when we complete the rectangles which have these segments for altitudes and the lengths $x'_1x''_1$ and $x''_1x'''_1$ respectively for bases, the areas of these rectangles, $x'_1t'_1y''_1x''_1$ and $x''_1t''_1y'''_1x'''_1$ will be quantitatively proportional to the net yields from successive employments of £1,000 worth of capital on land No. 1, these net yields being measured, as before, in units of product and equal to 85 and 75 quarters respectively. This being understood, the second part of the demonstration amounts to saying that, since there cannot be two different rates of profit in agriculture, when it becomes necessary to employ a second £1,000 worth of capital on land No. 1, which will occur after land No. 2, but before land No. 3, has been brought under cultivation, the rent paid by reason of the employment of the first £1,000 worth of capital will be the difference between the two rectangles $Ot_1 y'_1 x'_1$ and $x'_1 t'_1 y''_1 x''_1$, i.e. the area $Lt_1 y'_1 t'_1$ corresponding to 15 quarters. And when it becomes necessary to employ a third £1,000 of capital on the same land No. 1, the rent paid by reason of the employment of the first £1,000 worth of capital will be the difference between the two rectangles $Ot_1 y'_1 x'_1$ and $x''_1 t''_1 y'''_1 x'''_1$, i.e. the area $Mt_1 y'_1 N$ corresponding to 25 quarters, and the rent paid by reason of the employment of the second £1,000 worth of capital will be the difference between the two rectangles $x'_1 t'_1 y''_1 x''_1$ and $x''_1 t''_1 y'''_1 x'''_1$, i.e. the area $Nt'_1 y''_1 t''_1$ corresponding to 10 quarters, so that in final analysis, the total rent paid for the use of land No. 1 will be the two areas $Mt_1 y'_1 N$ and $Nt'_1 y''_1 t''_1$, i.e. the area $Mt_1 y'_1 t'_1 y''_1 t''_1$, corresponding to 35 quarters.

354. But when the theory is put into mathematical form, it becomes immediately apparent that what Ricardo has to say about successive equal employments of capital either on different pieces of land or on the same piece, should be as true or as untrue of successive employments of £100, £10, or £1 worth of capital as it is of successive employments of £1,000 worth. In short, if the rate of yield from each piece of land is a decreasing function of the capital used, there is nothing to prevent us from supposing that every time the capital used is increased by an infinitely small quantity, the rate of yield must decrease by an infinitely small quantity. Of course this may not be true, but until we are shown either rationally or empirically that the case where it is not true is the general one, we are justified in arguing theoretically on the assumption that it is true. Consequently, in order to portray the sort of diminution we are now discussing, we shall have to replace the discontinuous curves like $t_1 y'_1 t'_1 y''_1 t''_1 y'''_1$ by continuous curves like $T_1 T'_1, T_2 T'_2, T_3 T'_3 \ldots$ of Fig. 33, drawn in such a way that with the capital employed on lands No. 1, 2... represented by the lengths Ox_1, $Ox_2 \ldots$, the net yields, in terms of [physical] units of product, are represented by the areas $OT_1 y_1 x_1$, $OT_2 y_2 x_2 \ldots$. Now, from the consideration that there cannot be two rates of profit from capital invested in agriculture, it follows that the areas of the rectangles $OPy_1 x_1$, $OQy_2 x_2 \ldots$, which represent the profits in question on lands No. 1, 2... in terms of [physical] units of product, are proportional to their bases Ox_1, $Ox_2 \ldots$, and that the altitudes of these rectangles $x_1 y_1$, $x_2 y_2 \ldots$ are all equal since they represent the rate of profit (i.e. the rate of yield) in terms of units of product. And, therefore, those partial areas $PT_1 y_1$, $QT_2 y_2$ which lie above the horizontal line PQR, represent

the rent on lands No. 1 and 2 in terms of [physical] units of product; but land No. 3 does not yield any rent if, as is shown in our figure, the horizontal line PQR does not cross the curve $T_3 T'_3$.

355.[7] To express this analytically, let n_1, n_2, n_3... be the number of hectares in lands No. 1, 2, 3... respectively.[b] Also let h_1, h_2, h_3... be the excess *per hectare*[c] of the total number of units of product over the number of units necessary for the payment of wages [on each kind of land, respectively]; let x_1, x_2, x_3 be the amount of capital goods expressed in terms of money ['numéraire'] which are employed per hectare; and let t be the rate of interest charges[8] expressed in terms of [physical] units of product. Then the rents [*per hectare*] r_1, r_2, r_3 expressed in the same terms will be given by the equations

$$r_1 = h_1 - x_1 t,$$
$$r_2 = h_2 - x_2 t, \qquad\qquad ..(1)$$
$$r_3 = h_3 - x_3 t,$$

· · · · · ·

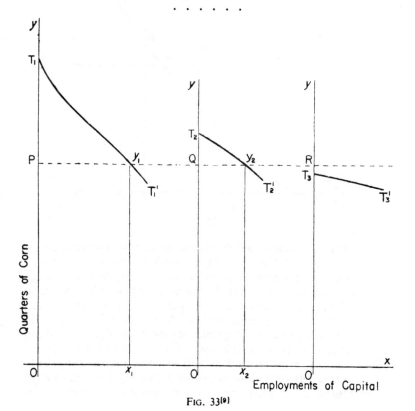

FIG. 33[9]

The relation between the net products and the capital employed may be expressed as

$$h_1 = F_1(x_1),$$
$$h_2 = F_2(x_2),$$
$$h_3 = F_3(x_3),$$
$$\cdots \cdots \cdots$$

..(2)

and the relation between the rate of interest charges and the capital employed is given by[d]

$$t = F'_1(x_1) = F'_2(x_2) = F'_3(x_3) = \cdots .$$

..(3)

Both sets of relations are represented by curves like $T_1 T'_1$, $T_2 T'_2$, $T_3 T'_3 \cdots$ [of Fig. 33] in which the variable x corresponds to the abscissas, the function t to the ordinates, and the function h to the areas [under the curves].

On close examination of the above equations it will be seen that for m [different kinds or] numbers of land, there are $3m+1$ unknowns[10] and only $3m$ equations. Another equation is needed. We can, without deviating in any way from a faithful interpretation of Ricardo's theory, write the following equation which is analogous to those given above in §§242 and 248:[e]

$$n_1 x_1 + n_2 x_2 + n_3 x_3 + \ldots = X.$$

..(4)

According to Ricardo, it seems that in every economy there is a certain amount of capital which is constantly increasing and with which it is possible to obtain a quantity of products that is constantly increasing, though not proportionately [to the capital], so that a constantly increasing population may be nourished. At any given moment, the amount of capital is determinate. Let us call such a determinate amount X,[f] and let us distribute it among the different kinds of land in such a way that the rate of yield is the same on all lands.

If we suppose equations (3) to be solved for x, they may be rewritten as

$$x_1 = \psi_1(t), \qquad x_2 = \psi_2(t), \qquad x_3 = \psi_3(t) \ldots,$$

and then t can be found from equation (4) in the form[e]

$$n_1 \psi_1(t) + n_2 \psi_2(t) + n_3 \psi_3(t) + \ldots = X.$$

Once t has been determined, x_1, x_2, x_3 can be found from equations (3) as rewritten above. The lands for which $F'(O) < t$ will not be cultivated; only those for which $F'(O) > t$ will be brought under cultivation.[g] With $x_1, x_2, x_3 \ldots$ determined, we can now solve for $h_1, h_2, h_3 \ldots$ by means of equations (2). And then $r_1, r_2, r_3 \ldots$ are determined by equations (1). Thus in final analysis rent depends on the capital of a country, and is determined without regard to wages, interest or the prices of products. This is the essence of the English theory of rent.[h]

356. The need for restating Ricardo's reasoning in terms of infinitesimals is so imperative that a number of authors have succumbed to it even though they continued to use ordinary language. Hence the rigorous formulation which we have just given to this reasoning is the true formulation of the English theory of rent. We shall, therefore, always refer to this formulation in our discussion and thus avoid the necessity of stopping to consider the defects in exposition and deduction resulting from the cruder modes of expression which were used by Ricardo and Mill. It becomes unnecessary, then, to show how Mill's first theorem, which is in essence based on the assumption that the worst land yields no rent, is intrinsically erroneous and formally contradicts the second theorem. As a matter of fact, in the mathematical statement of the theory, this error disappears. It is only necessary to inspect Fig. 33 to perceive at once that the worst lands under cultivation do, in general, yield a rent, except in the unusual case of a discontinuous productivity curve which cuts the horizontal line (representing the rate of production) only at its starting-point.

357. Let us now go back to the general equation:

$$r = h - xt.$$

In conformity with our usual notation, let (B) designate the product under consideration; let p_b be its price; let (T) designate the kind of land on which this product is harvested; let H be the total number of units of output per hectare; and, consequently let $b_t = \dfrac{1}{H}$ be the coefficient of production representing the amount of the productive service (T) utilized in the production of a unit of (B). Furthermore, let p_t and i be respectively the rent and the rate of net income in terms of *numéraire*. Since r and t represent, as we have seen, the rent and the rate of interest charges expressed in terms of [physical] units of product, they may be replaced by the values $\dfrac{p_t}{p_b}$ and $\dfrac{i}{p_b}$ in the above equation which then reads

$$\frac{p_t}{p_b} = h - x\frac{i}{p_b}.$$

Moreover, let (P), (P'), (P'')... be the different kinds of personal capital or persons whose services also contribute to the production of (B); let b_p, $b_{p'}$, $b_{p''}$... be the corresponding coefficients of production; let p_p, $p_{p'}$, $p_{p''}$ be the prices of personal services, i.e. wages; and let P_p, $P_{p'}$, $P_{p''}$... be the prices of the personal capital goods, i.e. of the human beings themselves, these prices being expressed in *numéraire*. According to Ricardo, the net yield in units of product, h, will equal[11]

$$H - \frac{H}{p_b}(b_p p_p + b_{p'} p_{p'} + b_{p''} p_{p''} + \ldots),$$

or,[4] if depreciation and insurance are ignored for the sake of simplicity,[12]

$$H - \frac{Hi}{p_b}(b_p P_p + b_{p'} P_{p'} + b_{p''} P_{p''} + \ldots).$$

Finally let (K), (K'), (K'')... designate the various kinds of capital goods proper, the services of which also enter into the production of the product (B); let b_k, $b_{k'}$, $b_{k''}$... be the corresponding coefficients of production; let p_k, $p_{k'}$, $p_{k''}$... be the prices of the capital services, i.e. the interest charges; and let P_k, $P_{k'}$, $P_{k''}$... be the prices of the capital goods proper, these prices being expressed in *numéraire*. Then, according to Ricardo, the capital employed, x, measured in terms of *numéraire*, will be equal to

$$H(b_k P_k + b_{k'} P_{k'} + b_{k''} P_{k''} + \ldots),$$

or, ignoring depreciation and insurance,

$$\frac{H}{i}(b_k p_k + b_{k'} p_{k'} + b_{k''} p_{k''} + \ldots).$$

358. Now, in the light of these considerations, we are obviously justified in correcting the equation under discussion so as to give it the greatest possible rigour without otherwise affecting it. This correction consists in combining the prices of persons (P), (P'), (P'')... with the prices of the capital goods proper (K), (K'), (K'')..., in order to make the term x include the total employment of all capital, both human capital and capital proper; for unquestionably the rate of wages, like the rate of interest charges, is uniform,[13] and the rate of wages [i.e. the ratio of wages to the value of personal capital] is exactly equal to the rate of interest charges. Hence we may, and should, in fact, base our reasoning in this theory on the uniformity of both the rate of interest charges and the rate of wages, as, indeed, some English economists have done. Once this correction has been made, the net product h becomes

identical with the total product H and the capital employed becomes finally

$$x = H(b_p P_p + b_p' P_p' + b_p'' P_p'' + \ldots + b_k P_k + b_k' P_k' + b_k'' P_k'' + \ldots)$$

$$= \frac{H}{i}(b_p p_p + b_p' p_p' + b_p'' p_p'' + \ldots + b_k p_k + b_k' p_k' + b_k'' p_k'' + \ldots).$$

359. H and x thus defined are functions of each other and are represented respectively by the areas and abscissas of the TT' curves of Fig. 33. And now nothing could be easier than to find out whether H is a function which does not increase proportionally with x, or, in other words, whether the TT' curves are negatively inclined. We need only inquire whether the ratio

$$\frac{H}{x} = \frac{1}{b_p P_p + b_p' P_p' + b_p'' P_p'' + \ldots + b_k P_k + b_k' P_k' + b_k'' P_k'' + \ldots}$$

$$= \frac{i}{b_p p_p + b_p' p_p' + b_p'' p_p'' + \ldots + b_k p_k + b_k' p_k' + b_k'' p_k'' + \ldots}$$

decreases when x and H increase.

It is an indubitable fact of experience that when increasing quantities of personal services and services of capital proper are combined with a given amount of landed capital, one does not obtain proportionally increasing quantities of product; otherwise it would be possible to obtain an unlimited quantity of products simply by applying an unlimited quantity of personal services and services of capital proper on a single hectare of land or on an even smaller area. Thus, in precise terms, one can say, as we have already done in §325, that b_p, b_p', b_p''... b_k, b_k', b_k''... are not constants but decreasing functions of b_t, that is to say,[14] increasing functions of H.[1] But what Ricardo and the English economists assert is something altogether different. They say that when more and more applications of personal capital and capital proper are made on a piece of land, the output of products does not increase proportionately; and the applications of capital of which they speak are evaluated in terms of *numéraire*. To make their statement identical with the preceding one, it must be assumed that the [successive] applications are not only equal in terms of the quantities of *numéraire* by which they are expressed, but are also equal in terms of the quantities of personal and capital services which they represent; for otherwise, if we supposed equal quantities of *numéraire* to correspond to larger and larger quantities of productive services, it is conceivable that the product may vary proportionately with the applications of

---

[1] For simplicity in this context, we shall disregard the circumstance that the technical coefficients are functions not only of b_t or of H, but also of one another.

capital. In precise terms, for H to be a function that does not increase proportionately with x either at a given instant of time or at different [successive] instants, we must suppose that $P_p, P_{p'}, P_{p''}\ldots$ $P_k, P_{k'}, P_{k''}\ldots i$, and consequently $p_p, p_{p'}, p_{p''}\ldots p_k, p_{k'}, p_{k''}\ldots$ are not only determinate at a given instant but are also constant from one instant to the next.

On rereading Ricardo, we observe that this twofold hypothesis is implicitly, if not explicitly, assumed from beginning to end. Ricardo obviously could not have argued that the product obtained depended on the capital employed no matter how this capital was employed, even if it was employed absurdly. Consequently he must have meant that these applications of capital, whether simultaneous or successive, whether made on different pieces of land or on the same piece, represent certain determinate quantities of definite kinds of capital goods. Since each application always amounts to £1,000, it follows that the prices of the capital goods in question are determinate and constant. By and large, however, output depends on the kind and the quantity of the productive services.[j] Consequently, it must be admitted that Ricardo considered the employment of certain determinate quantities of definite kinds of capital goods to entail the application of certain determinate quantities of definite kinds of services.[k] With each employment of capital always reckoned at £1,000, if we let the rate of interest charges be 5 per cent, then each application of services will always be worth £50; and thus the prices of the services are determinate and constant.

360. This hypothesis has important consequences to which we must now call attention. It led Ricardo to base the existence, the origin and the growth of rent on the increasing dearness of products. Indeed, in his view, cost of production determines selling price. Moreover, as we have just seen, the expenses necessary for the production of the net yield are determinate and constant, amounting to £50. If in addition to cultivating land No. 1 on which an employment of £50 yields a net produce of 100 quarters, we find it necessary to cultivate land No. 2 on which an employment of £50 yields a net produce of 90 quarters, the cost of production and consequently the selling price will increase from $£\frac{50}{100}$ to $£\frac{50}{90}$ [per quarter]. Or again, if to the first £50 employed on land No. 1, it becomes necessary to add another £50 and this second £50 yields 85 quarters net, the cost of production, which is also the selling price, will rise from $£\frac{50}{100}$ to $£\frac{50}{85}$ [per quarter]. The fact that we add the wage outlays to the interest charges in our particular mathematical restatement of

Ricardo's theory does not affect the result in the slightest. In fact, the price of the product, p_b, is equal either to the ratio of the total outlay on rent, wages and interest charges, p_t+xi, to the total quantity of product H; or to the ratio of the outlay on rent alone, p_t, to the rent in terms of [physical] units of product, r; or, finally, to the ratio of the outlay on wages and interest, xi, to the wages and interest in terms of [physical] units of product xt, that is to say, to the ratio $\frac{i}{t}$.[16] Now, if we ignore variations in i, this last ratio will increase indefinitely as t decreases, which is the basis of the theory. It follows from this, finally, that rent in *numéraire* is subject to a twofold increase from one moment to the next: first by reason of the increase in the number of units of output, r, which is related to the increase of rent in *numéraire*; and second by reason of the rise in the price of the product, p_b. That Ricardo understood this consequence[1] perfectly and accepted it can be seen in the special note at the close of his chapter *On Rent*.

361. Thus, the English theory can only determine the price of land-services and demonstrate its residual character on the twofold assumption that the prices of personal capital, the prices of capital goods proper and the rate of net income are predetermined and constant, and that, therefore, the prices of the services of personal capital and capital goods proper are also predetermined and constant. As we shall see in the following two Lessons, the economists of the English School actually determined neither the wages nor the interest charges; but, for the present, let us stretch a point and suppose that they did. *A priori*, however, we cannot attribute to this school the hypothesis that the prices of productive services are fixed. Hence the curves or equations representing the product as a function of the capital employed are completely useless either for a comparison of rents over an interval of time during which the successive applications of capital are made, or for enunciating a law of the variation of rent in a progressive society. At best, these curves or equations can only serve to determine rent at a given instant of time with reference to different alternative employments of capital at that instant or to enunciate a law of the establishment of rent. It is only within these limits that one can make use of the curves and equations under discussion. As long, then, as $p_p, p_p', p_p'' \dots p_k, p_k', p_k'' \dots$ are supposed already determined, the rent will be given *in terms of units of product* by the equation

$$\frac{p_t}{p_b} = H - \frac{H}{p_b}(b_p p_p + b_p' p_p' + b_p'' p_p'' + \dots + b_k p_k + b_k' p_k' + b_k'' p_k'' + \dots), \quad \dots(5)$$

and *in terms of numéraire* by the equation:

$$p_t = Hp_b - H(b_p p_p + b_{p'} p_{p'} + b_{p''} p_{p''} + \ldots$$
$$+ b_k p_k + b_{k'} p_{k'} + b_{k''} p_{k''} + \ldots). \qquad ..(6)$$

If,[m] in accordance with our previous discussion in §358. we substitute H for h and write

$$H = F(x)$$

and therefore[16]

$$\frac{H}{p_b}(b_p p_p + b_{p'} p_{p'} + b_{p''} p_{p''} + \ldots + b_k p_k + b_{k'} p_{k'} + b_{k''} p_{k''} + \ldots)$$
$$= xF'(x),$$

then we can put equation (5) in the form[17]

$$\frac{p_t}{p_b} = F(x) - xF'(x).$$

It is now clear how the equation

$$r = h - xt$$

and the corresponding curve TT', when corrected and completed as far as can be, give rent in units of product as a decreasing function of the quantity employed of personal capital and capital proper or their services. We may ask, even at this stage of the argument, why the English School determines rent by the quantities of labour and capital-services employed, rather than wages and interest by the quantities of land-services employed; or why this school does not try to formulate a unified general theory to determine the prices of all productive services in the same way. The fact remains, however, that, by introducing the above equation and curve (which can only be accepted subject to the qualifications already mentioned and to an even more serious qualification to which we are now coming), the English School somehow[n] introduces into the general problem of the determination of prices a number of equations equal to the number of unknowns which are the rents reckoned in units of product. Moreover, the problem, thus formulated in theory, is solved in practice by competition among entrepreneurs. Once the problem of rent [in kind] has been solved, wages, interest charges and the rate of net income in terms of *numéraire*, which are still unknowns, remain to be determined. After that, the rate of production[18] is determined, as was shown above in §355, by the quantity of capital available. Furthermore, the price of the product is determined by the ratio of the rate of net income to the rate of production;[19] and finally the rent in *numéraire* is determined by multiplying the rent in units of product by the price of the product. Thus, to be sure, the English School succeeded in demonstrating that *rent does not enter into cost of production*, but this proposition proved to be the rock on which the English theory of rent finally foundered, as we shall now proceed to show.

362. If we replace H by $\dfrac{1}{b_t}$ in equation (6), then multiply through by b_t, and finally transpose the quantity in parentheses to the left-hand side of the equation, we obtain

$$b_t p_t + b_p p_p + b_{p'} p_{p'} + b_{p''} p_{p''} + \ldots$$
$$+ b_k p_k + b_{k'} p_{k'} + b_{k''} p_{k''} + \ldots = p_b.$$

This equation is simply the equation of cost of production of the product (B), as it appears in system (4) of our production equations in §203—with one qualification, however, namely that, whereas different kinds of labour-services (P), (P'), (P'')... and capital-services (K), (K'), (K'')... are used in the production of (B), only one kind of land-service (T) is so used. Thus, the English theory of rent is based on the further assumption that no more than one kind of land-service ever enters into [any given branch of] production. This hypothesis is no more appropriate to agriculture than to industry. For example, the wheat in Ricardo's illustration does not fit into this hypothesis, since the production of wheat requires fertilizer as a raw material which is derived from cattle that graze on grass-lands, and these grass-lands are different from wheat land. When to this reason we add the further fact, which will be shown in the next Lesson, that the English School does not directly determine either wages or interest charges, it becomes necessary to complete the equation of the cost of production of the product (B) as follows:

$$b_t p_t + b_{t'} p_{t'} + b_{t''} p_{t''} + \ldots + b_p p_p + b_{p'} p_{p'} + b_{p''} p_{p''} + \ldots$$
$$+ b_k p_k + b_{k'} p_{k'} + b_{k''} p_{k''} + \ldots = p_b;^{[0]}$$

and to add to it the production equation

$$Q = \phi(Qb_t \ldots Qb_p \ldots Qb_k \ldots) \ (\S 326),$$

with which the other production equations will have to be combined in order to determine not only the prices of products, but also the prices of productive services. The marginal productivities are taken into account, not, in the inept and incorrect way of the English School, for the determination of the prices of land-services, but for the determination of the coefficients of production, just as costs of production are taken into account for the determination, not of the prices of products as the English School would have it, but of the quantities of output.[1] Thus, all that remains of Ricardo's theory after a rigorous critical analysis is that rent is not a component part, but a result, of the price of products. But the same thing can be said of wages and interest. Hence, rent, wages, interest, the prices of products, and the coefficients of production are all unknowns within the same problem; they must always be determined together and not independently of one another.

[1] If we let (B) be a product of two services, (T) and (K), then from the equations of marginal productivity (1) and (3) in §326, [viz.

$$Qp_b = Tp_t + Kp_k \qquad\qquad ..(1)$$

$$\text{and } \frac{\partial\phi}{\partial K} = \frac{p_k}{p_b} \Big] \qquad\qquad ..(3)$$

we obtain

$$T\,\frac{p_t}{p_b} = Q - K\,\frac{\partial\phi}{\partial K}\,.$$

If, now, we let $Q = H$, so chosen that $T = Hb_t = 1$ and if we let $K = x$, then the function $Q = \phi(T, K)$ becomes $H = F(x)$, the partial derivative $\frac{\partial\phi}{\partial K}$ becomes $F'(x)$ and the above equation becomes

$$\frac{p_t}{p_b} = F(x) - xF'(x),$$

which is identical with the equation of the Ricardian theory of rent (mathematically expressed). (1902)

Lesson 40

EXPOSITION AND REFUTATION OF THE
ENGLISH THEORIES OF WAGES AND INTEREST

363. Turning now to the English theory of wages, we shall cite John Stuart Mill, not because he was the first to enunciate it, but because his proof is the fullest that has been given. This proof consists of two theorems which were formulated in Mill's *Principles of Political Economy*: the first in Book I, Chapter V, §9, reads, *To purchase produce is not to support labour;*[1] and the second in Book II, Chapter XI, §1, reads, *Wages depend on the proportion between population and capital.*[2] We shall now examine each of these two propositions in turn.

The singular phrasing of the first of these two theorems strikes us at once. This initial impression is by no means unfounded, for the theorem in question is nothing but a long and tedious quibble. What can so vague and so unscientific a term as *support* ['*alimenter*'] signify? Mill himself tells us: "To purchase produce is not to support labour" means that "the demand for labour is constituted by the wages which precede the production, and not by the demand which may exist for the commodities resulting from the production".[3] Consequently, "To purchase produce is not to support labour" means that "demand for commodities does not constitute demand for labour".[4] Then why not state the theorem in these terms, or better still, instead of this negative form, why not use a positive form, as Mill does only as an afterthought? We must look more closely into the matter to obtain light on these questions.

Mill imagines a consumer and alternatively supposes him to expend his income either in the direct purchase of productive services when, for example, he has a house built, or in the purchase of final products such as velvet and lace.[5] Then he tells us that these two operations are different, and he attempts to define exactly what this difference is, but fails lamentably. What he ought to have done was to contrast either a man who has a house built with a man who buys one already constructed, or else a man who buys lace and velvet already manufactured with a man who has lace and velvet made for him. Then Mill might clearly have shown us that there is an important difference between the direct purchase of productive services, which provides working capital for the manufacture of a product, and the purchase of the finished products, which simply replenishes this capital for subsequent production. It appears, indeed, that Mill himself was not quite satisfied with the example given in the text, for he offers another comparison in a note.[6] A rich man, A, who expends a certain amount daily in wages or alms, which the labourers or the poor spend on coarse foods, dies, leaving his property to B, who spends the same sum on himself for table delicacies. This example is even more puzzling than the first. Mill ought to have made up his mind whether it was alms or wages [on which A expended a portion of his income], for they are by no means the same thing; and if it was the latter, Mill should have informed us how the labour paid for by these wages was employed. If, for instance, the labour is that of gardeners growing table delicacies for A, we simply revert to the distinction already drawn between the purchase of productive services and the purchase of finished products, and to the observation that a supply of working capital is created in the first case and not in the second.

This is sufficient to show where the vagueness of the word *support* leads Mill. Owing to the double meaning which he gives the word, he tells us that he is going to prove one thing and then proves something entirely different. What he undertook to prove was that to purchase produce is not to support labour, in the sense that to purchase produce is not to demand labour, but what he did prove, more or less satisfactorily, was that to purchase produce is not to support labour in the sense that to purchase produce is not to supply [additional] working capital for the labour employed in manufacturing the produce. Thus we may consider the first theorem as null and void.

364. Let us now examine the second theorem.

Wages, then, depend mainly upon the demand and supply of labour; or, as it is often expressed, on the proportion between population and capital. By *population* is here meant the number only of the labouring class, or rather of those who work for hire; and by *capital* only circulating capital, and not even the whole of that, but the part which is expended in the direct purchase of labour. To this, however, must be added all funds which, without forming a part of capital, are paid in exchange for labour, such as the wages of soldiers, domestic servants, and all other unproductive labourers. There is unfortunately no mode of expressing by one familiar term, the aggregate of what has been called the wages-fund of a country; and as the wages of productive labour form nearly the whole of that fund, it is usual to overlook the smaller and less important part, and to say that wages depend on population and capital. It will be convenient to employ this expression, remembering, however, to consider it as elliptical, and not as a literal statement of the entire truth.

With these limitations of the terms, wages not only depend upon the relative amount of capital and population, but cannot, under the rule of competition, be affected by anything else. Wages (meaning, of course, the general rate) cannot rise, but by an increase of the aggregate funds employed in hiring labourers, or a diminution in the number of the competitors for hire; nor fall, except either by a diminution of the funds devoted to paying labour, or by an increase in the number of labourers to be paid.[7]

This theory of wages lends itself more easily to mathematical formulation than the theory of rent. We are told that the population under consideration does not include idle people; it does not even include all who work, but only all those who work for a wage, i.e. *the number of wage-earning workers*. Let this number be *T*. Mill tells us, moreover, that the capital he has in mind does not include fixed capital; it does not even include all the circulating capital, but only that part of it which is expended on the payment of wages, i.e. *the amount of working capital used for hiring labourers*. Let this amount be *K*. There is one other point over which he passes much more rapidly, but which we must not overlook. It appears that the rate to be determined is only *the average rate of wages*. Let *s* be this rate. To say, then, that *the wage rate is governed by the proportion between population and capital* means that $s = \dfrac{K}{T}$, or that *the average rate of wages is equal to the quotient of the sum total of wages paid divided by the number of the population who receive wages*. Surely, it is not surprising that a proposition of this kind does not require long-drawn-out proof. Nor is it surprising that such a proposition is not very useful.

365. It should be noted, first of all, that what we want is not the average rate of wages but the different rates of wages paid in various employments. These latter rates are all the more important because, according to the theory of the English School, we must have the prices of the productive services in order to determine the prices of the final products. If the products are excavations or embankments, what we want to know is the wage rate of common labourers; if the products are clocks or watches, what we want to know is the wage rate of clock- and watch-makers. Thus, even supposing that the average rate of wages is determined by the above formula, it is of no use to us. Then again, is the average rate really determined in that way? It would be, if we knew the population and the capital required by the formula, i.e. the amount of working capital expended on labour and the number of wage-earning workers. Unfortunately, these quantities, though perfectly definable, are completely undetermined. Their ratio does not determine the rate of wages, but rather the other way round, for the quantities in the ratio depend on this rate.

As the wage rate rises or falls, the number of wage-earners will inevitably increase or decrease through a decrease or increase in other groups of workers [i.e. workers who are not wage-earners] and the leisure class; and, furthermore, the amount of working capital expended on labour will necessarily increase or decrease through a decrease or increase not only in other items of circulating capital, but also in fixed capital. It is as impossible to distinguish the working capital expended on labour from the working capital expended on land-services or that expended on capital-services, as it is to distinguish, in the case of a tank equipped with three outlets, the water that will flow through one outlet from the water that will flow through the other two. What determines the quantity of water flowing through each outlet from such a tank is the size of the outlet. The problem is exactly the same in the case of the distribution of circulating capital in the form of wages, rent and interest payments among workers, land-owners and capitalists. If wages are high and the working capital to be expended on labour is inadequate, this fund will first increase at the expense of the working capital to be laid out on land-services and capital-services. Then, perhaps, the total amount of circulating capital may prove inadequate. In that case, the rate of interest charges on circulating capital will be very high as compared with the rate of interest charges on fixed capital; and savings in the process of formation will go into circulating rather than fixed capital. People will buy fewer stocks and bonds on the stock exchange and will make larger bank deposits. If, on the other hand, wages are low, and the working capital destined for labour excessive, this fund will shrink at first in favour of the working capital to be laid out on land-services and capital-services. There may, then, be too much circulating capital. In that case, the rate of interest charges on this capital will fall relatively to the rate on fixed capital, and savings in the process of formation will go into fixed rather than circulating capital. People will withdraw bank deposits in order to make investments in securities.

The fund of working capital expended on wages, instead of determining the rate of wages, is itself determined by that rate. What, then, determines the rate of wages, and likewise the rate of rent and of interest? In final analysis, notwithstanding Mill, it is the price of the products of labour, land-services and capital-services; in other words, competition among consumers in the market for products and not competition among entrepreneurs in the market for services. Though it is true that productive services are bought and sold in their own special markets, nevertheless the prices of these services are determined in the market for products. But there is no need to restate here our theory of the determination of the price of productive services. Enough has been said to show what the English theory of wages is worth.[a]

366. The theory of interest is no less important than the theories of rent and wages. It has been a favourite target for socialists; and the answer which economists have given to these attacks has not, up to the present, been overwhelmingly convincing.

The theory of interest, especially that of the English School, starts out with an error that beclouds the whole issue. It fails to distinguish between the role of the capitalist and the role of the entrepreneur. Under the pretext that it is difficult in reality to be an entrepreneur without being a capitalist at the same time, English economists do not differentiate between the two functions. That is why the term *profit*, as they use it, signifies simultaneously *interest* on capital and *profit* of enterprise.[b]

This confusion is unfortunate. In reality, it is admittedly difficult but not impossible to be an entrepreneur without being a capitalist. It frequently happens that men who have no capital of their own, but whose intelligence, honesty, and experience are known, obtain loans for agricultural, industrial, commercial, or financial enterprises. At any rate, even supposing that there are very few entrepreneurs who are not also capitalists, there are large numbers of capitalists who are not entrepreneurs. They are the holders of mortgage debentures, unsecured debts, shares in limited partnerships and bonds. Moreover, even if the two roles were combined in practice more frequently than they actually are, it would still be important for theory to distinguish between them.

So far as profit is concerned, in the sense of profit of enterprise ['bénéfice de l'entreprise'], the English School fails to see that it is the correlative of possible loss, that it is subject to risk, that it depends upon exceptional and not upon normal circumstances, and that theoretically it ought to be left to one side. Profit in the sense of interest charges on capital is defined as "a remuneration for the abstinence of the capitalist who has saved the capital". I shall now proceed to relate how the English School determines each of these two things which it presents under the same name of profit. Once again John Stuart Mill will be my authority for the statement of the English doctrine that follows.

367. Building on the Ricardian theory of rent, Mill begins by establishing, or, at least he establishes as an afterthought, that *the advances of capital consist solely in wages* or that *rent does not enter into the cost of production of agricultural products.*

I undertook (Mill says) to show in the proper place, that this is an allowable supposition, and that rent does not really form any part of the expenses of production, or of the advances of the capitalist. The grounds on which this assertion was made are now apparent. It is true that all tenant farmers, and many other classes of producers, pay rent. But we have now seen, that whoever cultivates land, paying a rent for it, gets in return for his rent an instrument of superior power to other instruments of the same kind for which no rent is paid. The superiority of the instrument is in exact proportion to the rent paid for it. If a few persons had steam-engines of superior power to all others in existence, but limited by physical laws to a number short of the demand, the rent which a manufacturer would be willing to pay for one of these steam-engines could not

ELEMENTS OF PURE ECONOMICS

be looked upon as an addition to his outlay because by the use of it he would save in his other expenses the equivalent of what it cost him; without it he could not do the same quantity of work, unless at an additional expense equal to the rent. The same thing is true of land. The real expenses of production are those incurred on the worst land, or by the capital employed in the least favourable circumstances. This land or capital pays, as we have seen, no rent; but the expenses to which it is subject cause all other land or agricultural capital to be subjected to an equivalent expense in the form of rent. Whoever does pay rent gets back its full value in extra advantages, and the rent which he pays does not place him in a worse position than, but only in the same position as, his fellow-producer who pays no rent, but whose instrument is one of inferior efficiency.[1]

Rent having thus been eliminated from the expenses of production, the only expense that remains, apart from interest charges, is wages, the rate of which is determined, according to the English School, by the ratio of capital to population. Hence interest charges (or, as the English say, profit, which includes interest charges properly speaking and profit of enterprise) is easy to determine.

The capitalist, then (Mill concludes), may be assumed to make all the advances and receive all the produce. His profit consists of the excess of produce above the advances; his *rate* of profit is the ratio which that excess bears to the amount advanced.[2]

This, in short, is the English theory of the determination of prices of productive services. The capitalists are entrepreneurs: they pay the land-owners by remitting to them, in the form of rent, the excess of products attributable to the relative superiority of their land; they pay the workers by distributing to them, in the form of wages, the wages fund; and then the final products are the capitalists' to do with as they please. Whatever is left to these capitalist-entrepreneurs, after all the outlays have been deducted, represents at one and the same time the interest charges on their capital and their business gains, i.e. their profit. We must now discuss the theory mathematically in order to show how illusory it is.

368. Let P be the aggregate price received for the products of an enterprise; let S, I and F be respectively the wages, interest charges and rent laid out by the entrepreneurs, in the course of production, to pay for the services of personal faculties, capital and land. Let us recall now that, according to the English School, the selling price of products is determined by their costs of production, that is to say, it is equal to the cost of the productive services employed. Thus we have the equation

$$P=S+I+F,$$

and P is determined for us. It remains only to determine S, I and F.

[1] John Stuart Mill, *Principles of Political Economy*, Book II, Chapter XVI, § 6 [*op. cit.*, pp. 433–434].
[2] John Stuart Mill, *Principles of Political Economy*, Book II, Chapter XV, § 5. [This passage is found in § 5 of the 1848 edition of Mill's *Principles of Political Economy*; but in the Ashley edition cited above it is found in § 6, pp. 417–418.]

Surely, if it is not the price of the products that determines the price of productive services, but the price of productive services that determines the price of the products, we must be told what determines the price of the services. That is precisely what the English economists try to do. To this end, they construct a theory of rent according to which rent is not included in the expenses of production, thus changing the above equation to

$$P=S+I.$$

Having done this, they determine S directly by the theory of wages. Then, finally, they tell us that "the amount of interest or profit is the excess of the aggregate price received for the products over the wages expended on their production", in other words, that it is determined by the equation

$$I=P-S.$$

It is clear now that the English economists are completely baffled by the problem of price determination; for it is impossible for I to determine P at the same time that P determines I. In the language of mathematics one equation cannot be used to determine two unknowns. This objection is raised without any reference to our position on the manner in which the English School eliminates rent before setting out to determine wages.

369. Such is the pass in which economics still finds itself in the matter of the determination of prices of productive services. Jean Baptiste Say had said in Book I, Chapter V, of his *Treatise on Political Economy*:[8]

An industrious person may lend his industry to another possessed of land and capital only.

The owner of capital may lend it to an individual possessing land and industry only.

The landholder may lend his estate to a person possessing capital and industry only.

Whether the thing lent be industry, capital, or land, inasmuch as all three concur in the creation of value, their use also bears value, and is commonly paid for.

The price paid for the loan of industry is called *wages*.

The price paid for the loan of capital is called *interest*.

And that paid for a loan of land is called *rent*.

J. B. Say had a tolerably clear and accurate idea of the combination of the three productive services in the process of production. The terminology he employed was good; we have therefore adopted it ourselves.[9] But there were large gaps in his work which needed to be filled. In the first place, J. B. Say did not fully understand the specific role of the entrepreneur. In fact, this person is absent from his theory. In the second place, Say did not give an adequate explanation of the services for which wages, interest charges and rent are paid; and he goes no further than the Physiocrats in showing how the prices of these services are determined. In this connection, he ought to have introduced a satisfactory theory of value and of the mechanism of exchange, an acceptable theory of capital and income and of the mechanism of production, as well as definitions of the entrepreneur and of the market for products and services. In the last fifty years the economists of the French School have not made a single contribution along these lines; they have not added a single doctrine to pure economics; in fact, they still do not know how interest charges, wages and rent are determined.

As evidence of this incompetence, I need only cite the work of P. A. Boutron entitled, *Théorie de la rente foncière*,[10] which was awarded a prize by the Académie des sciences morales et politiques. The author sets out to prove that the selling price of products is determined by their cost of production. Then he defines rent as "the excess of the price of products over the interest and wages expended on their production". If he had undertaken to present a theory of wages, he would obviously have defined it as "the excess of the price of products over the interest and rent expended on their production". And if the Académie had chosen the theory of interest charges as the subject for this contest, he would undoubtedly have won the prize by defining it as "the excess of the selling price over the rent and wages expended on their production".

370. We have replaced these unsatisfactory systems by one made up of three principal elements: (1) a description of the mechanism of free competition in exchange (effective offer and effective demand; increasing price, decreasing price and current equilibrium price) in Parts II and III; (2) a description of the mechanism of free competition in production (land and land-services, persons and personal services, capital proper and capital-services; land-owners, workers and capitalists; entrepreneurs; profit, loss and equality between selling price and cost of production) in Part IV; and (3) a description of the mechanism of free competition in capital formation and credit (new capital proper and the excess of income over consumption; and the ratio of total net income from new capital goods to the total excess of income over consumption) in Part V. These fundamental concepts give us: (1) a market for services in which the services of land, persons and capital proper are offered respectively by competing land-owners, workers and capitalists and demanded competitively not only by entrepreneurs in their capacity as producers but also by land-owners, workers and capitalists in

their capacity as consumers; (2) a market for products in which consumers' goods are supplied competitively by entrepreneurs and demanded competitively by land-owners, workers and capitalists; and (3) a market for capital goods in which new capital goods proper are supplied competitively by entrepreneurs and demanded competitively by capitalist-savers. Hence, we have also: (1) the prices of services, i.e. rent, wages and interest charges; (2) the prices of products; and (3) the rate of net income, and consequently, the prices of landed capital, personal capital and capital goods in the narrow sense. The demand for services and the supply of consumers' goods and new capital goods on the part of entrepreneurs are governed by their desire to make profits and avoid losses. The offer of services and the demand for consumable products and new capital goods on the part of land-owners, workers and capitalists are governed by their desire for maximum satisfaction.[c]

Perhaps, as has already happened, I shall be asked, whether it is really necessary, and whether it does not do more harm than good, to use mathematical symbols in presenting a doctrine which seems simple and clear enough as it stands. This is my answer.

To state a theory is one thing; to prove it is another. I know that in economics so-called proofs which are actually nothing more than gratuitous assertions are doled out and find acceptance again and again. And precisely for this reason, I submit that economics will not attain the status of a science until economists are compelled to demonstrate that which they have hitherto been content, in the main, merely to assert. Now, in order to demonstrate that commodity prices, in other words the quantities of *numéraire* exchangeable against other commodities, result effectively from such and such givens or conditions, it is absolutely indispensable, as I see it: (1) to formulate, in conformance with these givens or conditions, a system of equations which will be exactly equal in number to the unknowns, and of which the unknowns are the roots; and (2) to show that the sequence of actual events gives us, in fact, an empirical solution of this system of equations. This is what I have done first with regard to exchange, then with regard to production and finally with regard to capital formation. The use of the language and method of mathematics has thus enabled me to demonstrate not only the laws of the establishment of current equilibrium prices but also the laws of change in these prices. It has made it possible for me to analyse the facts, and thus to set the principle of free competition on firm foundations. I readily grant that to describe a system is not the same thing as to investigate its rational structure. Though both the description and the rational analysis are combined in my work, they could, if necessary, be separated from each other. I shall not object, if those of my readers who are economists without being mathematicians pass over the rational proofs and simply make good use of the descriptions. Very few of us are capable of reading Newton's *Philosophiae Naturalis Principia Mathematica* or Laplace's *Mécanique céleste*; and yet, on the word of competent scientists, we all accept the current description of the universe of astronomical phenomena based on the principle of universal gravitation. Why should the description of the universe of economic phenomena based on the principle of free competition not be accepted in the same way? There is no reason why the proof of the system, once established, may not be taken for granted, nor why the assertions involved may not be used in the study of questions of applied or practical economics. For my part, however, I have felt bound to give both the proof and the assertions, in order to present the main outlines of a truly scientific theory of social wealth.[d]

PART VIII
Price Fixing, Monopoly, Taxation

PRICE FIXING AND MONOPOLY

371. All the conclusions we have reached so far relate to one and only one hypothesis: that of absolutely free competition in exchange, production and capital formation. Thus, what we have found out are simply the effects of free competition. No matter what economists may say, or frequently seem to say, free competition is not the only possible system of economic organization; there are other systems like those of public regulation, price fixing, special privileges, monopolies, etc. In order to make a choice between free competition and the other systems, or, if we are so inclined, to express a preference for free competition as against its alternatives, and do so intelligently, we must consider the effects of the other systems as well. And quite apart from practical considerations, we should, I repeat, still have to inquire into the natural and necessary consequences of various possible types of social organization, if only to satisfy our scientific curiosity.

372. We have now to draw a clear distinction between restrictions on *laisser-faire, laisser-passer* in matters pertaining to the production or circulation of wealth, and State intervention in the distribution of wealth. Maximum and minimum prices, prohibitive or protective tariffs, monopolies and the issuance of paper money are comprised in the first category; while taxes and fiscal dues are comprised in the second. Varied as the topics are in this part of pure economics, they are at present completely ignored, but they will be developed little by little as a fuller knowledge of the general case makes possible a more detailed study of every kind of exception. All we can do here is to broach a few salient problems in order to show how such problems should be treated. Their elucidation is of importance for the elaboration of the elements of applied and social economics.

It is unnecessary, however, to go into any great detail in order to understand the effects of various disturbing influences on the mechanism of free competition. We may neglect mutually compensating variations and those variations which are secondary or inappreciable as compared with the major variations.[1] For this purpose, the price curves of §§229 and 230 are very useful.[a]

373. Let us suppose that the price of a productive service or of a product is regulated. We must differentiate now between two cases: (1) the case of a *maximum* [price], when it is forbidden to sell a service or a product at a price higher than the fixed price which

has been [arbitrarily] set below the level that would have been determined by free competition; and (2) the case of a *minimum* price, when it is forbidden to sell a service or a product at a price lower than the fixed price which has been [arbitrarily] set above the level that would have been determined by free competition. In actual practice it is generally very difficult to enforce such restrictions; but it is not impossible. At all events, we propose to inquire into the effects of substituting an artificial for a natural price, quite apart from the question of ways and means of enforcing such a price. We shall examine the consequences of price fixing first in relation to productive services and then in relation to products.

374. Let $\delta_t(p_t)$ and $\omega_t(p_t)$ be respectively the purchase and sales functions of the productive service (T) [i.e. land-service], and let these functions be represented by the curves T_dT_p and MN in Fig. 34. If the price of (T) is fixed at a maximum $p'_t < p_t$ or at a minimum $p''_t > p_t$, the equation

$$\delta_t(p_t) = \omega_t(p_t)$$

will be replaced, in the case of a maximum, by the inequality

$$\delta_t(p'_t) > \omega_t(p'_t),$$

resulting [geometrically] in a higher ordinate $p'_t T'$ than the ordinate $p'_t t'$ so long as the possibility of a rise in price which would normally have resulted from the excess of effective demand over effective offer is ruled out; and, in the case of a minimum, by the inequality

$$\delta_t(p''_t) < \omega_t(p''_t),$$

resulting [geometrically] in a lower ordinate $p''_t T''$ than the ordinate $p''_t t''$ so long as the possibility of a fall in price which would normally have resulted from the excess of effective offer over effective demand is ruled out. In the case of the maximum price, either a certain number of entrepreneurs would find it impossible to purchase any land-services at all, or they would all have to do with less land-services than they would like. A profit would be realized on whatever land-services were purchased, since the selling price of the products would be higher than their cost of production. In the case of the minimum [price], either a certain number of land-owners would be unable to sell any land-services at all, or they would all find it impossible to sell as much as they would like. In the same way, if, for example, a maximum [rate of] interest charges were established, entrepreneurs would not be able to borrow as much capital as they would like, in spite of the profit they might make. And finally, if the State established a minimum wage by legislation or if certain private organizations did the same by the use of threats and violence,[b] either a certain number of workers would not be able to sell any

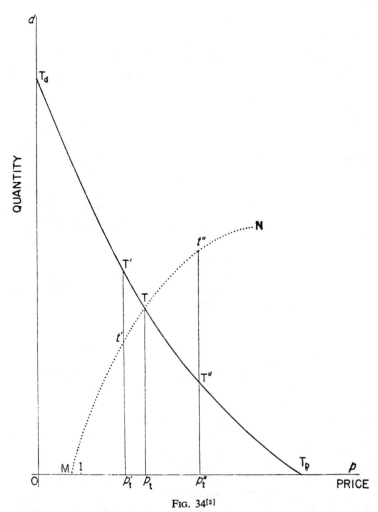

Fig. 34[2]

labour at all, or all of them would find it impossible to sell as much of their labour as they would like—which has nothing to do with the question whether or not it is of benefit to the workers to work more hours at a lower wage or fewer hours at a higher wage. This leads us to a consideration of the theory of monopoly, for at this point the theory of price fixing comes into contact with the theory of monopoly. In the case of price fixing, we have just seen that the price of commodities is set arbitrarily and the volume of sales is determined in consequence; in the case of monopoly, as we shall see presently, the volume of sales is set arbitrarily and the price of commodities is determined in consequence. In either case, it is possible to aim at maximizing the quantity sold multiplied by the price. This may be the guiding principle of *The International*, a principle which has neither been refuted by the adversaries of the organization nor adequately defended by its partisans.

375. If the price of the product (B) is fixed at a maximum $p'_b < p_b$ or at a minimum $p''_b > p_b$, the equation

$$b_t p_t + b_p p_p + b_k p_k + \ldots = p_b$$

will be replaced, in the case of a maximum, by the inequality

$$b_t p_t + b_p p_p + b_k p_k + \ldots > p'_b,$$

since there cannot be any rise in the price of (B), which would be the normal consequence of the withdrawal of entrepreneurs when cost exceeded selling price; and, in the case of a minimum, by the inequality

$$b_t p_t + b_p p_p + b_k p_k + \ldots < p''_b,$$

since there cannot be any fall in the price of (B), which would be the normal consequence of the entry of [new] entrepreneurs when selling price exceeded cost. In the case of a maximum [price], the entrepreneurs, rather than incur the loss $D_b(p_b - p'_b)$, which is represented by the area $p'_b B' b' p_b$ in Fig. 35, would stop producing altogether. In the case of a minimum [price], those entrepreneurs who were still able to sell their products would enjoy a profit of $D''_b(p''_b - p_b)$, which is represented by the area $p_b b'' B'' p''_b$. Thus, if a maximum limit were set on the price of bread, no more bread would be baked; and if a minimum limit were set, bakers would sell at a profit. Under these conditions, there would hardly be any justification for establishing an [arbitrary] maximum or minimum price. But the situation is different if we suppose the State itself to assume the role of an entrepreneur and then either to set a minimum price in order to make a profit in lieu of a tax, or to set a maximum price, thereby incurring a loss to be compensated by some tax or other. Whether such schemes turn out to be satisfactory or not, we have no right to declare them impossible and thus evade the responsibility of subjecting them to critical examination. It is perfectly conceivable that in a given country the State might, for example, manufacture the primary necessaries of life at a loss and luxuries at a profit; but it remains to be shown, in applied economics and social economics, that such a system would be inconsistent with public welfare and social justice.[e]

376. The economic theory of *monopoly* has been formulated mathematically, which is the clearest and most precise way of presenting

it, by Cournot in Chapter V of his *Researches into the Mathematical Principles of the Theory of Wealth*, published in 1838, and by Dupuit in two memoirs, the first of which entitled, "De la mesure de l'utilité des travaux publics", and the second, "De l'influence des péages sur

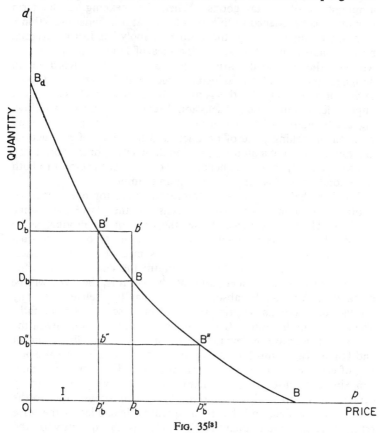

FIG. 35[3]

l'utilité des voies de communication", were published respectively in 1844 and 1849 in the *Annales des Ponts et Chaussées*. Unfortunately, economists have not thought it worth their while to look into this theory, with the result that their ideas on the subject of monopoly are reduced to a state of confusion which is accurately reflected in their verbal obfuscations. They have given the name of monopoly to enterprises [i.e. industries] which are not under a single control, but under the [divided] control of a limited number of persons. And, by analogy, they have even applied the term monopoly

to the ownership of certain productive services that are limited in
quantity like, for example, land. But all productive services are
limited in quantity; so that, if land-owners have a monopoly of land,
labourers have a monopoly of personal faculties, and capitalists have
a monopoly of capital goods. When the meaning of the term
monopoly is broadened to this extent, so that it includes everything,
it means nothing. In fact, the word monopoly has lost its original
meaning and is used to express the idea of limitation in quantity
whence value and wealth arise. And now there is no word left to
designate the idea of an exclusive single control over a productive
service or a product. But this is precisely the idea which is of capital
importance in our present discussion, because it nullifies the following two conditions of free production: the condition of equality
between the selling price of products and their cost of production,
and the condition of a uniform price on the market [for each product].
In order to study the consequences of monopoly with respect to both
these conditions, it is best to consider an example.

377. We shall imagine an entrepreneur who, for one reason or
another, has a monopoly (in our sense of the word) over some
product. He has the power to set the price of his product as he
pleases; but he has no control over the quantity of the product
which will be demanded, sold, and consumed at any given price.
In this respect, only one thing is certain: the dearer the product
is, the less will be demanded, and the cheaper it is, the more will be
demanded. We can be absolutely sure that the demand for any
product decreases as its price rises and increases as its price falls.
The only thing that differs from product to product is the law of the
increase or decrease in demand as the price rises or falls. Cournot
and Dupuit called this law the *law of the demand, sales, or consumption* of each product. For every product there is, on the one hand,
a maximum limit to price, and that is the price at which the quantity
demanded is zero; and, on the other hand, a maximum limit to the
quantity demanded, and that is the quantity demanded at the price
zero. This maximum quantity demanded is the quantity of the
product which would be taken and consumed if the product were
free and if there were enough of it for everybody. Let us suppose
that the quantity demanded of our [monopolized] product is zero
when the price is 100 francs per unit, and that the quantity taken at
the price zero is 50,000 units. Let us suppose, furthermore, that at
different prices ranging from 100 to 0 francs and taking on [succes-
sively] the values 50, 20, 5, 3, 2, 1 and 0·50 francs, the corresponding
quantity demanded ranges from 0 to 50,000 units, amounting
respectively to 10, 50, 1,000, 2,500, 5,000, 12,000 and 20,000 units,
in accordance with the following table:

PRICE	DEMAND	GROSS RECEIPTS	EXPENSES	NET RECEIPTS
in francs	[no. of units]	in francs	in francs	in francs
100	0	0	0	0
50	10	500	20	480
20	50	1,000	100	900
5	1,000	5,000	2,000	3,000
3	2,500	7,500	5,000	2,500
2	5,000	10,000	10,000	0
1	12,000	12,000	24,000	−12,000
0·50	20,000	10,000	40,000	−30,000
0	50,000	0	100,000	−100,000

Our entrepreneur's gross receipts will then be 0, 500, 1,000, 5,000, 7,500, 10,000, 12,000, 10,000, and 0 francs respectively. Thus the gross receipts, which start at zero when the price is at the maximum corresponding to a demand for zero units, increase to a maximum and then diminish finally reaching zero again when the price is zero and the quantity demanded has attained its maximum. In our example, maximum gross receipts are realized when the price is 1 franc and the corresponding quantity demanded is 12,000 units. At this point the gross receipts amount to 12,000 francs. If our entrepreneur had no costs of production, he would choose the selling price of 1 franc for his product; and this price would yield him the maximum profit. But how would he discover this price? By the simplest kind of groping. He would first try very high prices and he would observe that the quantity demanded was zero or very small and that his receipts were also zero or very small. Then gradually lowering his price, he would observe that both the quantity demanded and his receipts increased. In this way he would come to the price of 1 franc. If he lowered his price still further, he would find that although the quantity demanded increased, his receipts would start diminishing. And he would immediately raise his price to 1 franc again and hold it there. This is not a difficult operation; in fact, it is done all the time in ordinary business.

378. Generally, however, our entrepreneur will have certain costs of production. These are divided between overhead and direct costs, or, more precisely, between some costs that are more or less fixed and others that are more or less proportional to the quantity sold. These latter costs increase either exactly in proportion to sales or in a greater or smaller proportion, all depending on the special conditions of the particular industry in question. Let us suppose, for simplicity, that the expenses incurred in the manufacture of the

ELEMENTS OF PURE ECONOMICS

product under consideration are all proportional and that they amount to 2 francs per unit. The [total] costs corresponding to different prices in our hypothetical schedule, when the correlated quantities demanded are taken into account, will be respectively 0, 20, 100, 2,000, 5,000, 10,000, 24,000, 40,000, and 100,000 francs. The corresponding net receipts, which are equal to the excess of gross receipts over costs of production, will be 0, 480, 900, 3,000, 2,500, 0, −12,000, −30,000, and −100,000 francs. Thus, in our example, maximum net receipts are earned when the price is 5 francs per unit at which 1,000 units are demanded. At this point the net receipts are 3,000 francs. Consequently, our entrepreneur would set the price at 5 francs. He would discover this price by the same sort of groping which we described above.

379. In order to simplify our discussion, we assumed that our entrepreneur had no fixed overhead costs. If there were such costs amounting, let us say, to 1,000 francs, we should have to deduct these 1,000 francs from the net receipts earned at each price; and this would reduce the maximum net receipts by that amount, but would not change the position of this maximum. The price that would maximize profits would remain unchanged. It is important to note that the price yielding maximum [total] profits is completely independent of the [total] fixed costs.

380. Having thus found the price 5 francs which yields maximum profits, our entrepreneur would keep it there in so far as he had exclusive control over the product. If the product were not monopolized, the profits of the firm would attract competitors, the quantity sold and consumed would increase to 5,000 units and the price would fall to 2 francs which is equal to the cost of production. Hence the consequence of monopoly is that consumers have only 1,000 units at 5 francs each instead of 5,000 units at 2 francs each. We now see the difference between monopoly and free competition. The principle of *laisser-faire, laisser-passer*, when applied to an industry operating under the régime of unlimited competition, enables consumers to obtain the greatest possible satisfaction of their desires consistent with the condition of uniformity of price for each product in the market, the price in each case being equal to the cost of production so that producers make neither profit nor loss. The same principle of *laisser-faire, laisser-passer*, when applied to a monopolized industry, enables consumers to obtain [only] that maximum satisfaction which is consistent with the [double] condition that selling price be higher than cost of production and that the producers make the greatest possible profit. We shall see presently what becomes of uniformity of prices [under monopoly conditions]. In the case of unlimited competition, the entrepreneur is an intermediary whom we may

disregard, while land-owners, workers and capitalists are exchanging productive services with one another on the basis of equal value for equal value. In the case of monopoly, entrepreneurs intervene not only to combine the productive services and convert them into products, but to levy a certain portion of the wealth exchanged for their own benefit.

381. The theory of monopoly price yielding maximum profits can be applied to services as well as products. We can go further and formulate a more abstract and more scientific expression of the theory than we have done up to this point, if we start with Cournot's equation showing sales as a function of price

$$D=F(p).$$

Since (as Cournot tells us) the function $F(p)$ is continuous, the function $pF(p)$ which expresses the total value of the quantity annually sold must be continuous also. This function would equal zero, if p equals zero, since the consumption of any article remains finite even on the hypothesis that it is absolutely free; or, in other words, it is theoretically always possible to assign to the symbol p a value so small that the product $pF(p)$ will vary imperceptibly from zero. The function $pF(p)$ disappears also when p becomes infinite, or, in other words, theoretically a value can always be assigned to p so great that the demand for the article and the production of it would cease. Since the function $pF(p)$ at first increases, and then decreases as p increases, there is therefore a value of p which makes this function a maximum, and which is given by the equation

$$F(p)+pF'(p)=O \qquad \qquad ..(1)$$

in which F', according to Lagrange's notation, denotes the differential coefficient of function F.

If we lay out the curve *anb* (Fig. 36) of which the abscissas Oq and the ordinates qn represent the variables p and D, the root of equation (1) will be the abscissa of the point n from which the triangle Ont, formed by the tangent nt and the radius vector On, is isosceles, so that we have $Oq=qt$.[1][d]

In fact, the maximum of a function is given by the root of its derivative set equal to zero. The derivative of a product like $pF(p)$ equals the sum of two products: the factor $F(p)$ multiplied by the derivative of p, plus the factor p multiplied by the derivative of $F(p)$. The derivative of p is equal to unity.

The equation of a tangent to the curve $D=F(p)$ at a point with co-ordinates (D, p) is

$$y-D=F'(p)(x-p).$$

If we substitute into this equation the value $F'(p)=-\dfrac{F(p)}{p}$ from equation (1), and then try to find the intercept of this tangent on the x axis by setting $y=O$, we get $x=2p$.

[1] A. Cournot, *Researches into the Mathematical Principles of the Theory of Wealth*, Chapter IV, [*op. cit.*, §24, pp. 52–53. In Cournot, the diagram is referred to as Fig. 1.]

Cournot founds his theory of monopoly on this determination of a maximum. He passes from the case of a product freely given by nature to that of a manufactured product and from maximum gross receipts to maximum net receipts; then he makes the transition from the case of a single monopolist to that of two monopolists [duopoly], and, finally, from monopoly to unlimited competition. I have preferred, for my part, to start with unlimited competition as the

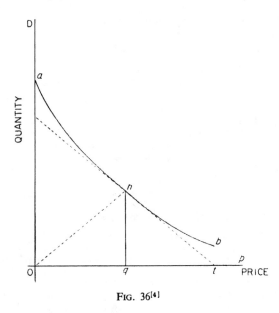

FIG. 36[4]

general case, and then to work towards monopoly as a special case. Pursuing this course, I was able, in §§154 and 230, to relate the rational and rigorously exact equations of exchange and production to the empirical and approximative equation of sales written as a function of price.[6]

382. We have just seen how monopoly impairs the condition that the selling price of a product equal its cost of production; and now it remains for us to see how monopoly impairs the condition of uniformity of price in the market.

Let us return to the example that we have just been considering and let us suppose, for simplicity, that each consumer takes only one unit of the commodity. At 50 francs a unit, 10 units can be sold; therefore, out of the 50 units which are sold at 20 francs a unit, there would be at most 40 units for which 20 francs was a maximum price and which, under all circumstances, could be sold at this price. If we deduct in this way, from any total quantity demanded at a given price, the quantity demanded at the price immediately above, we obtain [the marginal increment of quantity demanded, or] that layer of the quantity for which the given price is a maximum and which, under all circumstances, could be sold at this price. Let us now suppose that instead of a uniform price there are several [coexisting] prices on the market and that a layer of the total quantity demanded is sold at each of these prices. If we keep the prices of our original example unchanged and compel every consumer to pay the price which, for him, is a maximum, it will be possible to sell 0 units at 100 francs per unit; 10 units at 50 francs; 40 at 20 francs; 950 at 5 francs; 1,500 at 3 francs; 2,500 at 2 francs; 7,000 at 1 franc; 8,000 at 0·50 francs; and 30,000 at 0 francs, according to the following table:

Price	Layers [or marginal increments] of demand	[Marginal receipts] or gross receipts from each successive layer	Aggregate gross receipts	Cost of each successive layer [or marginal increment of cost]	[Marginal net receipts] or net receipts from each successive layer	Aggregate net receipts
frcs.	[no. of units]	frcs.	frcs.	frcs.	frcs.	frcs.
100	0	0	0	0	0	0
50	10	500	500	20	480	480
20	40	800	1,300	80	720	1,200
5	950	4,750	6,050	1,900	2,850	4,050
3	1,500	4,500	10,550	3,000	1,500	5,550
2	2,500	5,000	15,550	5,000	0	5,550
1	7,000	7,000	22,550	14,000	− 7,000	−1,450
0·50	8,000	4,000	26,550	16,000	−12,000	−13,450
0	30,000	0	26,550	60,000	−60,000	−73,450

The gross receipts from each layer of sales thus affected would be respectively 0, 500, 800, 4,750, 4,500, 5,000, 7,000, 4,000 and 0 francs. If only 50 and 20 francs, the first two prices at which the quantity demanded is not zero, were charged, the aggregate gross receipts would be 1,300 francs. But if, in addition to these two prices, the third, fourth, fifth, sixth, and seventh prices at which the demand is not zero were successively included [in the schedule], the aggregate gross receipts at each of these prices would be respectively 6,050, 10,550, 15,550, 22,550, and 26,550 francs. In addition, 30,000 units could be disposed of free of charge.

442 ELEMENTS OF PURE ECONOMICS

383. The cost of production being 2 francs per unit, the expenses incurred in the production of each layer of quantity demanded at the different prices would be respectively 0, 20, 80, 1,900, 3,000, 5,000, 14,000, 16,000, and 60,000 francs. Subtracting these expenses from the gross receipts we obtain the following net receipts for each layer: 0, 480, 720, 2,850, 1,500, 0, −7,000, −12,000, and −60,000 francs. The sixth of these nine figures is zero; the last three are negative and represent losses. Hence, by eliminating all prices like 0, 0·50 and 1 francs, which are lower than the cost of production and by retaining only the others, we arrive at the following result. If there were only two prices, 50 and 20 francs, the aggregate net receipts would amount to 1,200 francs. And if, in addition to these two prices, the prices 5 francs and 3 francs were also included [in the schedule], the aggregate net receipts at each of these prices would be respectively 4,050 francs and 5,550 francs. Thus, if we suppose that the expenses of production are 2 francs per unit, the maximum net receipts would be 5,500 francs. In addition, 2,500 units could be sold at cost.

384. These observations do not pertain exclusively to the monopoly case. Clearly, even under free competition, an entrepreneur may profit by price discrimination, if, taking his cost of production as the lower limit, he sets up a scale of prices and is successful in inducing each consumer to pay the highest price he would be willing to pay for the product. This hypothetical situation is realized in the actual world of trade and industry more frequently than one generally supposes. The art of selling the same commodity at different prices —in fact, at the highest possible price to each class of consumers—is highly developed among manufacturers and merchants. The practice of this fine art is very often facilitated by the thoughtlessness, vanity and caprice of consumers. Sometimes it is only necessary to use a variety of labels in order to differentiate prices and to find customers at each price. More often, the commodity, while remaining essentially the same, is given a slightly different form to sell at different prices. For example, a manufacturer who sells chocolate wrapped in plain glazed paper and modestly labelled "Superfine" at 3 francs a pound, will charge 4 francs a pound for the same chocolate with a little vanilla flavour added, wrapped in gilt paper and advertised as "Royal". In the case of theatre seats, their various prices are in no way proportional to the cost of production. It is readily seen, however, that, under a régime of free competition, it is much more difficult to continue playing these artful tricks, precisely because the differences in price, which are appreciably greater than the costs of producing discriminative forms and labels, tend constantly to be narrowed by competition. A competitor will soon enter the field of our chocolate manufacturer and sell "Royal" chocolate at

3 francs 80 centimes a pound, which will compel our original manufacturer to offer it at 3 francs 60 centimes, so that the competitor, in turn, will bring his price down to 3 francs 40 centimes and force the original manufacturer to lower his price to 3 francs 20 centimes. Under a monopoly, however, nothing could be easier than to perpetuate the current and well-known practice of price discrimination without let or hindrance. It happens very often that a publisher, who has exclusive rights over a sensational book written by a famous author, sells a first edition in octavo at 7 francs 50 centimes, then two or three editions in smaller format at 3 francs, and finally a popular edition at 1 franc. The difference in the price of the paper and the printing is negligible. The only significant difference is that one edition can be had sooner than another. Since some readers are more impatient than others to have the books, they automatically classify themselves with respect to the maximum price they are willing to pay; and the publisher profits by this classification. Hence the importance under monopoly, of operating with multiple prices instead of a uniform price so that the consumer is compelled to pay the highest possible price.

385. As we have already pointed out, Cournot was the first to enunciate a scientific theory of the fact that demand decreases as the price of a commodity increases, and to show the consequences of this fact in his formulation of the mathematical conditions of maximum gross receipts and maximum net receipts in the case of a monopoly. In this connection, Dupuit only repeated under the name of *law of consumption* the propositions and corollaries which Cournot had originally presented under the name of *law of sales* ['*loi du débit*']. Dupuit's own contribution consisted in his observations on multiple prices for one and the same commodity. He made a very thorough and ingenious study of this phenomenon in the two memoirs cited above. While we have no need to do more than refer the reader to these memoirs, we must, none the less, call attention to an egregious error which Dupuit committed in a matter of capital importance.

386. The diverse considerations regarding utility which we have just presented (Dupuit says) can be portrayed geometrically in a very simple fashion.

If we suppose that the lengths Op, Op', Op''... laid off on an unbounded line OP (Fig. 37) represent the price of an article and that the perpendicular line-segments pn, $p'n'$, $p''n''$... represent respectively the number of units of the article consumed at these prices, a curve $Nnn'n''P$ will result, which we shall call a consumption curve. ON represents the quantity consumed when the price is zero, and OP represents the price at which the consumption becomes zero.

Since pn represents the number of units of the article consumed at the price Op, the area of the rectangle $Ornp$ represents both the expenses of production of np units, and, according to J. B. Say, their utility. We have proved, we believe, that the utility of these *np* units for all [consumers] is at least *Op*, and that for all but very few consumers it is something greater than *Op*. For example, if we erect a perpendicular at *p'*, we have *n'p'* units of the article, each with a utility at least equal to *Op'*, since these units will be bought at that price. Consequently, of the *np* units consumed at the price *Op* there are only *np−n'p'=nq* units, whose utility is really no greater than *Op* (or rather a mean between *Op* and *Op'*), the utility of any one of the other units being at least *Op'*. We conclude, therefore, that, so far as these *nq* units are concerned, their utility is represented by the area *rnn'r'*, and that the utility of the remaining *qp* or *n'p'* units is greater than the

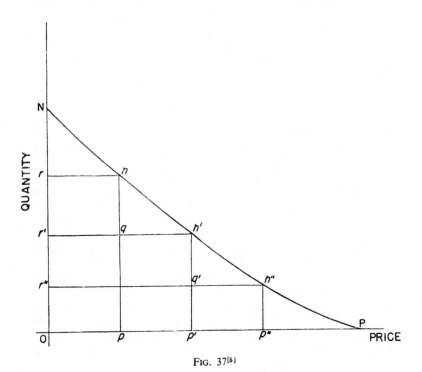

FIG. 37[5]

rectangle *r'n'p'O*. If we supposed the price to be further increased by *p'p''*, we could demonstrate that the utility of the *n'p'−n''p''=n'q'* units was equal to a mean between *Op'* and *Op''* [per unit] and was proportional to the area *r'n'n''r''*, etc., etc. We could then prove that the absolute utility of these *np* units for the consumer is the [mixtilinear] trapezoid *OrnP*. To find the relative utility, we need only subtract the expenses of production, i.e. the rectangle *rnpO*, which, according to our theory, leaves the [mixtilinear] triangle *npP* to represent the utility remaining to the consumers of the *np* units after they have been paid for. It is obvious that the area of this [mixtilinear] triangle to the right of the line *np* has no relation whatsoever to the area of the rectangle to the left of this line.

If the product under consideration is a natural product entailing no expenses of acquisition, the utility is represented by the large mixtilinear triangle *NOP*.

We observe that as the price of a good increases, its utility diminishes, but it diminishes more and more slowly; and that as the price diminishes, the utility increases, but it increases more and more rapidly, since the utility is represented by a triangle which is being shortened or lengthened.[1]

387. This geometric representation expresses Dupuit's theory of utility very precisely and very clearly. Instead of measuring utility, as J. B. Say did,[6] by the pecuniary sacrifice which the consumer actually does make once he knows the price, Dupuit measures utility by the sacrifice which the consumer is willing to make. The maximum pecuniary sacrifice which a consumer is willing to make in order to procure a unit of product being the measure of the utility of this unit of product for the given consumer, it follows that the sum total of the maximum pecuniary sacrifices which all consumers together are willing to make in order to obtain the largest number of units of a product that can be sold is the measure of the utility of this product for the totality of consumers or for society as a whole. Thus, the measure of total utility is geometrically represented by the area under the demand curve drawn as a function of price; and arithmetically it is represented by the total gross receipts calculated, in the manner described above, by aggregating layers of gross receipts. Unfortunately, all these statements are erroneous, and Dupuit's theory is no improvement on J. B. Say's. To be sure, the maximum pecuniary sacrifice which a consumer is willing to make in order to obtain a bottle of wine, for instance, depends, in part, on the utility of this bottle of wine for this consumer; for, according as this utility increases or decreases, the maximum sacrifice in question will increase or decrease. But Dupuit did not perceive that this maximum sacrifice depends, in part, also on the utility which bread, meat, clothes and furniture have for the consumer; for, as the utility he derives from other commodities increases or decreases, the maximum sacrifice that he will be willing to make for wine will decrease or increase. Moreover, Dupuit failed to see that the maximum pecuniary sacrifice in question depends, in part again, on the quantity of the wealth (measured in terms of *numéraire*) which the consumer possesses; for, according as this quantity is larger or smaller, the sacrifice which he will be ready to make for wine will be larger or smaller. In general, the maximum pecuniary sacrifice which a consumer is willing to make to obtain a unit of a product depends not only on the utility of the product in question, but also on the utility of all the other products in the market, and, finally, on the consumer's means. We have already given sufficient attention to the interrelations among the

[1] *Annales des Ponts et Chaussées*, 2nd series, 1844, 2nd semester, p. 373 [Jules Dupuit, *De l'utilité et da sa mesure. Ecrits choisis et republiés par* Mario de Bernardi, Turin, La riforma sociale, 1933, in the *Collezione di scritti inediti o rari di economisti*, edited by Luigi Einaudi, pp. 62–63].

phenomena of utility, effective demand, effective supply and current price, to make it unnecessary to repeat the argument here. We may, therefore, without further discussion, definitely reject all Dupuit's statements in his two memoirs which bear upon the variation of utility as price varies and as the quantity demanded varies from price to price. It is true that these statements constitute the principal part of his argument, but it is no less true that they rest on a confusion of ideas resulting from Dupuit's complete failure to distinguish between utility or want curves on the one hand, and demand curves on the other.[1]

Lesson 42

TAXATION

388. To complete our theory of monopoly, we should have to show how, in the absence of perfect competition, those who have services or products to sell tend to combine in order to profit by a monopoly position. Moreover, a fuller treatment of the effects of different modes of organization of the production and circulation of wealth would require that we analyse, also, the effects of prohibitive tariffs, protective tariffs and paper money. All such questions, however, will find their appropriate place in our studies of applied economics, where we propose to discuss exceptions to the principle of *laisser-faire, laisser-passer*, and special applications of this principle.[1] The question of combinations will then be taken up in the course of our investigation of the great industrial monopolies in mines and railways; the problem of prohibitive and protective tariffs will be treated as part of our discussion of the freedom of foreign trade; and the subject of paper money will be examined in connection with the general problem of the free issue of bank notes. For the present, let us pass to a study of the effects of different systems of distribution of wealth.

389. In our description of the mechanism of exchange, production and capital formation, we have not only assumed perfect freedom of competition in the markets for products, services and capital goods, but we have also abstracted from two things: first, the method of appropriation of services concerning which we made no special assumptions, and, second, the role of the State, its services and its needs. It is manifest, however, that an economy cannot function without the intervention of an authority empowered to maintain order and security, to render justice, to guarantee national defence, and to perform many other services besides. The State, however, is not an entrepreneur; it does not sell its services in the market either on the principle of free competition (at a selling price equal to the cost of production), or on the principle of monopoly (in pursuit of maximum net receipts). It often sells its services at a loss and sometimes gives them away without charge. As we shall see in a later work, this is as it should be, because the services of the State are meant for collective, and not individual, consumption. There remains now to consider two ways of providing for the needs of the State, that is, for public expenditures: the first is to let the State participate along with individuals in the distribution of social wealth by holding *property* of its own; the second is to make a levy on the incomes of

individuals by *taxation*. Which of these two systems is preferable? Can they not be fused into a single system? We shall deal with such questions in our study of social economics.[2] Our problem will then be to work out simultaneously a theory of property and a theory of taxation. For the present, however, we need only inquire into the natural and necessary effects of different kinds of taxes. Even if we supposed taxation to be abolished, it would still be useful to determine the effects of taxation, if only to understand the nature of, and the reasons for, the action taken. Moreover, we are again in the presence of one of those questions which we have a right to study in the interests of science, quite apart from practical applications. All economists who, like Ricardo, James Mill and Destutt de Tracy, have written on the subject of pure economics, have devoted important chapters to taxation.

390. Let us consider again the hypothetical country to which our economic table in §319 refers. There were 80 milliards worth of land yielding annually 2 milliards in rent; there were 50 milliards worth of personal faculties yielding 5 milliards in wages; and there were 60 milliards worth of capital proper yielding 3 milliards in interest. And now let us suppose that there is a question in this country of raising annually a sum of 1 milliard for public expenditures or for expenditures in the public interest. This figure may, upon examination, be found too large or too small in view of the needs of the State; but such considerations are outside the scope of pure economics. The essential thing here is to come to [conceptually] clear conclusions by the simplest possible calculations. Hence I take 1 milliard, for convenience, in order to sharpen our analysis.

391. To define the problem of taxation properly, we shall have to begin by making several preliminary observations.

The first is that capital should never be used for consumption, whether public or private. It may very well be that some individuals consume their capital as they are free to do, but this deplorable fact is happily compensated by the circumstance that other individuals save out of their incomes. The State, however, ought not systematically to destroy the source of national wealth. Land, personal faculties and capital goods proper constitute the fund available for production. Land-services, labour-services, and capital-services constitute the fund available for consumption, and it is only from this latter fund that taxes ought to be drawn.

392. We have seen[3] that there are three types of income or services: the services of land, the labour of personal faculties, and the services of capital goods proper. These are sometimes consumed directly in the form of consumers' services and sometimes combined with one another in the form of productive services for the purpose

of producing a certain amount of products made up of income goods and new capital goods proper. The total value of consumers' services and products is 10 milliards, two-tenths of which or 2 milliards are derived from the land-services, five-tenths or 5 milliards from labour, and three-tenths or 3 milliards from the service of capital goods. We must not fail to include among the consumers' services, i.e. among the items of income subject to taxation, the income from the personal faculties of the members of the leisure class who do not work, as well as the income from the land of those land-owners who do not rent their land to others and the income from the capital goods of those capitalists who do not lend their capital goods to others. While we propose that taxes be levied on income only, it must be on all [categories of] income. Neither governments nor the general run of theorists view the matter in this light, for, on the basis of classifications made solely by rule of thumb, they are determined to tax workers, but it never occurs to them to tax idlers as owners of personal faculties.

In the economy under consideration, there are three classes of consumers: land-owners, workers and capitalists, corresponding to the three factors of production. The land-owners receive as rent 2 milliards in the form of services or products in return for 2 milliards worth of land-services; the workers receive as wages 5 milliards in the form of services or products in return for 5 milliards worth of labour; and the capitalists receive as interest 3 milliards in the form of services or products in return for 3 milliards worth of capital-services. The figures 2, 5 and 3 represent proportions in consumption as well as in production. Entrepreneurs are not considered in this connection, because they do not earn anything *qua* entrepreneurs; and consequently they are subject to taxation only in so far as they are land-owners, labourers, or capitalists.

We may now observe that whatever system of taxation the State may adopt, the various possible methods of taxation can be classified under four heads. As a matter of fact, the State has the alternative of stepping in either after the completion of the exchange of [productive] services for consumers' goods and services or before that exchange takes place. If the State steps in after this exchange, it will collect the tax directly, either from land-owners by taking away part of their rent, or from workers by taking away part of their wages, or, again, from capitalists by taking away part of their interest. This makes in all three kinds of *direct taxation*. If, on the other hand, the State steps in prior to the exchange of [productive] services for consumers' goods and services, then the social income from which the State takes its share must be considered as an aggregate of 10 milliards of consumers' goods and services and not as a composite of 2 milliards of rent, 5 milliards of wages, and 3 milliards of interest. Under these circumstances the State collects the tax in advance from the entrepreneurs, it being clearly understood that they will reimburse themselves by adding the amount of the tax to the prices of the products which they sell to land-owners, workers and capitalists. In this way, the reduction in rent, wages and interest is made indirectly. And so we have *indirect taxation*.[a] Direct taxes are levied on services and indirect taxes are levied on products. We are speaking here only of the taxation of *property* and not of *persons*, for the latter sort of taxes cannot be assessed, nor can their incidence be traced.

393. Finally, it should be noted that for present purposes we are ignoring the question of the right of the State to levy one or the other of these four kinds of taxes, as well as the questions of the relative advantage accruing to the State and of the ease or difficulty experienced by the State in adopting any one of these methods. Thus we are ignoring the same sort of questions we left to one side in the foregoing discussion of price fixing. Actually, a direct tax on land is easy to administer, though it entails great labour and much expense; but a direct tax on wages (apart from taxes on the salaries of public officials) or a direct tax on income from capital (apart from taxes on house rentals and on public debt interest) is quite impossible to assess with any accuracy, no matter how much effort or money is expended for that purpose. An indirect tax is easy to impose on certain products and hard to impose on others. These are practical considerations with which we shall not concern ourselves here. If we suppose that the State is invested with the power not only to collect the three kinds of direct taxes but to levy indirect taxes as well and that it has recourse successively to all four methods, what will the consequences be? That, strictly speaking, is the question with which we are here concerned.[b]

394.[c] In our hypothetical country the total annual wage bill amounts to 5 milliards. If we suppose that the State undertakes to impose a proportional tax of 1 milliard on the income from personal faculties only, then the immediate effect of such a tax will be the diversion to the State of one-fifth of the wages of each worker. Now, the price of labour is determined, as we have seen, by the offer and demand for labour-services used in consumption and in production. The imposition of the tax does not change these conditions in any way. The State simply takes the place of the taxed workers in the consumption of 1 milliard worth of goods and services. It is impossible to say [*a priori*] what services or goods will be more in demand or less in demand than before. It is equally impossible to predict whether the offer of labour will increase or decrease and whether, if the offer increases or decreases, the total wage bill will be larger or smaller. Consequently, we must either renounce taking account of these eventualities or imagine that they mutually compensate one another and assume that the rate of wages will be the same after the tax as before. That being the case, the workers will find it impossible to shift the tax to others by raising the price of their labour. Each worker will simply be deprived of one-fifth of his income. If, for example, a worker labours ten hours and earns five francs a day, it can be said either that the State takes from him one franc every day or that he works two hours every day for the benefit of the State. Only in one case can the tax have a different effect and that is the case where the wages barely suffice to cover the strict minimum of subsistence for the workers. Then the imposition of a tax on wages will inevitably result in a diminution of the working population, and consequently the conditions of the effective offer of labour on the market for productive services will change. If this offer diminishes, wages will rise and the amount of the tax will, in reality, be included in the cost of production of the products. Hence, it will be paid in this case by the consumers of the final products. In all other cases, the burden will fall on the workers.

395.[d] Let us now state mathematically some of the more important conclusions. In the first place, we see that generally: *A direct tax on wages constitutes an act of appropriation by the State of a definite fraction of the workers' personal incomes.*

If s is the tax rate on gross income, then any gross wage [say p_p] becomes

$$p'_p = p_p(1-s).$$

396. A direct tax on rent would be a land-tax, which, in contradistinction to the sort of land-taxes which have always been levied and are still levied today, would fall exclusively on the income from land and not on the income from those capital goods proper which are combined with land in agriculture. The argument developed above in our discussion of a tax on wages shows that a tax on rent would result in the diversion to the State of a portion of the income of land-owners, who would, however, find it impossible to shift the burden of the tax to the consumers of their products by raising the price of their land-services. This principle was correctly stated, if not rigorously proved, by Ricardo in Chapter X of his *Principles of Political Economy and Taxation*. Taking Ricardo as his starting-point, Destutt de Tracy in Chapter XII of his *Traité d'économie politique* argued with no less reason that when land is taxed in perpetuity, it is equivalent in every respect to a confiscation of a part of the land corresponding to the rate of the tax.

ELEMENTS OF PURE ECONOMICS

In his own words:[4]

As to a tax on land income, it is evident that he who owns the land at the time the tax is established really pays the whole tax without being able to shift it to any one else. For the tax does not help him increase his output, since it adds nothing either to the demand for the product or to the fertility of the soil; nor does it in any way diminish the cost of production. Everyone agrees that this is true. But what has not been sufficiently noticed is that the land-owner in question ought to be considered not so much as having been deprived of a portion of his yearly income, but as having lost that part of his capital which would produce this portion of income at the current rate of interest. The proof of this lies in the fact that a farm, which yields a net rent of five thousand francs and is worth one hundred thousand francs [before the tax], will only fetch eighty thousand francs on the market, other things being equal, the day after the rent has been charged with a perpetual tax of one-fifth of its value; and this same farm will then be reckoned at only eighty thousand francs in the inventory of any estate the other items of which have not changed in value. When, indeed, a State declares that it takes in perpetuity a fifth of the income of lands, it is as if it had declared itself proprietor of a fifth of the capital, for no property is worth more than the utility which can be derived from it. When the State levies a new tax and then floats a loan for the interest of which it pledges the proceeds of the new tax, then surely the process [of seizure] is completed. The State, in that case, really converts the capital it has seized into cash and uses it up all at once instead of gradually spending the annual income from the capital. This is what Mr. Pitt did when he made a once-for-all levy of the capital value of the land tax. The landed proprietors found themselves liberated [from all future payments of the tax], and Mr. Pitt ate up the capital.

It follows, therefore, that once all the land has changed hands after the establishment of the tax, no one really pays the tax. Purchasers pay only for what is left and lose nothing; heirs succeed only to what they find [in the inheritance], and must consider the rest of the estate as spent or lost by their predecessors who have indeed lost it. In case of inheritances abandoned as of no value, it is the creditors who lose the capital which the State took out of the property serving as security for the loan.

It follows, also, that when the State remits the whole or part of a land tax which had previously been established in perpetuity, it simply makes the current land-owners a gift of the capital value of the income which it no longer exacts. From the point of view of the present land-owners, it is an absolutely free gift, to which they have no more right than any one else, for not one of them counted on this capital in the transaction by which he became a land-owner.

The results would not be altogether the same, if the tax had originally been established only for a given number of years. In that case, what is really taken from the land-owners is that part of their capital which corresponds to the given number of *annual tax payments*. The State, furthermore, could not borrow more than this amount from lenders, to whom it pledges the tax in payment of their principal and interest; and in any sale the value of land would fall only by this same amount. When, in such a case, the last tax instalments and the corresponding interest coupons on the loan are paid, the debt is extinguished on both sides, because it is paid off. On the whole, the principle is the same as in the case of a perpetual tax and a perpetual loan.

It is always true then, that when a tax is laid on land, a value equal to the capital value of this tax is thereupon taken from those who own the land at that time, but after all the land has changed hands, the tax is, in reality, no longer paid by any one. This observation is, indeed, curious, but important.

Destutt de Tracy is entirely mistaken in applying this observation to a tax on the income from buildings, and partly mistaken, as we shall see, in applying it to a tax on government bond interest; but his observations relating to a tax on land income are quite correct and are confirmed by history. It has always been known that taxes on land income, whether levied by the State, feudal lords, the Church or any religious community, affect the value of the landed capital, and reduce it exactly by the ratio of the amount of the tax to the amount of the rent. There have been times when taxes completely absorbed all the rent; and then the value of the land to the owner was reduced to zero. This leads us to another observation which has been entirely overlooked, but is no less important than the last.

397. The value of land and of land-services rises steadily in a progressive economy, a fact which is mathematically deducible from our theory of social wealth. From this, it follows, first of all, that the loss suffered by those who owned the land at the time the tax was introduced continually diminishes, while those who acquired the land later and who had never lost anything enjoy the full benefit of the increasing value of landed capital and land income. It follows, also, that it is preferable for the State to levy a tax calculated as a definite ratio of the rent rather than as a lump sum, for then the State's proportional part will increase *pari passu* with that of the land-owners. The establishment of a proportional land-tax will thus result definitely either in making the State a co-proprietor of the soil or in dividing landed property between private individuals and the State. It is now clear that the two problems of property and taxation are intimately related to each other.

398. If, now, instead of supposing a [lump sum] tax of 1 milliard, we suppose that a tax amounting to half the total rent is levied exclusively on rent in our hypothetical country, then the following consequences will ensue:

(1) the land-owners, possessing the land at the time of the intro-duction of the tax will, in the first instance, be deprived of half their capital as well as half their income. The State will become a co-proprietor, holding half the land;

(2) once all the land has changed hands by sale, gift or inheritance, the tax will no longer be paid by anyone;

(3) as soon as economic progress has raised the total rent from 2 to 4 milliards, the original owners who held on to their land will recuperate their losses completely and the new owners will see their income double.

(4) the revenue of the State will increase from 1 to 2 milliards.

There is no doubt, therefore, that it is preferable for the State to become a co-proprietor of the land than to be entitled simply to a lump-sum tax assessed on the land, provided, however, that the economy is progressive and that it keeps careful account of the increases in land values and land income. We shall return to this question on a later occasion, in our discussion of the cadastre.

Such, then, are the conclusions to be drawn from a study of taxes on rent. The effects of a tax on wages are the same in the first instance; but they soon become intermingled with other phenomena, in consequence of two facts: (1) that personal faculties cannot be bought and sold like land in countries that forbid slavery, and (2) that the steady rise in the value of land and land-services in a progressive economy is a characteristic peculiar only to this type of wealth.[e]

399.[d] Thus: *A direct tax on rent is an act of appropriation by the State of a determinate fraction of income from land and, at the same time, of a corresponding fraction of the landed capital belonging to land-owners.*

If s is the tax rate relative to gross or net rent or to the capital value of land, any rent [say p_t] becomes

$$p'_t = p_t(1-s)$$

and the price of the land [say P_t] becomes

$$P'_t = P_t(1-s).$$

400.[f] Now let us suppose that a tax is imposed directly on the interest charges on capital proper, and let us inquire what will happen. I maintain in this case that if the tax is imposed on the interest charges on all kinds of capital goods without exception, all capitalists would be affected in proportion to their incomes, just as if there had been a reduction in the rate of income. Moreover, since a fall in the rate of income may lead either to an increase or to a decrease in savings (§242), we cannot trace this effect any further and we may as well assume that the incidence of the tax falls on the capitalists. Granting this, I have an observation to make, which is applicable to taxes on land and personal faculties up to a certain point, but more so to taxes on income from capital goods proper, because: (1) it is difficult, if not impossible, to reach all capital goods by taxation and (2) capital goods are products, the price of which, under normal conditions, must equal their cost of production. The observation I have in mind is that if the tax is imposed on the interest charges on certain kinds of capital only, such a tax on interest charges would be, in part, a consumption tax. In order to prove this, I propose to show the effects of passing from a situation where only some kinds of capital goods are taxed to one where all capital goods are taxed, by starting with a tax levied first on one kind of capital goods and then allowing the tax to be gradually extended to all kinds of capital goods.

Let us return to our hypothetical country in which there are 60 milliards worth of produced capital goods yielding annually 3 milliards in interest. We shall assume that in this country the decision is taken to impose a proportional tax of 1 milliard on the income from produced capital goods exclusively, and that at the start a levy is made of one-third of the house rents. Let us single out the owner of a house worth 60,000 francs, yielding annually 3,000 francs in house rent. Out of these 3,000 francs the tax will take 1,000 francs per annum. If this measure entailed nothing but immediate effects, the house in question would thereafter yield only 2,000 francs in income and would consequently not be worth more than 40,000 francs. We know, however, that the 60,000 francs corresponds to the cost of production of the house. Now, if houses cost 60,000 francs to construct and, upon completion, are not worth more than 40,000 francs, entrepreneurs will lose 20,000 francs on each house. Under these conditions the building of houses will stop at once; old houses will deteriorate and fall into ruins and no replacements will be made. Thus little by little, in consequence of the laws of the market, house rents will rise and the value of the houses will rise accordingly. Both rents and houses will recover their lost value. Production will be resumed and events will once more take their natural and normal course. From the point of view of the particular house-owner whom we are discussing, the return to normal will be complete when the house is worth 60,000 francs and yields 4,500 francs in annual interest, out of which the State takes 1,500 francs in taxes. Who will then pay the tax? The tenants. These tenants will be of two sorts. Some will rent the house in order to live in it; in technical terms, they will buy the capital-service for use as a consumers' good. Others will rent the house for industrial use; in technical terms, they will buy the capital-service for use as a productive service. In the first case, the tax will be paid directly; in the second case, the tax will be included in the expenses of production incurred by the industrial enterprise and will be paid, in final analysis, by the purchasers of the products of the industry.[g]

Hence a tax on house rent would work out like a tax on consumption—at least in part, for, if we look at the matter closely, we observe that a portion of the burden is borne by the capitalist. Since some of the capital goods previously employed in the construction of houses will be transferred to all sorts of other employments, a general decline in the rate of income [from capital goods] will result, and this decline will be to the detriment of all capitalists including house-owners, and to the advantage of all consumers including tenants. One could, therefore, inquire into the extent to which the consumers thus recover, through the decline in the prices of other services and products, what they lose by the rise in house rents.

Having now established these two facts, we can easily understand that if we pass from [a tax on] houses to [a tax on] railways and then, in turn, to [a tax on] capital goods of all kinds without exception, the original distribution of savings among the various types of capital goods will be restored, so that, finally there will be the same number of houses, railways, and all other capital goods as there were at the start. The only lasting effect will be a general and continuous decline in the rate of income. Consequently the burden of the tax will gradually cease to be borne by the consumers and will rest finally on the shoulders of the capitalists alone.

401. The case of a direct tax levied in perpetuity on State *rentes* deserves special consideration. If, after the tax has once been introduced, the State does not float any additional loans, the *rentes* will behave very much like natural wealth [e.g. land] and the holders of *rente* certificates will lose capital as well as income. The quotation on the Exchange for these *rente* certificates will fall the very day the tax is introduced. If, however, the State does float additional loans, the *rentes* will behave like produced wealth, for subscribers to the new certificates will take them only at a price corresponding to the current rate of interest. Should the subscribers have reason to believe that the State will [subsequently] impose additional taxes on the *rentes*, they will [then and there] deduct another proportional amount from the subscription price. When such a tax is actually levied, there will be little or no further decline in the value of the securities, since the fall in value has already been anticipated.

402.[d] The mathematical expression of the foregoing argument is as follows.

First: *A direct tax on only one category of interest charges is, in effect, a tax on consumption.*

Let s be the tax rate on the gross income and let us suppose that the capital good (K) is the only kind of capital taxed. Then, in the first instance, the gross interest charge [say p_k] becomes

$$p'_k = p_k(1-s).$$

Eventually, however, as the quantity manufactured of the capital good (K) diminishes, the gross interest charge will become[5]

$$p''_k = p_k + sp''_k = \frac{p_k}{1-s}.$$

Then all costs of production will change, p_b changing, for example, to

$$p'_b = b_t p_t + b_p p_p + b_k p''_k \ldots.$$

403.[d] Secondly: *A direct tax on all categories of interest charges resolves itself into a reduction of the rate of net income.*

Thus, in effect, so long as the gross interest charge stays at

$$p'_k = p_k (1-s)$$

the net interest charge [say π_k] becomes approximately

$$\pi'_k = \pi_k (1-s)$$

(§§232 and 233); and when the aggregate amount of net interest charges is

$$(1-s)(D_k \pi_k + D_{k'} \pi_{k'} + D_{k''} \pi_{k''} + \ldots),$$

then the rate of net income itself becomes

$$i' = i(1-s)$$

(§§266 and 267) approximately.

404.[d] We have now to inquire into the effects of this reduction in the rate of net income.

In the first place, the price of land becomes

$$P'_t = \frac{p_t}{i'} = \frac{p_t}{i(1-s)}.$$

Hence: *A direct tax on all categories of interest charges raises the price of land in the same proportion that the rate of net income falls.*

In the second place, as the rate of net income falls, the demand for net income D_e (which is a decreasing function of the price of net income $p_e = \dfrac{1}{i}$)[6] diminishes.

Hence: *Since a direct tax on all categories of interest charges encourages consumption and discourages capital formation, it thwarts economic progress.*

405. From a tax on interest charges we pass now to a tax on products. Let us suppose, therefore, that, in our hypothetical country, it has been decided to impose a proportional tax of 1 milliard to be assessed on the 10 milliards worth of annual output, rather than on any part of the 10 milliards worth of services. The fiscal authority then collects the tax from the entrepreneurs in proportion to the value of their output. It is evident that since entrepreneurs are presumed to make neither profit nor loss when exchange and production are in general equilibrium, they will necessarily consider the amount of the tax as an addition to their cost of production and

increase *pro tanto* the price of their products. If this cannot be effected at once, then, as production is closed down, output diminished and the prices of products raised, it will be effected, in the long run precisely as in the case of houses. Thus, sooner or later, the total output will be sold to the consumers for 11 milliards, and the consumers will pay the tax.[h] In this discussion we are reckoning consumers' services among the products, because we consider such services as products created by a single productive service the owner of which is always an entrepreneur.

406. Thus far, however, we have traced only part of the complete incidence of a tax on consumption. It cannot, indeed, be supposed that the prices of all goods and services will rise equally by 10 per cent. Some of these goods and services are commodities of prime necessity, their effective demand falling very little in consequence of such a rise in price; others are luxury articles, for which the effective demand will fall considerably as the price increases. Hence, the immediate effect of the tax, if levied, as we have assumed, on all products in proportion to their value, will be, above all, to diminish the consumption and consequently the production, of particular luxury articles. It follows therefore that, in the market for services, the prices of those services which are employed specifically in the production of these [luxury] articles are bound to fall. Thus a tax on consumption resolves itself into a diminution in the value of certain productive services. We may observe, then, that since the effect of a tax on consumption is to restrict the demand for goods and services, an overall tax of 10 per cent [on consumption] will not yield the required 1 milliard, so that it will be necessary to raise the tax rate.

407.[d] The formula for a tax on consumption paid wholly by the consumers of any product [say (B)] would be

$$p_b(1+s)=b_t p_t+b_p p_p+b_k p_k+sp_b.$$

The formula for a tax paid wholly by the owners of the productive services employed in manufacturing this product would be

$$sp_b=b_t(p_t-p'_t)+b_p(p_p-p'_p)+b_k(p_k-p'_k).$$

408. Usually, a consumption tax is not imposed on all products, any more than a direct tax is imposed on all categories of interest charges.[i] Certain commodities, the consumption of which is widespread and assured, are selected to bear the tax. Thus, in our hypothetical country the 1 milliard [of revenue required] may be derived from taxes on salt, beverages and tobacco. In this case the effects of the tax will be those we have just described, but restricted naturally to the products on which it is imposed; in other words, it

is borne partly by the consumers of these products and partly by the owners of the productive services which are employed in their manufacture. The extent to which the owners of services are affected will depend upon whether the products of their services are more in the nature of prime necessities or of luxuries. It will also depend upon the degree to which the productive services in question are specialized. A tax on wheat would weigh more heavily on consumers of bread and less on land-owners, because bread is an article of prime necessity; a tax on wine, however, would weigh much more on the land-owners, first, because wine is, to a certain degree, a luxury, and, secondly, either because the land suited for vineyards cannot be used for any other kind of agriculture, or because a transfer to other uses simply for the purpose of counteracting the effects of the tax cannot be made with advantage. Obviously, the incidence of consumption taxes is extremely complex and the effects of such a tax imposed on any specific product will have to be studied separately. This is what needs to be done when practical policies are contemplated; but the general principles which we have considered here are more than enough for the elaboration of the theories of social economics and applied economics which we have in view.[1]

APPENDIX I[a]

GEOMETRICAL THEORY
OF THE DETERMINATION OF PRICES[1]

Part I

The Exchange of Several Commodities for One Another

1. When, in the course of writing my *Eléments d'économie politique pure*, I passed from the theory of exchange of two commodities for each other to the theory of exchange of several commodities for one another, and realized that the demand or offer of each commodity by each of the trading parties is a function, not only of the price of that commodity, but also of the prices of all the other commodities, I felt that it was necessary to adopt the analytical mode of expression exclusively, and to forgo the help of diagrams. Subsequently, however, I found a way of elaborating the theory in question by means of a geometrical method which I shall now describe in brief.

Let us suppose that, over a certain period of time, a trader holds the quantities $q_a, q_b, q_c, q_d \ldots$ of the commodities (A), (B), (C), (D)..., represented by the lengths $Oq_a, Oq_b, Oq_c, Oq_d \ldots$ in Fig. 38, and that his wants for these commodities during the same period are expressed by the curves $\alpha_q \alpha_r, \beta_q \beta_r, \gamma_q \gamma_r, \delta_q \delta_r \ldots$. I shall proceed now to explain the nature, and to describe the law, of these curves which constitute the essential and fundamental basis of the whole mathematical theory of social wealth.

We may say in ordinary language: "The want which we have for things, or the utility which things have for us, diminishes gradually as consumption increases. The more a man eats, the less hungry he is; the more he drinks the less thirsty, at least in general and apart from certain deplorable exceptions. The more hats and shoes a man has, the less need he has of a new hat or a new pair of shoes; the more horses he has in his stables, the less effort he will make to procure

[1] Of the three parts of which this theory is composed, the first is a revised version of a memoir read before the *Société des ingénieurs civils de Paris* on the 17th of October 1890, and printed in the *Bulletin* of that society for January 1891. I have made certain changes, one of which is particularly important, because it simplifies the fundamental proof of the theorem of maximum satisfaction. The last two parts are taken, with certain modifications necessitated by these changes, from a paper contributed to the *Recueil Inaugural* of the University of Lausanne (1892). "The Geometrical Theory of the Determination of Prices" which appeared in English translation in the *Annals of the American Academy of Political and Social Science* for July 1892 is quite similar to this appendix.

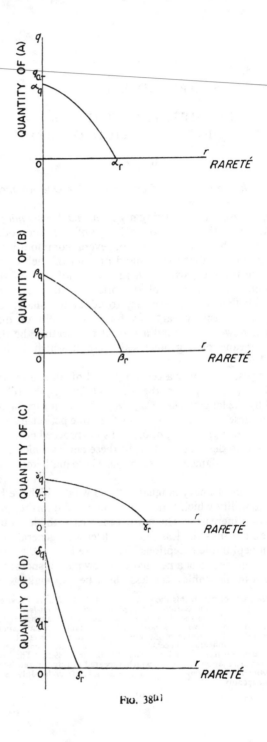

Fig. 38[1]

another horse, provided we neglect impulsive acts which our theory may ignore except when accounting for special cases." But in mathematical terms, we say: "The intensity of the last want satisfied is a decreasing function of the quantity of the commodity consumed"; and we represent these functions by curves, the *quantities consumed* being measured by the ordinates and the *intensities of the last want satisfied* by the abscissas. For example, take commodity (A): the intensity of the want for this commodity on the part of our consumer would be $O\alpha_r$ at the beginning of his consumption, and zero after he has consumed the quantity $O\alpha_q$, the consumer having reached satiety. For brevity, I call the intensity of the last want satisfied *rareté*. The English call it the *final degree of utility*, the Germans *Grenznutzen*. It is not a measurable quantity; yet we have only to form a conception of it to found the demonstration of the fundamental laws of pure economics upon the fact of its diminution.

2. Now let $p_b, p_c, p_d\ldots$ be respectively the prices of (B), (C), (D)$\ldots$ in terms of (A) cried at random on the market. The first problem we have to solve consists in determining the quantities $x, y, z, w\ldots$ of (A), (B), (C), (D)$\ldots$ respectively, some positive representing the quantities demanded, others negative representing the quantities offered, which our party to the exchange will add to or subtract from the quantities $q_a, q_b, q_c, q_d\ldots$ he already possesses, so as to consume the quantities $q_a+x, q_b+y, q_c+z, q_d+w\ldots$ represented by the lengths $Oa, Ob, Oc, Od\ldots$. In addition to the afore-mentioned general hypothesis of a party to the exchange for whom the *rareté* decreases with the quantity consumed, we shall now make the further general assumption that our party seeks in the exchange the greatest possible satisfaction of his wants. The sum, then, of the wants satisfied by a quantity Oa of the commodity (A), for example, is the area $Oa\varrho_a\alpha_r$ (Fig. 39). The *effective utility* is the definite integral of the *rareté* with respect to the quantity consumed. Consequently, in final analysis, the problem which we are trying to solve consists in determining $Oa, Ob, Oc, Od\ldots$ by the condition that the sum of the shaded areas $Oa\varrho_a\alpha_r, Ob\varrho_b\beta_r, Oc\varrho_c\gamma_r, Od\varrho_d\delta_r,\ldots$ be a maximum.

In order to present that solution very simply in geometrical form, I subject the utility or want curves $\beta_q\beta_r, \gamma_q\gamma_r, \delta_q\delta_r\ldots$ to the following transformation. Starting at the origins O, I lay off on the horizontal axes new abscissas equal to $\frac{1}{p}$ of the original abscissas. Also on lines parallel to the vertical axes drawn through the extremities of the new abscissas, I lay off from the horizontal axes new ordinates equal to p times the original ordinates. In Fig. 39, let $p_b=2, p_c=3, p_d=\frac{1}{2}\ldots$. As is easily seen, the new curves $\beta'_q\beta'_r, \gamma'_q\gamma'_r, \delta'_q\delta'_r\ldots$ represent the utility of (A) to be spent on (B), (C), (D)$\ldots$ respectively, or, in other

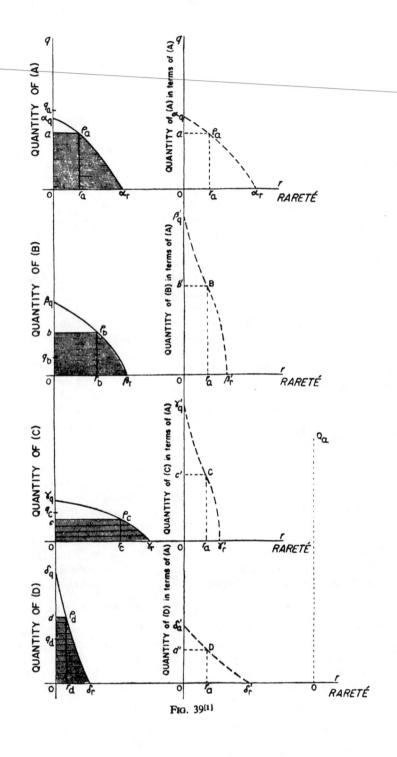

Fig. 39[1]

words, the want which our party has for (A) with which to buy himself some of (B), (C), (D). . . . If, indeed, we consider the areas $O\beta_q\beta_r$, $O\gamma_q\gamma_r$, $O\delta_q\delta_r$... as the limits of sums of infinitely minute rectangles, the areas $O\beta'_q\beta'_r$, $O\gamma'_q\gamma'_r$, $O\delta'_q\delta'_r$... must then be considered as the limits of equal sums of infinitely minute rectangles with bases p times smaller, and altitudes p times greater [than the bases and altitudes of the original rectangles]. Since each of the rectangles of the former sums represents the effective utility of an increment of commodity, each of the new rectangles in the latter sums, given the process of transformation, must represent the same effective utility of p increments of (A) with which that increment of commodity may be bought.

The curves $\alpha_q\alpha_r$, $\beta'_q\beta'_r$, $\gamma'_q\gamma'_r$, $\delta'_q\delta'_r$... being placed one underneath the other, I take a vertical length OQ_a, representing the equivalent, in terms of (A), of the quantities q_a, q_b, q_c, q_d... of (A), (B), (C), (D)... at the prices 1, p_b, p_c, p_d..., viz. $q_a+q_bp_b+q_cp_c+q_dp_d$..., and I move this line from right to left [under each of the curves], in such a way as to satisfy the various wants in the order of their intensity, until it is subdivided among the curves into the ordinates $r_a\varrho_a=Oa$, $r_aB=Ob'$, $r_aC=Oc'$, $r_aD=Od'$..., corresponding in each case to a like abscissa, Or_a. This abscissa Or_a represents the particular *rareté* r_a of (A) in the form of (A), (B), (C), and (D)... respectively, which corresponds to maximum effective utility. The ordinates Oa, Ob', Oc', Od'... represent the respective quantities of (A) to be consumed in the form of (A), (B), (C), (D)..., the only commodities consumed being those for which the intensity of the first want to be satisfied is greater than r_a.

If we carry back the abscissas $Or_a=r_a$, $Or_b=p_br_a$, $Or_c=p_cr_a$, $Or_d=p_dr_a$... to the [original] curves $\alpha_q\alpha_r$, $\beta_q\beta_r$, $\gamma_q\gamma_r$, $\delta_q\delta_r$..., we obtain the ordinates Oa, Ob, Oc, Od... representing the quantities of (A), (B), (C), (D)... to be consumed.[1] Our party to the exchange will, therefore, finally offer the quantities x, z... of (A), (C)...,

---

[1] It is possible, also, to construct a total curve, as I did in the memoir I read before the Société des ingénieurs civils, by adding vertically the separate transformed utility curves of (B), (C), (D)... to the original separate utility curve of (A). This is done by adding all the ordinates corresponding to like abscissas. As is easily seen, this total curve would represent the total utility of (A) to be used as (A), (B), (C), (D)...; in other words, it would represent the total want of our party for (A) to be spent on (A), (B), (C).... If, indeed, we consider the areas under the separate curves as the limits of sums of infinitely minute rectangles, we may regard the area under the total curve as the limit of the sum total of all these rectangles superimposed on one another in the order of their horizontal lengths. And, on finding the ordinate of the total curve equal to OQ_a, we obtain the corresponding abscissa Or_a representing the particular *rareté* r_a of (A) in the form of (A), (B), (C), (D)... respectively which corresponds to maximum effective utility. This diagrammatic device, which can be constructed not only for the case of the exchange of several commodities for one another but also for the case of the exchange of products and services for each other, makes it possible to demonstrate rigorously the gains in utility realized in exchange and production.

represented by $q_a a, q_c c \ldots$ and will demand the quantities $y, w \ldots$ of
(B) (D)..., represented by $q_b b, q_d d$.... And so, in a state of *maximum
satisfaction, the* raretés *are proportional to the prices,* according to
the equations

$$\frac{r_a}{1} = \frac{r_b}{p_b} = \frac{r_c}{p_c} = \frac{r_d}{p_d} = \ldots.$$

3. Thus, given the quantities possessed and the utilities of the
commodities, it is possible to determine for any trading party the
particular demand or offer of each of the commodities which will
afford maximum satisfaction of his wants, at prices cried at random.
Having found the demand and offer of commodities at random prices
by all the participants in an exchange, we still have to determine the
current equilibrium prices at which the total effective demand and
total effective offer are equal. The solution of this second problem
can also be obtained geometrically.

For the moment, let us neglect $p_c, p_d \ldots$ and first try to determine
p_b provisionally. Accordingly, let us inquire how ($p_c, p_d \ldots$ being
supposed constant) variations in p_b affect the demand and offer
of (B).

If y is positive, that is to say, if a given party to the exchange is
demanding (B), an increase in p_b can only diminish y. Surely, if our
party to the exchange were to purchase the same quantity at a higher
price [as he did at p_b], he would have to make a greater outlay,
and he could not do this without reducing the quantities he holds of
(A), (C), (D). . . . But then he would increase the *raretés* of these
other commodities; and consequently he would be so much further
from the condition of maximum satisfaction. Hence the quantity
demanded y is too great for a price higher than p_b. It follows, there-
for that *the demand curve is negatively inclined.*

If y is negative, that is, if our party is offering (B), there are three
possibilities. Let us suppose that our party sells the same quantity
at a higher price [as at the lower price]. Then he will receive in
return an additional amount, with which he can increase the quantities he holds of (A), (C), (D)..., thereby lowering their *raretés* for
him. Now, one of three things will occur: either the surplus will be
insufficient to restore the condition of maximum satisfaction, or it
will be just sufficient, or it will be more than sufficient; and, in
consequence, at a price higher than p_b, our party must offer a
quantity of (B) which is either greater than, equal to, or less than y.
We can be sure that he will find himself in one of these three cases,
depending on the extent of the rise in p_b.

Let us, therefore, imagine a party who, at the prices $p_b, p_c, p_d \ldots$ of
(B), (C), (D)... in terms of (A), offers a quantity o_b of (B), and

demands or offers (A), (C), (D)... with a view to attaining the maximum satisfaction of his wants in conformity with the equations

$$\frac{r_a}{1} = \frac{r_b}{p_b} = \frac{r_c}{p_c} = \frac{r_d}{p_d} = \dots$$

If, under these circumstances, p_b increases, while p_c, p_d... remain constant, and if our party continues to offer the same quantity o_b of (B), using, as he must, the additional amount paid to him for the purchase of (A), (C), (D)..., the ratio $\frac{r_b}{p_b}$ will diminish by reason of the increase in the denominator p_b, whereas the ratios $\frac{r_a}{1}$, $\frac{r_c}{p_c}$, $\frac{r_d}{p_d}$ ... will decrease as the numerators r_a, r_c, r_d... diminish. The first ratio cannot fall to zero unless p_b becomes infinite; but, provided: (1) that the prices p_c, p_d... are not infinite, (2) that the number of commodities involved is not infinite and (3) that our party to the exchange cannot consume an infinite quantity of any one of them, the other ratios will become zero at a certain price of (B), which need not be infinite, though it must be sufficiently high for the additional amount paid to our party to permit him to satisfy all his desires for (A), (C), (D)... completely. When that happens and the ratios of *raretés* to prices are respectively $\frac{0}{1}$, $\frac{r_b}{p_b}$, $\frac{0}{p_c}$, $\frac{0}{p_d}$ ..., our party will have to resell some of his (A), (C), (D)... in order to repurchase a certain quantity of (B), that is to say, he will have to diminish his offer o_b of (B), in order to recover maximum satisfaction.

It is, therefore, certain that the rise in p_b, which causes our party to pass from the side of demand to the side of offer, will also cause his offer to increase at first and then to decrease. In other words, *the offer curve, considered positively, first rises and then falls.* It is, also, possible to suppose the offer o_b to be infinitely small at a certain price of (B); but this price will have to be infinitely large for r_a, r_c, r_d... to be zero. Then maximum satisfaction will be attained by virtue of the equations

$$\frac{0}{1} = \frac{r_b}{\infty} = \frac{0}{p_c} = \frac{0}{p_d} = \dots,$$

that is to say, the offer will become zero again when the price is infinite. In other words, *the offer curve is asymptotic to the price axis.*

The variation of p_b, from zero to infinity, therefore, causes our party to the exchange to pass first from the demand side to the offer side, and then from an increasing to a decreasing offer. At the price zero, the demand is equal to the excess of the quantity necessary for the complete satisfaction of wants over the quantity possessed; at the price infinity, the offer is zero. In the case of the exchange of several commodities for one another, as in the case of the exchange of two commodities for each other, these propensities of a given party can be represented geometrically by the curve $b_d b_p b_o$ (Fig. 40). This curve is referred to $q_b p$, which serves as the *price axis* and to $b_d O$, which serves as the *quantity axis*, the portion of $b_d O$ lying above the

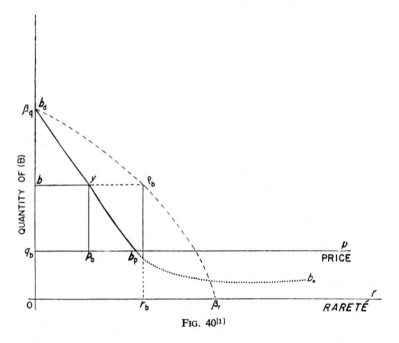

FIG. 40[1]

origin q_b being the *axis of the quantity demanded*, and the portion lying below the origin q_b being the *axis of the quantity offered*. Thus, at the price zero, our party would demand a quantity of (B) represented by $q_b b_d$; at the price p_b represented by $q_b p_b$, he would demand a quantity of (B) represented by $p_b y = q_b b$; at the price b_p represented by $q_b b_p$, he would neither demand nor offer (B); at higher prices, he would offer quantities represented by the [vertical] distances from the axis $q_b p$ to the curve $b_p b_o$; and at the price infinity, he would offer no (B) at all, the curve $b_p b_o$ being asymptotic to the axis $q_b p$.

Since all parties to the exchange are not identical, but similar in their propensities, it is clear that, so far as commodity (B) is concerned, all the individual demand curves must be added together to form a total curve $B_d B_p$ (Fig. 41) which is negatively inclined throughout its whole length. In like manner, all the individual offer curves must be added together to form a total curve NP', which, if taken positively by rotating it on the horizontal axis so as to bring

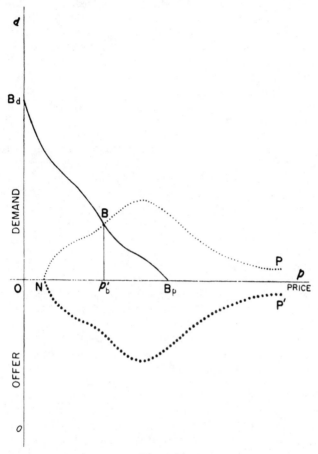

FIG. 41[2]

it into the position of NP, first rises from zero and then falls to zero again, being asymptotic to the price axis. Provisionally, the abscissa Op'_b of the point of intersection B of the two curves $B_d B_p$ and NP will be the current equilibrium price at which the total effective demand and offer of (B) are equal. Moreover, the intersection of the two curves $B_d B_p$ and NP may take place on either the ascending or the descending segment of the latter curve.

It follows from the nature of the two curves that the provisional current price of (B) will be arrived at by a rise in the price of (B) in the case of an excess of effective demand over effective offer and by a fall in the price of (B) in the contrary case of an excess of effective offer over effective demand. The same procedure is followed in passing to the determination of the current price of (C), then to that of the current price of (D) .... It is quite true that in determining the price of (C), we may destroy the equilibrium with respect to (B), that in determining the price of (D), we may destroy the equilibrium both with respect to (B) and with respect to (C), and so forth. But since the determination of the prices of (C), (D) ... will, on the whole, entail certain compensating effects on the relationship between the demand and offer of (B), in all probability equilibrium will be approximated more and more closely at each successive step in the groping process. We enter here on the theory of groping ['tâtonnement'] which I have developed in my book and by virtue of which *equilibrium is arrived at in the market by raising the price of those commodities, the demand for which is greater than the offer, and by lowering the price of those commodities, the offer of which is greater than the demand.*

4. The concurrent use of analytical expressions and geometric figures now gives us simultaneously both the idea and the pictorial representation of the phenomenon of the determination of prices on the market in the case of the exchange of several commodities for one another. And with this, as I see it, we at last have the theory. Some critics, however, poke fun at the number of pages I use in proving that the price must rise when demand exceeds offer, and fall in the contrary case, if the current price is to be reached.—"And you," I once said to such a critic, "how would you prove it?" "Well," he replied, a little surprised and even somewhat embarrassed, "does it need to be proved? It seems to me to be self-evident." "Nothing is self-evident except axioms and this is not an axiom. But you have in mind, I suppose, the reasoning which Jevons formulated so clearly in his little treatise on *Political Economy*, that a rise in price, which necessarily decreases demand and increases offer, brings about equality between the two in case the demand is greater than the offer...." "Precisely." "But there is an error here. A rise in price necessarily diminishes the demand but it does not necessarily augment the offer. If you are selling wine, it may well be that you will offer less at a million francs a cask than at a thousand, and still less at a milliard than at a million, simply because you will prefer to drink the wine yourself rather than consume the superfluous things you could procure by selling more than a certain amount of your wine. The same holds true of labour. It is perfectly conceivable

that a man, who would offer ten hours a day of his time at 1 franc
an hour, would not offer more than four hours at 10 francs or more
than one hour at 100 francs. It is a matter of common observation
in large cities that workmen, when they earn 20 or 25 francs a day,
do not work more than three or four days a week." "But, if that is
so, how can a rise in price bring about the current price?" "This is
what the theory explains. Two individuals, starting at some distance
from each other, can come together either by walking towards each
other from opposite directions, or by walking in the same direction if
one walks faster than the other. Offer and demand become equal to
each other sometimes by the former method and sometimes by the
latter."

Is it, or is it not worth while to demonstrate rigorously the fundamental laws of science? There are today heaven knows how many
schools of political economy: the *deductive* school and the *historical*
school, the school of *laisser-faire* and the school of *State intervention*
or *Socialism of the Chair*, the *Socialist* school properly so-called, the
Catholic school, the *Protestant* school, etc. For my part, I recognize
only two: the school of those who do not demonstrate, and the school,
which I hope to see founded, of those who do demonstrate their
conclusions. By demonstrating rigorously first the elementary
theorems of geometry and algebra, and then the resulting theorems
of the calculus and mechanics, in order to apply them to experimental
data, we have achieved the marvels of modern industry. Let us
follow the same procedure in economics, and, without doubt, we
shall eventually succeed in having the same control over the nature of
things in the economic and social order as we already have in the
physical and industrial order.

Part II

The Exchange of Products and Services for one Another

5. I propose now to apply to the theory of production and the
theory of capital formation the same purely geometric method of
demonstration which I used above in sketching the theory of
exchange. However, instead of assuming, as we did in the theory
of exchange, that the [total] quantities of commodities are given and
not unknown elements of the problem, we shall have to begin, in the
theory of production, by considering these commodities as products
which result from the combination of productive services, and
we must consequently introduce the quantities of manufactured products into the problem as so many unknowns, adding, as is proper,

an equal number of mathematical conditions to determine them. That is what I wish to do here, referring to my *Elements of Pure Economics* for definitions and notations.

6. Let there be, then, services of land, persons and capital goods [proper], (T), (P), (K) . . ., utilizable either directly as consumers' services, or indirectly as productive services, the latter being embodied in products of all sorts (A), (B), (C), (D). . . . The first problem we have to solve consists in determining, for each consumer, the demand and offer of services in the form either of consumers' services or of products, at certain prices of (T), (P), (K)... and (B), (C), (D)... cried at random in terms of (A). Actually, the solution of this problem is found in the theory of exchange. Given, for example, a consumer in command of the quantities q_t, q_p, q_k... of the services (T), (P), (K) . . . during a certain interval of time, and having certain wants, during the same interval of time, not only for these services, but also for the products (A), (B), (C), (D). . . . These wants can be expressed by utility or want curves. As before, the abscissas of such curves represent the *raretés* or *intensities of the last wants satisfied*, which are decreasing functions of the *quantities consumed* represented by the ordinates. And let p_t, p_p, p_k... π_b, π_c, π_d... be respectively the prices of (T), (P), (K)... and (B), (C), (D)... in terms of (A) cried in the market at random. We shall transform the utility or want curves of all the services and products, other than (A), into utility curves of (A) designed to be used as (T), (P), (K)... and (B), (C), (D)..., that is to say, designed for the purchase of (T), (P), (K)... and (B), (C), (D).... This transformation is effected by dividing the abscissas and multiplying the ordinates by the above prices, just as was done in §2 in the case of the exchange of several commodities for one another. The utility or want curve of (A) and the transformed utility or want curves of (T), (P), (K)... and (B), (C), (D)... being placed one underneath the other, let us take a vertical length $Q_a = q_t p_t + q_p p_p + q_k p_k + \ldots$ and move it from right to left [under each of the curves] until it is subdivided among all the curves into ordinates corresponding, in each case, to a like abscissa. This abscissa represents r_a, i.e. the particular *rareté* of, or the particular intensity of the last want satisfied by (A) which corresponds to maximum effective utility when (A) is considered in the form of (T), (P), (K) . . . (A), (B), (C), (D). . . . By carrying back the abscissas $p_t r_a, p_p r_a, p_k r_a . . . r_a, p_b r_a, p_c r_a, p_d r_a . . .$ to the original curves, we obtain [corresponding] ordinates which represent the quantities of the services (T), (P), (K) . . . and of the products (A), (B), (C), (D) . . . to be consumed. It is evident that, *in a state of maximum satisfaction, the* raretés *will be proportional to the prices according to the following equations:*

$$\frac{r_t}{p_t} = \frac{r_p}{p_p} = \frac{r_k}{p_k} = \cdots = \frac{r_a}{1} = \frac{r_b}{p_b} = \frac{r_c}{p_c} = \frac{r_d}{p_d} = \cdots$$

7. The prices of services and products with which we started p_t, $p_p, p_k \ldots \pi_b, \pi_c, \pi_d \ldots$ were assumed to be cried at random. We shall now suppose that the quantities manufactured of (A), (B), (C), (D)… are random quantities, say Ω_a, Ω_b, Ω_c, Ω_d…. Leaving p_t,

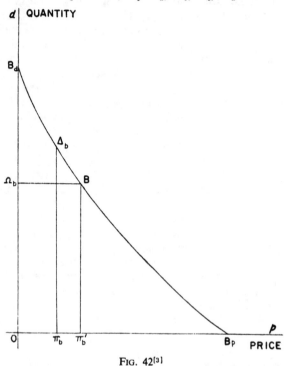

FIG. 42[3]

$p_p, p_k \ldots$ as they were, let us determine the prices of (B), (C), (D)… consistent with the condition that the demand for these products be equal to their supply, i.e. to the quantity manufactured. The solution of this second problem is also to be found in the theory of exchange. Let Δ_b, represented in Fig. 42 by the ordinate $\pi_b \Delta_b$, be the total demand for (B), at the above-mentioned prices of services and products. We know from the theory of exchange that if we first neglect the prices of (C), (D)… and attempt to determine the price of (B) provisionally, then, as this price varies from zero to infinity, the demand for (B) will diminish according to the curve $B_d B_p$. Hence there exists a price π'_b, corresponding to the condition of equality between the demand for (B) and its supply Ω_b [which, as we have seen, is determined at random along with Ω_c, Ω_d...]. π'_b is either $>\pi_b$, if, at the price of π_b, the demand for (B) is greater than the supply; or $<\pi_b$, if, at the price π_b, the supply of (B) is greater than the demand. In the same way, we could find a price π'_c corresponding to the condition of equality between the demand for (C) and its supply Ω_c; also a price π'_d corresponding to the condition of equality between the demand for (D) and its supply Ω_d; and so forth. After this first trial in groping [towards general equilibrium], we proceed to a second, then to a third, and so on, until we have obtained a series of prices π''_b, π''_c, π''_d... at which the demands for (B), (C), (D)... are equal respectively to the supplies Ω_b, Ω_c, Ω_d.... We conclude, then, that *equilibrium is reached in the market for products by raising the prices of those products, the demand for which is greater than the supply, and by lowering the prices of those products, the supply of which is greater than the demand.*

8. π''_b, π''_c, π''_d... are thus the *selling prices* of the quantities Ω_b, Ω_c, Ω_d... of (B), (C), (D).... But the prices p_t, p_p, p_k... of the services (T), (P), (K) ... give rise to certain *costs of production* of the products (B), (C), (D)..., viz. p_b, p_c, p_d....[1] And the difference, positive or negative, between the selling price and the cost of production in the manufacture of (B), (C), (D)..., results in gains or losses, viz. $\Omega_b(\pi''_b-p_b)$, $\Omega_c(\pi''_c-p_c)$, $\Omega_d(\pi''_d-p_d)$.... It is now necessary to determine the quantities manufactured of (B), (C), (D)... consistent with the condition that price and cost of production be equal, so that there may be neither gain nor loss to the entrepreneurs. This third problem is the special problem of the theory of production, which may also be solved geometrically, as follows.

Let Op_b in Fig. 43 be an abscissa representing the cost of production p_b. And let $O\pi''_b$ be an abscissa representing the selling price

---

[1] It is true that when we assume the cost of production to be the same for all entrepreneurs, we also have to assume that the [total] *fixed costs* [i.e. overhead or supplementary costs] are spread over the same amount of output [for each entrepreneur], thus making it possible to put fixed costs on the same footing as the *proportional costs* [i.e. variable or prime costs]. In other words, we must assume that all entrepreneurs manufacture equal quantities of products. This hypothesis has no more objective reality than the assumption that profits and losses are zero, but it is just as rational. If, now, at a given moment, a certain output corresponds to the absence of profit or loss, entrepreneurs who manufacture less than this output will incur losses, cut down their production and finish by liquidating; while those who manufacture more will make profits, expand output and draw to themselves the business of the unsuccessful entrepreneurs. Thus, in consequence of certain characteristic properties of fixed and variable costs, an industry, which starts out under free competition with a large number of small enterprises, tends to be divided among a smaller number of enterprises of medium size, and then among a still smaller number of large-scale enterprises—to end, finally, in a *monopoly first selling at cost of production and then selling at a price yielding a maximum profit.* This statement is confirmed by facts. But during the whole period of competition and even during the period in which monopolies sell at cost of production it is always permissible to simplify the theory by assuming that all entrepreneurs manufacture the same quantities of products and by putting the fixed costs on the same footing as the variable costs.

π''_b. Furthermore, let $\pi''_b B'$ be an ordinate representing the quantity Ω_b of (B) manufactured at random and demanded at the price π''_b. If we suppose $p_t, p_p, p_k \ldots \pi''_c, \pi''_d \ldots$ determined and constant, and if we allow the price of (B) to vary from zero to infinity, we may be certain that the demand for (B) will decrease continuously, as indicated by the curve $B'_d B'_p$. Consequently, there exists a demand Ω'_b for (B) corresponding to a selling price equal to its cost of production p_b. Ω'_b will be $\gtreqless \Omega_b$ according as π''_b is $\gtreqless p_b$. Similarly,

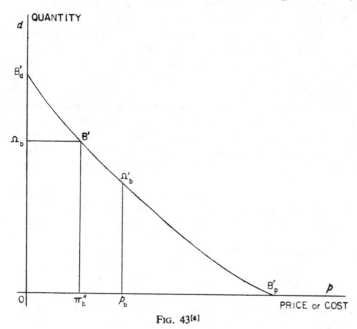

FIG. 43[a]

we might also find a demand Ω'_c for (C) corresponding to a selling price equal to its cost of production p_c; a demand Ω'_d for (D) corresponding to a selling price equal to its cost of production p_d; and so forth. If, then, we substitute the quantities $\Omega'_b, \Omega'_c, \Omega'_d \ldots$ for the quantities $\Omega_b, \Omega_c, \Omega_d \ldots$ [originally manufactured at random], and offer the new quantities for sale according to the mechanism of competitive bidding among buyers and sellers which we described earlier, we obtain new selling prices which will still be slightly different from $p_b, p_c, p_d \ldots$. After that, we make a second, and then a third trial and so on, in groping towards both [equilibrium] prices and quantities, until finally we obtain certain quantities $D_b, D_c, D_d \ldots$ of (B), (C), (D)... which sell at prices equal to their costs of production p_b, p_c, p_d.... We may, then, enunciate the following proposition which is specific to the theory of production: *equality between the selling price of products and the cost of the productive services employed in their manufacture is attained by increasing the quantity of those products the selling price of which exceeds the cost of production and by decreasing the quantity of those products the cost of production of which exceeds the selling price.* From this it can be seen that, strictly speaking, the consideration of cost of production determines not the *price*, but the *quantity* of the products.[1]

9. We have been assuming all along that the prices of services p_t, p_p, p_k... are determined at random. There remains, consequently, a fourth and last problem for us to solve, namely, the problem of so determining these prices that the quantities demanded and the quantities offered may be equal. Up to this point in our analysis, the quantities offered U_t, U_p, U_k... of (T), (P), (K)... have been determined by the condition of maximum satisfaction, in conformity with the solution of our first problem. Over against these quantities offered, the quantities demanded are made up of two elements: first, the quantities demanded by consumers for use as consumers' services, namely, u_t, u_p, u_k..., which are determined, like the quantities offered, by the condition of maximum satisfaction; and secondly, the quantities demanded by entrepreneurs for use as productive services, namely D_t, D_p, D_k..., which are determined by the quantities manufactured of the products (A), (B), (C), (D)..., the demand for which is equal to their supply and the selling prices equal to their costs of production, in conformity with the solution of our second and third problems. It could be demonstrated, exactly as in the theory of exchange, that if, all other things remaining equal, we allow the price p_t to vary from zero to infinity, (1) the demand for (T), $D_t + u_t$, will diminish along a curve $T_d T_p$ (Fig. 44); and (2) the offer of (T) starting from zero will increase, then diminish and finally return to zero following a curve QR. Consequently, there exists a price p'_t at which the offer and the demand for (T) are equal. This p'_t will be $> p_t$ if, at the price p_t, the demand for (T) is greater than

[1] Let us imagine that Robinson Crusoe, instead of being the sole survivor, came ashore with a hundred or so sailors and passengers, some of whom had salvaged rice, others rum, etc. If all these survivors held a market on the beach in order to exchange their commodities with each other, the commodities would have current prices perfectly determined and entirely independent of the costs of production. This is the problem of exchange and shows how prices depend only on the *rareté*, i.e. the utility, and the quantity possessed of the commodities. But if afterwards, upon discovering the requisite productive services on the island, they proceeded to manufacture the same kinds of commodities and carried them to the market, those products whose selling prices exceeded their costs of production would be produced in larger quantities and those products whose cost of production exceeded the selling price would become scarcer until equality was established between selling prices and costs of production. This is the problem of production, and shows how cost of production determines the quantity and not the price of the products.

the offer, and will be $<p_t$ if, at p_t, the offer of (T) is greater than the demand. Similarly there exists a price p'_p at which the offer and demand for (P) are equal; a price p'_k at which the offer and demand for (K) are equal, and so on. After a first series of adjustments of the prices p_t, p_p, p_k... in the process of groping, which includes, of course, the successive adaptations [of the prices of products and the

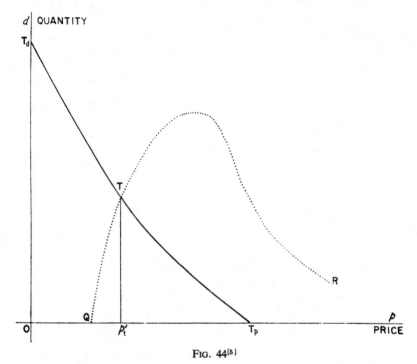

FIG. 44[5]

quantities manufactured] described in the second and third problems, there will be a second series of adjustments, this time of the [new] prices p'_t, p'_p, p'_k..., then a third, and so on. Hence, *equilibrium in the market for services, as in the market for products, is attained by raising the prices of those services the demand for which is greater than the offer and by lowering the prices of those services the offer of which is greater than the demand.*[1]

10. We must remember that all these operations take place simultaneously, although, for purposes of demonstration, we had to imagine them as taking place successively. In other words, in the

---

[1] The prices of raw materials given by nature would be determined in the same way as the prices of productive services.

market for services as in the market for products, demanders outbid one another when demand exceeds offer and suppliers underbid one another when offer exceeds demand; and, at the same time, entrepreneurs increase their output when selling price exceeds cost of production and reduce output in the contrary case. Here, too, thanks to the geometrical method of representation, we have an exact and complete picture of the general phenomenon of the emergence of economic equilibrium under the rule of free competition. Nevertheless, the analytical form of expression is necesssary for a strictly scientific statement of the matter. From this point of view, once the elements of the system or the quantities that come into play have been defined, it is necessary to distinguish the knowns from the unknowns, to express by equations the economic conditions of equilibrium, to make certain that these equations are exactly equal in number to the number of unknowns, to show that successive trials in the process of groping converge towards a solution at each step, and to explain the special conditions of equilibrium with respect to the product (A) which serves as *numéraire*. For all these topics which are not treated here, I take the liberty of referring the reader to Part IV of my *Eléments*.

This Appendix is, therefore, only a résumé, which may serve, it is hoped, to make the general outlines of the theory somewhat clearer. It is evident, now, that the theory of production, like that of exchange, starts with the problem of the attainment of the maximum satisfaction of wants by each trading party, and ends with the problem of the establishment of equality between supply and demand in the market. The only difference is that *services* take the place of commodities. In fact, in the mechanism of production, services are exchanged for services. But, whereas one part of the services we buy is composed of services as such, another part is composed of services in the form of *products*. Consequently, our theory had to be expanded to include the transformation of a portion of the services into products. This is what I did in the second and third problems. And I did it as simply as possible, only to find that practically all the criticisms levelled against me have consisted in calling my attention to complications which I had left to one side. I find it very easy to reply to these criticisms. So far as I am concerned, since I was the first to elaborate a pure theory of economics in mathematical form, my aim has been to describe and explain the mechanism of production in terms of its bare essentials. It is for other economists who come after me to introduce one at a time whatever complications they please. They in their way and I in mine will then, I think, have done what had to be done.

Part III

The Exchange of Savings for New Capital Goods

11. For simplicity, we shall now suppose equilibrium to be established not only with respect to the prices of products and services, but also with respect to the quantities of products manufactured. Moreover, we shall neglect any disturbances of the assumed equilibrium in exchange and production which may result from the special adjustments towards equilibrium in capital formation. We shall also ignore the depreciation and insurance of capital goods.

12. The components of equilibrium in capital formation are the quantities produced of new capital goods and the rate of income i. From these the prices of capital goods can be derived according to the general formula $\Pi = \frac{p}{i}$. Let us suppose, then, that certain random quantities $D_k, D_{k'}, D_{k''} \ldots$ of new capital goods of the types (K), (K'), (K'')... are produced and that a certain rate of income i is cried at random. Knowing this rate, each party to the exchange will determine the excess of his income over his consumption, and the total of these individual excesses forms a total excess E which is the quantity of *numéraire* offered in the purchase of new capital goods, or the demand for new capital goods in terms of *numéraire* at the rate i. On the other hand, at the current prices of the productive services of these new capital goods, viz. $p_k, p_{k'}, p_{k''}$, which are supposed, *ex hypothesi*, to have been already determined and constant, the quantities $D_k, D_{k'}, D_{k''} \ldots$ of new capital goods of the types (K), (K'), (K'')... will yield an aggregate income of $D_k p_k + D_{k'} p_{k'} + D_{k''} p_{k''} + \ldots$ and will have a total value of $\dfrac{D_k p_k + D_{k'} p_{k'} + D_{k''} p_{k''} + \cdots}{i}$, which is the quantity of *numéraire* demanded in exchange for the new capital goods or the offer of new capital goods in terms of *numéraire* at the rate i. If, by chance, the above two quantities of *numéraire* [E and $\dfrac{D_k p_k + D_{k'} p_{k'} + D_{k''} p_{k''} + \cdots}{i}$] happen to be equal, the rate i will be the equilibrium rate of income; but generally they will not be equal, and then they will have to be rendered equal. Now, we may take it for granted that the excess of income over consumption starts at zero when the rate of income is zero; and that it will make its appearance [as a positive value] at some rate of income above zero, increasing as the rate rises, and finally diminishing and returning to zero as the rate tends to become infinitely great, that is to say, as it becomes possible to procure a very great increase in income with

a very small amount of savings. In other words, the rate of income being measured on the *OI* axis (Fig. 45), the excess of income over consumption can be represented by the ordinates of a curve *ST* that rises from zero and then decreases to zero (at infinity). As for the value of the new capital goods, it evidently increases or decreases according as the rate of income decreases or increases. In other

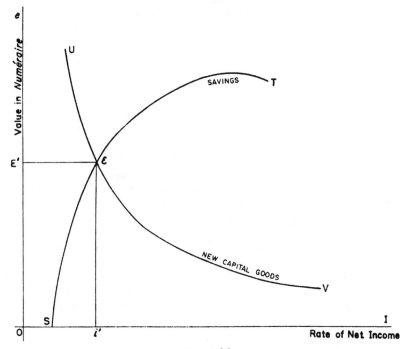

FIG. 45[6]

words, the rate of income being measured on the axis *OI*, the value of new capital goods can be represented by the ordinates of the curve *UV* which is negatively inclined throughout its whole length. Hence, it is clear, without further discussion, *that it is necessary to raise the price of new capital goods by lowering the rate of income if the demand for new capital goods in terms of* numéraire *is greater than the offer, and to lower the price of new capital goods by raising the rate of income if the offer of new capital goods in terms of* numéraire *is greater than the demand.*

13. At this juncture we must take into account the costs of production P_k, $P_{k'}$, $P_{k''}$... which correspond to the selling prices Π_k, $\Pi_{k'}$, $\Pi_{k''}$... of the new capital goods (K), (K′), (K″).... The

problem is to reduce these selling prices and costs of production to an equality which generally does not exist between them. We may consider as established, according to the law of the variation of the prices of services developed earlier in §9 of this Appendix, that if the prices of the productive services required in the manufacture of a capital good (K), and consequently its cost of production, are augmented indefinitely, the offer of these services and hence the

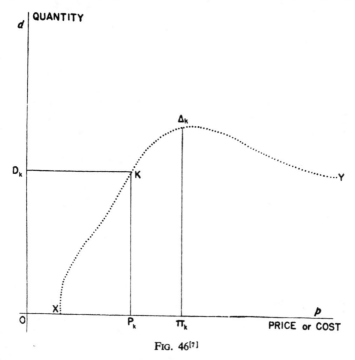

FIG. 46[7]

amount of this capital good manufactured would increase from zero and then diminish to zero again (at infinity). In other words, the curve XY in Fig. 46, representing the quantity manufactured of new capital goods as a function of the cost of production, first rises from zero and then falls to zero again (at infinity). Therefore, if a selling price $\Pi_k \gtrless P_k$ results from the determination of a rate of income i, it is immediately evident that *it is necessary to raise the price of the productive services [employed in the manufacture] of those new capital goods whose selling price exceeds their cost of production, and to give up producing those capital goods whose cost of production exceeds their selling price.*

14. Once equilibrium in capital formation has been established, the following relation will obtain:

$$P_k = \Pi_k = \frac{p_k}{i}, \qquad P_{k'} = \Pi_{k'} = \frac{p_{k'}}{i}, \qquad P_{k''} = \Pi_{k''} = \frac{p_{k''}}{i} \, \dots,$$

or:

$$\frac{p_k}{P_k} = \frac{p_{k'}}{P_{k'}} = \frac{p_{k''}}{P_{k''}} = \dots.$$

That is to say, the rate of income will be the same for all capitalized savings. It could be demonstrated geometrically in a very simple manner, at least as far as capital goods yielding direct consumers' services are concerned, that *this uniformity in rate of return is the condition of maximum utility derived from new capital goods.*

There are two problems of maximum utility relating to the services of new capital goods: one connected with the distribution by an individual of his income among his different kinds of wants, and the other connected with the distribution by the economy as a whole of its excess of income over consumption among the numerous varieties of capital to be created. The first is solved by means of a model, which was devised in the theory of exchange and which was referred to again at the beginning of the theory of production, involving the proportionality of the *raretés* to the prices of the services, as expressed by the equations

$$\frac{r_k}{p_k} = \frac{r_{k'}}{p_{k'}} = \frac{r_{k''}}{p_{k''}} = \dots.$$

It will be understood, without difficulty, that the second problem can be solved by means of an exactly similar model (except that the want curves for services, instead of being transformed by dividing their abscissas and multiplying their ordinates by the prices p_k, $p_{k'}$, $p_{k''}$... of the services, are transformed by dividing the one and multiplying the other by the costs of production P_k, $P_{k'}$, $P_{k''}$... of the capital goods), a model involving the proportionality of the *raretés* to these costs, as expressed by the equations

$$\frac{r_k}{P_k} = \frac{r_{k'}}{P_{k'}} = \frac{r_{k''}}{P_{k''}} = \dots.$$

If we divide this latter system of equations by the former, we obtain

$$\frac{p_k}{P_k} = \frac{p_{k'}}{P_{k'}} = \frac{p_{k''}}{P_{k''}} = \dots$$

thus giving the uniformity in rates of income from all capital goods as a solution of the second problem.

OBSERVATIONS ON THE AUSPITZ AND LIEBEN PRINCIPLE OF THE THEORY OF PRICES[1]

1. According to Messrs. Auspitz and Lieben, the price of a commodity is determined by the slope of the radius vector Oc which is common to the two curves ON' and OA' of Fig. 47. These two curves are *derived* (*abgeleiteten Kurven*) from ON and OA respectively; that is to say, the radius vectors of the former are parallel to the tangents of the latter. Hence, whatever meaning may be attached to the curves ON and ON', and to the curves OA and OA', it is evident, on the one hand, that the first pair can be replaced by a single curve vv' (Fig. 48), so drawn that the areas under it are proportional to the ordinates of ON and its own ordinates are proportional to the slopes of radius vectors to ON'; and, on the other hand, that the second pair can be replaced by a single curve $\alpha\alpha'$ (Fig. 48), so drawn that the areas under it are proportional to the ordinates of OA and its own ordinates are proportional to the slopes of radius vectors to OA'. Thus, with their disguises removed, the two curves vv' and $\alpha\alpha'$ at once reveal themselves as Cournot's[2] and Mangoldt's[3] *supply and demand curves* which a number of English economists, following the lead of Mr. Marshall of Cambridge, are wont to employ. The curve vv' is drawn so that its abscissas represent the *demand* as a function of the *selling price* which is represented by the ordinates; while the curve $\alpha\alpha'$ is drawn so that the ordinates represent the *cost of production* as a function of the *supply* which is represented by the abscissas. It follows, then, that the abscissa Oa of the point of intersection p gives the demand equal to the supply, and that the ordinate $O\pi$ of the same point gives the selling price equal to the cost of production.

2. The first observation we shall make on the subject of these curves is that since their ordinates represent prices in money, the use of a *numéraire* is implicitly assumed in this construction; in other

---

[1] Reprinted from the *Revue d'économie politique* for May–June 1890. The principle under discussion was developed in the first chapter (pp. 1–24) and in the corresponding appendix (pp. 431–435) of the *Untersuchungen über die Theorie des Preises* by Rudolf Auspitz and Richard Lieben, Leipzig, Verlag von Duncker & Humblot, 1889.

[2] *Researches into the Mathematical Principles of the Theory of Wealth* (1838), Chapters IV and VIII [*op. cit.*].

[3] *Grundriss der Volkswirthschaftslehre* (ed. 1, [Stuttgart, Engelhorn] 1863), §§ 62–67. It should be noted that in the second edition of this work, which was published posthumously, Friedrich Kleinwächter, the editor, saw fit to omit the curves.

words, it is assumed that there is a commodity in terms of the value of which the value of all other commodities are expressed and the price of which is unity. It is not good scientific procedure to introduce a condition in this way without first analysing it.

3. The *demand* curve vv', i.e. the curve representing the *quantity sold* as a function of the *selling price*, cannot be regarded as a rigorously exact curve. The quantity sold of any product is a function not only of its own selling price, but also of the selling prices of all other products and the prices of all productive services. Messrs. Auspitz and Lieben assume that the selling prices of other products and the prices of all productive services can be held constant, while the selling price of the product under consideration varies. Theoretically, they have no right to do this. The selling prices of products and the prices of productive services are mutually interrelated.

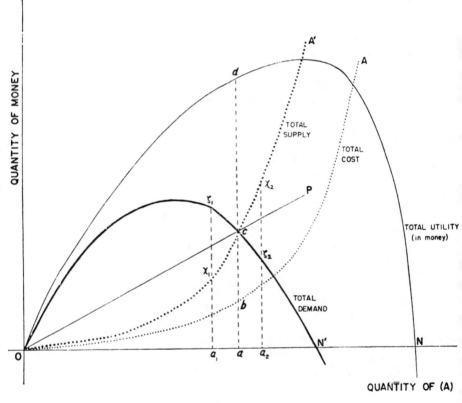

FIG. 47[1]

PRICE or COST

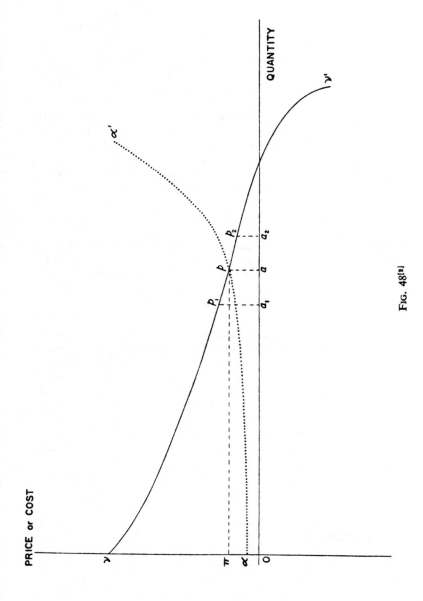

QUANTITY

FIG. 48[2]

Whenever the price of a given product is changed, the prices of the productive services and consequently the selling prices of the other commodities are also changed. Strange as it may seem, these very authors, Messrs. Auspitz and Lieben, have quite wrongly taken me to task, in their preface, for a fault which I have good reason here to lay at their door, namely, that of treating demands which are functions of several variables as functions of a single variable.

4. The definite integral of the demand function does not represent the total utility; and, therefore, if the curve ON' in Fig. 47 is a *demand curve* (*Nachfragekurve*), then the curve ON is not a *total utility curve* (*Gesammtnützlichkeitskurve*). Here Messrs. Auspitz and Lieben fall into the very error to which I called attention in Lesson 41 of my *Eléments* in the course of my criticism of Dupuit. It follows that the *consumers' surplus* (*Nutzen der Konsumtion*) is not measured by the expression which they give.

5. Their *supply* or *cost of production curve*, $\alpha\alpha'$, which is drawn as a function of the *quantity of output*, is not admissible either. The cost of production of a product is a function of the prices of the productive services employed in the manufacture of this product; and it is because the prices of the productive services increase or decrease that the cost of production increases or decreases with the quantity produced. But as the prices of the productive services increase or decrease, the costs of production of all the products in the manufacture of which these services are used will also increase or decrease; and the entire economic equilibrium will be disturbed. It is, therefore, theoretically impossible to construct a cost of production curve for a product as a function of the quantity produced of this product on the supposition that economic equilibrium will maintain itself indefinitely so far as the costs of production and the quantities of output of other products are concerned.

6. The definite integral of the supply function does not represent the total cost of production of the quantity manufactured. In a system of free competition, every unit in the quantity Oa (Fig. 48) must be considered as having the same cost of production ap, whence it follows that the total cost is represented not by the area $O\alpha pa$, but by the area $O\pi pa$. Consequently, if the curve OA' of Fig. 47 is a *supply curve* (*Angebotskurve*), the curve OA is not a *total cost of production curve* (*Gesammtherstellungskostenkurve*). Hence a *producers' surplus* (*Nutzen der Produktion*) which would be measured by the given expression does not exist.

7. We have still to examine the proposed construction as an approximation. If, however, we refer back to the production equations in §§202 and 203 of my *Eléments*, we perceive that even from

this point of view Auspitz and Lieben's construction is needlessly contradictory and complex.

In order to draw a demand curve for product (B), we must consider the following equation taken from our system (2) [§202]:

$$D_b = F_b(p_t, p_p, p_k \ldots p_b, p_c, p_d \ldots).$$

We suppose $p_t, p_p, p_k \ldots p_c, p_d \ldots$ to be determined and constant. We then assign all possible values to p_b and we derive from this equation all the corresponding values of D_b.

In order to draw a supply curve for the same product, we have to make use of all the equations of systems (1) and (3), and eliminate $O_t, O_p, O_k \ldots$ to obtain

$$a_t D_a + b_t D_b + c_t D_c + d_t D_d + \ldots = F_t(p_t, p_p, p_k \ldots p_b, p_c, p_d \ldots),$$
$$a_p D_a + b_p D_b + c_p D_c + d_p D_d + \ldots = F_p(p_t, p_p, p_k \ldots p_b, p_c, p_d \ldots),$$
$$a_k D_a + b_k D_b + c_k D_c + d_k D_d + \ldots = F_k(p_t, p_p, p_k \ldots p_b, p_c, p_d \ldots),$$
$$\cdot \; \cdot$$

and then we must take from system (4) the equation

$$b_t p_t + b_p p_p + b_k p_k + \ldots = p_b$$

for substitution in the above equations. Furthermore, we suppose $D_a, D_c, D_d \ldots p_c, p_d \ldots$ to be determined and constant. Assigning all possible values to D_b, we first derive $p_t, p_p, p_k \ldots$ from the above equations after the aforementioned substitutions, and then we derive all the corresponding values of p_b. The cost of production curve constructed in this way as a function of the quantity of output has abscissas that first increase and then decrease as the ordinates increase. This curve is asymptotic to the axis itself and not, as Messrs. Auspitz and Lieben think, to a line parallel to the price axis.

The intersection of the two curves of demand and supply gives the value of D_b at which the selling price is equal to the cost of production.

Now, on the one hand, it is evident that, in the second operation, in which $p_t, p_p, p_k \ldots$ are allowed to vary, $p_c, p_d \ldots$, which are considered as determined and constant in the first operation, must vary in consequence. On the other hand, in so far as we suppose $p_t, p_p, p_k \ldots$ to be determined and constant, it suffices to deduce p_b from them and then substitute this value of p_b into the equation of the demand curve in order to derive D_b.

Let $p_b = O\pi = ap$ [Fig. 48]. If a quantity $Oa_1 < Oa$ be manufactured, the selling price will be $a_1 p_1 > O\pi$. Profits will be earned and output will expand. If a quantity $Oa_2 > Oa$ be manufactured, the selling price will be $a_2 p_2 < O\pi$. There will be losses and output will be reduced.

Moreover, this demand curve, showing demand as a function of the cost of production, is at the same time a price curve showing price as a function of the quantity supplied.

Let Oa [Fig. 48] be the quantity supplied. If a price $a_1 p_1 > ap$ be cried, the corresponding demand will be $Oa_1 < Oa$. The price must fall. If a price $a_2 p_2 < ap$ be cried, the corresponding demand will be $Oa_2 > Oa$. The price must rise.

A demand curve conceived in this way is none other than my *price curve*.[1] I am not saying that for this or that specific problem there is no advantage to be gained in utilizing a supply curve as well; but I insist that these two curves cannot serve as a starting-point for a complete and rigorously exact theory of the determination of prices.

----

[1] If we assume that the market is in the state of complete equilibrium apart from the production of (B), the curve vv' represents the two curves $B_d B_p$ (Fig. 42) and $B'_d B'_p$ (Fig. 43) of Appendix I rolled into a single curve, of which the abscissas represent the quantities, and the ordinates the prices.

APPENDIX III[1][a]

NOTE ON MR. WICKSTEED'S REFUTATION OF THE ENGLISH THEORY OF RENT[2]

1. The description and refutation of the English theory of rent, which forms the subject-matter of Lesson 31 [of ed. 3, cf. Lesson 39 of ed. 4 def.] of my *Eléments d'économie politique pure*, is among those problems of mathematical economics which have given me the greatest trouble. Nevertheless, that Lesson has so far found very few readers, notwithstanding that it represents an attempt to formulate in mathematical language a terse and rigorous criticism of a theory which has been the subject of so much confused and sterile discussion as to give rise to a plethora of books, a list of whose titles alone would fill a volume. I was, however, sure from the very start that this effort would eventually excite the interest of mathematical economists, when they had had enough of the inane commonplaces which still clutter the criticisms of pure economics. That is why I took so much interest in Mr. Wicksteed's short treatise on this subject; and I was very pleased to find that, using exactly the same methods as I did, he arrived at conclusions that were precisely the same as mine.

2. System (4) of my [*cost of*] *production equations* is a system of equations of the form

$$b_t p_t + \ldots + b_p p_p + \ldots + b_k p_k + \ldots = p_b$$

expressing the fact that "the selling prices of the products are equal to the cost of the productive services employed in their manufacture" (*Eléments*, §199 [of ed. 3, cf. §203 of ed. 4 def.]). These equations, when multiplied by the appropriate quantity manufactured, e.g. by D_b, take the form

$$D_b b_t p_t + \ldots + D_b b_p p_p + \ldots + D_b b_k p_k + \ldots = D_b p_b.$$

This system of equations needs to be supplemented by still another system of equations of the form

$$\phi(b_t \ldots b_p \ldots b_k \ldots) = 0,$$

expressing the relation among the coefficients of production (§274 [of ed. 3, cf. §325 of ed. 4 def.] of the *Eléments*).

---

[1] Reprinted [except for the postscript] from the *Recueil publié par la Faculté de Droit de l'Université de Lausanne* (1896).

[2] This refutation was published in a book entitled *An Essay on the Coordination of the Laws of Distribution* by Philip H. Wicksteed (author of *The Alphabet of Economic Science*) London, Macmillan & Co., 1894. [No. 12 in *Series of Reprints of Scarce Tracts in Economic and Political Science*, London School of Economics and Political Science, 1932.]

Mr. Wicksteed in his *Essay on the Coordination of the Laws of Distribution* (Prefatory Note and §6) writes the equation

$$P = F(A, B, C \dots)$$

subject to the condition that

$$mP = F(mA, mB, mC \dots)$$

whence he derives

$$P = \frac{dP}{dA} A + \frac{dP}{dB} B + \frac{dP}{dC} C \dots$$

(Essay, §6). Designating "the product" by P and "the factors of production" by $A, B, C \dots$, he regards "the product" as a "function of the factors of production". The notation of these equations is deliberately ambiguous; for the author reserves the right to interpret P *ad libitum* either as a quantity or as a value. But this is a minor matter. If $P = D_b$ and is the *quantity of output*, his $\frac{dP}{dA}, \frac{dP}{dB}, \frac{dP}{dC} \dots$ correspond respectively to my $\frac{p_t}{p_b} \dots \frac{p_p}{p_b} \dots \frac{p_k}{p_b} \dots$. If $P = D_b p_b$ and is the *value of output*, his $\frac{dP}{dA}, \frac{dP}{dB}, \frac{dP}{dC} \dots$ correspond respectively to my $p_t \dots p_p \dots p_k \dots$. In either case, $A = D_b b_t$, $B = D_b b_p$, $C = D_b b_k \dots$, always subject to the condition

$$\phi(b_t \dots b_p \dots b_k \dots) = 0,$$

so that his equation differs from mine, if it really differs at all, only by being more general in form.

3. Having posited this equation, Mr. Wicksteed launches into a detailed criticism of the English theory of rent (Essay, §5), which is identical with the criticism I developed in Lesson 31 [of ed. 3, cf. Lesson 39 of ed. 4 def.] of my *Eléments*.

I altered the English theory in order to express it in a mathematical formula

$$p_t = F(x) - x F'(x)$$

which I identified with the equation

$$b_t p_t + \dots + b_p p_p + \dots + b_k p_k + \dots = p_b.$$

Mr. Wicksteed, starting with the equation

$$P = \frac{dP}{dA} A + \frac{dP}{dB} B + \frac{dP}{dC} C + \dots,$$

derives from it the following reformulation of the English theory:

$$p_i = F(c) - c F'(c).$$

For the benefit of discriminating readers, I wish to call attention to a slight difference between Mr. Wicksteed's and my own modifications of the English theory.

In my restatement, the variable x is "the value, in terms of *numéraire*, of the different kinds of personal capital and capital goods proper (P), (P'), (P'')... (K), (K'), (K'')... applied to a unit of land (T)", according to the equation

$$x = H(b_p P_p + \ldots + b_k P_k + \ldots) = \frac{H}{i}(b_p p_p + \ldots + b_k p_k + \ldots),$$

where

$$H = \frac{1}{b_t} = \frac{1}{\theta(b_p \ldots b_k \ldots)}$$

is the number of units of product obtained per unit of quantity of land (*Eléments*, §306 [of ed. 3, cf. §358 of ed. 4 def.]). It follows, then, that my $F(x) = Hp_b$, that my $F'(x) = i$, that my $xF'(x) = H(b_p p_p + \ldots + b_k p_k + \ldots)$, and finally that my $p_t = Hp_b - H(b_p p_p + \ldots + b_k p_k + \ldots)$.

In Mr. Wicksteed's restatement, the variable c would represent, in my notation, "the number of units of *capital-plus-labour* (K) applied to a unit of land (T)", according to the equation

$$c = Hb_k$$

(*Essay*, p. 24). From this it follows that his $F(c) = Hp_b$, that his $F'(c) = p_k$, that his $cF'(c) = Hb_k p_k$ and that his $p_i = Hp_b - Hb_k p_k$.

For Mr. Wicksteed as for myself, the whole area under the curve representing $F(x)$ or $F(c)$ is, therefore, "the total amount of output in terms of *numéraire*" and the upper [residual] area, representing $F(x) - xF'(x)$ or $F(c) - cF'(c)$ is "the amount of rent measured in terms of *numéraire*" and not in *units of product* as the English theory would have it. On the other hand, while I, in my attempt to go further than Ricardo and Jevons along their own lines, took as my abscissa the *value in terms of numéraire of the personal capital and capital goods proper applied to land*, and as my ordinate the *rate of net income in terms of numéraire*, which permitted me to assume any number of services, Mr. Wicksteed took as his abscissa the *number of units of capital-plus-labour applied to land* and as his ordinate the *price of this [composite] service*, which compelled him not merely to reduce all the different varieties of personal capital to a single category and all the different varieties of capital goods proper to another single category, but to lump these two single categories together. Mr. Wicksteed's procedure can be explained by his desire: (1) to represent the law of the variation of rent geometrically and

(2) to reverse the relation between the two factors, *land* and *capital-plus-labour*, in order to formulate a theory of capital-plus-labour symmetrical with the theory of land. But whatever intrinsic merit this arrangement may have, it differs from mine only in form; for the substance of his criticism consists, as I have already said, in deducing the formula of the English theory of rent from an equation similar to my cost of production equation, in the same way that I reduced the formula of the English theory of rent to my cost of production equation.

4. Whether we proceed in one direction or the other, the aim of the operation is the same. We see at once, upon completion of this operation, that neither Mr. Wicksteed's nor my own mathematical reformulation of the English theory of rent applies with any more right to the determination of the price of land-services $\left(p_t \text{ or } \dfrac{dP}{dA}\right)$ than it does to the determination of the price of personal services $\left(p_p \text{ or } \dfrac{dP}{dB}\right)$ or the price of capital-services $\left(p_k \text{ or } \dfrac{dP}{dC}\right)$. This is what I meant when I wrote: "thus all that remains of Ricardo's theory after a rigorous critical analysis is that rent is not a component part, but a result, of the price of products. But the same thing can be said of wages and interest" (*Eléments*, §310 [of ed. 3, cf. §362 of ed. 4 def.]). Mr. Wicksteed expresses the same idea on p. 47 of his *Essay* where he writes: "'Rent is not the cause but the effect of the exchange value of the product' we read in books. Precisely so, and since the law of rent is also the law of wages and the law of interest, it is equally true that 'wages are not the cause but the effect of the exchange value of the product'. And so too with interest." I could cite to the same effect several other passages in Mr. Wicksteed's *Essay* (p. 18, l. 14; id., l. 6), which, like the preceding passage, seem to have been translated from the *Eléments* (p. 367, l. 18; p. 369, l. 18 [ed. 3]) and which the author might well have put in quotation marks while using this opportunity to mention my work.

5. There are, however, several differences between Mr. Wicksteed's *Essay on the Coordination of the Laws of Distribution*, which he published in 1894, and my book, in which I have endeavoured, since 1874–1877, "to show how a certain distribution of products results from a given allotment of services" (*Eléments*, p. 254 [of ed. 3, cf. p. 234 or §223 of ed. 4 def.].

After proving that what is true of rent is equally true of wages and interest, I added: "Consequently, rent, wages, interest, the prices of products, and the coefficients of production are all unknowns within the same problem; they must always be determined together and not independently of one another" (*Eléments*, p. 358 [of ed. 3, cf. p. 414 or §362 of ed. 4 def.]). In consequence, I combined my system of equations expressing *equality between selling price and cost of production* not only with the system of equations expressing *equality between the demand and offer of services* but also with the systems of equations relating the *offer of services* to the *demand for products*; and I showed how free competition, by solving all these equations, determines thereby all the unknowns. Mr. Wicksteed has done nothing of the sort. As I pointed out earlier, he leaves his equation

$$P=F(A, B, C...)$$

in a form capable of expressing either the quantity or the value of the product, or, as he puts it, either the "physical product" or the "commercial product". He then shows within what limits, in one case as in the other, the function is equal to the sum of the products of the partial differential coefficients multiplied by the [independent] variables; and he demonstrates, in consequence, that the rate of remuneration of each factor is the differential coefficient of the product with respect to the quantity of that factor. Finally he develops a geometrical theory of the rate of remuneration of the services of *capital-plus-labour* which is perfectly symmetrical with the very theory of rent he disproves. It is not my purpose to evaluate this part of Mr. Wicksteed's work. However interesting it may be, I doubt if it warrants his saying, as he does on p. 3 of his *Essay*, that, so far as he was aware, no "satisfactory attempt has been made to state what might be called the new theory of Distribution in its entirety; and *still less have its relations to the old theory been defined*". I doubt, too, if he is justified in proffering his little treatise to fill the gap.   September 1894.

P.S. The aforementioned doubt was well founded. In a note which has just been brought to my attention, Enrico Barone has criticized a part of Mr. Wicksteed's work on which I had reserved judgement; and the following is my understanding of this criticism.

Mr. Wicksteed rigorously defined his proposition for the case where his equation was linear and homogeneous, and identical with my own. In this case, to be sure, the differentials are respectively proportional to their variables: and since we have

$$dP= \frac{\partial P}{\partial A} dA + \frac{\partial P}{\partial B} dB + \frac{\partial P}{\partial C} dC+...,$$

it follows that

$$P= \frac{\partial P}{\partial A} A + \frac{\partial P}{\partial B} B + \frac{\partial P}{\partial C} C+....$$

He did not, however, give any proof applicable to the case where his equation is neither linear nor homogeneous, that is, to the case where the coefficients of production vary with the quantity produced. Mr. Barone, on the other hand, has given such a proof applicable to this case, by utilizing my equation

$$D_b p_v = D_v b_t p_t + \ldots + D_v b_v p_v + \ldots + D_v b_k p_k + \ldots$$

or

$$P\pi = Ap_a + Bp_b + Cp_c + \ldots \qquad \qquad ..(1)$$

and my equation

$$\phi(b_t \ldots b_v \ldots b_k \ldots) = 0.$$

This last equation, already modified by Pareto through the introduction of D_b, becomes

$$\phi(b_t \ldots b_v \ldots b_k \ldots D_b) = 0$$

which Mr. Barone writes in the form

$$D_b = \phi(D_v b_t \ldots D_v b_v \ldots D_v b_k \ldots)$$

or

$$P = \phi(A, B, C \ldots). \qquad \qquad ..(2)$$

This is Mr. Wicksteed's equation which may be supposed non-linear and non-homogeneous and in which P is a physical quantity, not a value, of the product.

If we differentiate equations (1) and (2) to minimize the cost of production, we obtain

$$\frac{d\phi}{dA} = \frac{p_a}{\pi}, \qquad \frac{d\phi}{dB} = \frac{p_b}{\pi}, \qquad \frac{d\phi}{dC} = \frac{p_c}{\pi} \ldots. \qquad ..(3)$$

Now, the entrepreneur, proceeding, as is his wont, by groping, adds to or subtracts from the quantity of each productive service according as the value of the [marginal] increment of this service is less than or greater than the value of the [marginal] increment of the product which this increment of service produces, until, finally, the following equalities are reached:

$$\Delta A\, p_a = \frac{d\phi}{dA} \Delta A\, \pi, \qquad \Delta B\, p_b = \frac{d\phi}{dB} \Delta B\, \pi, \qquad \Delta C\, p_c = \frac{d\phi}{dC} \Delta C\, \pi \ldots$$

or, as we saw before,[1]

[1] To bring out the meaning of the differentiation and to reveal the concordance between theory and practice, I need only advance the proposition conceived along the lines of the proof I gave for the theorem of maximum satisfaction of new capital goods, viz. *that in equilibrium minimum cost of production equals selling price* when the partial differential increments of cost assignable to each of the productive services are: (1) equal to one another, since, in the absence of such equality, it would be profitable for the entrepreneur to substitute certain services for others; and (2) equal to the partial differential increments of receipts assignable to each service, since in the absence

$$\frac{d\phi}{dA}=\frac{p_a}{\pi}, \qquad \frac{d\phi}{dB}=\frac{p_b}{\pi}, \qquad \frac{d\phi}{dC}=\frac{p_c}{\pi}\ldots \qquad ..(3)$$

From equations (1) and (3), we derive

$$P=\frac{d\phi}{dA}A+\frac{d\phi}{dB}B+\frac{d\phi}{dC}C+\ldots \qquad ..(4)$$

Therefore, (1) *free competition leads to minimum cost of production*; (2) *under the rule of free competition, the rate of remuneration for each service is equal to the partial derivative of the production function, i.e. to its marginal productivity*, according to the equations of system (3); and (3) *the total quantity of the output is distributed among the productive services* according to equation (4).

This triple proposition constitutes the "Theory of Marginal Productivity".[1] This is a highly important theory, first, because it introduces into the problem of production a system of equations (3), in which the number of equations is equal to the number of coefficients of production and in which these coefficients are represented as unknowns; and, secondly, because it makes possible a definitive criticism and refutation of the English theory of rent, by showing that the consideration of marginal productivity is relevant to the determination of the coefficients of production, but is not relevant to the determination of the prices of services.

This is precisely what I said in Lesson 31 (p. 385, l. 20 [of ed. 3, cf. §362 of ed. 4 def.]). M. Barone deduced this proposition with logical rigour from my theory of economic equilibrium. Mr. Wicksteed, however, fell short of establishing it for the more general case and would have been better inspired if he had not made such efforts to appear ignorant of the work of his predecessors.

October 1895.

of this latter equality, the entrepreneur would have occasion either to expand or to contract his output. In other words equality between the minimum cost of production and selling price is attained in equilibrium when

$$\pi\Delta P=p_a\Delta A=p_b\Delta B=p_c\Delta C=\ldots$$

or when

$$\frac{d\varphi}{dA}=\frac{p_a}{\pi}, \qquad \frac{d\varphi}{dB}=\frac{p_b}{\pi}, \qquad \frac{d\varphi}{dC}=\frac{p_c}{\pi}\ldots,$$

that is *when*, finally, *the marginal productivities are equal to the rates of remuneration.*

[1] This theory has been taken up on several occasions by various American economists, notably by Wood, Hobson and Clark, in the *Quarterly Journal of Economics* published by Harvard University, and in the publications of the American Economic Association. As for Barone's note, it will appear in extended form in the *Giornale degli Economisti.*

TRANSLATOR'S NOTES[1]

Lesson 1

[1] Adam Smith, *Inquiry into the Nature and Causes of the Wealth of Nations*, edited by Edwin Cannan, London, Methuen, 1930, vol. I, p. 395.

[2] cf. Auguste Walras, *De la nature de la richesse et de l'origine de la valeur*, p. ix (1831) or p. 57 (1938): "Non que je prétende, ce qu'à Dieu ne plaise, que le droit naturel et l'économie politique soient une seule et même science. Je sais que chacune d'elles se fonde sur des considérations diverses, et qu'elles se forment et se développent dans deux ordres d'idées bien distincts et bien délimités, dont l'un a pour objet l'utile, et l'autre le juste. Jamais je ne confondrai l'intérêt avec le devoir, ou le sensible avec le rationnel."

[3] These quotations are found in Germain Garnier's translation of Adam Smith's *Wealth of Nations*, *Recherches sur la nature et les causes de la richesse des nations*, ed. 5 (*Collection des principaux économistes*), Paris, Guillaumin, 1881, vol. II, pp. 1–2, note 2.

[4] *A Treatise on Political Economy: or, The Production, Distribution, and Consumption of Wealth*, translated from ed. 4 of the French by C. R. Prinsep, M.A., with notes by the translator; fifth American edition, Philadelphia, Gregg and Eliott, 1832.

[5] Charles Coquelin and Gilbert U. Guillaumin, *Dictionnaire de l'économie politique*, ed. 3, Paris, Guillaumin, 1864.

[6] cf. Auguste Walras, *op. cit.*, pp. iii and iv (1831) or pp. 54–55 (1938): "Qu'on juge, si on le peut en ce moment, du désappointement que j'éprouvai, lorsque ayant entrepris de consulter les principaux ouvrages qui traitent de l'économie politique . . . je crus apercevoir, entre les différentes écoles d'économistes, des divergences si remarquables, et, dans les ouvrages même d'un seul auteur, des contradictions si palpables, qu'elles me firent soupçonner, avec juste raison, qu'elles tenaient à une ignorance générale sur les premiers principes de la science et sur la nature même de l'objet qui sert de base aux théories économiques."

Lesson 2

[1] Charles Coquelin, *Traité du crédit et des banques*, Paris, Guillaumin, 1848.

[2] See above Translator's Note [5] of Lesson 1.

Lesson 3

[1] In this Lesson the terms '*rare*' and '*rareté*' are used in the general sense of scarce and scarcity. See below, Lesson 8, Translator's Note [9], and §101.

[2] See §75.

[3] cf. Francis Bacon, *Novum Organum*, I, 129: "Naturae enim non imperatur, nisi parendo."

[1] The symbols in parentheses following each quotation from unpublished letters are the reference numbers identifying the manuscripts preserved in the classified *Fonds Walras* at the Bibliothèque Cantonale et Universitaire de Lausanne (Switzerland), as they are listed there in a typewritten "Inventaire Sommaire". The letters to Walras are those he actually received; those from Walras are his own rough copies, which he retained and which are always difficult to decipher. In the quotations from the latter letters only the final version is given below, the crossed out passages being ignored. (See my note describing these manuscripts in "La correspondance complète de Cournot et Walras", *Economie Appliquée*, vol. v, no. 1, January 1952, pp. 5–7.)

LESSON 4

[1] See § 19.

[2] cf. John Stuart Mill, *Principles of Political Economy*, Book II, Chapter I, § 1.

[3] P. J. Proudhon, *Système des contradictions économiques ou philosophie de la misère*, ed. 2, Paris, Garnier Frères, 1850, vol. I, pp. 63–64: "Pour le surplus, je suis prêt à reconnaître les effets heureux du mécanisme propriétaire; mais j'observe que ces effets sont entièrement couverts par les misères qu'il est de la nature de ce mécanisme de produire: en sorte que, comme l'avouait naguère devant le parlement anglais un illustre ministre, et comme nous le démontrerons bientôt, dans la société actuelle, le progrès de la misère est parallèle au progrès de la richesse. . . ."

[4] Frédéric Bastiat, *Harmonies économiques*, Paris, Guillaumin, 1850, translated from ed. 2 (1851) by Patrick James Stirling under the title *Harmonies of Political Economy*, London, J. Murray, 1860: ". . . *all legitimate interests are in harmony. That is the predominant idea of my work* . . .", p. 1.

LESSON 5

[1] cf. V. Pareto, *Manuel d'économie politique*, Paris, 1909, reprinted Paris, Giard, 1947, pp. 242–246; Antonio Osorio, *Théorie Mathématique de l'échange*, Paris, Giard, 1913, pp. 194–195. Walras's definition of "value in exchange" was assailed by Pareto as unmeaningful, because it defines an unknown "value in exchange", in terms of an equally unknown "property". He finds it useless to refer to this metaphysical entity, when its concrete manifestation, price, i.e. ratio of exchange, is all that is needed in the theoretical development that follows. This is not altogether true, for, as Cournot pointed out, while *value in exchange* "necessarily implies the idea of a ratio between two terms . . . an accomplished change in the ratio is a relative effect, which can and should be explained by absolute changes in the terms of the ratio", Augustin Cournot, *Researches into the Mathematical Principles of the Theory of Wealth*, p. 24. But apart from the question of the justness of the criticism, the acerbity of Pareto's remarks directed against Walras's definition seems entirely uncalled for. Walras was not responsible for introducing any term into economic literature, but he proved conclusively, as is seen in §§ 101–102, that the only meaning "value in exchange" could possibly have was that of a term in a ratio with no autonomous existence outside of that ratio. To this Pareto added nothing by his criticism.

[2] Throughout the theory of exchange, the French word '*offre*' is translated as "offer", whenever it refers exclusively to offers for sale out of stocks of commodities or securities already existing in the hands of prospective sellers. Only when the word '*offre*' refers to a flow of products from the prospective sellers' fields, factories or workshops (or to new issues of securities) is "*offre*" rendered as "supply". It is in the theory of production (see Part IV) that '*offre*' characteristically bears this latter connotation.

[3] 'Chaque agent vendeur ou acheteur trouve exactement ce qu'on appelle sa *contre-partie* chez un autre agent acheteur ou vendeur.' The word *contre-partie* has no technical equivalent in English. It designates the broker with whom a broker deals, for French brokers do not trade with dealers or jobbers, but only with other brokers. cf. J. O. Ketteridge, *French-English and English-French Dictionary of Business Terms, Phrases and Practice*, London, Routledge, n.d., *sub verbo* '*contre-partie*'.

[4] John Stuart Mill, *op. cit.*, Book III, Chapter II, § 1.

[5] In the case of so-called bilateral monopoly, as Edgeworth was the first to point out, price is indeterminate. cf. F. Y. Edgeworth, *Mathematical Psychics*, London, C. Kegan Paul & Co., 1881 (Reprint No. 10 published by the London

School of Economics and Political Science, 1932), p. 20ff.; *Papers Relating to Political Economy*, London, Macmillan, 1925, vol. II, pp. 315–317; Alfred Marshall, *Principles of Economics*, ed. 8, London, Macmillan, 1920, Appendix F and Mathematical Appendix Note 12 *bis*; Knut Wicksell, *Ueber Wert, Kapital und Rente*, Jena, Gustav Fischer, 1893 (Reprint No. 15 published by the London School of Economics and Political Science, 1933), pp. 36–43; *Lectures on Political Economy*, London, Routledge, 1934, vol. I, pp. 49–51.

[6] This concept of value in exchange as a term in a ratio which is inversely proportional to the ratio of the quantities exchanged was adumbrated quite early in Achille Nicolas Isnard's *Traité des richesses*, Lausanne, François Grasset, 1781. For example, we read on pp. 16 and 17 of this treatise: "Si l'on suppose que la monnaie n'existe pas, l'échange est plus difficile, il est néanmoins possible. Il arrive alors qu'une certaine quantité de marchandises d'une espèce équivaut à une certaine quantité de marchandises d'une autre espèce; qu'un nombre a de mesures déterminées d'une marchandise équivaut à un nombre b de mesures déterminées d'une autre; on peut conclure que la valeur de la première est à la valeur de la seconde dans le rapport de b à a. Si les marchandises ont un rapport entre elles prises deux à deux, elles ont aussi des rapports prises ensemble. Si on a trois mesures, M, M', M'' telles que $M:M''::1:2$ et $M':M''::3:5$ on aura $M:M': M''::3:6:10$. Ces rapports sont les valeurs de ces mesures. Le mot de valeur exprime donc le rapport de deux choses que l'on compare pour les échanger." And again on p. 18: "Nous considérerons ici les échanges immédiats des marchandises en général contre marchandises dans un même lieu, pour rechercher quelles valeurs elles ont entr'elles sans l'intermède des monnaies . . . . Il est facile de voir que ce qui arriveroit dans un échange entre propriétaires isolés de deux marchandises, dont les besoins du superflu de l'un equivaudroient aux besoins du superflu de l'autre. Si l'on suppose, par exemple, que le superflu des premiers est une quantité a de mesures M d'une marchandise, et que celui des seconds est une quantité b de mesures M' d'une autre; ces choses ne pouvant être échangées que l'une contre l'autre, puisqu'on les suppose seules, la quantité a de mesures M equivaudra à la quantité b de mesures M': ainsi on aura $aM=bM'$, et par conséquent $M:M'::\frac{1}{a}:\frac{1}{b}$. La valeur de chaque mesure sera donc en raison inverse de la quantité qui est exposée en échange."

Walras's definition of price corresponds more closely to Isnard's "valeurs" expressed "sans l'intermède des monnaies" than to Cournot's concept of price. That Walras's definition was broader than Cournot's has been shown by Dr. Lilly Hecht in her study, *A. Cournot und L. Walras, ein formaler und materialer Vergleich wirtschaftstheoretischer Abhandlungen*, Heidelberg, Verlag der Weiss'-schen Universitätsbuchhandlung, 1930, vol. I, no. 6 of the Heidelberger Studien aus dem Institut für Sozial-u. Staatswissenschaften, p. 41. Cournot finds it necessary to invent "a fictitious and invariable modulus", as he calls it (*op. cit.*, p. 27), to the value of which all other values are referred in determining the relative values between commodities. "But," he tells us (p. 26) "if no article exists, having the necessary conditions for perfect fixity, we can and ought to imagine one which, to be sure, will only have an abstract existence." He suggested a "*corrected money*" for this purpose. Walras's procedure is more general and makes it unnecessary, in his theory of exchange, to have recourse to the concept of money, which is introduced later (Part VI) in its proper place in the methodical development of the theory of general equilibrium.

There is, however, no essential difference between the two. If we let an imaginary commodity (Z) be Cournot's *tertium comparationis*, then as is seen in §§111ff., $p_{a,b}=\frac{p_{a,z}}{p_{b,z}}$ and $p_{b,a}=\frac{p_{b,z}}{p_{a,z}}$.

[7] Multiplying the first two equations that follow in the text we obtain

$$D_a D_b = O_b O_a p_b p_a,$$

and using the fact that $p_a p_b = 1$, we derive the third equation.

[8] cf. Cournot, *op. cit.*, p. 46: "The sales or the demand generally, we say, increases when the price decreases." Neither Cournot's nor Walras's proposition possesses the quality of absolute generality implied. Only barring certain exceptions is it a "universal rule" that the demand curve "is negatively inclined throughout the whole of its length" (Alfred Marshall, *op. cit.*, p. 99, note 2). Cases of positively inclined segments of the demand curve have long been known empirically as Pareto has pointed out in his *Cours d'économie politique*, Lausanne, F. Rouge and Paris, F. Pichon, 1897, vol. II, §§977–978. Pareto demonstrates, further, that in cases of competing goods "quand le prix hausse, la demande peut augmenter et ensuite diminuer . . ." (*Manuel*, p. 273, Appendice §§47–48, 121–125). On the other hand, exceptions to this downward slope of the demand curve are "rare and unimportant", appearing only when the commodity in question is an inferior good, and even then under very stringent conditions, as has been clearly demonstrated by J. R. Hicks in his *Value and Capital*, ed. 2, Oxford, Clarendon Press, 1946, p. 35.

[9] The clause, '. . . quand il était plus riche', referring evidently to the individual demander's condition before the price rose, strikingly adumbrates the later theory of income effects of changes in price. *Vide* J. R. Hicks, *op. cit.*, p. 32, and Henry Schultz (who attributes the concept to Eugen Slutsky), *The Theory and Measurement of Demand*, Chicago, University of Chicago Press, 1938, pp. 41–42.

LESSON 6

[1] 'dispositions à l'enchère'.

[2] Walras's diagrams, unlike those usually found in Anglo-American economic literature, measure price on the horizontal axis and quantity on the vertical axis. In this respect Walras follows Cournot, whose law of demand

$$D = F(p)$$

and whose corresponding diagrams represent the individual purchaser under competition as a quantity adjuster. Walras's diagrams reflect this conception more clearly than the Marshallian diagrams.

Moreover, since Pareto and most other continental European economists have also followed Cournot's example in their diagrams, it is well to heed Philip H. Wicksteed's observation: "It is of great importance not to become dependent on any special convention as to the position, etc., of the curves" (*Alphabet of Economic Science*, London, Macmillan, 1888, p. 13).

[3] From Fig. 1 of ed. 4. In this and all subsequent curves, the descriptive labels of the axes have been inserted by the translator.

[4] cf. Cournot, *op. cit.*, pp. 49–50: "We will assume that the function $F(p)$, which expresses the law of demand or of the market, is a *continuous* function, i.e. a function which does not pass suddenly from one value to another, but which takes in passing all intermediate values. It might be otherwise if the number of consumers were very limited. . . . But the wider the market extends, and the more the combinations of needs, of fortunes, or even of caprices, are varied among consumers, the closer the function $F(p)$ will come to varying with p in a continuous manner. However little may be the variation of p, there will be some consumers so placed that the slight rise or fall of the article will affect their

consumptions, and will lead them to deprive themselves in some way or to reduce their manufacturing output, or to substitute something else for the article that has grown dearer, as, for instance, coal for wood and anthracite for soft coal."

[5] From Fig. 2 of ed. 4.

[6] '*à tout prix*'.

[7] Equal in the sense described in the following paragraph of the text.

[8] From Fig. 2 of ed. 4; shading inserted.

[9] In §45 we have seen that $O_b = D_a p_a$. Where O_b equals D_b we may substitute D_b for O_b and obtain $D_b = D_a p_a$, whence $p_a = \dfrac{D_b}{D_a}$ whenever p_a is the equilibrium price.

[10] Again starting with the equation $O_b = D_a p_a$, we obtain $p_a = \dfrac{O_b}{D_a}$. Now substituting $D_a p_a$ for O_b and $O_b p_b$ for D_a (§46), we obtain $p_a = \dfrac{D_a p_a}{O_b p_b}$. Where $D_b = O_b$, $\dfrac{D_a p_a}{O_b p_b} = \dfrac{D_a p_a}{D_b p_b}$ which is true whenever p_a and p_b are equilibrium prices.

[11] The alternative translation of Walras's term, '*établissement*' by the word *emergence* was suggested by the following passage in Philip H. Wicksteed's *The Common Sense of Political Economy*, edited by Lionel Robbins, London, George Routledge & Sons Ltd., 1933, vol. II, p. 516 (Book II, Chapter IV): "In the higgling of the market the price *emerges* as the result of the play of a conflict between buyers and sellers as such, which is not relevant to the ultimate facts and forces which *constitute* that price." The laws of the *emergence* or *establishment* of equilibrium price refer to the laws of those operations of the market which result in equilibrium, whereas the laws of the *determination* of equilibrium price take into account "the ultimate facts and forces which *constitute* that price".

[12] cf. Alfred Marshall, *op. cit.*, Book V, Chapter II. The type of equilibrium here described by Walras can only be compared with Marshall's "temporary equilibrium of supply and demand" by which "market values" are determined. At this stage of their argument both Walras and Marshall are concerned exclusively with fixed aggregate *stocks* of goods already in existence, and consequently neither the rate of output nor the cost of production is taken into account. In his corn market example Marshall describes 36s. as "the true equilibrium price, because if it were fixed on at the beginning and adhered to throughout, it would exactly equate demand and supply (i.e. the amount which buyers were willing to purchase at that price would be just equal to that for which sellers were willing to take that price); . . ." (*op. cit.*, p. 333). In a letter to F. Y. Edgeworth, Marshall explains why he refrained from illustrating market equilibrium by means of curves: "You know I never apply curves or mathematics to market values. For I don't think they help much. And market values are, I think, either absolutely abstract or terribly concrete and full of ever-varying (though individually vital) side-issues. Also Ox [i.e. the quantity axis] for market values measures a stock and not a 'flow'; and I found that, if I once got people to use Demand and Supply curves which discussed *stocks* along the axis of x, they could not easily be kept from introducing the notion of stock when flow was essential." (*Memorials of Alfred Marshall*, p. 435.)

[13] The London silver market offers perhaps a clearer example than the stock exchange of a real market in which price determination most closely approximates the theoretical establishment of *static* equilibrium prices under competitive conditions. The functioning of this market has been described in the following terms: "The London price is fixed once a day by four bullion firms which have for many years constituted the market. Representatives of these four

firms meet at about 2 p.m. on weekdays and at about 11 a.m. on Saturdays. All orders to sell or buy are placed with these brokers. They compare the orders, and the price is then fixed where it will move the greatest amount of 'at market' orders. In short, the price is determined according to demand and supply. This is called 'fixing' the price. As presumably the only interest of the brokers is the one-eighth of 1 per cent commission they make on purchases (there is no commission for selling silver) they have no interest in fixing the price at any but its economic level. Once determined, the price is immediately cabled to the banking centres of the world." (H. M. Bratter, "Silver—Some Fundamentals", *Journal of Political Economy*, June 1931, vol. xxxix, no. 3, pp. 362–363.)

LESSON 7

[1] The discussion which follows to the end of Lesson 7, while essentially geometrical and not analytical, indicates unmistakably that Walras was perfectly aware of the fact that his system of equations developed up to this point, though still confined to the plane of exchange, did not suffice to determine a unique price solution. It is possible, as he proceeds to show, that there may be either no solution at all or a multiplicity of solutions. Surely Léon Walras should *not* be numbered among those economists who "Gleichungen bloss *aufgestellt* haben, ohne sich um *Existenz* und Eindeutigkeit ihrer Lösungen zu kümmern, und bestenfalls darauf sahen, dass die Anzahl der Unbekannten mit der Anzahl der Gleichungen übereinstimme (was für Existenz und Unizität von Lösungen natürlich weder notwendig noch hinreichend ist)" (Karl Menger, *Ergebnisse eines mathematischen Kolloquiums*, Heft 6, Leipzig and Vienna, Franz Deuticke, 1935, p. 20, concluding the discussion of Karl Schlesinger's paper "Über die Produktionsgleichungen der ökonomischen Wertlehre" and of Abraham Wald's paper "Über die eindeutige positive Lösbarkeit der neuen Produktionsgleichungen"). See Lesson 10, note [1].

[2] Such curves would take the form shown in Fig. 49 opposite. OK is the reciprocal of OB_p; and ON is the reciprocal of OA_p.

[3] In other words, referring to the diagram in the preceding note, the most eager buyer of (A) holding (B) will not give more than θ_a ($\gtrless A_p$ in Fig. 49a) units of (B) for one of (A) and will only give one of (B) if he can obtain at least λ_b ($\lessgtr N$ in Fig. 49b) units of (A) in exchange; while the most eager buyer of (B) holding (A) will not give more than θ_b ($\gtrless N$ in Fig. 49b) units of (A) for one of (B) and will only give one of (A) if he can obtain at least λ_a ($\lessgtr A_p$ in Fig. 49a) units of (B) in exchange.

[4] From Fig. 2 of ed. 4. The broken line rectangles have been inserted.

[5] The propriety of calling these stability conditions Walrasian has been called in question. Alfred Marshall first laid claim to priority with regard to this theory in a private letter he sent to Walras on November 1, 1883, in which he wrote: "It happens, however, that in order to explain the use of a machine that a pupil of mine had made for me to construct a series of rectangular hyperbolas, I read on October 20, 1873 before the Cambridge Philosophical Society a short paper anticipating incidentally your doctrine of stable equilibrium. A brief note of it is contained in Part XV of the 'Proceedings' (not the 'Transactions') of that Society." (F.W. II, 935.) But the "brief note" published in the *Proceedings* of that date (pp. 318–319) reveals nothing more than the bare statements that "under some circumstances, there may be more than one point of intersection" between supply and demand curves, and that "only at every alternative point of intersection can the exchange value remain in *stable* equilibrium: at other points it is in *unstable* equilibrium." Later on, in the first edition of his *Principles of Economics* (1890), where Marshall formulated a definitive version of his characteristic theory

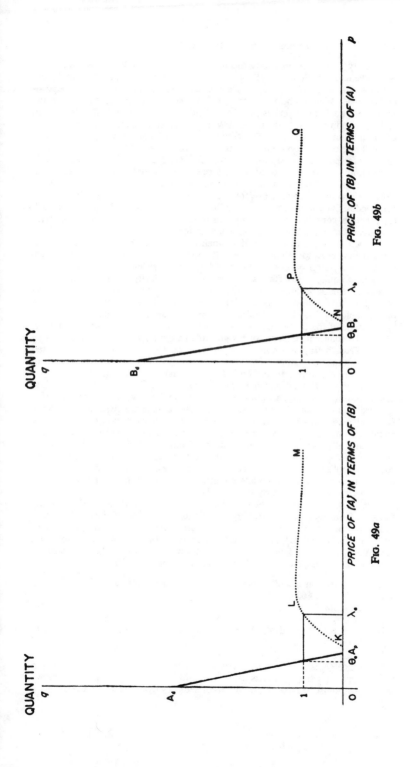

QUANTITY

q

A_4

1

O $\theta_a A_9$ λ_a

K

L

M

PRICE OF (A) IN TERMS OF (B)

Fig. 49a

QUANTITY

q

B_4

1

O $\theta_b B_9$ λ_b p

N

P

Q

PRICE OF (B) IN TERMS OF (A)

Fig. 49b

of stability conditions in a long footnote on pp. 424–425 (cf. pp. 806–807 n. of ed. 8), he ended with a bracketed paragraph, which he omitted from subsequent editions, reading: "*This* theory of unstable equilibrium was published independently by M. Walras and the present writer" (italics inserted). More recently, Professor Paul Samuelson has called the identification of the "so-called Walrasian stability conditions" with the name of Walras "an historical error" ("The Stability of Equilibrium: Comparative Statics and Dynamics", *Econometrica*, vol. IX, no.2, April, 1941, p. 103, footnote 9). It is true, as Professor Samuelson points out, that "as far back as in the *Pure Theory of Foreign Trade* Marshall defined stable equilibrium, in which a so-called backward rising supply curve was involved, exactly as in the Walrasian case." Indeed, in Marshall's *Pure Theory of Foreign Trade* printed originally for private circulation in 1879 and reprinted in 1930 by the London School of Economics and Political Science, we find that his Figure 4, for example, contains an interesting pair of reciprocal-demand curves, each with a segment representing inelastic demand for one of the two commodities exchanged; and it is easily seen that when these curves are geometrically transformed into corresponding price-supply curves referred to conventional Marshallian axes, each of them becomes a "backward rising supply curve" of the other commodity. Nevertheless, before denying priority to Walras in the discovery of this type of stability, two things should be noted. For one thing Marshall's first published elaboration of a theory of instability did not appear in print before 1879, whereas Walras's definitive version was published in the first half-volume of the first edition of the *Eléments* (§§ 66–67) in 1874; for another, Marshall's economic analysis of his graphs in Chapter II of his *Pure Theory of Foreign Trade* betrays a confusion which is reflected again in the footnote quoted above from the first edition of his *Principles* where he implies that his theory and Walras's are the same. In the *Pure Theory* Marshall did not perceive that the criterion of positive or negative excess profits, which is appropriate for the determination of the type of instability characterized by the intersection of a forward falling supply curve (really a long-run cost curve) with a *less* steeply falling demand curve, is not appropriate for the determination of the type of instability characterized by the intersection of a backward rising supply curve (really an "offer" curve) with a *more* steeply falling demand curve. Nowhere did he refer to the criterion of positive or negative excess demand which Walras correctly applied to the second type. Walras, on the other hand, never mentioned the first type, but he did formulate a consistent theory of the second type, which may, therefore, quite properly be called Walrasian.

cf. R. F. Kahn, "The Elasticity of Substitution and the Relative Share of the Factor", *Review of Economic Studies*, vol. I, 1933–1934, pp. 74–75; Jacob Marschak, "Identity and Stability in Economics", *Econometrica*, vol. X, no. 1, January 1942, pp. 70–74; Melvin Warren Reder, *Studies in the Theory of Welfare Economics*, New York, Columbia University Press, 1947, pp. 112–116; William J. Baumol, *Economic Dynamics*, New York, Macmillan, 1951, pp. 117–120.

[6] By hypothesis μ and $\dfrac{1}{\mu}$ represent the equilibrium prices at which $D_a = O_a$ and $O_b = D_b$. See §60.

[7] See §156.

[8] See §54.

[9] From Fig. 2 of ed. 4; the π_a and π_b rectangles and the Q_a hyperbola inserted.

[10] See §55.

[11] Since Q_b is the numerical value of any rectangular area inscribed within the Q_b hyperbola and represents the total quantity of (B) on the market, it follows that $Q_b \div p_a$ must be an ordinate which coincides by hypothesis with the ordinate

of the demand curve for (A) and must equal $F_a(p_a)$. Substituting $Q_b \dfrac{1}{p_a}$ in (1) of §62 for its equivalent $F_a(p_a)$, we obtain the equation given in the text.

[12] Multiplying both sides of the previous equation

$$Q_b \frac{1}{p_a} = F_b\left(\frac{1}{p_a}\right)\frac{1}{p_a}$$

by p_a and substituting p_b for $\dfrac{1}{p_a}$, we have

$$Q_b = F_b(p_b).$$

Since the previous equation is a special case of equation (1) of §62 and since equation (2) of §62 is simply another form of equation (1), the equation derived above is the same as equation (2).

[13] We have seen above in note [11] of this Lesson that $Q_b \div p_a = F_a(p_a)$. But $F_a(p_a) = Q_a$, since $F_a(p_a) = D_a$ and $D_a = Q_a$. The offer of (A) always being Q_a whatever the price may be, it follows that $Q_b \div p_a = Q_a$. Similarly $Q_a \div p_b = Q_b$.

LESSON 8

[1] 'utilité *d'extension* ou *extensive*'.

[2] cf. Auguste Walras, *De la nature de la richesse*, p. 150 (1831) or p. 175 (1938): "Après avoir considéré l'utilité dans son *intensité*, on peut et on doit même la considérer encore dans son *extension*. Les besoins auxquels nous sommes soumis ne se distinguent pas seulement par leur plus ou moins grande urgence; ils se distinguent aussi par leur étendue, ou par le nombre des hommes qui les éprouvent." Three years later, Montifort Longfield wrote in his *Lectures on Political Economy*, delivered the year before at Dublin: "By the extent of utility I of course mean the number of persons whose wants and wishes can be satisfied by the object, and the imperiousness of those desires in demanding their proper gratification." (Reprint No. 8 published by the London School of Economics and Political Science, 1931, p. 26.)

While Léon Walras endows his father's vague notions of "extensive utility" with mathematically precise meaning, defining it as the intercept of the demand curve (individual or collective?) on the quantity axis, his use of the word "utility" and his reference to any "number of people ('selon que plus ou moins d'hommes les éprouvent')" in this connection are unfortunate, for, by his own subsequent use of the term utility, he properly restricted it to individual psychological reactions to goods. Since little further reference is made to this concept and no other use is made of it, the damage is negligible.

[3] This is only true provided that an individual's demand for (A) and for (B) are independent of each other. If (A) and (B) were completing or competing goods, then their respective "extensive utilities" would not be autonomous phenomena, because the "extensive utility" of each would depend upon the terms on which the other could be procured. cf. Vilfredo Pareto, *Manuel d'économie politique*, Chapter IV, §§ 9–20; Henry Schultz, *The Theory and Measurement of Demand*, pp. 569–582.

[4] 'utilité *d'intensité* ou *intensive*'.

[5] From Fig. 1 of ed. 4.

[6] See §55.

[7] It should be noted that the arbitrary unit which Walras adopts for measuring the imponderable utility of commodities is a unit of *intensity* of want. This is not altogether appropriate. The intensity of desire, represented on Walras's utility curves by the length of the abscissas, is a derived and not a fundamental

dimension. As is seen a little farther on (§75) it is measured by the derivative of total (effective) utility with respect to the quantity of the commodity affording the utility. In other words, it is a complex magnitude composed of two magnitudes, the utility and the quantity of the commodity, which are set in such a relation to each other as to indicate the rate of increase of utility per unit of the commodity acquired. Since Walras was seeking a standard that might be applied "not only to similar units of the same kind of wealth but also to different units of various kinds of wealth", he ought to have defined this standard in terms of a fundamental dimension, viz. utility itself. This is, in effect, what Wicksteed does when he arbitrarily takes a small square of a given size to represent a unit to which different satisfactions can be reduced, and in which they can be expressed for diagrammatic comparison with each other. (Philip H. Wicksteed, *The Common Sense of Political Economy*, edited by Lionel Robbins, vol. II, pp. 440–441.) cf. W. S. Jevons, *Theory of Political Economy*, ed. 4, London, Macmillan, 1911, pp. 61–69, on the "Theory of Dimensions of Economic Quantities" and P. H. Wicksteed's article "Dimensions of Economic Quantities" in Robert H. I. Palgrave's *Dictionary of Political Economy*, London, Macmillan, 1926.

[8] From Fig. 3 of ed. 4.

[9] After careful consideration of alternatives, the translator decided to leave Walras's term '*rareté*' in French and italicize it whenever the word is used in the technical sense to denote the derivative of the total utility of a commodity to an individual with respect to the quantity he possesses of that good. In English this mathematical concept was called "final degree of utility" by Jevons and "marginal degree of utility" by Marshall; but to translate '*rareté*' into either one of these terms, or into the usual current abbreviation "marginal utility" would be to rob the text of its characteristic Walrasian flavour. In practically all references to Walras's utility theory in the English language, the word '*rareté*' is retained in the French, so that the word can now be said to be traditionally associated with Walras. Only when '*rareté*' is used in the ordinary literary sense, as in §21 of the *Elements*, is it translated as "scarcity". See above Lesson 3, Translator's Note [1] and §21.

It may be contended that Léon Walras would have done better to have chosen a word less vague and less ambiguous to express his mathematically precise concept; but it was clearly out of filial piety that he perpetuated in his own work his father's favourite term '*rareté*'. Auguste Walras had made significant use of the term in his *De la nature de la richesse*, where he defines it as the "disproportion naturelle entre la somme de ces biens [limités dans leur quantité] et la somme des besoins qui en réclament la possession" (p. 41).

'*Rareté*', when used to designate the intensity of the last want satisfied, or the derivative of total utility with respect to the quantity possessed, has exactly the same significance as Jevons's "final degree of utility", which Jevons defines as the differential coefficient of total utility considered as a function of quantity. (W. S. Jevons, *The Theory of Political Economy*, p. 51.) Walras acknowledged Jevons's prior use of this concept in his letter to Jevons of May 23, 1874, published in the *Théorie mathématique de la richesse sociale*, Lausanne, Corbaz, 1883, pp. 28–31. Unquestionably Wicksteed is right in identifying Gossen's "Werth der letzten Atome" with Walras's '*rareté*' (see P. H. Wicksteed's article, "Final Degree of Utility", in Palgrave's *Dictionary of Political Economy*), since Gossen means by that expression "die Grösse der Genüsse bei ihrem Abbrechen" (Hermann Heinrich Gossen, *Entwickelung der Gesetze des menschlichen Verkehrs und der daraus fliessenden Regeln für menschliches Handeln*, Berlin, R. L. Prager, 1927, ed. 3, p. 15), or better "der Differential-Coëfficient $\frac{dW}{dE'}$", W being the sum total of satisfactions and E' being the time during which the source of satisfaction is being consumed at a uniform rate (*ibid.*, p. 18). It is, however, erroneous to state as Wicksteed (*loc. cit.*), Lilly Hecht (*op. cit.*, p. 46), and Walras himself (see Appendix I, §1) have stated, that the Austrian term "Grenznutzen" means precisely the same thing as Walras's '*rareté*' or Jevons's "final degree of utility". The earliest appearance of the Austrian concept of "Grenznutzen"—in all but the name—is found in Carl Menger's *Grundsätze der Volkswirtschaftslehre*, Vienna, Braumüller, 1871 (Reprint No. 17 published by the London School of Economics and Political Science, 1934), p. 99. There he says that the value of any given portion of the stock of a commodity in the hands of an individual is equal to the "Bedeutung, welche die am wenigsten wichtigen der durch die Gesamtquantität noch gesicherten und mit einer gleichen Teilquantität herbeizuführenden Bedürfnisbefriedigungen für [diese Person] haben". That this is the accepted Austrian conception of "Grenznutzen" can be seen in the approval with which Eugen von Böhm-Bawerk quotes the foregoing passage in support of his own theory of value. He himself defines the "Grenznutzen" of a good as "die an der Grenze des ökonomisch zulässigen stehenden kleinsten Nutzen" (*Grundzüge der Theorie des wirtschaftlichen Güterwerts*, Conrad's *Jahrbücher für Nationalökonomie und Statistik*, Neue Folge, Band 13, 1886; Reprint No. 11 published by the London School of Economics and Political Science, 1932, p. 29). In the same place Böhm-Bawerk refers also to p. 128 of Friedrich von Wieser's *Über den Ursprung und die Hauptgesetze des wirtschaftlichen Werthes*, Vienna, Hölder, 1884, where the term "Grenznutzen" is first used and defined as follows: "Ich werde im Folgenden den für den Werth des Gütereinheit entscheidenden Güternutzen, weil er an der Grenze der wirtschaftlich zugelassenen Verwendungen steht, den wirtschaftlichen Grenznutzen oder auch kurzweg den Grenznutzen nennen (vergl. die Ausdrücke '*final degree of utility*' und '*terminal utility*' bei Jevons)." It is evident that "Grenznutzen", as used by the Austrians and as the German word itself indicates, means the marginal increment of utility afforded by a "Teilquantität der verfügbaren Gütermenge" (Menger), by a "Gütereinheit" (von Wieser) or by a "Güterexemplar" (Böhm-Bawerk). Although von Wieser implied that his "Grenznutzen" was the same thing as Jevons's "final degree of utility", and even though he states "Der Nutzen müsste graphisch durch eine Linie . . . dargestellt werden" (*op. cit.*, p. 129), still it is clear from the context that—mathematically speaking—he means not the derivative of utility with respect to quantity but the differential increment of utility, and that by a "Linie" for representing "Grenznutzen" graphically he cannot mean a mathematical straight line without thickness but rather what Marshall, using more careful language, called a "very thin parallelogram" or a "thick straight line" of which the breadth measured the unit affording the marginal satisfaction (Marshall, *op. cit.*, ed. 8, p. 128, note 1). If the Austrians really meant to designate a degree of utility by "Grenznutzen", Böhm-Bawerk at least might have defined it in terms of the "Wichtigkeitsgraden" which he uses in his famous table (*op. cit.*, pp. 25–31). cf. Marshall *Principles*, ed. 8, Mathematical Appendix, note 1, p. 838.

[10] For mathematical proof of this proposition, see below Translator's Note [16] of this Lesson.

[11] Starting with $o_b = d_a p_a$ and substituting $\frac{r_{a,1}}{r_{b,1}}$ for p_a, we obtain $o_b = d_a \frac{r_{a,1}}{r_{b,1}}$ whence by clearing of fractions, we derive the equation referred to in the text.

[12] Multiplying each side of the inequality $r_a > p_a r_b$ by corresponding sides of the equality $\frac{d_a}{s} p_a = \frac{o_b}{s}$, we obtain $\frac{d_a}{s} p_a r_a > p_a r_b \frac{o_b}{s}$, from which p_a may be eliminated to give the equation referred to in the text.

[13] From Fig. 3 of ed. 4; broken lines inserted.

[14] See §§86–89.

[15] We know from §76 that $r_{a,1}=\varphi_{a,1}(d_a)$ and $r_{b,1}=\varphi_{b,1}(y)$; and from §77 that $o_b=d_a p_a$.

[16] To prove that this equation is a condition of maximum satisfaction, let it be recalled that in the expression $\Phi_{a,1}(d_a)+\Phi_{b,1}(q_b-o_b)$, which measures the total effective utility to be maximized, d_a and o_b are the only variables. Hence

$$\Phi_{a,1}(d_a)+\Phi_{b,1}(q_b-o_b)=f(d_a,o_b). \qquad ..(1a)$$

It is only necessary to set the total differential of this equation equal to zero for a maximum (or minimum), thus:

$$df(d_a,o_b)=\Phi'_{a,1}(d_a)dd_a+\Phi'_{b,1}(q_b-o_b)d(q_b-o_b)=0. \qquad ..(1b)$$

We are now in a position to demonstrate the proposition taken for granted in §76, that the equation $\dfrac{r_{a,1}}{r_{b,1}}=p_a$ is a condition of maximum satisfaction. Substituting $r_{a,1}$ for $\Phi'_{a,1}(d_a)$ and $r_{b,1}$ for $\Phi'_{b,1}(q_b-o_b)$ in equation (1b) above, we obtain

$$r_{a,1}\,dd_a+r_{b,1}d(q_b-o_b)=0, \qquad ..(2a)$$

whence

$$\frac{r_{a,1}}{r_{b,1}}=\frac{-d(q_b-o_b)}{dd_a}. \qquad ..(2b)$$

Now taking the differential of equation (1) in the text,

$$d_a p_a+(q_b-o_b)=q_b,$$

in which q_b and p_a are constants, we have

$$p_a dd_a+d(q_b-o_b)=0, \qquad ..(3a)$$

whence

$$p_a=\frac{-d(q_b-o_b)}{dd_a}. \qquad ..(3b)$$

Since p_a and $\dfrac{r_{a,1}}{r_{b,1}}$ are equal to the same thing, in (2b) and (3b), it follows that $p_a=\dfrac{r_{a,1}}{r_{b,1}}$ when $\Phi_{a,1}(d_a)+\Phi_{b,1}(q_b-o_b)$ is a maximum subject to the budget equation (1) in the text.

[17] Obtained by taking differentials of equation (1) in which p_a is a constant. The differential of q_b is zero, because q_b is, by hypothesis, a constant. In the second term of the equation the price factor is not indicated because the price of (B) in terms of (B) is unity.

[18] This equation is derived from the two preceding equations by substituting $\varphi_{a,1}(d_a)$ for $\Phi'_{a,1}(d_a)$, $\varphi_{b,1}(q_b-d_a p_a)$ for $\Phi'_{b,1}(q_b-o_b)$ (§§75 and 77) and $-p_a dd_a$ for $d(q_b-o_b)$. Then it is only necessary to transpose and divide through by dd_a.

[19] $\dfrac{d[\Phi_{a,1}(d_a)]}{dd_a}=\Phi'_{a,1}(d_a)=\varphi_{a,1}(d_a)$

and

$$\frac{d[\Phi_{b,1}(q_b-d_a p_a)]}{dd_a}=\Phi'_{b,1}(q_b-d_a p_a)\frac{d(q_b-d_a p_a)}{dd_a}$$
$$=-p_a\varphi_{b,1}(q_b-d_a p_a).$$

[20] Since the successive increments of (A), $d_a d''_a$ and $d_a d'''_a$ are each equal to unity by hypothesis, it follows that $d_a \mathbf{a}$ and $d'''_a \mathbf{a}'''$ designate respectively the numerical values of the areas $d_a d''_a \times d_a \mathbf{a}$ and $d_a d'''_a \times d''_a \mathbf{a}'''$. The inequalities in the text mean, therefore, that the decrement in effective utility resulting from the relinquishment of the last parcel of (B), yy'', given up in exchange, is less than the increment of effective utility received from the last unit of (A), $d_a d''_a$, obtained in exchange; and that the decrement in effective utility that would result if another equal parcel of (B), yy''', were given up would be greater than the increment of effective utility that would be gained from another unit, $d_a d'''_a$, of (A) obtained in exchange.

[21] By adding the two equations immediately above and dividing both sides by $m'' + m'''$.

[22] Since m'' is a little shorter than $y\beta$ and m''' is a little longer than $y\beta$.

[23] Since the numerator $\varepsilon'' - \varepsilon'''$ is the difference between very small quantities.

[24] From Fig. 3 of ed. 4.

[25] Because $p_a = yy'' = yy'''$.

[26] The **r** symbols are printed in a distinctive type in the original text of this passage in order to indicate, it may be surmised, that the *raretés* of (A) are constant over finite intervals in the case of a discontinuous *rareté* function for this commodity.

[27] Since the series $q_b - p_a$, $q_b - 2p_a$ ... is cumulative as well as successive, it would have been more consistent with what precedes to write the limits of the integrals expressing the effective utilities of (B) relinquished as 1, 2 ... units of (A) are acquired, as follows:

$$\int_{q_b - p_a}^{q_b} \varphi_{b,1}(q)dq \qquad \int_{q_b - 2p_a}^{q_b} \varphi_{b,1}(q)dq \dots.$$

[28] For a discussion of the effect of discontinuous *rareté* curves on price determination, see §§ 133–137.

LESSON 9

[1] See § 81.

[2] From Fig. 3 of ed. 4. Broken lines inserted.

[3] All editions read $a_{d,1}$, which is obviously a typographical error.

[4] From Fig. 4 of ed. 4.

[5] i.e. the lengths $q_{a,1} a_{p,1}$ and $q_{b,1} b_{p,1}$.

[6] This is simply another form of the equation

$$d_a v_a = o_b v_b$$

or

$$d_b v_b = o_a v_a.$$

If we substitute a positive x_1 for d_a or a negative x_1 for o_a and if we substitute a positive y_1 for d_b and a negative y_1 for o_b, the equations reduce to $x_1 v_a + y_1 v_b = 0$.

[7] Remembering that $\dfrac{v_a}{v_b} = p_a$ and $\dfrac{v_b}{v_a} = p_b$ from § 44, and that $y_1 = -x_1 p_a$, and $x_1 = -y_1 p_b$ from § 94.

[8] Even if the price of one of the commodities, say (A), is such as to make a given holder wish that he had more of that commodity to sell than he possesses, he will, of course, not be able to sell more than he has. Consequently he will be compelled to stop selling before $\varphi_{a,1}(q_{a,1} + x_1) = p_a \varphi_{b,1}(q_{b,1} - x_1 p_a)$. In fact, $p_a \varphi_{b,1}(q_{b,1} - x_1 p_a)$ will be indeterminably greater than $\varphi_{a,1}(q_{a,1} + x_1)$. In other

words, it becomes otiose, under these circumstances, to formulate the solution
in terms of *raretés*, the only relation determinable being the quantitative ones,
$x_1 = -q_{a,1}$ and $y_1 p_b = q_{a,1}$.

[9] This simply makes explicit the fact that in the first equation, which may
be written

$$\varphi_{a,1}(q_{a,1}+x_1) - p_a \varphi_{b,1}(q_{b,1} - x_1 p_a) = 0,$$

where $q_{a,1}$ and $q_{b,1}$ are taken to be constants, x_1 is an implicit function of p_a.
Similarly in the second equation y_1 is an implicit function of p_b. See § 81.

[10] Where p_a is an equilibrium price the sum of the positive $f_a(p_a)$'s, i.e. of
the d_a's, must equal in numerical value the sum of the negative $f_a(p_a)$'s, i.e. of the
o_a's, so that their algebraic sum must equal zero. Likewise where p_b is an equilibrium price the algebraic sum total of the $f_b(p_b)$'s, some positive (i.e. the d_b's)
and some negative (i.e. the o_b's), must equal zero.

[11] The positive x lengths are measured above the $q_{a,1}p$, $q_{a,2}p$, $q_{a,3}p$...
axes for given values of p_a; and the positive y lengths are measured above the
$q_{b,1}p$, $q_{b,2}p$, $q_{b,3}p$... axes for given values of p_b, as seen in Fig. 16.

[12] The negative x and y lengths are measured below the $q_a p$ and the $q_b p$ axes
respectively in Fig. 16.

[13] cf. J. R. Hicks, *Value and Capital*, ed. 2, p. 63, where "the difference
between demand and supply at any price" is called "excess demand". Walras's
X and Y are, in Hicks's terminology, the "excess demand" for (A) and (B)
respectively.

[14] See § 64.

LESSON 10

[1] Wicksell interprets this passage to mean that: "under free competition and
under the existing laws of property, each of the exchanging parties obtains the
maximum amount of satisfaction for his needs with *any* system of *uniform* price
in the market". Then he proceeds to criticize this doctrine of maximized utility
under free competition on two grounds: first, since multiple equilibria are possible,
as Walras himself admits (§§ 65–68), they cannot all represent positions of
maximum satisfaction; and second, given social differences and an unequal
distribution of property, it is possible for exchange at suitably determined prices
prescribed by public authorities to yield a higher sum total of satisfactions than
would be obtained under free competition (*Knut Wicksell Lectures on Political
Economy*, vol. I, pp. 73–83).

The first criticism is not as serious as it appears. The want of a unique solution
(see above Translator's Note [1] of Lesson 7) is not fatal to the theory as an
economic theory. In judging the validity of economic conclusions mathematically
arrived at, there are cases where it might well be misleading to confine oneself to
criteria that are purely mathematical. Professor Edwin B. Wilson, in his review
of Pareto's *Manuel d'économie politique*, indicated the difference between pure
mathematics and its applications as follows: "To many modern mathematicians
the fear that the equations might be either redundant or incompatible would
probably be so strong as to deter them from seeing much of value in the analysis.
But it should be remembered that not so very long ago the method of counting
constants was widely used in pure mathematics even though the science was then
much more highly developed towards arithmetic equations than is now the case
with economics. Moreover, in a physical science the question of rigour is very
different from that in mathematics; to be ultra-rigorous mathematically may be
to be infra-rigorous physically. To throw out Gibb's phase because its proof,
being essentially a count of constants, is no proof at all, would be equally good
mathematics and equally bad physics. On the other hand, setting up exact

mathematical relations, compatible and uniquely soluble, over the whole range of variation of the variables might be a wonderful mathematical *tour de force* while being viciously misleading physics in the neighbourhood of certain critical points where a slight change of the variables introduces such wide variations in the functions as to make the problem just as indeterminate physically as it has become determinate mathematically." (*Bulletin of the American Mathematical Society*, June 1912, p. 470, cited by Professor Henry Schultz in his review of Griffith C. Evans's "Mathematical Introduction to Economics" in the *Journal of the American Statistical Association*, December 1931, p. 487.)

Whether Wicksell's second criticism is valid or not depends on the interpretation placed on the obscure passage under discussion. If, as Wicksell appears to interpret it, this passage means that when the utilities of all the individuals in the market are added up, the sum total is greater under perfect competition than under any other régime, then Walras's generalization is clearly wrong. Only if all incomes were approximately equal (and only if it is assumed that all utilities are susceptible of interpersonal comparisons and all utility functions relating to income are the same for all individuals) would such a maximum result from the free play of offer and demand. Otherwise, a system of administered uniform prices can usually be found at which exchanges will produce a larger sum total of utility for society as a whole. Walras, however, makes no assumption of equality of income or of '*quantités possédées*', but takes the distribution of property or income as he finds it. Hence, Walras's unqualified generalization is an error —"almost tragic", according to Wicksell.

On another interpretation, Walras was not wrong at all. In fact, there is very little justification for following Wicksell in attributing to Walras any hypothesis of interpersonal comparisons of utility. Though Walras supposes that *rareté* can be defined as a cardinal magnitude (§74), nowhere does he allude to any actual addition of the utilities enjoyed by different persons; and though he later refers to average *raretés* for the market as a whole (§101) and makes use of this concept in his theory of money (§279), the addibility implied in the averaging process is always purely formal, never real. It seems, therefore, more in accord with the whole tenor of Walras's utility analysis to assume that he precludes interpersonal comparisons of utility. If, then, we reject Wicksell's interpretation, two possibilities remain. Either Walras means by maximum utility for society as a whole a situation in which it is impossible to increase the utility of any one party without decreasing that of another once competitive equilibrium has been attained or he means something so vague as to defy any clear interpretation at all. The acceptance of the first possibility presupposes that Walras had a premonition of the Paretian welfare principle (Vilfredo Pareto, *Manuel d'économie politique*, pp. 617–618). There is nothing in Walras that would contradict such a generous interpretation. Given any predetermined distribution of property or income, an "optimum" position is automatically reached under perfect competition in which no individual can be made better off without making someone else worse off. So long as interpersonal comparisons are not admitted, it is impossible to add algebraically the positive and negative increments of utility accruing to different persons as the result of a shift from this position. That some other distribution of property or income could yield a better "optimum" may be freely granted, but Walras was not concerned with such problems here. Moreover, since multiple equilibria may very well coexist under the Paretian welfare principle, Wicksell's first criticism relating to multiple equilibria is disposed of at once.

[2] When the missing term $r_{b,3}$ is replaced by $(p_b r_{a,3})$ in the table of ratios of *raretés*, we have

$$v_a : v_b :: r_{a,3} : (p_b r_{a,3})$$

which reduces to the identity

$$\frac{v_a}{v_b} = \frac{r_{a,2}}{p_b r_{a,2}} = \frac{1}{p_b} = p_a \quad (\S 44).$$

This preserves symmetry in the system of equations; but the economic signifi-cance of such a solution is not clear.

The problem is important, because the extension of the principle of maximum satisfaction to the theories of production and capitalization depends, in part, upon its solution. Pareto examined the problem in relation to these theories, but his argument, like that of Walras, was developed in terms of the theory of exchange (Vilfredo Pareto, *Cours d'économie politique*, vol II, pp. 212–214, §859, note 3). Wicksell also refers to this same problem in his *Lectures*, vol. I, pp. 68–69, in connection with his discussion of the discontinuity which occurs at those points of the demand and supply curves which correspond to prices of the commodity in question "so *high* that some buyers cease to purchase it, or some sellers dispose of the whole of their stocks" or "so *low* that some sellers will not dispose of any of their stocks, whilst not yet appearing as purchasers. . . ." He then concludes that "in such circumstances, of course, marginal utility has ceased to regulate the quantities of goods demanded or supplied by such persons Yet the mathematical treatment of the problem raises no difficulties, for these quantities now enter into the equations as constants." Thus Wicksell's procedure is not unlike that adopted by Pareto in the above-mentioned note, where the quantity of any commodity or productive service which would have been offered by an individual without change at higher prices than the prevailing one is set down as a constant, its "weighted ophelimity" not appearing among the equations until the quantity becomes again a function of price. See below, Lesson 12, Trans-lator's Notes [5] and [6].

[3] This passage elicited critical comment from Pareto, who quoted only the latter part of Walras's sentence, '. . . il est certain que la rareté est la cause de la valeur d'échange', as if it were the whole sentence (Vilfredo Pareto, *Manuel*, p. 246, note 1). Pareto thought that Walras had strayed from his solitary narrow path of general equilibrium because he was momentarily tempted by the broad highway crowded with literary economists all vainly seeking a *causa causans* of value. It seems more probable that this lapse from mathematical virtue was simply a gesture of deference to Léon Walras's revered father who first pro-pounded the doctrine that *rareté* was the "cause de la valeur" in 1831 (Auguste Walras, *De la nature de la richesse et de l'origine de la valeur*, p. 41 (1831) or p. 95 (1938).

When we take account of Walras's conditional clause, 'Or, s'il est certain que la rareté et la valeur d'échange sont deux phénomènes concomitants et propor-tionnels . . .', which Pareto omitted from his quotation, the passage under consideration appears no less vulnerable. Difficulties still remain, for, in general, even if we are sure that there are no more than two otherwise perfectly independent phenomena linked by a relationship of concomitance and proportionality, we still cannot tell anything about the direction of the causal nexus in a static model. It is impossible to say which of the two phenomena is the cause and which the effect. Moreover, when we are not sure that there are only two otherwise independent phenomena involved in the system, or when, as in this case, we know that there are additional elements intimately connected with the two under consideration, then mere concomitance and proportionality without any indica-tion of logical sequence subject to empirical verification, give no clue at all to the nature of the causal relation. Not only are *raretés* invariably proportional to prices in a freely competitive market at equilibrium, but costs of production are, in most instances, proportional as well. Which of the three—*rareté*, cost of production, or value—is *the* cause and which are the effects? This turns out to be a meaningless question, for there is no conceivable way of refuting any one of the three possible answers under static assumptions. Walras's pious restatement of his father's doctrine is, therefore, untenable; but fortunately it plays no essential role in his system. Actually it is no more than an *obiter dictum.* Later on, he makes it perfectly plain that "theoretically all the unknowns of the economic problem are determined by all the equations of general equilibrium" (§266). In such a system the concept of causality is an anomaly.

LESSON 11

[1] The following diagram illustrates two of the possible six surfaces in space referred to a universe of three commodities. The surface $MLRST$ in Fig. 50a depicts the quantity of (A) demanded in exchange for (B) as a function of the prices of (A) and (C) in terms of (B); while the surface $M'L'R'S'T'$ in Fig. 50b depicts the quantity of (B) demanded in exchange for (A) as a function of the prices of (B) and (C) in terms of (A). The equations of the two surfaces are respectively

$$D_{a,b}=F_{a,b}(p_{a,b}, p_{c,b}),$$
$$D_{b,a}=F_{b,a}(p_{b,a}, p_{c,a}).$$

The curves MS and $M'S'$ are vertical sections found by cutting the surfaces by planes perpendicular to the $Op_{c,b}$ and $Op_{c,a}$ axes at the arbitrarily fixed points K and K' respectively. The equations of the curves MS and $M'S'$ are

$$D_{a,b}=F_{a,b}(p_{a,b}, K),$$
$$D_{b,a}=F_{b,a}(p_{b,a}, K').$$

The curve MS is, therefore, the demand function of (A) in exchange for (B), when the price of (C) in terms of (B) is assigned a value K; while the curve $M'S'$ is the demand function of (B) in exchange for (A), when the price of (C) in terms of (A) is assigned a value K'.

The curves RST and $R'S'T'$ are simply the loci of pairs of prices at which in the one case no (A) is demanded in exchange for (B) and in the other no (B) is demanded in exchange for (A). They are both negatively inclined with respect to their corresponding horizontal (east-west) axes, because, to take one instance, the higher the price of (C) in terms of (B), the lower the price of (A) in terms of (B) at which the demand for (A) in exchange for (B) falls to zero.

Under these conditions equilibrium is attained when the base of the shaded rectangle inscribed within MS in the plane MSK is the reciprocal of the base of the shaded rectangle inscribed within $M'S'$ in the plane $M'S'K'$ and at the same time the number of units of altitude of one rectangle equals the number of units of area of the other rectangle in accordance with the equations $D_{a,b}=D_{b,a}p_{b,a}$ and $D_{b,a}=D_{a,b}p_{a,b}$. As Walras indicates in §111, the equilibrium here illustrated is not general, for it is established only between commodities (A) and (B), the price of (C) in terms of either (A) or (B) being altogether arbitrary. At this stage in the argument, this is all that can be done, for general equilibrium involving all three commodities cannot be determined until the six equilibrium price functions are determined on the basis of the theorem of maximum satisfaction, given the *rareté* curves of the three commodities (see Lesson 12).

[2] i.e. assuming that $p_{o,b}$ is greater than the ratio of $p_{c,a}$ to $p_{b,a}$.

[3] $\dfrac{p_{c,b}}{\alpha}$ is less than $p_{c,b}$, since $\alpha>1$.

[4] In the equation $p_{c,b}=\alpha\dfrac{p_{c,a}}{p_{b,a}}$, let $p_{c,b}=4, p_{c,a}=6$, and $p_{b,a}=2$, then $4=\alpha 6/2$, which makes $\alpha=4/3$ or $1\cdot33$.

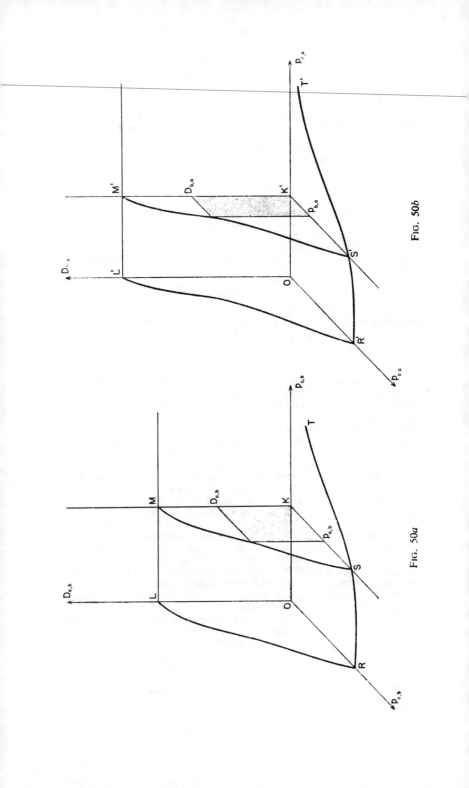

FIG. 50b

FIG. 50a

[5] cf. F. Y. Edgeworth, *Papers Relating to Political Economy*, vol. II, pp. 311–312: "He [Walras] describes *a* rather than *the* way by which economic equilibrium is reached. For we have no general *dynamical* theory determining the path of the economic system from any point assigned at random to a position of equilibrium. We only know the statical properties of the position; . . . Walras's laboured description of prices set up or 'cried' in the market is calculated to divert the attention from a sort of higgling which may be regarded as more fundamental than his conception, the process of *recontract*. . . ." Pareto, while admitting that Walras only describes *a* way of arriving at equilibrium, maintains that "the way indicated by Mr. Walras is indeed the one that represents the major part of the economic phenomena" (*Cours*, p. 25). This defence of Walras is weak, for it carries the argument to the empirical plane, whereas Edgeworth's criticism is essentially formal in character. What Edgeworth objects to is Walras's implicit assumption that the *path followed* by the arbitrage operations does not influence the result.

[6] As in the case of the word *rareté* (see above, Translator's Note [9] of Lesson 8), *numéraire* is left untranslated in order to retain the peculiar Walrasian flavour associated with the special use to which Walras put the term. He was probably the first to employ *numéraire* to designate a commodity, which in all other respects is like any other commodity (having a *rareté* function of its own for each and every individual), except that it also serves as a standard in terms of which the prices of all the other commodities are expressed. John R. Hicks, in a passage obviously inspired by Walras, calls this commodity a "standard commodity" (*Value and Capital*, p. 58); but other recent books and articles dealing with general equilibrium economics and econometrics in English simply use the term *numéraire* as such in the sense of a "standard commodity" (e.g. Jacob L. Mosak, *General Equilibrium Theory in International Trade*, Bloomington, Indiana, Principia Press, 1944, p. 9; and Paul Anthony Samuelson, *Foundations of Economic Analysis*, Cambridge, Harvard University Press, 1947, *passim*), so that the French word bids fair to become part of the English language. For a fuller discussion of Walras's concept of a *numéraire* and for an apposite warning against confusing this concept with that of an *abstract* money-of-account, see Arthur W. Marget, "Monetary Aspects of the Walrasian System", *Journal of Political Economy*, vol. XLIII, no. 2, April 1935, pp. 170–175.

[7] See § 116.

[8] For example, supposing only three commodities in our system, (A), (B) and (M), we should have

$$D_{a,b} + D_{a,m} = D_{b,a}p_b + D_{m,a}p_m,$$

$$D_{b,a} + D_{b,m} = D_{a,b}\frac{1}{p_b} + D_{m,b}\frac{p_m}{p_b},$$

$$D_{m,a} + D_{m,b} = D_{a,m}\frac{1}{p_m} + D_{b,m}\frac{p_b}{p_m}.$$

Now multiplying both sides of the second equation of this system by p_b and both sides of the third by p_m, we obtain

$$D_{b,a}p_b + D_{b,m}p_b = D_{a,b} + D_{m,b}p_m,$$
$$D_{m,a}p_m + D_{m,b}p_m = D_{a,m} + D_{b,m}p_b.$$

Adding the two equations and cancelling equal terms on both sides of the sum, we have:

$$D_{b,a}p_b + \cancel{D_{b,m}p_b} + D_{m,a}p_m + \cancel{D_{m,b}p_m} =$$
$$D_{a,b} + \cancel{D_{m,b}p_m} + D_{a,m} + \cancel{D_{b,m}p_b}$$

or

$$D_{a,b} + D_{a,m} = D_{b,a}p_b + D_{m,a}p_m,$$

which is the same as the first equation in the system we started with. Hence the first equation is redundant.

LESSON 12

[1] See §§79–82. Since $\varphi_{b,1}(q_{b,1}+y_1)=r_{b,1}$ and $\varphi_{a,1}(q_{a,1}+x_1)=r_{a,1}$, $p_{b,a}$ must equal $\dfrac{r_{b,1}}{r_{a,1}}$ or $\dfrac{\varphi_{b,1}(q_{b,1}+y_1)}{\varphi_{a,1}(q_{a,1}+x_1)}$ after the final exchange resulting in maximum satisfaction.

[2] The following illustrates the mathematical procedure by which $m-1$ of the unknown quantities exchanged are successively eliminated. For purposes of simplification, let us suppose that there are only three commodities in our system: (A), (B), (C); and let us designate the quantities of each of these commodities which party (1) gives up or receives by the unknowns x_1, y_1, and z_1 respectively. Then the m equations with which we start will be

$$x_1+y_1p_b+z_1p_c=0$$

and

$$\varphi_{b,1}(q_{b,1}+y_1)=p_b\varphi_{a,1}(q_{a,1}+x_1),$$
$$\varphi_{c,1}(q_{c,1}+z_1)=p_c\varphi_{a,1}(q_{a,1}+x_1).$$

From the first of these equations we know that

$$x_1=-(y_1p_b+z_1p_c).$$

Substituting in the next two equations and transposing we obtain

$$\varphi_{b,1}(q_{b,1}+y_1)-p_b\varphi_{a,1}(q_{a,1}-y_1p_b-z_1p_c)=0,$$
$$\varphi_{c,1}(q_{c,1}+z_1)-p_c\varphi_{a,1}(q_{a,1}-y_1p_b-z_1p_c)=0.$$

From this system of two equations with two unknowns we may suppose it possible now to eliminate one of the unknowns. In the first, for example, z_1 is an implicit function of y_1 which we may express explicitly by $\psi_{b,1}(y_1)$. Substituting in the second of the above equations we have

$$\varphi_{c,1}[q_{c,1}+\psi_{b,1}(y_1)]-p_c\varphi_{a,1}[q_{a,1}-y_1p_b-p_c\psi_{b,1}(y_1)]=0.$$

Solving now for y_1 and remembering that p_b and p_c are variables while $q_{a,1}$ and $q_{c,1}$ are constants, we obtain

$$y_1=f_{b,1}(p_b, p_c).$$

In like manner we see that y_1 is an implicit function of z_1 which may be expressed explicitly by $\psi'_{c,1}(z_1)$. Substituting in the first of our system of two equations we have

$$\varphi_{b,1}[q_{b,1}+\psi_{c,1}(z_1)]-p_c\varphi_{a,1}[q_{a,1}-p_b\psi_{c,1}(z_1)-p_cz_1]=0.$$

Solving now for z_1 and remembering that p_b and p_c are variables while $q_{a,1}$ and $q_{b,1}$ are constants, we obtain

$$z_1=f_{c,1}(p_b, p_c).$$

[3] Starting with $x_1+y_1p_b+z_1p_c+w_1p_d+\ldots=0$ and substituting $-q_{b,1}$ for y_1, we have

$$x_1+z_1p_c+w_1p_d+\ldots=q_{b,1}p_b.$$

By substituting for p_b, $p_c\ldots$ the values given by $p_b=\dfrac{\varphi_{b,1}(0)}{\varphi_{a,1}(q_{a,1}+x_1)}$;

$p_c=\dfrac{\varphi_{c,1}(q_{c,1}+z_1)}{\varphi_{a,1}(q_{a,1}+x_1)}\ldots$ and then multiplying both sides of the equation by

$\varphi_{a,1}(q_{a,1}+x_1)$, we obtain the equation referred to in the text.

[4] cf. italicized the proposition in §88, which is simply a special case of this theorem. The areas to be equated are, on the one hand, the sum of the rectangular utility areas of commodities (A), (C), (D)..., like the shaded area $\overline{q_{a,1}+x_1 q_{a,1} a\alpha'}$ of commodity (A) in Fig. 51a; and, on the other hand, the utility area $q_{b,1} O\beta_{r,1} B$ in Fig. 51b relating to commodity (B) of which the entire original stock is being offered.

[5] The meaning of the qualifying phrase, 'dans certains cas', is vague. What Walras may have had in mind was the case of a commodity which has no *direct* utility for the party in question. Our individual would then give up all he had of this commodity. This interpretation is inferred, not from the text, but from an unpublished letter Walras addressed to Pareto on June 3, 1893. This was a reply to the latter's question asking how Walras calculated the *rareté* of capital goods which yielded no consumable services and had no *rareté* of their own. Pareto felt that equations involving *rareté* functions for such goods were indispensable to a system of equations of production. Walras, on the other hand, argued as follows: "Pour vous donner l'explication que vous me demandez je dois m'appuyer sur l'observation que je vous ai déjà faite, il y a quelques jours, au sujet du *processus* exact de la détermination du prix courant et qui est celle-ci: 'La considération de la rareté et l'équation de satisfaction maxima dans laquelle entrent la rareté et le prix ne déterminent pas les *prix courants* mais la *quantité demandée ou offerte à un prix crié au hasard*. Le prix courant est déterminé par l'équation exprimant l'égalité des quantités totales demandées et offertes.' Cela posé, lorsque l'utilité est nulle, il y a constamment offre (et non demande) et *offre égale à la quantité possédée*. Cette offre s'ajoute aux autres offres pour fournir l'inégalité puis l'égalité des quantités totales demandées et offertes d'où résulte le prix-courant. Il ne manque donc aucune équation pour la résolution du problème. Cette observation est générale et s'applique aux services comme aux produits et aux services producteurs comme aux services consommables.

"Pour vous mettre à même de vous édifier à fond sur ce point, je dois vous faire remarquer: (1) que le cas particulier de l'offre égale à la quantité possédée par suite *d'utilité nulle*, est compris dans le cas général d'offre égale à la quantité possédée avec utilité réelle; *que le prix de la marchandise à demander est égal ou inférieur au rapport de l'intensité du dernier besoin qui peut être satisfait de cette marchandise à l'intensité du besoin maximum de la marchandise à offrir* et (2) que ce dernier cas se traite mathématiquement en vertu de la théorie et de la formule de la satisfaction maxima.

"Dans mon volume j'ai fait cette discussion avec soin pour l'échange de deux marchandises entre elles (pp. 111–112 [of ed. 2; §§85–87 of ed. 4 def.]) et pour l'échange d'un nombre quelconque de marchandises entre elles (pp. 145–146 [of ed. 2; §§119–120 of ed. 4 def.]). Mais la question devient beaucoup plus simple et plus claire si l'on emploie pour l'établissement d'une théorie de la satisfaction maxima, dans le cas de l'échange d'un nombre quelconque de marchandises entre elles, le mode géométrique de mon petit mémoire américain (pp. 49–50) [see Appendix I, §2]. Je vous engage beaucoup à le traiter ainsi.

"Non seulement j'ai discuté cette éventualité de l'offre égale à la quantité possédée, mais j'en ai tenu compte dans les tableaux des raretés à l'état d'équilibre soit des produits (pp. 157–158 [of ed. 2; §134 of ed. 4 def.]) soit des services (p. 255 [of ed. 2; §225 of ed. 4 def.]). Je crois qu'après vous être reporté à ces divers passages vous comprendrez parfaitement que les services producteurs n'ont pas d'utilité ni de rareté directes et que cette circonstance n'introduit aucun défaut de conditions mathématiques dans l'établissement de l'équilibre économique." (F.W., I, 428.)

The essence of this reply is that a commodity with no direct utility for a given individual is a special case of those commodities with an initial *rareté* so low that

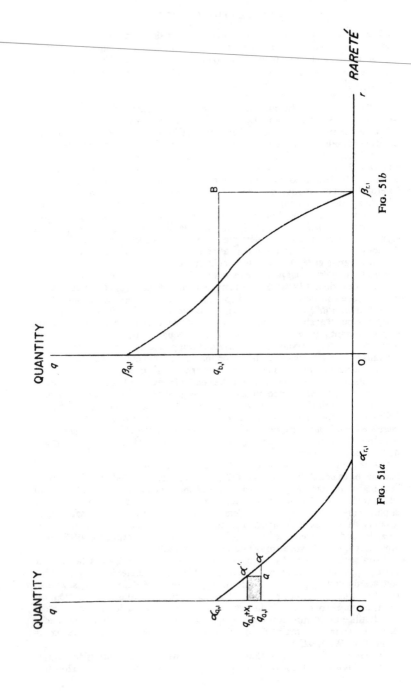

QUANTITY

q

$\alpha_{q,1}$

$q_{q,1}+x_1$
$q_{0,1}$

α'
α
a

O

$\alpha_{r,1}$

Fig. 51a

QUANTITY

q

$\beta_{q,1}$

$q_{b,1}$

B

O

$\beta_{r,1}$

Fig. 51b

RARETÉ

r

TRANSLATOR'S NOTES519

the ratio of the *rareté* of the commodity demanded to the *rareté* of the commodity offered is equal to or greater than the price (§87). Under such circumstances, it would be superfluous to invoke the condition of maximum satisfaction in order to determine the quantity our individual will offer. This quantity is a constant and is predetermined by the quantity possessed. The equilibrium price of such a commodity is, nevertheless, perfectly determinate, for it is the price at which the aggregate quantity demanded is just equal to the fixed aggregate quantity offered. It would be an error to include an equation involving the *rareté* function, for the system would then be over-determined.

Pareto appears to have been satisfied with this reply, for on the same day he wrote the following note to Walras: "Merci. C'est très clair, et c'est bien ainsi que j'entends la résolution du problème. Mais je craignais de n'être pas d'accord avec ce que vous disiez de la production. Je suis maintenant heureux de voir que je suivais entièrement votre manière de voir." (F.W., II, 1777.)

[6] The equation $\varphi_{c,1}(q_{c,1}+z_1)=p_c\varphi_{a,1}(q_{a,1}+x_1)$ has no place in a system where $z_1=-q_{c,1}$, as long as party (1) feels that in order to attain maximum satisfaction at the price p_c, he would have to supply more than $q_{c,1}$. Under these circumstances $z_1=-q_{c,1}$ only because it is materially impossible for z_1 to be greater. In that case $\varphi_{c,1}(q_{c,1}+z_1)$, or the *rareté* of (C) after the exchanges are completed, is indeterminate, and must remain indeterminate until p_c rises (or falls) to such a level that party (1) is only just persuaded to give up his total quantity of (C) to attain maximum satisfaction. Then $\varphi_{c,1}(0)$ would be determinate, p_c would equal $\dfrac{\varphi_{c,1}(0)}{\varphi_{a,1}(q_{a,1}+x_1)}$ and $\varphi_{c,1}(0)=p_c\varphi_{a,1}(q_{a,1}+x_1)$ would find a place in the system.

Pareto describes an analogous case and adopts a similar solution in his *Cours*, §859, note 3 (see above, Translator's Note [2] of Lesson 10). He imagines a labourer working 6 hours a day, who would have been willing to work 7 hours at the same rate of pay. If we let (T) represent labour, and (translating Pareto's notation into Walras's) if we let $U_{t,1}$ or 7 hours represent the amount of labour this individual (1) would have been willing to offer to attain maximum satisfaction within the given price structure, while $-q_{t,1}$ or 6 hours represents the amount of labour actually given, which for one reason or another he may not exceed, then $U_{t,1}$ must be reduced until

$$U_{t,1}=-q_t,$$

i.e.

$$U_{t,1}=6 \text{ hours.}$$

Had $U_{t,1}$ been equal to 7 hours, then

$$\varphi_{t,1}(q_{t,1}+U_{t,1})=p_t\varphi_{a,1}(q_{a,1}+x_1);$$

but when $U_{t,1}$ is reduced to 6 hours

$$\varphi_{t,1}(\dots)<p_t\varphi_{a,1}(\dots)$$

and $\varphi_{t,1}(\dots)$ has no place in a system of equations describing the condition of maximum satisfaction any more than $\varphi_{c,1}(\dots)$ has a place in Walras's system of equations to which this note refers. Only if conditions of employment change so that our individual (1) may offer 7 hours, will

$$\varphi_{t,1}(\dots)=p_t\varphi_{a,1}(\dots),$$

and this equation will again return to the fold.

[7] This equation is derived from the preceding system by summating all the equations in the system after multiplying both sides of the second by p'_b, both

sides of the third by p'_c, etc., and after substituting $p'_b r'_{a,1}$ for $r'_{b,1}$, $p'_c r'_{a,1}$ for $r'_{c,1}$, etc., by virtue of the fact that maximum satisfaction requires that $r'_{b,1} = p'_b r'_{a,1}$, $r'_{c,1} = p'_c r'_{a,1}$, etc. (§79).

[8] Since the p's and q's are supposed to be known *ex hypothesi*, $r'_{a,1}$ is the only unknown and is consequently given by the solution of the equation.

[9] See §80.

[10]
$$y_1 + y_2 + y_3 + \ldots = Y = f_{b,1}(p_b, p_c, p_d \ldots) + f_{b,2}(p_b, p_c, p_d \ldots) = F_b(\ldots)$$
which must equal zero since $Y = 0$.

[11] In the original, this sentence reads: 'Si c'est la demande qui est supérieure à l'offre, on fait la hausse du prix de la marchandise en le numéraire; si c'est l'offre qui est supérieure à la demande, on fait la baisse.' A literal rendering of 'on fait la hausse du prix' and 'on fait la baisse' would be "one raises the price" and "one lowers it". This is the way Richard M. Goodwin translates these words found in a similar passage at the end of §217 of the *Eléments*; and then he protests: "Unfortunately for the theory, no one raises or lowers any price under perfect competition." (See p. 5 of Goodwin's article cited in the next Translator's Note.) From a purely grammatical point of view, Walras's expression is ambiguous in the French, but in the light of the total context of the *Eléments*, such a literal translation as Goodwin suggests is misleading. Surely Walras never supposed for a moment that there was any one person or corporate entity that raised or lowered prices under perfect competition. This is clear from §§41 and 42 of the *Eléments* where Walras succinctly describes, in realistic terms, the mechanism of price adjustments in a competitive market. What may, however, be implied in Walras's ambiguous expression 'on fait . . .'—one cannot be sure of this—is another matter, which, had Goodwin perceived it, might have elicited his praise rather than his blame. When Walras discusses the mathematical *determination* of equilibrium prices on a purely theoretical plan, he seems to be imagining a theorist operating a mathematical machine and moving price levers upwards or downwards until demand equals offer. When, however, Walras is discussing the actual *establishment* of equilibrium prices in a real, competitive market, then the competitive mechanism described in §§41 and 42 comes into play. In the first case, there is someone who raises or lowers prices; in the second case, there is no such person for the rise or fall in prices takes place in the course of the competitive bidding process.

[12] Here Walras introduces his characteristic theory of '*tâtonnement*' which literally translated means 'groping'. It is a theory of the process by which the market mechanism solves the equilibrium equations—not only the equations of exchange, but also the equations of production (Lesson 21) and the equations of capitalization (Lesson 25). The market does this, not as a rational, sentient entity, but rather as a blind mechanism so constituted that it automatically makes continual trial and error adjustments towards equilibrium. Hence Walras's term '*tâtonnement*', the meaning and spirit of which is best rendered in English by the word "groping" rather than "approximations", as Professor Stigler suggests (George J. Stigler, *Production and Distribution Theories*, New York, Macmillan, 1941, p. 244). For a discussion of Walras's theory of '*tâtonnements*' in relation to more recent developments in dynamic analysis, see Richard M. Goodwin, "Iteration, Automatic Computers, and Economic Dynamics", *Metroeconomica*, vol. III, no. 1, April 1951, pp. 1–7.

[13] See §123.

LESSON 13

[1] See §100.

[2] From Fig. 5 of ed. 4.

[3] The factor 2 in the right member of this equation is the *rareté* of (A). 2·5 is the price of (C) in terms of (A), and is equal to the ratio between the underlined *rareté* of (C), $\underline{5}$, and the *rareté* of (A), 2. $2 \cdot 5 = \underline{5}/2$ or $\underline{5} = 2 \times 2 \cdot 5$.

[4] $6 = r_{a,2}$ and $2 = p_b$, so that $12 = r_{a,2} p_b = r_{b,2}$.

[5] $6 = r_{a,2}$, and $2 \cdot 5 = p_c$, so that $15 = r_{a,2} p_c = r_{c,2}$.

[6] See § 101.

[7] $4 = r_{a,3}$ and $2 \cdot 5 = p_c$, so that $10 = p_c r_{a,3} = r_{c,3}$.

[8] See § 102.

[9] See § 103.

[10] We know from § 135 that when the market is in equilibrium,

$$p_b = \frac{R_b}{R_a}, \qquad p_c = \frac{R_c}{R_a}, \qquad p_d = \frac{R_d}{R_a} \ldots$$

where, it will be recalled, R_a, R_b, R_c, R_d... stand for average *raretés*. Since these equations may be written

$$R_a = \frac{R_b}{p_b}, \qquad R_a = \frac{R_c}{p_c}, \qquad R_a = \frac{R_d}{p_d} \ldots$$

it follows that

$$\frac{R_a}{1} = \frac{R_b}{p_b} = \frac{R_c}{p_c} = \frac{R_d}{p_d} = \ldots.$$

If, after the establishment of this equilibrium, the tastes of some of the consumers of (B) were to change autonomously in such a way that the *raretés* of (B) rose for them, then the simple arithmetic average of $r_{b,1}$, $r_{b,2}$, $r_{b,3}$... some increasing and others remaining constant, would have to increase from R_b to say R'_b. This being the only change in the first instance, R_a will remain constant to start with, so that the original equilibrium price of (B), $p_b = \frac{R_b}{R_a}$ will rise to $p'_b = \frac{R'_b}{R_a}$. This increase in the price of (B) will affect the quantities of (A), (C), (D)... given up, at least in the case of some of the traders. Since the r_a, r_c, r_d... will change for such traders, the average *raretés*, R_a, R_c, R_d..., will have to change also. Consequently, the equation

$$\frac{R_a}{1} = \frac{R_b}{p_b} = \frac{R_c}{p_c} = \frac{R_d}{p_d} = \ldots$$

with which we started will no longer hold, and all terms being *ex hypothesi* variables, an indefinite variety of changes are possible in re-establishing equality between the ratios.

[11] cf. A. Cournot, *op. cit.*, pp. 44–45.

LESSON 14

[1] Since $q_{a,1} - q'_{a,1} = x'_1 - x_1$; $q_{b,1} - q'_{b,1} = y'_1 - y_1$; etc.

[2] See § 118.

[3] See § 123.

[4] See § 139.

[5] From § 141.

[6] See above, Translator's Note [6] of Lesson 11.

[7] "Avec un peu plus d'apparence de raison, mais non pas avec plus de fondement, on a nommé le numéraire, ou la monnaie, une *mesure des valeurs*. On peut apprécier la valeur des choses; on ne peut pas la mesurer, c'est à dire la comparer avec un type invariable et connu, parce qu'il n'y en a point. ... C'est

ce qui rend impossible la comparaison qu'on a quelquefois tenté de faire des richesses de deux époques ou de deux nations différentes. Ce parallèle est la quadrature du cercle d'économie politique, parce qu'il n'y a point de mesure commune pour l'établir." Jean Baptiste Say, *Traité d'économie politique*, ed. 7, Paris, Guillaumin, 1861, pp. 273–275.

[8] These letters are more clearly defined in §108 of ed. 1 where:

$$M=D_{a,b}, \quad P=D_{a,c}, \quad R=D_{a,d}\cdots$$
$$N=D_{b,a}, \quad F=D_{b,c}, \quad H=D_{b,d}\cdots$$
$$Q=D_{c,a}, \quad G=D_{c,b}, \quad K=D_{c,d}\cdots$$
$$S=D_{d,a}, \quad J=D_{d,b}, \quad L=D_{d,c}.$$

[9] By definition, $N+F+H\ldots$ is the total quantity of (B) given in exchange for (A) at the price μ per unit of (B) in terms of (A). The items of this sum, $N, F, H\ldots$, are the respective amounts of (B) to be ultimately exchanged for M units of commodity (A), G units of commodity (C), J units of commodity (D).... In the initial transaction, where all $N+F+H+\ldots$ units of (B) are exchanged for the money commodity (A), the total receipts in terms of (A) can be broken up into separate items making up the sum $M+F\mu+H\mu+\ldots$. By definition, the M units of (A) in this sum constitute the definitive acquisition of commodity (A), say for use as a consumable commodity (since we are abstracting at this juncture from any use of the money commodity as a store of value), whereas the item $F\mu$ units of (A) is acquired only to be exchanged again for G units of commodity (C) at the price π per unit of (C) in terms of (A). Hence $F\mu=G\pi$. Likewise the item $H\mu$ units of (A) is acquired only to be exchanged again for J units of commodity (D) at the price ϱ per unit of (D) in terms of (A). Hence $H\mu=J\varrho$. And so on.

If we refer back to §44 and let $N+F+H+\ldots=n$ and $M+F\mu+H\mu=m$, we have

$$\frac{M+F\mu+H\mu+\ldots}{N+F+H+\ldots}=\frac{m}{n}=\frac{v_b}{v_a}=p_{b,a}=\mu.$$

The equations of the form $(F\mu=G\pi)v_a=Gv_c$ merely express the fact that equal exchange values are traded for equal exchange values. When $F\mu$ units of (A) are traded for G units of (C) at the price π per unit of (C) in terms of (A), we may write

$$\frac{F\mu}{G}=\frac{v_c}{v_a}=p_{c,a}=\pi.$$

[10] See Lessons 29 and 30. cf. Arthur W. Marget, "The Monetary Aspects of the Walrasian System", *op. cit.* pp. 179–186.

LESSON 15

[1] From Fig. 7 of ed. 4.
[2] From Fig. 7 of ed. 4.
[3] From Fig. 8 of ed. 4.
[4] From Fig. 8 of ed. 4.
[5] cf. Cournot, *op. cit.*, Chapter IV, especially pp. 47–52.

LESSON 16

[1] Adam Smith, *op. cit.*, vol. I, pp. 32–33.
[2] *Œuvres diverses de J. B. Say contenant: Catéchisme d'économie politique*, Paris, Guillaumin, 1848, p. 9.

[3] *Œuvres complètes de Condillac*, tome IV, *Le commerce et le gouvernement*, Paris, Ch. Honel, an IV-1798 (E. Vulg., pp. 16-17).

[4] Jean Jacques Burlamaqui, *Eléments du droit naturel*, nouvelle édition, Paris, chez Delestre-Boulage, 1821, pp. 211-213.

[5] Antonio Genovesi, *Lezioni di commercio o sia d'Economia Civile*, Milan, Società Tipogr. de' Classici Italiani, 1824 (a collated reprint of the 1765 and 1768 editions), Part II, Chapter I.

[6] Nassau William Senior, *An Outline of the Science of Political Economy* (offprint from *Encyclopaedia Metropolitana*), London, W. Clowes & Sons, 1836; new edition: *Library of Economics*, London, George Allen & Unwin, 1938, pp. 115-139.

[7] "*Es muss jeder der beiden Gegenstände nach dem Tausche unter A und B der Art sich verteilt finden, dass das letzte Atom, welches jeder von einem jeden erhalt, beiden gleich grossen Werth schafft.*" Hermann Heinrich Gossen, *op. cit.*, p. 85.

Gossen arrives at this proposition by a devious argument found on pp. 83 to 85 of his *Entwickelung*. He postulates a universe of two individuals interchanging two commodities by a process of barter. Then, assuming a one-to-one ratio of exchange between the two commodities, he shows that either individual, considered by himself, can trade with advantage up to the point where the "value of the last atom" (i.e. marginal degree of utility or *rareté*) of each of the two commodities traded is the same for him. It is possible, however, that one of the two individuals may reach this point of maximum satisfaction before the other at the given rate of exchange. In that case, it will pay the individual who is anxious to go on trading, after the other has reached equilibrium, to make tempting price concessions and so persuade the other individual to resume trading. Price concessions and exchange will continue until both individuals simultaneously discover that any further price concession which either individual might be willing to make would be unacceptable to the other. Gossen perceives that such a point of equilibrium is indeterminate in the case of isolated exchange, since an indefinite variety of transaction paths are possible depending upon the concessions made by whichever party is not the first to reach relative maximum satisfaction at the initial rate. The only determinate elements are the limits within which all possible terminal transactions may take place. Gossen defines two such limits, one for each individual. For one as for the other, the limit is found where the individual considered has acquired enough of the commodity received in exchange to afford him complete satiety of his wants for that commodity on terms that would leave him no better off or worse off than he might have been had he not acquired any of this commodity at all by trading.

Thus far, the argument is an anticipation of Edgeworth's theory of the contract curve (F. Y. Edgeworth, *Mathematical Psychics*, pp. 20-30; *Papers Relating to Political Economy*, vol. II, pp. 306-307; 315-318). In Walras's notation (§§ 81, 82 and 163), Edgeworth's equation of the locus of terminal transactions, i.e. his contract curve, would read

$$\frac{\dfrac{\partial \Phi_{a,1}(q_a - d_a)}{\partial d_a}}{\dfrac{\partial \Phi_{b,1}(d_b)}{\partial d_b}} = \frac{\dfrac{\partial \Phi_{a,2}(d_a)}{\partial d_a}}{\dfrac{\partial \Phi_{b,2}(q_b - d_b)}{\partial d_b}}, \qquad ..(1)$$

where the Φ's, it will be recalled, are integrals of the φ's or *rareté* functions. This result does not depend on any assumptions of interpersonal comparisons of utility.

Gossen is not content with this result, for he is interested not only in the problem of defining the relative maximum utility which each individual can obtain via the barter process, but also in the problem of defining the maximum sum of utility obtainable by both individuals together from the division of the given total existing amounts of the two commodities between them. While Gossen's solution of the first problem implies the assumption of a cardinal measure of utility which need only serve to make comparisons between commodities for the *same* individual, his solution of the second problem implies the much more daring assumption of a cardinal measure of utility adaptable for interpersonal comparisons.

Without this stronger assumption, Gossen could not speak of the value of the last atom (i.e. the *rareté*) of each commodity as being the same for one barterer as for the other. Under the stronger assumption, it follows mathematically that such an interpersonal equality is necessary for a maximum sum of utility. If we write the sum of utility to be maximized as

$$\Phi_{a,1}(q_a-d_a)+\Phi_{b,1}(d_b)+\Phi_{a,2}(d_a)+\Phi_{b,2}(q_b-d_b),$$

where q_a and q_b are constants, the necessary (not sufficient) condition of a maximum is found by setting the partial derivatives of this function with respect to d_a and d_b equal to zero, so that

$$\frac{\partial\Phi_{a,1}(q_a-d_a)}{\partial d_a}+\frac{\partial\Phi_{a,2}(d_a)}{\partial d_a}=0,$$

$$\frac{\partial\Phi_{b,1}(d_b)}{\partial d_b}+\frac{\partial\Phi_{b,2}(q_b-d_b)}{\partial d_b}=0. \qquad ..(2)$$

This reduces to Walras's representation of the Gossen conclusion in §162. Moreover, if we transpose the second term in each of the above equations and then divide the first equation by the second, we obtain equation (1) of this note again. The equation derived in this way would, however, be a special case of equation (1) because the indicated proportionality results from the fact that both the numerators and both the denominators are equal, a sufficient but not a necessary condition for that equation. We see, therefore, that the Gossen condition of maximum aggregate satisfaction must be satisfied somewhere on the Contract Curve, though there is no reason to suppose that this point will be found within the limits of the Contract Curve which enclose all possible final transactions that can be reached on terms subject to the mutual consent of the contracting parties. Gossen concludes lamely that as a rule unequal quantities of the two commodities must be exchanged for each other if a point of aggregate maximum is to be attained.

Walras, on the other hand, delves more deeply into the problem in the passage of the *Études d'économie sociale* referred to in note 1 of §162 of the *Elements*. There he points out that in order to insure the achievement of a maximum sum of utility, the intervention of an authority will be necessary. All that voluntary barter can do on terms mutually acceptable to both barterers is to permit them simultaneously to reach a point of relative maximum utility for each barterer. Only by accident could such a point coincide with that of a maximum sum of utilities for both parties taken together. If the latter maximum is set up as a social goal, the only way to attain it with any assurance is through the intervention of an authority who may compel the requisite division of the commodities between the barterers, irrespective of their consent to the terms on which the exchanges are made. This violates Walras's conception of the right of private property.

[8] W. Stanley Jevons, *Theory of Political Economy*, ed. 4, p. 95.

[9] "When we speak of the ratio of exchange of pig-iron and gold, there can be no possible doubt that we intend to refer to the ratio of the number of units

of the one commodity to the number of units of the other commodity for which it exchanges, the units being arbitrary concrete magnitudes, but the ratio an abstract number." *ibid.*, pp. 81–82.

[10] The pertinent passage in Jevons reads as follows: "By a *trading body* I mean, in the most general manner, any body either of buyers or sellers. The trading body may be a single individual in one case; it may be the whole inhabitants of a continent in another; it may be the individuals of a trade diffused through a country in a third." *ibid.*, p. 88.

[11] "In such circumstances the average laws applying to them [i.e. persons differing widely in their powers, wants, habits, and possessions] will come under what I have elsewhere (*Principles of Science*, ed. 1, [London, Macmillan, 1874] vol. I, p. 422; ed. 3, [1879], p. 363) called the 'Fictitious Mean', that is to say, they are numerical results which do not pretend to represent the character of any existing thing. But the average laws would not on this account be less useful, if we could obtain them; for the movements of trade and industry depend upon averages and aggregates, not upon the whims of individuals." *ibid.*, p. 90.

LESSON 17

[1] '*loi des frais de production ou du prix de revient*'.

[2] The translation of '*rente*' as land-service and of '*profit*' as capital-service needs to be explained. In his Theory of Production Walras employs these terms not in the usual sense of categories of distributive shares or of "component parts of price" (Adam Smith), but rather to designate categories of tangible or intangible returns in kind from productive resources. It would, therefore, be disconcerting, if not positively misleading, to translate '*rente*' and '*profit*' in this context as "rent" and "profit". Moreover, it would be intolerably awkward in the later development of the Theory of Production to translate Walras's 'prix . . . de la rente' and 'prix . . . du profit' (§185) as "price of rent" and "price of profit" instead of "price of land-service" and "price of capital-service".

This peculiar terminology was taken over, with slight modifications, from Auguste Walras's *Théorie de la richesse sociale* (Paris, Guillaumin, 1849), pp. 71–72:

"La terre donne lieu à un *revenu* qu'on appelle la *rente foncière* ou le *loyer du sol*.

"Les *facultés humaines* donnent lieu à un *revenu* qui s'appelle le *travail*.

"Les *capitaux* proprement dits, les *capitaux artificiels* donnent lieu à un *revenu* qui s'appelle le *profit*.

"Le prix débattu, le prix à forfait de la *rente foncière* ou du *loyer du sol* s'appelle le *fermage*.

"Le prix débattu, le prix à forfait du *travail* s'appelle le *salaire*.

"Le prix débattu, le prix à forfait du *profit* s'appelle *intérêt de l'argent*."

[3] 'tout bien fongible'.

[4] cf. following passages from Auguste Walras's *Théorie de la richesse sociale*, pp. 53–55: "J'appelle *valeur capitale* ou *capital* toute richesse sociale qui ne se consomme point ou qui ne se consomme qu'à la longue, toute utilité limitée qui survit au premier service qu'elle nous rend, qui se prête plus d'une fois au même usage. . . . J'appelle *revenu* toute richesse sociale ou toute valeur échangeable qui ne sert qu'une fois, qui se consomme immédiatement, qui ne survit point au premier service qu'on en retire. . . . Un grand nombre de valeurs échangeables se prêtent à plusieurs usages, et . . . dès lors on peut en faire des *capitaux* ou des *revenus*, suivant qu'on les emploie de façon à ne les consommer qu'à la longue ou suivant qu'on s'en sert de manière à les consommer sur-le-champ. Un arbre planté dans un verger et qui donne des fruits tous les ans, est un *capital*; un arbre qu'on abat pour en faire du bois à brûler, est un *revenu*. . . ."

On this point cf. George Stigler, *Production and Distribution Theories*, p. 233. While Stigler regards the Walrasian distinction between resources and their services as "fundamental to production theory", he points quite rightly to the inadequacy of Walras's criterion. "The number of services", according to Professor Stigler, "is incidental from an economic point of view; the fundamental difference relates to the time period over which the services of a capital good are spread. If this period is short, the consumption of the capital good and its service merge. If the period is considerable, and the test is whether the discounted value of the services differs significantly from their total value, services must be treated separately."

[5] *'service d'approvisionnement'*, literally 'service of storage'.

[6] The idler is here conceived as capital yielding income to himself.

[7] *'capitaux mobiliers* ou *capitaux* proprement dits'. The expression 'capitaux mobiliers' is here omitted from the translation and wherever it occurs by itself in later passages is translated as 'capital proper' or 'capital goods proper'. Since Walras obviously means to designate more than is included under the English term 'movables', there is no appropriate English equivalent for the expression in this context.

[8] Professor Stigler, *op. cit.*, p. 234, regards "these hoary distinctions" as "indefensible in the form Walras proposes them".

<h2 style="text-align:center">LESSON 18</h2>

[1] See §272.

[2] See above, Lesson 17, Translator's Note [2].

[3] Whenever Walras uses the term 'intérêt' in the sense of a payment for capital-services, it will be rendered throughout this translation as "interest charge". Only when used in the sense of a payment for the service of money or, in special cases, for the service of *numéraire*, e.g. in loans, will 'intérêt' be rendered simply as "interest".

[4] See Lessons 37–40.

[5] "Si les produits sont plus demandés qu'offerts. . . ." Here 'offerts' is translated as 'supplied' rather than as 'offered', in accordance with our convention described above in Lesson 5, Translator's Note [2], since the word in this context refers to a rate of output which finds its way to the market.

[6] The Walrasian doctrine of the gainless entrepreneur was severely criticized by Edgeworth on repeated occasions as is seen in his review of Walras's second edition of the *Eléments* which appeared in *Nature*, No. 1036, vol. 40, September 5, 1889, pp. 434–436, and in several passages of his *Papers Relating to Political Economy*, referred to in the index under "Entrepreneur", "Pareto" and "Walras". One can only echo Barone's astonishment, which was recorded by Edgeworth himself, that "any difficulty whatever can arise as to the validity . . . of this conception which is indeed most simple". Surely the conception is now commonplace in the current theory of the individual firm as developed by Joan Robinson, Edward Chamberlin and a host of others, that *at equilibrium, under conditions of pure and perfect competition* (certainly Walras's conditions!), the entrepreneur neither gains anything above and beyond "normal profits" which are implicit in Walras's cost of production function, nor does he lose. This by no means precludes the doctrine that the pursuit of profits and the avoidance of loss are the mainspring of all entrepreneurial activity.

<h2 style="text-align:center">LESSON 19</h2>

[1] The translator is indebted to Dr. W. Collings, M. Gerard Debreu of the Cowles Commission and Professor Stewart Y. McMullen of Northwestern

University who very kindly read this Lesson in manuscript and offered helpful suggestions in rendering the French accounting terms into English.

[2] Throughout this Lesson such expressions as *'capital fixe* ou . . . *fonds de premier établissement'* or *'capital fixe* ou *frais* de premier établissement' (§193) are translated simply as "fixed assets", because, as J. O. Kettridge informs us (*op. cit.*, p. 59), *"premier établissement* is a loose and indeterminate term in French and fortunately has no equivalent in English".

[3] Strictly speaking, the lenders, including the entrepreneur considered as a lender to his own business, are merely creditors and not silent partners ['*commanditaires*'].

LESSON 20

[1] See §§79–82. Since $\varphi_t(q_t-o_t)=r_t$ and $\varphi_a(d_a)=r_a$, $p_{t,a}$ must equal $\dfrac{r_t}{r_a}$, or $\dfrac{\varphi_t(q_t-o_t)}{\varphi_a(d_a)}$ after the final exchange of (T) for (A) resulting in maximum satisfaction.

[2] The method of performing these successive eliminations is described in Lesson 12, Translator's Note [2].

[3] The special *a priori* assumption of constant coefficients of production, which, it should be stressed, is purely provisional, is made at this point for no other reason than to avoid introducing any more variables than are strictly necessary for the solution of the problem of the determination of the prices of productive services. To achieve this simplicity of exposition, Walras considers all the productive services (or "factors") as "limitational"; and this implies not only that all the production functions throughout the economy are homogeneous of the first degree, but also that the cross partial derivatives are zero. Hence the adjustment of the aggregate demand for these services to their offer is reached through variations in the number of firms, which are assumed, again for simplicity, to be all equal (and presumably constant) in size, and free to enter or leave as profit or loss may dictate. This fiction remains internally consistent so long as the service-yielding resources are taken to be fixed in total amount. When, however, Walras considers the consequences of net aggregate capital formation with the total amount of land remaining constant, then a new type of production function becomes inevitable involving substitutability between the different kinds of productive services. The coefficients must now be variable. It is for this reason that Walras delays introducing the marginal productivity theory until Part VII where he is concerned with economic progress (§324); and there he insists that the object of this theory is to determine the magnitudes of the variable coefficients, not their prices. (cf. N. Georgescu-Roegen, "Fixed Coefficients of Production and Marginal Productivity Theory", *Review of Economic Studies*, vol. III, No. 1, October 1935, pp. 40–49; Wassily W. Leontief, *The Structure of American Economy, 1919–1929*, Cambridge, Harvard University Press, 1941, pp. 36–41; and see below Translator's Note [1] of Lesson 36 and Collation Note [*f*] of Lesson 20.)

[4] cf. George J. Stigler, *op. cit.*, p. 240, footnote 1. Professor Stigler, having misconstrued the word *'proportionnels'* in this context and having mistranslated it as 'proportional', is quite naturally exasperated with Walras for not telling us to what all the expenses are proportional. Had Professor Stigler referred to p. 476, footnote 1 of ed. 4 def. (see above, p. 474, footnote 1), he would have noted that Walras there contrasts the term *'frais proportionnels'* with the term *'frais fixes'* precisely in the same way that 'prime costs' are contrasted with 'supplementary costs' in Alfred Marshall's *Principles of Economics* (p. 359) or, alternatively, in the same way that 'variable costs' are contrasted with 'fixed costs'

528   ELEMENTS OF PURE ECONOMICS

in the current theory of the firm. The adjective 'proportionnels' wherever it describes 'frais' must, therefore, be translated as 'prime' or 'variable' in this context.

Walras's statical assumption of fixed technical coefficients of production carries with it the implication that all firms producing a given homogeneous product must have identical production functions, which is a sufficient (though not necessary) condition for equal rates of output for all firms at equilibrium under conditions of pure and perfect competition. Moreover, with fixed coefficients of production, the distinction between prime and supplementary costs or between variable and fixed costs is blurred out. cf. Robert Triffin, *Monopolistic Competition and General Equilibrium Theory*, Cambridge, Harvard University Press, 1940, pp. 108–109; and Alfred Marshall, *op. cit.*, p. 395. No economic rent appears in this static model; in fact, Walras finds no place for this concept until he considers the consequences of differences in elasticity of supply of certain resources as the aggregate economy expands (Lesson 39).

[5] In passing from the laws of the *determination* of a given equilibrium to those of the *establishment* or *emergence* of that equilibrium, Walras changes his entire method of analysis. His purely theoretical solution, like Homer's epic of the Trojan wars, starts *in medias res* and attains a beautiful poetic simplicity. On the other hand, his description of the actual groping of the market towards a will-o'-the-wisp equilibrium, of necessity takes into account the whole complex of changing antecedent circumstances, and loses its sharpness of outline, as would a tale of the fall of Troy that went back to Leda's egg.

Walras begins his discussion of the emergence of the equilibrium price *ab ovo* by assuming some disequilibrium price taken at random as a starting-point. It is fashionable among institutionalists to criticize this procedure, because it throws no light on the ultimate origin of price itself (*vide* François Simiand, *La méthode positive en science économique*, Paris, Alcan, 1912, p. 92, and L. H. Haney, *History of Economic Thought*, ed. 3, New York, Macmillan, 1936, p. 652). This criticism is entirely beside the point, which is not to trace the historic or prehistoric beginnings of the phenomenon of price, but to trace the process by which the market, starting from an initial disequilibrium position, arrives at equilibrium price. The "institutionalists" would have a theory of price begin *ex nihilo*. Their own theory of price only serves to confirm the medieval doctrine *ex nihilo nihil*.

[6] These '*tickets*' or '*bons*', as Walras calls them, are provisional contracts to buy or to sell given quantities of goods or services at stated prices. What makes them provisional is the stipulation that the contracts are binding only if the stated prices turn out to be equilibrium prices for the economy as a whole; otherwise they become null and void. The translation of '*bons*' in this sense as 'tickets' is suggested by the fact that tickets often read "bon pour . . ." in French, or "good for . . ." in English. The 'tickets' Walras has in mind might be thought of as reading, for example, "Good for the sale of $o_{b,1}$ units of product (B) by producer (1) at the price p'_b, provided the market is in equilibrium at this price. At any other price this ticket is null and void." *Mutatis mutandis* the tickets issued by buyers of products as well as by buyers and sellers of services are similarly worded.

Walras's '*bons*' might also be thought of as 'chips' that are only cashable in terms of goods and services on the completion of the market game when equilibrium is fully achieved. cf. Nicholas Kaldor, "A Classificatory Note on the Determinateness of Equilibrium", *Review of Economic Studies*, vol. I, no. 2, February 1934, pp. 126–127.

The purpose of this imaginary device, particularly in the theory of production, is to make possible the attainment of "true" equilibrium prices, without the distortion which might otherwise result from the production of other than equilibrium quantities corresponding to "false" prices that might be quoted before equilibrium is reached through the groping process of the market. Thus the "problem of the path" is evaded.

LESSON 21

[1] This **r**, representing income ['revenu'] has been put in bold-face type in the translation to distinguish it from the r representing *rareté*.

[2] i.e. if the elasticity of demand for (B) were unity.

[3] The Ω_a in each equation is explained by the assumption that the quantity of the *numéraire* is a parameter, while the quantities of (B), (C), (D) . . . are allowed to vary until equilibrium is reached.

[4] By subtracting the above equation from the one given just previously.

[5] i.e. quantities of productive services incorporated in the products they sell.

[6] This follows from the third equation above, since the right-hand side of that equation has now been shown to equal zero when the markets for (B), (C), (D)... are in equilibrium and $p_a=1$.

[7] See §203.

[8] It will be recalled that the technical coefficients are provisionally assumed to be constant. See §204.

[9] See curve T_dT_p in Fig. 44 on p. 477.

[10] This assumes that (T) is not employed in the fabrication of (A), (B), (C), (D)....

[11] See curve QTR in Fig. 44.

[12] The process of deriving this equation is analogous to that described in §213.

LESSON 22

[1] See §134.

[2] Remembering from §224 that

$$v_t : v_p : v_k$$
$$:: r_{t,1} : r_{p,1} : r_{k,1}$$
$$:: . \quad . \quad . \quad . \quad .,$$

it follows that

$$\frac{v_t}{v_a} : \frac{v_p}{v_a} : \frac{v_k}{v_a}$$
$$:: r_{t,1} : r_{p,1} : r_{k,1}$$
$$:: . \quad . \quad . \quad . \quad .;$$

but since

$$\frac{v_t}{v_a} = p_t, \quad \frac{v_p}{v_a} = p_p \quad \text{and} \quad \frac{v_k}{v_a} = p_k,$$

the prices quite properly replace the v's in the first row of the numerical table of proportionality at equilibrium.

[3] From Fig. 6 of ed. 4.

[4] cf. §135.

[5] From Fig. 9 of ed. 4.

[6] From Fig. 10 of ed. 4.

[7] See §§154 and 155.

Part V

[1] The French word 'capitalisation' is as awkward to translate in this context as it is easy to transliterate into its English equivalent "capitalization". In both languages the word is defined in the same way, but in English as well as in French

it has two definitions. According to one definition, capitalization or 'capitalisa-tion' means a process of computing the present value of a periodical income; while according to another, it means a process of forming or creating capital. Evidently Walras uses the word in both senses in his theory of the determination of the prices of capital goods. Within the wider framework of his general equilibrium theory, the dominant idea is that of the determination of the rate at which the capital value of periodical income is computed; and this rate depends largely upon the rate of capital formation. Hence, except where the word is used in the narrow computational sense, it has been found preferable to render 'capitalisation' as "capital formation".

Lesson 23

[1] i.e. the term income ('*revenu*'), which previously referred to physical services rendered per unit of time, is henceforth used in the wider sense of such services multiplied by their prices. Until we come to the theory of money, these prices are always expressed in terms of *numéraire*.

[2] Care should be taken not to confuse Walras's 'rate of net income' ['*taux du revenu net*'] or its symbol i with the monetary rate of interest. See §255 and Part IV *passim*, especially §281.

[3] Derived from the preceding equation in the text as follows:

$$p = iP + (\mu + \nu)P = P(i + \mu + \nu).$$

[4] 'capital numéraire'.

[5] Since it is assumed throughout Part V that the aggregate quantity of personal capital is to be kept constant, provision must be made for the mainte-nance not only of the wives and children of workers but also of the workers themselves. In that case, the expression $(\mu_p + \nu_p)P_p$, in which μ_p and ν_p are respectively the special rates of depreciation and insurance applicable to personal capital, must include provision for what Alfred Marshall called the "productive consumption" of the individual worker himself in addition to provision for the support of his wife and of enough children to assure his eventual replacement. Using Walras's notation of §§238–240 and neglecting (K'), (K'')... for simplicity, we may write a generalized individual worker's maintenance budget as follows:

$$(q_t - o_t)p_t + (q_p - o_p)p_p + (q_k - o_k)p_k + d_a$$
$$+ d_b p_b + d_c p_c + \ldots = q_p[(\mu_p + \nu_p)P_p],$$

where q_p represents the quantity of personal faculties the individual keeps intact.

Obviously the standard of consumption necessary for maintaining the efficiency of a unit of personal capital differs in different places and at different times and even for different individuals at the same time and place. The required amount and pattern of consumption are not determined economically, but physiologically, psychologically and sociologically. Such consumption must, therefore, be taken by the economist as a datum similar to the utility functions.

[6] It will be observed that Walras uses the symbols p_k, $p_{k'}$, $p_{k''}$... to denote both the gross incomes (in terms of the *numéraire*) derived from single units of capital goods (K), (K'), (K'')... respectively (§§232 and 233), and the prices per unit of these incomes. These two uses may be readily reconciled by defining a unit of each type of income as the amount of income yielded by a single unit of the corresponding type of capital. This is a matter of definition involving no question of principle.

[7] Walras's e, representing the difference between the value of the services offered and the value of the products and services demanded, or what amounts to the same thing, the excess of gross income over consumption, has been put into

bold-face type in the translation to avoid confusion with the E and e which are introduced later in §242.

[8] For **r** meaning income ('revenu') see §212 and Translator's Note [1] of Lesson 21.

[9] The only possible way of expressing d_e in terms of units of *numéraire* is to assume that each unit of (E) consists of *one unit of numéraire per annum payable in perpetuity*. Thus, if we assume that the *numéraire* is also money, that each unit of (E) consists of 1 franc per annum payable in perpetuity and that the current rate of interest i is 4 per cent, then the price of 1 franc per annum payable in perpetuity becomes $\frac{1}{i}$ or 25 francs. Under this interpretation, if an individual demands 20 francs per annum payable in perpetuity, and if the current rate of net income is 4 per cent, then $d_e p_e = 20$ francs $\times$ 25 francs.

An alternative and, in some respects, a more convenient way of expressing d_e would be to regard it as a quantity or number of *perpetual annuity shares* each entitling the holder to *any* fixed number of francs per annum payable in perpetuity. In certain parts of the subsequent argument a strict adherence to Walras's definition would lead to unnecessarily arduous reasoning. This is clearly apparent in Translator's Note [11] of this Lesson where Walras's demand and offer function of (E) is described geometrically.

[10] The expression 'denier (au denier 20, au denier 25)' may also be translated as "penny (twentieth penny, twenty-fifth penny)".

[11] In effect, this amounts to a geometrical description of the relationship between the net quantity demanded of (E) (i.e. the excess of the *number* of perpetual annuity shares demanded over the *number* offered), and the price per share p_e which is equal to the rate of capitalization $\frac{1}{i}$. This is shown graphically in the following diagram (Fig. 52), the heavily dotted curve drawn below the price axis portraying the net negative demand (i.e. the net offer) of these perpetual annuity shares as a function of the reciprocal of i.

It will be observed that the same diagram can also be used to show the amount of net savings E offered in exchange for perpetual annuity shares as a function of the rate of perpetual net income i. This offer is measured geometrically by the areas of rectangles inscribed within the net demand curve for perpetual annuity shares. When p_e is zero and i is therefore infinite, the offer of savings is zero. As p_e increases, the increase in positive savings available for investment in perpetual annuity shares, viz. $D_e p_e$, is proportional to the increase in the corresponding areas of the rectangles inscribed within the curve $E_d E_p$. After reaching at least one maximum these areas will decrease, falling to zero when $p_e = OE_p$. At this point, p_e is very high and i is consequently very small (cf. William Jaffé, "Léon Walras's Theory of Capital Accumulation", published in *Studies in Mathematical Economics and Econometrics*, edited by Oscar Lange et al., the University of Chicago Press, Chicago, 1942, pp. 45–47).

As i becomes still smaller and p_e increases beyond OE_p, perpetual annuity shares will be offered for sale instead of being purchased. The economy will then do the very opposite of saving: it will consume its own savings and it may even consume the savings of others. In other words, it may resell foreign perpetual annuity shares which it had previously acquired by purchase; and it may even offer new rights to perpetual net income, by floating abroad a new issue of fixed yield bonds without maturity. The negative ordinates of the heavily dotted curve (taken positively under the lightly dotted curve) indicate the total net offer of perpetual annuity shares as a function of the price of these shares. It is unnecessary to go into further detail in the matter of this offer function, for

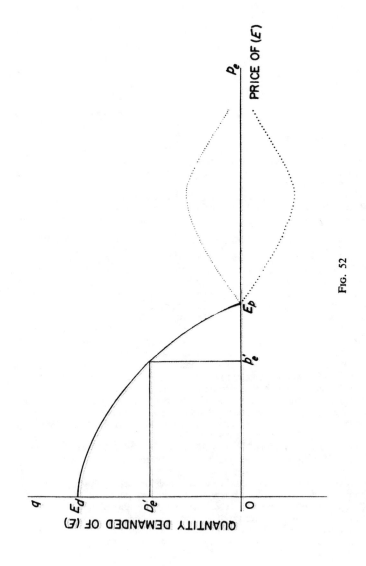

Fig. 52

Walras arbitrarily excludes the hypothesis of consumption of capital from his theory of capital formation, confining his attention to a progressive economy in which there is an uninterrupted increase in the accumulation of capital goods.

[12] Remembering that $p_e = \dfrac{1}{i}$ (§242), we see that by appropriately transforming F_e into F_e, we may eliminate the factor p_e and substitute the variable i for p_e in the function. The reader must be careful to distinguish between E, the sum total of savings in the community in question, and (E), the designation of the fictive commodity consisting of perpetual net income, for the purchase of which E is accumulated.

[13] See Lessons 26 and 27.

LESSON 24

[1] See §§125–130 and 207.

LESSON 25

[1] Eds. 4 and 4 def. read D_k, $D_{k'}$, $D_{k''}$... instead of D'_k, $D'_{k'}$, $D'_{k''}$..., as at the beginning of this Lesson and in the following equations; doubtless a misprint.

[2] For the significance of Ω_a, see above, Lesson 21 *passim*, and Translator's Note [3] of that Lesson.

[3] Reducing, for simplicity, our list of commodities to (A) and (B) and our list of productive services to (T), (P) and (K), we write the two derived systems as follows:

$$\left.\begin{aligned}
\Omega_a p'_a &= \Omega_a a_t p'_t + \Omega_a a_p p'_p + \Omega_a a_k p'_k \\
D'_b p'_b &= D'_b b_t p'_t + D'_b b_p p'_p + D'_b b_k p'_k \\
D'_k P'_k &= D'_k k_t p'_t + D'_k k_p p'_p + D'_k k_k p'_k
\end{aligned}\right\} \quad ..(1)$$

$$\left.\begin{aligned}
p'_t a_t \Omega_a + p'_t b_t D'_b + p'_t k_t D'_k &= p'_t O'_t \\
p'_p a_p \Omega_a + p'_p b_p D'_b + p'_p k_p D'_k &= p'_p O'_p \\
p'_k a_k \Omega_a + p'_k b_k D'_b + p'_k k_k D'_k &= p'_k O'_k
\end{aligned}\right\} \quad .(2)$$

from which we obtain

$$\Omega_a p'_a + D'_b p'_b + D'_k P'_k = O'_t p'_t + O'_p p'_p + O'_k p'_k,$$

which is obviously an abbreviated version of Walras's equation.

[4] cf. the last equation of system (2) and equation (7) of Lesson 24.

[5] See §§210 and 211.

[6] See §212.

LESSON 26

[1] The text here is vague and ambiguous. The pairs in question cannot be all possible pairs, for this would entail a contradiction. If we set any sum equal to zero, e.g.

$$a_1 + a_2 + a_3 = 0$$

and then postulated that the sums of all possible pairs of the terms in the left-hand side were equal to zero, so that

$$a_1 = -a_2,$$
$$a_1 = -a_3,$$
$$a_2 = -a_3,$$

it would follow that

$$-a_2 = -a_3,$$

which contradicts the third equation in the system. The pairs Walras has in mind are pairs composed of one term relating to the *numéraire* (A) and another term relating to each of the other commodities in succession, as is seen in system [δ] in the text.

[2] The s in equation (1) and the prices being constants, the differential equation may be written

$$p_t d\delta_t + \ldots + p_p d\delta_p + \ldots + p_k d\delta_k + p_{k'} d\delta_{k'} + p_{k''} d\delta_{k''} + \ldots$$
$$+ d\delta_a + p_b d\delta_b + p_c d\delta_c + p_d d\delta_d + \ldots = 0.$$

Of the possible solutions of this equation only one is consistent with the assumption that the prices are all expressed in terms of (A); and that solution implies system of equations [ε] in the text.

[3] System of equations [ε] may be rewritten

$$p_t = -\frac{d\delta_a}{d\delta_t}, \ldots \quad p_p = -\frac{d\delta_a}{d\delta_p}, \ldots \quad p_k = -\frac{d\delta_a}{d\delta_k}, \quad p_{k'} = -\frac{d\delta_a}{d\delta_{k'}}, \ldots$$

Now from system [δ] in the text

$$-\frac{d\delta_a}{d\delta_t} = \frac{\Phi'_t(\delta_t)}{\Phi'_a(\delta_a)} = \frac{r_t}{r_a}$$

$$\cdot \quad \cdot \quad \cdot \quad \cdot \quad \cdot \quad \cdot \quad \cdot$$

$$-\frac{d\delta_a}{d\delta_p} = \frac{\Phi'_p(\delta_p)}{\Phi'_a(\delta_a)} = \frac{r_p}{r_a}$$

$$\cdot \quad \cdot \quad \cdot \quad \cdot \quad \cdot \quad \cdot \quad \cdot$$

$$-\frac{d\delta_a}{d\delta_k} = \frac{\Phi'_k(\delta_k)}{\Phi'_a(\delta_a)} = \frac{r_k}{r_a}$$

$$-\frac{d\delta_a}{d\delta_{k'}} = \frac{\Phi'_{k'}(\delta_{k'})}{\Phi'_a(\delta_a)} = \frac{r_{k'}}{r_a}$$

$$\cdot \quad \cdot \quad \cdot \quad \cdot \quad \cdot \quad \cdot \quad \cdot$$

by definition, so that substituting in the first system of equations of this note, we get

$$p_t = \frac{r_t}{r_a}, \ldots \quad p_p = \frac{r_p}{r_a}, \ldots \quad p_k = \frac{r_k}{r_a}, \quad p_{k'} = \frac{r_{k'}}{r_a}, \ldots$$

whence

$$\frac{r_t}{p_t} = \ldots = \frac{r_p}{p_p} = \ldots = \frac{r_k}{p_k} = \frac{r_{k'}}{p_{k'}} = \ldots$$

[4] Again (see Translator's Note [1] above), these pairs cannot be all possible pairs, but pairs composed of a term relating to any one capital good, say (K), and a term relating to each of the other capital goods in succession, as is seen in systems [ζ] [η] and [θ] in the text.

[5] For example, the first equation of system [η] may be rewritten

$$\frac{P_k}{P_{k'}} = -\frac{d\delta_{k',1}}{d\delta_{k,1}};$$

and, since $\Phi'_{k,1}(\delta_{k,1}) = r_{k,1}$, $\Phi'_{k',1}(\delta_{k',1}) = r_{k',1}, \ldots$ by definition, the first equation of system [ζ] in the text may be rewritten

$$-\frac{d\delta_{k',1}}{d\delta_{k,1}} = \frac{r_{k,1}}{r_{k',1}}.$$

Now, remembering that $\dfrac{r_{k,1}}{r_{k',1}} = \dfrac{p_k}{p_{k'}}$, by substituting in the first equation of this note, we get

$$\frac{P_k}{P_{k'}} = \frac{p_k}{p_{k'}}$$

or

$$\frac{p_k}{P_k} = \frac{p_{k'}}{P_{k'}}.$$

[6] For example,

$$P_k + \frac{\mu_k + \nu_k}{i_k} P_k = P_k \left(1 + \frac{\mu_k + \nu_k}{i_k}\right).$$

From §238 we know that $\dfrac{\pi_k}{i_k} = \dfrac{p_k}{i_k + \mu_k + \nu_k}$ or $\dfrac{i_k}{\pi_k} = \dfrac{i_k + \mu_k + \nu_k}{p_k}$; and multiplying both sides of this last equation by $\dfrac{p_k}{i_k}$, we obtain

$$\frac{p_k}{\pi_k} = 1 + \frac{\mu_k + \nu_k}{i_k}.$$

Substituting in the first equation of this note, we have

$$P_k + \frac{\mu_k + \nu_k}{i_k} P_k = \frac{p_k}{\pi_k} P_k.$$

[7] For example, rewriting the first equation of system [θ]

$$\frac{\dfrac{p_k}{\pi_k} P_k}{\dfrac{p_{k'}}{\pi_{k'}} P_{k'}} = - \frac{d\delta_{k',1}}{d\delta_{k,1}}$$

and remembering from Note [5] of this Lesson that $\dfrac{P_k}{P_{k'}} = \dfrac{p_k}{p_{k'}}$, and hence

$$- \frac{d\delta_{k',1}}{d\delta_{k,1}} = \frac{p_k}{p_{k'}},$$

we obtain

$$\frac{\dfrac{p_k}{\pi_k} P_k}{\dfrac{p_k}{\pi_{k'}} P_{k'}} = \frac{p_k}{p_{k'}},$$

or, multiplying both sides by $\dfrac{p_{k'}}{p_k}$, and inverting fractions

$$\frac{\dfrac{\pi_{k'}}{P_{k'}}}{\dfrac{\pi_k}{P_k}} = 1$$

which yields

$$\frac{\pi_k}{P_k} = \frac{\pi_{k'}}{P_{k'}}.$$

For an account of F. Y. Edgeworth's difficulties in attempting to understand these equations as they appeared in ed. 2 (see Collation Notes [b], [c] and [d] of this Lesson), and for a summary statement of his objections to Walras's postulate that the quantities manufactured of capital goods are also the quantities consumed of the services of those goods, see William Jaffé, "Unpublished Papers and Letters of Léon Walras", *Journal of Political Economy*, vol. XLIII, No. 2, April 1935, p. 203. The economic significance of these equations is discussed below in Translator's Notes [2] and [3] of Lesson 27.

Lesson 27

[1] See above, Translator's Notes [1] and [4] of Lesson 26.

[2] This sentence and the rest of the mathematical exposition in §263 is obscure to the point of almost complete incomprehensibility. It is possible, however, to reconstruct the argument and render it intelligible in Walras's own terms, as can be seen from the following analysis. I am especially indebted to Mr. G. Th. Guilbaud (Assistant Director of the Institut de Science Economique Appliquée of Paris) for helpful comments on the mathematical development of the argument and to Professor Paul A. Samuelson whose penetrating questions have contributed to a clarification of the issues treated in the next note.

The object of the demonstration is to relate the demand for capital goods to the utility functions of the ultimate consumers' goods which these capital goods help to produce. It is clear that for the sum of effective utilities enjoyed by individual (1)

$$\Phi_{a,1}(\delta_{a,1}) + \Phi_{b,1}(\delta_{b,1}) + \Phi_{c,1}(\delta_{c,1}) + \ldots$$

to be a maximum, it is necessary that

$$\Phi'(\delta_{a,1})d\delta_{a,1} + \Phi'_{b,1}(\delta_{b,1})d\delta_{b,1} + \Phi'_{c,1}(\delta_{c,1})d\delta_{c,1} + \ldots = 0 \qquad ..(1)$$

for all admissible values of $d\delta_{a,1}$, $d\delta_{b,1}$, $d\delta_{c,1}$..., subject to the budget constraint of the individual in question. It follows that any change, such as $\pm d\delta_{a,1}$, in individual (1)'s consumption of (A), for instance, necessarily entails a change opposite in sign, such as $\mp d\delta_{b,1}$, in his consumption of at least one other commodity, say (B). In the simplest conceivable case, therefore, where the compensating changes in consumption take place only between pairs of commodities, the criterion for admissible values of differentials in equation (1) above is given by

$$\Phi'_{a,1}(\delta_{a,1})d\delta_{a,1} = -\Phi'_{b,1}(\delta_{b,1})d\delta_{b,1},$$
$$\Phi'_{a,1}(\delta_{a,1})d\delta_{a,1} = -\Phi'_{c,1}(\delta_{c,1})d\delta_{c,1}, \qquad ..(2)$$
$$\cdots \cdots \cdots \cdots \cdots$$

It is important to note, now, that any differential increment in individual (1)'s consumption of (A) involves corresponding differential increments in the capital-services utilized, and hence in the capital goods employed in the production of the increment of (A) consumed by individual (1). For the sake of completeness, we shall not confine our attention to capital goods proper (K), (K'), (K")..., as Walras does, but we shall also take into account personal capital (which Walras defines in §237) and consider, for simplicity, only one kind of personal capital (P). We shall, however, neglect landed capital (T), because its aggregate amount is, by definition, invariant. Though, in the absence of slavery, there can be no market for personal capital, there is nothing to prevent an individual in his private economy from investing more or less of his savings in his own or his family's capacity to produce, either by devoting an increase in his total savings to this purpose or by allocating a larger proportion of given savings to (P) at the expense of (K), (K′), (K″).... Since the aggregate amount of (P) may, unlike (T), increase or decrease in the economy as a whole, personal capital becomes a significant variable in our problem. We may, therefore, write

$$\begin{aligned}
d\delta_{p,1,a} &= a_p d\delta_{a,1}, \\
d\delta_{k,1,a} &= a_k d\delta_{a,1}, \\
d\delta_{k',1,a} &= a_{k'} d\delta_{a,1}, \\
d\delta_{k'',1,a} &= a_{k''} d\delta_{a,1},
\end{aligned} \qquad ..(3)$$

. . . .

where the left-hand side of these equations expresses differential increments in the amounts (P), (K), (K′), (K″)... required for a given increase in the consumption of (A) by individual (1), and where the coefficients of production in the right-hand side of the equations are considered as constants. Similar equations could be written relating differential increments in (1)'s consumption of (B), (C)... to the capital goods employed in their production. Hence any change in (1)'s direct consumption of (A) and the compensating changes in, let us say (B), entail changes in the indirect consumption of (P), (K), (K′), (K″)... via (A), denoted by $d\delta_{p,1,a}$, $d\delta_{k,1,a}$, $d\delta_{k',1,a}$, $d\delta_{k'',1,a}$... and compensating changes, opposite in sign, in the indirect consumption of (P), (K), (K′), (K″)... via (B), denoted by $d\delta_{p,1,b}$, $d\delta_{k,1,b}$, $d\delta_{k',1,b}$, $d\delta_{k'',1,b}$.... The problem, therefore, as Walras clearly states it, is to sort out from the above differential equations (1) and (2) the interrelated differentials of (P), (K), (K′), (K″)... implicit in the differentials of (A), (B), (C)... in such a way as to show how the distribution of a given aggregate excess of income over consumption among the various types of investment (P), (K), (K′), (K″)... is governed, in last analysis, by the actions of individuals in their pursuit of maximum utility within the limits of their incomes. In this note and the following note, the aggregate excess of income over consumption will be called "savings" for the sake of brevity, even though the present argument relates exclusively to the stationary state in which there is no net difference between income and consumption above and beyond what is required simply to maintain the capital equipment of the economy intact. Walras, it will be recalled, restricts his use of the term *savings* to net excesses only (§241).

Remembering that $\Phi'(...) = r$, we may rewrite equation (1) of this note in the form

$$r_a d\delta_{a,1} + r_b d\delta_{b,1} + r_c d\delta_{c,1} + ... = 0. \qquad ..(4)$$

By successive substitution into equation (4): first of the prices of (A), (B), (C)... for the *raretés* to which they are proportional at equilibrium according to

$$\frac{r_{a,1}}{1} = \frac{r_{b,1}}{p_b} = \frac{r_{c,1}}{p_c} = ...,$$

and then of unit costs of production for the prices to which they are equal at equilibrium (ignoring, for simplicity, the land-service costs), we obtain

$$\begin{aligned}
(a_p p_p + a_k p_k + a_{k'} p_{k'} + a_{k''} p_{k''} + ...) d\delta_{a,1} \\
+ (b_p p_p + b_k p_k + b_{k'} p_{k'} + b_{k''} p_{k''} + ...) d\delta_{b,1} \\
+ (c_p p_p + c_k p_k + c_{k'} p_{k'} + c_{k''} p_{k''} + ...) d\delta_{c,1} + ... = 0. \qquad ..(5)
\end{aligned}$$

Removing parentheses and rearranging terms, we have

$$\begin{aligned}
a_p p_p d\delta_{a,1} + a_k p_k d\delta_{a,1} + a_{k'} p_{k'} d\delta_{a,1} + a_{k''} p_{k''} d\delta_{a,1} + ... \\
+ b_p p_p d\delta_{b,1} + b_k p_k d\delta_{b,1} + b_{k'} p_{k'} d\delta_{b,1} + b_{k''} p_{k''} d\delta_{b,1} + ... \\
+ c_p p_p d\delta_{c,1} + c_k p_k d\delta_{c,1} + c_{k'} p_{k'} d\delta_{c,1} + c_{k''} p_{k''} d\delta_{c,1} + ... = 0.
\end{aligned} \qquad ..(6)$$

Adding columns and factoring, we obtain

$$P_p(a_p d\delta_{a,1} + b_p d\delta_{b,1} + c_p d\delta_{c,1} + \dots) + p_k(a_k d\delta_{a,1} + b_k d\delta_{b,1} + c_k d\delta_{c,1} + \dots)$$
$$+ p_{k'}(a_{k'} d\delta_{a,1} + b_{k'} d\delta_{b,1} + c_{k'} d\delta_{c,1} + \dots) \qquad \dots (7)$$
$$+ p_{k''}(a_{k''} d\delta_{a,1} + b_{k''} d\delta_{b,1} + c_{k''} d\delta_{c,1} + \dots) + \dots = 0.$$

But if we write

$$a_p d\delta_{a,1} + b_p d\delta_{b,1} + c_p \, d\delta_{c,1} + \dots = d\delta_{p,1},$$
$$a_k d\delta_{a,1} + b_k \, d\delta_{b,1} + c_k \, d\delta_{c,1} + \dots = d\delta_{k,1},$$
$$a_{k'} d\delta_{a,1} + b_{k'} d\delta_{b,1} + c_{k'} d\delta_{c,1} + \dots = d\delta_{k',1},$$
$$\cdot \quad \cdot \quad \cdot \quad \cdot \quad \cdot \quad \cdot \quad \cdot \quad \cdot \quad \cdot \quad \cdot \quad \cdot$$

(which differs from Walras's system [ι] in the text), and then substitute into (7), we obtain

$$p_p d\delta_{p,1} + p_k d\delta_{k,1} + p_{k'} d\delta_{k',1} + p_{k''} d\delta_{k'',1} + \dots = 0 \qquad \dots (8)$$

as a necessary condition of maximum effective utility for individual (1). Similar equations could be derived for individuals (2), (3). . . .

If we let

$$d\delta_{p,1} + d\delta_{p,2} + d\delta_{p,3} + \dots = dD_p,$$
$$d\delta_{k,1} + d\delta_{k,2} + d\delta_{k,3} + \dots = dD_k,$$
$$d\delta_{k',1} + d\delta_{k',2} + d\delta_{k',3} + \dots = dD_{k'},$$
$$\cdot \quad \cdot \quad \cdot \quad \cdot \quad \cdot \quad \cdot \quad \cdot \quad \cdot \quad \cdot \quad \cdot \quad \cdot \quad \cdot$$

we may write

$$p_p dD_p + p_k dD_k + p_{k'} dD_{k'} + p_{k''} dD_{k''} + \dots = 0 \qquad \dots (9)$$

for the economy as a whole.

On the macro-economic side, the stationary state we are assuming requires that there be annual "savings" exactly equal to the cost of maintaining the capital equipment of the economy intact. If we designate such constant "savings" by E^*, we may write

$$P^*_p D_p + P^*_k D_k + P^*_{k'} D_{k'} + P^*_{k''} D_{k''} + \dots = E^* \qquad \dots (10)$$

where $P^*_p, P^*_k, P^*_{k'}, P^*_{k''} \dots$ represent the *costs to the consumer* (by no means necessarily equal to Walras's $P_p, P_k, P_{k'}, P_{k''} \dots$, as will be seen in the next note) of the corresponding capital goods, and $D_p, D_k, D_{k'}, D_{k''} \dots$ represent the aggregate annual quantities demanded of the different varieties of new capital goods. Assuming that $P^*_p, P^*_k, P^*_{k'}, P^*_{k''} \dots$ as well as E^* are already determined and constant, so that the quantities demanded alone are variables in our present problem, we have

$$P^*_p dD_p + P^*_k dD_k + P^*_{k'} dD_{k'} + P^*_{k''} dD_{k''} + \dots = 0. \qquad \dots (11)$$

The differentials in equation (11) must be such that, *at least for pairs* involving any one capital good with each of the others in succession, the following equations are satisfied

$$P^*_k dD_k + P^*_p \, dD_p = 0,$$
$$P^*_k dD_k + P^*_{k'} \, dD_{k'} = 0, \qquad \dots (12)$$
$$P^*_k dD_k + P^*_{k''} dD_{k''} = 0,$$
$$\cdot \quad \cdot \quad \cdot \quad \cdot \quad \cdot \quad \cdot \quad \cdot \quad \cdot \quad \cdot$$

Inasmuch as the quantities of capital goods are always assumed to be numerically equal to quantities of the corresponding services yielded by these capital goods and the prices of the services are assumed at this stage to be already determined, we may also write

$$p_k dD_k + p_p \, dD_p = 0,$$
$$p_k dD_k + p_{k'} \, dD_{k'} = 0,$$
$$p_k dD_k + p_{k''} dD_{k''} = 0, \qquad \dots (13)$$
$$\cdot \quad \cdot \quad \cdot \quad \cdot \quad \cdot \quad \cdot \quad \cdot$$

which constitutes an additional constraint on (9) expressing the fact that, from the aggregate or macro-economic point of view, individuals can only maximize their sums of effective utility within the limits prescribed by the aggregate amount of "savings" to be invested in the various capital goods required for the production of consumers' goods. Thus, the maximization of utility expressed in equations (1) and (9) is subject to a double constraint: the micro-economic constraint given by the individual budget equations and the macro-economic constraint given by a comprehensive "savings"-investment equation. Since the macro-economic constraint on (11) could also be expressed by other systems in which algebraic sums involving any one capital good with all possible combinations of two, three or more of the others are equated to zero, system (12) constitutes a sufficient, but not a necessary condition of the maximum in question.

From (12) and (13) we have

$$\frac{p_p}{P^*{}_p} = \frac{p_k}{P^*{}_k} = \frac{p_{k'}}{P^*{}_{k'}} = \frac{p_{k''}}{P^*{}_{k''}} = \dots \qquad ..(14)$$

for each and every individual, from which Walras's italicized conclusion at the close of §263 follows. In other words, from the standpoint of each individual who consumes the services of capital goods directly or indirectly, for his total effective utility to be a maximum, it is necessary that the rate of return over cost be the same for all new capital goods.

Thus the demands for the productive services of capital goods and hence for capital goods without any utility of their own are not "adventitious" elements in Walras's system, as I once asserted, but are rigorously related to the utility functions which constitute, as it were, the primary motive for the entire system (cf. my "Leon Walras's Theory of Capital Accumulation", *op. cit.*, pp. 47–48).

[3] The juxtaposition of Walras's equations

$$\frac{\pi_k}{P_k} = \frac{\pi_{k'}}{P_{k'}} = \frac{\pi_{k''}}{P_{k''}} = \dots \qquad ..(1.1)$$

with his

$$\frac{p_k}{P_k} = \frac{p_{k'}}{P_{k'}} = \frac{p_{k''}}{P_{k''}} = \dots \qquad ..(2.1)$$

gave his early readers and critics a great deal of trouble, as can be seen in a long series of unpublished letters which Walras exchanged with von Bortkiewicz and Edgeworth between the dates January 9 and September 14, 1889, when finally Walras wrote to von Bortkiewicz: ".... j'ai en ce moment la tête fatiguée" (F.W., I, 66). It will be shown in this note that neither the difficulty his readers had in understanding him nor the mental fatigue Walras suffered in trying to make himself understood was necessary, for the difficulty lay not in any inherent contradiction in his argument, but in a slip of the pen and in the peculiar clumsiness of his exposition.

Whether Walras's system designated as (2.1) in this note is arrived at by Walras's undecipherable method of analysis in §263 or whether it is arrived at, as in Lesson 26 for the special case where capital goods yield consumers' services only, one is inevitably faced with the problem of reconciling this system, which is a necessary condition of maximum effective utility for the individual consumer, with Walras's system of equations designated above as (1.1), which is the condition of equilibrium in the capital goods market resulting from arbitrage. It should be noted that although no ratio $\frac{\pi_p}{P_p}$, corresponding to $\frac{p_p}{P^*{}_p}$, in system (14)

of the previous note, figures explicitly in (1.1) because there is no market for
~~personal capital in the absence of slavery, such a ratio may still be considered as~~
virtually existing in consequence of each individual's private allocation of his
"savings" among non-marketable as well as marketable investments.

Indeed, if the terms P_k, $P_{k'}$, $P_{k''}$... are defined simply as the market prices of
the corresponding capital goods, as Walras actually defines them in §§ 262 and 263
—and this was his slip—then the two systems (1.1) and (2.1), with or without
$\frac{\pi_p}{P_p}$ and $\frac{P_p}{P_p}$, are irreconcilable unless the π's and the p's are proportional to each
other. If each π_k were equal to the corresponding p_k, which would be the case
supposing all capital goods to be infinitely durable and indestructible, the problem
would be automatically solved; but the theorem would be trivial, for then all
capital goods would reduce to landed-capital and there would be no "capital
goods proper" at all—in Walras's terminology (§§ 174–176). The only way to
retain "capital goods proper" and preserve proportionality between the π_k's and
the p_k's is to assume that the combined rates of depreciation and insurance,
i.e. $(\mu_k + \nu_k)$, $(\mu_{k'} + \nu_{k'})$, $(\mu_{k''} + \nu_{k''})$..., are the same for all varieties of capital
goods. This would be a purely fictitious assumption, having no applicability
whatsoever to the real world where these rates often differ very widely from one
kind of capital good to another, and it would have the further disadvantage of
concealing the very relations which are the crux of the present problem. There remains, then, a formal contradiction when the $(\mu_k + \nu_k)$'s are neither zero nor equal
to one another for all varieties of capital goods. Since $\pi_k = p_k - (\mu_k + \nu_k)P_k$,
$\pi_{k'} = p_{k'} - (\mu_{k'} + \nu_{k'})P_{k'}$, $\pi_{k''} = p_{k''} - (\mu_{k''} + \nu_{k''})P_{k''}$ (§ 232), system (1.1) may
be rewritten

$$\frac{p_k - (\mu_k + \nu_k)P_k}{P_k} = \frac{p_{k'} - (\mu_{k'} + \nu_{k'})P_{k'}}{P_{k'}} = \frac{p_{k''} - (\mu_{k''} + \nu_{k''})P_{k''}}{P_{k''}} = \cdots \qquad ..(1.2)$$

which is obviously incompatible with system (2.1) if at least two of the parenthetical expressions in (1.2) are not equal.

As Walras developed the argument, however, this incompatibility was only
formal and not one of substance, for at the very point where the danger of
a contradiction appeared he made appropriate additions to the denominators in
system (2.1). Here is where the clumsiness of his exposition becomes only too
apparent. In the previous note the whole difficulty was avoided by choosing
a different set of symbols P^*_k, $P^*_{k'}$, $P^*_{k''}$... to represent Walras's P_k, $P_{k'}$, $P_{k''}$...
plus the additional capital provision consumers must make per unit of each new
capital good in order to assure a steady flow of income sufficient to cover the
recurrent depreciation and insurance charges pertaining to that capital good.
That is why the P^*_k's were defined in the previous note as *costs to the consumer*.
Since the *cost to the consumer* of a new non-permanent capital good in a
stationary state is not the same as the market price received by the producer of
such a good, only the P^*_k's, and not the P_k's, are relevant in the consumer's
calculus of maximum effective utility. On the other hand, all that the producer
of a new capital good needs to consider in his pursuit of maximum profit are
the P_k's. Hence the P_k's, and not the P^*_k's, are alone appropriate to system (1.1)
which is a necessary condition of equilibrium in the capital goods market.
What Walras's awkward procedure amounted to was first to assume that all
capital goods were permanent or that the depreciation and insurance charges
were paid by a *deus ex machina*, so that Walras had, to begin with, the same
denominators in (1.1) and (1.2) which did not matter since, in this case, the p_k's
and the π_k's were equal. Then, dropping this assumption, he added the appropriate $\frac{(\mu_k + \nu_k)P_k}{i}$'s to each of the denominators in (2.1). These additions turn

out to be the differences between the P^*_k's and the P_k's of this note. Once system (2.1) is replaced by

$$\frac{p_k}{P_k+\dfrac{(\mu_k+\nu_k)P_k}{i}}=\frac{p_{k'}}{P_{k'}+\dfrac{(\mu_{k'}+\nu_{k'})P_{k'}}{i}}=\frac{p_{k''}}{P_{k''}+\dfrac{(\mu_{k''}+\nu_{k''})P_{k''}}{i}}=\ldots, \quad ..(3.1)$$

the desired reconciliation is achieved, for, as can be easily seen from Translator's Notes [5] and [6] of Lesson 26, system (3.1) reduces to system (1.1).

To explain the new denominators in the ratios of system (3.1), let us imagine that at the beginning of a given year a unit of one of the capital goods, say (K), needs to be replaced in order to preserve the steady flow of consumers' goods characteristic of a stationary state. Consumers, then, must not only pay P_k for the new unit of (K) out of their "savings", but they must also provide "savings" annually and for ever which are sufficient to replace this unit as it is recurrently used up or destroyed. This annual provision which must be made in perpetuity, if the stationary state is to be preserved, is equivalent to a once-and-for-all investment of a capital sum large enough to yield this annual provision. Adding this capital sum to the market price of the new unit of capital good (K), we obtain $P_k+\dfrac{(\mu_k+\nu_k)P_k}{i}=P^*_k$, which is the total capital cost consumers must incur, directly or indirectly, in order to receive a flow of annual services worth p_k for ever.

It is for this reason that the ratio $\dfrac{p_k}{P^*_k}=\dfrac{p_k}{P_k+\dfrac{(\mu_k+\nu_k)P_k}{i}}$ was designated in the

previous note as a rate of return over cost for each consumer. It follows, moreover, that

$$P^*_k-P_k=\frac{(\mu_k+\nu_k)P_k}{i}, \qquad ..(4.1)$$

for (K), and similarly for the other capital goods (K'), (K'')....

There still remains a gap in the argument which needs to be filled. When the transition is made from the micro-economic equilibrium of the individual to the macro-economic condition of the stationary state, it is by no means evident from Walras's discussion in Lessons 26 and 27 how the additional capital funds required for the maintenance of the economy's new capital goods are accounted for in the "savings"-investment constraint. Walras expressed this constraint by his equation (2) in §§262 and 263

$$D_kP_k+D_{k'}P_{k'}+D_{k''}P_{k''}+\ldots=E, \qquad ..(5.1)$$

which could equally well have been written

$$D_pP_p+D_kP_k+D_{k'}P_{k'}+D_{k''}P_{k''}+\ldots=E \qquad ..(5.2)$$

if Walras had thought fit to take non-marketable personal capital into consideration. In either case, this equation could only serve his purpose so long as he assumed that the burden of depreciation and insurance was not borne by the consumer. When, however, this assumption is dropped, equation (5.1) or (5.2) is no longer adequate. A different equation, like equation (10) of the previous note, is now required. The difference between that equation and equation (5.2) of this note

$$E^*-E=D_p(P^*_p-P_p)+D_k(P^*_k-P_k)+D_{k'}(P^*_{k'}-P_{k'})+D_{k''}(P^*_{k''}-P_{k''})+\ldots$$

is exactly equal to

$$D_p\left[\frac{(\mu_p+\nu_p)P_p}{i}\right]+D_k\left[\frac{(\mu_k+\nu_k)P_k}{i}\right]+D_{k'}\left[\frac{(\mu_{k'}+\nu_{k'})P_{k'}}{i}\right]$$
$$+D_{k''}\left[\frac{(\mu_{k''}+\nu_{k''})P_{k''}}{i}\right]+\ldots,$$

as can be seen from (4.1) above.

LESSON 28

[1] See §135.

[2] Thus, when Léon Walras broaches questions of applied economics, he recognizes, no less clearly than Alfred Marshall, that there is a hierarchy of interrelationships among economic variables, some sets being more closely inter-related than others. In his pure theory of general equilibrium, Walras considers all interrelationships *ex aequo*, but in passing to applied problems he is just as aware as Marshall of the existence of changes "of the second order of smallness" (to use Marshall's phrase), which may therefore be neglected for all practical purposes. Surely Professor Milton Friedman drew too sharp a contrast between Marshall and Walras in his article, "The Marshallian Demand Curve", which appeared in the *Journal of Political Economy*, vol. LVII, no. 6, December 1949, pp. 463–495. There one gets the impression that Walras's sole preoccupation was the achievement of "abstractness, generality and mathematical elegance" (p. 490), while Marshall sought "an engine for the discovery of concrete truth". A more valid and important distinction between Walras and Marshall resides in the fact that the former always took great care not to confuse pure theory with applied theory, while the latter gloried in fusing the two.

LESSON 29

[1] See §169 and Translator's Note [5] of Lesson 17.

[2] What Walras apparently has in mind here is a stationary state, i.e. an economy operating under stationary conditions. For a defence of Walras's inclusion of money and cash balances within the stationary framework, see Arthur W. Marget, "The Monetary Aspects of the Walrasian System", *op. cit.*, pp. 158–163. This was in answer to J. R. Hicks's contention that money has no proper place in a model of general equilibrium characterized by "perfect fore-sight" ("Gleichgewicht und Konjunctur", *Zeitschrift für Nationalökonomie*, Band IV, Heft 4, 1933, pp. 446–448). The subject-matter of Lesson 29 itself constitutes, by anticipation, Walras's own answer to Hicks's objections. cf. Jacob Marschak, "The Rationale of the Demand for Money and of 'Money Illusion'", *Microeconomica*, vol. II, August 1950, pp. 71–100, especially §2 and the bibliography on p. 100; and Eraldo Fossati, "A Note about the Utility of Money", *ibid.*, pp. 112–120. See below, Translator's Note [4] of Lesson 30.

[3] See above, Translator's Note [6] of Lesson 20; and §§207, 251 and 257.

[4] The substance, though not the words, of this quotation is found in §235.

[5] See above, Translator's Note [5] of Lesson 20.

[6] The distinction between p_u and $p_{u'}$ is sometimes overlooked, despite its crucial importance. Certainly it is wrong to define $p_{u'}$ as Don Patinkin does on p. 144 of his article "Relative Prices, Say's Law and the Demand for Money", *Econometrica*, vol. 16, no. 2, April 1948, as "the price of money in terms of some commodity (i.e. some measure of the price level)". What Patinkin has in mind is Walras's p_u which is the price per unit of money in terms of an arbitrarily chosen *numéraire*, and not $p_{u'}$ which is the price of the service of availability of a unit of money per unit of time. The relationship between the two prices is defined by $p_{u'} = p_u i$ (see below, Translator's Note [4] of Lesson 30).

[7] This equation differs from previous versions of the equation of exchange of services against consumers' goods and net income (or securities) by the addition of new terms which are written after the first three in the left-hand side of the equation (cf. §244). To understand these new terms, which appear obscure at first sight, it is helpful to interpret them concretely. For example, let us imagine

a farmer who makes butter on his farm and let us consider him exclusively as a consumer living strictly within his income. This implies that he keeps the value of his real capital assets constant. His purchases of consumers' goods and securities must then be exactly equal to his expendable income, which is here defined as the value of all the services he sells. We assume that our farmer consumes some of his butter, stores some of it in his larder because he finds it convenient to have a certain amount constantly available for consumption, and has a balance of butter for which he has no use at all. Following Walras, we shall call the butter consumed (B), the butter in the larder (B') and the butter he has no use for (M). It should be noted that both (B') and (M) are categories of capital, albeit circulating capital, in Walras's terminology. Let us say, now, that at a given moment our farmer finds it advantageous to reduce the amount of butter he is accustomed to keep in his larder and, therefore, sells part of it. This gives rise to an essentially positive $o_{b'}$. He cannot, however, spend all he receives in exchange for $o_{b'}$ on consumers' goods and securities without alienating some of his real capital assets or reducing his income which is the value of the services of these real assets. If he is to keep the value of his real capital assets constant, all he can spend of the proceeds from the sale of part of his larder butter on consumers' goods and securities is the value of the service of availability rendered by the larder butter sold, in other words, $o_{b'}p_{b'}$. This always was part of his income, the rest of the value received being part of the value of his real capital assets. All he can do, therefore, without affecting the value of his real capital assets, is to convert some of his virtual income into expendable income.

If, on the other hand, our farmer wished to increase the amount of butter in his larder, $o_{b'}$ would become essentially negative. The foregoing argument would apply *mutatis mutandis* to this case also, even if we transposed $o_{b'}p_{b'}$ to the right-hand side of the equation with the appropriate change in sign and then substituted $d_{b'}p_{b'}$ for $-o_{b'}p_{b'}$, since $-o_{b'}=d_{b'}$. This would amount to a conversion of some of our farmer's expendable income into virtual income, and of some other form of capital asset into larder butter having the same value.

As for the butter we have designated as (M), since our farmer neither consumes it nor stores it, he will, as Walras tells us, sell all of it, i.e. q_m; but, again, the only portion of the value received which can consistently find a place in the equation of exchange under consideration is the portion which represents the market value of the service of availability of (M), above and beyond the replacement value of the butter itself. This replacement value must be used to replenish the real capital assets after the sale of q_m of (M) in order to keep the value of the real capital assets constant. Hence q_m is multiplied by $p_{m'}$ and not by p_m. The *raison d'être of* $p_{m'}$ is found in the fact that manufacturers, food processors for example, need to keep certain stocks of this raw material on hand in order to assure the smooth functioning of the productive process. This explains the demand for the service of availability of (M).

Since o_u is by definition a quantity of money and $p_{u'}$ is really the price per unit of the service of availability of money, $o_u p_{u'}$ is the amount of interest received in terms of *numéraire* for the loan of o_u units of money and is obviously an item of expendable income.

[8] Although α, β... are defined as quantities of services rather than quantities of (A'), (B')... themselves, these two quantities must be considered numerically equal, like the quantities of capital goods and their services in §262. The meaning of the offer equation of money then becomes clearer if we subject it to the following transformation. Substituting $p_a i$ for $p_{a'}$, $p_b i$ for $p_{b'}$, etc., we have

$$o_u = q_u - \frac{\alpha p_a i + \beta p_b i + \ldots + \varepsilon p_a i}{p_u i}.$$

Cancelling out i, we obtain

$$o_u = q_u - \left(\alpha \frac{p_a}{p_u} + \beta \frac{p_b}{p_u} + \ldots + \varepsilon \frac{p_a}{p_u} \right),$$

which may be rewritten

$$o_u = q_u - (\alpha p_{a,u} + \beta p_{b,u} + \ldots + \varepsilon p_{a,u}),$$

where $p_{a,u}, p_{b,u} \ldots$ represent respectively the prices of (A), (B)... in terms of (U).

[9] It is readily seen that d_α, d_β... represent summations of the α's, β's... which all the individuals in the economy taken together wish to hold.

[10] This sentence begins in French with the words "Ce montant..." which have been translated as "The value . . ." rather than "This value . . .", because the original is ambiguous and appears to refer to O_u, whereas only the last term in the right-hand side of the equation

$$\frac{d_\alpha p_{a'} + d_\beta p_{b'} + \ldots + d_\epsilon p_a}{p_u'}$$

could possibly be the '*encaisse désirée*' of the individual party to the exchange, here considered exclusively in his role as a consumer.

Though the expression '*encaisse désirée*' is peculiarly Walrasian, like '*rareté*' and '*numéraire*', it was found preferable to translate the term literally as "*desired cash balance*" rather than leave it in the French. It will, however, be italicized through this translation in order to mark it clearly as a distinctively Walrasian term.

As for the meaning of the term, Arthur W. Marget ("Leon Walras and the 'Cash Balance Approach' to the Problem of the Value of Money", *Journal of Political Economy*, vol. xxxix, No. 5, October 1931, pp. 587–588) has pointed out that, depending upon the context, the *desired cash balance* may represent either the "quantity of money" or the "demand for money". This distinction is important only in the absence of equilibrium, for at equilibrium the aggregate *actual* cash balance equals the aggregate *desired* cash balance (cf. Alvin H. Hansen, *Monetary Theory and Fiscal Policy*, New York, McGraw Hill, 1949, pp. 56, 61 and 77). In the context to which this note refers the *desired cash balance* may be interpreted, to paraphrase Marget (*loc. cit.*), as the "real" value of the individual consumer's monetary stock—the amount of real wealth which he is prepared to give up in order to possess himself of a cash balance of the desired amount.

[11] Thus δ_α, δ_β... δ_μ... δ_κ... represent the aggregate quantities demanded of the services of availability of (A'), (B')... (M)... (K)... in the form of money. Each of these quantities can be broken down into the components indicated in the left-hand side of the equations which consists of sums of "real" coefficients of production rendering their services of availability in the form of money multiplied by the aggregate demand for their respective products. This aggregate demand is, in turn, made up of two quantities in the case of consumers' goods—the quantity demanded for consumption, e.g. D_b, and the quantity demanded for storage in larders, wardrobes and bins, e.g. $D_{b'}$.

[12] What this boils down to is that a_u, b_u... m_u... k_u... are the values in *numéraire* of the cash reserves which producers of (A), (B)... (M)... (K)... hold in the form of money per unit of output. Each of these monetary coefficients of production can be broken down into the components indicated in the right-hand side of the equations where we have sums, evaluated in *numéraire*, of the services of availability of the "real" coefficients of production held in the form of money rather than in kind.

[13] Utilizing the relations indicated in Translator's Note [8] of this Lesson and the additional relations $p_k = P_k i$, etc., we may rewrite this equation in the form

$$\delta_\alpha p_{a,u} + \delta_\beta p_{b,u} + \ldots + \delta_\mu p_{m,u} + \ldots + \delta_\kappa P_{k,u} + \ldots = O_u.$$

[14] In other words, equations (3) and (7) of Lesson 24 are now expanded in order to include the quantities demanded of the different varieties of circulating as well as fixed capital; and, consequently, the excess of aggregate production (or income) over aggregate consumption must be a function of the prices of the services of circulating as well as fixed capital.

[15] The equations and unknowns counted in the remainder of this paragraph can be set out as follows:

a first group of $m+s+1$ equations consisting of
  m equations

$$\frac{p_a'}{i} = p_a, \qquad \frac{p_b'}{i} = p_b \ldots;$$

  s equations

$$\frac{p_m'}{i} = p_m \ldots;$$

  1 equation

$$\frac{p_u'}{i} = p_u;$$

a second group of $m+1$ equations (in which it should be recalled from §242 that $p_e = \frac{1}{i}$) consisting of
  m equations

$$O_{a'} = F_{a'}(p_t, p_p, p_k \ldots p_b, p_c, p_d \ldots p_a \ldots p_{a'}, p_{b'} \ldots p_{m'} \ldots p_{u'}, p_e),$$
$$O_{b'} = F_{b'}(. \quad . \quad . \quad . \quad . \quad . \quad . \quad . \quad . \quad . \quad . \quad . \quad . \quad . \quad .),$$

  1 equation

$$O_u = Q_u - \frac{d_\alpha p_{a'} + d_\beta p_{b'} + \ldots + d_\epsilon p_{a'}}{p_{u'}};$$

and a third group of $m+s+1$ equations consisting of
  m equations

$$a_{a'}(D_a + D_{a'}) + b_{a'}(D_b + D_{b'}) + \ldots + m_{a'}D_m + \ldots + k_{a'}D_k + \ldots = D_{a'},$$
$$a_{b'}(D_a + D_{a'}) + b_{b'}(D_b + D_{b'}) + \ldots + m_{b'}D_m + \ldots + k_{b'}D_k + \ldots = D_{b'},$$

  where $D_{a'}, D_{b'} \ldots$ are the aggregate quantities demanded of the services (A'), (B') $\ldots$;

  s equations

$$a_m(D_a + D_{a'}) + b_m(D_b + D_{b'}) + \ldots + m_m D_m + \ldots + k_m D_k + \ldots = Q_m,$$

  1 equation

$$\frac{\delta_\alpha p_{a'} + \delta_\beta p_{b'} + \ldots + \delta_\mu p_m + \ldots + \delta_\kappa P_k + \ldots}{p_{u'}} = D_u$$

  where D_u is the aggregate quantity demanded of (U).

Corresponding to these $3m+2s+3$ equations there are exactly the same number of unknowns, viz.

a first group of $m+1$ unknowns consisting of
  m unknowns
    $D_{a'}, D_{b'}\ldots$;
  1 unknown
    D_u;
a second group of $m+s+1$ unknowns consisting of
  m unknowns
    $p_{a'}, p_{b'}\ldots$;
  s unknowns
    $p_{m'}\ldots$;
  1 unknown
    $p_{u'}$;
and a third group of $m+s+1$ unknowns consisting of
  m unknowns
    $O_{a'}, O_{b'}\ldots$;
  s unknowns
    $Q_m\ldots$;
  1 unknown
    p_u.

[16] In other words, if $D_{a'}=O_{a'}$, $D_{b'}=O_{b'}\ldots$ and $D_u=O_u$, the $2m+s+2$ equations of the second and third groups of equations in the previous note reduce to $m+s+1$ equations, viz.

  m equations

$$a_{a'}(D_a+D_{a'})+b_{a'}(D_b+D_{b'})+\ldots+m_{a'}D_m+\ldots+k_{a'}D_k+\ldots=$$
$$F_{a'}(p_t, p_p, p_k\cdots p_b, p_c, p_d\cdots p_{a'}, p_{b'}\cdots p_{m'}\cdots p_{u'}, p_e);$$
$$a_{b'}(D_a+D_{a'})+b_{b'}(D_b+D_{b'})+\ldots+m_{b'}D_m+\ldots+k_{b'}D_k+\ldots=$$
$$F_{b'}(.\qquad\qquad\qquad\qquad\qquad\qquad\qquad\qquad);$$
$$\cdots\cdots\cdots\cdots\cdots\cdots\cdots\cdots\cdots\cdots\cdots\cdots\cdots\cdots\cdots;$$

  s equations

$$a_m(D_a+D_{a'})+b_m(D_b+D_{b'})+\ldots+m_m D_m+\ldots+k_m D_k+\ldots=Q_m$$
$$\cdots\cdots\cdots\cdots\cdots\cdots\cdots\cdots\cdots\cdots\cdots\cdots\cdots$$

in which D_a, $D_{a'}$, D_b, $D_{b'}\ldots D_m\ldots D_k\ldots$ are functions of all the prices in the system;

  1 equation

$$\frac{\delta_\alpha p_{a'}+\delta_\beta p_{b'}+\ldots+\delta_\mu p_{m'}+\ldots+\delta_\kappa p_k+\cdots}{p_{u'}}=$$
$$Q_u-\frac{d_\alpha p_{a'}+d_\beta p_{b'}+\ldots+d_\epsilon p_{a'}}{p_{u'}}.$$

LESSON 30

[1] See §275.

[2] i.e. *circa* 1900.

[3] Though Walras always assumes, implicitly or explicitly, that the quantity of services of any capital asset, be it fixed capital, circulating capital or money, is numerically equal to the quantity of the capital asset yielding the services, it is important here to interpret D_α as the quantity of *services* of availability

rendered by the aggregate cash balances held by the consumers in lieu of stores of consumers' goods, Δ_α as the quantity of such *services* rendered by the aggregate cash balances held by producers in lieu of inventories, stocks of raw materials and fixed capital, and E_α as the quantity of the same *services* held generally in lieu of perpetual annuity shares (or securities)—all of these quantities of services being measured in terms of (A). Unless these items are strictly interpreted as quantities of *services* and not as quantities of cash held in the balances, we shall not be prepared to understand the distinction between H_α and H_α made at the close of §278.

[4] This passage, taken in conjunction with Walras's assumption of a money 'sans utilité propre' (§275), i.e. without any utility of its own, constitutes, according to Don Patinkin ("Relative Prices, Say's Law and the Demand for Money", *op. cit.*, pp. 143–144, and his article, "The Indeterminacy of Absolute Prices", *Econometrica*, vol 17., no. 1, January 1949, p. 12), the Achilles' heel of the whole Walrasian system. Patinkin's argument, so far as it relates to Walras, hinges on Walras's alleged exclusion of money from the utility function. We are told that since Walras "assumed that money is not in the utility function", $o_u p_{u'}$ cannot be in "the budget equation", i.e. in the equation of exchange (§275). There are two errors of fact in Patinkin's account of Walras's "error" in logic. The first is Patinkin's misinterpretation of $p_{u'}$ already referred to in Translator's Note [6] of Lesson 29; and the second is his misapprehension of Walras's money 'sans utilité propre'. Actually, though a money, like paper money, may well be "without any utility of its own", the price of its service of availability $p_{u'}$ stands, according to Walras, in a definite and unique relationship to the utility functions of the various services of availability which money (U) performs. Thus in the fifth paragraph of §275 Walras gives the *rareté* functions $\varphi_\alpha(\alpha)$, $\varphi_\beta(\beta)$... which are none other than the *rareté* functions of each of the services of availability rendered by (U) in the individuals' *desired cash balance*. Moreover, on the aggregative, or macro-economic side, as seen in §279, Walras clearly writes $R_{u'}$ to designate the conventional "average *rareté*" (cf. §135) of the service of availability of (U). These are devices for relating a money which admittedly has no utility of its own to services which actually do enter into the utility function, thus rendering the Walrasian system, on this score at least, both consistent and determinate (cf. Karl Brunner, "Inconsistency and Indeterminacy in Classical Economics", *Econometrica*, vol. 19, no. 2, April 1951, pp. 169–171).

[5] The word '*agio*' in this context refers to any differences in the value of money at different times or in different places.

[6] Here H_α is the aggregate value in (A) of the *desired cash balances* themselves, as distinguished from H_α which is the aggregate value in (A) of the services of these cash balances. The two are related by the capitalization equation $\frac{H_\alpha}{i} = \mathrm{H}_\alpha$. It follows that $\frac{\mathrm{H}_\alpha}{p_u}$ is the aggregate value of the same cash balances in terms of (U). See above, Translator's Note [3] of this Lesson.

[7] See §§135 and 226.

[8] i.e. in the same proportion as Q_u. If this proportion be θ, then in the special case considered all the individual q_u's are multiplied by the proportionality factor θ.

[9] If each q_u is multiplied by θ ($\theta > 0$), all other things remaining the same, then $p_{u'}$ will have to be multiplied by $\frac{1}{\theta}$ by virtue of the fact that $p_{u'}$ varies inversely with q_u. That being the case, it follows that

$$\theta q_u \frac{p_{u'}}{\theta} = q_u p_{u'}.$$

Moreover, under the assumed circumstances, it follows from the *ceteris paribus* condition that in each individual case the demand for money $q_u - o_u$ and the offer o_u are linear functions of the total quantity, so that each of them must be multiplied by θ, giving

$$\theta(q_u - o_u)\frac{p_u'}{\theta} = (q_u - o_u)p_u'$$

and

$$\theta o_u \frac{p_u'}{\theta} = o_u p_u'.$$

[10] This cryptic sentence becomes intelligible when interpreted to mean that the "rectangular utility" H of varying quantities of the money commodity in money use will remain constant provided that the price elasticities of demand for each of the cash balance items involved in H are equal to unity and provided that there are no changes in the offer functions of these items. The latter proviso restricts the variations in the quantities desired of the components of H to variations resulting from increases or decreases in the quantity of the money commodity in money use. Thus from Walras's definition of H (§279)

$$Q_u \frac{R_u'}{R_a} = d_\alpha \frac{R_a'}{R_a} + \delta_\alpha \frac{R_a'}{R_a} + d_\epsilon \frac{R_a'}{R_a} + d_\beta \frac{R_b'}{R_a} + \dots$$

which may be rewritten

$$Q_u p_u' = d_\alpha p_a' + \delta_\alpha p_a' + d_\epsilon p_a' + d_\beta p_b' + \dots,$$

the prices being expressed in terms of (A), it is obvious that if the elasticity of each of the demands itemized in the right-hand side of the equation is equal to unity, each of the quantities demanded multiplied by the corresponding prices will be constant and the sum of these separate constant quantities will equal a constant $Q_u p_u'$, provided, however, that the only changes in d_α, δ_α, d_ϵ, $d_\beta \dots$ are those corresponding to changes in Q_u. In other words, given

$$d_\alpha + \delta_\alpha + d_\epsilon = q_\alpha - o_\alpha, \quad d_\beta + \delta_\beta = q_\beta - o_\beta \dots \quad \delta_\mu = q_\mu - o_\mu \dots \quad \delta_\kappa = q_\kappa - o_\kappa \dots,$$

all of the o's must be constant. These are sufficient (but not necessary) conditions for a constant $Q_u p_u'$.

[11] It should be remembered that E'_α and E''_α are respectively fixed and circulating capital in the form of money and not in kind. Hence j' and j'' must be interpreted as long rates and short rates of interest on money loans.

[12] cf. Léon Walras, *Etudes d'économie politique appliquée*, p. 316.

[13] From Fig. 15 of ed. 4.

Lesson 31

[1] Giving

$$Q'_o = F_o(\omega P_a) \qquad \qquad \text{..modified (4),}$$
$$Q''_a = P_a + Q''_o \omega P_o = H \qquad \qquad \text{..modified (5).}$$

[2] The order of exposition in this and the following two paragraphs differs slightly from the original to accord with the new presentation of the geometrical figures.

[3] The economic interpretation of the equilateral hyperbola in this context is different from what it was in §283 of Lesson 30. Originally it was drawn for the monometallic case and the ordinates measured quantities of monetized (A); in Lesson 31 the bimetallic case is under discussion, and the ordinates measure both the quantities of monetized (A) and monetized (O), the latter quantity being multiplied by the ratio of the value of (O) to the value of (A), i.e. $Q''_a + \omega Q''_o$.

[4] From Fig. 17 of ed. 4.

[5] From Fig. 16 of ed. 4.

Lesson 32

[1] From Fig. 18 of ed. 4.
[2] From Fig. 19 of ed. 4.
[3] cf. Walras's "Monnaie d'or avec billon d'argent régulateur", reprinted from the *Revue de droit international*, December 1, 1884, in the *Etudes d'économie politique appliquée*, pp. 1–19.

Lesson 33

[1] cf. Walras's "Note sur la 'Théorie de la Quantité'" and his "Théorie mathématique du billet de banque" in the *Etudes d'économie politique appliquée*, pp. 154–158 and pp. 339–375.

Lesson 34

[1] London, Effingham Wilson, 1864, Chapter II.

Lesson 35

[1] See §232.

Lesson 36

[1] The purpose of this note is to elucidate the theoretical argument presented in §§325 and 326 and in the postscript to Appendix III of which §326 of ed. 4 and ed. 4 def. is a revised summary. No attempt will be made here to clarify or adjudicate the delicate question of Walras's priority *vis-à-vis* Philip Wicksteed in the discovery of the marginal productivity theory. Nor, apart from occasional comments, will anything be said here about the evolution of Walras's own conception of the theory, as revealed in his unpublished correspondence particularly with Enrico Barone. Though these matters have already been discussed at some length in the literature, there is good reason to suppose that the last word has not been said and will not be said until a full documentation far exceeding the dimensions of a note has been published. The following are some of the more recently published items dealing with Walras's theory of marginal productivity: Henry Schultz, "Marginal Productivity and the General Pricing Process", *Journal of Political Economy*, vol. XXXVII, no. 5, October 1929, pp. 505–551; "Marginal Productivity and the Lausanne School", *Economica*, no. 37, August 1932, pp. 285–296; John R. Hicks, "Marginal Productivity and the Principle of Variation", *Economica*, no. 35, February 1932, pp. 79–88; "A Reply", *ibid.*, no. 37, August 1932, pp. 297–300; *The Theory of Wages*, London, Macmillan, 1932, pp. 232–239; H. Neisser, "A Note on Pareto's Theory of Production", *Econometrica*, vol. 8, no. 3, July 1940, pp. 253–262; George Stigler, *Production and Distribution Theories*, Chapter XII; Paul Samuelson, *Foundations of Economic Analysis*, Chapter IV.

Up to this point in the *Elements*, it has been assumed that the coefficients of production are fixed, i.e. not subject to any compensatory or other variation, but technically given. See §204 and Translator's Note [3] of Lesson 20. Nevertheless, as was shown in Part IV of the *Elements*, the prices of the productive services (as well as the amounts employed in each industry) were perfectly determined under conditions of pure and perfect competition (cf. J. R. Hicks, "Marginal Productivity and the Principle of Variation", *op. cit.*, pp. 80–83.) The marginal productivity theory had no part to play in the simple theory of production with fixed coefficients. In as early a version of the *Eléments* as the first edition, before there was any mention of the marginal productivity theory as such, Walras clearly intimated in a passage (§343 of ed. 1, cf. §362 of ed. 4 def.), which does not appear to have been noticed by any of the commentators so far, that the sole purpose of production functions was to determine the coefficients of production, when, of course, these coefficients were not technically given. The prices of the productive services could then be determined very much as they had been before: by solving the four systems of equations given in the theory of production (§§245–246 of ed. 1 or §§202–203 of ed. 4 def.), with this difference, however, that the equations

$$b_t = \theta(b_p, b_k \ldots); \qquad b_p = \psi(b_t, b_k \ldots); \qquad b_k = \chi(b_t, b_p \ldots); \ldots$$

must now be added to determine the variable coefficients. This was the state of the theory in the text of the first three editions. The niche for the marginal productivity theory was prepared and properly situated, but it was still empty.

In ed. 4 the niche was filled when the marginal productivity theory was finally integrated into the text after Walras had first presented it in Appendix III of ed. 3 as an adjunct to his polemic against Wicksteed and as a joint product of his discussions with Barone and Pareto. In ed. 4, as in the earlier editions, the variability of the coefficients of production was postulated as a dynamic phenomenon peculiar to economic progress. When population and capital increase on a fixed territory, though the state of the industrial arts remains unchanged, the coefficients of production must change. Nevertheless, the theoretical model Walras devised for the study of this phenomenon was not, properly speaking, dynamic. His method was that of comparative statics. What is implicitly assumed is a once-for-all increase in capital and population on a fixed amount of land, entailing readjustments in the coefficients of production. Then the marginal productivity theory, in conjunction with the other conditions of economic equilibrium, defines the new stationary equilibrium, so far as the new coefficients of production are concerned.

Walras's exposition of the theory is extremely difficult to follow. As John R. Hicks put it in his *Theory of Wages*, p. 234: ". . . Unfortunately Walras expressed himself in so crabbed and obscure a manner that it is doubtful if he conveyed his point to anyone who did not possess some further assistance. Anyone who knows the answer can see that Walras has got it, but anyone who does not must find it almost impossible to get it from Walras." Hence the need for further elucidation.

Though §§325 and 326 are considered together in this note, the key to the understanding of Walras's theory is found by separating the two sections. A comparison of editions (cf. Collation Notes [c]–[f] of this Lesson) shows that the two sections are really the fruits of separate and unco-ordinated layers of Walras's development, the first layer having been retained, in all probability, in order to preserve the vestigial evidence of his earlier contribution to the theory before the advent of Wicksteed. This explains Walras's "mathematical error" to which Henry Schultz has called attention in his article "Marginal Productivity and the General Pricing Process" (*op. cit.*, pp. 515 and 545–546), where he criticized Walras for using the same symbol φ to represent two quite different functions,

$$\varphi(b_t, b_p, b_k \ldots) = 0$$

and

$$Q = \varphi(Qb_t, Qb_p, Qb_k \ldots).$$

As Neisser pointed out (*op. cit.*, p. 256, note 11), the "error" is harmless, if we consider the first function simply as "an introductory formulation designed to set forth the principle of substitution" and if we regard the second function as the *definitive* one and the only one which is actually used in the subsequent analysis.

A careful and detailed study of the mathematical implications of Walras's peculiar exposition has already been made by Henry Schultz in the above-mentioned article and need not be repeated here. Moreover, Neisser has shown (op. cit., pp. 256–258) how Walras's theory can be generalized so as to remove certain objections to it which Pareto first made and Henry Schultz later echoed. Both of the major difficulties, viz. "(a) the restriction to homogeneous production functions of the first degree . . . and (b) the existence of limitational factors which impair the general existence of the production function . . ." can be overcome within the framework of the Walrasian system (cf. also J. R. Hicks, *The Theory of Wages*, pp. 236–239).

It remains now only to reconstruct the Walrasian demonstration of his marginal productivity theorem, which becomes more intelligible when an additional ambiguity in Walras's symbolism is removed and the mathematical procedures suggested by Paul A. Samuelson (op. cit., pp. 57–66) are followed. Since p_b has hitherto been generally used to designate the selling price per unit of (B), it is less confusing to introduce a new symbol π_b to represent the cost of production per unit of (B) and write Walras's equation (1) of §326 as:

$$Q\pi_b = Qb_t p_t + Qb_p p_p + Qb_k p_k + \dots \qquad \qquad ..(1.1)$$

where the symbols, apart from π_b which we have just defined, have the significance attributed to them by Walras and where $Q, p_t, p_p, p_k \dots$ are considered as given in advance and fixed. In accordance with Walras's definitions of $T, P, K \dots$, (1.1) may be rewritten

$$Q\pi_b = T p_t + P p_p + K p_k + \dots \qquad \qquad ..(1.2)$$

The problem is to minimize (1.2) subject to Walras's "definitive" production function

$$Q = \varphi(T, P, K \dots). \qquad \qquad ..(2.1)$$

This problem is equivalent to minimizing a new function

$$\Pi = T p_t + P p_p + K p_k + \dots - \lambda [\varphi(T, P, K \dots) - Q] \qquad ..(3.1)$$

where $-\lambda$ is a Lagrangean multiplier. Π is thus a function of all the coefficients of production considered as independent variables and is nothing else than the total cost function plus an additional term equal to zero. To minimize the total cost, therefore, it is necessary to equate to zero each of the partial derivatives of (3.1) with respect to the coefficients of production implicit in T, P, K . . .:

$$\frac{\partial \Pi}{\partial T} = p_t - \lambda \frac{\partial \varphi}{\partial T} = 0,$$

$$\frac{\partial \Pi}{\partial P} = p_p - \lambda \frac{\partial \varphi}{\partial P} = 0, \qquad \qquad ..(4.1)$$

$$\frac{\partial \Pi}{\partial K} = p_k - \lambda \frac{\partial \varphi}{\partial K} = 0,$$

$$\cdot \quad \cdot \quad \cdot \quad \cdot \quad \cdot \quad \cdot$$

whence

$$\lambda = \frac{p_t}{\frac{\partial \varphi}{\partial T}} = \frac{p_p}{\frac{\partial \varphi}{\partial P}} = \frac{p_k}{\frac{\partial \varphi}{\partial K}} = \dots, \qquad \qquad ..(4.2)$$

which is identically Walras's system (4) of §326, the additional equation involving λ giving simply the factor of proportionality which, as will be seen, is not without definite economic meaning. The second order conditions of a relative minimum are assumed to be satisfied. Thus, all the marginal productivity theorem shows, when taken by itself, is that the total (or average) cost of producing *a given output* of a given product is minimized (provided second order conditions are satisfied), when the coefficients of production are so adjusted that their marginal productivities $\left(\dfrac{\partial \varphi}{\partial T}, \dfrac{\partial \varphi}{\partial P}, \dfrac{\partial \varphi}{\partial K} \dots \right)$ are proportional to the prices of the productive services.

The foregoing theorem holds for any given output and is independent of the selling price of the product. Consequently, its validity does not depend—as Walras apparently imagined—on any assumptions regarding the competitiveness of the product market. Unless we think of Walras as momentarily blinded by his ardent advocacy of the policy of "free competition" it is hard to explain why he should have made such a point of "free competition" in this connection, in the first italicized conclusion of §326 and Appendix III, as if it were essential to his theorem. Certainly, on logical grounds, it is all the more surprising that he should have fallen into this error since he had the perspicacity to reject Barone's suggestion, made in an unpublished letter to Walras dated September 20, 1894, that the marginal productivity theorem be derived by maximizing the "produit net", i.e. the net profits, of the entrepreneur. Walras wrote in pencil on the margin of this letter: "Voilà bien la formule des productivités marginales. Mais le fondement économique est mauvais." (F.W., II, 1848.) Apparently Walras understood that minimizing cost and maximizing profit were not the same thing: the first is implied in the second, but the second is not implied in the first and may be considered independently.

Of course, "free competition" in the product market is not involved in the determination of minimum cost; but if, as a totally separate proposition external to the marginal productivity theorem, the assumption is arbitrarily made that the product market is governed by pure and perfect competition, so that the operation of the market mechanism equates cost of production to selling price, then the selling price p_b per unit of (B) will be such that

$$p_b = \pi_b. \qquad \qquad ..(5.1)$$

Under these special circumstances, the total outlay on (B) (i.e. the total revenue from (B)) will be equal to the total cost, so that, referring back to (1.1) we may write

$$Q p_b = Q \pi_b = Q b_t p_t + Q b_p p_p + Q b_k p_k + \dots \qquad ..(5.2)$$

Now, returning to (3.1) and partially differentiating $\varPi$ this time with respect to Q we get

$$\frac{\partial \varPi}{\partial Q} = \lambda, \qquad \qquad ..(6.1)$$

and it turns out, as Samuelson has rigorously demonstrated (*op. cit.*, pp. 65–66), that λ or $\dfrac{\partial \varPi}{\partial Q}$ is the marginal cost of (B). Substituting from (6.1) into (4.1) and transposing, we get

$$
\begin{aligned}
p_t &= \frac{\partial \varphi}{\partial T}\, \frac{\partial \varPi}{\partial Q}, \\
p_p &= \frac{\partial \varphi}{\partial P}\, \frac{\partial \varPi}{\partial Q}, \\
p_k &= \frac{\partial \varphi}{\partial K}\, \frac{\partial \varPi}{\partial Q},
\end{aligned}
\qquad ..(7.1)
$$

$$. \quad . \quad . \quad . \quad .$$

As is well known from the theory of the individual firm, under pure and perfect competition, selling price equals marginal cost as well as average cost at equilibrium, so that

$$p_b = \frac{\partial \Pi}{\partial Q} = \pi_b, \qquad \qquad ..(7.2)$$

and (7.1) may be written

$$p_t = \frac{\partial \varphi}{\partial T} \pi_b,$$

$$p_p = \frac{\partial \varphi}{\partial P} \pi_b, \qquad \qquad ..(7.3)$$

$$p_k = \frac{\partial \varphi}{\partial K} \pi_b,$$

$$. \quad . \quad . \quad .$$

This is identically Walras's system (3) of §326 of ed. 4 def., but it is true only when (7.2) is true and is thus a corollary of the marginal productivity theorem instead of being part of its proof, as Walras supposed.

Substituting from (7.3) into (5.2) we obtain

$$Q\pi_b = Qb_t \frac{\partial \varphi}{\partial T} \pi_b + Qb_p \frac{\partial \varphi}{\partial T} \pi_b + Qb_k \frac{\partial \varphi}{\partial K} \pi_b \qquad ..(8.1)$$

or, remembering Walras's definitions of T, P, K...,

$$Q = T\frac{\partial \varphi}{\partial T} + P\frac{\partial \varphi}{\partial P} + K\frac{\partial \varphi}{\partial K} + ... \qquad ..(8.2)$$

This is identically Walras's equation (4) of Appendix III and of §326 in ed. 4 (see Collation Note [ƒ] of this Lesson), and is again a corollary, whose validity depends upon the assumption of a purely and perfectly competitive product market and all that that implies with regard to freedom of entry, etc.

Walras's own method of deriving his equations (3) of ed. 4 def. (our system (7.3)) and (4) of ed. 4 (our equation (8.2)), which he describes in a footnote to his postscript of Appendix III (see p. 494, footnote 1) was vitiated by his confusion of the problem of minimizing cost with that of equating minimum cost to selling price. Having rejected Barone's suggestion that the marginal productivity theorem be derived by maximizing the net profit function, because, as Walras said in an unpublished letter to Barone, dated October 30, 1895, " . . . l'entrepreneur qui ne connaît pas la fonction φ [the demand function for (B)] ou θ [the production function] ne s'amuse pas à faire la différentiation . . ." (F.W., I, 27), he envisages the solution of the theorem as taking place in practice through a double set of finite adjustments made by the entrepreneur in the process of groping towards minimum cost and towards equality between marginal cost and marginal revenue. Unfortunately, he implies that these are conditions of equality between minimum cost and selling price, without noticing that this last equality is not sought by the entrepreneur but imposed from without by the market structure.

[2] Vilfredo Pareto's *Economie pure* cited in Walras's footnote has long eluded the search of economists. Henry Schultz had made diligent efforts to find it in 1929, but without success ("Marginal Productivity and the General Pricing Process", *op. cit.*, p. 459). A copy has now been located in the library of the University of Algiers, to which Professor G. H. Bousquet, who very kindly furnished me with a photostat reproduction, had donated it. It is a brochure of 16 pages, entitled *L'ECONOMIE PURE, Resumé du cours donné à l'Ecole des Hautes Etudes de Paris* (1901-1902), *par M. Vilfredo Pareto, professeur d'économie politique à l'Université de Lausanne*. There is no indication of any

publisher, date or place of publication. The following passage found on pages 9 and 10 is all there is in the brochure relating to the marginal productivity theory:

"Un autre groupe de conditions concerne les transformations des biens économiques et exprime les rapports en lesquels se trouvent les quantités de biens sujets aux transformations avec les produits qu'on en obtient. Il faut observer que ces rapports ne sont pas seulement techniques, ils sont aussi économiques. Ainsi, pour obtenir 1000 kg. de blé il faut une certaine étendue de terres et certaines dépenses de main-d'œuvre, d'engrais, etc. Mais ces quantités ne sont pas fixes; il est bien connu que l'on peut, en de certaines limites, réduire l'étendue de la surface cultivée, pourvu qu'on augmente les dépenses de main-d'œuvre, etc.; et c'est en cela que se trouve la différence entre l'agriculture extensive et l'agriculture intensive. Pourtant ce ne sont pas tous les rapports qui sont ainsi économiquement variables, il en est de fixes ou d'à peu près fixes. Ainsi, pour faire un habit, il faut une certaine quantité de drap, et le tailleur pourrait augmenter indéfiniment la surface de ses ateliers que cela ne diminuerait nullement cette quantité de drap. Un sous-groupe de conditions détermine les rapports qui sont variables. Ces rapports, lorsqu'on considère l'unité de marchandise, ont reçu un nom spécial; M. Walras les a nommé *coefficients de fabrication*; ce sont les quantités de certaines choses nécessaires pour produire une unité d'une marchandise déterminée. Sous un régime de libre concurrence, une des fonctions principales des entrepreneurs est de déterminer ceux de ces coefficients de fabrication qui sont variables économiquement. Sous un régime de propriété collective, cette fonction devrait être remplie par les mandataires de la communauté; on ne saurait la négliger sans courir le danger de réduire considérablement la production."[1]

The footnote referred to at the end of the foregoing paragraph reads:

"[1] Nous avons donné, *Cours*, §719 note, les équations pour déterminer ces coefficients de fabrication.

"La théorie qui prétend les déterminer par la considération des productivités marginales est erronée. On y traite comme des variables indépendantes des quantités qui ne le sont pas, et les équations que l'on écrit pour déterminer le minimum ne sont pas admissibles. Telles sont les équations (3) des *Eléments d'écon. pol. pure*, de M. Walras, 4e édition, p. 375."

[3] cf. Jean Baptiste Say, *Traité d'économie politique*, Book II, Chapters II and III, pp. 318-337.

LESSON 39

[1] James Anderson, *Inquiry into the Nature of the Corn Laws*, Edinburgh, Mrs. Mundell, 1777, pp. 45-50, note (*a*).

[2] Sir Edward West, *An Essay on the Application of Capital to Land*, London, Underwood, 1815.

[3] Thomas Robert Malthus, *Inquiry into the Nature and Progress of Rent, and the Principles by which it is regulated*, London, Murray, 1815.

[4] James Mill, *Elements of Political Economy*, London, Baldwin, Cradock and Joy, 1821, Chapter II, Section I, pp. 13-23.

[5] John Ramsay McCulloch, *The Principles of Political Economy*, Edinburgh, William and Charles Tait, 1825, Part III, Section V, pp. 264-287.

[6] From Fig. 13 of ed. 4.

[7] For a critical discussion of Walras's restatement and criticism of the classical rent theory, see George J. Stigler, *Production and Distribution Theories*, pp. 255-260.

[8] 'Taux de l'intérêt' here translated as 'rate of interest charges' for reasons given above in Translator's Note [3] of Lesson 18.

TRANSLATOR'S NOTES 555

[9] From Fig. 14 of ed. 4.

[10] Let $m=3$; then the equations are as given in systems (1), (2) and (3), nine in number. The unknowns are: r_1, r_2, r_3; h_1, h_2, h_3; x_1, x_2, x_3; and t, in all ten.

[11] This is more clearly seen when rewritten

$$h = H - \left(Hb_p \frac{p_p}{p_b} + Hb_{p'} \frac{p_{p'}}{p_b} + Hb_{p''} \frac{p_{p''}}{p_b} + \ldots \right),$$

where, if we consider only one type of labour-service (P),

Hb_p = the total output of (B) per hectare × the amount of (P) employed in producing a unit of (B) = the total employment of (P) in the production of H on a hectare of land; and

$\frac{p_p}{p_b}$ = the price in *numéraire* per unit of service of (P) ÷ the price in *numéraire* per unit of (B) = the price per unit of (P) in terms of (B); so that

$Hb_p \frac{p_p}{p_b}$ = the total cost in (B) of the labour-service (P) employed in producing H units of (B) on a hectare of land;

and similarly for (P'), (P'')…. Hence h is the total produce per acre less the total wage bill, all expressed in terms of (B).

[12] Remembering from §237 that $P_p i = p_p$, when $p_p = \pi_p$.

[13] By the rate of wages is here meant $\frac{p_p}{P_p}$, $\frac{p_{p'}}{P_{p'}}$, $\frac{p_{p''}}{P_{p''}}$ …, and by the rate of interest charges $\frac{p_k}{P_k}$, $\frac{p_{k'}}{P_{k'}}$, $\frac{p_{k''}}{P_{k''}}$ …. Just as $\frac{p_k}{P_k} = \frac{p_{k'}}{P_{k'}} = \frac{p_{k''}}{P_{k''}} = \ldots$ at equilibrium ($\S263$), so $\frac{p_p}{P_p} = \frac{p_{p'}}{P_{p'}} = \frac{p_{p''}}{P_{p''}} = \ldots$. Moreover, $\frac{p_k}{P_k} = \frac{p_{k'}}{P_{k'}} = \ldots = \frac{p_p}{P_p} = \frac{p_{p'}}{P_{p'}} = \ldots$.

[14] Remembering that H is defined as the number of units of product per hectare, whence $b_t = \frac{1 \text{ hectare}}{H}$, it follows that if b_p is a function of b_t such that $\frac{\partial b_p}{\partial b_t} < 0$, b_p must also be a function of H such that $\frac{\partial b_p}{\partial H} > 0$.

The "vestigial" production function of §325 (see above, Translator's Note [1] of Lesson 36), to which the sentence in the text refers is one in which the output does not figure explicitly. The function is, therefore, a homogeneous function of the first degree in the coefficients of production, as Henry Schultz proved in his article, "Marginal Productivity and the General Pricing Process", *op. cit.*, pp. 543–545.

[15] These three ratios may be set out thus:

$$p_b = \frac{p_t + xi}{H}, \qquad ..(1)$$

$$p_b = \frac{p_t}{r}, \qquad ..(2)$$

$$p_b = \frac{xi}{xt} = \frac{i}{t}. \qquad ..(3)$$

Remembering that $H = h$ in this context and that personal capital is now included with capital goods proper in x, the second equation of §357 may be rewritten

$$\frac{p_t}{p_b} = H - x \frac{i}{p_b},$$

whence the first of the above equations. The second of these equations is derived from

$$r = \frac{p_t}{p_b}$$

since the rent per hectare in terms of (B) = the rent per hectare in *numéraire* ÷ the price in *numéraire* per unit of (B). The third is derived from

$$xt = \frac{xi}{p_b}$$

where xt is the total investment of capital proper and personal capital × the rate in (B) of the interest charges on this capital, i.e. the total interest charges in (B) on all the capital employed on a hectare of land, which is equal to the same total interest charges in terms of *numéraire* (i being the rate expressed in such terms) ÷ the price in *numéraire* per unit of (B).

[16] The left-hand side of this equation represents the total outlay in (B) on labour and capital-services. Remembering that $t = \dfrac{dF(x)}{dx} = F'(x)$, we see that the right-hand side of the equation in the text represents the total capital employed in terms of *numéraire* × the rate of interest charges in terms of (B).

[17] Remembering from §357 that

$$r = h - xt$$

and substituting H for h, we may write

$$r = H - xt.$$

Substituting into this last equation $\dfrac{p_t}{p_b}$ for r (§357), $F(x)$ for H (§355 and 358), and $F'(x)$ for t (§355), we obtain the equation referred to in the text.

[18] By the "rate of production" ('taux de production'), Walras obviously means t which was shown in the last equation of §355 to be a function of the aggregate X.

[19] i.e. $p_b = \dfrac{i}{t}$, as seen in Translator's Note [15] of this Lesson.

Lesson 40

[1] Walras writes: '*Acheter le produit n'est pas alimenter le travail*', which is, in all probability, quoted from Dussard and Courcelle-Seneuil's French translation of J. S. Mill's *Principles*, *Principes d'économie politique*, Paris, Guillaumin, 1854, p. 94. The nearest English equivalent in the section cited is found on p. 80 of the Ashley edition (*op. cit.*) of Mill's *Principles*: ". . . to purchase produce is not to employ labour . . .". In the translation from Walras, the word "support" is substituted for "employ", because it is a better rendering of "alimenter", which becomes a crucial word in the argument that follows, and because Mill in the same context uses the expression "supports and employs productive labour" in such a way that the two verbs may be taken as practically synonymous.

[2] Walras writes: '*Le taux des salaires se règle par le rapport de la population aux capitaux*' (cf. above-mentioned French translation, p. 390), to which the nearest English equivalent in the section cited is found in the original, *op. cit.*, p. 343, reading as follows: "*Wages*, then, depend mainly upon the demand and supply of labour; or as it is often expressed, on the proportion between population and capital."

[3] cf. p. 96 of the French translation, or p. 80 in the original of Mill's *Principles*.

[4] Walras writes: 'Acheter le produit n'est pas demander le travail.'

[5] cf. p. 97 of the French translation, or p. 81 in the original of Mill's *Principles*.

[6] cf. pp. 101–103 of the French translation or pp. 85–86 in the original.

[7] Mill, *op. cit.*, pp. 343–344 or pp. 390–391 of the French translation; the italics are those of the French translation.

[8] Jean Baptiste Say, *A Treatise on Political Economy*, p. 18.

[9] See §185.

[10] P. Auguste Boutron, *Théorie de la rente foncière*, Paris, Guillaumin, 1867, "ouvrage couronné par l'Institut".

Lesson 41

[1] See above, Translator's Note [2] of Lesson 28.

[2] From Fig. 9 of ed. 4.

[3] From Fig. 10 of ed. 4.

[4] From Fig. 11 of ed. 4.

[5] From Fig. 12 of ed. 4.

[6] *Traité d'économie politique*, pp. 55–56 and 307–310.

Lesson 42

[1] The future tense of the verb in this sentence was retained from ed. 1 of the *Eléments* where Walras promised to treat the topics enumerated at a later date. By the time ed. 4 of the *Eléments* appeared, the promise had been fulfilled (see Walras's *Etudes d'économie politique appliquée, passim*).

[2] See Walras's *Etudes d'économie sociale*, which appeared in 1896, the same year as ed. 3 of the *Eléments*.

[3] See above, Lesson 17.

[4] Paris, Bouguet et Lévi, 1823, pp. 278–281. The translation in the text is adapted from "*A Treatise on Political Economy. . .* by the Count Antoine Louis Claude Destutt de Tracy . . ., translated from the unpublished French original", pp. 206–209, Georgetown, D.C., Joseph Milligan, 1817. This translation was revised by Thomas Jefferson.

[5] It will be noted that the validity of this mathematical argument is not general, but depends upon the cost of production of capital good (K) remaining constant in the long run as well as in the short run after the tax. Thus, if we let

p_k = the price per unit of service of capital good (K) before the tax,
P_k = the price per unit of capital good (K) before the tax, such that

$$\frac{p_k}{i} = P_k, \text{ and}$$

Π_k = the cost of production per unit of capital good (K) before the tax, then, since price equals cost of production at equilibrium, we have

$$P_k = \frac{p_k}{i} = \Pi_k, \qquad ..(1)$$

where i is here considered a constant rate of return on capital investments.

The immediate or short run effect of a proportional tax on p_k is to reduce the net selling price of the service of (K) to

$$p'_k = p_k(1-s),$$

where s is the proportional tax rate. Consequently, the price of the capital good (K) will fall immediately to

$$\frac{p'_k}{i} = \frac{p_k(1-s)}{i} = P'_k.$$

Since $P'_k < P_k$, if Π_k is constant in the short run, it follows that

$$P'_k < \Pi_k.$$

In that case the output of (K) will be reduced in the long run and the unit price of its service will rise in consequence. Since i is assumed constant, the price of the capital good itself must also rise. The new price of the service p''_k and the new price of the capital good P''_k will be in long run equilibrium when

$$\frac{p''_k}{i} = P''_k = \Pi'_k, \qquad ..(2)$$

where Π'_k is the long run cost of production of (K) after the tax. If, however, $\Pi'_k = \Pi_k$, i.e. if the cost of production of (K) is a constant not affected by any changes in the quantity produced of (K), then and only then do we have from (1) and (2)

$$\frac{p_k}{i} = \frac{p''_k(1-s)}{i}, \qquad ..(3)$$

whence Walras's equations

$$p''_k = p_k + sp''_k$$

and

$$p''_k = \frac{p_k}{1-s}$$

which obviously hold only when the cost of production of (K) is constant.

[6] See §242.

Appendix I

[1] From Fig. 20 of ed. 4. The curve $\beta_q\beta_r$ in Fig. 40 is simply an enlargement of the same curve found in Fig. 39.

[2] From Fig. 21 of ed. 4.
[3] From Fig. 22 of ed. 4.
[4] From Fig. 23 of ed. 4.
[5] From Fig. 24 of ed. 4.
[6] From Fig. 25 of ed. 4.
[7] From Fig. 26 of ed. 4.

Appendix II

[1] From Fig. 27 of ed. 4.
[2] From Fig. 28 of ed. 4.

TABLE OF CORRESPONDING SECTIONS
LESSONS AND PARTS
for all editions
of Léon Walras's *ÉLÉMENTS*

Italicized section numbers indicate that the parallelism with corresponding sections of the previous edition is found only in the general character of the subject matter. Section numbers in parentheses indicate partial or overlapping parallelism. The bold-face figures in square brackets of varying lengths are the numbers of the Leçons in which the sections enumerated immediately to the left are found.

Ed. 4 def. (1926) and Ed. 4 (1900)[1]		Ed. 3 (1896)[2] and Ed. 2 (1889)[2]		Ed. 1 (1874–1877)	
Part I[3]		*Part I*[3]		*Part I*[3]	
§§	Leçon	§§	Leçon	§§	Leçon
1–5	[1]	1–5	[1]	1–5	[1]
6–9		6–9		6–9	[2]
10–15	[2]	10–15	[2]	10–15	[3]
16–20		16–20		16–20	[4]
21–26	[3]	21–26	[3]	21–26.	[5]
27–30		27–30		27–30	[6]
31–34	[4]	31–34	[4]	31–34	[7]
35–39		35–39		35–39	[8]
Part II		*Part II*[4]		*Part II*[4]	
40–43	[5]	40–43	[5]	40–43	[9]
44–48		44–48		44–48	[10]
49–55	[6]	49–55	[6]	49–55	[11]
56–61		56–61		56–61	[12]
62–70	[7]	62–70	[7]	62–70	[13]
71–75		71–75		71–75	[14]
76–81	8	76–81	8	76–81	[15]
82		(81)		—	
83–84		82–83			
85–91	9	84–90	9	82–88	[16]
92–98		91–97		89–95	[17]
99–103	[10]	98–102	[10]	96–100	[18]
Part III		—		—	
104–110		103–109		101–107	[19]
111–114	11	110–113	11	*108–114*[5]	[20]
115		114		123	
116		115		—	
117		116		*116*[6]	21
118		117		*117–118, 121*[6]	
119–120	12	118–119	12	*119–120*[6]	
121		120		—	
122		—		—	
123		121		*122*[6]	
124–130		122–128		*124–131*[7]	[22]

559

Ed. 4 def. (1926) and Ed. 4 (1900)[1]		Ed. 3 (1896)[2] and Ed. 2 (1889)[2]		Ed. 1 (1874–1877)	
§§	Leçon	§§	Leçon	§§	Leçon
Part III		—		—	
131		129		132	[23]
132		130		(115)[8]	[20]
133	13	131	13	133	
134–135		132–133		—	[23]
136–138		134–136		134–136	
139–144	14	137–142	14	137–142	[24]
145–150		143–148		143–148	[25]
151		149		149–150	
152–154	15	150–152	15	151–153	26
155		153		—	
156		154		154	
157–161		155–159		155–159	[27]
—	16	—	16	160–165	[28][9]
162–164		160		—	
Part IV		*Part III*		*Part IV*[10]	
165–169	17	161–165	17	208–212	[35]
170–177		166–173		213–220	[36]
178–181	18	174–177	18	221–224	[37]
182–188		178–184		225–231	[38]
189–194	19	185–190	19	232–237	[39]
195–199		191–195		238–242	[40]
200–206	20	196–202	20	243–249	[41]
207		203		—	
208		204		250	
209		205		251–252	42
210–212		206–208		253	
213	21	209	21	254	
214–218		210–214		255–259	
219		215		260–261	43
220		216		262	
221–224		217–220		263–266	
225–226		221–222		—	44
227	22	223	22	267	
—		—		(*from Part VI*)	
228–230		224–226		(353)–355[11]	|59|
Part V		*Part IV*		*Part V*[12]	
231–235		227–231	23	268–272	[45]
236–241	23	232–237		273–278	46
242–243		238–239[13]		279–280[13]	
244–245		241–242	[14]	282–283	
246	24	240	24	281	47
247–250		243–246		284–287	
251		247		—	

Ed. 4 def (1926) and Ed. 4 (1900)[11]		Ed. 3 (1896)[2] and Ed. 2 (1889)[2]		Ed. 1 (1874–1877)	
Part V		*Part IV*		*Part V*[12]	
§§	Leçon	§§	Leçon	§§	Leçon
252		248		288	[ ][15]
253–255		249–251		—	
256		252		289–290	48
257	25	(253)	25	(291)	
258		(253)–254		(291)	
259		255			
—		—		292	[49]
260		256		293	
261–262	[26]	257–258		—	
263	[27]	259		—	
264		260	26	298	[50]
—		261		—	
265–267	[28]	—		—	
268–271		262–265	[27]	294–297	[49]
Part VI[16]		*Part V*[16]		*Part III*[16]	
272–277	[29]	*319–323*[17]	33	*172–178*[17]	[30]
278–282	[30]	324–325		—	
283		326–331	[34]		
284–289	[31]	332–339	[35]		
290–297	[32]				

Ed. 4 def. and Ed. 4		Ed. 3		Ed. 2		Ed. 1	
§§	Leçon	§§	Leçon	§§	Leçon	§§	Leçon
298–302	[ ]	340–344	[ ]	340–344		192–196	[ ]
303		—					33
304	33	345		345		*197* [18]	
305		—	36	—	36		
306–311		346–351		346–351		198–203	
312	34	352		—		—	34
313–316		353–356		352–355		204–207	
—		—		356–358	[17]	166–168	[17]
—		—		359		170	
—		—		360		169	29
—		—		—	37	171	
—		—		361–362		—	
—		—		363–365		179–181	[17]
—		—		366		182–183	31
—		—		367		184	
—		—		—		185	[17]
—		—		368	[17]	186	
—		—		369–371		*187–189*	32
—		—		372–374	38	—	
—		—		375–376		*190–191*	
- -		—		377–379		—	

Ed. 4 def. (1926) and Ed. 4 (1900)[1]		Ed. 3 (1896)[2] and Ed. 2 (1889)[2]		Ed. 1 (1874–1877)	
Part VII		*(Part IV resumed)*		*(Part V resumed)*	
§§	Leçon	§§	Leçon	§§	Leçon
317–322	[35]	266–271	[27]	299–304	[50]
323–325	⎡	272–274	⎡	305–307	⎡
326		—		—	
327	36	(274)–275	28	(307)–308	51
328–329		276–277		309–310	
330–335	⎣	278–283	⎣	311–316	[52]
336–341	[37]	284–289	[29]	317–322	[53]
342–349	[38]	290–297	[30]	323–330	[54]
350–355	⎡39	298–303	⎡31	331–336	[55]
356–362	⎣	304–310	⎣	337–343	[56]
363–365	⎡40	311–313	⎡32	344–346	[57]
366–370	⎣	314–318	⎣	347–351	[58]

Ed. 4 def. and Ed. 4		Ed. 3		Ed. 2		Ed. 1	
Part VIII		*Part VI*		*Part VI*		*Part VI*[19]	
§§	Leçon	§§	Leçon	§§	Leçon	§§	Leçon
371	⎡	357	⎡	403	⎡	352	⎡
372		358		404		(352)–(353)[20]	59
373–375	41	359–361	37	405–407	41	356–358	⎣
376–381		362–367		408–413		359–364	[60]
382–387	⎣	368–373	⎣	414–419	⎣	365–370	[61]
388–393	⎡	374–379	⎡	420–425	⎡	371–376	[62]
394		380		426		377	⎡
395		—		—		—	63
396–398		381–383		427–429		378–380	⎣
399		—		—		—	⎡
400–401	42	384–385	38	430–431	42	381–382	
402–404		—		—		—	
405–406		386–387		432–433		383–384	64
407		—		—		—	
408	⎣	388	⎣	434	⎣	385	⎣
Appendix I		Appendix I		—		—	
Appendix II		Appendix II		—		—	
—		Appendix III		—		—	

(1) The order of the Parts, Lessons and sections is exactly the same throughout the fourth and the definitive editions.

(2) Where the order of the Parts, Lessons and sections of eds. 2 and 3 is the same, the numbers have been combined in a single column. Between the author's 'Préface' and the text, the second and third editions contain a mathematical prelude (pp. 3–21), entitled 'Des fonctions et de leur représentation géométrique. Théorie mathématique de la chute des corps'. This was omitted from the subsequent editions probably as a result of the criticisms Walras received from Maurice d'Ocagne in an unpublished letter dated May 7, 1891 (F.W. II, 1623).

(3) 'SECTION' in the original is translated as PART in order to avoid confusion with the numbered subdivisions of the Lessons, here called sections. The title page of Part I of the first three editions is headed 'Théorie de la richesse sociale'.

(4) In ed. 1 the title of Part II reads 'Théorie mathématique de l'échange'; changed in ed. 2 to read 'Théorie de l'échange'; and finally changed as translated in ed. 4.

(5) See Collation Note [h] of Lesson 11.
(6) See Collation Note [a] of Lesson 12.
(7) See Collation Note [i] of Lesson 12.
(8) See Collation Note [b] of Lesson 13.
(9) The 28ᵉ Leçon of ed. 1, entitled 'Examen critique de la doctrine de M. Cournot sur les changements de valeur, absolus et relatifs', was omitted from all subsequent editions.
(10) In ed. 1 the title of Part IV reads 'Théorie naturelle de la production et de la consommation de la richesse'; changed in ed. 2 and subsequent editions for the corresponding Part.
(11) See below footnote [20] and Collation Note [h] of Lesson 22.
(12) In ed. 1 the title of Part V reads 'Conditions et conséquences du progrès économique'; changed in ed. 2 (where the corresponding Leçons form Part IV) to read 'Théorie de la capitalisation et du crédit'. In ed. 4 and ed. 4 def. the latter title applies to Part V which comprises only those Leçons which correspond to Leçons 45–49 of ed. 1 (Leçons 23–28 of ed. 2). The Leçons corresponding to the remainder of Part V of ed. 1 were shifted to Part VII in ed. 4.
(13) See Collation Note [h] of Lesson 23.
(14) See Collation Note [a] of Lesson 24.
(15) See Collation Note [a] of Lesson 25.
(16) In ed. 1 the title of Part III reads 'Du numéraire et de la monnaie'; changed in ed. 2 to read 'Théorie de la monnaie' and in ed. 4 to read 'Théorie de la circulation et de la monnaie' as the title of the corresponding Part.
(17) See Collation Note [a] of Part VI.
(18) See Collation Note [d] of Lesson 33.
(19) In ed. 1 the title of Part VI reads 'Effets naturels et nécessaires des divers modes d'organisation de la société'; changed as translated in ed. 2.
(20) See above, footnote (11)

COLLATION OF EDITIONS[1]

Lesson 1

[a] End of 1re Leçon in ed. 1.

[b] In ed. 1 this sentence reads: 'Et, pour cela, nous allons, au préalable, distinguer l'art de la science et la science morale de la science naturelle.' Changed in ed. 2. End of 2e Leçon in ed. 1.

Lesson 2

[a] In ed. 1 the final clause of this sentence reads: '... il oublie complètement de signaler aussi celle [la distinction] à faire entre l'art, la science et la morale'. Changed in ed. 2.

[b] End of 3e Leçon in ed. 1.

[c] Ed. 1 reads: 'Il est clair que, pour ce qui est des effets des forces naturelles, il n'y a rien autre chose à faire qu'à les reconnaître, les constater, les expliquer, et que, quant aux effets de la volonté humaine, au contraire, il y a lieu de les gouverner.' Changed in ed. 3.

[d] End of 4e Leçon in ed. 1.

Lesson 3

[a] In place of the two preceding sentences, ed. 1 reads: 'De même ici la rareté et l'abondance ne s'opposent pas l'une à l'autre: la rareté n'est qu'une abondance moindre, ou, pour mieux dire, l'abondance n'est qu'une moindre rareté. Une chose est rare, en économie politique, dès qu'elle est utile et limitée en quantité, exactement comme un corps a de la vitesse, en mécanique, dès qu'il parcourt un certain espace en un certain temps.' Changed in ed. 2.

[b] End of 5e Leçon in ed. 1.

[c] Sentence appears first in ed. 2.

[d] In place of the two preceding sentences ed. 1 reads: 'Les sciences naturelles proprement dites décrivent purement et simplement la nature, elles ne sortent pas de l'expérience.' Changed in ed. 2.

[e] End of 6e Leçon in ed. 1.

Lesson 4

[a] In ed. 1 the remainder of this sentence reads: 'jusqu'à un certain point'. Deleted in ed. 4.

[b] End of 7e Leçon in ed. 1.

[c] Ed. 1 reads: '. . . que je ne veux pas dissimuler'; changed in ed. 4 to 'que je veux signaler'.

[d] End of 8e Leçon in ed. 1.

Part II

[a] Ed. 1 reads: 'Théorie Mathématique de l'Echange'; changed in ed. 2 to read: 'Théorie de l'Echange'. In the first three editions, the theory of the exchange between two commodities only (Part II of ed. 4) and the theory of exchange among several commodities (Part III of ed. 4) were combined in Part II.

[1] See above, p. 497, footnote 1.

LESSON 5

[a] This sentence appears first in ed. 2.

[b] End of 9ᵉ Leçon in ed. 1.

[c] 'd'échange' appears first in ed. 2.

[d] This sentence appears first in ed. 4.

[e] In ed. 1 the remainder of this paragraph reads: 'Nous avions à la Bourse des acheteurs de rente et des vendeurs de rente, des demandeurs et des offreurs; une hausse dans le prix de la rente ne pouvait que diminuer la demande et augmenter l'offre; une baisse ne pouvait qu'augmenter la demande et diminuer l'offre. Ici, nous avons des échangeurs, des demandeurs de (A) contre (B) et des demandeurs de (B) contre (A), pour qui cette demande est le fait principal, et pour qui l'offre, comme nous l'avons fait remarquer, n'est qu'un fait accessoire. Or cette circonstance modifie tout.' Changed in ed. 2.

[f] The passage translated into the following three sentences appears first in ed. 4.

[g] End of 10ᵉ Leçon in ed. 1.

LESSON 6

[a] Ed. 1 reads: 'La courbe $a_{d,1}a_{p,1}$ s'obtient par le *procédé graphique*, l'équation $d_a = f_{a,1}(p_a)$ s'obtient par la *méthode d'interpolation*; l'une et l'autre sont empiriques.' Changed in ed. 2.

[b] The following sentence in ed. 1 reads: 'Si, par exemple, l'avoine coûtait 1 milliard en blé, il est à croire qu'à moins de circonstances très exceptionnelles, personne ne nourrirait plus de chevaux.' Omitted from subsequent editions.

[c] End of 11ᵉ Leçon in ed. 1.

[d] End of 12ᵉ Leçon in ed. 1.

LESSON 7

[a] The next four sentences in ed. 1 read: 'Lorsqu'on cherche l'équation empirique d'une courbe par la méthode d'interpolation, on essaye successivement de l'obtenir algébriquement du premier, du second, du troisième degré, et ainsi de suite. Nous avons supposé, dans notre figure, les courbes A_dA_p, B_dB_p algébriques du second degré, par conséquent continues, et n'offrant aussi qu'un seul maximum pour les rectangles des coordonnées D_ap_a, D_bp_b entre le point pour lequel $D_a = OA_d$, $p_a = O$, et celui pour lequel $p_a = OA_p$, $D_a = O$, entre le point pour lequel $D_b = OB_d$, $p_b = O$, et celui pour lequel $p_b = OB_p$, $D_b = O$. Nous n'avons d'ailleurs à considérer que la partie de ces courbes comprise dans l'angle des coordonnées positives, et, dans cet angle, que la partie comprise entre les points A_d et A_p, entre les points B_d et B_p. Cela ressort très évidemment de la nature même du fait de l'échange. Dans cette hypothèse, les courbes *KLM*, *NPQ* sont des courbes algébriques du troisième degré, continues, et n'offrant qu'un seul maximum pour les ordonnées.' Changed in ed. 2.

[b] Ed. 1 reads: 'Maintenant, après le cas où il n'y a, entre les courbes de demande et les courbes d'offre, qu'un seul point d'intersection, et celui où il n'y a aucun point d'intersection, l'inspection attentive de la forme des courbes fait apercevoir le cas où il y aurait trois points d'intersection.' Changed in eds. 2 and 3 to read: 'Maintenant, après le cas où il n'y a, entre les courbes de demande et les courbes d'offre, qu'un seul point d'intersection, et celui où il n'y a aucun point d'intersection, l'inspection attentive de la forme des courbes fait apercevoir le cas où il y aurait plusieurs points d'intersection.' And finally changed in ed. 4 to read as translated in the text.

COLLATION OF EDITIONS 567

[c] '$=\mu$' does not appear in ed. 1.

[d] '$=\dfrac{1}{\mu}$' does not appear in ed. 1.

[e] Ed. 1 reads: 'relativement grand'; changed in ed. 4 to read 'fort'.

[f] Ed. 1 reads: 'relativement petit'; changed in ed. 4 to read 'faible'.

[g] Ed. 1 reads: 'Théoriquement, nous sommes forcés d'admettre l'éventualité comme possible pour deux marchandises s'échangeant l'une contre l'autre en nature; nous verrons plus tard si elle l'est encore pour plusieurs marchandises s'échangeant les unes contre les autres avec intervention de monnaie.' Changed in ed. 4.

[h] Ed. 1 reads: 'Sans sortir des données de notre hypothèse générale, il convient d'examiner le cas extrême où les courbes de demande, se confondant avec l'hyperbole de la quantité existante, seraient asymptotes à ces axes.' Changed in ed. 4.

[i] End of 13ᵉ Leçon in ed. 1.

LESSON 8

[a] In ed. 1 this paragraph reads: 'L'étude que nous avons poursuivie jusqu' ici de la nature du fait de l'échange rend possible l'étude de la cause même du fait de la valeur d'échange. Si, en effet, les prix ou les rapports des valeurs résultent mathématiquement des courbes de demande, pour connaître les causes et conditions premières d'établissement et de variation des prix, il faut rechercher les causes et conditions premières d'établissement et de variation des courbes de demande.' Changed in ed. 4.

[b] In ed. 1 the remainder of this paragraph reads: 'Sur le premier Oq, je porte, à partir du point O, les longueurs successives Oq, qq', $q'q''$... représentant les nombres d'unités ou fractions d'unités de (B), q, q', q''... d'une même intensité d'utilité que le porteur (1) consommerait successivement s'il les avait à sa disposition. Et, sur le second axe Or, et sur des parallèles à cet axe menées par les points q, q', q''..., je porte, à partir du point O et de ces points q, q', q''..., des longueurs $O\beta_{r,1}$, qr', $q'r''$... représentant les *utilités intensives* $\beta_{r,1}$, r', r''... de chacun des groupes d'unités ou fractions d'unités q, q', q''.... Je forme les rectangles $OqR\beta_{r,1}$, $qq'R'r'$, $q'q''R''r''$... représentant les produits $q\beta_{r,1}$, $q'r'$, $q''r''$.... J'obtiens ainsi la courbe $\beta_{r,1}Rr'R'r''R''$... $\beta_{q,1}$. Cette courbe est continue ou discontinue: elle est discontinue si q, q', q''... ne sont pas des quantités infiniment petites; elle est continue dans le cas contraire, et se confond alors avec la courbe $\beta_{r,1}r'r''$... $\beta_{q,1}$. J'obtiendrais de même la courbe $\alpha_{r,1}\alpha_{q,1}$ continue ou discontinue. Dans le cas de continuité, comme dans le cas de discontinuité, d'ailleurs, je suppose les intensités d'utilité décroissantes depuis l'intensité $\beta_{r,1}$ ou $\alpha_{r,1}$ de la première unité ou fraction d'unité jusqu'à l'intensité zéro de la dernière unité ou fraction d'unité consommée.' Fig. 3 of ed. 1 to which this passage refers appears as Fig. 53 on p. 569.

This diagram was changed in ed. 2, in which Walras no longer considers successive unequal increments in quantity ($Oq>qq'<q'q''$ in Fig. 53), each having a uniform *rareté*. The defects of his first presentation in ed. 1 were discussed in the unpublished correspondence between Ladislas von Bortkiewicz and Léon Walras. In a letter dated November 23, 1887, L. von Bortkiewicz wrote: ". . . Dans vos *Eléments* [ed. 1], §74 je lis ce qui suit: 'Sur Oq, je porte, à partir de O, des longueurs successives Oq, qq', $q'q''$... représentant les nombres d'unités de (B), q, q', q'' . . . d'une même intensité que le porteur consommerait successivement. Et sur le second axe etc., je porte des longueurs $O\beta_{r,1}$, qr', qr''... représentant les *utilités intensives* de chacun des groupes d'unités q, q', q'' etc.' Eh bien, c'est

ce que j'avoue ne pas comprendre. Les quantités représentées par $Oq, qq', q'q''$, etc. ayant une même intensité d'utilité, comment se peut-il que cette même intensité d'utilité soit représentée tantôt par $O\beta_{r,1}$, tantôt par qr, etc.? Tout serait clair si vous aviez dit 'des longueurs $O\beta_{r,1}$, qr', $q'r''$ représentant les utilités intensives *d'une unité* de chacun des groupes'. Encore une remarque. Les longueurs $Oq, qq', q'q''$ ... représentant les quantités d'une même intensité d'utilité, la longueur qq' doit être plus grande que Oq, $q'q''>qq'$, et en général $q_{m-1}q_m<q_mq_{m+1}$. La loi psychologique qui sert de base à votre théorie de la rareté l'exige nécessairement. . . ." (F.W. II, 1317.) To this Walras replied on December 6: "La phrase de mes *Eléments* (§74) que vous me citez . . . est très mauvaise. Je vous ferai seulement observer que je l'avais déjà corrigée en disant dans ma *Théorie mathématique de la richesse sociale* (p. 20): '. . . un certain nombre de quantités successives $Oq, qq', q'q''$ ... *chacune d'une intensité uniforme d'utilité.*' J'ajoute que cette correction ne .n'a pas paru suffisante et que, dans la seconde édition des *Eléments* dont je viens de commencer l'impression, je substitue aux quantités quelconques q, q', q'' des unités de marchandise, comme vous le désirez, et comme je le fais depuis plusieurs années déjà dans mes cours. . . ." (F.W. I, 66.) In ed. 2, the first sentence of the passage in question reads: 'Sur le premier, Oq, je porte, à partir du point O, des longueurs successives $Oq', q'q'', q''q'''$ ... représentent les unités de (B) que le porteur (1) consommerait successivement [dans un certain temps], s'il les avait à sa disposition'; the phrase in brackets was added in ed. 4. In conjunction with this phrase there appeared for the first time in ed. 4 the subsequent sentences of the same paragraph setting forth the static assumptions implied in the argument. The remainder of the passage under discussion, which had taken its definitive form in ed. 2, was then made into a new paragraph.

It will be observed, furthermore, that the *rareté* curves in Fig. 3 of ed. 1 (reproduced here as Fig. 53) are drawn as straight lines like those of Gossen. They were replaced in ed. 2 by curvilinear *rareté* functions. Walras explained the change in an unpublished letter to W. Stanley Jevons dated August 17, 1878, in which he wrote: "J'ai aussi modifié sur la figure 3 les courbes d'utilité. J'avais d'abord pris des lignes droites afin d'obtenir exactement par le calcul la courbe de demande qui s'en déduit; mais je trouve, toutes réflexions faites, qu'il vaut mieux n'avoir qu'une courbe de demande approximative et ne pas risquer d'en donner cette idée fausse que la rareté variait toujours en raison inverse de la quantité possédée ou selon quelque loi simplement analogue." (F.W. I, 278.)

[c] Ed. 1 reads: 'quantité possédée'. Changed in ed. 2.

[d] Ed. 1 does not contain this paragraph, which in ed. 2 reads: 'Analytiquement, les raretés étant données en fonction des quantités consommées par les équations $r=\varphi_{a,1}(q)$, $r=\varphi_{b,1}(q)$, les utilités effectives seraient données par les intégrales définies de O à q de ces fonctions:

$$\int_o^q \varphi_{a,1}(q)dq, \qquad \int_o^q \varphi_{b,1}(q)dq.'$$

Changed in ed. 4.

[e] End of 14[e] Leçon in ed. 1. This paragraph appears as the second paragraph of §75 of ed. 1, as the third paragraph of §75 of ed. 2, and as the first paragraph of §76 of ed. 4, the first words reading: 'Tout cela posé' in ed. 1, changed to 'Cela posé' in ed. 4.

[f] Ed. 1 reads: 'On est fondé à dire en principe qu'il opérera l'échange de manière à satisfaire la plus grande somme totale de besoins possible, et que, par conséquent, p_a étant donné, d_a est déterminé par la condition que l'ensemble des deux surfaces $Oy\beta\beta_{r,1}$, $Od_a\alpha\alpha_{r,1}$ soit maximum.' Changed in ed. 2. It is to be observed that the principle of maximization of utility in exchange, which had

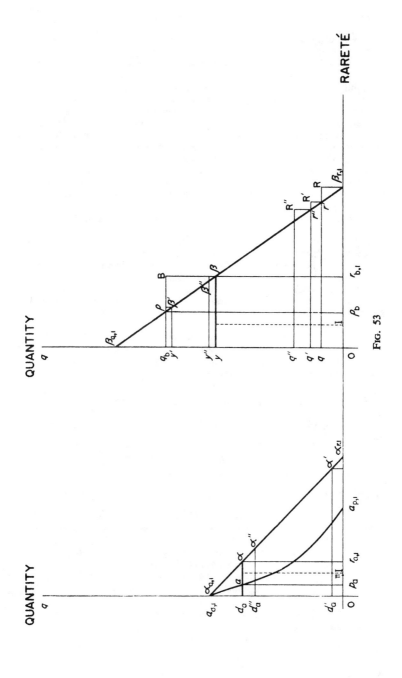

QUANTITY

QUANTITY

RARETÉ

Fig. 53

been enunciated as a broad empirical observation in the first edition, was reduced to a hypothetical proposition in the second and subsequent editions.

[g] In ed. 1 this is followed by a paragraph which reads: 'Notre figure suppose les courbes de besoin continues; il y aurait lieu de discuter le cas où elles seraient discontinues. Cette discussion montrerait notamment qu'en ce cas, il pourrait y avoir, à la limite, un certain nombre d'échanges élémentaires indifférents, c'est-à-dire qui ne seraient ni avantageux ni désavantageux. Les quantités o_b et d_a seraient alors indéterminées entre certaines limites; mais le théorème n'en serait pas moins vrai par la raison que, dans ces limites, la satisfaction serait toujours maximum du moment où le rapport des intensités dernières serait égal au prix.' Omitted in ed. 2. In §82 of ed. 2 (equivalent of §§83 and 84 of ed. 4) Walras first presents a developed demonstration of the theory of equilibrium quantities and rigorously defines the narrow limits within which such an equilibrium is indeterminate when the utility curve of one of the commodities exchanged is discontinuous.

[h] Ed. 1 reads: '$r_a=\varphi_{a,1}(q_a)$, $r_b=\varphi_{b,1}(q_b)$'. The subscripts to the r's and q's were omitted in ed. 2.

[i] End of 15e Leçon in ed. 1. The remainder of this Lesson, consisting of the last paragraph of §81 and §§82–84, appears first in ed. 2.

[j] In ed. 2 this paragraph reads: 'Ainsi se résoudrait le problème qui consiste —Etant données deux marchandises (A) et (B) et les courbes d'utilité ou de besoin de ces deux marchandises pour chacun des échangeurs, [ou les équations de ces courbes,] ainsi que la quantité possédée par chacun des porteurs, à déterminer les courbes de demande [ou leurs équations].' In the definitive edition of 1926 the bracketed words were omitted.

[k] This sentence is included in the previous paragraph of eds. 2 and 3. In ed. 4 it forms a separate paragraph, the first in §82. In ed. 4 the next paragraph reads: 'Soient d_a la quantité à demander de (A), o_b la quantité à offrir de (B), au prix p_a de (A) en (B), conformément à l'équation

$$d_a p_a = o_b,$$

q_b étant la quantité de (B) possédée par le porteur.' Changed in the definitive edition of 1926.

[l] The phrase 'en vertu de l'équation [1]' appears first in the definitive edition of 1926.

[m] The passage constituting §82 in ed. 4 does not appear as a separate section in eds. 2 and 3, but in abbreviated form as part of §81, reading: '$\varphi_{a,1}(q)$ et $\varphi_{b,1}(q)$ étant les raretés décroissantes de (A) et (B) pour le porteur (1) de (B) en fonction des quantités consommées, les intégrales définies $\int_o^q \varphi_{a,1}(q)dq$ et $\int_o^q \varphi_{b,1}(q)dq$ sont, comme nous l'avons dit (§75), les utilités effectives des mêmes marchandises pour le même porteur en fonction des mêmes quantités consommées. Après l'échange de $o_b=d_a p_a$ de (B) contre d_a de (A), à un prix p_a de (A) en (B), c'est-à-dire avec des quantités d_a de (A) et $q_b-o_b=q_b-d_a p_a$ de (B), l'utilité effective totale des deux marchandises pour le porteur en question est

$$\int_o^{d_a} \varphi_{a,1}(q)dq + \int_o^{q_b-d_a p_a} \varphi_{b,1}(q)dq.$$

Et cette utilité effective totale atteint son maximum quand sa dérivée par rapport à d_a est nulle, soit quand

$$\varphi_{a,1}(d_a)-p_a\varphi_{b,1}(q_b-d_a p_a)=0$$

ou quand

$$\varphi_{a,1}(d_a)=p_a\varphi_{b,1}(q_b-o_b).'$$

Changed in ed. 4.

The change in the fourth edition embodied almost verbatim the observation made by L. von Bortkiewicz in an unpublished letter dated May 9, 1888, which was sent in response to Walras's letter of May 5 enclosing the proof sheets of parts of the forthcoming second edition of the *Eléments*. Von Bortkiewicz argued that the phrase "$\varphi_{a,1}(q)$ et $\varphi_{b,1}(q)$ étant les raretés *décroissantes*", mentioned simply in passing, as it were, might still leave the uninformed reader with the false impression that proportionality between the *raretés* and the prices was a necessary and sufficient condition of maximum satisfaction whether or not the *rareté* functions were decreasing functions of the quantities possessed. He went on to suggest: "Or, quelques lignes insérées à la page 106 [of eds. 2 and 3] suffiraient pour éliminer toute possibilité d'un pareil malentendu. L'équation

$$\varphi_{a,1}(d_a)-p_a\varphi_{b,1}(q_b-d_ap_a)=0$$

correspond au maximum de

$$\int_0^{d_a} \varphi_{a,1}(q)dq \;+\; \int_0^{q_b-d_ap_a} \varphi_{b,1}(q)dq$$

seulement à la condition que la dérivée du second ordre de

$$\int_0^{d_a} \varphi_{a,1}(q)dq \;+\; \int_0^{q_b-d_ap_a} \varphi_{b,1}(q)dq$$

par rapport à d_a soit une quantité négative. Donc le théorème de la satisfaction maxima ne tient debout qu'à cette condition qui s'exprime par l'inégalité suivante:

$$\varphi'_{a,1}(d_a)+p^2_a\varphi'_{b,1}(q_b-d_ap_a)<0.$$

Il est évident que cette condition sera remplie si nous avons $\varphi'_{a,1}(d_a)<0$ et $\varphi'_{b,1}(q_b-d_ap_a)<0$, soit en général $\varphi'(q)<0$, ce qui veut dire que la rareté doit être une fonction décroissante de la quantité possédée." (F.W. II, 1355.) Walras accepted this correction with gratitude, but the final proof having already been sent to the printer, it was too late to make any change. In fact, the correction was not made, perhaps because of an oversight, until the fourth edition.

[n] Ed. 2 reads: 'Ainsi dans le cas de l'échange d'une marchandise à courbe de besoin continue contre une marchandise à courbe de besoin discontinue, quand a lieu la satisfaction maxima, ce n'est pas le rapport des intensités des derniers besoins satisfaits des deux marchandises, mais *le rapport de la moyenne des intensités du dernier besoin satisfait et du premier besoin non satisfait de la marchandise achetée à l'intensité du dernier besoin satisfait de la marchandise vendue* qui est (du moins à peu près) *égal au prix*.' Changed in ed. 4.

[o] Ed. 2 reads: 'et renoncera à des utilités effectives de (B)'; changed in ed. 4 to read 'et renoncera aux utilités effectives de (B)'.

LESSON 9

[a] End of 16e Leçon in ed. 1. The following sentence appears first in ed. 2. The footnote, however, does not appear until ed. 4.

[b] Ed. 1 reads: '$r_a=\varphi_{a,1}(q_a)$, $r_b=\varphi_{b,1}(q_b)$'.

[c] This paragraph appears first in ed. 2.

[d] End of 17e Leçon in ed. 1.

LESSON 10

[a] Ed. 1 reads: 'De ces éléments résultent mathématiquement en premier lieu les courbes de demande partielle et totale', to which the phrase 'en raison de ce

fait que chaque porteur cherche à obtenir la satisfaction maxima de ses besoins' was added in ed. 2.

[b] Ed. 1 reads: '*obtiennent*'; changed in ed. 2 to read '*peuvent obtenir*'.

[c] In ed. 1 this paragraph reads: '$p_a = \dfrac{v_a}{v_b}$ et $p_b = \dfrac{v_b}{v_a}$ étant les prix courants ou d'équilibre, $r_{a,1}$, $r_{b,1}$, $r_{a,2}$, $r_{b,2}$, $r_{a,3}$, $r_{b,3}$ ... étant les raretés des marchandises (A) et (B) ou les intensités des derniers besoins satisfaits de ces marchandises chez les porteurs (1), (2), (3)... on a

$$p_a = \frac{v_a}{v_b} = \frac{r_{a,1}}{r_{b,1}} = \frac{r_{a,2}}{r_{b,2}} = \frac{r_{a,3}}{r_{b,3}} = \ldots$$

$$p_b = \frac{v_b}{v_a} = \frac{r_{b,1}}{r_{a,1}} = \frac{r_{b,2}}{r_{a,2}} = \frac{r_{b,3}}{r_{a,3}} = \ldots,$$

Changed in ed. 2.

[d] This paragraph appears first in ed. 2.

[e] Ed. 1 reads: '... et le terme $r_{b,3}$ devrait être remplacé par un dénominateur $\dfrac{1}{p_a}$ $r_{a,3} = p_b r_{a,3} \ldots$' Changed in ed. 2.

[f] The sentence from which the next two sentences in the text were translated appears first in ed. 2.

[g] Ed. 1 reads: 'La rareté, pourrait-on dire, est *individuelle*.' Changed in ed. 4.

[h] In ed. 1 this paragraph reads: 'Les causes et conditions premières d'établissement des prix étant connues, les causes et conditions premières de variation de ces prix sont connues par cela même.' Changed in ed 2.

[i] In ed. 1 this passage, including the two previous paragraphs, reads: 'Quant aux effets respectifs des changements dans l'utilité ou des changements dans la quantité sur les prix, il y a quelques précautions à prendre pour énoncer à cet égard des propositions générales, du moins en ce qui concerne les changements dans l'utilité, par la raison que ces changements peuvent s'effectuer de façons très diverses. Toutefois, en réservant les expressions *d'augmentation* et de *diminution de l'utilité* aux déplacements de la courbe de besoin qui ont pour résultat d'augmenter ou de diminuer l'intensité des derniers besoins satisfaits, ou la rareté, après l'échange, on peut dire que l'augmentation ou la diminution de l'utilité, la quantité restant la même, a pour conséquence nécessaire l'augmentation ou diminution du prix. En effet, la rareté d'une des deux marchandises augmentant ou diminuant chez un ou plusieurs échangeurs, et devenant, par conséquent, plus grande ou plus petite que le produit de son prix par la rareté de l'autre, il y a avantage, pour ces échangeurs, en vertu du théorème de la satisfaction maximum (§ 80), à acheter ou à vendre de la première marchandise, en vendant ou en achetant de la seconde. De là une demande ou une offre effective de la première marchandise, accompagnée d'une offre ou d'une demande effective de la seconde, d'où résulte finalement une hausse ou une baisse du prix de l'une en l'autre. Au contraire, l'augmentation ou la diminution de la quantité, l'utilité restant la même, a pour conséquence nécessaire, d'après ce que nous avons dit de la nature des courbes (§ 75), la diminution ou l'augmentation de la rareté, et, par suite, la diminution ou l'augmentation du prix. Cela étant, on pourrait donc énoncer les deux propositions suivantes:' Changed in ed. 2.

[j] The phrase 'à l'état d'équilibre sur un marché' appears first in ed. 2.

[k] End of 18e Leçon in ed. 1.

Part III

[a] See above, Collation Note [a] of Part II.

LESSON 11

[a] Ed. 1 reads: 'Il va nous suffire, pour cela, de généraliser convenablement nos formules.' Changed in ed. 2.

[b] Ed. 1 reads: '. . . et les 2 équations d'échange. . . .' Changed in ed. 2.

[c] In ed. 1 the following paragraphs are found at the beginning of §107 (corresponding to §110 in ed. 4 def.):

'On peut donc poser le problème général de l'échange d'un nombre quelconque de marchandises entre elles en ces termes:

'*Etant données m marchandises* (A), (B), (C), (D)*... et les équations de demande de ces m marchandises l'une en l'autre, déterminer les prix respectifs d'équilibre.*

'Et, en principe, ce problème est toujours susceptible d'une solution par la résolution de $2m(m-1)$ équations à $2m(m-1)$ inconnues qui sont les $m(m-1)$ prix des m marchandises les unes en les autres et les m $(m-1)$ quantités totales de ces m marchandises échangées les unes contre les autres.'

These three paragraphs were omitted in ed. 2.

[d] Ed. 1 reads: 'équations'; changed in ed. 2 to read 'fonctions'.

[e] Ed. 1 reads: 'deux variables'; changed in ed. 2 to read 'une variable'.

[f] Ed. 1 reads: 'trois variables'; changed in ed. 2 to read 'deux variables'.

[g] End of 19e Leçon in ed. 1. The following sentence appears first in ed. 2.

[h] The description of the mechanism of arbitrage in ed. 1 differs so radically from that of the subsequent editions that it is impracticable to include the original version found in ed. 1 in our collation of texts so far as it relates to the remaining sections of this Lesson. For example, in the 20^e Leçon of ed. 1, the process of arriving at general equilibrium through arbitrage operations was described in a very summary fashion, the notations used being those found below in §148 of the definitive edition. There was no recourse to the expository device of hypothetical, isolated markets where only pairs of commodities are exchanged for each other. More important than this is the fact that in ed. 1 Walras had not introduced his *numéraire* until a later stage of the argument, in the 25e Leçon which corresponds to Lesson 14 of the subsequent editions. See Arthur W. Marget, "Monetary Aspects of the Walrasian System", *op. cit.*, p. 179, note 67. The result was that in the first edition, Walras passed immediately from the conclusion that a state of general equilibrium in exchange required that the price of either one of any two commodities in terms of the other must equal the ratio of the prices of these two in terms of any third commodity to the corollary found in §132 of the definitive edition that the ratios between the *raretés* of any two commodities must be the same for all traders. He could do this without the aid of a *numéraire* by supposing three parties to be in the market, party (1) holding (A), party (2) holding (B) and party (3) holding (C). Then he supposed isolated trading to take place between pairs of such traders until, by virtue of the theorem of maximum satisfaction,

$$\frac{r_{b,1}}{r_{a,1}} = p_{b,a} = \frac{1}{p_{a,b}} = \frac{r_{b,2}}{r_{a,2}},$$

$$\frac{r_{c,1}}{r_{a,1}} = p_{c,a} = \frac{1}{p_{a,c}} = \frac{r_{c,3}}{r_{a,3}}, \qquad\qquad ..(1)$$

$$\frac{r_{c,2}}{r_{b,2}} = p_{c,b} = \frac{1}{p_{b,c}} = \frac{r_{c,3}}{r_{b,3}}.$$

When, however, arbitrage transactions were introduced, the result was

$$\frac{r_{b,2}}{r_{a,2}} = p_{b,a} = \frac{p_{c,a}}{p_{c,b}} = \frac{r_{b,3}}{r_{a,3}},$$

$$\frac{r_{c,2}}{r_{b,2}} = p_{c,b} = \frac{p_{c,a}}{p_{b,a}} = \frac{r_{c,1}}{r_{b,1}}. \qquad ..(2)$$

Now, from the second line of system (1) we know that $\dfrac{r_{c,1}}{r_{a,1}} = \dfrac{r_{c,3}}{r_{a,3}}$. If in place

of $r_{c,3}$ we put $\dfrac{r_{c,2}r_{b,3}}{r_{b,2}}$ from the third line of system (1), and in place of

$r_{a,3}$ we put $\dfrac{r_{a,2}r_{b,3}}{r_{b,2}}$ from the first line of system (2), then we obtain

$$\frac{r_{c,1}}{r_{a,1}} = \frac{r_{c,2}}{r_{a,2}}. \qquad ..(3)$$

It is to be noted, moreover, that in the "20ᵉ Leçon" of ed. 1 Walras did not combine the system of equations defining general equilibrium after arbitrage with the previously derived system of equations of offer and demand as he did in the later editions at this juncture of his argument, for example, in §116 of the edition here translated. See below, Collation Note [a] of Lesson 12.

[i] The 20ᵉ Leçon of ed. 1 ends at a corresponding point in the argument with the following sentences: 'Que si, maintenant, on voulait qu'il n'y eût pas lieu à arbitrages sur le marché et que l'équilibre des prix des *m* marchandises deux à deux fût en même temps équilibre général, il faudrait alors introduire les équations exprimant cet état du marché dans le système des équations de demande et d'échange. C'est ce que nous allons faire en fournissant la formule générale de solution mathématique du problème de l'échange de plusieurs marchandises entre elles.' Changed in ed. 2.

[j] Ed. 2 reads: '. . . l'égalité de la demande et de l'offre de chaque marchandise contre chacune des autres . . .'; changed in ed. 4 to read ". . . l'égalité de la demande et de l'offre de chaque marchandise en et contre chacune des autres . . .'.

LESSON 12

[a] The 21ᵉ Leçon of ed. 1, like the 20ᵉ Leçon of that edition, cannot be included in our detailed collation of texts without undue extension of these notes, for here again the original mathematical argument took no account of a *numéraire* (see above, Collation Note [h] of Lesson 11). The fact that the value of all commodities demanded on a given market by a given individual must equal the value of all commodities offered by that individual was first expressed in ed. 1 by

$$x_1 v_a + y_1 v_b + z_1 v_c + w_1 v_d + \ldots = 0,$$

which, when divided through by v_a, ultimately became

$$x_1 + \frac{y_1}{p_{a,b}} + \frac{z_1}{p_{a,c}} + \frac{w_1}{p_{a,d}} + \ldots = 0.$$

This resembles the first equation of §118 of the translated edition, with the sole difference that the above prices are expressed in terms of $m-1$ commodities instead of being expressed in terms of a *numéraire*. Furthermore, the individual demand for each commodity was originally described as a function of the prices of that commodity in terms of all the other commodities and not as a function of the prices of all the other commodities in terms of a *numéraire*. The following m equations of offer and demand

$$F_a(p_{a,b},\ p_{a,c},\ p_{a,d}\cdots)=0,$$
$$F_b(p_{b,a},\ p_{b,c},\ p_{b,d}\cdots)=0,$$
$$F_c(p_{c,a},\ p_{c,b},\ p_{c,d}\cdots)=0,\qquad\qquad ..(1)$$
$$F_d(p_{d,a},\ p_{d,b},\ p_{d,c}\cdots)=0,$$
$$\cdots\cdots\cdots\cdots$$

reduced to $m-1$ equations by virtue of

$$Xv_a+Yv_b+Zv_c+Wv_d+\ldots=0.$$

To this system of $m-1$ equations Walras then added $(m-1)(m-1)$ equations of general equilibrium resulting from arbitrage operations:

$$p_{a,b}=\frac{1}{p_{b,a}},\qquad p_{c,b}=\frac{p_{c,a}}{p_{b,a}},\qquad p_{d,b}=\frac{p_{d,a}}{p_{b,a}}\cdots$$

$$p_{a,c}=\frac{1}{p_{c,a}},\qquad p_{b,c}=\frac{p_{b,a}}{p_{c,a}},\qquad p_{d,c}=\frac{p_{d,a}}{p_{c,a}}\cdots\qquad ..(2)$$

$$p_{a,d}=\frac{1}{p_{d,a}},\qquad p_{b,d}=\frac{p_{b,a}}{p_{d,a}},\qquad p_{c,d}=\frac{p_{c,a}}{p_{d,a}}\cdots$$

$$\cdots\cdots\cdots\cdots\cdots\cdots$$

and obtained, in all, $(m-1)+(m-1)(m-1)$ or $m(m-1)$ equations to determine the $m(m-1)$ prices of m commodities expressed in terms of one another. The combined systems of equations of offer and demand and of general equilibrium prices resulting from arbitrage in §§122 and 123 of ed. 1 find their counterpart in §§115 and 116 at the end of Lesson 11 of the translated edition; but they differ from the latter in that the argument in ed. 1 contained no mention of either the $m(m-1)$ unknown total quantities exchanged implicit in system (1) or of the virtual introduction of a *numéraire* implicit in system (2).

[*b*] Ed. 2 reads: 'le rapport des raretés de deux marchandises' to which the word 'quelconques' was added in ed. 4.

[*c*] The phrase 'pendant un certain temps' was added in ed. 4.

[*d*] In ed. 2 the passage immediately after the equations reads: '. . . soit $m-1$ équations formant avec la précédente un système de m équations entre lesquelles on peut éliminer successivement $m-1$ des inconnues $x_1, y_1, z_1, w_1\ldots$ de manière à n'avoir plus qu'une équation . . .'. Changed in ed. 4 in which the possibility of elimination is stated conditionally, probably to account for the fact that not all systems of simultaneous equations have a solution, even where the number of equations equals the number of unknowns.

[*e*] In ed. 2 the passage immediately after the equations reads: '. . . soit en tout $m-1$ équations entre lesquelles on pourrait éliminer $m-2$ inconnues telles que $x_1, w_1\ldots$, de manière à n'avoir plus qu'une équation...'. Changed in ed. 4 presumably for reasons indicated in Collation Note [*d*] above.

[*f*] In ed. 2 the passage immediately after the equations reads: '. . . soit toujours $m-1$ équations entre lesquelles on pourrait éliminer $m-2$ inconnues telles que $z_1, w_1\ldots$ de manière à n'avoir plus qu'une équation . . .'. Changed in ed. 4, again presumably for reasons indicated in Collation Note [*d*] above.

[*g*] The passage constituting §122 appears first in ed. 4.

[*h*] The corresponding point in the 21e Leçon of ed. 1 is followed by §123 already referred to in Collation Note [*a*] above; and then this Leçon ends.

[*i*] The 22e Leçon of ed. 1 must be omitted from our detailed collation of texts for the same reason that the 20e and 21e Leçons were omitted (see Collation

Note [a] above). The first and subsequent editions all deal with the same general idea that equilibrium prices are established empirically in the market by a trial and error process, but this idea was developed in ed. 1 without reference to a *numéraire*, which appears first at this stage of the argument in ed. 2. Since the prices in ed. 1 were not expressed in terms of a *numéraire*, Walras found it necessary to make use of arbitrary factors α, β, γ, δ... by which he multiplied the various prices of (A), (B), (C), (D)... respectively, in order to show how the quantities offered and demanded of each commodity changed, as each of the corresponding factors, α for the prices of (A), β for the prices of (B), etc., was made to vary from zero to infinity, while the other arbitrary factors remained constant. General equilibrium was then approached by an appropriate adjustment of all these factors simultaneously. Thus, if all but the (A) markets are in equilibrium so that

$$F_a(p_{a,b},\ p_{a,c},\ p_{a,d}...)\gtreqless 0,$$

i.e. if the prices of (A) are such that the offer of (A) does not equal the demand for (A), then by multiplying the $p_{a,b}, p_{a,c}, p_{a,d}...$ by a suitable α we may obtain

$$F_a(\alpha p_{a,b},\ \alpha p_{a,c},\ \alpha p_{a,d}...)=0.$$

In all likelihood this will throw the (B) market out of its original equilibrium and hence

$$F_b\left(\frac{p_{b,a}}{\alpha},\ p_{b,c},\ p_{b,d}...\right)\gtreqless 0.$$

Then by the use of an appropriate β, we may obtain

$$F_b\left(\frac{\beta p_{b,a}}{\alpha}\ \beta p_{b,c},\ \beta p_{b,d}...\right)=0,$$

and so forth.

General equilibrium is reached by a series of adjustments in the values of all these factors simultaneously. Such adjustments actually take place in the market where prices, or, to use the Walrasian fiction of ed. 1, variable adjustment factors, increase or decrease according as the quantity demanded is greater or less than the quantity offered.

[j] In eds. 2 and 3 this sentence closed with the following phrase indicating that there is no occasion for arbitrage when the equilibrium price of one of any two commodities in terms of the other is equal either to the ratio of these two commodities in terms of any third commodity, 'soit au rapport inverse des prix d'équilibre d'une troisième quelconque en l'une et l'autre'. This phrase was omitted in ed. 4.

[k] In eds. 2 and 3, the conclusion following the conditional clause reads: '... les autres sont nécessairement négatives, et réciproquement', from which the word 'nécessairement' was omitted in ed. 4.

[l] Eds. 2 and 3 read 'fonction'; changed in ed. 4 to read 'inégalité'.

[m] The parenthetical expression '... mais qui ne se présente pas, quand parmi les échangeurs, il y en a qui sont porteurs de plusieurs marchandises ...' was inserted in ed. 4.

Lesson 13

[a] Ed. 1 reads: 'obtiennent'; changed in ed. 2 to read 'peuvent obtenir'.

[b] The whole of §132 first appears at this point as §130 in ed. 2, becoming §132 in ed. 4. The substance of this section is found in §115 of the '20e Leçon' of ed. 1 (see above, Lesson 11, Collation Note [h]).

[c] In ed. 1 the passage from the beginning of §133 up to this point reads:

'v_a, v_b, v_c, v_d... étant les valeurs d'échange des marchandises (A), (B), (C), (D)... dont les rapports constituent les prix courants d'équilibre; $r_{a,1}$, $r_{b,1}$, $r_{c,1}$, $r_{d,1}$ ... $r_{a,2}$, $r_{b,2}$, $r_{c,2}$, $r_{d,2}$ ... $r_{a,3}$, $r_{b,3}$, $r_{c,3}$, $r_{d,3}$ ... étant les raretés de ces marchandises, ou les intensités des derniers besoins satisfaits, chez les échangeurs (1), (2), (3)... après l'échange; on a dans ces conditions (115):

$$
\begin{aligned}
& v_a \;:\; v_b \;:\; v_c \;:\; v_d \;:\; \cdots \\
&:: r_{a,1} : r_{b,1} : r_{c,1} : r_{d,1} : \cdots \\
&:: r_{a,2} : r_{b,2} : r_{c,2} : r_{d,2} : \cdots \\
&:: r_{a,3} : r_{b,3} : r_{c,3} : r_{d,3} : \cdots \\
&:: \quad . \quad . \quad . \quad . \quad . \quad .
\end{aligned}
$$

'Ici encore il est possible qu'un ou plusieurs termes manquent parmi les raretés d'un échangeur donné. Cela arrivera toutes les fois que cet échangeur, n'étant pas porteur d'une marchandise, n'en sera pas demandeur au prix courant, ou qu'en étant porteur, il en sera offreur de toute la quantité possédée. Les riches seront ceux chez lesquels les derniers besoins satisfaits seront nombreux et peu intenses, et les pauvres ceux chez lesquels ils seront peu nombreux et intenses.

'A cette première réserve il en faut joindre une autre relative au cas de discontinuité des courbes d'utilité ou de besoin. Ce cas est très fréquent. C'est d'abord le cas de toutes les marchandises qui se possèdent et qui se consomment par unités naturelles, telles que meubles, vêtements, etc.' Changed in ed. 2. The clause 'dont les rapports constituent les prix courants d'équilibre' and the words 'ou les intensités des derniers besoins satisfaits' of the first sentence were omitted in ed. 4.

[d] In ed. 1, the passage from this point to the end of the paragraph reads: 'Même pour les marchandises qui se possèdent et se consomment par unités artificielles, telles que les aliments par exemple, le cas de discontinuité des courbes de besoins est un cas fréquent. Ainsi, pour un homme sobre, une certaine quantité de bouchées de pain et de viande, de gorgées de vin, nécessaires à sa subsistance quotidienne, sont d'une utilité très intense et à peu près uniforme, et, cette limite atteinte, toute bouchée ou gorgée supplémentaire est inutile. Dans tous ces cas, le rapport des raretés ne sera pas rigoureusement égal au prix, il sera seulement aussi rapproché que possible de l'égalité. On rentrerait dans les données mathématiques en substituant aux courbes discontinues des courbes continues en différant infiniment peu. Après cette substitution, les quantités cédées ou acquises seraient sensiblement les mêmes qu'auparavant, et les termes de rareté seraient rigoureusement proportionnels aux termes de valeur d'échange.' Changed in ed. 2.

[e] This paragraph appears first in ed. 2.

[f] This section appears first in ed. 2.

[g] This section appears first in ed. 2.

[h] The final clause reading 'qui sont tout à fait décisives pour la solution des principaux problèmes économiques' was added in ed. 4.

[i] In ed. 1 the clause here translated as a separate sentence reads: '. . . et dont, par conséquent, les rapports seuls, égaux aux rapports communs et identiques des raretés de deux marchandises quelconques chez un porteur quelconque, soit au prix de ces deux marchandises l'une en l'autre, sont susceptibles de recevoir une expression numérique'. Changed in ed. 2.

[j] The modifying phrase 'ayant toujours sa cause dans la rareté qui seule est un fait absolu' appears first in ed. 2.

[k] The following sentence in ed. 1 reads: 'C'est ce que nous avons fait notamment pour poser les équations d'équivalence des quantités partielles (§117) ou des quantités totales (§122) demandées et offertes.' Omitted from subsequent editions.

[l] In ed. 1 the italicized conclusion reads: '*chaque marchandise n'a qu'une valeur*

d'échange sur le marché'. The words *'par rapport à toutes les autres'* were added after the word *'échange'* in ed. 2.

[*m*] The word 'peut-être' was added in ed. 2.

[*n*] This paragraph appears first in ed. 2. In ed. 1 the remainder of §135 reads: 'L'augmentation ou la diminution de la quantité possédée par un ou plusieurs porteurs d'une marchandise, l'utilité restant la même, a toujours pour conséquence nécessaire, d'après la nature même des courbes d'utilité (§75), la diminution ou l'augmentation de la rareté. Que si, d'autre part, nous réservons toujours les expressions d'*augmentation* et de *diminution de l'utilité* aux déplacements de la courbe de besoin qui ont pour résultat d'augmenter ou de diminuer la rareté, on voit que les variations de l'utilité ont des effets contraires à ceux des variations de la quantité. D'ailleurs, la rareté d'une marchandise augmentant ou diminuant chez un ou plusieurs échangeurs, et devenant, par conséquent, plus grande ou plus petite que les produits de ses prix par les raretés de toutes les autres marchandises, il y a avantage pour ces échangeurs à acheter ou à vendre de cette marchandise, en vendant ou en achetant de toutes les autres (§80). De là une demande ou une offre effective de la même marchandise, accompagnée d'une offre ou une demande effective de toutes les autres, d'où résulte finalement une hausse ou une baisse des prix de l'une en toutes les autres. On peut donc énoncer cette double proposition:

—*Plusieurs marchandises étant données, si, toutes choses restant égales d'ailleurs, l'utilité d'une de ces marchandises augmente ou diminue pour un ou pour plusieurs des échangeurs, la valeur de cette marchandise par rapport à la valeur de toutes les autres, ou son prix en chacune des autres, augmente ou diminue.*

Si, toutes choses restant égales d'ailleurs, la quantité d'une des marchandises augmente ou diminue chez un ou chez plusieurs des porteurs, les prix de cette marchandise diminuent ou augmentent.

'Il convient de remarquer que l'utilité ou la quantité d'une marchandise variant ainsi, la variation de sa valeur ou de ses prix en toutes les autres, qui sera le phénomène principal, sera nécessairement accompagnée, comme d'un phénomène accessoire, de variations des prix de toutes les autres marchandises les unes en les autres. En effet, les raretés de ces marchandises étant changées, et les rapports de ces raretés l'étant aussi, le plus souvent, les prix devront changer. On ne saurait donc supposer un changement de valeur d'une marchandise, sur le marché, sans supposer en même temps un changement de valeur de toutes les marchandises. Nous reviendrons sur ce point un peu plus loin.

'On peut ajouter aux deux propositions ci-dessus les deux suivantes:

—*Plusieurs marchandises étant données, si l'utilité et la quantité d'une de ces marchandises à l'égard d'un ou de plusieurs des échangeurs ou porteurs varient de telle sorte que les raretés ne varient pas, la valeur de cette marchandise par rapport à la valeur de toutes les autres, ou son prix en chacune des autres, ne varie pas.*

Si l'utilité et la quantité de toutes les marchandises à l'égard d'un ou de plusieurs des échangeurs ou porteurs, varient de telle sorte que les rapports des raretés ne varient pas, les prix de toutes les marchandises ne varient pas.' Changed in ed. 2.

[*o*] 'ou virtuelle' was added in ed. 2.

[*p*] Ed. 1 reads: 'scientifiquement'. Changed in ed. 2.

[*q*] End of 23ᵉ Leçon in ed. 1. The next two sentences appear first in ed. 2.

LESSON 14

[*a*] In ed. 1 the general equilibrium prices read: '$p_{a,b}, p_{a,c}, p_{a,d} \cdots p_{b,a}, p_{b,c}, p_{b,d} \cdots p_{c,a}, p_{c,b}, p_{c,d} \cdots p_{d,a}, p_{d,b}, p_{d,c} \cdots$'. Changed in ed. 2 where these prices are expressed in terms of the *numéraire* (A).

[b] In ed. 1 the system of equations (1) reads:

$$'q_{a,1}v_a+q_{b,1}v_b+q_{c,1}v_c+q_{d,1}v_d+\ldots$$
$$=q'_{a,1}v_a+q'_{b,1}v_b+q'_{c,1}v_c+q'_{d,1}v_d+\ldots$$
$$q_{a,2}v_a+q_{b,2}v_b+q_{c,2}v_c+q_{d,2}v_d+\ldots$$
$$=q'_{a,2}v_a+q'_{b,2}v_b+q'_{c,2}v_c+q'_{d,2}v_d+\ldots$$
$$q_{a,3}v_a+q_{b,3}v_b+q_{c,3}v_c+q_{d,3}v_d+\ldots$$
$$=q'_{a,3}v_a+q'_{b,3}v_b+q'_{c,3}v_c+q'_{d,3}v_d+\ldots;$$
$$\ldots\ldots\ldots\ldots\ldots\ldots\ldots$$

Changed in ed. 2, where the *numéraire* is introduced. One version is translatable into the other by dividing each of the above equations by v_a and substituting p_b for $\dfrac{v_b}{v_a}$, p_c for $\dfrac{v_c}{v_a}$, p_d for $\dfrac{v_d}{v_a}$, etc.

[c] In ed. 1 this system of equations reads:

$$'\varphi_{a,1}(q'_{a,1}+x'_1)=p_{a,b}\,\varphi_{b,1}(q'_{b,1}+y'_1),$$
$$\varphi_{a,1}(q'_{a,1}+x'_1)=p_{a,c}\,\varphi_{c,1}(q'_{c,1}+z'_1),$$
$$\varphi_{a,1}(q'_{a,1}+x'_1)=p_{a,d}\varphi_{d,1}(q'_{d,1}+w'_1);$$
$$\ldots\ldots\ldots\ldots\ldots\ldots\ldots\ldots$$

Changed in ed. 2 where the *numéraire* is introduced.

[d] In the corresponding section of ed. 1 (§139) v_a is found in place of the implicit $p_a=1$, and v_b, v_c, v_d... are found in place of p_b, p_c, p_d.... Changed in ed. 2.

[e] End of 24ᵉ Leçon in ed. 1.

[f] In ed. 1 this series reads: '1, p_b, p_c, p_d...'. Changed in ed. 2.

[g] In place of this sentence, ed. 1 reads: 'De ces prix, on déduit successivement les suivants: $p_{a,b}=\dfrac{1}{\mu}$, $p_{a,c}=\dfrac{1}{\pi}$, $p_{a,d}=\dfrac{1}{\varrho}$... $p_{c,b}=\dfrac{\pi}{\mu}$, $p_{d,b}=\dfrac{\varrho}{\mu}$... $p_{b,c}=\dfrac{\mu}{\pi}$, $p_{b,d}=\dfrac{\mu}{\varrho}$... $p_{d,c}=\dfrac{\varrho}{\pi}$, $p_{c,d}=\dfrac{\pi}{\varrho}$.... A tous ces prix d'équilibre général correspondent, en vertu de la condition de satisfaction maximum, les quantités demandées: N, Q, S... M, P, R... G, J... F, H... L... K....' Changed in ed. 2.

[h] End of 25ᵉ Leçon in ed. 1.

LESSON 15

[a] In ed. 1 the corresponding passage from the beginning of §149 to this point reads: 'Pour définir le rôle d'un instrument de mesure et d'un intermédiaire d'échange de la richesse sociale, nous avons supposé les prix courants d'équilibre général déterminés antérieurement au choix de cet instrument et de cet intermédiaire.' This passage was omitted in eds. 2 and 3; but in ed. 4 §151 begins with the words: 'Il ressort déjà de notre résolution des équations de l'échange (§§127, 128, 129, 130) que l'adoption . . .'. The remainder of this paragraph is substantially the same in all editions, though the last sentence was changed in ed. 4 from: 'C'est cette simplification qu'il nous faut étudier à présent, d'autant plus qu'en nous plaçant dans cette hypothèse de l'usage d'un numéraire et d'une monnaie, nous nous rapprochons de plus en plus de la réalité des choses.'

[b] In §150 of ed. 1 this paragraph reads: 'Soit donc (A) le numéraire et la

monnaie. Soient à présent, d'un côté, les marchandises (A), (C), (D)... s'échangeant ou prêtes à s'échanger entre elles aux prix déterminés d'équilibre général π, ϱ... de (C), (D)... en (A), suivant les équations

$$(Q'+K'+...)v_c=(P'+K'\pi+...)v_a,$$
$$(K'\pi=L'\varrho)v_a=L'v_d...$$

$$(S'+L'+...)v_d=(R'+L'\varrho+...)v_a,$$
$$(L'\varrho=K'\pi)v_a=K'v_c....$$

Et soit, d'un autre côté, la marchandise (B) se présentant sur le marché pour s'y échanger contre les marchandises (A), (C), (D)....' In ed. 2 the passage preceding the equations was changed to read: 'Soit donc (A) le numéraire et la monnaie. Soient à présent, d'un côté, les quantités effectivement demandées, égales aux quantités effectivement offertes: P', R'... Q', K'... S', L'... des marchandises (A), (C), (D)... s'échangeant ou prêtes à s'échanger entre elles aux prix déterminés d'équilibre général $p_c=\pi$, $p_d=\varrho$... de (C), (D)... en (A), suivant les équations....' And in ed. 4 the whole paragraph underwent a final revision and was made part of §151.

[c] Ed. 1 reads $p_{b,a}$ and $p_{a,b}$ where subsequent editions read p_b and $\dfrac{1}{p_b}$ throughout this paragraph.

[d] Ed. 1 reads '*monnaie*' where subsequent editions read '*numéraire*' throughout this italicized paragraph.

[e] This section appears first in ed. 2.

[f] In ed. 1, the corresponding section (§154) begins with the following paragraph: 'Enfin, au lieu de supposer déterminés les prix de $m-1$ quelconques d'entre les marchandises, pour déterminer le prix de la $m^{\text{ième}}$ nous pourrions supposer les m marchandises se présentant à la fois sur le marché. L'adoption d'un numéraire et d'une monnaie équivaudrait alors purement et simplement à l'introduction de la condition d'équilibre général, et les prix courants se détermineraient d'ailleurs conformément aux deux conditions de satisfaction maximum des besoins et d'égalité de la demande et de l'offre totales effectives de chaque marchandise. L'intervention du numéraire et de la monnaie ne change donc rien à la loi de l'offre et de la demande, dont l'énoncé reste tel quel, sauf qu'au lieu de parler des prix des marchandises en toutes les autres, il suffit de parler de leur prix en numéraire.' Omitted in ed. 2.

[g] End of 26e Leçon in ed. 1.

LESSON 16

[a] Eds. 1, 2 and 3 read: 'et en la défendant contre toutes doctrines opposées'. Omitted in ed. 4.

[b] End of 27e Leçon in ed. 1. The remainder of this Lesson appears first in ed. 2.

[c] In eds. 2 and 3 the following footnote is referred to at this point: 'Je répète, pour éviter tout malentendu, que j'ajoute ce paragraphe à la seconde édition de mon livre et que si je n'ai pas cité, dans la première édition, en 1874, les trois ouvrages ici mentionnés parus antérieurement au mien, c'est que j'ignorais entièrement leur existence.' Omitted in ed. 4.

[d] The remainder of this paragraph reading '. . . et d'égalité de l'offre et de la demande effectives à ce prix et qui, ainsi, supprime la propriété' appears first in ed. 4.

[e] This paragraph was first designated as a separate section (§163) in ed. 4.

[*f*] In eds. 2 and 3 the opening words of this sentence read: 'C'est ce que Jevons n'a pas fait et c'est précisément ce qu'il s'est interdit de faire. . . .' Changed in ed. 4.

[*g*] In eds. 2 and 3 the following paragraph appears at this point: 'Je n'ai critiqué qu'un point spécial de la doctrine de mes devanciers. Je dois ajouter tout de suite que la conception de l'intensité du dernier besoin satisfait par Gossen sous le nom de *Werth des letzten Atoms* et par Jevons sous le nom de *Final Degree of Utility* leur a permis d'éclaircir d'autres points importants, et que leurs ouvrages doivent être lus avec le plus grand soin par les économistes désireux de travailler à la constitution définitive de l'économie politique pure.' Omitted in ed. 4.

[*h*] This paragraph was first designated as a separate section (§ 164) in ed. 4.

[*i*] In eds. 2 and 3 these authors are referred to more fully as follows: 'Je dirai seulement que lui et les auteurs qui l'ont suivi, comme M. le professeur Frédéric de Wieser, de Prague, dans son ouvrage: —*Ueber den Ursprung und die Hauptgesetze des wirtschaftlichen Werthes* (1884) et M. le professeur Eugène de Boehm-Bawerk, dans ses *Grundzüge der Theorie des wirtschaftlichen Güterwerts* (1886). . . .'

[*j*] Eds. 2 and 3 read 'peut-être'; omitted in ed. 4.

[*k*] Eds. 2 and 3 read 'économistes en Allemagne'; the last two words were omitted in ed. 4.

[*l*] In eds. 2 and 3 this sentence reads: 'J'en ai tiré, comme on l'a vu, la théorie de la détermination des prix des marchandises.' Changed in ed. 4.

[*m*] The remainder of this paragraph was added in ed. 4.

Lesson 17

[*a*] In ed. 1 the corresponding section (§ 208) is found at the beginning of the 35ᵉ Leçon entitled 'Du capital et du revenu'. The intervening Leçons of ed. 1 were made up of the 28ᵉ Leçon, entitled 'Examen critique de la doctrine de M. Cournot sur les changements de valeur, absolus et relatifs', which was omitted from all subsequent editions, and the 29ᵉ to the 34ᵉ Leçons, which were devoted to the formal theory of money and constituted Part III of ed. 1 under the general title 'Du numéraire et de la monnaie'. In the later editions the special treatment of the theory of money was deferred to Part VI.

[*b*] This sentence appears first in ed. 4.

[*c*] In ed. 1 the following sentence reads: "Elle se précisera bientôt tout à fait pour nous.' Omitted in ed. 4.

[*d*] End of 35ᵉ Leçon in ed. 1.

[*e*] In ed. 1 there is another sentence at the close of this paragraph, just at the end of the 36ᵉ Leçon, reading: 'L'importance de cette étude n'apparaît-elle pas suffisamment si l'on songe qu'en économie politique il y a actuellement cinq ou six théories de la rente, ce qui revient exactement à dire qu'il n'y a pas de théorie de la rente, pas plus qu'il n'y a, du reste, de théories du salaire ou de l'intérêt.' Omitted in ed. 4.

Lesson 18

[*a*] End of 37ᵉ Leçon in ed. 1.

[*b*] Ed. 1 reads '*services producteurs*'. Changed in ed. 2.

[*c*] This and the previous sentence appear first in ed. 2.

[*d*] This sentence appears first in ed. 4.

[*e*] End of 38ᵉ Leçon in ed. 1.

LESSON 19

[*a*] In ed. 1 the remainder of this paragraph reads: 'Si je prends de l'argent pour acheter de la matière première ou des marchandises en gros, j'inscrirai la somme au crédit de Caisse et au débit d'un compte *Marchandises*; si pour payer mon loyer ou mes ouvriers, et d'une façon générale pour payer des fermages, des salaires ou des intérêts, je l'inscrirai au crédit de Caisse et au débit d'un compte *Frais généraux*. Et si je .nets dans ma caisse de l'argent provenant de la vente de mes produits, j'inscrirai la somme au débit du compte Caisse et au crédit du compte Marchandises.' Changed in ed. 2.

[*b*] End of 39ᵉ Leçon in ed. 1.

[*c*] End of 40ᵉ Leçon in ed. 1.

LESSON 20

[*a*] Throughout this Lesson the term 'services producteurs' used in ed. 1 was changed in ed. 2 to read simply 'services'.

[*b*] The phrase 'à recueillir pendant une certaine période de temps' was added in ed. 4.

[*c*] The phrase 'à consommer pendant la même période' was added in ed. 4.

[*d*] The appositional phrase 'soit les excédents des o_t, o_p, o_k... positifs sur les o_t, o_p, o_k... négatifs' appeared first in ed. 2.

[*e*] The principal clause, here translated as a sentence, reads in ed. 1: '. . . on aurait déjà, en vue de la détermination des quantités cherchées, le système suivant de *n* équations d'offre totale des services producteurs'. Changed in ed. 2.

[*f*] Ed. 1 reads: 'Il serait facile d'exprimer cette condition par un système d'autant d'équations qu'il y a de coefficients de fabrication à déterminer; mais comme ce système serait en quelque sorte indépendant des autres que nous considérons, nous en faisons abstraction, pour plus de simplicité, en supposant que les coefficients ci-dessus figurent parmi les données et non parmi les inconnues du problème.' In ed. 2, the clause 'mais comme ce système serait en quelque sorte indépendant des autres que nous considérons' was omitted and the remainder of the sentence appeared as a separate sentence. The version translated in this text appears first in ed. 4. Actually, even in the earlier editions the concept of variable coefficients of production was enlarged upon mathematically in the 51ᵉ Leçon of ed. 1 and the 28ᵉ Leçon of eds. 2 and 3, where the discussion had every appearance of being an adumbration of the marginal productivity theory which was then explicitly developed in Appendix III of ed. 3 and later in the 36ᵉ Leçon of the subsequent editions when Appendix III was omitted.

[*g*] End of 41ᵉ Leçon in ed. 1. The following section appears first in ed. 2 as §203 (equivalent of §207 in ed. 4 def.), where the opening sentences read: 'Il s'agit d'arriver à l'équilibre de la production de la même façon que nous sommes arrivés à l'équilibre de l'échange, c'est-à-dire en supposant les données du problème invariables pendant tout le temps que dureront nos tâtonnements, sauf à supposer ensuite ces données variables en vue d'étudier les effets de leur variations. Mais le tâtonnement en matière de production rencontre une complication qui n'existait pas en matière d'échange.' Changed in ed. 4.

[*h*] In ed. 2 the remainder of this paragraph reads: 'Acceptant cette nécessité, nous devons supposer que, pour chaque reprise de tâtonnement, nos entrepreneurs trouveront, dans le pays, des propriétaires fonciers, travailleurs et capitalistes possédant les mêmes quantités de services et ayant les mêmes besoins des services et des produits. Une reprise de tâtonnement consistera en ceci. A des prix de services criés d'abord au hasard, et ensuite en hausse ou en baisse suivant les circonstances, les entrepreneurs emprunteront aux propriétaires

fonciers, travailleurs et capitalistes les quantités de ces services nécessaires pour fabriquer certaines quantités de produits déterminées d'abord au hasard, et ensuite en augmentation ou en diminution suivant les circonstances. Puis ils viendront vendre ces produits sur le marché des produits, suivant le mécanisme de la libre concurrence, à ces propriétaires fonciers, travailleurs et capitalistes possédant toujours les mêmes quantités de services et ayant toujours les mêmes besoins des services et des produits. Le tâtonnement sera fini lorsque, en échange des produits qu'ils auront fabriqués, les entrepreneurs obtiendront des propriétaires fonciers, travailleurs et capitalistes précisément les quantités de rentes, travaux et profits qu'ils leur devront et qu'ils auront fait entrer dans la confection des produits; de telle sorte qu'ils pourront ou s'acquitter et en rester là, ou plutôt continuer indéfiniment la production dont la marche sera dès lors réglée pour autant qu'aucune variation ne surviendra dans les données, c'est-à-dire dans les quantités possédées des services et dans les utilités des services et des produits.' This was changed in ed. 4 where the device of '*bons*', i.e. of *tickets* was introduced.

[*i*] The following two paragraphs appear first in ed. 4.

LESSON 21

[*a*] In ed. 1 this first paragraph reads: 'Pour cela, venons sur le marché, et supposons qu'on y détermine au hasard n prix de services producteurs p'_t, p'_p, p'_k.... Afin de mieux faire saisir les opérations qui vont suivre, nous les partagerons en deux phases au moyen de la double hypothèse que voici. Nous supposerons d'abord que les entrepreneurs de (A), (B), (C), (D)... vont acheter leurs services producteurs (T), (P), (K)... sur un marché étranger, en s'engageant à restituer plus tard des quantités de ces services non pas égales mais simplement équivalentes. Nous supposerons ensuite qu'ils s'engagent à restituer plus tard des quantités non plus seulement équivalentes mais égales, auquel cas nous pourrons supposer aussi qu'ils achètent leurs services producteurs sur le marché du pays aux propriétaires fonciers, travailleurs et capitalistes auxquels ils vendent leurs produits. On voit assez comment cette manière de procéder fait abstraction sinon du numéraire au moins de la monnaie.' Changed in ed. 2 to read: 'Venons donc sur le marché, et supposons qu'on y détermine au hasard n prix de services p'_t, p'_p, p'_k... et m quantités à fabriquer de produits $\Omega_a, \Omega_b, \Omega_c, \Omega_d$.... Afin de mieux faire saisir les opérations qui vont suivre, nous les partagerons en deux phases au moyen de la double hypothèse que voici. Nous supposerons d'abord que les entrepreneurs de (A), (B), (C), (D)... achètent leurs services producteurs (T), (P), (K)... en s'engageant à restituer plus tard des quantités de ces services non pas égales mais simplement équivalentes, et nous déterminerons ainsi les quantités $\Omega_a, \Omega_b, \Omega_c, \Omega_d$... de façon à ce que les entrepreneurs ne fassent ni bénéfice ni perte. Nous supposerons ensuite que les entrepreneurs s'engagent à restituer plus tard des quantités non plus seulement équivalentes mais égales, et nous déterminerons ainsi les quantités p'_t, p'_p, p'_k... de façon à ce que l'offre et la demande effectives des services soient égales. On voit assez comment cette manière de procéder fait abstraction sinon du numéraire au moins de la monnaie.' This was changed in ed. 4 where the fiction of the 'marché étranger', abandoned in ed. 2, was replaced by that of the 'bons', i.e. 'tickets'.

[*b*] The phrase 'sauf à faire voir plus tard que le prix de revient de la marchandise numéraire tend de lui-même à être égal à l'unité sous le régime de la libre concurrence' appears first in ed. 2.

[*c*] In ed. 1 the passage beginning with the previous paragraph and ending at this point reads (apart from the equations which have remained unchanged): 'Maintenant, il faut supposer que les entrepreneurs trouvent sur le marché étranger, aux prix p'_t, p'_p, p'_k... des services producteurs (T), (P), (K)... en

quantités indéfinies, et qu'ils produisent, aux prix de revient p'_a, p'_b, p'_c, p'_d...
des quantités déterminées au hasard Ω_a, Ω_b, Ω_c, Ω_d... de (A), (B), (C), (D)...
exigeant des quantités Δ_t, Δ_p, Δ_k... de (T), (P), (K)... conformément aux
équations

$$. \quad . \quad . \quad . \quad . \quad . \quad . \quad . \quad . \quad . \quad .$$

'Les quantités Ω_a, Ω_b, Ω_c, Ω_d... étant alors apportées sur le marché du pays
que nous considérons y seront vendues par les entrepreneurs suivant le mécanisme
de la libre concurrence.' Changed in ed. 2.

[d] This paragraph appears first in ed. 2.

[e] The passage beginning with the second paragraph of §211 and ending at
this point appears first in ed. 2.

[f] Ed. 1 reads 'par tâtonnement'. Omitted in ed. 2.

[g] The phrase 'sous forme de bons' appears first in ed. 4.

[h] The remainder of this sentence reading 'en multipliant les m équations du
premier respectivement par Ω_a, D'_b, D'_c, D'_d... et les n équations du second
respectivement par p'_t, p'_p, p'_k... additionnant les deux systèmes ainsi obtenus et
remarquant que les seconds membres des deux sommes sont identiques...'
appears first in ed. 2.

[i] In ed. 1 the remainder of this section, which closes the 42ᵉ Leçon of that
edition, reads: 'Il faut, pour cela, que les quantités de services producteurs
achetées sur le marché étranger et les quantités reçues sur le marché du pays par
les entrepreneurs soient équivalentes, puisque, par hypothèse, les entrepreneurs
de (B), (C), (D)... ne font ni bénéfice ni perte. Ainsi il faut que

$$(O'_t - D'_t)p'_t + (O'_p - D'_p)p'_p + (O'_k - D'_k)p'_k + ... = 0,$$

soit que

$$D'_a = \Omega_a p'_a;$$

et comme il faut, pour l'équilibre, que la demande de (A), D'_a, et l'offre de (A),
Ω_a, soient égales, il faut que p'_a soit égal à 1, c'est-à-dire que le prix de revient
du numéraire soit égal à son prix de vente. C'est ce qui aura lieu, si l'on a pris soin
de poser tout d'abord

$$p'_a = a_t p'_t + a_p p'_p + a_k p'_k + ... = 1.$$

'En dehors de cette équation, il n'y a pas d'équilibre possible. Et, cette équation
supposée satisfaite, l'équilibre existera quand Ω_a sera égal à D'_a. Ainsi, pratique-
ment, lorsqu'on aura fixé le prix des services producteurs de manière à ce que le
prix de revient du numéraire soit égal à l'unité, il suffira, pour obtenir l'équilibre
partiel que nous cherchons, que les entrepreneurs de (A) fabriquent à ce prix de
revient égal au prix de vente, par conséquent sans bénéfice ni perte, toute la
quantité de (A) qu'on leur demandera. Alors sera remplie cette première condition que les entrepreneurs s'engagent à restituer des quantités de services
producteurs non pas égales mais simplement équivalentes. En d'autres termes,
alors seront satisfaites toutes les équations de la production, sauf toutefois le
système (1) des équations d'offre totale de services producteurs.' Changed in ed. 2.

[j] In ed. 2 the remainder of this paragraph reads: 'Alors sera remplie cette
première condition que les entrepreneurs s'engagent à rendre des quantités de
services producteurs non pas égales mais simplement équivalentes à celles qu'ils
ont empruntées. En d'autres termes, alors seront satisfaites toutes les équations
de la production, sauf toutefois le système [1] des équations d'offre totale des
services.' Changed in ed. 4.

[k] Ed. 1 reads: 'Ainsi, le moment est venu de fermer, pour ainsi dire, le cercle
de la production en éliminant la supposition du marché étranger (§250 [§208 of
ed. 4 def.]) et en introduisant celle, conforme à la réalité, que les entrepreneurs

achètent les services producteurs aux propriétaires fonciers, travailleurs et capitalistes du pays auxquels ils vendent leurs produits.' Changed in ed. 2 to read: 'Ainsi, le moment est venu de fermer, pour ainsi dire, le cercle de la production en introduisant la condition, conforme à la réalité, que les produits s'échangent contre les mêmes quantités de services qui entrent dans leur confection.' Changed again in ed. 4.

[*l*] In ed. 1 the paragraph up to this point reads: 'La condition d'égalité dont nous venons de parler serait remplie si on avait

$$D'_t = O'_t, \qquad D'_p = O'_p, \qquad D'_k = O'_k, \ldots$$

mais, généralement, on aura

$$D'_t \gtreqless O'_t, \qquad D'_p \gtreqless O'_p, \qquad D'_k \gtreqless O'_k, \ldots'$$

Changed in ed. 4.

[*m*] In ed. 1 all Greek symbols in the section have one less prime. Changed to its final form in ed. 2.

[*n*] Ed. 1 reads: 'la loi d'établissement des prix d'équilibre de l'échange et de la production'. Changed in ed. 4.

[*o*] End of 43ᵉ Leçon in ed. 1.

LESSON 22

[*a*] Ed. 1 reads: '*La libre concurrence en matière d'échange et de production est une opération par laquelle les services producteurs se combinent en les produits de la nature et de la quantité propres à donner la plus grande satisfaction possible des besoins dans les limites de cette condition que chaque service producteur comme chaque produit n'ait qu'un seul prix sur le marché.*' Changed in ed. 2 to read: '*La production et l'échange sur un marché régi par la libre concurrence est une opération par laquelle les services peuvent se combiner en les produits de la nature et de la quantité propres à donner la plus grande satisfaction possible des besoins dans les limites de cette condition que chaque service comme chaque produit n'ait qu'un seul prix sur le marché.*' Amplified finally in ed. 4 to include the condition of equality between price and cost of production as well as that of uniformity of price.

[*b*] In ed. 1 the end of the sentence reads: 'à l'agriculture, à l'industrie, au commerce, au crédit'; 'au crédit' was omitted in ed. 2.

[*c*] The statement and refutation of this first objection found in the following four sentences appear first in ed. 2.

[*d*] In ed. 1 the last clause of this sentence reads: '. . .; et, quelles que puissent être ces causes, on en aura suffisamment tenu compte en concluant qu'il faut les supprimer autant que possible'. Changed in ed. 4.

[*e*] These reservations appear first in ed. 2. In ed. 1 this paragraph reads simply: 'Et ainsi, on doit généraliser, en l'étendant aux services producteurs comme aux produits, la proposition que: —*Les valeurs d'échange sont proportionnelles aux raretés.*'

[*f*] This section appears first in ed. 2.

[*g*] This section appears first in ed. 2.

[*h*] End of 44ᵉ Leçon in ed. 1. In ed. 2 the remainder of this Lesson was transferred to this place, almost verbatim, from §§353–359 of the 59ᵉ Leçon of ed. 1 where it originally formed part of the discussion of price fixing (see below, §372 of Lesson 41 and Collation Note [*a*] of that Lesson). The few changes of any importance that were made in the transposition are noted below.

[*i*] In §354 of ed. 1 the remainder of this paragraph reads: 'Ce raisonnement consiste, on le voit, à faire abstraction de l'intervention des entrepreneurs dans

la production et à considérer les services producteurs comme des marchandises s'échangeant les unes contre les autres. Mais c'est surtout en ce qui concerne les produits que les courbes d'achat et de vente sont utiles à considérer, par la raison qu'elles se ramènent alors à des courbes de prix.' Omitted in ed. 2.

[*j*] In §355 of ed. 1 the remainder of this paragraph reads: 'On peut remarquer qu'au point de vue que nous avons adopté, mais à ce point de vue seulement, il est exact que *le prix des produits est déterminé par le montant des frais de production*. Ainsi, l'école anglaise, en posant son principe, a pris une vérité d'approximation pour une vérité absolue.' Omitted in ed. 2.

Part V

[*a*] In ed. 1 the Leçons dealing with the theory of capitalization (i.e. capita formation) and credit were found in Part V, which was then entitled 'Conditions et conséquences du progrès économique'. In eds. 2 and 3 this same material was shifted to Part IV and the title was changed to 'Théorie de la capitalisation et du crédit'. Finally in ed. 4, the Leçons describing the conditions and consequences of economic progress and those criticizing other systems of pure economics were separated out to form the present Part VII.

Lesson 23

[*a*] Ed. 1 reads 'revenus producteurs'; changed in ed. 2 to 'services'. This same change was made throughout wherever 'revenu producteur' occurred in ed. 1.

[*b*] In ed. 1 this paragraph reads: 'Soit p le prix du revenu, y compris les deux primes d'amortissement et d'assurance; c'est le revenu *brut*. Soit μ la prime d'amortissement, v la prime d'assurance. Ce qui reste du revenu brut après qu'on a retranché ces deux primes, soit $\pi = p - (\mu + v)$, est le revenu *net*.' Changed in ed. 2. In view of the modification in the meaning of μ and v, which first designated the absolute values of depreciation and insurance in ed. 1, and subsequently designated the corresponding rates, the later editions read μP and vP where the first edition reads simply μ and v. This change in notation resulted in concordant changes in the algebraic formulation of the theory of capital formation and credit throughout Part V which are here noted once for all.

[*c*] In ed. 1 the remainder of this section reads: 'Car comment n'achèterait-on pas à des prix égaux deux capitaux rapportant des revenus nets égaux? Et comment n'achèterait-on pas à des prix deux ou trois fois plus élevés l'un que l'autre deux capitaux rapportant des revenus nets deux ou trois fois plus élevés l'un que l'autre? Du moins doit-il en être ainsi à un certain état normal et idéal qui sera l'état d'équilibre du marché des capitaux.

'Soit donc P le prix du capital. Le rapport $\frac{\pi}{P}$, ou le *taux* du revenu net, est un rapport commun, à l'état d'équilibre. Soit i ce rapport; quand nous l'aurons déterminé, nous aurons déterminé par cela même le prix de tous les capitaux fonciers, personnels et mobiliers.' Changed in ed. 2.

[*d*] In ed. 1 the last clause in this sentence reads: '. . . et cette opération ne fournirait aucun prix en numéraire'; changed in ed. 2 to read: '. . . et cette opération, qui n'aurait théoriquement aucune raison d'être, ne fournirait non plus aucun prix en numéraire si le numéraire n'était pas lui-même un capital, et s'il était un produit ou un service ayant une rareté à laquelle on pût rapporter les raretés des autres produits ou services, comme il le faudrait pour que l'établissement de l'équilibre de la production fût possible.' Changed to its final form in ed. 4. The remainder of this section reads in ed. 1: 'Pour avoir une offre et une demande de capitaux, il faut substituer à la conception d'un état économique

stationnaire celle d'un état économique progressif. Il faut supposer des entrepreneurs qui, au lieu de fabriquer des produits consommables, ont fabriqué, pour les vendre, des capitaux producteurs neufs. En regard, il faut supposer des propriétaires fonciers, travailleurs ou capitalistes qui, ayant acheté des produits consommables pour une somme inférieure au montant de leurs revenus producteurs, ont le moyen d'acheter ces capitaux producteurs neufs. Avec ces données nouvelles, nous possédons tous les éléments de solution du problème, si nous songeons que les capitaux producteurs neufs sont des produits soumis à la loi des frais de production. En effet, à l'état d'équilibre, le prix de vente de ces capitaux producteurs neufs doit être égal à leur prix de revient; et, d'autre part, le prix de vente des capitaux producteurs déjà existants doit être égal au prix de vente de ces capitaux producteurs neufs. Si donc nous connaissons le prix de revient des capitaux producteurs neufs, nous connaîtrons le prix de vente des capitaux producteurs neufs ou déjà existants, et, par consequent, le taux du revenu net. Ici comme ailleurs, nous avons à exprimer mathématiquement cet état d'équilibre et à montrer comment il se réalise sur le marché. Auparavant, toutefois, nous devons mentionner une circonstance importante que nous avions réservée (250) pour l'introduire à present.' Changed in ed. 4.

[e] In ed. 1, where the wording of this sentence is slightly different, only new capital goods are mentioned; reference to already existing capital goods in this connection is first made in ed. 2. The remainder of this section in ed. 1 reads: 'Nous montrerons, au surplus, comment le problème de la détermination du taux du revenu net se résout aussi bien dans une hypothèse que dans l'autre, sur le marché, par le mécanisme de la libre concurrence. Remarquons seulement dès à présent qu'il ne faut pas confondre le marché des capitaux, c'est-à-dire le marché où les capitaux producteurs se vendent et s'achètent, avec le marché du capital, c'est-à-dire avec le marché où se loue le capital monnaie et qui n'est autre que le marché des services producteurs. Nous trouverons ces deux marchés distincts l'un de l'autre dans le cours de notre démonstration. Remarquons aussi que, faisant abstraction de la monnaie, nous devons parler dorénavant non du capital *monnaie*, mais du capital *numéraire*.' Changed in ed. 2 to read as translated in the text except for the last part of the last sentence which appears first in ed. 4.

[f] End of 45e Leçon in ed. 1.

[g] In ed. 1 this sentence ends with the clause 'ce qui n'est pas un cas normal'. Omitted in ed. 2.

[h] From this point on, the changes made in ed. 2 and in ed. 4 in the theory of capital formation and credit were so substantial that any detailed collation of texts becomes impracticable apart from certain minor revisions noted below.

It had not occurred to Walras until his fourth edition (§242) to introduce the imaginary commodity (E). In the first three editions he presented the individual savings function

$$e = f_e(p_t \ldots p_p \ldots p_k, p_{k'}, p_{k''} \ldots p_b, p_c, p_d \ldots i)$$

which he described as an empirical datum in the following terms (§279 of ed. 1 and §238 of eds. 2 and 3):

'Nous posons cette équation d'épargne empiriquement, comme nous avons posé, au début, l'équation de demande effective. Peut-être y aurait-il lieu de rechercher les éléments mathématiques constitutifs de la fonction d'épargne, comme nous avons recherché ceux de la fonction de demande effective. Il faudrait évidemment, pour cela, considérer l'utilité sous un aspect nouveau, la distinguer en utilité *présente* et utilité *future*. Nous ne ferons pas cette recherche, et nous laisserons à la fonction d'épargne son caractère empirique, sans prétendre aucunement, pour cela, qu'il soit impossible de remonter à ses éléments, mais parce que cette opération ne nous est pas nécessaire pour le moment.'

588   ELEMENTS OF PURE ECONOMICS

The reason for this reluctance to pursue any further the analysis of time preference in its relation to the savings function was given partly in the Preface (see above, pp. 45–46), and principally in Walras's correspondence with von Bortkiewicz and Böhm-Bawerk. To the former he wrote in an unpublished letter, dated February 20, 1889: "Et quand on considère l'intérêt comme le prix du service du capital, ou du profit, ainsi que je le fais aussi, il n'y a nul besoin de l'expliquer par la différence de valeur d'un bien présent et d'un bien futur, comme font Jevons et Böhm-Bawerk. Leurs théories et la mienne sont entièrement divergentes à cet égard." (F.W. I, 66.) To the latter he wrote on May 5 of the same year: "Vous déduisez le taux de l'intérêt de la différence de valeur entre les biens présents et les biens futurs; et moi je crois que la différence de valeur entre les biens présents et les biens futurs ne saurait se déterminer directement, et qu'elle ne peut se tirer que du taux de l'intérêt qui, lui, se détermine directement par le rapport du revenu net total des capitaux neufs au montant des épargnes. . . . Je crois que la question est une question mathématique, qui ne peut se vider que mathématiquement. . . ." (F.W. I, 58.) See William Jaffé, "Unpublished Papers and Letters of Léon Walras", op. cit., pp. 203–204; and "Léon Walras's Theory of Capital Accumulation", op. cit. p. 43.

In the fourth edition, the introduction of perpetual net income as commodity (E) enabled Walras to avoid the dilemma of either continuing to use an empirical function or of complicating his postulates with considerations of differences between present and future utilities.

[i] In the first three editions a function

$$E=F_e(p_t\ldots p_p\ldots p_k, p_{k'}, p_{k''}\ldots p_b, p_c, p_d\ldots i)$$

was simply derived by summating the empirical individual functions. The nature of the F_e function was not directly considered. We were merely told in ed. 1 that the individual savings function f_e is such that: 'Il nous suffira de poser en fait que cette fonction est croissante ou décroissante pour des valeurs croissantes ou décroissantes de i, par la raison qu'il serait absurde de supposer qu'un homme, disposé à faire une certaine épargne dans de certaines conditions de revenu net à obtenir, ne soit pas disposé à faire une épargne au moins égale dans des conditions encore plus favorables.' This was radically changed in eds. 2 and 3 to read: 'Il nous suffira de poser en fait que cette fonction est successivement croissante et décroissante pour des valeurs croissantes de i par la raison que l'offre des services en échange de capitaux neufs, non plus que celle en échange de produits consommables, n'augmente pas indéfiniment avec la quantité à obtenir, mais tend à redevenir nulle si le prix devient infiniment grand, c'est-à-dire si avec une épargne minime on peut obtenir un supplément de revenu extrêmement considérable.' Finally in ed. 4, with the introduction of commodity (E) and with the substitution of the function

$$d_e=f_e(p_t\ldots p_p\ldots p_k, p_{k'}, p_{k''}\ldots p_b, p_c, p_d\ldots p_e)$$

for

$$e=f_e(p_t\ldots p_p\ldots p_k, p_{k'}, p_{k''}\ldots p_b, p_c, p_d\ldots i)$$

the whole raison d'être of any special discussion of $f_e(\ldots)$ disappeared and a discussion of $D_e=F_e(\ldots)$ and of $E=D_e p_e=F_e(\ldots)p_e$ took its place.

[j] In ed. 1 there is no further development of this section. The next sentence which closes the 46e Leçon in ed. 1 reads: 'Et il ne nous reste plus qu'à introduire convenablement ces équations dans le système des équations de la production pour résoudre le problème de la capitalisation ou de la détermination du taux du revenu net.'

[k] In eds. 2 and 3 this sentence ends with the clause: '. . . comme nous avions, en matière d'échange (117) [§ 118 in ed. 4 def.] et de production (197) [§ 201 in

ed. 4 def.], des systèmes de m et $n+m$ équations de distribution d'une somme de richesse ou de revenu possédée par un individu entre ses m ou $n+m$ espèces de besoins, de façon à ce que le rapport de la rareté au prix fût le même pour toutes les marchandises.' This is followed by the sentence: 'Cette condition d'égalité des rapports des raretés aux prix des services et des produits est la condition du maximum d'utilité effective pour chaque échangeur, vu que, si elle n'est pas remplie, pour deux marchandises quelconques, il y a avantage à demander moins de celle pour laquelle le rapport est plus faible et plus de celle pour laquelle ce rapport est plus fort.' Omitted in ed. 4.

LESSON 24

[a] In general form, the equations of capital formation and credit are similar in all five editions, but in detail these equations underwent so many changes between eds. 3 and 4, as a consequence of the introduction of (E) in the previous Lesson (see above, Lesson 23, Collation Note [h]), that once again the usual collation of texts becomes impracticable. Some of the more significant differences may, however, be noted.

In the first three editions the individual exchange equation with which Walras starts his discussion in §244 of the text translated, reads:

$$o_t p_t + \ldots + o_p p_p + \ldots o_k p_k + o_{k'} p_{k'} + o_{k''} p_{k''} + \ldots$$
$$= f_e(p_t \ldots p_p \ldots p_k, p_{k'}, p_{k''} \ldots p_b, p_c, p_d \ldots i) + d_a$$
$$+ d_b p_b + d_c p_c + d_a p_a + \ldots;$$

while, in ed. 4, the function $f_e(\ldots)$ was replaced by $d_e p_e$. Then in the system of equations of maximum satisfaction which followed, the first three editions gave only $n+m+1$ equations, since $\varphi_e(q_e+d_e)=p_e\varphi_a(d_a)$ could not be introduced until ed. 4. The n equations of the positive or negative supply of productive services are the same in all editions except for the final variable which reads i in the first three editions and was changed to p_e in the fourth. Prior to the introduction of commodity (E), there were only $m-1$ equations of demand for products in eds. 1 to 3, equation

$$d_e = f_e(p_t \ldots p_p \ldots p_k, p_{k'}, p_{k''} \ldots p_b, p_c, p_d \ldots p_e)$$

appearing first in ed. 4. Moreover, in these equations as in the previous system, p_e was substituted in ed. 4 for i of the earlier editions. In the equation of the individual demand for (A), as in the individual exchange equation, the expression

$$f_e(p_t \ldots p_p \ldots p_k, p_{k'}, p_{k''} \ldots p_b, p_c, p_d \ldots i)$$

of eds. 1 to 3 was replaced in ed. 4 by $d_e p_e$.

The sequence of the sections having been changed apparently in order to group together the eight systems of equations determining the general equilibrium in capital formation, the order of the first three systems was changed, system (1) of the first three editions becoming system (3) in ed. 4. This system reads $E=F_e(p_t \ldots p_p \ldots p_k, p_{k'}, p_{k''} \ldots p_b, p_c, p_d \ldots i)$ in eds. 1 to 3, changed in ed. 4 to read as in the translation. The remaining systems are the same in all editions, except that wherever ed. 4 reads p_e the first three editions read i as the last variable. In ed. 1, furthermore, system (8) reads $P_k = \dfrac{p_k - (\mu_k + \nu_k)}{i}$, etc., for reasons already noted (see above, Lesson 23, Collation Note [b]).

[b] The remainder of this section, except for the last two sentences, appears first in ed. 2.

590   ELEMENTS OF PURE ECONOMICS

[c] Ed. 1 reads: 'le taux du revenu net'; changed in ed. 4 to read 'le prix ou le taux du revenu net'.

[d] End of Lesson 47 in ed. 1. The next section appears first in ed. 2.

[e] Ed. 2 reads: 'pendant tout le temps que dureront nos tâtonnements'; changed in ed. 4 to read 'pendant un certain temps'.

[f] In ed. 2 the remainder of this section reads: 'Acceptant cette nécessité, nous devons supposer que, pour chaque reprise du tâtonnement, nos entrepreneurs de produits et de capitaux neufs trouveront, dans le pays, des propriétaires fonciers, travailleurs et capitalistes, possédant les mêmes quantités de services, ayant les mêmes besoins des services et des produits et les mêmes dispositions à l'épargne. Une reprise de tâtonnement consistera en ceci, en ce qui concerne la capitalisation envisagée isolément. A un taux du revenu net crié d'abord au hasard, et ensuite en hausse ou en baisse suivant les circonstances, les entrepreneurs de capitaux neufs fabriqueront certaines quantités de capitaux neufs déterminées d'abord au hasard, et ensuite en augmentation ou en diminution suivant les circonstances. Puis ils viendront vendre ces capitaux neufs sur le marché des capitaux suivant le mécanisme de la libre concurrence, c'est-à-dire à un prix de vente égal à leur revenu net divisé par le taux du revenu net (234). Le tâtonnement sera fini lorsque, au taux crié du revenu net et avec les quantités fabriquées de capitaux neufs, 1° le montant total de l'excédent du revenu sur la consommation sera égal au montant total des capitaux neufs, et que 2° le prix de vente des capitaux neufs sera égal à leur prix de revient. La production et la capitalisation pourront alors continuer, mais, bien entendu, avec les changements provenant de l'existence des capitaux neufs.' Changed in ed. 4 where the device of 'bons' or *tickets* was first introduced to read as translated in the text.

LESSON 25

[a] While the argument of this Lesson is fundamentally identical in all five editions, several important revisions in detail were made between the first and second editions and again between the third and fourth editions. A brief review of the more significant changes between eds. 1 and 2 will take the place of what would otherwise have been a lengthy and tedious juxtaposition of texts.

In all five editions Walras begins with systems of equations leading up to two conditions of equilibrium in capital formation: (1) equality between the total surplus of income over consumption and the aggregate value of new capital goods; and (2) equality between the cost of production of each new capital good and the capitalized value of its net income. Since it is highly improbable that the initial random determination of the rate of net income and of other relevant data would immediately result in a comprehensive equilibrium, Walras resumes, with appropriate amplifications, his discussion of the process of groping towards equilibrium in a free competitive market. In all five editions it is argued that equality between the cost of production of new capital goods and their selling price is arrived at by increasing or decreasing the quantities produced of new capital goods according as the capitalized value of the net income is greater or less than the cost of production of these goods.

The first edition differs, however, from the later editions both in the order of exposition of the varieties of trial adjustments by which the market converts an inequality between $D_k P_k + D_{k'} P_{k'} + D_{k''} P_{k''} + \ldots$ and E into an equality and in the very meaning of the equation. In ed. 1 formal precedence is given to the discussion of the trial adjustments between cost of production and selling price of new capital goods, whereas in ed. 2 this discussion is made to follow that of the trial adjustments between the total excess of income over consumption and the aggregate value of new capital goods.

This difference between ed. 1 and ed. 2 in formal arrangement is not as important as the reinterpretation of the equation

$$D_k P_k + D_{k'} P_{k'} + D_{k''} P_{k''} + \ldots = E.$$

In §292 of ed. 1 Walras assumed a rate of net income i' such that

$$D''_k \frac{p''_k - (\mu_k + \nu_k)}{i'} + D''_k \frac{p''_{k'} - (\mu_{k'} + \nu_{k'})}{i'} + D''_{k'} \frac{p''_{k''} - (\mu_{k''} + \nu_{k''})}{i'} + \ldots$$

$$\gtreqless F_e(p''_t \ldots p''_p \ldots p''_k, p''_{k'}, p''_{k''} \ldots p''_b, p''_c, p''_d \ldots i'),$$

and interpreted the left member of this inequality to represent 'la demande du capital numéraire par les entrepreneurs de produits *qui aiment autant emprunter du capital numéraire que de louer des capitaux existants* (K), (K'), (K'')...' (italics inserted), and the right member to represent 'l'offre du capital numéraire par les créateurs de l'excédent du revenu sur la consommation'. This implied an identification of the market for *numéraire* capital with the capital goods market. Such an identification would be justified if, as was further implied, all of (A) not used as a consumers' good were immediately converted into new capital goods. Under these implicit assumptions Walras correctly regarded

$$D_k P_k + D_{k'} P_{k'} + D_{k''} P_{k''} + \ldots = E$$

as expressing equality between the effective demand and offer of *numéraire* capital. Furthermore, D_a could only mean the demand for (A) as a consumers' good. Hence the equation

$$D'_a = O'_t p'_t + \ldots + O'_p p'_p + \ldots + O'_k p'_k + O'_{k'} p'_{k'} + O'_{k''} p'_{k''} + \ldots$$
$$- (E' + D'_b p'_b + D'_c p'_c + D'_a p'_a + \ldots)$$

was included in the system of equations determining the quantities demanded of consumers' goods, there being m such equations in §288 of ed. 1.

It is apparent that in his second edition Walras realized that the demand for (A) as *numéraire* capital had been overlooked in the previous edition. Hence, in §§250 and 251 of ed. 2 (§§254–255 of ed. 4 def.) he made a clear distinction between the market for *numéraire* capital and the new capital goods market, showing at the same time the relationship between the two. The reasons for a "liquidity preference" (to use J. M. Keynes's expression) in terms of (A) were not developed until the monetary theory was reached in Part VI of ed. 4; but granted the existence of some demand for (A) not destined for consumption, it follows that D_a, the total demand for (A), could no longer be determined within a system of equations of demand for consumers' goods, but could only be determined along with the demand for new capital goods. Hence the absence of an equation with the term D_a among the equations of demand for consumers' goods, there being $m-1$ such equations in §248 of ed. 2 (§252 of ed. 4 def.). The determination of D_a was then incorporated in the discussion of equilibrium in capital formation, as shown in the equation

$$\Omega_a p'_a + D'_k P'_k + D'_{k'} P'_{k'} + D'_{k''} P'_{k''} + \ldots = D'_a + E'$$

which appeared first in ed. 2.

Another noteworthy innovation in the second edition was the insertion of the last paragraph of §253 and of a new §254 (§258 of ed. 4 def.) in which Walras described the process of trial adjustments by groping towards equality between the selling price and cost of production of new capital goods.

Ed. 2 differs from ed. 1 also in the omission from this part of the theory of capital formation of all but passing reference (§243 of ed. 4 def.) to existing, as contrasted with new, capital goods. The passage on the subject cited in Collation Note [d] of Lesson 23 appeared only in the first three editions. Ed. 1 alone contained the following version of § 289 (§ 256 of ed. 4 def.) where the selling prices of new capital goods,

$$\Pi_k = \frac{p'_k - (\mu_k + \nu_k)}{i'}, \qquad \Pi_{k'} = \frac{p'_{k'} - (\mu_{k'} + \nu_{k'})}{i'},$$

etc., were set down as equal to the 'prix de vente des capitaux existants sur le marché des capitaux, comme il est facile de le démontrer en les supposant demandés soit par les capitalistes soit par les entrepreneurs'. The argument then continued: 'Car si ces prix de vente s'établissaient plus haut, il y aurait avantage pour les capitalistes créateurs d'épargnes à acheter des capitaux déjà existants (K), (K'), (K'')... plutôt que des capitaux neufs, et pour les entrepreneurs de produits à louer des capitaux existants aux prix de location $p'_k, p'_{k'}, p'_{k''}$... plutôt que d'emprunter du capital numéraire au taux de i' afin d'acheter des capitaux neufs. Les entrepreneurs de capitaux neufs seraient alors obligés d'offrir ces capitaux neufs au rabais. Et si, au contraire, ces prix de vente s'établissaient plus bas. . . .' This passage is not found in ed. 2. In fact, from the second edition on, practically the whole discussion of the pricing of old capital goods was deferred until after the problem of maximum utility in capital formation had been treated (§§ 268, 269 of ed. 4 def.).

Finally ed. 2 progressed beyond the arbitrary description of the supply of new capital in terms of *numéraire* as a monotonically increasing function of the rate of net income to one more in conformity with Walras's psychological theory of offer functions generally. Thus in § 292 of ed. 1 (cf. § 253 of ed. 4 def.) we are referred to the passage discussed in Collation Note [i] of Lesson 23, and we are told that F_e 'est une fonction croissante de i''. In § 249 of ed. 2, on the other hand, this function was described as 'une fonction successivement croissante et décroissante de i', de zéro à zéro'. It is all the more astonishing, therefore, that no change at all was made in § 253 of eds. 2 and 3 (cf. § 257 of ed. 4 def.) where the cost functions of capital goods were described as monotonically increasing functions of the volume of output of these goods (see below, Collation Note [n] of this Lesson).

Walras himself enumerated the principal changes made in ed. 2 in an unpublished letter to P. H. Wicksteed, dated April 9, 1889 (F.W. I, 612). So far as the theory of capital formation is concerned, the list reads as follows:

"§ 229 [§ 233 of ed. 4 def.] J'ai rectifié des formules mathématiques du revenu net et du taux du revenu net.

"§ 239 [§ 243 of ed. 4 def.] J'ai mis en évidence les $l+1$ équations spéciales de la capitalisation.

"§ 246 [§ 250 of ed. 4 def.] J'ai expliqué la réduction de $2m+2n+2l+2$ équations générales de la capitalisation à $2m+2n+2l+1$.

"§ 247 [§ 251 of ed. 4 def.] J'ai défini le tâtonnement en matière de capitalisation.

"§§ 248–256 [Lesson 25] J'ai rectifié sur plusieurs points la démonstration de la loi d'établissement du taux du revenu net, et spécialement, j'ai justifié (§ 250 [§ 254 of ed. 4 def.]) le tâtonnement en vue de l'égalité de l'offre et de la demande des capitaux neufs, distingué l'un de l'autre et relié l'un à l'autre (§ 251 [§ 255 of ed. 4 def.]) le marché du capital numéraire et celui des capitaux neufs, et justifié (§ 254 [§ 258 of ed. 4 def.]) le tâtonnement en vue de l'égalité du prix de vente et du prix de revient des capitaux neufs."

The last change indicated in this letter, viz. "§§ 257–260 J'ai démontré le théorème de l'utilité maxima des capitaux neufs", relates to the following two Lessons of ed. 4 def.

All the foregoing changes in the order and contents of the argument preclude the establishment of any parallelism between Lesson 25 of the translation and corresponding Leçons in ed. 1. All that can be said is that, taken as a whole, the subject-matter of this Lesson in the second and subsequent editions is to be found in the 48^e Leçon and in §§292 and 293 of the 49^e Leçon of ed. 1.

The changes in Lesson 25 between eds. 3 and 4 will be indicated by the usual collation of texts, except where the only differences are those which obviously follow from the modifications already indicated in Collation Notes [b], [h] and [i] of Lesson 23 and in Collation Note [a] of Lesson 24. For example, no special notice will be taken of the substitution of p_e for i or for $\frac{1}{i}$ in ed. 4 resulting from the introduction of the imaginary commodity (E) in Lesson 23 of that edition.

[b] Prior to ed. 4 systems of equations (1), (2) and (3) of this section were presented in a different order, viz. (3), (1), (2), with a correspondingly different enumeration.

[c] In ed. 2 the Ω_a's read Ω'_a; the primes were deleted in ed. 4.

[d] Ed. 2 reads: 'exprimant l'égalité des m prix de revient . . .'; changed in ed. 4 to read 'exprimant les m prix de revient. . . '.

[e] The numbers designating the systems of equations were changed in ed. 4 to conform to the revisions in the order of presentation of these systems in the previous Lesson (see above, Collation Note [a] of Lesson 24).

[f] Ed. 2 reads: 'Et quant au second membre, bien que nous ne connaissions pas la fonction F_e, nous savons qu'elle est une fonction, successivement croissante et décroissante de i, de zéro à zéro.' Changed in ed. 4 where F_e is no longer an empirically given function (see above, Collation Note [i] of Lesson 23).

[g] The final clause of this sentence appears first in ed. 4.

[h] In ed. 2 this paragraph reads: 'Or le tâtonnement indiqué est exactement celui qui se fait sur le marché des capitaux alors que les capitaux neufs s'y vendent suivant le mécanisme de l'enchère et du rabais, au prorata de leurs revenus nets (234); c'est-à-dire alors que le montant du revenu net des capitaux neufs s'échange contre le montant de l'excédent du revenu sur la consommation suivant l'équation

$$D_k\pi_k+D_{k'}\pi_{k'}+D_{k''}\pi_{k''}+\ldots$$
$$=iF_e(p_t\ldots p_p\ldots p_k, p_{k'}, p_{k''}\ldots p_b, p_c, p_d\ldots i)$$

i étant le taux de revenu net, et $\frac{1}{i}$ le *prix de l'unité de revenu net*.' Changed in ed. 4. This passage from ed. 2 is remarkable in that it gives the first adumbration of Walras's concept of a unit of net income with a given price, later called $p_e=\frac{1}{i}$ (§242 of ed. 4 def.).

[i] Ed. 2 reads simply 'en partie'; changed in ed. 4 to read 'en tout ou en partie'.

[j] Ed. 2 reads: 'ce taux d'intérêt . . . ne saurait différer en rien du taux du revenu net tel que nous venons de le déterminer'. Changed in ed. 4 where the coincidence of the two rates is described not as the consequence of an identity, but as the result of a tendency.

[k] In ed. 2 the beginning of this sentence reads: 'Le marché du capital numéraire n'ayant ainsi qu'un intérêt pratique et non théorique. . .'; made stronger in ed. 4.

[l] Ed. 2 reads: 'dans les équations des systèmes (1), (2) et (3) . . .', but since the order and content of these systems of equations were changed as indicated in Collation Note [a] of Lesson 24, the system omitted from this passage in ed. 4 was

$$E=F_e(p_t\ldots p_p\ldots p_k, p_{k'}, p_{k''}\ldots p_b, p_c, p_d\ldots i).$$

This omission was the consequence of the change in the meaning of E (see above, Collation Note [h] of Lesson 23).

[m] The remainder of this sentence in ed. 2 reads: '. . . et en éliminant succes-sivement $n-1$ d'entre ces inconnues, on obtiendrait finalement n équations de la forme suivante, donnant les prix des services en fonction des quantités à fabriquer de capitaux neufs et du taux de revenu net.' Changed in ed. 4.

[n] The discussion of the adjustments in price and quantity resulting from these inequalities was substantially modified in ed. 4, so that a simple collation of texts is impracticable. Briefly, the argument in ed. 2 starting from these inequalities is as follows. The cost of production of a capital good, say (K),

$$P_k = k_t p_t + \ldots + k_p p_p + \ldots + k_k p_k + k_{k'} p_{k'} + k_{k''} p_{k''} + \ldots$$

was assumed to be a monotonically increasing function of the output of (K); and its selling price, $\Pi_k = \dfrac{p_k}{i + \mu_k + \nu_k}$ was regarded as a monotonically decreasing function of the volume of sales. Hence, if $P_k \gtrless \Pi_k$, all that was needed to bring about equality was to diminish or increase the output of (K), thus reducing the output or increasing Π_k and increasing or reducing P_k. A similar argument was applied to capital goods (K'), (K'').... But changes in the quantities produced of (K'), (K'')... would upset any independently established equilibrium between P_k and Π_k. Nevertheless, Walras maintained that continued multipartite adjustments along the same lines would be convergent and would result finally in equality between the costs and selling prices of all new capital goods.

To demonstrate this point, Walras imagined the case where the output of *all* capital goods was simultaneously increased. An increase in the quantity manu-factured of (K) would bring about a rise in $p_t \ldots p_p \ldots p_{k'}, p_{k''} \ldots$ and a fall in the price p_k; an increase in the quantity manufactured of (K') would bring about a rise in $p_t \ldots p_p \ldots p_k, p_{k''} \ldots$ and a fall in $p_{k'}$; and so on. Centering our attention on (K), it is seen that the increases in the output of (K'), (K'')... would raise certain costs of production of (K) considerably, e.g. $p_t \ldots p_p \ldots$, while slightly lowering other costs, e.g. $p_{k'}, p_{k''} \ldots$ (assuming the coefficients of produc-tion to be constant). At the same time, the selling price Π_k would rise as a result of the increase in p_k. These complex movements in the component cost of production and in the selling price of (K) would, according to ed. 2, destroy any equality independently established between P_k and Π_k; but the resulting inequality would be closer to equality than the initial inequality had been. What is true of (K) is equally true *mutatis mutandis* of (K'), (K'')....

In ed. 4 the argument underwent three fundamental changes: (1) the supply function of a capital good was described as an increasing-decreasing function (with at least one maximum) as the cost of production increased; (2) the product (A) serving as *numéraire* was included in the list of capital goods; and (3) instead of assuming the supply of all capital goods to increase in the course of the trial adjustments, Walras now supposed the increase in the quantity produced of some capital goods so to raise the price of certain productive services used in the manufacture of other capital goods that the supply of these other capital goods might, at times, fall to zero.

The movements in price and quantity being more or less self-compensating, Walras argued (without offering any rigorous proof) that the secondary effects of adjustments in the quantity of one capital good would probably not seriously affect the costs of production and the selling prices of other capital goods.

[o] From here on the argument resumes in ed. 4 the same course it had taken in the two previous editions.

[p] The words 'à les supposer tous opérés dans le même sens' found at this point in ed. 2 omitted from ed. 4.

[*q*] The remainder of this sentence appears first in ed. 4.

[*r*] The words 'comme nous l'avons vu (248) [§252 of ed. 4 def.]' found in ed. 2 at this point omitted from ed. 4.

[*s*] 'en numéraire' appears first in ed. 4.

[*t*] The adjective 'proportionnelle' found in ed. 2 after 'hausse' and 'baisse' omitted from ed. 4.

[*u*] Ed. 2 reads: 'conformément à la loi de l'offre et de la demande'. Changed in ed. 4. The following passage with which the 25e Leçon ends in ed. 2 was omitted from ed. 4: 'Faisons seulement, avant de terminer, deux observations sur ces deux points.

'Remarquons d'abord, en ce qui concerne la détermination des prix des capitaux proprement dits neufs, que les entrepreneurs de ces produits, connaissant d'avance les prix des services et le taux du revenu net, connaissent d'avance le prix de revient et le prix de vente de leurs produits, et se trouvent, théoriquement, dans la même situation que les entrepreneurs du produit numéraire qui sont libres de ne produire qu'en cas de bénéfice et de s'abstenir en cas de perte (215).

'Rappelons ensuite, en ce qui concerne le taux du revenu net, que ce taux étant déterminé, le taux de l'intérêt, qui est le prix de location du capital numéraire, se trouve déterminé lui aussi et n'a plus qu'à se manifester sur le marché de ce capital numéraire (251). Et remarquons que, du moment où le capital fixe se loue sous forme de numéraire, rien n'empêche que le capital circulant ne se loue sous la même forme et (abstraction faite de circonstances d'un intérêt pratique et non théorique) au même prix, vu qu'il est tout à fait indifférent au capitaliste prêteur de numéraire que l'entrepreneur emprunteur transforme ce numéraire en machines, instruments, outils ou en matières premières en magasin et produits fabriqués en vente à l'étalage. Ainsi le problème de la location du capital est entièrement resolu par la détermination du taux du revenu net.'

LESSON 26

[*a*] Both in his letter to P. H. Wicksteed cited above in Collation Note [*a*] of Lesson 25, and in his Preface to ed. 2 (which was reproduced practically verbatim in ed. 3), Walras announced the formulation of a new theorem of maximum utility of new capital goods which appeared first in ed. 2. He explains in the following terms (ed. 2, p. xi) how the idea of the new theorem occurred to him: 'J'ai établi, dans un théorème nouveau, que la condition d'égalité du taux du revenu net était aussi la condition d'utilité maxima pour les capitaux neufs. Quand je publiai ma première édition, je n'avais encore aperçu qu'un seul des deux problèmes de maximum d'utilité relatifs aux services des capitaux neufs: celui qui se présente, si on suppose les quantités des capitaux données par la nature même des choses ou déterminées au hasard, à propos de la distribution par un individu de son revenu entre ses diverses espèces de besoins, que j'appelle pour abréger problème *de la satisfaction maxima des besoins*, et qui se résout mathématiquement par la proportionnalité des raretés aux prix des services des capitaux. Mais, en préparant cette seconde édition, j'en ai aperçu un autre: celui qui se présente, quand on cherche à déterminer les quantités de capitaux neufs en vue du maximum d'utilité effective de leurs services, à propos de la distribution par une société de l'excédent de son revenu sur sa consommation entre les diverses variétés de capitalisation, que j'appelle problème *de l'utilité maxima des capitaux neufs*, et qui se résout mathématiquement par la proportionnalité des raretés aux prix des capitaux eux-mêmes; d'où il résulte que le double maximum a lieu par la proportionnalité des prix des services aux prix des capitaux, ce qui est précisément, et sous une seule réserve, le résultat amené par la libre concurrence.'

The new theorem, which constitutes the subject-matter of Lessons 26 and 27 of the last two editions, originally appeared in ed. 2 as a single Lesson, the 26e Leçon. In ed. 4, Walras made two separate Lessons of the theorem, the first dealing with new capital goods yielding consumers' services and the second with new capital goods yielding production services.

Ed. 1 is, therefore, not included in the collation of texts of this and the following Lesson.

[b] In ed. 2 the remainder of this paragraph and the whole of the following paragraph read: 'Les dérivées de ces fonctions étant essentiellement décroissantes, le maximum d'utilité effective des services et produits aura lieu, pour notre individu, quand les accroissements différentiels relatifs aux quantités consommées de chacune des marchandises seront égaux, puisque, si on suppose inégaux deux quelconques d'entre ces accroissements, il y aura avantage à demander moins de la marchandise pour laquelle l'accroissement différentiel est plus faible pour demander plus de celle pour laquelle il est plus fort. La condition de satisfaction maxima des besoins peut donc s'exprimer par le système d'équations

$$\Phi'_t(\delta_t)\partial\delta_t = \ldots = \Phi'_p(\delta_p)\partial\delta_p = \ldots$$
$$= \Phi'_k(\delta_k)\partial\delta_k = \Phi'_{k'}(\delta_k)\partial\delta_{k'} = \Phi'_{k''}(\delta_{k''})\partial\delta_{k''} = \ldots$$
$$= \Phi'_a(\delta_a)\partial\delta_a = \Phi'_b(\delta_b)\partial\delta_b = \Phi'_c(\delta_c)\partial\delta_c = \Phi'_d(\delta_d)\partial\delta_d = \ldots$$

'Or, d'une part, les dérivées des fonctions d'utilité effective par rapport aux quantités consommées ne sont autre chose que les *raretés*; et, d'autre part, au point de vue du problème de la distribution par un individu d'un certain revenu entre ses diverses espèces de besoins, les différentielles de ces quantités consommées sont inversement proportionnelles aux prix, qui sont eux-mêmes les rapports inverses des quantités de marchandises échangées, suivant les équations

$$p_t\partial\delta_t = \ldots = p_p\partial d_p = \ldots$$
$$= p_k\partial\delta_k = p_{k'}\partial\delta_{k'} = p_{k''}\partial\delta_{k''} = \ldots$$
$$= \partial\delta_a = p_b\partial\delta_b = p_c\partial\delta_c = p_d\partial\delta_d = \ldots'$$

Changed in ed. 4.

It should be observed that in ed. 2 Walras employed two different symbols for differential increments: the symbol ∂ for increments in the services of capital goods and the symbol d for increments in the capital goods themselves as seen in the following quotation and the next note. Walras explained this difference in unpublished letters to Foxwell (February 13 and March 13, 1889), Bortkiewicz (February 20, 1889) and Edgeworth (March 22, 25 and April 14, 1889). To quote from his letter to Bortkiewicz: "Le nœud de la démonstration consiste en ce que les *quantités fabriquées de capitaux* sont aussi les *quantités consommées de services*, mais que les rapports des différentielles des premières quantités et les rapports des différentielles des secondes ne sont pas les mêmes. Ces dernières différentielles sont inversement proportionnelles *aux prix des services* suivant les équations

$$p_k\partial\delta_{k,1} = p_{k'}\partial\delta_{k',1} = p_{k''}\partial\delta_{k'',1} = \ldots$$

Les premières sont inversement proportionelles *aux prix des capitaux* suivant les équations

$$P_k d\delta_{k,1} = P_{k'} d\delta_{k',1} = P_{k''} d\delta_{k'',1} = \ldots" \text{ (F.W. I, 66)}$$

[c] In ed. 2 the remainder of this paragraph reads: 'Les dérivées de ces fonctions étant essentiellement décroissantes, le maximum d'utilité effective des capitaux neufs aura lieu, pour notre échangeur, quand les accroissements différentiels relatifs aux quantités fabriquées de chacun des capitaux neufs seront égaux, puisque, si on suppose inégaux deux quelconques d'entre ces accroissements, il y aura avantage à fabriquer moins du capital pour lequel l'accroissement

différentiel est plus faible, pour fabriquer plus de celui pour lequel il est plus fort. La condition d'utilité maxima des capitaux neufs pour l'échangeur (1) peut donc s'exprimer par le système d'équations

$$\Phi'_{k,1}(\delta_{k,1})d\delta_{k,1}= \Phi'_{k',1}(\delta_{k',1})d\delta_{k',1}= \Phi'_{k'',1}(\delta_{k'',1})d\delta_{k'',1}= \ldots.'$$

Changed in ed. 4.

[d] In ed. 2 the remainder of this paragraph reads: '. . . les différentielles des quantités fabriquées des divers capitaux sont inversement proportionnelles aux prix de ces capitaux P_k, $P_{k'}$, $P_{k''}$... suivant les équations

$$P_k d\delta_{k,1}=P_{k'}d\delta_{k',1}=P_{k''}d\delta_{k'',1}= \ldots.'$$

Changed in ed. 4.

[e] In ed. 2 the next sentence (which is a clause in the original) reads: 'Alors les différentielles des quantités fabriquées des divers capitaux, au lieu d'être inversement proportionnelles aux prix P_k, $P_{k'}$, $P_{k''}$... suivant les équations

$$P_k d\delta_{k,1}=P_{k'}d\delta_{k',1}=P_{k''}d\delta_{k''}= \ldots$$

le seraient aux sommes $P_k+\dfrac{\mu_k+\nu_k}{i_k}P_k$, $P_{k'}+\dfrac{\mu_{k'}+\nu_{k'}}{i_{k'}}P_{k'}$, $P_{k''}+\dfrac{\mu_{k''}+\nu_{k''}}{i_{k''}}P_{k''}$...

soit aux produits $\dfrac{p_k}{\pi_k}P_k$, $\dfrac{p_{k'}}{\pi_{k'}}P_{k'}$, $\dfrac{p_{k''}}{\pi_{k''}}P_{k''}$,... suivant les équations

$$\frac{p_k}{\pi_k}P_k d\delta_{k,1}=\frac{p_{k'}}{\pi_{k'}}P_{k'}d\delta_{k',1}=\frac{p_{k''}}{\pi_{k''}}P_{k''}d\delta_{k'',1}= \ldots.'$$

Changed in ed. 4.

LESSON 27

[a] See above, Collation Note [a] of Lesson 26. This section corresponds to §259 of Lesson 26 of eds. 2 and 3 which begins with the following sentences: 'Nous avons supposé, dans le paragraphe précédent, que les capitaux neufs étaient destinés à donner des profits consommables. Il nous faut supposer maintenant qu'ils sont destinés à donner des profits producteurs, c'est-à-dire des profits consommés non plus directement, mais dans la fabrication de produits, et voir quelle est, dans ce cas, la condition de maximum.' Changed in ed. 4.

[b] The adjective 'neufs' modifying 'profits' added in ed. 4.

[c] The next sentence (a clause in the original) was added in ed. 4.

[d] The phrase 'd'utilité' modifying 'accroissements différentiels' added in ed. 4 both here and in the rest of this paragraph.

[e] The phrase 'deux à deux en même temps que de signe contraire' modifying 'accroissements différentiels' added in ed. 4. In eds. 2 and 3 the condition of maximum utility was expressed simply by equating all the differential increments with respect to the quantities manufactured of each of the new capital goods (cf. Collation Note [c] of Lesson 26).

[f] The words 'et de signe contraire' added in ed. 4.

[g] In eds. 2 and 3, there is an additional clause immediately after the system of equations [t] describing the differentials of the quantities manufactured of each of the new capital goods, taken two at a time, as inversely proportional to the prices of the capital goods, and reading 'et inversement proportionnelles aux prix des capitaux, d'un capital à l'autre, suivant les équations

$$P_k d\delta_{k,1}=P_{k'}d\delta_{k',1}=P_{k''}d\delta_{k'',1}= \ldots$$

d'où il résulte que, au point de vue du problème qui nous occupe, les différentielles des quantités consommées de produits sont inversement proportionnelles aux

produits des coefficients de fabrication par les prix des capitaux P_k, $P_{k'}$, $P_{k''}$....'
The passage, which replaces the three translated paragraphs after system [ι] then
continues:
'Les accroissements différentiels partiels d'utilité effective relatifs aux quantités
fabriquées de chacun des capitaux neufs (K), (K'), (K'')... chez l'échangeur (1),
sont donc, pour chacune des marchandises (A), (B), (C), (D)... directement
proportionnels aux produits des coefficients de fabrication par les prix des
profits et inversement proportionnels aux produits des coefficients de fabrication
par les prix des capitaux; et la condition d'utilité maxima des capitaux neufs
pour cet échangeur peut s'exprimer par le système d'équations

$$\frac{a_k p_k}{a_k P_k} + \frac{b_k p_k}{b_k P_k} + \frac{c_k p_k}{c_k P_k} + \frac{d_k p_k}{d_k P_k} + \dots$$

$$= \frac{a_{k'} p_{k'}}{a_{k'} P_{k'}} + \frac{b_{k'} p_{k'}}{b_{k'} P_{k'}} + \frac{c_{k'} p_{k'}}{c_{k'} P_{k'}} + \frac{d_{k'} p_{k'}}{d_{k'} P_{k'}} + \dots$$

$$= \frac{a_{k''} p_{k''}}{a_{k''} P_{k''}} + \frac{b_{k''} p_{k''}}{b_{k''} P_{k''}} + \frac{c_{k''} p_{k''}}{c_{k''} P_{k''}} + \frac{d_{k''} p_{k''}}{d_{k''} P_{k''}} + \dots$$

$$= \quad . \quad . \quad . \quad . \quad . \quad . \quad . \quad . \quad . \quad . \quad . \quad . \quad .$$

lequel exprimerait également la condition du maximum d'utilité effective des
capitaux neufs pour les échangeurs (2), (3)....
'Cela étant, l'égalité des sommes des accroissements différentiels partiels
relatifs aux quantités fabriquées de chacun des capitaux neufs qui forme la
condition du maximum d'utilité effective des services de ces capitaux neufs, dans
le cas où ils sont destinés à donner des profits producteurs et non plus consommables, s'exprime toujours par le système d'équations

$$\frac{p_k}{P_k} = \frac{p_{k'}}{P_{k'}} = \frac{p_{k''}}{P_{k''}} = \dots,'$$

Changed in ed. 4.
[h] In ed. 1 the corresponding section (§298) is found at the beginning of the
50e Leçon entitled 'Du Marché Permanent' (see Lesson 35), where the first two
paragraphs read:
'La libre concurrence en matière de création de capitaux neufs constituant
bien la résolution par tâtonnement des équations de la capitalisation et du crédit
telles que nous les avons posées, il s'ensuit que:
'La capitalisation des épargnes par le crédit sur un marché régi par la libre
concurrence est une opération par laquelle l'excédent du revenu sur la consommation
se transforme en les capitaux neufs de la nature et de la quantité propres à donner
la plus grande satisfaction possible des besoins dans les limites de cette condition
qu'il n'y ait qu'un seul taux du revenu net pour tous les capitaux producteurs sur le
marché.'
[i] In eds. 2 and 3, the remainder of this paragraph reads: 'dans les limites de
cette condition qu'il n'y ait qu'un seul taux du revenu net pour tous ces capitaux sur
le marché, autrement dit, que l'amortissement et l'assurance des capitaux proprement
dits soient à la charge du consommateur du profit et non du propriétaire du capital.'
Changed in ed. 4.
[j] Ed. 1 reads: 'capital numéraire sur le marché de ce capital'; changed in
ed. 2 to read 'revenu net sur le marché des capitaux'.
[k] End of §298 in ed. 1. Additional paragraphs were added in subsequent
editions.
[l] In ed. 2 the 26e Leçon ends with the following section:
'261. Les quantités à fabriquer D_k, $D_{k'}$, $D_{k''}$... des capitaux neufs (K),

(K'), (K'')... se déterminant ainsi proprement par le système des équations

$$\frac{\pi_k}{P_k} = \frac{\pi_{k'}}{P_{k'}} = \frac{\pi_{k''}}{P_{k''}} = \ldots$$

le taux du revenu net *i* se détermine proprement par l'équation

$$i = \frac{D_k \pi_k + D_{k'} \pi_{k'} + D_{k'} \pi_{k''}}{E} + \ldots.$$

Si donc on fait abstraction du fait que l'excédent du revenu sur la consommation, *E*, est lui-même fonction du taux du revenu net, *i*, et qu'on le suppose donné par la nature des choses, on peut énoncer cette loi très simple d'établissement et de variation du taux du revenu net:

'*Le taux du revenu net est égal au rapport du revenu net total des capitaux neufs à l'excédent total du revenu sur la consommation.*

'*Si, toutes choses restant égales d'ailleurs, le revenu net d'une ou de plusieurs espèces de capitaux augmente ou diminue, le taux du revenu net augmente ou diminue.*

'*Si l'excédent du revenu sur la consommation augmente ou diminue, le taux du revenu net diminue ou augmente.*'

This section was omitted in ed. 4, but the discussion of the laws of the establishment and variations of the rate of net income was carried over, after complete revision, to §§265–268 of the following Lesson.

Lesson 28

[*a*] §§265–268 appear first in ed. 4 (see above, Collation Note [*l*] of Lesson 27).

[*b*] In ed. 2 the corresponding paragraph appears as the first paragraph of §262 at the beginning of the 27ᵉ Leçon of that edition and reads: 'Le taux du revenu net et les prix des capitaux neufs étant déterminés, restent à déterminer les prix des capitaux existants: fonciers, personnels et mobiliers.' Changed in ed. 4. No such paragraph is found in ed. 1.

[*c*] In ed. 1 the corresponding passage immediately preceding the equations appears in §294 of the 49ᵉ Leçon of that edition and reads: 'Quant aux prix des capitaux proprement dits, nous avons vu (289) comment ils étaient égaux à ceux des capitaux neufs et s'établissaient, sur le marché des capitaux, suivant les équations. . . .' Changed in ed. 2 (see above, Collation Note [*a*] of Lesson 25). The equations are substantially the same in all editions (see above, Collation Note [*b*] of Lesson 23).

[*d*] Ed. 1 reads: 'capitaux producteurs'. In ed. 2 the adjective 'producteurs' was omitted here and elsewhere in this Lesson.

[*e*] In ed. 1 this sentence reads: '*Si, toutes choses restant égales d'ailleurs, le taux du revenu net augmente ou diminue sur le marché des services producteurs, les prix de tous les capitaux producteurs diminuent ou augmentent sur le marché de ces capitaux.*' Changed in ed. 2.

[*f*] The rest of this sentence added in ed. 4.

[*g*] Ed. 1 reads: 'l'échange de ces produits'. Changed in ed. 4.

[*h*] 'des capitaux existants' added in ed. 4.

[*i*] Ed. 1 reads simply '$\frac{1}{i}$'. Changed to '$p_e = \frac{1}{i}$' in ed. 4.

[*j*] Sentence appears first in ed. 2.

[*k*] Ed. 1 reads: 'capitaux neufs'. The adjective 'neufs' omitted in ed. 4.

[*l*] 'par la considération du taux du revenu net' added in ed. 4.

[*m*] Ed. 1 reads: 'Restent donc les capitaux proprement dits dont le revenu brut est généralement assez loin d'être fixe, et pour lesquels les primes d'amortissement et d'assurance sont elles-mêmes aussi peu fixes que les chances de détérioration par l'usage et de disparition accidentelle auxquelles elles se rapportent, dont le prix est, par conséquent, très variable. . . .' Changed in ed. 4.

[*n*] Ed. 1 reads 'circulation'; changed in ed. 2 to 'échange' in consequence of the shift of the Lessons on the Theory of Circulation and Money to the latter part of the book after the Lessons on the Theory of Capital Formation.

[*o*] Ed. 1 reads: 'en numéraire'. Omitted in ed. 4.

[*p*] End of 49ᵉ Leçon in ed. 1; but in eds. 2 and 3 this is simply the end of §265 of the 27ᵉ Leçon which then continues with §§266–271 corresponding to Lesson 35 below.

Part VI

[*a*] As Walras himself indicated in his Preface (pp. 38–39), his theory of money underwent several fundamental changes between 1876 and 1899. He even shifted the position of the Part in which he expounded his monetary theory and altered its number accordingly in the transition from ed. 1 to ed. 2 and again in the transition from ed. 3 to ed. 4. In ed. 1, the Part entitled '*Du Numéraire et de la Monnaie*' appeared as '*Section III*' immediately after the Part dealing with the mathematical theory of exchange and before the Parts concerned with the theories of production and capital formation. In ed. 1 this '*Section III*' consisted of the following six Leçons:

29ᵉ Leçon. *Conditions du numéraire et de la monnaie.*
30ᵉ Leçon. *Problème de la valeur de la monnaie.*
31ᵉ Leçon. *Qualités des métaux précieux.*
32ᵉ Leçon. *Système rationnel de numéraire et de monnaie.*
33ᵉ Leçon. *De la monnaie fiduciaire.*
34ᵉ Leçon. *Du change.*

In eds. 2 and 3, on the other hand, the Part entitled '*Théorie de la Monnaie*' appeared as '*Section V*' of the *Eléments*, after the Part dealing with the theory of capital formation and credit and just before the last Part dealing with price fixing, monopoly and credit. In ed. 2 this '*Section V*' consisted of eight Leçons:

33ᵉ Leçon. *Problème de la valeur de la monnaie.*
34ᵉ Leçon. *Théorie mathématique du bimétallisme.*
35ᵉ Leçon. *De la fixité relative de valeur de l'étalon bimétallique.*
36ᵉ Leçon. *De la monnaie fiduciaire et des paiements par compensation. Du change.*
37ᵉ Leçon. *Conditions du numéraire et de la monnaie. Qualités des métaux précieux.*
38ᵉ Leçon. *Système rationnel de numéraire et de monnaie.*
39ᵉ Leçon. *Examen critique des doctrines de Cournot et de Jevons sur la mesure des variations de valeur de la monnaie. Détermination du prix de la richesse sociale en monnaie.*
40ᵉ Leçon. *Régularisation de la variation de valeur de la monnaie. Le quadrige monétaire.*

Of these only the first four were retained in ed. 3. In ed. 4 the position was again shifted to the place found in the present translation.

The text of Lessons 29 and 30 of the translated edition is not comparable with the text of the corresponding Leçons on the theory of money in the first three editions. On the other hand, the texts of these Lessons in ed. 4 and ed. 4 def. are identical. Hence the usual collation of the texts is precluded so far as Lessons 29 and 30 are concerned.

The various transformations through which Walras's monetary theory passed and the various refinements which were added in the successive editions of the *Eléments* and in the rest of Walras's writings were carefully collated and discussed in great detail in Arthur W. Marget's two articles, "Léon Walras and the 'Cash Balance Approach' to the Problem of the Value of Money", *op. cit.*, pp. 569–600, and "The Monetary Aspects of the Walrasian System", *op. cit.*, pp. 145–186. Any further enumeration of the minutiae of these changes would be redundant. It is sufficient here simply to note the broader lines of development of Walras's monetary theory between 1871 and 1899.

The first important change occurred in ed. 2 when Walras substituted the notion of an *'encaisse désirée'* for his earlier notion of a *'circulation à desservir'*. This was fundamental, for from the second edition on—or rather from the publication of his *Théorie de la monnaie*, Lausanne, Corbaz et Cie, 1886—Walras based his monetary theory on the individual demands for a *desired cash balance*, and no longer on the aggregate demand for whatever money was required to subserve the *"circulation à desservir"*, i.e. the circulation of goods. This led him, as Marget points out in the first of the above articles, to replace his earlier "Fisherian" equation of exchange by an equation essentially Keynesian in form. Nevertheless, in both eds. 2 and 3, the monetary theory was still not effectively integrated with his general equilibrium theory. Walras apparently contented himself in these two editions with a vague institutional explanation of the demand for *desired cash balances*, which he expressed as follows: 'Sans nous demander quelles circonstances naturelles peuvent obliger les propriétaires fonciers, travailleurs et capitalistes et les entrepreneurs à avoir, à un moment donné, une encaisse plus ou moins considérable, en vue de faire des achats ou une épargne plus ou moins considérables, nous poserons en fait, pour plus de simplicité, que le montant de cette encaisse dépend non-seulement de la situation, mais encore du caractère et des habitudes de chacun' (§ 321 of eds. 2 and 3). It is not surprising that, with his passion for symmetry and over-all coherence, he was not satisfied to leave his monetary theory so loosely and precariously attached to his utility functions which are the *primum mobile* of the entire system. The problem of incorporating the equations representing the demand for cash balances into his more general system of equations proved, however, to be extremely difficult—if we judge the difficulty by the time it took him to solve the problem. Indeed, it was not until 1899 that Walras first published his solution and presented it as the capstone of his whole theoretical structure. This he did in a memoir entitled *Equations de la circulation*, which he had read on May 3 of that year to the Société Vaudoise des sciences naturelles. When ed. 4 of the *Eléments* appeared in 1900, the memoir was reproduced with very few changes, replacing the 33e Leçon of ed. 3, and extending in the translated edition from §272 to §283. In this final version Walras identified cash balances with circulating capital yielding services of availability; and this enabled him to link the value of money to utility functions in the same way that the values of other categories of circulating capital goods were linked to these functions.

Another noteworthy change in the transition from ed. 3 to ed. 4 relates to the role played by the interest rate in equating the demand for cash balances to the existing quantity of money. In §322 of eds. 2 and 3 this role was described as follows: 'L'intérêt du capital circulant paie le service de la monnaie pendant qu'on la garde et celui des approvisionnements en matières premières et produits fabriqués, exactement comme l'intérêt du capital fixe paie le service des machines, instruments, outils. . . . Si, au taux crié de l'intérêt, la demande [de monnaie] est supérieure à l'offre [previously indicated as 'égale à la quantité existante de la monnaie'], on fera la hausse et les producteurs et consommateurs réduiront leur encaisse désirée. Si l'offre est supérieure à la demande, on fera la baisse et les producteurs et consommateurs augmenteront leur encaisse désirée. Le taux courant de l'intérêt sera celui auquel la demande et l'offre du capital monnaie seront égales.' To this Walras adds the following observation which is as relevant to the last editions as it is to the second and third: 'Il est donc naturel que le prix à crier sur le marché de la monnaie soit le taux de l'intérêt du capital monnaie. A côté de ce taux, subsiste celui du revenu net qui est toujours le rapport du prix du service des capitaux neufs au prix de ces capitaux eux-mêmes. Et ces deux taux tendent à l'égalité par la raison que, suivant que le premier est supérieur ou inférieur au second, les créateurs d'épargnes et les emprunteurs ont également intérêt à laisser ou à prendre du capital monnaie sur le marché; mais ils n'en sont pas moins distincts.' In ed. 4 the rate of interest, instead of being defined as the price of the service of circulating capital in general, is defined as the price of the service of only those cash balances which are held in lieu of fixed capital. Its role as an equilibrating factor is restricted to the special long-term money market described in §281 of the translated edition. Thus the rate of interest is no longer *the* rate which equates the demand for cash balances *in toto* to the quantity of money at equilibrium, but is only one of a complex of rates (the rate of discount being another), which together bring about this equality in the aggregate by means of separate adjustments that are not always concurrent or of the same degree.

As for the remaining Lessons in Part VI of this translation, the texts of Lessons 31 and 32 are comparable with the texts of the corresponding Leçons in ed. 2 and the intervening editions, while the texts of Lessons 33 and 34 are comparable with those of the equivalent Leçons in ed. 1 and the intervening editions. Since the text of Lesson 31 is identically the same in all of the last four editions, the Collation Notes will not be resumed until Lesson 32.

LESSON 32

[a] In ed. 2 this paragraph contains an additional sentence, omitted in ed. 4, reading: 'Cette courbe PP_1P_2... est remarquablement horizontale dans notre exemple, ce qui vient de ce que nous avons supposé la quantité de l'argent et la quantité de l'or variant généralement en sens inverse; et cependant, telle qu'elle est, elle permet très bien de reconnaître les limites de l'action compensatrice du bimétallisme.' Moreover, Walras's footnote refers to a further paragraph originally published in eds. 2 and 3 immediately after the paragraph under consideration, but dropped in ed. 4. This omitted passage was reprinted verbatim as the first paragraph of §19 of the *Théorie de la monnaie* both in the original version of 1886 and in the version found in the *Etudes d'économie politique appliquée* (1898). The passage relates to a graph (Fig. 22 in ed. 2) which was replaced in ed. 4 by our Fig. 30 (Fig. 19 in ed. 4).

[b] In ed. 2 this sentence reads: 'Mais nous reviendrons plus loin sur ces questions d'économie politique appliquée et d'économie politique pratique; et il nous suffira pour l'instant d'avoir fixé les points les plus importants de la théorie pure de la monnaie.' Changed in ed. 4 when Walras apparently recalled that in ed. 3 he had deleted from the *Eléments* the four Leçons dealing with the applied theory of money.

LESSON 33

[a] In the 33e Leçon of ed. 1 the next sentence reads: 'A la section du *crédit*, dans la théorie ['appliquée' added in ed. 2] de la *production de la richesse*, nous étudierons en détail les conditions de ce fonctionnement; pour le moment, nous prenons le fait en lui-même et au point de vue des conséquences qui en résultent touchant l'usage et la valeur de la monnaie métallique.' Omitted in ed. 4.

[*b*] The next sentence was added in ed. 4.

[*c*] This section was added in ed. 4.

[*d*] The remainder of this Lesson and the corresponding passages in eds. 2, 3 and 4 cannot be compared with ed. 1, so that any further collation of the text of this Lesson as it appeared in the later editions with that found in the first edition is impracticable. As already explained in Collation Note [*a*] of Part VI, the whole tenor of Walras's monetary theory was fundamentally changed in the interval between ed. 1 and ed. 2 with the consequence that his discussion of fiduciary money had to be modified accordingly. In ed. 1 Walras considered credit instruments in terms of a "flow" of additional circulating media supplementing the "flow" of non-fiduciary money required to assure the circulation of goods. From ed. 2 onwards, while the same symbol F was used as before to represent credit instruments, it was conceived in terms of a "stock" in conformity with his new notion of a *desired cash balance*. The equations and the entire argument were then changed (cf. Arthur W. Marget, "Léon Walras and the 'Cash Balance Approach' . . .", *op. cit.*, pp. 579–586).

[*e*] Ed. 2 reads 'billets de banque'; changed to 'titres' in ed. 4.

[*f*] The remainder of this sentence was added in ed. 4.

[*g*] In eds. 2 and 3, where the subject-matter of this Lesson does not constitute a separate Leçon, but is found in the first part of the 36e Leçon which then continues on the subject of Foreign Exchange, the remainder of the discussion of Fiduciary Money and Payments by Offsets reads as follows: 'Qu'on le remarque bien, je concède parfaitement que, d'un moment à l'autre, toutes les données du problème se modifiant, il n'y a plus de rapport nécessaire de proportionnalité entre la quantité de la monnaie et les prix; que, par exemple, la quantité de la monnaie diminuant, mais la monnaie de papier suppléant de plus en plus la monnaie métallique, ou les compensations se développant de jour en jour, les prix se maintiendraient au lieu de baisser; mais je soutiens que, à un moment donné, ou d'un moment à l'autre toutes choses restant égales d'ailleurs, si la quantité de la monnaie augmente ou diminue, les prix hausseront ou baisseront en proportion. Qu'on réfute ma démonstration, je m'inclinerai; mais quant à citer purement et simplement les chiffres des compensations effectuées aux *clearing-houses* de Londres et de New York pour conclure que "nous ne sommes plus à l'époque où il y avait corrélation entre la quantité des métaux précieux et les prix", c'est montrer qu'on n'a aucune idée de la manière dont une quantité qui est fonction de plusieurs variables peut dépendre de chacune de ces variables en particulier.' Changed in ed. 4.

LESSON 34

[*a*] This section was added in ed. 3.

[*b*] In ed. 1 this sentence reads: 'Les idées ont notablement changé à cet égard; et cependant il est bon de savoir qu'un pays qui a le change contre soi, alors que la perte atteint la limite déterminée par les frais de transport des métaux précieux, sort une partie de sa monnaie métallique, ce qui peut avoir des conséquences graves au point de vue des prix des marchandises et de la circulation de la richesse.' Changed in ed. 3.

[*c*] End of 34e Leçon in ed. 1 and of the 36e Leçon in eds. 2 and 3.

Part VII

[*a*] See above, Collation Note [*a*] of Part V.

LESSON 35

[a] The subject-matter of this Lesson is found in §§299–304 of the 50ᵉ Leçon of ed. 1 (cf. Collation Note [h] of Lesson 27) and in the latter part (§§266–271) of the 27ᵉ Leçon of eds. 2 and 3 (cf. Collation Note [p] of Lesson 28). In the first three editions, the Continuous Market ('Du marché permanent') was discussed immediately after the description of the operations of the capital goods market; in ed. 4 this discussion was restored to the place it held in ed. 1, in so far as it was situated again in the Part entitled 'Conditions et conséquences du progrès économique' and just before Walras's dynamic analysis of expanding output. Though the text was modified considerably, especially in ed. 4, in order to adapt the discussion to the new position in the book and to certain alterations in the symbols made in the earlier Lessons, most of the changes were inconsequential. Only the more important changes will be listed in the following notes.

[b] In ed. 1 the first sentence of the next paragraph reads: 'Nous supposons toujours un marché d'échange et de production sur lequel il s'agit de transformer certains services producteurs en produits, en capitaux fixes et enfin en capitaux circulants.' Omitted in ed. 4.

[c] The remainder of this sentence was first added in ed. 2, reading: '. . . qui, théoriquement, peut être considéré comme se prêtant et s'empruntant sur le marché du capital numéraire au taux de l'intérêt *i* égal au taux du revenu net (256).' Changed in ed. 4.

[d] This paragraph appears first in ed. 4.

[e] In ed. 1 the remainder of this sentence reads: '. . . et l'on verra qu'on pourrait d'autant mieux les réprimer ou les prévenir qu'on connaîtrait mieux les conditions de l'équilibre idéal de l'échange et de la production. Mais, au surplus, et quel que soit le résultat de la science à ce point de vue, elle n'en est pas moins fondée à se rendre compte de ces conditions dans l'intérêt de la vérité pure: lui contester ce droit, c'est lui refuser l'existence.' Changed in ed. 2, which reads substantially like ed. 4 except for a first clause in the first sentence: 'Nous étudierons ces crises . . .', which was omitted in ed. 4.

[f] End of the 50ᵉ Leçon in ed. 1, and of the 27ᵉ Leçon in eds. 2 and 3.

LESSON 36

[a] In ed. 1 the title of the 51ᵉ Leçon, which corresponds to §§323–329 of this Lesson, reads 'De l'augmentation dans la quantité des produits', to which 'Lois de variation générale des prix dans une société progressive' was added when the 52ᵉ Leçon of ed. 1 was combined with the 51ᵉ Leçon to form a single Leçon 28 in ed. 2. The significant heading 'Théorème des productivités marginales' was not added until ed. 4.

[b] Ed. 1 reads simply 'équation'; changed to the italicized expression '*équation de fabrication*' in ed. 4.

[c] In eds. 1, 2 and 3, the paragraph does not end here, but continues, reading: 'Nous ne fournirons pas ici cette expression plus que nous ne l'avons fait dans la théorie de la production; nous poserons seulement en fait que. . . .' What follows then is the second clause of the first sentence of §327 of the translated edition and the rest of that section. In ed. 4, there is only one additional sentence in this paragraph, reading: 'Voici ce système.' Omitted in ed. 4 def.

[d] This section appears first in ed. 4 but reads there quite differently from ed. 4 def. Though footnote 1 on the first page of the Preface of ed. 4 def. calls attention to the new footnote in this section, it does not apprise the reader at all of the changes in the text of §326, which could hardly be called 'petits remaniements' (cf. Henry Schultz, "Marginal Productivity and the General Pricing

Process", *op. cit.*, p. 516). In ed. 4 this section begins: 'Introduisons une quantité fabriquèe Q du produit (B) . . .'. Changed in ed. 4 def. to read: 'Introduisons une quantité déterminée à fabriquer Q du produit (B) . . .'.

[*e*] The first two sentences of this paragraph were added in ed. 4 def.

[*f*] In ed. 4 the remainder of § 326 reads:

'Or l'entrepreneur qui tâtonne ajoute ou retranche de chaque service producteur selon que la valeur de l'incrément de ce service est inférieure ou supérieure à la valeur de l'incrément de produit qu'il sert à obtenir, de façon à arriver aux égalités

$$\Delta T . p_t = \frac{\partial \varphi}{\partial T} \Delta T . p_b, \qquad \Delta P . p_p = \frac{\partial \varphi}{\partial P} \Delta P . p_b, \qquad \Delta K . p_k = \frac{\partial \varphi}{\partial K} \Delta K . p_b \ldots$$

soit toujours

$$\frac{\partial \varphi}{\partial T} = \frac{p_t}{p_b}, \qquad \frac{\partial \varphi}{\partial P} = \frac{p_p}{p_b}, \qquad \frac{\partial \varphi}{\partial K} = \frac{p_k}{p_b} \ldots \qquad ..(3)$$

Des équations (1) et (3), on tire

$$Q = \frac{\partial \varphi}{\partial T} T + \frac{\partial \varphi}{\partial P} P + \frac{\partial \varphi}{\partial K} K + \ldots \qquad ..(4)$$

'Donc: 1° *La libre concurrence amène le prix de revient minimum;*

2° *Sous ce régime, le taux de rémunération de chaque service est égal à la dérivée partielle de la fonction de fabrication, soit à la productivité marginale;*

3° *Toute la quantité fabriquée du produit est distribuée entre les services producteurs.*

'Cette triple proposition constitue *la théorie de la productivité marginale,* théorie capitale en économie politique pure, parce qu'elle introduit dans le problème de la production le système des équations (3) en nombre égal à celui des coefficients de fabrication et dans lesquelles ces coefficients figurent à titre d'inconnues, et parce qu'elle fournit ainsi le ressort de la demande des services et de l'offre des produits par les entrepreneurs, tout comme la *théorie de l'utilité finale* fournit le ressort de la demande des produits et de l'offre des services par les propriétaires fonciers, travailleurs et capitalistes, mais que j'ai préféré ne pas introduire dans ma théorie générale de l'équilibre économique, déjà suffisamment compliquée, de peur que celle-ci ne devînt trop difficile à saisir dans son ensemble.

'Cette théorie de la productivité marginale, dont le germe se trouve dans les chapitres VI et VII de la *Theory of Political Economy* de Jevons, a été abordée par divers économistes américains et italiens, notamment par MM. Wood, Hobson, Clark et Montemartini. Mais elle était demeurée empirique, jusqu'à ce que MM. Pareto et Barone l'eussent rattachée à l'équation de fabrication (325) en modifiant d'abord cette équation de façon à y faire entrer la quantité fabriquée de produit, afin de pouvoir supposer les coefficients de fabrication variant avec cette quantité fabriquée, puis en différentiant les équations de prix de revient et de fabrication modifiée, en vue du minimum de prix de revient du produit. M. Barone m'a communiqué les équations (1), (2), (3), et (4) en 1894 et 1895; je les ai discutées avec lui, et nous sommes tombés d'accord pour déduire la troisième des deux premières comme ci-dessus. Je les ai fait figurer de cette manière dans ma *Note sur la réfutation de la théorie anglaise du fermage de M. Wicksteed,* insérée dans le *Recueil publié par la Faculté de Droit de l'Université de Lausanne* (1896). Et je les fais, à présent, figurer ici suivant la notation la plus conforme à la mienne.'

The footnote referred to at the end of this passage reads: 'J'ajoute ce numéro 326 à la 4e édition des *Eléments* dont je retranche, par contre, l'appendice III de la 3e édition qui contenait la *Note sur la réfutation de la théorie anglaise du fermage de M. Wicksteed.*'

The significance of the differences between the above text and that of ed. 4 def. was discussed by Henry Schultz in the article mentioned above in Collation Note [d] of this Lesson (cf. the postscript to Appendix III of ed. 3, translated below, pp. 493–495).

[g] In ed. 1 this sentence reads: 'Mais il paraît également hasardé d'énoncer que l'augmentation dans la quantité des moyens de subsistance résultant de la découverte du blé ou de la pomme de terre, de l'invention des machines ou des perfectionnements du crédit, a lieu suivant une fonction logarithmique plutôt qu'exponentielle, et que celle résultant du développement du capital a lieu suivant une progression arithmétique dont la raison est l'unité.' Changed in ed. 2.

[h] End of 51ᵉ Leçon in ed. 1.

[i] End of 52ᵉ Leçon in ed. 1 and of 28ᵉ Leçon in eds. 2 and 3.

Lesson 37

[a] End of 53ᵉ Leçon in ed. 1 and of 29ᵉ Leçon in eds. 2 and 3. The remainder of this sentence appears first in ed. 4.

Lesson 38

[a] Ed. 1 contains an additional clause reading: '. . .; elles ne font partie de la richesse sociale qu'à cette condition'. Omitted in ed. 2.

[b] In ed. 1 this sentence reads: 'On raisonnerait de même pour la baisse.' Changed in ed. 2.

[c] In ed. 1 the "rise or fall in the prices of productive services" is modified by a clause reading: 'qui résulte de la hausse ou de la baisse originaire des produits'. Omitted in ed. 2.

[d] Ed. 1 contains a further sentence reading: 'Ainsi la distinction fondamentale de l'école anglaise n'a nullement la valeur que ses auteurs lui attribuent.' Omitted in ed. 4.

[e] End of the 54ᵉ Leçon in ed. 1 and of the 30ᵉ Leçon in eds. 2 and 3.

Lesson 39

[a] In ed. 1 the remainder of this sentence reads: '. . . avant de la discuter; car c'est la seule manière de s'en rendre compte'. Omitted in ed. 4.

[b] This sentence appears first in ed. 4 def. This change and other changes noted below which were made in the definitive edition of this section are not indicated in the first footnote of the Preface.

[c] In ed. 1 the first part of this sentence reads: 'Algébriquement, soient h_1, h_2, h_3... les produits nets des terres Nos 1, 2, 3... ou les excédents . . .'. Changed in ed. 4 def., where, it is to be noted, the words 'par hectare' were added in italics.

[d] In ed. 1 the symbols φ_1, φ_2, φ_3... are found in place of F'_1, F'_2, F'_3.... Changed in ed. 2 where an intervening passage introducing system (3) reads: '. . . et si l'on pose

$$\varphi_1(x)=F'_1(x), \qquad \varphi_2(x)=F'_2(x), \qquad \varphi_3(x)=F'_3(x),$$

il y a, entre le taux de l'intérêt et les capitaux employés, les relations

$$t=\varphi_1(x_1)=\varphi_2(x_2)=\varphi_3(x_3)= \ldots .' \qquad \qquad ..(3)$$

Changed in ed. 4.

[e] The factors n_1, n_2, n_3... appear first in ed. 4 def. See above, Collation Note [b] of this Lesson.

[*f*] The remainder of this sentence appears first in ed. 2.

[*g*] See above, Collation Note [*d*] of this Lesson.

[*h*] End of 55ᵉ Leçon in ed. 1.

[*i*] The remainder of this sentence, including the next equation, appears first in ed. 2.

[*j*] Ed. 1 reads: 'Mais, à tout prendre, c'est de la nature et de la quantité des revenus producteurs, et non pas de la nature et de la quantité des capitaux producteurs, que dépend le produit.' Changed in ed. 4.

[*k*] Ed. 1 reads 'revenus'; changed to 'services' in ed. 2.

[*l*] In ed. 1 'conséquence' is followed by 'd'une cherté croissante des produits'. Omitted in ed. 2.

[*m*] In ed. 1 the remainder of this section reads: '. . . qu'on peut traduire en ces termes: —*Le fermage est égal à l'excédent du prix des produits sur le prix de revient en salaires et intérêts.* Bien que l'école anglaise détermine le prix des produits au moyen du prix des services producteurs, il n'y a pas, pour elle, de pétition de principe à déterminer ici le fermage au moyen du prix des produits, à la condition qu'on suppose les salaires, les intérêts et le taux du revenu net en numéraire déterminés d'autre part. Alors, en effet, le taux de production se détermine, comme il a été dit précédemment (336 [cf. §355 of ed. 4 def.]), en raison de la quantité de capital disponible; et le prix des produits se détermine par le rapport du taux du revenu net au taux de production. En ce sens, l'école anglaise réussirait bien à établir que: —*Le fermage ne fait pas partie des frais de production,* n'était ce dernière difficulté qu'il nous reste à signaler.' Changed in ed. 2 to read: 'Ainsi, en résumé, par l'introduction des courbes $T_1T'_1$, $T_2T'_2$, $T_3T'_3$... (introduction qu'on ne doit admettre que sous la réserve qui précède et que sous une autre plus grave qui va suivre), l'école anglaise introduit bien, . . .' The rest of this section reads in ed. 2 as in the edition translated from the point marked by the Collation reference [*n*] to the end. The intervening mathematical discussion appears first in ed. 4.

[*n*] Ed. 1 reads 'bien'; changed in ed. 4 to read 'tant bien que mal'.

[*o*] In ed. 1 the remainder of this section reads: '. . . et, cela fait, la réunir aux autres équations de la production pour déterminer à la fois, comme nous l'avons fait, les prix des produits et des services producteurs. Les fonctions de fabrication serviront à la détermination des coefficients de fabrication. Les fermages, les salaires, les intérêts, les prix des produits et les coefficients de fabrication sont autant d'inconnues d'un même problème, qui doivent être déterminées toutes ensemble et non pas indépendamment les unes des autres.' This is the end of the 56ᵉ Leçon in ed. 1 and of the 31ᵉ Leçon in eds. 2 and 3. In ed. 4 the beginning of this passage reads: '. . . y joindre l'équation de la fabrication

$$\varphi(b_t \ldots b_p \ldots b_k \ldots) = 0,$$

et, cela fait, la réunir aux autres équations de la production pour déterminer à la fois, comme nous l'avons fait, les prix des produits et des services producteurs.' Changed in ed. 4 def., where it will be noted the "definitive" production function replaced the "vestigial" function (see Translator's Note [1] of Lesson 36). The remainder of this Lesson in ed. 4 is uniform with ed. 4 def. except for Walras's new footnote which was added, as indicated, in 1902.

Lesson 40

[*a*] End of 57ᵉ Leçon in ed. 1.

[*b*] Ed. 1 contains an additional sentence reading: 'Il ne faut pas perdre ce détail de vue quand on lit leurs ouvrages.' Omitted in ed. 4.

ELEMENTS OF PURE ECONOMICS

[c] In ed. 1 this paragraph reads:

'C'est à ces systèmes insuffisants que nous substituons celui dont les deux éléments principaux sont l'exposition du mécanisme de la libre concurrence en matière d'échange (offre et demande effectives: hausse, baisse, prix courant d'équilibre) faite à la section II [equivalent to Parts II and III of the translated edition], et celle du mécanisme de la libre concurrence en matière de production (terres et rentes, personnes et travaux, capitaux proprement dits et profits; propriétaires fonciers, travailleurs et capitalistes; entrepreneurs, bénéfice, perte, égalité du prix de vente et du prix de revient) faite à la section IV [equivalent to Part IV of the translated edition]. Grâce à ces conceptions fondamentales, nous avons: 1° un marché des services producteurs sur lequel des rentes de terres, des travaux de personnes et des profits de capitaux proprement dits sont offerts au rabais par des propriétaires fonciers, travailleurs et capitalistes et demandés à l'enchère par des entrepreneurs; et 2° un marché des produits sur lequel ces produits sont offerts au rabais par des entrepreneurs et demandés à l'enchère par des propriétaires fonciers, travailleurs et capitalistes. Et, dès lors, nous avons aussi: 1° les prix des services producteurs ou les fermages, salaires et intérêts; et 2° les prix des produits. La demande des services producteurs et l'offre des produits sont déterminées, pour les entrepreneurs, par la considération de bénéfice ou de perte; l'offre des services producteurs et la demande des produits sont déterminées, pour les propriétaires fonciers, travailleurs et capitalistes, par la considération de satisfaction maximum des besoins. Je ne dis rien ici de l'exposition du mécanisme de la libre concurrence en matière de capitalisation faite à la section V et grâce à laquelle nous avons: 1° sur le marché des services producteurs, un marché du capital numéraire; 2° sur le marché des produits, un marché des capitaux proprement dits neufs; et enfin 3° un marché des capitaux producteurs; ce qui nous donne: 1° le taux du revenu net; et 2° les prix des terres, des personnes et des capitaux proprement dits.' Changed in ed. 2. This change is significant as evidence of Walras's growing sense of integration of his entire system between the first and second editions.

[d] End of the 58e Leçon in ed. 1 and of the 32e Leçon in eds. 2 and 3.

LESSON 41

[a] In ed. 1, §§ 228, 229 and 230 of the translated edition were all found at this place. See above, Collation Notes [h]–[j] of Lesson 22.

[b] Ed. 1 reads 'par des procédés à la façon des *Molly Maguires*'; changed in ed. 2 to read 'par des procédés d'intimidation et de violence'.

[c] End of 59e Leçon in ed. 1.

[d] In ed. 1 the next two paragraphs are found in Walras's footnote following the reference to Cournot. When transposed to the text in ed. 2, the final sentence of the footnote, 'Donc $Oq = qt$', was omitted.

[e] End of 60e Leçon in ed. 1 where the final sentence reads: 'Mais, comme on voit, le point de départ de toute cette étude se trouve dans une application de calcul différentiel; et c'est pourquoi, plutôt que de suivre l'auteur dans cette voie, qu'il vaut mieux éviter, si possible, dans un traité élémentaire, nous avons donné la théorie du monopole dans la forme arithmétique et non analytique.' Changed in ed. 2.

[f] End of 61e Leçon in ed. 1.

LESSON 42

[a] In ed. 1, the remainder of this section reads: 'On peut dire que ces quatre espèces d'impôts diffèrent quant à *l'assiette*, les impôts directs étant assis sur les

services producteurs et l'impôt indirect étant assis sur les produits.' Changed
in ed. 2.

[*b*] End of 62ᵉ Leçon in ed. 1.

[*c*] In ed. 1 the first sentence of this paragraph reads: 'Nous commencerons
par les effets de l'impôt direct sur les salaires.' Omitted in ed. 2.

[*d*] This section appears first in ed. 4.

[*e*] End of 63ᵉ Leçon in ed. 1.

[*f*] In place of the first paragraph of this section, ed. 1 reads:

'Si, maintenant, on impose directement les intérêts des capitaux proprement
dits, que va-t-il arriver? Les capitalistes seront-ils atteints dans leur capital comme
les propriétaires fonciers, et leurs successeurs demeureront-ils exempts de toute
charge? Ou bien seront-ils frappés à perpétuité dans leur revenu comme les
travailleurs? Rien de tout cela. On peut énoncer ce principe:— L'impôt direct
sur les intérêts est un impôt indirect de consommation.

'Que les capitalistes aient tout d'abord le ferme désir de s'exonérer de l'impôt,
c'est à quoi il faut s'attendre: ils l'auront comme auraient pu l'avoir les propriétaires fonciers et les travailleurs; ils l'auront même d'autant plus vivement que,
dans une société progressive, la valeur du profit s'abaisse constamment. Mais la
question est de savoir si les lois naturelles et nécessaires de la richesse sociale
viennent en aide au capitaliste mieux qu'au travailleur et au propriétaire foncier.
Or c'est effectivement ce qui arrive.

'La fécondité et la solidité de la terre, ou la rente, l'activité intellectuelle et
physique de l'homme, ou le travail, sont des richesses naturelles: l'une et l'autre
de ces deux forces sont utiles, l'une et l'autre sont limitées en quantité parmi
beaucoup d'autres forces naturelles qui sont également utiles, mais qui existent
dans le monde en quantité illimitée. De là leur valeur. Cette valeur se détermine
en dernier ressort par la loi de l'offre et de la demande; et l'impôt ne la fait ni
plus haute ni plus basse. Il en est autrement du capital: le capital est une richesse
artificielle, les capitaux sont des produits, et leur valeur se détermine par le
principe des frais de production; c'est-à-dire que leur prix de vente concorde
avec leur prix de revient.' Changed in ed. 3.

[*g*] In ed. 1 the remainder of this section reads: 'Ce raisonnement pouvant
être reproduit à l'occasion de tous les capitaux proprement dits, il en résulte que
l'impôt sur les intérêts du capital est payé par les consommateurs du profit ou
par les consommateurs des produits à la production desquels concourt le profit.
C'est donc bien un impôt indirect de consommation.' Changed in ed. 3.

[*h*] In ed. 1 there is another sentence following this, which reads: 'C'est pourquoi l'impôt sur les produits s'appelle aussi impôt indirect de consommation.'
Omitted in ed. 4.

[*i*] In ed. 1 this sentence reads: 'En général, on n'établit pas l'impôt de consommation sur tout l'ensemble des produits comme on cherche à établir l'impôt
direct sur tous les salaires, sur tous les fermages et sur tous les intérêts.' Changed
in ed. 3.

[*j*] End of the 64ᵉ Leçon in ed. 1, and of the 38ᵉ Leçon in ed. 3.

Appendix I

[*a*] This Appendix appears first in ed. 3.

Appendix II

[*a*] This Appendix appears first in ed. 3.

ELEMENTS OF PURE ECONOMICS

Appendix III

[a] This Appendix appeared in ed. 3 only and was omitted from the later editions (see above, p. 386, footnote 1, and Collation Notes [d]–[f] of Lesson 36). On the page proofs of the version of this Note which was published in the *Recueil* mentioned in Walras's footnote, there is the following pencilled notation in Walras's own hand: "J'avais écrit ces quelques pages pour moi seul. J'ai saisi l'occasion de les publier en apprenant que la direction de l'*Economic Journal* avait refusé à M. Barone l'insertion de sa Note." Mlle Aline Walras communicated to me this annotated copy of the proof. Barone's Note, which Edgeworth first praised and then refused to publish in the *Economic Journal*, was entitled "Sopra un recente libro del Wicksteed" (see George G. Stigler, *Production and Distribution Theories, op. cit.*, pp. 361–362).

INDEXES

The ordinary Arabic numerals refer to *pages*, not sections, of the translated text. The page number sometimes indicates the beginning, sometimes the whole of the relevant passage. The bold-faced numerals refer to Lessons; and the numbers or letters in square brackets designate respectively the Translator's or Collation Notes of the Lesson indicated by the preceding bold-faced numeral.

INDEX OF SUBJECTS

(See also the analytical table of contents, pp. 13–28)

INDEX OF NAMES

THE END